T0366563

CALIFORNIA, A SLAVE STATE

CALIFORNIA, A SLAVE STATE

JEAN PFAELZER

Yale

UNIVERSITY PRESS

New Haven and London

Published with assistance from the John R. Bockstoce Endowment
Fund, and from the foundation established in memory of Amasa
Stone Mather of the Class of 1907, Yale College.

Yale University Press books may be purchased in quantity for
educational, business, or promotional use. For information, please
e-mail sales.press@yale.edu (U.S. office) or sales@yaleup.co.uk
(U.K. office).

Set in Janson type by Integrated Publishing Solutions.
Printed in the United States of America.

Library of Congress Control Number: 2022945967
ISBN 978-0-300-21164-1 (hardcover : alk. paper)

A catalogue record for this book is available from the
British Library.

This paper meets the requirements of ANSI/NISO Z39.48-1992
(Permanence of Paper).

10 9 8 7 6 5 4 3 2 1

For
Peter Panuthos

Slavery exists in the life of slaves.

—KEVIN BALES

Great streams are not easily turned from channels, worn deep
in the course of ages. They may sometimes rise in quiet and
stately majesty, and inundate the land, refreshing and fertilizing
the earth with their mysterious properties. They may also rise
in wrath and fury, and bear away, on their angry waves, the
accumulated wealth of years of toil and hardship. They, however, gradually flow back to the same old channel, and flow
on as serenely as ever. But, while the river may not be turned
aside, it may dry up, and leave nothing behind but the withered
branch, and the unsightly rock, to howl in the abyss-sweeping
wind, the sad tale of departed glory. As with rivers so with
nations.

—FREDERICK DOUGLASS

Contents

CALIFORNIA, A SLAVE STATE

Crescent City
Del Norte
Yreka
Siskiyou
Modoc

Arcata
Eureka
Humboldt
Trinity
Shasta
Redding
Lassen
Susanville

Red Bluff
Tehama
Plumas
Corning
Chico
Glenn
Butte
Oroville
Sierra
Yuba
Nevada
Truckee
Mendocino
Ukiah
Lake
Colusa
Sutter
Yuba City
Placer

Healdsburg
Yolo
South Lake Tahoe
El Dorado
Sonoma
Napa
Sacramento
Alpine

Napa
Fairfield
Amador
Vallejo
Solano
Marin
Contra Costa
Stockton
Calaveras
Tuolumne
Mono
San Joaquin

San Francisco
Oakland
San Francisco
Fremont
Alameda
Modesto
Mammoth Lakes
Stanislaus
Mariposa
San Mateo
Santa Clara
San Mateo
San Jose
Santa Clara
Merced
Madera
Madera
Santa Cruz
Santa Cruz
Hollister
Fresno
Monterey
Salinas
San Benito
Fresno

Monterey

Prologue

"That's [the] Reason I Tell It"

THE WAILAKI SPENT THEIR long summers along the Eel River in a remote village tucked under the dark sandstone peaks of the Coastal Range in Northern California. They called themselves and their village "Kenesti," a oneness of person and place.[1] There the Wailaki and Lassik people had lived in the shade of the alder forest for thousands of years.[2] Few had ever seen white people.

For three years, the U.S. military had ridden along the coast and across the foothills of the Sierra Nevada Mountains, slaughtering Indians and torching villages. Now the troops had reached the remote inland valleys between the coast and the Sierras and had built small forts near the banks of the Eel, Klamath, and Russian rivers.

In the autumn of 1861, three miles away at Fort Seward, hundreds of federal troops were departing to join the Union Army in the blood-drenched Civil War and, ultimately, the fight against plantation slavery. They would leave it to the soldiers who remained to complete the massacres of the Indigenous California tribes who lived inland, capture the refugees, and sell them in a "slave-raiding boom."[3] Enthusiastic vigilantes and brigades of the California Volunteers were on the way to the raw outpost at Fort Seward, eager to clear the land for white settlers and capture and sell the women and children as unpaid workers for California's new ranchers and homesteaders.

On October 24, 1861, thirty soldiers and volunteers rode out from Fort Seward through the narrow canyon on the sandy banks of the Eel to

Kenesti. They were one small battalion in what came to be known as the "California Genocide," a decade of kidnap and slaughter that had begun when California joined the United States in 1850.

On that autumn day, T'tc~tsa, a ten-year-old Wailaki girl, her little sister, Gotibintci, and their mother, Yeltas, watched the white soldiers charge through her fishing village; by sunset, the military had slaughtered over one hundred men. T'tc~tsa saw the soldiers kill her father and her brother. She saw the militia set fire to the Wailaki encampment, abandon the charred village, and march their captives three miles back to Fort Seward.[4]

A few soldiers split off to chase the women and children who were frantically trying to escape.[5] Forced to abandon the bodies of her husband and son, Yeltas fled with her daughters. When they reached the woods, Yeltas hid the girls inside a hollow redwood tree. She sat watch. For two days the hushed trio saw the soldiers ride by, searching for runaways. Under California's 1850 Act for the Government and Protection of Indians, Yeltas, T'tc~tsa, and Gotibintci were now "vagrants," legally available in the new state for capture, forced indenture, or sale.[6]

The three fugitives managed to stay just ahead of the soldiers. They crossed familiar sand bars and waded through riffles in the Eel River. They caught crayfish with their hands and dodged deadly rattlesnakes sunning themselves on warm rocks along riverbanks. They foraged for berries and fallen acorns and edible bulbs. One day, to get their bearings, Yeltas, T'tc~tsa, and Gotibintci dared to leave the dark redwood forest behind and climb snowy Lassik Peak in the Coastal Range. Here they came upon other Indian refugees also in flight from the military.

California had just entered the United States with a state constitution that promised never to "tolerate" slavery. But within months the new legislature legalized the profitable capture, indenture, and bondage of California's Indigenous people.[7] In 1861 George Hanson, then superintendent of Indian Affairs for Northern California, untangled the seeming paradox of murdering thousands of the only available labor pool, reporting: "Kidnappers follow at the heels of the soldiers to *seize* the children when their parents are murdered and sell them to the best advantage."[8]

The massacre at Kenesti (renamed Alderpoint) added more widows and orphans to the thousands of California Natives available for sale from a decade of occupation and slaughter. The Modoc War on the searing lava beds in Northeastern California and southern Oregon drove the Modoc toward the Klamath Reservation, where Modoc women would be available for kidnap and sale. The powerful Modoc Chief Kientpoos ("Captain

Jack") was hanged and his head was removed and shipped to the Army Medical Museum in Washington, DC.[9]

Each week, from 1857 to about 1863, soldiers entered the inland valleys and hunted and killed fifty or sixty California Indians at a time, and then marched the survivors to a fort or reservation. There, under the eye of the U.S. military, slave traders or brokers, here called "traffickers" or "baby hunters," collected women and children and loaded them into wagons. They sold the refugees across the state, deliberately far from their families and tribes. In this fraught decade, slave brokers bought twenty thousand "vagrant" Indians at the reservations or removed them from local jails; three thousand were displaced children. Ranchers or Indian agents bought the children to plow settlers' fields, dig holes for fence posts, and serve as wetnurses and nannies to white babies.[10]

For a few months Yeltas, T'tc~tsa, and Gotibintci survived in the mountains until the soldiers found their camp and marched them down to Fort Seward. One day, a trafficker whom the Wailaki children called the "Bald Man" was traveling up and down Northern California taking "vagrants" from the Indian reservations and military forts. Mostly he wanted young girls. He loaded the children into a wagon, hid some under blankets, and tied others onto pack mules. He traveled over one hundred miles, delivering his human cargo to ranchers and homesteaders in Humboldt and Mendocino counties, where they would legally serve as field hands and nannies until they were twenty-five years old. Locked in domestic indentures, the girls often became sexual slaves. In 1861 the going rate for a young girl was between $45 and $300 (about $1,200 to $9,400 today).[11]

One day the "Bald Man" came for T'tc~tsa. He tied her to his saddle and rode with her into the Siskiyou Mountains, where he sold the ten-year-old girl to a hog farmer. Although the farmer was recently married, he wanted T'tc~tsa to "stay as his woman." After a week of flogging and abuse, T'tc~tsa made her escape. She took a matchbox, a loaf of bread, and some meat from the cabin. Then she opened the barn door and let the horses loose, so the farmer could not chase her. On the run again, she encountered other child fugitives. But she trekked on alone for eighty miles, following ancient Indian trails etched into mountain meadows, until at last she made her way back to her mother, still a captive at the fort.[12]

The hog farmer found T'tc~tsa at Fort Seward, forced her into his wagon, and drove her back to his ranch. For a time, he kept her.[13] T'tc~tsa's freedom had been only an interlude between captivities. But each time she was sold and delivered, she found a way to bolt and find her mother still

A Native American wetnurse breastfeeds a white infant.
Studio photograph, Sacramento.
(Courtesy of the Beinecke Rare Book and Manuscript Library,
Yale University Library, New Haven.)

trapped by the military that shuttled her between Fort Seward and Fort Baker. On one return, T'tc~tsa followed the stench of the scorched corpses of the men from her tribe who had been seized by the soldiers and then burned on a vast funeral pyre at the military fort.[14]

When she was about fourteen, T'tc~tsa was "taken" by Abraham Rogers to his homestead in the Shasta Mountains. He changed her name to Lucy and, for twenty years, held her as his "wife." With Rogers, she bore three children, all of whom died, and he left her for a white woman; soon another farmer seized her and kept her chained up. She said she had many "dead babies" (miscarriages).[15] Sometime around 1907 she escaped and moved back to the banks of the Eel River, about fifty miles from her childhood village.

Finally free, in her late forties, T'tc~tsa moved to Hayfork, a Wintu village in the foothills of the Trinity Mountains, where she cared for two elderly cousins, Kai'ital and Ouneil, who told her Lassik legends of loss and return—how Panther and Crow survived deadly rains and lived to repopulate the world, and how Grandfather convinced the sun to return light to a darkened world. She learned how Coyote rescued stolen children who were hidden in a tree, and how he saved the sun by burying it in a deep hole in the ground. She heard how Frog found lost people by following the sounds of their songs.

In 1910 T'tc~tsa, then age fifty, met and married Sam Young, of Wintu, Lassik, and white descent, and the couple brought T'tc~tsa's mother, Yeltas, to live with them in the mountains. However, she never reunited with her sister. After a white man took "Li'l sister" away, said T'tc~tsa, "I never see her no more. If I saw her, maybe I wouldn't know her. Mother lost her at Fort Seward."[16]

In the 1930s anthropologists from the University of California, Berkeley, were collecting pottery shards, baskets, human bones, and stories of the inland tribes. They approached T'tc~tsa, who agreed to teach them Wailaki and Lassik words and describe their food customs and burial rituals; she refused to answer questions about her tribe's sexual practices.[17]

T'tc~tsa wanted to tell the "whole story" of her bondage and her freedom herself, rather than just respond to anthropologists' requests for data "which does not contain any personality."[18] In 1939, at about age ninety and nearly blind, she traveled from her farm on the Round Valley Reservation to tell her history to her friend Edith Van Allen Murphey, a public health nurse and botanist whom she called "Seed Seeker."[19] Murphey transcribed T'tc~tsa's story as she told it in creolized English, focusing on her years of captivity.[20]

T'tc~tsa catches the tense memories of a fugitive child caught between Native American ways and white captivity. The ninety-year-old woman's telling of the survival skills of her tribe and her own endurance is immediate and insistent, unfiltered, and filled with gaps. She recognizes the bark of hound dogs brought west to hunt fugitives from slavery. She eats familiar seeds in the grasses and uproots nourishing blue camas bulbs in the meadows. She licks water from the underside of ferns. She always carries a hot coal to start her next fire and she burns brush to release and roast grasshoppers. California Natives were walking people. T'tc~tsa coolly describes trekking thirty miles a day as a young girl.

She explains she survived by using white ways—she gathered handfuls of wheat from an abandoned field and pounded the chaff into flour to bake bread in an old pan she found in the woods. Her story draws an ecological timeline of the impact of white settlement. She recalls how one afternoon, in flight from the farmer, she watched a grizzly bear devour a hog it had seized from a settler's farm. By the time of her telling in the early 1930s, decades had passed and settlers had killed off the California grizzly.

Because T'tc~tsa's narrative is oral, we become another generation who learns California history by listening to Native American elders tell of a people and a land. Despite distortions of transcription, her clipped voice and clear memories preserve her urgency. She comes upon a half-sister in a remote cabin and watches the diseased girl die; she tells how the family cremates the body and traditionally burns down the house. She describes how Yeltas knows where to hide her daughters and, later, keeps her runaway child alive. It is a creation story of California.[21]

T'tc~tsa tells us what we cannot otherwise know.[22] Her telling offsets a better-known story of Indian extinction. Like African American runaway and orator Frederick Douglass, she believes that bondage has given her the responsibility to speak strongly and truly.[23] By telling us of her fears and defiant escapes in her own words, T'tc~tsa prevents her history from becoming a spectacle that we see from a safe distance.[24]

T'tc~tsa is a witness. The Lassik and Wailaki people called her a "seer." Her tale traveled with me as I researched this history. Like her grandfather, she is a California historian who speaks backward and forward in time. She begins with people gathering to listen to her grandfather tell of his dream of the time "before white people came." Then he foresees his people carrying white people's baskets. Weaving their voices together she recalls him telling her, "Those White Rabbit (he meant white people) got lotsa everything." Her grandfather insists, "I not crazy. You young people gonta see this." Then he predicts what is to come.[25]

T'tc~tsa (Lucy Young), Zenia, California, July 1, 1922.
C. Hart Merriam Collection of Native American Photographs,
BANC PIC 1978.008—PIC A/1j/P1 no.1, v.3, Bancroft Library,
University of California, Berkeley.

T'tc~tsa's horrors of slavery and escape, confinement and rape, were never unspeakable. "If you could only know the truth of [how] the Indian has been treated since the first white man came into his part of the country it would make an ordinary man shake and shudder. I would like to tell you the whole story. I am afraid it would not be allowed to be put in print."[26]

"White Rabbit Got Lotsa Everything"

by T'tc~tsa

My grandpa, before white people came, had a dream. He was so old he was all doubled up. Knees to chin and eyes like indigo. His grown son carried him in a great basket on his back. My grandpa said: "White Rabbit"—he meant white people—"gonta devour our grass, our seed, our living. We won't have nothing more in this world."

The first soldiers I ever saw was when my li'l sister was 'bout three feet high. They took us to Fort Baker down Van Duzen River.

Mother ran away. I ran off, too. Many times. In August, the soldiers gathered Indians to take us to Hoopa Reservation. Mother ran away when we hit the redwoods. She hid us in a hollow log.

For two days we lay in a hollow log. I heard a soldier. I go li'l ways, listen. I go li'l further, listen. Way down in a gulch, we found lots of hazelnuts and we ate. Then we traveled on.

We saw a horse track. We hid again. Somebody whistled. We dropped into the ferns and saw a soldier's hat go by. Mother began to get sick. I packed water for poor mother. Poor little sister was tired, can't hardly walk. I pack her by hand. Got pretty close to our own grass country. We made a little hole and lay down to sleep. Mother never slept. I never slept. Li'l sister slept.

I am starving for water. We feel too hungry. I want to go back on road and let the soldiers catch us. But then we found many sunflowers and ate dry seeds. We went down to the creek and caught crawfish. We stayed one night. That's all. We keep moving up hill.

"Come, children. We make it tonight." "I 'fraid I step on snake," I say. Mother got deerskin, made us high moccasin, up to knee, but no moccasin for mother; hide ain't big enough.

We stay on South Fork Mountain 'bout month, eat hazelnuts, camas bulbs, too. Then came the rain. We built a bark house. We were happy there. Our cousins came there, them that ran off from military, dressed in soldiers' clothes: "We are sick, nothing to eat but grasshoppers." Lots of Indians were dying on the road, starving.

Soon the white people find us. They take us all to Fort Seward. But only Indian women were there. All the Indian men killed.

One white man came and he take me up South Fork Mountain. His woman had a li'l baby. He wanted me to stay as his woman. He herded hogs to take to Weaverville. His Indian woman whipped me all the time. She didn't talk my language.

'Bout a week was all I stayed. It began to rain pretty hard. The man told me go get water. I went down to the river. The water was muddy. He threw out the water and began to whip me. Told me again, "go get water."

I went back down to the river; the hill was pretty steep. I threw the bucket in river and I ran off. I had on soldier's shoes, took them off and tied them around my neck. The water was knee deep. I just had a thin dress. I can run good and came up a big high bank.

I saw a big fire and lots of downed timber and tree tops. Same time, there was an awfully funny smell. Everybody was crying. Mother told me: "All our men are killed now." White men from there and others from Round Valley killed our old uncle, Chief Lassik, and all our men. They stood about forty Indians in a row with rope around their necks. "What this for?" Chief Lassik asked. White men say, "To hang you, dirty dogs." Lassik said, "Hanging, that's dog's death. We've done nothing to be hung for. If we must die, shoot us." So they shoot. All our men. Then they build a fire with the wood that Indian men had been cutting for days. They never knew they were making their own funeral fire. All them bodies burned. That was the funny smell before I get to our house.

That white man, that same evening, got me, and took me to his house. I rode behind him. He had a cowhide rope. A short one. He stayed all night, next morning he goes back Fort Seward. An Indian boy he tells me: "Tomorrow, 'nother white man come, gonta take you off, way down."

So it did happen. He took me, this white man did. He took me down low [south]. I rode a packsaddle. I had a big blanket hiding me. We ride up to the gate. White man takes me off. I can't walk. Ride all day. Take li'l boy off too.

I half cry all the time for my mother. Next morning another man was there, washing his face. He came in, counted my fingers: "One, two, three, four, days you are going down close to ocean." Two Indian women come in. Talk quick to me: "Poor my li'l sister, where you come from?" "I come from the north. That bald-headed man bring me." "That's way all Indian children come here," they say. "He bring them all."

After a while, the bald-headed man left to gamble. I think: the only show is for me to run off now. I ran into the house. A match box was on the shelf. I put it in my pocket. In the kitchen, I take a loaf of bread. I take boiling meat. I take a big blanket from my bed. I went out so quick, I never shut the door. Then I went out to the barn, opened the door, let all his horses out.

All day I travel on edge of valley. I forgot that I've got to swim the Eel River. I'm 'fraid then. Stop and listen, every little while. Pretty soon I found the footbridge. Just getting dark. Good. Star coming up. I cross in water knee-deep. Owl commence to holler, coming daylight. I pack shoes on one shoulder, blanket on other shoulder, pack grub in hand. Lots of snow by that time on Bell Springs Mountain. There I put on shoes and went over the big mountain. I saw the white man hunt for me on a white horse. I traveled all night. I find a big log, dry underneath. I slept right there, all day.

Then I am home, not far from Alder Point. Three days I stay there, afraid go down to Fort Seward. Think 'bout mother all time. Two nights I stay alone, then I go to Fort Seward.

Lots of women there. Men all killed. I drink water out of a basket setting there. After a while I see woman coming. "Who's you," she says. "That you, my daughter?" I say: "Yes." I told her. "Don't fetch grub out, they might follow you, find me."

My uncle found me. He say: "Poor li'l thing, hunted, starving. 'Bout midnight I will put you 'cross river in boat." He say two li'l girls been taken away from 'nother woman. Cry all time. Midnight, I watch the stars for the time.

My uncle makes no tracks; he walks in leaves and river. Had a big boat. Put my aunt and me 'cross river. If mother let li'l sister go, white men would kill mother. We travel all night, sleep all day.

I see old man on look-out. He went into big bark house. I look in door, big fire in middle of house. Young girl lay there, sick, my half-sister. That night she died. Snowing, raining hard. They dig a hole right by house, put her body in. Tore all house down, set it afire. Midnight, snow whirl, wind howl.

White man name Rogers came after this. Rogers took me that summer. Marry me by and by when I get old enough. 'Bout size ten year girl, I guess, when I first see soldier. I stay there at Hayfork long time. My mother come there too. She died after a while.

Li'l sister, white man took her away. I never see her no more. If I saw her, maybe I wouldn't know her. Mother lost her at Fort Seward.

Father and brother got killed in soldier war, before the soldiers captured us. Three days fight. Three days running. Just blood, blood, blood.

A young woman had been stolen by white people, come back. Shot through liver. Her front skin hangs down like apron. She tied it up with cotton dress. Never die, neither. Only two man of all our tribe left after that battle.

White people want our land, want to destroy us. Break and burn all our baskets, break our pounding rock. Destroy our ropes. No snares, no deerskin, flint knife, nothing. Some old lady wears a moss blanket she peeled off of a rock.

All long, long ago. My white man die. My children all die but one. Oldest girl, she married, went way off. Died a few years ago. Left a little girl. All I got left. Flu take rest of them. About twenty-five years ago I marry Sam by preacher. Sam, he's good man. Hay-fork Indian. We get old age pension, buy li'l place here in Round Valley, keep our horses, keep cow, keep chickens, dogs, cats too. We live good.

I hear people tell 'bout what Indian do early days to white man. Nobody ever tell it what white man do to Indian. That's [the] reason I tell it. That's history. That's truth. I seen it myself.[27]

Introduction

In the summer of 2013, I read in the local Eureka *Times-Standard* that a fifteen-year-old girl had escaped from a nearby marijuana farm. She was a runaway, drifting in Hollywood when a man lured her into his car with the promise of a place to stay. He drove her the length of the state to his home in Northern California, where he chained the girl in a large metal toolbox; since that April, he had let her out to sexually serve the workers or tend the lucrative plants. The captor had drilled two holes in the box, one so he could zap her with a cattle prod, the other so he could hose her down. On a rare day trip to Sacramento, the teenage girl saw a telephone and, in an unattended moment, dialed 9-1-1. She was free. The captive child had endured a brutal year at the crossroads of labor trafficking and sex trafficking.[1]

How could I not have noticed that this was happening in a state that I thought I knew so well?

I spend months of each year in nearby Humboldt County, where the redwoods meet the Pacific Coast, where crab boats spark the winter sky and egrets guard the fern prairies. It is here that I hike and here that I write. I researched and wrote much of this book from a cabin at the edge of Big Lagoon. This is Yurok land. About 170 years ago, Yurok clans lived along the sandy banks of the lagoon that they call "Oketo," "There Where It Is Calm." A meadow at the edge of the lagoon is a sacred ceremonial site the Yurok call "O-pyuweg," "There Where We Dance."

It was in Humboldt, over a decade ago, that I was shown a photograph, likely taken in the late 1870s, of a Chinese girl displayed in a caged brothel in San Francisco. What had happened to the Thirteenth Amendment? Hadn't it abolished slavery at the end of the Civil War?: "Neither slavery nor involuntary servitude, except as a punishment for crime whereof the party shall have been duly convicted, shall exist within the United States, or any place subject to their jurisdiction."

These questions took me to the origins of the state itself. The story of California is a history of 250 years of uninterrupted human bondage. California thrived because it welcomed, honed, and legalized numerous ways for humans to own humans. Its braided history unsettles the mythology that slavery ended; its history disrupts the color of slavery in the United States.

"Slavery," observed Frederick Douglass, is a "hydra-headed monster." The mythical water snake has many heads; as soon as one head is cut off, two others grow in its place.[2] Throughout the history of California, the hydra has gorged on numerous systems of both illegal and legal slavery. It has slithered across a bountiful landscape. The hydra is insatiable—it has grown many heads. Slavery secured the conquest of California; it settled the land and fostered its wealth. Here brutal regimes of human bondage have appeared, disappeared, and reappeared. Slavery in California is polymorphous. Here an array of regimes of slavery built a state that today represents the fifth-largest economy in the world.[3] Here slavery was signed in race.

Under four empires—Spain, Russia, Mexico, and finally the United States—770 miles of land along the Pacific Coast grew as a slave state. Starting in 1769, four empires found an unclaimed utopia—*terra nullius*, "nobody's land." California was rich in fertile soil and long days of sunshine, a destination awaiting occupation and settlement of its fertile soil, the plunder of its ore and ocean. But who would work this plentiful land?

Sea otters nested in cold kelp beds along the shore. Ancient forests were dense with redwood, its lumber splitting easily into long, rose-hued planks. Nearly two centuries ago, flecks of gold sat in the riverbeds of the Sierra Nevada Mountains. Wheat flourished. Now peach and cherry orchards grow in the hot inland valley. Grapevines thrive in the moist coastal hills. Tall marijuana plants flourish in the fields and federal forests, hidden behind spruce and redwood trees. The hydra mutated and returned so that generations of settlers and investors might enjoy the fruits of the land.

A popular 1857 map of slavery in the United States (see page 18) is wrong. Once we recognize the origins and growth of California as a slave state, the partition of U.S. slavery into storylines of a free North and plantation South recedes. The South did not have a monopoly on U.S. slavery;

Henry D. Rogers and A. K. Johnson, *General Map of the United States
Showing the Area and Extent of the Free and Slave-Holding States,* 1857.
This popular map of slavery in the United States, drawn four years
before the Civil War, shows California as a "free state."
Library of Congress, Washington, DC.

the North did not impede its spread. The history of slavery in California
sits right beneath the surface of what we thought we knew. Today, the
national Black Lives Matter protests in California have exposed how slavery metastasized in the West. This history presses us to listen to the voices
of those who were owned, transported, silenced. Voices that many have
not wanted to hear. In writing this book, I have turned to the voices of the
enslaved. The voices of the ancestors.

Birth of a State

California was named for the fictional Black virgin Queen Calafia (or Califia), who ruled over a paradise of Black women in the sixteenth-century

Spanish novel *Las Sergas de Esplandián* (The Adventures of Esplandián). Popular at the time of Spain's first explorations of North America, it tells of a distant island protected by steep rocks and sharp ravines. Any man who managed to penetrate the natural barriers was fed to Queen Califia's pet, a fantastical "griffin," part eagle and part lion.[4]

Spain, Russia, Mexico, and the United States would each learn, in turn, that the reverie of California was flawed. In reality, it had no easy treasure, available women, or willing laborers. A land without people to work it was worthless; a land without children was barren. Before each empire could profit from California's natural bounty, it imported, transported, or captured a labor force to till its fertile meadows, slaughter its marine mammals, and mine its golden ore. Each empire imposed a distinct system of human bondage for its role in a global economy. Like the fault lines and cracks in the geologic plates of the state itself, slavery created California. As in the silver mines of Mexico, the sugar plantations in Cuba, and the guano mountains in Peru, this last colony in the Americas depended on unfree labor.

This is an American story. Our vocabulary is rich in words for human beings who are trapped in human bondage in distinct ways: chattel, debt peons, unwilling prostitutes, indentured field hands, convict laborers, and victims of human trafficking. Each empire imported its own systems to possess diverse human beings—California Native Americans, Alaska Natives, African Americans, Chinese girls, and convicts. Slavery, writes historian Walter Johnson, is the system of "world-making violence" that involves "kidnapping, dispossession, and labor extraction"—usually for economic, political, and imperial purposes. Slavery is a system that turns humans into "profits, fancies, sensations, and possessions." California was populated by what Andrés Reséndez calls "the other slaves" who were sold, distributed, transported, and used to create profitable and disposable workforces. This history brings together what Kevin Bales labels the "old slavery" based on legal ownership of human beings and the "new slavery" in which brutal mechanisms of control—debt, threats of violence, and human trafficking—replaced formal ownership. Reséndez points out that the "new slavery" did not replace the "old slavery" but has been here all along. Marisa Fuentes exposes how archives duplicate and disrupt the silences, meanings, perceptions, and, hence, the political structures of enslaved women; she shows how history has redefined the brutality of the labor and involuntary sexual work of enslaved women and she exposes distinct forms of their flights and insurrections.[5]

Legal and extralegal slavery thrived side by side in California, where

brutal forces of involuntary servitude and human trafficking have endured
for centuries; these forces have often been substitutes for state-sanctioned
slavery. What Frederick Douglass called the "evil hydra," Reséndez calls
"the other slavery"—the many forms of human bondage, particularly of
Native Americans, that have endured, even when banned by law.[6] The
hydra—bold and adaptive—has slithered across the state and across centuries, gorging itself on new groups of vulnerable people, but the enslaved
have always resisted entrapment and sale.

By having a slave population that was forced to reproduce itself, North
America was unique in the world of global slavery. In some iterations the enslaved in California endured forms of the "old slavery" or "chattel slavery"—
the system of enslaving and owning human beings and their offspring, of
keeping men, women, and children as property who could be bought, sold,
trapped, and forced to work without wages. But California also had other
systems of forced, unpaid, or unfree people.

In the United States' first major legal dictionary, from 1839, lexicog-
rapher John Bouvier identified how slavery braids emotional and legal ter-
rors into "civil death." He wrote that not only is a slave "by law deprived
of his liberty for life and becomes the property of another," but he is also
expelled from the safety contract that binds a nation together. Unlike the
"savage," Bouvier said a slave possesses "natural life"; yet without political
rights, he enters a state of "civil death" and, indeed, "is considered dead"—
just like a felon who faces a life sentence.[7] Ironically, this fictional death
brings a person who is both a criminal and a slave back under the civilized
cover of the world of law. Saidiya Hartman notes that the "civilly dead
slave and prisoner are incapacitated legal insiders"; they share one form of
agency—"criminal liability."[8]

Each type of human bondage in California prompted diverse forms
of resistance; each prompted revolts, flights, and organized calls for abolition; each exposed its presence by resisting its evils. Historian Walter
Johnson defines slavery through its "epochal barbarities and quotidian
tortures, its corruptive tyranny and degrading license, its economic and
moral backwardness, its unfreedom." It was in the nineteenth century, he
says, that the term "slavery" became the antithesis of the term "freedom."[9]
California's intractable struggle with slavery, writes historian Stacey Smith,
did not end with its entrance into the Union as a free state as part of the
Compromise of 1850, nor with its constitution that promised that slavery
would never be tolerated.[10] Indeed, its lineage is long.

Throughout the history of Indigenous California, freedom preceded slavery. The Thirteenth Amendment, writes Andrés Reséndez, failed to cover the forced indenture of Native Americans: California was "a major bastion of 'the other slavery' in the 1850s and early 1860s," when Indians who could not prove that they were employed were given to the highest bidder.[11]

Each empire that occupied California created legal shelters for a slave-owner, who, as Frederick Douglass observed, was free to "work him, flog him, hire him out, sell him, and . . . kill him, with perfect impunity."[12] The hydra-headed monster finds countless ways to extract profit from a human body. Chattel slavery—the purchase and sale of human beings—is typically thought of in terms of southern plantations. Yet freedom is more than a practice that involves the right to work for a wage. California had a vast collection of tools of enslavement. Threats and violence and whips, water-boarding and chains subsidized California's great wealth. Rapes and star-vation ensured that the enslaved remained in bondage.

Four empires invaded the Native lands of California and sought to remain. Settler colonialism involves the invasion, removal, and occupation of Indigenous lands and resources. It permanently dispossessed Native peo-ples' homelands and cultures through slaughter, displacement, and disease, and then through building enduring "settlements." In California, it also cohabited with slavery.[13] Unlike plantation slavery, which forcibly grew or reproduced the enslaved workforce, the invaders of California initially sought to remove or destroy the Indigenous population. Settler colonial-ism is not an event, such as the Gold Rush; its impact cannot be canceled or undone. It lives forever.

In a historical paradox, the new state slaughtered its potential work-force. In the first century after the Spanish invasion and the founding of the first Franciscan mission in 1769, a population of 310,000 Native Cali-fornians fell to 18,000. But the invaders still needed an agrarian workforce. The invaders, mostly male, sought sexual partners and domestic workers. In terrifying symmetry, colonialism turned both California's land and people—men, women, and children—into property.[14]

As priests, settlers, and the U.S. military occupied California, they wove race hatred into Church dogma, economic policy, and law. Race scripted Catholic *testimonias;* it deformed court cases and legalized bills of sale.[15] Bigotry mated with biological forces of extinction, such as measles, syphilis, and cholera, that devoured Native Californians at rates far more aggressive than the contagions of more immune and robust invaders and travelers. Through slaughter and diseases of empire, over 90 percent of

California's Native people died, leaving populations of children available for capture and sale.[16]

Slavery is a state of dread.

Empires of Slavery in California

In California, the enslaved rarely stayed where they were born; they often faced forced transport and were scattered. The enslaved in California were kept on the move. Slavery severed the emotional, family, and tribal ties necessary for intimacy, community, and cohesive strength. Catholic priests and Spanish soldiers looped ropes around the necks of thousands of Native Americans and marched them to the Franciscan missions. Russian fur traders hired Boston ship captains and leased their clipper ships to carry captive Alaska Natives to hunt and slaughter otters along the Pacific Coast, never to return home. To provide a labor force for the vast lands bestowed by the new Mexican regime, wealthy ranchers such as José Maria Amador, Salvador Vallejo, and John Sutter hired private armies to capture nearby Indians, subdued them to ready their own lands for raising cattle, and leased or sold them to neighbors eager for unpaid workers.[17] Plantation owners crossed the plains for the Gold Rush, bringing enslaved African Americans who walked beside the wagon train. Brokers kidnapped Chinese girls in Guangdong (Canton) for prostitution, shipped them in padded cargo crates seven thousand miles across the Pacific Ocean and sold them from the docks of San Francisco. Presently, modern human traffickers transport migrants across the border in the trunks of cars, the holds of ships, or, more boldly, in airplanes.

Slavery usurps choice. The enslaved cannot select where to work or when to quit. The men, women, and children in this history did not choose to plow the fields of early Los Angeles with their feet bound into wooden shackles. They could not select a mate nor decide how to parent their children. They did not choose to wet-nurse the babies of white women at new homesteads and ranches in Northern California.

Slavery severs the unfree from the products of their labor—otter pelts or wheat—and the products of their bodies—their children or even their breast milk. Like the bondsmen that Douglass observed on a southern plantation, "To eat the fruit of his own toil, to clothe his person with the work of his own hands, is considered stealing. He toils that another may reap the fruit; he is industrious that another may live in idleness."[18] The enslaved may own nothing.

To Families.

FOR SALE—A valuable NEGRO
GIRL, aged eighteen, bound by indentures for two years. Said girl is of an amiable disposition, a good washer, ironer and
cook. For particulars inquire at the *Van-
dorn Hotel*, of [apl-tf] J. H. HARPER.

This 1850 advertisement for the sale of a "valuable" and
"amiable" Negro girl for domestic service in Sacramento
was posted just one year after California adopted a constitution promising the state would never "tolerate" slavery.
In the *Sacramento Transcript*, April 1, 1850.
Center for Bibliographical Studies and Research,
University of California, Riverside.

The Body Politic

The West Coast perimeter of American slavery sat three thousand miles
from southern slave hunters and paddy rollers. In 1850 California adopted
a constitution that declared that the state would not "tolerate" slavery, but
"tolerate" was not a legal standard. California was a unique state—far from
law, far from East Coast institutions. In this bachelor society in the West,
white privateers, miners, soldiers, and landless veterans were a long way
from a population of white women; they were not accountable to families
or churches or inhibited by their traditional mores. The 1850 and the
revised 1860 Act for the Government and Protection of Indians defined
vagrancy and indenture in ways that permitted the capture and sale of
Indigenous women and children.

During the 1850s, white brokers, or slave traders, took California Native girls from military forts and Indian reservations and sold them in
legal indentures to new households, soldiers, ranchers, and farmers who
eagerly crossed racial lines for domestic help and sex workers.[19] Rancher
John Sutter sold Pomo people to new settlers; "baby-stealers" delivered
Wailaki and Yurok children across Mendocino County. The "Indian Acts"
left these slave dealers free to carry on the trade in human beings.

From the Spanish Invasion on, Indigenous women were vulnerable to
theft and sale—they were stolen people. During the Gold Rush, women
were kidnapped, bought, and shipped from port towns of China to San

Francisco and auctioned to madams and pimps or sold into brothels. Miners, ranchers, and prison wardens bought or forced Indian, Chinese, and African American women to wash muddy clothes and cook food that would not come out of a tin. A series of business models for the trade in women subsidized California's great wealth.

From the moment of statehood in 1850, California extracted enslaved laborers from its prisons and the hydra disgorged another form of slavery into the state's economy. In 1851 the state gave $100,000 to a profiteer to convert abandoned ships into jails and build a state penitentiary. Since then, California convicts have worked in factories built inside prison walls. Its prison system has offered up inmates to dig sewage systems, operate dangerous looms, and fight raging wildfires. For nearly two hundred years, prison guards have herded convicts into mills and onto roads, and tortured them on behalf of private corporations—even for the infraction of talking as they worked. Prison guards still sell female convicts to inmates for sex. A sex trade thrives inside the carceral state.

California let slavery thrive because the U.S. Constitution said it could. The Constitution, passed in 1789, allowed U.S. slaveholders to enjoy the global trade in Africans until 1808. The Bill of Rights then allowed each state to hold on to slavery as long it wished; the Ninth Amendment promised that "the enumeration in the Constitution, of certain rights, shall not be construed to deny or disparage others retained by the people." Slave ownership was one of those certain rights.[20] The Tenth Amendment was the ticket to states' rights and assured slaveholding states that "the powers not delegated to the United States by the Constitution, nor prohibited by it to the States, are reserved to the States respectively, or to the people."[21]

Since Congress "could make no law" to bestow or limit the right to own human beings, California was free to improvise. The U.S. Constitution never mentions slavery by name, but the Fifth Amendment guarantees that private property may not be taken "without just compensation"; enslaved people were legal property. Indeed, although the Constitution never included the word "slave" or "slavery," "We the People" separated "free Persons" from "other persons" who were only partially counted for purposes of taxation or Congressional representation.[22] This exclusion from legal identity shaped the public personhood, civil standing, and political access of the enslaved.[23] Although the Thirteenth Amendment finally acknowledged slavery's presence by abolishing it, it did not deliver liberty, equality, or the right to own land, marry, vote, or testify. Without these rights, the

Convicts work at a jute mill inside the walls of
San Quentin Prison, making burlap bags for California
farmers. In "Jobbery in the Products of State Prison,"
San Francisco Call, January 12, 1898.
Center for Bibliographical Studies and Research,
University of California, Riverside.

free, freed, or formerly enslaved African American remained a legal person
but a civil nonentity.[24] Freedom was not a straight path to citizenship.

Slavery endured in California after the Civil War because the state
copied repressive Jim Crow codes from the U.S. South. California made
the unlawful lawful. Unfettered, it gave itself the sovereign right to legalize human bondage and enjoy the revenue from unpaid labor.

Today, California is one of the top three markets for modern human
trafficking.[25] Slavery is a shape-shifting monster that takes cover in gated
communities, conference centers, luxury hotels, casinos, sweatshops, and
marijuana fields.[26] Trafficked girls, lured as nannies or housekeepers, enter
at Los Angeles International Airport dressed as tourists.[27] Smugglers wait
to snag frightened migrants at California's border at Tecate and Tijuana
just as they begin to trek across the Ojai Desert or cross the border in the
wheel bed of a truck. Refugees pay thousands of dollars to "coyotes" to

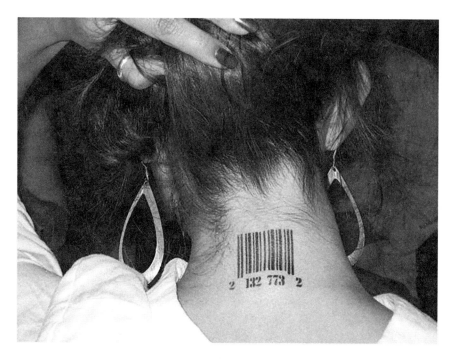

A barcode tattoo has become a global mark of
human ownership, usually on young women.
In Paul Peachey, "Symbolic Tattoos Assert Ownership over 'Assets' That
Can Be Sold for Thousands of Pounds," *Independent*, September 30, 2014.

crawl through a tunnel in northern Mexico and surface in San Diego, only
to discover that they have arrived in the state of lifelong debt peonage.[28]

Most victims of modern sex trafficking work for online escort agencies
or independent pimps. In California, their average age is twelve years old.[29]
Nineteenth-century fantasies of passive Chinese girls have morphed into
twenty-first-century illusions of submissive Thai and Korean women promoted through social media's private pornography empires. Latinas are
marketed as hypersexual and willing. Behind darkened windows garment
workers toil in lofts that are surrounded with razor wire. Often with babies strapped to their backs, unfree women stitch the athletic attire that
reflects the carefree brand of the "golden state."[30] Traffickers snare women
and girls at immigration detention centers and snag them from truck stops
and foster homes for the sex trade, domestic work, and field labor.[31]

Slavery in California is mundane.

Escapes, Uprisings, and Revolts

Resilient and resistant voices beckon us from the litany of horror stories. They call out from explorers' logs, early wax recordings of Alutiiq ancestors, private letters, ship manifests, immigration documents, court cases, sheet music, petitions, ads offering rewards for the return of enslaved runaways, and the minutes of three Colored Conventions—the first Civil Rights movement in California.

The forgotten history of slave revolts in California began in 1769 when the Kumeyaay swooped in and freed their brethren from the first Franciscan mission, founded in San Diego. Revolts at the missions along the central Pacific Coast coalesced into a fierce civil war against the Spanish regime. "Mission Indians" burned dormitories and barracks to the ground. In the nineteenth century, indentured Indians attacked their owners and fled, Chinese prostitutes escaped from locked brothels, and convict laborers went on strike.

The records of slave revolts in California unsettle a history of abolition that has often ignored these acts of resistance in the West. When the new state preserved slavery through a series of codes, enslaved Blacks joined free Blacks to build a West Coast Underground Railroad. The victims of all the regimes of slavery fought for their freedom, yet were always fearful that their families, still in bondage, would be in danger. Slave revolts mark each scourge of human bondage in California and defy images of helplessness that historically have marked the enslaved as capable of rage but not resistance; this story of resilience and revolt challenges white narratives of the "vanishing tribes" and of submissive Asians.[32] For thousands of enslaved, survival itself is a form of resistance.

Unfree people defied the silences of bondage and found ways to tell their own histories. Slaveholders depicted Alaska Natives, California Natives, African Americans, Chinese women, and convicts as debased, savage, exotic—only fractionally legal humans. But when we listen to the enslaved, we hear a different version of California history. Confessions transcribed at the Catholic missions and diaries written from prison cells reveal life stories of bondage and defiance.[33] A faded photograph of the cemetery behind Fort Ross shows a Dena'ina burial pole, long ago pounded into the graves to mark the way for Yega, the human spirit, to travel to the afterworld. The pole stood near Russian Orthodox crosses that mark the scattered gravesites of Alaska Natives captured to kill otters, of men and women who died far from home.[34]

The hydra lay coiled in the sun, ready to attack. Slavery in California was visible and familiar. White gold miners saw enslaved Blacks hauling rocks, building sluices, and panning for gold, wading waist-deep in the icy waters of the Feather River. By day, San Francisco residents saw chain gangs digging sewage systems. At night, they heard the wailing of convicts chained to the bunks in the fetid hull of the prison brig *Euphemia* that was docked next to a ship that had been converted into a saloon. Nearby, in Chinatown, teenage girls gazed blankly through caged doors in a thriving netherworld of forced sex. Slavery was upheld in the courts. It was affirmed in California's laws, even its own Fugitive Slave Act of 1852. It is visible today at truck stops, foster homes, and on our computer screens.

African American fugitive slave William Wells Brown declared in 1847 that "slavery never has been represented; slavery never can be represented."[35] Yet this is exactly what T'tc~tsa managed to do. The history of slavery in California dwells in monks' ledgers and transcripts of California Native dream visions. It is represented in graves in the barren and abandoned cemeteries behind the Indian boarding schools. It lives in the testimonies of African American runaways Archy Lee and Charles Perkins. Free Blacks who came West to escape the national Fugitive Slave Act expose its presence and the bold flights of runaways in the *Pacific Appeal*, the *Elevator*, and the *Mirror of the Times*, California's earliest Black newspapers.[36] Today, pimps force victims of sex trafficking to advertise themselves on Craigslist and Pornhub; they are compelled to represent their own bondage.

I was born in Los Angeles and went to Hamilton High School on Robertson Boulevard, a sprawling public high school with several thousand Latino, Chinese, Japanese, African American, and white students. We were "tracked," untested but segregated by "ability"—and by race. At age seventeen I entered the University of California at Berkeley. There I studied with generous and gifted scholars in American History and American Literature. I read histories of plantation slavery and the "peculiar institution" with Kenneth Stampp and the autobiographies of Frederick Douglass with Henry Nash Smith.

During the academic year 1964–65, I went on my first civil rights demonstration in Oakland's Jack London Square; the Black Panthers were demanding that the fish restaurants at the pier hire African American waiters. It was nighttime, dark by San Francisco Bay; the American Nazi Party flanked one side of the marchers, and the "Blue Meanies" (like the enemies of the Beatles' Yellow Submarine), or deputies of the Alameda County Sheriff's Department, flanked the other. The restaurants and the

Oakland Tribune were all owned by the powerful former senator Bill Knowland. The next week, card tables sprang up on the campus with flyers announcing the next demonstration. Knowland and the University of California's Board of Trustees insisted that the tables be removed—an order that launched the historic Free Speech movement and years of campus "teach-ins." Even so, I was blind to the origin story—the fact that segregation throughout California and in the progressive Bay Area is a durable legacy of the state's history of slavery.

Perhaps this book took seed on that frightening night in Oakland. At some point in those transforming undergraduate years, I earned my Red Cross Life Saving Certificate. I swam hundreds of laps each week at the magnificent Phoebe Hearst pool on the Berkeley campus; only recently did I learn from historian Tony Platt that I was swimming above ten thousand bones of California Natives, collected by University of California anthropologists and stashed for decades beneath that pool. I was unschooled.

As a Californian, I have been altered by this journey through a state that I believed I knew well. For the past seven years, I have traveled up and down California to find these stories, to excavate archives—ads for runaway slaves in San Francisco and photographs of Chinese girls sold from caged brothels. It seems like I never truly lived in this state. Like one who seeks to enter a boarded-up house, I have tried the doorknobs of long-locked rooms and have worked to open windows that are often still nailed shut. History has not yet fully told what happened inside this beautiful house of horrors.

Slavery in California is at odds with The Mamas and the Papas' mellow "California Dreamin'," an anthem of my early adult years. My doctoral dissertation and my early writings were on utopian history and fiction. I explored the politics of hope and read inspiring tales of a future perfect. I pondered whether humans have an innate drive toward fairness. I had the deep pleasure of discovering and teaching American women authors—mountain women working in textile mills, enslaved Black women hiding on steamships sailing north, child prostitutes, girls shipped to Indian boarding schools, trick riders, and women living in lesbian utopian communities. In writing about the purges of Chinese Americans that spread across the West in the nineteenth century, the roundups that became the basis of my history, *Driven Out: The Forgotten War against Chinese Americans*, I found a counternarrative of resistance and resilience that shapes this history too. I remain a card-carrying optimist.

We are powerless to intervene in the past. But we can challenge the notion of inevitability and alter the outcome. Settlers and slavers in California created cunning regimes of human bondage. What do these regimes reveal about human nature? What is the urge to dominate another person? Who were these men who wrote the laws that sanctioned slavery? As urgently, I wanted to know: Why did I not know the histories of those who defied the armed invaders and enslavers and rewrote the crushing laws? The ones who challenged racist assumptions that categorize human beings as unworthy of freedom? Where are California's monuments to Toypurina and Archy Lee—the enslaved who confronted cruelty? Forceful opposition arose in every community of the enslaved in California. Under inhuman conditions, from whence appeared the human spirit of hope?

The voices of the enslaved are deeply angry. The enslaved believe that their telling will produce change, that their stories may close what Saidiya Hartman calls the "distance from the human." T'tc~tsa's truth rejects our fears of listening to their harsh histories in what historian John Ernest calls the "soundscape" of slavery.[37]

T'tc~tsa reveals the volatile fault lines that shake California—the deep and frightening cracks that wrench the state. A Wailaki girl's flight to freedom runs to the epicenter of our history and our future. The ghosts of slavery call out for reckoning. But there is no reckoning. Their legacy will never go away. Still, the ghosts of slavery prod us for redress and reparations—justice that repairs. That is what ghosts do.

Freedom is a struggle, not a status. This is a story of how California's distinct multiracial population arose from the ranks of the unfree. The shape of human bondage in California was altered by the defiance of the enslaved who believed, like Frederick Douglass, that slavery could not "kill the elastic spirit of the bondman. That spirit will rise and walk abroad, despite of whips and chains, and extract from the cup of nature, occasional drops of joy and gladness." The "spirit of the bondman stands before God as an accusing angel against his enslaver."[38] The "spirit of the bondman" is the history of slavery in California. The voice of the captive is its own defiance.

Said T'tc~tsa, the Wailaki woman who was kidnapped and sold, who escaped time after time, "Nobody ever tell it what white man do to the Indian. That's [the] reason I tell it. That's history. That's truth. I seen it myself."[39]

CHAPTER ONE

Wikamee

Darkness and Mist at the California Missions

The first people came from Wikamee. It is said that the place
can be seen still, but Wikamee is a place of darkness and mist. It
is to the east and is hard to find because of the darkness. When
tu-cha-pai and yo-ko-mat-is made the world, it was only for
Indians.

—KUMEYAAY MYTH

IN THE EARLY SUMMER of 1769, one hundred Spanish soldiers and a handful of Catholic priests gathered on a beach in San Diego. Four battered
expeditions of Franciscan friars and Spanish soldiers had taken six months
to travel by land and sea from Mexico. Commanded by the pope and the
Spanish, they were to convert the Indigenous people to Catholicism and
occupy California, defending the northern corner of the Spanish empire
for the glory of god.

From behind dunes and boulders in the arid hills, the Kumeyaay
("Those Who Face the Water from the Cliff") tribe had monitored the
land flanking the expedition as it moved north from Baja (Lower) California. They had warned their people near San Diego to expect the strangers.
The Kumeyaay had heard of tall soldiers who dragged Indians along the

31

ground to their church, "tightly, with a rope halter." The warriors in Baja California had fired arrows at the invaders but could not protect their people.[1] The Kumeyaay saw two boats land and watched the passengers struggle to disembark, wade to shore, and haul themselves onto the beach. Many were dying; half of the soldiers were perishing from dysentery and scurvy, diseases to which the Kumeyaay had never been exposed.

Now Kumeyaay (known by the Spanish as "Diegueño") and Quechnajuichom ("Luiseño") watched the Spaniards shoot fire weapons and explode cannonballs to celebrate the arrival of their brethren who had trekked from the south. Friar Juan Crespí wrote that the Spaniards saw Indians "naked, heavily armed, with their large quivers on their backs and bows and arrows in their hands, and all went running along the crests of the hill alongside of us."[2]

The Kumeyaay wondered why, in a land with year-round sun, some of the invaders had encased their bodies in heavy gray tubes. Other invaders had covered their bodies with thick, shiny shells, like beetles. There were no women. Was this a war party?

The Kumeyaay wondered why the visitors did not first seek out their chief to ask permission to camp on land where six hundred generations of their ancestors had lived.[3] What did it mean that the strangers pointed up at them? Were they casting witchcraft their way?[4] Perhaps these men were shamans.

Friar Junípero Serra led the "Sacred Expedition" to build a chain of missions along the coast of Alta (Upper) California, block invasions by British and Russian explorers, and profit from the labor of unpaid Native Americans. California Natives, he hoped, would transform their mesas, now covered in grasses and wild oak, into orchards and vineyards.

Despite a seeping wound on his leg, Friar Serra had hobbled barefoot from his home mission in Loreto, Mexico. A theologian from Majorca, zealous administrator, and fanatical priest, Serra had been determined to walk into Alta California in "holy poverty," with only one loaf of bread and a hunk of cheese. He would seek charity at missions in northern Mexico and sleep under the stars. Yet when he came upon hungry Cochimí and Kumeyaay in flight from those missions, he begged them for their food.

Friar Serra had trekked across seven hundred miles.[5] After four months, covered with fleas and ticks, he reached the town of Velicatá in northern Mexico, the staging area for the land invasion of California. From there, Gaspar de Portolá, military officer and governor of Baja California, would lead a small army, and Serra would lead a small group of priests and thirty

Ramundus á Murillo, *Dragon de Cuera*. Spanish soldiers
(*soldados de cuera*) guarded the Franciscan priests and
captured or chased Indians, dragging them to the missions.
(Courtesy of the Army Art Collection, U.S. Army Center of Military History.)

baptized Indians to serve as guides and translators—credible ambassadors
for god. Together they would fulfill the orders of Spaniard Don José de
Gálvez, the inspector general of New Spain (Mexico), to dispatch a royal
expedition and colonize the neglected ports of San Diego and Monterey.

With his leg painful and swollen, Serra trekked north with his party;
they climbed along steep ravines, crawled over hills covered with yuccas,
cardón cacti, and scrubby cirios trees, and stumbled along winding dry
riverbeds, at times passing abandoned missions. At last, he and Portolá
entered Alta California, with the friars wrapped in heavy, long robes, as well
as with servants for the padres, muleteers, a troop of *mestizo* guards, one
hundred *soldados*—conscripted Spanish soldiers—and an odd battalion of

twenty "leather jackets," Spanish militia known for their impregnable cow-hide armor.[6]

At last, from the beach of San Diego Bay, Serra beheld a bountiful new Eden, with willows and poplar trees, fragrant with Castilian rose bushes, ample water, and fields dotted with wild grapevines. Serra imagined a "harvest of souls that might easily be gathered into the bosom of our Mother the Church. . . . With apostolic zeal and the grace of God . . . at the mere sight of His sons . . . the gentiles will be converted."[7] The pagans in Wikamee, the land of the coastal Kumeyaay, would surely put aside their bows and arrows to greet him.[8] Despite noting the wary assembly on the hilltop, Serra concluded that the Kumeyaay were showing him Indian gestures of welcome.

Spain did not invade California with dreams of the gold or silver that it had found in Mexico and Peru. Instead, Spanish soldiers and Mexican settlers were ordered to form a human border to protect the silver mines in northern Mexico and block the Russians who were advancing from the north.[9] The Franciscans would capture and convert the Indians to Catholicism and force them to till the fields, as they had done in under a century at seventeen missions in Mexico.

In California, a trifecta of the Catholic Church, the Spanish army, and unfree Native American labor would create a rich economic and religious alchemy; the invaders would collect Indian souls and export cowhides.[10] Captive California Natives would grow fruits and grains to feed Spain's soldiers, priests, and thousands of conscripted Indian silver miners working across the Americas at a string of theological plantations of conversion and surveillance, forced labor camps designed to recruit and brutally confine field laborers.[11]

The Kumeyaay saw that the visitors traveled with beasts so large and mighty that they could carry tall men and heavy packs on their backs. Then they watched as the visitors turned these fantastic animals loose to graze. Cattle, horses, and roughly 150 mules, hungry from the overland trek, trampled the Kumeyaay seed fields, devoured the grasses, and fouled the creeks.[12]

The Spaniards were unwelcome. Bands of Kumeyaay shot arrows into the air threatening to block the intruders from coming onto the beaches of San Diego Bay. In reply, the Spanish exploded powerful sticks that could kill from greater distances than any arrow. The Indians had heard of these thundering fire sticks that could rip bloody holes in the flesh that no herb or ceremony could cure.[13]

Over the next days, the Kumeyaay came closer to the strangers, but the visitors gave off bad odors. They did not seem to bathe, nor did they protect their skin from insects or the sun with powdered minerals. The newcomers' bodies were rotting, penetrated by germs and bacteria that would soon wreak disease and death on their people.

After the ships unloaded the last Spanish corpses, the Kumeyaay let the friars know through sign language and translators that they "did not want to become like these men, for they 'feared that they would die immediately. . . . They did not know why they [the Spaniards] had come unless they wanted to take their lands away from them."[14]

Fifteen days after the priests crossed into Alta California, Friar Serra donned vestments embroidered with sparkling gold thread to conduct the first mass. At Cosoy, the Kumeyaay village where the Spanish ships had landed, Serra held up a tall cross and a glittering silver chalice. He was flanked by priests clad in gray robes whose faces were hidden under deep hoods. As Serra swirled the chalice of smoking incense to purify a make-shift altar, the priests rang small bells and then gave them wafers and wine.[15] Perhaps most astonishing to the Kumeyaay, wrote Friar Crespí, was the sight of the priests ritually flogging their own backs with barbed ropes. Yet Serra's golden threads and the soldiers' powerful weapons could not block the Indians' view of the new Spanish burial ground, which already held sixty graves.[16]

Two hundred and nineteen men had left Baja to invade California. Fewer than one hundred survived. Never had these trained soldiers imagined that they were joining a lowly expedition to work as carpenters and masons tasked with building churches and raising cattle.[17] Governor Portolá rode off with the healthy soldiers to locate the Bay of Monterey site for the expedition's central *presidio* (fort) and mother mission. Portolá left behind eight soldiers to help three padres set up a ragged infirmary and morgue on the beach. With these few men, Serra built a few huts, called one a church, and blessed the first mission in California, San Diego de Alcalá.

Mission San Diego de Alcalá: Born of Violence

The Kumeyaay saw the new structures rise up and desecrate their homelands. Twenty Indians fired arrows at the priests and then plundered the Spaniards' tents. In riposte, eight soldiers fatally shot three Native men. Kumeyaay warriors retaliated—the first battle between Native Americans and Spaniards in California. The Spaniards hastily salvaged driftwood and lumber from the ship and threw together a stockade around their camp.

Just five months after that first mass, an abashed Governor Portolá returned, as he and his battalion had failed to find the vast Bay of Monterey. Friar Serra had failed to convert even one *neófia*—neophyte, or "new believer"—at the ragged mission, but in 1770 he went north with Portolá, this time by sea. Standing on the beach of Monterey, Serra and Portolá claimed Alta California as a Spanish possession.[18]

At the time that the Spanish were praying on the beach in San Diego, roughly sixty to seventy thousand California Natives were living along the Pacific Coast in hundreds of villages organized by clan and language. The Kumeyaay lived near the Mexican border; up the coast were the Chumash, Salinan, Costanoan, and Miwok. Like a medieval crusade, Spain's "Sacred Expedition" moved north from San Diego as crusading friars and reluctant soldiers built missions and forts, fifty to one hundred miles apart along an eight-hundred-mile strip of California coast. The chain grew—eight in the first decade—at Carmel, at San Gabriel near the pueblo of Los Angeles, San Francisco, and Capistrano, and ten more by 1798. The missions were about one day apart by horseback, three days on foot. Along El Camino Real, a dirt road that began in San Diego, the Spanish attacked California Natives' spiritual rituals, their languages, their names, and their villages.

A theocracy of agricultural slave labor grew. Franciscans and soldiers recruited about seventy thousand California Indians whose ancestors had lived for between six thousand and twelve thousand years along the coast. By luring or forcing Native Californians into the missions, the Spaniards would dismantle Indian sovereignty. Initially, inquisitive Indians came into missions of their own free will, tempted by new foods, colored beads, and the novel performances of Catholic rituals. The priests' seemingly generous offers of seeds, iron tools, or woven cloth enticed them to work in the fields, rectories, and refectories or to construct barracks, dormitories, and churches.

California Natives did not yet have horses to chase deer, elk, and bear. Instead, they waited with drawn arrows as animals came to their seed fields. At each new mission site, the Spanish let their cattle and horses loose to graze and gorge, stomping and defiling Indians' game habitats and fields. Of great risk to their food chain was the priests' ban on their traditional practice of burning fields in order to regenerate the seeds. The Indians were forced to plant European crops over ancestral fields, becoming innocent collaborators in their own hunger and destruction.

By 1772, in San Diego, Friar Luis Jayme had managed to convert only

Mission guards march Yokut or Ohlone fieldworkers carrying
bundles of reeds at Mission Dolores, San Francisco.

In Louis Choris, *Voyage pittoresque autour du monde, avec des portraits de sauvages d'Amérique,
d'Asie, d'Afrique, et des îles du Grand océan* (Paris: Didot, 1822). (Courtesy of the Beinecke
Rare Book and Manuscript Library, Yale University Library, New Haven.)

a few Ipai or Kumeyaay; starvation was a force of empire. Wrote Jayme:
"We cannot make the natives around here work, and often we cannot teach
them the doctrine because they have to go hunting for food every day. Fifty-
five have been baptized counting both children and adults. . . . It grieves
me sorely to see that for lack of food we shall not be able to teach them.
The Indians are suspicious."[19] Deprived of the miracles of firewood and
meat, and forced to farm rather than hunt, the Kumeyaay were living on
atole, a corn or barley gruel. Until 1779 so little food was harvested at the
missions that the padres had to allow the neophytes to sleep and eat in their
own villages, intensifying the Franciscans' concern about the powerful hold
of Indian ways.

The Spanish deliberately planted the missions near traditional Native
springs and along riverbanks, next to Indian villages and often on sacred
sites. In 1775, for instance, Friar Fermín de Lasuén raised the cross for Mission San Juan Capistrano by San Mateo Creek, where the Acagchemem
people had once declared their independence from the Pubuiem tribe to
the north. During an epidemic in the Santa Clara Valley south of San Francisco, the padres went through the nearby villages performing baptisms on

Tilesius von Tilenau, *Dance of the Indians at Mission in San José, New California*,
1803–7. At Mission San José, ca. 1816–18, Yokut demanded their right to
fish, hunt, gather shellfish, wear regalia, and perform rituals as they had
done before captivity and conversion. They continued to dance and
paint their bodies, a spiritual practice that also warded off insect
bites and acted as sunscreen.
BANC PIC 1963.002:1023—FR, Bancroft Library, University of California, Berkeley.

children who had died, declaring that they were immediately redeemed.[20]
Without translation, it was unlikely that the Indigenous people knew what
was happening to their children. The Franciscan cross debased a hallowed
Native American site and superimposed Spanish authority over essential
events of tribal power and freedom.[21]

A standing military fortified the Catholic compounds with soldiers
from Catalonia and with prisoners conscripted from jails in Baja. Some
were of African descent. Others were born in Latin America. This mixed
militia was to capture California Natives, mete punishments, track fugitives, perform menial labor, build churches, dormitories, and barracks, and
also protect the priests whom they came to despise. Far from home and the

army's command, the soldiers resented the unnaturally spare life. They were casual, if not indifferent, about military order.[22] Instead of enjoying tithes and tariffs, as they had at the mines in Mexico and Peru, the soldiers gained nothing for themselves by controlling Indigenous fieldworkers, for there was no market or plan to sell "Mission Indians." The soldiers decided to make the Indigenous people build the compounds by themselves.

Before long, conquest and conversion were at odds with settler colonialism and slavery. The Franciscans sought to continue the Spanish empire's policy of assimilation through mass conversion and indoctrination, while the soldiers and Mexican settlers wanted to remove the Indigenous people, take their lands, and raise cattle and families.[23] Pedro Fages, the lieutenant governor of the Californias, wrote that Kumeyaay were "the most restless, stubborn, haughty, warlike, and hostile to us" and were "opposed to all rational subjection."[24]

Friar Serra planned to enslave California Natives through the two-step regime that Spain had developed over three centuries in its conquest of Peru and Mexico: *mita* was an involuntary "tribute," in the form of compulsory labor, that required the Incas to leave their villages and work in the silver mines; and *reducción*—literally, reduction—involved removing, regathering, and converting Indians into obedient, enslaved members of the empire.[25] In California, reducción would remove Indigenous people from their tribes, their food sources, and their spiritual practices. Mita and reducción—forced labor and ethnic cleansing—expedited the Spaniards' access to unpaid fieldworkers and opened the tribal land for Spanish agriculture.

To compel Native Californians to labor in the fields, soldiers armed with muskets and swords swept Indians onto the vast Catholic estates where the priests would teach them European-style leatherwork, weaving, and woodworking. The Spanish kept obsessive logs of births and baptisms, floggings, and detentions, but there are no documents of wages for Indian labor.[26] Soon the snare was hunger. Friar Pedro Font observed that most Indians were "caught by the mouth." Terrorized by musket and whip, or by threats of rape by soldiers and priests, before long California Natives often approached the mission compounds only because they were starving and attacked on their own lands.[27]

California Natives were enslaved from the moment that they were baptized—a ritual that they did not understand in a language they did not know. Once they let holy water be poured over their heads or let their heads be held underwater, they were never again free to leave the mission without a *paseo*—a slave pass. If they returned to their villages, they would be seized and whipped. Yet captives who passed time in their villages were

Native Americans in San Diego, likely Kumeyaay, were given a Catholic Spanish
identity and posed as Joseph leading a donkey, Mary, and baby Jesus.

Photo by Arthur Schott, 1857. Lithographed by Sarony, Major and Knapp, New York.
Library of Congress Prints and Photographs, Washington, DC.

more likely to thrive. When they returned, noted Serra, they would come "back to us so changed that we can hardly recognize them."[28]

Forced field labor transformed Native Californians' traditional workday of sunrise to sunset, new moon to new moon. To control Indians' time, the padres used sundials and bells; to control their mobility, the padres turned to whips and walls.[29] Mission bells ordered captives and converts to line up for breakfast, religious instruction, mass, morning work, midday meals, midday prayer, afternoon work, choir practice, catechism, and bed. Mission bells tolled their lost freedom.[30]

For fifty years the Franciscan priests sought to turn the California Natives into a peasant class and make the missions economically self-sufficient. Flogging and faith, Serra believed, would transform Indians into docile fieldworkers. None of these "simple and ignorant people," he said, could govern themselves.[31] To inculcate habits of submission and adherence, the Franciscans taught captives the concepts of sin and guilt, confession, expiation, and redemption in the ever after. Californian Natives who were held at the missions learned to identify acts of immorality and feelings of shame. Catechism and confession were the Church's only releases from that harrowing new emotion.

Empire and Rape

Rape was an instrument of bondage and empire; sexual attacks by soldiers and friars on Native women sparked outrage and revolts. Although the righteous friars opposed Indian polygamy and free sexual practices, they did nothing to stop sexual assaults by soldiers and priests on Indigenous women.

In 1772, one year after Friar Jayme arrived in San Diego, he warned the mother church in Loreto that rape was destroying Spain's dream of an empire in California. The priests, utterly dependent on the soldiers, responded to reports of sexual assaults only by sending letters two thousand miles, by mule, to Mexico City or fifteen hundred miles by ship to Loreto, which arrived months later. Meanwhile, the soldiers, unrestricted by military orders or Church code, assaulted Indigenous women in their villages, on their trails, or in mission dormitories. Kumeyaay women so feared the soldiers that whenever Friar Jayme visited the villages to recruit or plead with fugitives to return, the women hid in the woods. Many soldiers, Jayme reported, "deserve to be hanged on account of continuous outrages which they are committing in seizing and raping the women. There is not a single mission where all the gentiles [unconverted Indians] have not been scandalized, even on the roads."[32]

Nonetheless, the brutal Captain Pedro Fages refused to discipline the soldiers because the "heathen," wrote Friar Jayme in 1775, "had been on the point of coming here to kill us all [after] some soldiers went there and raped their women, and other soldiers who were carrying the mail to Monterey turned their animals into their fields and ate up their crops." Indeed, "as soon as they saw us they fled from their villages . . . so that the soldiers will not rape their women, as they have done so many times in the past."[33]

The Luiseño and Kumeyaay were stunned by the assaults. Why, they wondered, would Christians who taught that their god would send them to hell for adultery and sin still "have sexual intercourse with our wives"? Friar Jayme reported that three soldiers had seized an unmarried woman as she was walking to the mission in San Diego from the village of Rincón and "sinned with her," nearly blinding her in the assault. The woman became pregnant and tried many times to abort the fetus before eventually giving birth. Before Jayme could baptize the infant boy, she killed the baby. The padre later heard the baby "was somewhat white and gave every indication of being a son of the soldiers."[34]

According to Indian accounts, or *testimonios*, four soldiers once entered a Kumeyaay village saying they were hungry and demanded a cooking pot and some prickly pears. When a Native woman refused to give them her food, they grabbed her and carried her into a corral where one soldier after the next "sinned" with her. The four Spanish men then seized another woman and raped her in the same corral. Afterward, the soldiers gave ribbons to both women—the men had come prepared to try to purchase sex with Native women with trinkets, or perhaps, to try to placate the victims.

Within hours the Kumeyaay women arrived at Mission San Diego weeping and ready to report the assaults. The soldiers and priests had anticipated their arrival and had chained a Kumeyaay man who had witnessed the assault into stocks and banished all the other Indian witnesses.[35] "What the Devil does not succeed in accomplishing among the pagans, is accomplished by the Christians," tepidly complained Friar Jayme, who took no action against the soldiers.[36] The priests were afraid of the Indians but just as afraid of their own soldiers; the military refused to acknowledge the crimes or punish these men who resented their deployment to a remote bachelor wilderness at half the rations and half the pay they had received in Mexico.[37]

Routine gang rapes drove California Natives away from the missions. In letter after letter, Serra reported the assaults to the Franciscan motherhouse in Mexico City: "In the morning, six or seven soldiers would set out together . . . and go to the far distant rancherías, even many leagues away. When both men and women at the sight of them took to their heels . . . the soldiers, clever as they are at lassoing cows and mules, would catch an Indian woman with their lassos to become prey for their unbridled lust." In one of his few comments on Indian resistance, Serra dryly reported, "At times some Indian men would try to defend their wives, only to be shot down with bullets."[38] Serra was aware that the "leather jackets" were also molesting Kumeyaay boys and men. He knew that the rapes provoked Indian revolts, but he seemed more concerned that sexual assault was threatening his strategy of conquest through conversion.[39]

Serra continued to witness Spanish soldiers kill Indian men "to take their wives," but he did not demand they be punished because he knew that the padres relied on soldiers to seize the unconverted, chase runaways, and flog converts.[40] After 1810 and the start of the long Mexican struggle for independence, the priests feared that the military would abandon the expedition. The Indians understood the dynamic: the weakness of the priests and the power of the soldiers.[41]

The unchallenged assaults exposed Spaniards' assumption that they owned the Indigenous people, and they undermined the priests' posture as loving Catholic fathers. Several distraught priests pleaded to return to Mexico.[42] A priest at Mission San Gabriel was so horrified at the "deeds of shame" with Indian children that he abandoned the mission he had founded.[43]

Friar Fermín de Lasuén from Mission Santa Cruz blamed the rapes on Indian hypersexuality. He claimed that when Indians could not "entirely gratify their lust because of the vigilance of the missionaries," they returned to their homelands where they could "give full sway to their carnal desires." Driven by "lewdness," they wanted to "shamelessly pursue without restraint whatever their brutal appetites suggest to them" and enjoy "no superior but their own free will." The escapes also frustrated Lasuén's eugenic dream of Spanish dominance through Christian marriages between soldiers and Indian women. Mestizo children would realize his goal of assimilation through insemination.[44]

"Whipping . . . A Spiritual Benefit for Everyone"

Junípero Serra was an impressionable altar boy in Madrid during the Spanish Inquisition; later he witnessed brutal Church interrogations in Mexico City. Serra believed that whipping was a way for priests to show

god's fatherly love and also a tool for ensuring obedience.[45] "The spiritual
Padres," said the fanatical priest, were simply godly parents who flogged
"their children." The unholy whip, rather than the holy cross, he said, would
lead California Natives to accept salvation as they worked in the fields and
planted the new orchards.[46] Yet fearing that the Indian captives would reject
the brutal padres, he decided to outsource the floggings to the soldiers.[47]

Many priests were shocked by California Natives' displays of "extrav-
agant love" for their children. Friar Serra and Franciscan priests, who saw
their god as a ruthless and punishing father, insisted that Indian parents
would learn to love the whip once they could understand that the padres
were giving their children "birth in Christ."[48]

Serra's sadism was only surpassed by his masochism. He flagellated
himself daily. During sermons, he often burned his bare body with a lit
taper to intensify the theatricality of his own agonized contrition. Once
in Mexico City, he stopped a sermon midway to "scourge" himself with a
metal chain.[49]

The padres whipped both male and female converts for sins such as
adultery or leaving the mission to hunt and fish. Mission journals, kept over
the seventy years of Franciscan reign, record how baptized Indians were
routinely flogged for conspiracy, running away, stealing cattle, or simply
displaying a bad character.[50]

In September 1786, seventeen years after the founding of the first
mission, French scientist and naval explorer Jean-François de Galaup La
Pérouse sailed into Monterey Bay, anticipating a respite from his travels in
a Mediterranean-style hacienda where he would be served French meals,
like those he had enjoyed in Mexico City. Instead, he found fifty adobe huts
with roofs made of branches and one ragged fort held together with straw.

In a rare diary of mission life in California, La Pérouse wrote that he
had stumbled into a world of slavery: "We declare with pain that the re-
semblance [to slave colonies in Santo Domingo] is so exact that we saw
both men and women loaded with irons, while others had a log of wood on
their legs; and even the noise of the lash might have assailed our ears as that
mode of punishment is equally admitted." He noticed that for missing their
prayers, "women are never whipped in public but in an enclosed and somewhat distant place that their cries may not excite too lively a compassion,
which might cause the men to revolt." The men, he saw, were whipped
in "view of all their fellow citizens that their punishment may serve as an
example."

Most chilling to La Pérouse was the sight of Indians forced to whip
other Indians of both sexes—a cruel perversion imposed upon a peaceful

people—all in the name of Catholic conversion.[51] The friars, he wrote, separated the neophytes into male and female sleeping quarters and then forced terrified Indian "nuns" to orchestrate the friars' sexual assaults.

Even as the friars professed their celibacy and fetishized a doxology of a chaste Madonna, La Pérouse saw that each night the padres took unmarried women and young girls from their parents and locked them in sparse and putrid *monjeríos*—women's narrow dormitories. In these fetid chambers, the Indian women slept on narrow wooden pallets that ran along both walls. The French visitor sardonically observed that "the holy fathers have constituted themselves guardians of the virtues of women," but he saw Indian "women in irons for having eluded the vigilance" of these elderly procurers.[52] Women who had committed adultery were locked into a *corma*—a brace once used to hobble livestock, made from two pieces of wood hinged together, twenty-four inches long and ten inches wide—that allowed women to work, grinding corn or cleaning wheat, but not to spread their legs for sex.[53]

Sexual slavery was built into the architecture of the mission. Woqoch, a baptized Indian, reported that at Mission San Buenaventura, north of Los Angeles, the priests took all the "best-looking girls and they put them in the monjerío," or women's dormitory. At his appointed time, a priest nightly entered the monjerío. The *maestra*—or Indian female overseer—would begin to sing loudly and force the other girls to join in, which, reported Woqoch, "drowned out any other sounds" so the priest could "select the girl he wanted [and] carry out his desires." Then "the singing would stop."[54] Woqoch remembered that "the priest had sex with all of them down the line. The priest's will was law."[55]

The unrelenting horrors of sexual bondage and child rape defied California Natives' sexual practices. Indians did not assault women whom they seized as war prisoners; they punished incest with death. The rapes of Indigenous women and girls undermined the spirituality of the Indians' intimate traditions. The Yuma believed that sexual intercourse with an enemy contaminated their warriors. The Tongva, just north of Los Angeles, believed that a woman who had been raped by a Spaniard needed to be purified with sweats and herbal teas.[56] Indeed, rape spread venereal disease throughout the mission chain.

In letter after letter, Serra wrote of his fear that Indians' outrage at the assaults "exposed priests to the danger of a new uprising." At Mission San Juan Capistrano, he wrote, "The soldiers, without any restraint or shame, have behaved like brutes towards the Indian women. It may well be brought as a reproach to Christian men that some of the women, both gentile and

convert-Christian, would not consent to what they know to be evil." Serra
saw the "scandalous behavior" by the priests, which he feared could thwart
"the pacification of the Indians and the tranquility of their souls."[57] Yet he
never recorded that, as the ruling priest, he ever held any priest to account.

The priests viewed sex and, by implication, rape, as a eugenic strategy
of empire, and they urged Spanish soldiers to remain in California, marry
Indian women, and breed an enduring colony of mestizo Catholic settlers.
A Catholic wedding with a Spanish man would draw an Indian woman
into the empire while satisfying a soldier's lustful appetite. Soldiers who
agreed to remain in California were rewarded with gifts of horses, cattle,
two years' pay, and five years of rations.[58] For a fee of 500 *reales*, mestizo
settlers could get reclassified as "pure" Spaniards and become legally white.

Empire, Slavery, and Sex

Lorenzo Asisara, a Costanoan, offers one of the few California Native
voices from this early era. Asisara was born into bondage at Mission Santa
Cruz in 1819, and was chosen by the priests to become a child sacristan.
He lived within the compound for ten years until Mexico closed the missions. Asisara's tale reveals the Franciscans' obsessions with Indians' intimate life and their concern about the declining population at the missions.

As an attendant at confessions, Asisara overheard the priests interrogate
each convert about the "sin" of infertility. He recalled how Friar Ramón
Olbés punished an Indigenous couple who had not conceived a baby. Olbés
first summoned the husband and questioned if he had sex with his wife
and, if so, why they had no children. The husband pointed to the sky, suggesting that "only God knows." Olbés then ordered the couple to have sex
in front of him. When they refused, Olbés told the husband to pull down
his pants, whereupon he inspected the man's penis to affirm that "he had
it in good order" and sent the husband to the guardhouse.

Olbés then tried to inspect the wife's vagina, but she grabbed him by
the cord that hung from his waist and "tried to bury her teeth in his arm."
He sent her to the guardhouse to suffer fifty lashes and then be shackled
in the women's dormitory.[59] Afterward, he had her make a wooden doll,
"like a recently born child, and to carry it in front of all the people for nine
days. He obligated her to present herself in front of the church with that
doll as if it were her child."[60]

Attempts to control Indians' sexual practices, reproductive traditions,
and privacy were crucial to the Spanish takeover of the land and the dom-

ination over the people. Before contact with the Spanish, Native women comfortably initiated sex, divorced abusive husbands, and, according to some legends, ridiculed inadequate sexual partners.[61] All sorts of sexual and polygamous relationships were possible and uncensored; there was no prostitution.[62] Many tribes practiced polygamy; virginity was not a prerequisite to marriage. That said, both husbands and wives were expected to be faithful for the duration of a marriage.

Before an Indigenous couple could be baptized, they had to remarry in the Church. During the years of Spanish occupation, 2,374 Indian couples had second Catholic weddings. When several Chumash at Mission Santa Barbara renounced Catholic marriage and returned to traditions of polygamy, Friar Estevan Tapis ordered them to be returned to the missions to be whipped and shackled.[63]

The Franciscans justified harsh surveillance by claiming that California Natives were "savage, lewd people" who gave "sway" to carnal desires.[64] They rejected the missions' demand for chastity and refused to abandon their polygamous customs in order to receive baptism.[65]

Indigenous traditions of polyandry titillated the Catholic priests, who kept catalogues of their prurient interrogations. The priests banned sex in any position in which the woman was not under the man and forbade "mating after the fashion of animals."[66] They urged baptized men to dominate their wives, for if a Native woman accepted a subservient role in her family, she might similarly obey the padres.[67] Yet female submission was not an Indian ethic.[68] There were female tribal chiefs as well as male chiefs, whose role was not to issue orders; generally, the role of a chief was to distribute food and monitor exogamy—marriage outside the clan.

The need to control all aspects of the lives of the enslaved appears in the "*confesionarios*"—pornographic scripts of standardized questions for confessions—that required California Natives to describe their carnality, in Spanish or in their own languages; for some, the very act of confession violated their communal rituals. Implicit in the questions were gender hierarchy, heterosexual expectations, and judgments about birth control. In his confesionario at Mission La Purísima, Friar Mariano Payéras asked females to confess to violating the Biblical commandment "Thou shalt not kill" if they had an abortion, and he asked male penitents if they practiced *coitus interruptus* as a means of birth control. In sanctioned pornography, Payéras urged Indians to describe their acts of fornication, masturbation, sodomy, incest, or bestiality—all sins of adultery.

The Ventureño Confesionario is the only extant Act of Contrition written in a Chumash dialect. Transcribed by Friar José Señán, a linguist, it exposes the Church's fears about the shrinking mission population with questions such as: "Have you ever induced a woman to kill the child in her womb?," "Have you had intercourse improperly with your wife so she would not bear a child?," "Have you ever drunk anything or done anything else to avoid giving birth to a child?," and "In having sexual intercourse with your husband or any other man, have you ever 'scattered their own seeds in the field' in order to avoid having a child?"[69] Fearful that masturbation might limit the Indian population, the priest asked: "How many times have you spilled the seed of your body?," and, more bluntly, "Have you ever handled yourself?"[70] There are no records of the Indian responses.

Other questions sought to uncover the free sexuality of the Chumash: "With how many women have you sinned? How many times did you sin with each one? Is she married? Is she your relative? Is she your sister? Is the woman your wife's younger sister? Older sister? Are you related to the woman's husband? . . . Have you ever given a woman to a man? How many times?" The confesionarios posed questions about "taking pleasure in watching people or animals having intercourse."[71] The priests asked about sexual relations with multiple partners at one time and the role of procuring sexual partners for others.[72]

The confession scripts also reveal the priests' fear of Indian revolts. In forced confessionals, Señán solicited, "How many times did you become angry with the priests?," "How many times have you felt hatred toward the priests?," and "How many persons have you wished to die or become ill? Have you ever given anyone poison to cause his death?"

Spanish friars, men who had chosen to live in all-male communities, obsessively posed questions about homosexuality and presumed the right to this knowledge.[73] Señán's lurid translation inquires, "Have you ever sinned with a man?," and "Have you thought about or desired men while you spilled the seed from your body?" Friar Juan Cortés asked Native penitents if they ever wanted to "do something bad with a man, through the buttocks, with the hand alone."[74] *Las joyas*, or Indians with gender nonconforming identities, unwittingly provided titillating material for the prurient padres. Friar Crespí was puzzled to see Chumash men "wearing the dress of women, with buckskin petticoats, very well-tanned and clean. . . . We have not been able to understand what it means, nor what its purpose is; time and understanding of the language, when it is learned will make it clear."[75] Captain Pedro Fages reported that he saw two or three men wear-

This image by Louis Choris shows Indigenous Californians (Ohlone)
at Mission Dolores, San Francisco. Traditionally naked, they now wear
identical striped mission clothing as they play an Indian stick game.
Library of Congress, Washington, DC, via Wikimedia Commons.

ing women's clothing in every Chumash village: "They pass as sodomites
by profession (it being confirmed that all Indians are much addicted to
this abominable vice) and permit the heathen to practice the execrable,
unnatural abuse of their bodies. . . . They are called *joyas* [jewels] and are
held in great esteem."[76]

Slavery granted the priests free rein for their salacious power. Some
tribes believed that those with fluid gender identities were powerful vision-
aries, destined to become shamans. But in the eyes of the padres, transexual
and bisexual Indians were living devils marked by the Church as primitive,
primal, and close to nature.[77] At Mission Santa Clara, a priest observed an
adult with "undeveloped breasts" working among the women and ordered
the soldiers to take him to the guardhouse and pull down his loincloth to
reveal him to be a man. The Chumash saw a transgendered individual as
a welcome "third gender"—or *aki*, "two-spirit" people—a possibility that
horrified priests.[78]

"Births Are Few and Deaths Are Many"

During the era of mission slavery, the Indigenous population in California dropped by 50 percent. Between 1769 and 1834, when Mexico began to disband the missions, the Spanish enslaved over one hundred thousand California Natives at the twenty-one missions—a third of what was likely the pre-contact Indian population of about 310,000. In the two decades since the Spanish invasion, by 1789 three thousand baptized Indians had died at the missions; five thousand more died the following year. Likely about 110,000 to 150,000 California Natives died from hunger, alien diseases, and violent abuse that endured at the missions. During this evangelical period, Franciscans baptized 53,600 California Natives and buried 37,000. From 1779 to 1833, when Mexico "secularized" the missions, the priests recorded 62,600 deaths and 29,100 births. Nearly half the deaths were caused by disease, including two deadly epidemics of European measles. The padres were desperate to recruit more Indian initiates.[79]

In 1821 Mexico won control of California from Spain, and Luis Antonio Argüello, the first Mexican governor, continued the Spanish policy of *reducción de indio.* Few Indians still lived at the missions. The trinity of land, labor, and assault had failed to anchor Spain in California. With more Indigenous people dying than being born at the missions, the system hinged on neophytes' children and their children's children to work under the whip, as field laborers, cooks, blacksmiths, saddle makers, and sexual slaves. As in the plantation South, Indian mothers birthed enslaved children. Meanwhile, pregnant Indian women turned to abortions and infanticide, especially when a baby was born with light skin.[80]

Slavery was a deadly condition. Friar Ramón Olbés reported that "births are few and deaths are many," for virtually all the converts had syphilis. At Mission San Gabriel, when a Tongva woman delivered a stillborn child, a priest shaved her head and had her flogged for fifteen days. Afterward, he demanded that she wear "iron on the feet" (shackles) for three months and carry a wooden doll, painted red; the priests ordered the other Indians to jeer at her while she stood in silence at the door of the church on Sundays.[81] In the mere four years between 1811 and 1815, Mission Santa Cruz witnessed the death of 25 percent of its baptized Indians. At Mission San Diego, in 1814 alone, 118 Indian converts died, mostly from venereal disease; that year only seventy-five were baptized—unsustainable birth and mortality rates. One friar noted that at Mission San Gabriel, for every four children born, three died, and few lived to the age of twenty-five.[82] In 1806 a measles pandemic killed all the children under ten years old at Mission

San Francisco de Dolores; the infirmary at Mission San Gabriel housed about four hundred infected patients.[83] At Mission San Carlos, 37 percent of the babies did not live until their first birthday.[84]

Rape spread *el gálico*—venereal disease—throughout the mission chain. From 1791 onward, syphilis caused half of the deaths of converts trapped at the missions.[85] Some priests blamed the disease on visiting soldiers and fur trappers. As muleteers, friars, and settlers moved across a once healthy landscape, malaria, measles, and smallpox spread.[86] Although the padres were wont to blame the scourge on California Indians' free sexuality, modern cultural anthropologists and medical historians have identified a killer European strain that spread through the Franciscan compounds by rape, midwifery, and childbirth. Known in Spain as "syphilis of the innocents," it passed to Indian women who were nursing babies fathered by infected soldiers.[87] Piercings, tattoos, and circumcisions also spread the disease. Traditional tribal cures, similar to European practices of bloodletting and sucking, spread the disease further. The epidemic of syphilis lasted the entire reign of the California missions; all the compounds were infected, although priests' deaths by venereal disease were not recorded as such.

Contagion was a consequence of slavery and empire. Disease-bearing insects and microbes traveled across the globe in bodies and clothing or even in the damp wood of the ships. Malaria, smallpox, measles, trachoma, diphtheria, typhoid fever, scarlet fever, amebic dysentery, and influenza invaded the Franciscans' locked dormitories and shared beds. The missions had no provisions for dealing with human waste. Bacteria traveled in the streams and water systems. Indigenous Californians, trapped inside the compounds, were no longer able to follow their traditional cleansing practices such as sweathouses and hot springs.

"In a few years hence on seeing Alta California deserted and depopulated of Indians within a century of its discovery and conquest by the Spaniards, it will be asked where is the numerous heathendom that used to populate it?" wondered Friar Mariano Payéras. Like "beasts," he wrote, Indians thrive in the wild, but once they commit themselves to a Christian life, "they become extremely feeble, lose weight, get sick, and die." As Payéras traveled through the northern missions, he was unable to find even one Indian who had been living there twenty years before. He mournfully predicted, "I believe there is no human recourse to us," and he left the destiny of California Natives to the will of god.[88] By 1820 the Franciscan priests worried that no Indians would survive their rule and foretold a future of empty missions and full cemeteries.[89]

Desperately sick Indians went home to die. Unwittingly they carried contagions back to their villages. Indigenous immune systems were unprepared for the onslaught, and as the mission chain grew, the pace of infections quickened. By the 1830s half of California's population at the time of the Spanish invasion in 1769 had died. Nearly 50 percent of the converts died each year.[90] Like Wikamee, the lands of the Kumeyaay, California had become "a place of darkness and mist."[91]

For enslaved California Natives, survival depended upon return. In bondage, captive Indians knelt before the cross, but at times they escaped to be with their kin, where they gave birth and died. Here they danced to mark the cycle of the seasons, to invite healing, and to honor death. They embodied the animals that threatened them or fed them. Under the whip, they tended Spanish cattle and grew corn on Indigenous seed fields, yet in their own villages they lit fires together that lofted smoke to the moon and threw handfuls of seeds to the sun to assure the abundance of their own crops.[92]

California: A Slave Colony

As mission bells pealed in California, the Spanish Crown was absorbing the largest number of slaves in its history to labor on sugar and tobacco plantations in Latin America and the Caribbean.[93] From the time of Columbus to the end of the nineteenth century, Spain held between 2.5 and 5 million Native Americans in slavery in the "New World," human beings kidnapped, bartered, shipped, and sold to silver mines, to plantations on the Yucatán peninsula, and to the guano islands of Peru to dig the fertilizer that preserved the plantations.[94]

Regimes of slavery were toppling across the world. On the island of Saint-Domingue, five hundred thousand enslaved Africans won their freedom in the Haitian Revolution (1781–1804).[95] The turbulent slave trade in the British empire came to an end with an act of Parliament in 1807, though, as in the United States, not the practice of slavery itself. Spain's regimes of slavery in California arose just at the time that the United States and France faced revolutions for the right to freedom and equality.

When Spain invaded California, its missions and mines had depleted the pool of unpaid labor in Latin America. Spain turned to Portuguese firms to capture and ship enslaved Africans to work in its mines in Peru and on its vast plantations in Cuba and Mexico. In California, Spain imposed the lifelong ownership of human beings and the inescapable enslavement of their children.

Eighty percent of Spain's investment in California went toward the
military, whose small presence was supposed to guard the ports of San
Diego, Monterey, and San Francisco. The missions and presidios would
halt the advance of Russians who were sailing from the north with captive
Alaska Natives to hunt the sea otter along the coast. Spain feared that the
Russians might sail on and reach the rich gold and silver mines of Sonora
and Sinaloa in northern Mexico.

In 1716 Spain abolished the enslavement of Africans in its colonies in
the Americas, yet soldiers and priests in Mexico, Puerto Rico, and Cuba
continued to abduct Indians from their villages and sell them at slave
marts to work in the silver mines or to plant and harvest at sugar, coffee,
and tobacco plantations.[96] Spain only insisted that the priests and wealthy
planters limit floggings to twenty-five lashes at a time. Through overwork
and starvation, the Spanish had decimated the Indigenous people in the
Caribbean and Latin America.

By the time Spain invaded California in 1769, it had conquered 7.5
million square miles of territory, or about 13 percent of the landmass of
the earth, and the people who lived on this land.

CHAPTER TWO

"The Flame of Their Fury"

Slave Revolts at the California Missions

I hate the padres and all of you, for living here on my native soil, for trespassing upon the land of my forefathers and despoiling our tribal domain. . . . I came to inspire the dirty cowards to fight, and not to quail at the sight of Spanish sticks that spit fire and death, nor [to] retch at the evil smell of gunsmoke—and be done with you white invaders.

—TOYPURINA (TONGVA), medicine woman, San Gabriel Mission, 1785

It is highly useful to the service of the king and the public welfare that the heathen of these establishments do not learn to kill the soldiers.

—GOVERNOR FELIPE DE NEVE, 1782

WITHIN ONE YEAR OF the Spanish invasion of California, Wikamee, the land of the Kumeyaay, had become a place of bondage, suspicion, and darkness. A few months after the Spaniards' invasion, several padres told Junípero Serra that they wanted to return to Mexico. The water in the San Diego River had dried up and they were always thirsty. The Kumeyaay were unimpressed with the promise of salvation and a Christian afterlife. They were only in awe of the rifles and horses and only guilty of stealing "bits of sailcloth" from the wreckage of the Spaniards' ships. In a papal bull, the Dudum Siquidem of 1493, the pope had declared that Indians in the Americas possessed souls, and also announced that they could reason and make choices. Serra feared their "discouragement" would spread like the other contagions. The tribes held at the Catholic missions made a collective reasoned choice to resist. The Spanish invasion quickly incited the Indians to revolt against the violent and repressive military theocracy.

The Spanish brought disorder to an orderly world. The First Peoples of California lived on over 160,000 square miles of land plentiful with seeds and berries, camas bulbs, sturgeon, and deer.[1] Coastal tribes marked time with rituals of dance, food, and sex. They marked the year by the ripening harvests, the fall of acorns, the return of salmon and steelhead, the rutting of elk, the arrival of waterfowl, and the snowmelt that poured fresh into the rivers. California Natives walked hundreds of miles for friendship and to barter and lived in circles of intimacy with tribes that spoke several hundred languages and dialects.[2] They forged connections with their ancestors and bonds with their enemies. Could these ties challenge the invaders?

In August 1774 the Franciscans relocated Mission San Diego de Alcalá to Kumeyaay land, closer to the cluster of Native villages but six miles east of the presidio. Yet even five years after the invasion, senior priests Luis Jayme and Vicente Fuster had converted fewer than one hundred Natives. From this new base, the padres ruthlessly accelerated conscriptions and conversions, and by the next autumn they baptized four hundred new converts. Mexican settlers who followed the soldiers raided the Natives' food and delivered new deadly diseases. In July 1775 eleven Indians deserted the mission at Monterey, but the priests blamed their departure on Satan, who resented the priests for baptizing the new converts.

But with missions low on food, and Natives starving, the padres had to let the converts commute to their villages. They were right to worry that the *paseos*, or visits to their villages, would restore the hold of Native traditions.

"The Flame of Their Fury"

By early October, Kumeyaay chiefs from eight villages of baptized Natives joined with seven villages of "pagans," and several hundred men and women from diverse Kumeyaay clans came together to plan an attack on Mission San Diego de Alcalá, burn the church, and expel the priests.[3] Where once there had been stockpiles of food, now there would be stockpiles of sharpened shafts of black willow bows, piercing bones, and stone arrowheads. Owl and hawk feathers would steady arrows for speed and aim. Sinewy bowstrings would ensure snap. In hiding, the Kumeyaay hunters carved their arsenal.[4]

To thwart the brewing rebellion, Spanish soldiers hiked thirty miles to a gathering of *las cabecillas*, the village heads, in the high desert. The Spaniards seized the chiefs, locked them in leg irons, and shuffled them back down to the presidio at the beach. Under ruthless questioning, the captured chiefs told Commander José Francisco Ortega that they had seen captive Kumeyaay working in the mission fields. They feared that their own clans would also be forced into labor and had decided to "kill the fathers and soldiers to live as they did before."[5] Ortega replied that if the defiant Kumeyaay did "not accept the salutary waters of holy baptism they will die on Saturday morning, and if they do—they will die all the same."[6] Believing that the chiefs were fearful of their eternal destiny, the padres at Mission San Diego de Alcalá let them return to their villages to deliver Ortega's warning. But the Kumeyaay goal remained: free the neophytes and then reclaim their lands.

On the day of the revolt, the allied coastal rebels who lived by the ocean gathered on the beach at the Kumeyaay village Chiap; those who lived on the high desert met at the San Diego River. One flank would torch the Mission San Diego de Alcalá and free the captives, while the other would attack the presidio.

Just after midnight on Sunday, November 5, 1775, eleven Franciscan priests and four Spanish soldiers were asleep under a full moon while nearly eight hundred armed Kumeyaay from fifteen "Christian" villages entered California's first mission. They circled the compound and set fire to its thatched dormitories and granaries and, finally, to the brushwood church.

Fuster awoke in terror and "saw on all sides around me so many arrows that you could not possibly count them. There we were, surrounded on all sides by flames."[7] As the church and outbuildings burned, the frantic priests dashed between the granary and cookhouse. With a copper kettle for a shield, Fuster hid behind bales of cotton, trying to protect his bags of gunpowder.

Fuster promised god that if he would let the Spanish win, he would fast for nine Saturdays.[8] As California's first mission burned to the ground, he stopped a soldier to ask, "What is this all about? Were the Indians giving orders that they should once and for all make an end of us?" Friar Francisco Palóu believed the mission was under attack by the army of Satan, who was "resentful . . . because the heathen were being taken away from him." "*El Diablo*" knew that "the missionaries . . . were banishing his followers." Deluded by their sense of divine purpose, the priests had failed to notice that the Church's "children" had grown into a "host of enemies."[9] In six years of intimate surveillance at a mission built atop an Indian village, none of the Franciscan priests spoke any of the seventy-eight tribal languages, and few California Natives spoke Spanish.[10] Friar Serra, fluent in the dialects of torture, understood that "they meant to exterminate the whole white population and the Fathers in particular."[11] Amid volleys of Kumeyaay arrows, the three Spanish soldiers fired dozens of musket balls and discharged fifty pounds of gunpowder, but by dawn, the rebels had freed all the Kumeyaay. With their remaining strength, they carried home their dead and wounded.[12]

Only a few devout converts stayed with the surviving priests. As they inventoried the ruin, they came upon the corpse of Friar Luis Jayme—stripped naked, beaten, pierced by twenty-nine sharpened stone arrows, and flung into a ditch. His bludgeoned "face was one great bruise from the clubbing and stoning it had suffered."[13] Only the mission bells remained unbroken.

During the night, the Spanish soldiers deliberately stationed themselves at the beach six miles from the mission, but saw the flames. Only after daylight did they ride out, just to carry the wounded on planks, drive the few remaining animals, and help surviving priests trek on foot back to the fort. Over the next few months, a humiliated Captain Fernando Rivera y Moncada and Captain Ortega rode through the villages in pursuit of the Kumeyaay rebels, firing muskets and swinging whips, but most had fled into the mountains.[14] The avenging Spaniards seized nine Native men and several women and marched them down to the presidio. Captain Rivera ordered that each male be whipped fifty times to compel them to reveal their *compadres*. The whippings went on through winter; one Indian man died from the torture.[15]

A year after the revolt at Mission San Diego de Alcalá, thirteen Ku-

The Death of Friar Luis Jayme was depicted 150 years later by a Franciscan padre, Zephyrin Engelhardt, O.F.M. James H. Barry Co., San Francisco, 1920.
(Courtesy of San Diego History Center.)

meyaay were still in the presidio jail, flogged each day for refusing to sur- render their accomplices. The padres sent soldiers into the mountains to retrieve their "lost sheep" and whip them for the "spiritual benefit of every- one."[16] Other Kumeyaay fled to distant villages. One committed suicide. Only twenty devout Natives lived in the mission's ruins.[17]

At a safe and smug remove in Mission Monterey, Junípero Serra re- called his earlier prediction: "It is certain that the . . . gentiles (the uncon- verted) now as gentle as sheep, will turn on us as tigers."[18] But after the revolt, local Kumeyaay and Ipai avoided the mission. Neither ritual nor torment, slavery, disease, displacement, nor threats of death wiped out the Kumeyaay. They continued to speak their own languages, persisted in their traditional intimate and spiritual practices, and lived on the plentiful sus- tenance of their land.[19]

Serra waited a year to come back to San Diego to rebuild his first mission; he chose a spot where the Kumeyaay had built an elaborate rock dam to hold water on the fickle San Diego River. Serra thanked his god: since the ground of California "has been watered [with priests' blood] now certainly we will achieve the conversion of the Diegueños [Kumeyaay and

Ipai]." The priests were transformed into holy martyrs, and the villages of the unconquered Kumeyaay became sanctuaries from the Spanish.[20]

Between 1769 and 1834, the padres seized, lured, and baptized eighty-one thousand Indians at the California missions. Two years after the revolt of 1775, soldiers heard rumors from trappers, travelers, and spies that the Kumeyaay at three villages—La Punta, Meti, and Pamo—were planning another revolt. To preempt their action, the militia raided Pamo and threw the villagers into a funeral pyre. Then they moved on to La Punta and found that the tribe had abandoned their village.[21] Across the missions, California Natives were in flight.

Although the captives were starved, raped, and flogged, neófia often managed to live as unconquered people. During mission rule, 146 friars baptized 53,600 adult Indians.[22] Indians held in bondage at the missions managed to create small communities within the compounds, where they continued to dance and to marry. While they sang hymns at the church services, joined the choir, and wore Mexican-style clothes that covered their bodies, they venerated their ancient spirits. They played music on their traditional instruments and cooked their traditional foods. Meanwhile, forced labor systems at the missions evolved. As mission fields expanded, Native Californians turned to the compounds for food. Mexican independence from Spain opened California to global trade, and the padres pressured local Indians, increasingly skilled in metal and leatherwork, to step up production. Still, from the Kumeyaay in San Diego north to the Ohlone at Mission San Francisco, California Natives managed to escape the missions to join in defiant acts and elude recapture.

Serra continued to send troops to locate and seize the *huídos* (runaways) and march them to a presidio: "I am sending them to you . . . for punishment . . . a period of time in exile and two or three rounds of whipping . . . applied on different days. . . . This should be a good lesson for them as well as for the others, and it will be a spiritual benefit for everyone." If the fort does not "have shackles on hand, if you let us know, they can be sent from here."[23] Elder Maria Solares described her late grandmother as an "*esclava de la mission* [*sic*]"—a slave of the mission in Monterey who ran away, was captured, and was whipped until maggots crawled on her wounded buttocks. Her grandmother survived to "hand down her memories of the golden age before the white man came."[24]

During the occupation, most California Natives lived beyond Spanish control—to the north and east of the chain of missions, in the hot interior valleys, in the Sierra Nevada Mountains, and along the swift green rivers of Northern California. But those trapped in the compounds tirelessly fought for freedom. Friar Antonio María Osio warned that "the ultimate goal [of the Indians] was to kill the gente de razón [people of reason, or Hispanics], . . . those who did not belong to the Indian race."[25] The Mexican governor of Alta California, Luis Antonio Argüello, understood better than the padres that the "ultimate goal" of the Natives was not murder; their plan "was no other than to rid themselves of all of us . . . and remain in their own gentile [unconverted] liberty."[26]

Toypurina: A Shaman Warrior, Los Angeles, 1775

As a young Tongva girl in 1771, Toypurina watched the tall men enter the wide valley of the Los Angeles River basin on foot and on horse. They appeared to be spirits in human form who brought magical animals and carried firepower from the gods. In fact, the Spanish soldiers had come to consecrate La Misión San Gabriel de los Temblores, or Saint Gabriel of the Tremors (Earthquakes). Over time, Toypurina watched these men seize her people and tie their hands behind their backs; she saw priests lure others into the mission buildings with blankets and food. She watched as the padres baptized her relatives and then forced them to dig up their own fields to plant orchards, vineyards, and farms. That year, the Indigenous people around San Gabriel held a vast powwow of surrounding tribes; plumes of smoke signals revealed to the priests that tribes from the foothills of the Sierras to the coast had made peace, in order to confront their shared enemy.[27] Meanwhile, the fruits of Native labor would soon feed the entire military and civilian government of California, while year after year, Toypurina saw soldiers march her people to the prison at the garrison.

Toypurina was a shaman child. Her father had told her how the invaders let loose their cattle and sheep on the Tongva's sweet grasslands, how their wheat, barley, and corn choked the tribe's food plants, and how the strangers chopped down the wild oak plentiful with nourishing acorns to use for their firewood and buildings. He described the Spanish soldier who raped the wife of a chief and then killed the chief and mounted his head on a pole. She did not believe that the power of the Spanish soldiers came from a god.

As a shaman, Toypurina was taught to endure pain, and the tribe granted her the visionary power of the hallucinogen *toloache*, a tea infused from the datura plant. As she grew older, Toypurina led rituals, predicted the future, and claimed that she could kill at will.

In the autumn of 1785, Nicolás José, a young married Indian *alcalde* (acolyte), visited Toypurina, who was then twenty-five. Nicolás José was an insider: he administered the sacraments in church. Serra wrote that Nicolás José also had to provide "women to as many soldiers as asked for them." In 1783 Nicolás José's wife died, and he remarried; eight months later this wife, too, was dead. Their son died before he turned two. In fact, Nicolás José saw one-third of the baptized adults from his village and one-half of its baptized children die.[28] Nicolás José wanted to dance his grief at the annual Chinigchinich mourning ritual, now banned by the Church, and he offered Toypurina shell beads that she might send his boy's spirit to the land of the dead. Nicolás José lived in a perilous equilibrium between two worlds.

Toypurina drank toloache tea and had a vision of the death of the Spanish soldiers and the triumph of her people. With Nicolás José, she raised a guerilla band of chiefs and converts. Nicolás José knew the mission layout well. The Tongva rebels were ready. From village to village, they let it be known that on October 25, 1785, under the darkness of a new moon, they would burn down Mission San Gabriel and ignite a chain of revolts. Five rancherías in the nearby mountains and three from the valley agreed to send warriors. Toypurina prophesied that the Tongva would destroy all the missions and presidios in Alta California. She promised that with her sorcery, the padres would die just before the Indians burst into the mission.

The Spanish had been warned, and they set a trap. Two soldiers dressed in friars' habits lay on their backs on the floor of the mission, arms crossed across their chests, candles burning at their heads and feet, pretending to be dead while the padres hid in the sanctuary. In the darkness, Toypurina led dozens of men, decorated with war paint, over the adobe wall; they opened the heavy door of the friars' sleeping quarters and crept toward the men. The battle cry "Santiago!" rang out, and Spanish soldiers charged at the Indians with muskets and bayonets. The Tongva bolted back over the wall, but the soldiers captured two chiefs, eleven Natives, Toypurina, and Nicolás José. The Spaniards whipped all the captives to prove that "the sorceress and incantations of the woman Toypurina are powerless in the face of the True Faith." At her trial, the chiefs betrayed Toypurina: they declared she was a "witch" and a "serpent" who had enchanted them all. Nicolás José testified that he had mistakenly believed her supernatural claims.

In the hearing room at the presidio, Toypurina kicked aside the witness stool, choosing to stand and testify: "I hate the padres and all of you for living here on my native soil, for trespassing upon the land of my fore-fathers and despoiling our tribal domain. . . . I came to inspire the dirty cowards to fight, and not quail at the sight of Spanish sticks that spit fire and death, nor retch at the evil smell of gun smoke—and be done with you invaders." Then Toypurina blamed Nicolás José for planning the revolt and for bribing her with beads. Knowing that she could be executed, she asked to become a Christian.

The military court sentenced the chiefs to two years of prison labor. They exiled Nicolás José to a remote fort to serve six years of hard labor, bound in shackles. Toypurina was sentenced to exile for life from her tribe and one year in the jail at distant Carmel. Knowing she could never return to her tribe, she converted to Catholicism and was baptized at Mission San Gabriel by one of the priests whom she had tried to murder.[29] She met and married a Spanish soldier and died at age thirty-nine in 1799. Toypurina was the only Native woman in North America known to lead a revolt against the Spanish empire.

The Mission of Sorrows: San Francisco, 1795

By the 1790s, Mission Dolores, the Mission of Sorrows in San Francisco, had over nine hundred Ohlone captives. In three decades, six hundred Indian babies had been born in the compound, but 2,400 Indians had died.[30] Hungry and abused, in 1795 the Ohlone neophytes built tawny canoes from bundles of long tule reeds and paddled across San Francisco Bay. Found by the soldiers, they refused to return to the mission and killed seven Spaniards. Two hundred and eighty starving Ohlone (one-third of the mission's population) and fifty from Mission San José soon joined in escape. Knowing that the mission was surrounded by unconverted Ohlone, Friar Fermín de Lasuén, the senior priest, urged military restraint. A fraught truce lasted for two years. Then, in 1797 "Raymundo the Californian," known as the "mission executioner," led an expedition to capture the fugitives, but a united force of Ohlone, Saclan, and Huchiun fighters forced the Spanish troops to return across the windy bay. The captives were sentenced to labor at the San Francisco presidio.[31]

On the next expedition, Sergeant Pedro Amador seized twenty-three Ohlone fugitives whose confessions reveal their rage at the grievous brutalities and hunger suffered at Mission San Francisco. Ohlone Liberato Yree described the deaths of his captive mother, two brothers, and three nephews—and his terrified conviction that he would be the next to die.

Detail of Victor Arnautoff's 1935 Presidio fresco mural. This New Deal mural at the Chapel of the Presidio in San Francisco depicts a *soldado* assisting a padre who blocks the Ohlone men even as he appears to welcome them. Framed by the rifles and the presidio itself, the American soldier looks reverently at the blue-eyed priest while the Native American, shorter than the Spaniards, stares at the cold soldado and the fur hunter.

(Photo by Mark Vallen ©.)

Another Ohlone, Tiburcio, testified that he escaped after a friar had ordered him to be whipped for crying when his wife and daughter died. The wife of Otolón fled after she was raped by a *vaquero*—a cowboy—at the mission; the priests had ordered the soldiers to whip Otolón because he did not chase after her. He, too, ran away. Próspero fled after having been "stretched" on a rack because he went to the lagoon to hunt for ducks. Román fled because his wife and son had escaped from the mission after they were brutally whipped and now, he said, he was starving because there was no one to feed him.[32]

Resistance and retaliation spread through the missions. Friar Andrés Quintana tested his horsewhips on the Natives at Mission Santa Cruz. After Quintana tried out his new *carto de hierro* (a whip embedded with iron nails) on a neophyte, the Indians met to plan his murder. In 1812, when the priest gathered Yokut and Ohlone Natives to test the whip, several Indians seized the padre and told him he was about to die. They would test their new tool on him. They gagged Quintana with his cape and used it to strangle him. They mutilated one of his testicles, carried his body to his house, and put him to bed. Then three Natives filled a trunk with the mission's silver and buried it in the woods. Years later, soldiers overheard two Native women discussing their new wealth. They forced them to expose the men who had murdered Quintana and stolen the silver. They arrested the rebels, flogged them, and shipped them south to the jail in San Diego. Lorenzo Asisara remembered: "Spanish padres were very cruel to the Indians . . . and they made them work like slaves. I was also subjected to that cruel life."[33] His testimony indelibly impugned the priests' claim that California Indians had become addicted to being flogged.[34]

The Chumash Revolt: A Civil War in California, 1824

By 1816 Chumash in central California had begun to escape to the lands of the Yokut, a tribe that had fiercely held on to its independence. About twenty-one thousand of the Indigenous population chose to live in bands of fugitives who had fled from the twenty-one missions. On the run, they enjoyed the yields of the mission fields and orchards, raiding pastures and selling stolen horses, cattle, and gold to ranchers and settlers. Converts also sold cattle and rifles from their missions to the Yokut, whose vast territory began just to the east of the mission chain and had formed a Native blockade that stopped the Spanish from expanding inland. In San Francisco, Friar Mariano Payéras had lost control of Mission Dolores. Hundreds of Esselen and Ohlone converts were also in flight to the Yokut in the tule marshes along the bay and valleys between the Coastal Range and the Sierras.[35] Still, Spanish soldiers were raiding their villages to capture runaways from the mission.

In 1817 soldiers invaded Yokut lands, seeking to retrieve the fugitive converts and gang-rape the women. Lead balls from the Spanish muskets and Yokut arrows crisscrossed the air. When the Yokuts refused to give up the fugitives, the Spanish soldiers burned their village to the ground.[36] The Yokut hid in the marshes, knowing the Spaniards' horses would simply sink in the muck.

In 1819 Chief Tiisac from the San Joaquin Valley rode tall into Mission Soledad fully armed, guarded by three aides, all mounted on stolen horses. They were flanked by a dozen foot warriors. Chief Tiisac flaunted the ban on Indians riding horses outside the mission compounds and denounced the soldiers and the priests for raping Native women and spreading diseases to the tribes. He taunted the Spanish: Chumash fugitives were in hiding in nearly every Yokut village. Daring the Spanish, he declared that all refugees from missions were free to raid Spanish horses. The horse, he hoped, would change the dynamic of Indian bondage in California.[37]

The Spanish empire, fully dependent for nearly three hundred years on forced Indian labor, was unraveling across Cuba, Mexico, Peru, and now California. After Britain abolished its slave trade in 1808, it pressured other European nations to follow suit. California did not have rum, tobacco, cotton, or other manufactured goods that they might leverage. Under pressure to end slavery in the Americas, the Spanish Crown vowed to neither buy nor carry slaves from any part of the coast of Africa.

Spain, Britain, and the United States pledged to end the slave trade, but not slavery itself. In 1807–8 the profits in Africans were dropping. Newly minted industrialists in Britain saw that slavery was competing with paid labor. Others wanted to trade manufactured goods for African resources. The American and French revolutions and the rise of Protestantism were prompting belated moral qualms about slavery. Further, Black Americans—some formerly enslaved and some their descendants—were speaking out for abolition. However, a global web of traders, bankers, and shipbuilders had arisen around the slave trade. Britain would pay 300 billion pounds in "compensation" to the slaveholders—but none to the enslaved. Thus did freedom seep into the Spanish empire.[38]

As the missions grew to the size of modern counties, dislocation, disease, and starvation drew Indians toward the compounds where they were held in forced *congregación*.[39] Here Indian revolts were forged against the Franciscans, contributing to the end of mission slavery. In the first two decades of the nineteenth century, Chumash, Lakisamni, and Yokut coordinated a revolt that was capped by a mass escape of detained converts and gentiles.

Freedom for California Natives was also linked to anti-imperial movements for national independence and freedom for other Native Americans. California had lost its imperial funding in 1810, and after a ten-year war, Mexico won its independence from Spain in 1821. In that era, fewer goods arrived from Mexico, prompting more violence, more expectations of forced labor, and more demands for the conversion of California Natives.

Indians who fled carried their knowledge of the Spaniards' mechanical skills to the unconquered tribes. During the early decades of the nineteenth century, California Natives who lived in the interior, outside the missions' realm, acquired the horse; with the horse came mobility, military power, and a swifter way to connect tribes. These Indians coordinated their resistance to the invasions by missionaries and mounted a counteroffensive to the settlers along the Coastal Range. Soon they were able to help free California Natives trapped by the Spanish regime and threaten the lives and property of new Mexican and Anglo settlers.

The Plan de Iguala (1822) marked Spain's surrender to Mexico. It abolished slavery and granted citizenship to "all the inhabitants of New Spain, without any distinction between Europeans, Africans, nor Indians." All inhabitants of California became citizens with the "option to all employment depending on their merit and virtues."[40] The government would no longer classify people by race and promised social equality for all. However, California Natives' rights to their land or payment for years of bondage was not included.

Although converts were no longer bound to live and work at the missions, as migrants from Asia and Europe entered California in the next decades, Indians' poverty, dispersal, and dispossession kept them subject to coerced labor.[41] California Natives gained little from Mexican independence. Many Franciscan padres, understanding they would be replaced by traditional Catholic clergy, sought a swift exit from California.

California Natives expected the new ruler to honor the Plan de Iguala and let all Indians return to their homelands after ten years in captivity. They expected Mexico to close the missions, restore their land, and end their bondage. But at five missions along the central coast, the Chumash remained captive. Forced labor and brutal assault were the primary experience of Native Americans at the missions.[42] Even as the missions grew and thrived by slaughtering cattle to supply the growing arrival of ships, selling hides, grain, tallow, and shoes, and as Indigenous people consciously decided to move into the mission compounds to forge alliances, explore the religion, or survive, the Franciscan padres were on edge.

Spanish soldiers were also preparing to leave the presidios; many married Indigenous women and settled on the land. Thousands of Mexicans moved into Alta California and occupied coastal Indian and mission lands. All the settlers wanted unpaid but skilled labor. Freed from legal accountability to the Crown and the Church, the Spanish soldiers enjoyed an era of exuberant violence.

The sacred Chumash spirits had foretold the misery that was to come. The missions had been feeding the converts, albeit very little and

Louis Choris, *Bateau du port de S. Francisco.* Ohlone Natives
escape from Mission Dolores across San Francisco Bay in reed canoes
and into the marshes of present-day Berkeley, Oakland, and Orinda.
(Courtesy of the Beinecke Rare Book and Manuscript Library,
Yale University Library, New Haven.)

very poorly. With the abolition of slavery came the decay of California's
first agricultural economy, and the Natives at Mission Santa Barbara were
starving.

Before the Spanish invasion of California in 1769, 18,500 Chumash
lived at the edge of the Pacific—on barrier islands off Santa Barbara, in
villages on the beach, and in the coastal mountain range. By the beginning
of the nineteenth century, those numbers dwindled to a few thousand. Many
Chumash had entered the missions just to survive; they still maintained
communal ties through their kin; they built planked canoes and traded
in Native foods. Spiritual leaders from the Chumash '*antap* sect stitched
together tribes over hundreds of miles. Although few priests learned the
Native languages, through barter and ritual many Chumash understood
all six languages of their broader culture. Spiritual rituals preserved the
communities and the people. Despite the inevitable punishment by priests
for performing "dark superstitions," tribal rites of passage continued. The

coastal Chumash continued to paint their faces with ochre—a natural sun-screen. When Chumash youth reached puberty, the spiritual leaders taught them to drink toloache tea, which connected them to their supernatural guardians, their spiritual healers, and one another.[43]

Yet the Chumash remained captive at the coastal missions, toiling unpaid—as shepherds and butchers, field laborers and cooks—while the priests were determined to eradicate Native spiritual practices and convert them into diligent Christian slaves. The overcrowded missions could nei-ther feed nor house more Indian "recruits," and the padres had to permit many Chumash to leave to return to their villages. Native Californians who lived inland, like the Mohave, faced invasions from Spanish soldiers and gold and silver miners but they escaped conquest by the Franciscans. Their traditions of weapons, tattoos, body paint, attire, basket weaving, and dance endured.

On a December night in 1823, in the early winter when the Chumash celebrate their birth as a people, a large comet appeared in a dark sky over Southern California and streaked across the heavens for four months. Just the year before, Friar José Señán had become gravely ill, sparing the Chu-mash his humiliating and terrifying confesionarios. It was a hopeful time.

In February 1824 a spark was lit. A neophyte from Mission La Purí-sima walked eighteen miles to visit his cousin in the jail at Santa Inés. A guard, swaggering with the power of his new authority under Mexico, re-fused to let him inside. He declared: "There is no longer any king except the guards" and then flogged the man for having left his own mission.[44]

That year the Chumash launched a historic slave revolt at the triangle of missions at Santa Inés, La Purísima, and Santa Barbara.[45] Sparked by the flogging at Santa Inés, a civil war against the missions raged along the Cal-ifornia coast. Chumash at La Purísima joined a surprise attack and torched Mission Santa Inés. Friars and soldiers' families crouched in a storeroom as the Chumash took over the mission. Over the next days, they built a small fortress inside the compound and cut slits through which to take aim and fire through the thick adobe walls. The captive padres waited a month for the Mexican troops to arrive. The Chumash torched Mission Santa Inés, tore down the workrooms, dormitories, and barracks, seized cannons and rifles, and fled to La Purísima. The twelve hundred converts took pos-session of the weapons, horses, cattle, and granaries and occupied Mission La Purísima for a month. They imprisoned the soldiers, priests, and set-tlers. When the military retook the mission, the defiant Natives also fled to the lands of the Yokut.

As Native runners called out the news that eighteen miles away Mission Santa Inés was burning, the Chumash rushed on to set fire to other nearby missions. At Mission Santa Barbara the converts also took up arms and seized food. While the Chumash took knives from the kitchen and machetes from the storehouses, the Spanish commander dispatched more troops. In the first clash, the soldiers killed four Natives but, unable to dislodge the rebels, they withdrew. Most Chumash simply wanted to escape from bondage and began the trek into Yokut territories in the tules, driving a herd of cattle for sixty miles through the mud to an island in a large marsh where Spanish cavalry could not pass.

The arrival of the refugees strained the Yokut villages. Still, they welcomed the insurgent exiles. The priests had long feared a coordinated uprising, but the military's threat to starve out or slaughter all the remaining Natives forestalled further revolts.[46] Throughout the spring of 1824, Indigenous Californians joined the mass exodus.

At that time, free Natives from the Channel Islands, twelve to seventy miles offshore, were gathering with coastal Indians near Mission Santa Barbara to celebrate sacred Chumash rituals. The padres and soldados feared that the Natives would use the gathering to foment revolt, and after three days they raided the ceremonies and shut them down.[47] To mark their ruthless power, the soldiers chose an Indian man at random and cut off his tongue; then they amputated his feet, piled wood and brush around his body, and set him on fire. When the Chumash converts at Mission Santa Barbara heard of the unspeakable brutality—intended to have quashed their revolt—they ambushed a priest and fled with him into the marshes, bringing only acorn mush for food. Many died on the way into the canyons, while those who remained looted the mission, taking silver from the church, weapons from the arsenal, and food from the kitchen.

Then, in darkness, the Chumash at Santa Barbara retrieved two *tomol*—long wooden canoes—that they had hidden in the reeds. Stealthily they loaded fifty men and women and thirty-four children into the sturdy crafts. They launched silently, paddling straight out across the channel to Santa Cruz Island. Many Tongva and Chumash had been captured from these islands and shipped to the missions. Now the converts were returning to an archipelago that their ancestors had inhabited for more than twelve thousand years. There is no record that the fugitives who fled from Mission Santa Barbara ever returned to the mainland.[48]

Hundreds of Chumash had escaped. After four months in hiding in the tules, the fugitives heard that military scouts had located their encampment. Terrified by the news that the Mexican soldiers were armed with rifles, cannons, and nails embedded in leather straps, some Indian exiles saw no option but to return. They staggered back to the small Catholic triangle of missions hoping for sanctuary.[49]

That March, the Chumash heard that Spaniards meant to retake Mission La Purísima. The Indians holding the mission took clothing and silver from the storeroom and began a thirty-mile trek into the canyons. The Mexican governor of Alta California dispatched a large militia of infantry, cavalry, and artillery. The Indians who remained, still hoping to claim La Purísima, greeted the soldiers with arrows, firing the Spaniards' own muskets and small cannonballs that they had taken from the armory. But the Indians lacked the skill and experience to use the weapons. In the end, sixteen Chumash died at the battle for La Purísima, and the Natives who were trapped inside the mission surrendered.

Friar Antonio Ripoll, believing that the Chumash trusted him, hoped to retrieve the fugitives. He trudged through the canyons and followed a creek, but the Indians moved further into the tule weeds. The number of Chumash fugitives had grown to over four hundred men and women. In a historic message to Friar Ripoll, the Chumash declared their independence from the Church and announced that they could survive in the marshes from skills that they had been forced to learn during bondage: "We shall maintain ourselves with what God will provide us in the open country. Moreover, we are soldiers, stonemasons, carpenters . . . and we will provide for ourselves by our work."[50]

The Chumash were unable to capture the three missions, but their escape into the *tulares* reunited a tribe that had endured thirty years of diaspora and captivity. They spent their freedom in the mountains gathering food and gambling, and they relished having sex without distinctions between married or unmarried couples. They savored their escape, released for a time to revel in the celebration of freedom.[51]

But neither the governor of Alta California, the soldiers, nor the priests were prepared to let the Chumash remain free. Four months after the start of the revolt, a Mexican brigade of 130 soldiers dragged two cannons into the interior. On June 11 a neophyte at the front tried to negotiate a surrender, but most of the Chumash fugitives fled deeper into the mountains, never to return to the missions or the coast. In bold pan-tribal unity, the Chumash who stayed in the tules survived by their traditional knowledge of the land. Other fugitives traveled into the lands of the Yokut and settled in a mountain pass in what is today Kern County.

The slave revolt had exposed the magnitude and duration of Native bondage and hunger, torture and outrage. By 1827, as the Mexican military began to distribute both tribal lands and thousands of mission acres to wealthy *rancheros* and settlers, the Chumash revolt swelled into an all-out war for land and freedom. Muleteer Estanislao Cucunuchi (of the Lakisamni Yokut) was a trusted alcalde at Mission San José. For the post-harvest paseo, or visit home, he led four hundred converts to their ancestral villages up the Río de los Laquisimes (now the Stanislaus River, named after Estanislao). Mexico's "secularization"—a grand giveaway of Indian land to rancheros, settlers, and soldiers that lasted through the 1830s—ended the possibility that Native converts would ever find a place of true return.

As the paseo of 1827 came to an end, the Lakisamni returned to the mission without Estanislao, but brought his message: "We are rising in revolt. . . . We have no fear of the soldiers, for even now they are very few, mere boys, and not even sharpshooters." Many Indian converts took horses from nearby missions to help the rebel encampment of Chumash and Yokut grow.

In early November, Friar Narciso Duran of Mission San José pleaded with the Mexican government: "Publicly, without reserve . . . they have declared themselves in revolt. I beg you to send us the aid of ten soldiers." Duran ordered soldiers to retrieve the fugitives and deliver "a sample punishment of sound throttlings." But Natives from the missions at Santa Clara, San Juan Bautista, and Santa Cruz were rushing to join Estanislao's band. Revolt spread. By late November, the padres asked the Mexican military to double the troops.

The soldiers did not venture out of the missions in the winter of 1827, and the Indians in the tule marshes took the time to build forces and raid horses and cattle. The fugitives built a fort near a patch of low woods, surrounding it with a maze of trenches deep enough to allow the Indians to stand upright and fire. They cut tall logs for a palisade. Then they sent a messenger to the missions to warn "our good Father Duran that from now on our real exploits begin. We shall fall upon the very ranches and cornfields. . . . And for the troops . . . we have nothing but contempt and defiance!"

General Mariano Vallejo led one hundred soldiers and fifty captive Indians who he ordered to carry two heavy cannons through the marshes. The soldiers set fire to the fort and blasted it with cannonballs. The Natives returned gunfire with arrows, burning branches, and stolen musket balls. The Mexican cavalry held fast at the wall of fire.

During the night, as smoke hung over both camps, some of the Indians tried to escape in the river, but the soldiers overtook them. In the early morning light, the Mexican troops charged through the forest, slaughtering Chumash. Finally, Vallejo ordered his troops to fire randomly into the woods. They killed most of the Natives and captured several Indian women and men. They hanged them all on the spot. Blown by the winds, the fire at the fort spread, chasing the soldiers back toward San Francisco Bay.

Although many guerilla groups of fugitives were determined to remain free, overwhelmed by the slaughter, Estanislao rode back to Mission San José to surrender and negotiate a pardon for survivors. Two years after his surrender, in 1834 Estanislao again came back to the mission to teach the converts Yokut traditions and language. The leader of a pan-Indian movement of gentiles and neophytes, pagans and converts, died in 1839 during a malaria epidemic brought into the Central Valley by beaver trappers from the Hudson Bay Company.[52]

The Chumash tell histories of the war, passed down by those who were there. They tell of powerful resistance to prolonged bondage.[53] Lucretia Garcia describes their sustaining faith in powerful totemic objects such as the *atishwin*, woven of human hair, that could turn the soldiers into "a pack of babies," protect the exiles from bears, or give them strength to carry comrades on their shoulders over the mountains; the atishwin would show Indians where the Spanish had hidden a fresh horse and warn of incoming soldiers. The Chumash tell of the collective courage of the revolts and the unbearable choices of the exodus, leaving children along the road before they could be killed by the soldiers, as well as the collective energy of their people.[54]

In 1843, six hundred miles from the nearest Spanish mission, trapper Joseph Reddeford Walker came upon a thriving community of about eight hundred Chumash. That trappers' camp delivered to the Chumash refugees a strain of the malaria epidemic (1833–46) that would ultimately decimate the California Native population by 75 percent.[55] None of the local Chumash survived that scourge.[56] The vast tribe had survived captivity and bondage, only to be invaded by microbes brought by the conquerors. Genocide by germs.

Ambiguous Freedom

The new Mexican government reclaimed all the lands taken by the Franciscan missions. In 1826 Governor José María de Echeandía, the second

Mexican governor, issued a provisional emancipation proclamation and ordered the padres to free all the baptized Indians; then he ordered the soldiers to seek and return runaways to serve *Californios* (elites), on their ancestral lands.

On September 16, 1829, inspired by the promises of the Haitian Revolution, President Vicente Guerrero abolished the slave trade in Mexico. Guerrero, president of a country with the largest free Black population in the Western Hemisphere, emancipated all slaves in Mexico and those "held to service" in California. Word of Indian emancipation reached California in 1830. Indigenous women, however, were not considered Mexican citizens and had to apply for their freedom through a husband or father. Governor Echeandía invited all Native fugitives and "self-supporting" Christian Indian men to "disaffiliate" from the missions, yet he still allowed the government to whip adult Indians, limiting the brutal punishment to fifteen blows each week.[57] And with those harsh strictures, slave labor as propagated by the California missions came to an end.

In 1833 Mexico seized and "secularized" the missions' lands that by now occupied about one-third of California. Despite a series of "decrees of confiscation" purportedly designed to return homelands to Indigenous Californians, the new government auctioned, sold, or gave most of the mission property to ex-military officers and ranchers in large land grants— despite their dependence on the mission, and hence, on Natives, to supply wheat, beans, eggs, and vegetables.

In 1835 California governor José Figueroa heard that "the workers no longer recognize the voice de razón [of reason], or of authority. In one voice they yell, 'We are free, we don't want to obey, we don't want to work.'"[58] As powerful Mexicans clamored for the land that had been Indian for time immemorial—extending so far beyond the reach of memory that the residents could not legally have to prove how they came to possess it—California had to confront the many meanings of freedom.

In 1826 Gil Ricla applied to the new Mexican government for emancipation from Mission San Diego, after twenty-nine years of captivity and forced labor. Ricla received neither land, tools, nor seeds. Known as "Citizen Gil," for the rest of his life, Ricla and his wife, Pia, had to carry his *licencia* (freedom paper) with him at all times. Ricla had no option but to move to the presidio, the old Spanish garrison that still functioned as a military fort, and work as a carpenter.[59] In October 1836 the male population of Mission San Buenaventura north of Los Angeles collectively applied for their emancipation, signed their names, and listed occupations that would qualify as "self-supporting": cowboy, weaver, tile maker, soap maker, and laborer.

Mexico did not include the word "freedom" in its abolition decree, but those Indians who spoke Spanish invoked *"Libertad,"* as opposed to "segregated" or "disaffiliated." As emancipated Indians sought to define the scope of the new political terms of their lives, "solicitations for freedom" flowed to the governor. Five days after emancipation, the Indians at Mission San Buenaventura asked Governor Echeandía to convert the compound into a free pueblo and to give them its land, money, seeds, livestock, and tools. Echeandía refused.

The Emancipation and Secularization Decree of 1833, Mexico's second abolition act, did not actually free California Natives; it only allowed them to leave the missions with no fear of recapture. Now homeless, many remained at the compounds to work their trades.

For more than fifty years, a total of two hundred priests and one hundred soldiers (at a time) had seized and baptized 87,787 Indians and recorded 63,789 deaths. Altogether the missions had held about two hundred thousand Indians in slavery. This figure is nearly half the number of 470,000 enslaved Africans that Spain shipped from 1800 to 1866 to the Caribbean to work in the coffee, cocoa, tobacco, and cotton fields.[60] The bondage of California Native people had extended Spain's reach in the global slave trade. It enriched the empire.

The Treaty of Guadalupe Hidalgo between Mexico and the United States banned slavery in the new territories, promised citizenship to Indians and mestizos, and granted Indians the right to their own lands—a promise overwritten as lands turned into states. And by 1848, Mexico had already given tracts of land—up to fifty thousand acres each—to powerful Californios such as ranchers, farmers, and military officers. At the end of the swift U.S.–Mexican War in 1848, the United States seized nearly one-half of the land of its southern neighbor and claimed California, Nevada, Utah, Wyoming, Colorado, Texas, New Mexico, and Arizona—lands that had recently all belonged to Spain.

Freedom and Reparations

California Natives sought reparations: retroactive wages for all the churches and barracks they had built, fields they had planted and harvested, losses that countered the new sheep that brought wool, horses that transformed trade and contact, and the wheel.[61] Equally important, they sought to reclaim the mission compounds as Indigenous space. The Native Californians, so long trapped in the missions, had transposed their Native skills into the conquerors' ways: they appropriated the Spaniards' horse as a warm-blooded and companionable vehicle of freedom. They used the loom and wove their tribal patterns and clothed themselves. Over time they had learned to speak Spanish to protect themselves and to insert their demands and ideas into the mission vocabulary. They reclaimed their traditional designs in rugs, pottery, and baskets to be used in California's market economy; those novel artifacts of an "authentic" and unfamiliar civilization soon would attract tourists' dollars.

During the sixty-five years of mission rule, thousands of Natives perished far from their villages, clans, and families, even as the missions' land extended to absorb villages and clans. The true numbers are unknowable. Tribes believed that it dishonored the dead to talk about them; lineages were lost.

Freed from the religious fanatics who had been dispatched to California as a holy tool of empire, the Indians transmitted their cultures and histories, their dances and storytelling, to their children. Although they sought land, they refused to move onto homelands held by other tribes. The Indians who survived at Mission San Juan Capistrano demanded the mission's land for themselves and remained at the compound. The missions, writes historian Lisbeth Haas, became part of the Indigenous geography of California.[62] At the end of mission rule, most Native Californians sought to return to their ancestral lands or tried to reclaim them from Mexico.[63]

The history of human bondage at the missions initiates the history of the twin forces of human bondage and the globalization of California. After Indian emancipation, the United States and Mexico only distributed 6 percent of mission territory to California Natives. Neither Mexico's California Territorial Legislature nor the U.S. Congress granted Native Californians the right to their homelands. The loss of land meant the loss of ancestors and memory. Without land or water rights, they took jobs as servants for new settlers coming from New England, the mid-Atlantic, and the plantation South: a forced hybridity of slavery and freedom emerged in California.

Many Indians did return to their tribal villages. Others, displaced by poverty and homelessness, remained on small plots of mission land that once were theirs; at least the priests removed them from the Church rolls.[64] In 1849 California's new state constitution revoked Indians' rights to U.S.

Father Junípero Serra, 1785. Painting found
at Santa Cruz Convent, Querétaro, Mexico.

California Historical Society Collection at
the University of Southern California.

citizenship that had been promised by the Treaty of Guadalupe Hidalgo.
Being "Indian" became a marker of a new era of political violence and
ethnic cleansing. "Indian" was a racial sign that marked a resilient system
of apartheid in California. As the eyes of the United States looked west, the
term "Indian" shaped the politics of race, gender, and class—that is to say,
the politics of freedom.

In justifying turning Native lands into mission lands and settlers' lands,
American concepts of manifest destiny, westward expansion, and settler
colonialism need to be stretched to include the ownership of people as
well as of territory. The "inevitability of expansion" belied the revolts of

the Kumeyaay and the Chumash that undid the uncontested power of the padres and soldiers to occupy Native land and own Native people.

For the most part, the Spanish soldiers and the two hundred priests who served the missions conspired to continue to treat California Natives as savages in need of confinement, exploitation, and protocols that invited torturous "correction." Moreover, the Franciscan regime was a paradigm for the racial inequalities upon which an intractable carceral state was built.

Franciscan missions set in motion more than two centuries of labor trafficking and sex trafficking in California and intractable assumptions about the rights to own and to enact violence on Indigenous people in California. The missions produced the codes and the vocabulary that made it possible for the mere two hundred religious fanatics to appropriate the bodies and lands of California's First Peoples to seek to rename people and reduce myriad discrete tribal nations, names, and geographies into a single monolithic and homogenous imposed label—"Indian"—to distribute their territory and individuals, to splinter communities, and to erase knowledge. The missions made it possible for Native Californians and their lands and waters to become the patrimony of the state—an entitlement to be dispensed to the powerful, to be wasted and abused.

On September 22, 2015, the Catholic Church canonized Father Junípero Serra, the friar who led the Spanish invasion of California in an absolutist system of brutality and bondage, and he became the first Hispanic saint in the United States. Serra did not predict that California Natives would escape from the Franciscans' franchise of torture, forced labor, and slavery. He did not imagine that all he wrought would be exposed and his holy hagiography unraveled, effectively dismantled by those the Church and empire had once sought to subjugate and consume.

CHAPTER THREE

A Slave Rectangle in the Pacific

Ukut skuunat gui qiagkwaraatnga (These schooners are making me cry).

—SÚGUCIHPET (Alaska Native)

FOR OVER FOUR THOUSAND years, the Chugach people lived where steep glaciers ring the dark Prince William Sound. One day, long ago, a hunter bent down in the surf to pluck a tasty sea mollusk that had attached itself to the rocks on the ocean floor. Suddenly the tide came in. It toppled the man and swept him out into the sea. Fearful of drowning, the man said, "I wish I might turn into a sea otter." And he did.[1] The Chugach believed that the playful sea otter, covered in soft, dense fur, began with this man. Ever since, the Chugach hunted *ahnaq*, sea otters, in kayaks in roiling surf in the cold waters of the Gulf of Alaska.

Chugach and otters both hungered for sea urchins and crabs. In this frozen whiteness, three thousand miles across the Bering Strait from Russia, they lived and suffered together. They were kin. The Chugach hunter possessed virtually the same spine, ribs, and organs as the sea otter. But the otter was covered in silky fur, one million hairs per square inch.

To honor his prey, on the morning of a hunt the hunter stripped off his clothes, poured water over his head, and entered the cold, icy sea. Only then did he climb into his *iqaq*—a low kayak built from seal skins, sinew, and bone—waterproofed with rubs of shark and seal oil. Chugach women

78

Louis Choris, *View of St. Paul Island in the Sea of Kamchatka, with Sea Lions.*
A solitary otter hunter, likely Unangax̂ from the Aleutian Islands,
faces the wild seas of the North Pacific.

In Louis Choris, *Vues et paysages des régions équinoxiales/recueillis dans un voyage autour
du monde* (Paris: Paul Renouard, 1826). (Courtesy of the Beinecke Rare Book
and Manuscript Library, Yale University Library, New Haven.)

had scraped and cured the skins for the boat and tightly stretched, sewn, and oiled his *kanagluk* (parka) and his *akkuilitaq* (spray skirt)—both cut from seal intestines and stitched with sinews of bears or seals.

Almost of the sea, the hunter knelt on a pad of grass and otter pelts; the sides of his kayak were so transparent that he could see below the waterline. Armed with a spear and a throwing block, he joined a small flotilla from his village. He would return with more than two hundred kilograms of seal meat lashed to his kayak. From time immemorial Alaska Natives had worn the pelts of sea mammals for warmth and burned their rich blubber for lighting oil. Like sea otters who hold each other's forepaws while they sleep so they do not drift apart in the night sea, Native hunters strapped their kayaks together so they would not lose one another as they navigated by the stars and the tides.

In this coherent world, the otter selected its hunter and taught him a song, to beckon it for the kill; the Chugach man chanted, "Ohö . . . ohö."[2]

The hunt might last two to three days as the kayaks circled the otter that would dive again and again to escape, surfacing every two minutes for air. Sound travels well underwater, and the otter could hear the splash of the paddle and the kayaks slipping through the surf. The hunters all aimed their spears at the otter's head with respect and focus so that it might die quickly.[3] The first hunter to strike the otter claimed the kill with floats made of seal bladders attached to his arrow. When the waters were calm, he watched the animal's underwater struggle and saw tiny bubbles of air trail from its long fur. With dive after dive, the otter weakened and both otter and hunter tired.

After three days at sea, the hunter was thirsty. But he would not drink until he had, at last, beached his prey. To acknowledge the thirst that he had caused the otter as it struggled to die, the hunter poured fresh river water over the mouth of the animal before he quenched his own thirst, and the otter passed from the sea into the custody of its human hunter. Later, the hunter would return the otter's bones to the sea so that it could be reborn.[4]

Eons ago, when the glaciers melted into the ocean, the salmon tasted the fresh water and rushed up the new creeks to spawn. Sea otters chased the salmon into the mouths of the icy creeks. For coastal tribes along the northern Pacific Rim, the salmon and the otter were the givers of life.

Since the sixteenth century, Russia had sought to spread its empire into Siberia's vast tributaries and wetlands to the east, and it turned its muskets on the sparse tribes. The vast land seemed hard and barren, yet sable and ermine, marten and fox lived on the tundra and in the scrub forests. While Spanish monks and soldiers were invading the Americas in the sixteenth and seventeenth centuries, the Russians were marching thousands of serfs—legally bound peasants trapped in involuntary servitude—into Siberia. Their task was to trap and skin the mink and ermine whose fur grew thick and long in the cold tundra, close to the unyielding ground. In Siberia, Russian fur traders kidnapped Siberian Natives and forced them to bludgeon the small mammals and deliver a quota of pelts and also pay an annual tax, or *iasak*, to the emperor. Russian privateers forced Siberian Natives to build their forts and provide the invaders with women.[5]

The Russian empire stretched from Kyiv (Kiev, now Ukraine) near the Polish border in the west, across the barren steppes to the sea of Okhotsk in far eastern Siberia, and from the Arctic Ocean in the north down to the Manchurian and Chinese borders to the south. Siberian fur was the commodity that China would accept in exchange for its coveted porcelain, gold, silver, tea, silk, and ivory. In the middle of the eighteenth century, when the overhunted fox and marten became extinct, Russia's tax collectors seized the Natives' tools, traps, livestock, and horses. The population of dark sable, the most valuable of all the mammals, was dwindling, and in lieu of the prized pelts, the Russians took Siberian hostages, often in chains, as debtor and sex slaves to be redeemed by their kin.

Then the Russian empire looked east. At the closest point, only two and a half miles of sea separate Russia and Alaska; when the Bering Strait freezes in midwinter, it is possible to walk across the ice of the North Pacific.

In the winter of 1724–25, Emperor Peter the Great lay dying in St. Petersburg, and he wrote two orders to Vitus Bering, a Danish explorer: sail forth and claim for Russia all the land to the east, and find a land route to China to replace the long march across the ice fields of Siberia. Perhaps Bering's route could take him to America, where Russia could challenge the Spanish empire. Hauling carpentry tools, ships' anchors, and a year of food supplies, Bering conscripted three thousand men. It took three years for him to cross thirty-five hundred miles over the Ural Mountains, float a raft across the icy watershed of the Lena River, and reach the Kamchatka Peninsula and the Sea of Okhotsk. In 1728 he sailed east. Blocked by fog from even seeing North America, he turned back to Russia.

In the early summer of 1741, Bering sailed on the "Great Northern Expedition" at a cost of 1.5 million royal rubles—about one-sixth of the entire yearly income of the Russian government.[6] He outfitted two more ships. On their sixth day out, a dense ocean fog separated the ships, and each captain decided to sail on alone.

Bering dropped anchor by an island in the Aleutian chain and sent sailors ashore with gifts of tobacco and brandy. Through his spyglass he watched Native people, Unangax̂ (in Russian, Aleuts or Aleutian Islanders), seize his crew; he then fired a threatening blast from the ship's cannon. Fearful of the loud noise, the Unangax̂ dropped to the ground, and the Russian crew broke free and swiftly rowed back to the ship.

Still, Bering was disoriented in the fog. The sailors were dying from scurvy, thirst, and hunger. Just a few days out from the coast of Siberia, high seas and violent winds hurled his ship against a small volcanic island, and the boat shattered against the rocks. As arctic foxes gnawed on the bodies of the dead and dying, it took the sailors a week to carry the sick from the wreck onto the beach.[7] Bering and twenty-eight men from his crew died on the island, but forty-six managed to live through the winter by burrowing in caves that they dug into the snow.

During the short days of the northern winter, the crew discovered sea otters—"soft gold"—nesting in the shoals and kelp beds of the island, and the Russian sailors slaughtered thirteen hundred for their pelts. In May, when the ice finally melted, the survivors built a little boat from the wreckage, and on August 26, 1742, they sailed into port bringing otter pelts softer than sable or mink. Before Bering's ill-starred voyage led to the discovery of "soft gold," 200,000 to 300,000 sea otters lived in the cold waters along the shores of the northern Pacific Ocean.[8]

Lacking a layer of blubber, the otter's thick fur—the densest of any animal—keeps it warm even in the cold waters of the northern Pacific. It can close its nostrils and small ears, hold its breath for up to five minutes, and deliver its young underwater. The sea otter can use a rock to wedge open hard shellfish or pound the shells of abalone against a rock with a large stone.[9] Although Bering's survivors had failed to locate a land crossing to China, they presented the tsar with a precious gift that would underwrite a path to a global "New Russia" and launch an era of slavery in the Pacific Northwest.

The Otter, the Empire, and the Alaska Natives

The survivors of Bering's expedition sold the otter pelts to fur traders who transported them by caravan two thousand miles over the Ural Mountains to Kiakhta, a remote wooden fort on the Mongolian border that was China's only trading outpost with Russia. Russia had long wanted to enter China's lucrative markets, but its neighbor had banned Russian ships from its ports. Yet China craved Russian furs, and in 1728 had built a remote fort near Lake Baikal, guarded by twelve hundred Mongolian men.

With no common currency at the frigid station, the Russians bartered Manchurian camels, sables, muskrats, beavers, hunting dogs, and fabric for Chinese cotton, ginseng and loose tea, porcelain, ivory, copper, ink, pepper, jellied fruits, silver, and tight balls of tobacco. But what the Chinese brokers really desired were otter furs, and they paid eighty to one hundred rubles for each pelt (about $2,300 today). Then they loaded the furs onto sleds pulled by reindeer and carted them across the ice to Beijing. The tiny otter pelt had traveled about thirty-four hundred miles just to adorn the collars, cuffs, and hems of the silk robe of a Mandarin merchant.

For the next hundred years, *promyshlenniki*—ruthless and independent Russian fur hunters—slaughtered sea otters across the Aleutian Islands, in the bays and coves of mainland Alaska, and down the Pacific Coast. When the promyshlenniki realized that their greed exceeded their skills, they decided to chase the sea hunters rather than the otters. Only Alaska Natives knew what the otter ate and when it birthed; only Alaska Natives could build the skin kayaks and use bone needles to stitch together waterproof parkas from a seal's intestines, paint the visors that deflected the blinding glare of the water, and flip a throwing board and shoot stone-tipped spears. To slaughter the valuable little sea mammal, the Russians seized Alaska Native men and women. The Native hunters became tragic tools of Russian expansion, and the otter pelts covered all the expenses of the tsar's court.[10] In an unruly rush for the "soft gold," destitute Natives from Siberia, free peasants from Kamchatka, fugitive serfs, sailors, debtors, and convicts hurried to the rough ports of Siberia to find a ship that would carry them east, to Alaska. But the Russians were unprepared for a maritime "harvest" in utterly uncharted rough waters on ragged islands occupied by skillful Alaska Natives.[11]

The profiteering from a natural resource and a ruthless regime of human bondage were codependent throughout the history of slavery in the West. In Alaska, a regime of conscripted and forced labor, backed by hostage-taking and taxes, supported an invasion that created a moving frontier. The Russians moved east, island by island, building an unfree workforce to slaughter the valuable otters. Russian slavery in North America uniquely followed only one natural resource, but unlike sugar, cotton, or tobacco, the sea otter could not be cultivated or replenished. By 1780 some of the new fur traders carried shiploads of otter pelts worth about 480,000 rubles (or $500,000 today) per voyage.[12] The otter became Russia's boon in its belated entry in the global contest for colonies: it opened the China trade and became a ticket to empire in the Americas, one with irretrievable human and ecological sacrifice.

For their frenzied invasion of the Alaskan islands, promyshlenniki hired inept shipbuilders who hastily assembled ships from raw wood. Neither ships nor men were ready to face the gales and turbulent waters of the northern Pacific.[13] Ships leaked, longboats capsized, vessels shipwrecked, and men died of scurvy and starvation. Captained by despotic and incompetent masters, guarded by Cossack soldiers, the ships often crashed against submerged rocks. Emaciated Russian crews became all the more determined to conscript the skilled Alaska Natives and capture otters.[14]

The promyshlenniki sailed with an *ukaz*, a government certificate that permitted them to "search out unknown islands, bestow Russian citizenship upon the peoples living there, found a trading industry for every variety of land and sea animal, and establish pleasant and friendly trade with the Natives."[15] In return for each permit, they agreed to pay the emperor 10 percent of the profit from Alaskan otter pelts.

The Russian adventurers knew nothing about hunting a small sea mammal that hides in kelp beds and dives quickly when it feels any movement in the water or smells blood from a nearby kill. They did not know that when one otter slipped under the water, the whole "raft" of otters would follow. They did not know that only four hundred thousand sea otters lived in the Pacific—from the Aleutian Islands to Baja California—and that a female "dam" birthed only one small pup a year.[16] They did discover the doomsday news that the fur of a female was softer and worth more than that of a male.

Too greedy and impatient to study the habits of their shy prey, Russian captains searched for Native hunters, taking Alaska Native women and children hostage, and forcing Native hunters to ransom their kidnapped families with pelts. Russians compelled the Indigenous people to slaughter the population of sea otters of the North Pacific.

For fifty years, Russian fur traders sailed from Siberia, across the Kuril Islands to the Aleutian chain and eastward to Kodiak Island, finally reaching the coast of mainland Alaska. They invaded the islands with iron weapons, muskets, and cannons, kidnapping skilled Alaska Native men and women. In place of the Natives' normal routines of gathering ice cranberries, salting fish, oiling their kayaks, and birthing children, the fur traders instead forced them to slaughter hundreds of thousands of the sea otters that were their spirit animals. The otter hunt drove the species nearly to extinction and tore apart a communal world of earth and sea, animal and human, men and women. Further, without the hunters to provide seasonal halibut and seal meat, and without the women to dry the fish and dig for roots, the people starved. Without seal skins for warmth, Alaska Natives froze to death. As the otter built the Russian empire, the world of coastal Alaska shattered.

Here, in a subarctic climate with a short fishing and hunting season, Alaska Natives thrived as a community. They were maritime people who had likely migrated from Mongolia and had lived on these islands for over seven thousand years. Clans of about fifty people shared underground houses, *ulax̂* or *barabara*, up to 240 feet long. The earth itself protected them from ice and winds; bones and driftwood held up sod roofs, and the people entered down a wooden ladder from the sky.[17] Honoring the ecology and the animals they killed, Alaska Natives used every organ and every piece of skin; whale ribs supported the ceiling and shoulder blades became tables and seats.[18] Usually, Alaska Natives who lived on the islands buried their dead in high caves, protecting their bones and spirits from the rains and ravenous animals, from earthquakes and tsunamis.[19] Daunted by the winds, the Russian invaders called the treeless and barren islands "the place that god forgot."[20]

The Unangax̂ believed they could travel to the sky and live under the sea. They danced, often naked and often in masks, at a sanctified high place or by a tall pole.[21] They asked the healers to release the souls of the animals that died so that their spirits might live in another being. Many Alaska Natives heard voices in the ice and in the stones. The women dreamed the hunters into returning, sometimes in the form of a bear or another man or woman.[22]

For thousands of years, no species of animal had ever become extinct in the North Pacific. But in the first fifty years of conquest, the Russians slaughtered over ninety-six thousand sea otters, four hundred thousand seals, and over one hundred thousand foxes, decimating species and Native people whose souls traveled between people and gods, animals, and spirits.[23]

Counterattack

In 1745, only three years after Bering's crew returned with their hoard of otter furs, Russian ships sailed back into the Aleutian chain, often met by hundreds of Native warriors armed with harpoons and darts. Desperate for fresh water, a few armed Russians attempted to land on Agattu Island, but the men of Agattu tried to seize their longboats. For likely the first time, Russian gunfire thundered on an Aleutian island and a bullet wounded an Alaskan man. Although the Aleutian spears carved from whalebone failed to pierce the Russians' longboat, the invaders were daunted by the Alaskans' resistance and fled back to their ship.

Sailing between islands, the Russians slaughtered Alaskan men, fifteen or twenty at a time. They raped the women and held them for ransom, to be redeemed for otter pelts. Not until the crew was sick with scurvy and the captains feared a shipwreck in the winter winds did the Russian ships return to Kamchatka with cargos of hundreds of furs.

The *toiens*, or chiefs, at Umnak, the Fox Islands, and Unalaska planned a joint revolt. In an early invasion, they beckoned the Russians to land and ambushed the crews, as other Alaska Natives burned the ships anchored in the bays. When the Russians tried to seize Native women, Umnak men, armed with spears, chased them off their island. Across the vast chain of western islands, measured in days of paddling, revolts against the invaders spread between Native villages. Expecting the Russians to return, Alaska Natives planned more revolts. Aleuts from each island gathered an equal number of long wooden splinters; each day they threw one splinter into the fire, and when the last splinter burned, they would attack the Russians when they tried to step onto land.

Independent ragtag Russian fur hunters merged into companies and sailed from island to island, kidnapping hunters, slaughtering otters, and moving on. In 1758, lured by Natives' feigned offers of females and furs, the Russians let themselves be divided across several islands.[24] Then the Unangax̂ people, armed only with bone knives and axes, attacked Russian "detachments." On Unalaska, the Aleuts chased the Russian invaders back to their ships, and many of the invaders died at sea searching in the heavy fog for other Russian ships. When the Russian survivors sailed back into the harbor of Umnak, they found that their mother ship had been torched. Except for a few sailors who hid in caves, all the Russians on Unalaska were killed. When spring arrived in the western Aleutian Islands, the returning Russians found that their ships were in cinders. Across Alaska, the beaches were littered with Russian corpses.[25]

Captains Ivan Soloviev and Stepan Glotov were determined to break the uprising. In 1763 Glotov destroyed all the villages on the south side of Umnak. Two years later, Soloviev slaughtered every male he could find on the Fox Islands and massacred as many as three thousand Aleuts. Filling otter intestines with gunpowder, the Russians made small bombs and overpowered Native forts built of bones and driftwood.

In the logbooks of the ships *Sv. Vladimir Gavriil* and *Sv. Vladimir*, Soloviev and Glotov masked the brutality in the otter trade, writing: "The inhabitants [of Attu] were very friendly towards the Russians . . . and even gave their children as hostages [*amanats*]." In 1763 the ships returned to Siberia with nine hundred pelts of sea otters, valued at 53,000 rubles. Although the Russian government later acknowledged that this "company which went to the Aleutian Islands to hunt animals, committed indescribable abuses, ruin, and murder upon the Natives there," it allowed the pro-myshlenniki to return to Alaska if they agreed to "bring revenue to Her Imperial Majesty" and "refrain from barbarizing and plundering local inhabitants."[26]

During the last decades of the eighteenth century, sea otters and Alaska Natives—human property claimed by independent fur traders—were the twin engines of the Russian empire and invasion of North America. In Alaska, the Russians faced none of the political or ethical antislavery debates arising in Britain and the United States. The Alaska Natives lived thousands of miles from the Russian capital, and their servitude left few footprints of Russian opposition. Yet human bondage enabled Russia's economic expansion into China and its territorial expansion across Alaska. By 1772, moving east, island by island, the Russians controlled the whole chain of the Aleutians and the Alaska Natives whose ancestors had lived on the windswept lands for ten thousand years. With the otter gone in the islands nearest to Russia, the promyshlenniki sailed on east toward Kodiak Island and the Alaskan mainland.

The Russian regime of human bondage spread through the ecological catastrophe it created. In the years of the American and French revolutions, as the Spanish moved up the California coast, seizing land and Natives, the privately owned promyshlenniki forced Alaska Natives to abandon their islands, leaving only a few old men to hunt for seals and birds and a few women to gather a sparse diet of eggs and roots.

In 1783 the ruthless entrepreneur Grigory Shelikhov began to extend the borders of Mother Russia and transform Alaska into a true colony built upon a slave fiefdom. The next year Shelikhov founded a slave labor camp on Kodiak Island, six hundred miles to the east of the long Aleutian chain, and there he deposited his captives—Aleut, Alutiiq, and Sugpiaq men and women—whom he seized along the way.[27] On Kodiak, Shelikhov faced one of the largest uprisings in the history of the northern Pacific. On August 14, 1784, the men, women, and children tried to flee. In a great flotilla of kayaks and larger *baidarka*, captive people of different tribes and languages swiftly paddled to a cove on the far side of the island. Shelikhov's private troops turned muskets and cannons on the hundreds of Natives in flight. In the Awa'ug Massacre, one hundred armed Russians killed between one thousand and three thousand Alaska Natives hiding on a nearby island, captured one thousand more, and held four hundred as hostages.[28]

Arsenti Aminak, a Sugpiaq, remembered the "terrible blood bath" of his boyhood. Shelikhov, he recalled, captured the survivors, and "every chief had to surrender his children; I was saved only by my father's begging and many sea otter pelts. . . . Only a few [people] were able to flee to Ang-yahtalek in baidarkas; three hundred Koniags [from Kodiak] were shot by the Russians. This happened in April. When our people revisited the place in the summer the stench of the corpses lying on the shore polluted the air so badly that none could stay there, and since then the island has been uninhabited." The Alutiiq call the site of the massacre "Awa'ug"—"where one becomes numb."[29]

On Kodiak Island, Shelikhov and his wife, heiress and mapmaker Natalia Alekseevna Shelikhova, built their own armed colony of 130 guards and sailors. From this central base, Shelikhov forced the Sugpiaq (translated as the "real people") and other Alaska Natives to paddle out in six hundred double kayaks, with an armed Russian guard in back seats. In return for otters, a Native hunter received tobacco leaves or a few glass beads. Any Native who refused was to be imprisoned or "beaten and taken away to the tundra and killed with spears." Shelikhov took hundreds of children hostage to redeem them for otter furs.[30] In his greed, he ordered three hundred skilled otter hunters to paddle into a raging sea. All drowned in their light single-seat kayaks.

The Alutiiq and Dena'ina (people from Kodiak Island, the Cook Inlet, and the area around modern Anchorage) tried to block the Russians' drive and sought to slaughter Shelikhov's private soldiers. But the Natives were outgunned. Then, in a tragedy of empire, a ferocious germ—smallpox—had traveled among sailors and in the wood of the ships and killed 75 percent of the population of Alaska Natives. The Unangax̂ population fell from sixteen thousand to nineteen hundred men and women.[31]

Slaves, Otters, and Empire

Grigory Shelikhov ignored the order of military Governor-General Ivan Iakobii to pay "fair wages" to the Alaska Natives that would "inspire in them a will to be subjects under the Russian scepter."[32] In 1786 Shelikhov returned to St. Petersburg from Kodiak and told Empress Catherine II (Catherine the Great) that the otter population was shrinking. He urged her to seize control of the fur trade and expel the independent promysh-lenniki. Catherine agreed to consolidate the otter trade, found a Russian colony in Alaska, and form the Russian-American Company. In the name of empire, Catherine would seize all the Native hunters and their Alas-kan prisoners—*kalgi*—and turn them into the human property of the new

Russian-American Company. The Russian-American Company was born as a slave-holding company owned by the tsar.[33]

In the winter of 1789, on the eastern islands of Unimak and Sanak (Sanaĝax), the captain of the ship *Tula* captured several Native hunters and sent them out to sea in fierce winds; three men died. Still, the *Tula* sailed on, stopping at islands and sending armed men ashore in longboats to seize over one hundred men and women, along with their kayaks, weapons, parkas, and reserves of food. The Russians left behind only the very young and the very old; after four winters without their hunters, starving Alaska Natives threw themselves over the cliffs and into the sea in mass suicides.

In 1789–90 Russian ships circled the far islands, conscripting more Native hunters and their kayaks. The officers even swiped the seal throats that the Native hunters used as shoes. Algamalinag, an Aleut *toien*, or chief, denounced the private Russian companies that "keep us prisoners" and "use us against our will for hunting animals." Algamalinag reported to the tsar that the Russian overseer, Pshenichnoi, "seized Aleut girls and women and kept them for fornication; he mercilessly whipped them with straps and beat them with sticks." With high winds blowing at sea, explained Algamalinag, it was too late in the season to hunt for seals or to fish for salmon, and over three hundred people on Unalaska died from starvation. The Russians gave them clothing, but "of course it comes from our own hunting and is prepared by us." On the island of Ugamak, a Russian shipmaster whipped two women and two men to death, while the Russian work crews "pierced with lances all the women, without leaving any."[34]

The chain of islands appeared to be deserted, the otters decimated, and the tribes fractured. A Native woman chanted her loss,

Ukut skuunat gui qiagkwaraatnga
tan'uraruaqa piteklluku.
Qai-ciin kinguatni;
piciqsaanga tan'uraruaqa
aiwilluku.

These schooners are making me cry
because of my boyfriend.
What am I going to do afterwards;
they are taking my boyfriend
away (by boat).[35]

In July 1795 Grigory Shelikhov died, but the capricious and unstable Emperor Paul I had appointed Alexander Baranov as the governor of Russian America, with orders to establish the Russian-American Company as a joint-stock enterprise. Baranov's first task was to oversee the capture and conscription of unwilling Native hunters. Only because he was deeply in debt did Baranov accept the posting, but his reign turned into a brutal dictatorship that lasted from 1791 to 1818. By the time Baranov arrived on Kodiak Island, Shelikhov's base was sparse, otters were few, and morale was low. The new colonial governor turned to a ruthless style of discipline that he copied from European navies and the Russian army: flogging reluctant Alaska Natives and running them through a narrow gauntlet of sharp staves made of stiff whalebone—an agonizing and humiliating punishment. At his back was ruthless strongman Ivan Kuskov, commerce councilor, whom Baranov put in charge of conscripting Natives and implementing his threats of exile and torture.[36]

By the spring of 1792, Baranov launched the largest drive for otter fur in the history of the region.[37] For that, he conscripted thousands of Alutiiq men from Kodiak and sent them under guard as far east as the Kuril Islands near Japan, where they began to search for new otter fields.[38]

The toiens sent protests to the tsar expressing their rage: "We are obligated to tolerate our women, wives, daughters and sisters being taken away . . . and although we see how our women are inhumanly treated . . . we not only cannot prevent it, but cannot say anything against it . . . because we know how beastly are the ways of the promyshlenniki and we are afraid that they will do to us the same as did the foreman Soloviev who devastated the islands . . . [who] placed men, one next to the other . . . and tried to find out how many of them he could kill with one bullet from his gun."[39]

Shelikhov had hoped that the arrival of missionaries from the Russian Orthodox Church might bring faith, education, and "pacification" to the Indigenous people of Alaska.[40] During his trip to St. Petersburg to plead for the Russian-American Company, he had traveled to remote monasteries on the Russo-Finish border to recruit missionaries to come to Alaska.[41] Although the Russian Orthodox Church in Kodiak planted parishes across the islands and reported that it converted twelve thousand Natives in its first three years, it failed to protect the Alaska Natives from assault and captivity, poverty and deportation. By the beginning of the nineteenth century, the Russian-American Company had conscripted enough private ships to become the third-largest navy in the world, trading from Bombay (Mumbai) to Nootka (Vancouver Island), England, and Hawaii.

Mikhail Tikhanov, *Aleut at Sea Hunt,* 1818. The Russian-American
Company kidnapped skilled Alaska Native hunters and forced
them to enter raging seas to chase the valuable sea otter.
Russian Academy of Arts Museum, St. Petersburg.

Tsar Paul I copied the Hudson Bay Company—a leader in the global
fur trade—and the British East India Company, and he gave the Russian-
American Company twenty-year control of all the lands to the south of
Alaska and the rights to all the otters "from Alaska . . . to Japan, and all other
islands, without competition from Southern Asia and North America."

Of dire concern, Tsar Paul I also gave the Russian-American Company the "full and forced labor of fifty percent of the Native population
for a period of five years." Half of the entire male population of Alaska
who had lived free was compelled to work for the new monopoly. The
mass slaveholder, chartered by the government, won the right to "half of
all men, not older than fifty and not younger than eighteen" who "can be
called by the Company for this purpose." With this, it seized the youngest
men, leaving the women, children, and older people to fend for themselves
in a world where food and survival were highly gendered. Unlike the Hudson Bay Company, which relied on Native traditions of barter, the Russian-
American Company could enslave the old men, women, and children. Alaska
Natives could not "absent themselves" without permission from the company; they could not barter or sell otters to anyone but the company.[42]

After the Russian conquest, Alaska Natives were forbidden from wearing
their traditional clothing made from the warm pelts of sea mammals.
Louis Choris, a watercolorist, traveled with several Russian expeditions
and depicted a couple caught in the forced transition of empire. A man from
the Aleutian Islands wears a parka, waterproofed by a layer of bird feathers.
His wooden visor, decorated with his chosen spirit animal, protects his face
and deflects the glare of the sun on the sea. The Alutiiq woman, by contrast,
has accepted Russian clothing and wears a Russian Orthodox Church cross.

In Louis Choris, *Voyage pittoresque autour du monde, avec des portraits de sauvages d'Amérique,*
d'Asie, d'Afrique, et des îles du Grand océan (Paris: Didot, 1822).
(Courtesy of Artokoloro/Alamy Stock Photo.)

By 1803 men from the Russian-American Company were allowed to
force Native women into "concubinage." On the Fox Islands, a Native man
reported that the Russians "act like barbarians with us. They seize our wives
and children as hostages, they send us early in the spring, against our will,
five hundred versts [about 330 miles] away to hunt otters, and they keep us

Louis Choris, *Jeunes lions marine mène par les enfants Aléoute* (Young sea lions guarded by Aleutian children). After the Russians forced Alaska Native otter hunters to spend most of the year at sea, the women, children, and elderly from the Aleutian Islands tried to survive by guarding the seals and sea lions, a precious source of food for families starving after the hunters were kidnapped by the Russians.

In Louis Choris, *Vues et paysages des régions équinoxiales/recueillis dans un voyage autour du mond* (Paris: Paul Renouard, 1826). (Courtesy of the Beinecke Rare Book and Manuscript Library, Yale University Library, New Haven.)

there until fall, and at home they leave the lame, the sick, the blind, and these, too, they force to process fish for the Company and to do other Company work without receiving any pay. . . . The remaining women are sent out on Company labor and are beaten to death. They are removed by force to deserted islands; the children are taken away from those who walk with crutches so there is no one to feed them."[43]

Any Alaska Native who refused to hunt for the new company could be whipped, even to death. As more otters were killed off, the Russian-American Company sent the Alaskan hunters to paddle further out from Sitka, at times to islands nearly one thousand miles from their villages. Native women were left to gut and smoke fish, dry otter skins, and stitch kayaks to ready them for the rest of the year. Otter hunters fell into impossible debt to the company. As captives and debt peons,[44] Alaska Natives were owned by the company, and the Russians now called them all "*kaiuri*"— captive laborers or slaves.[45]

During the frozen winter of 1804–5, Russian naval officer Gavriil Ivanovich Davidov was trapped by sea ice on Kodiak Island, and he spent the long winter months trekking across the island. Davidov recorded his horror in a diary: "Whenever the Company establishes a new settlement or a fort, it always takes hostages, *amanaty*, from the local Natives who serve as a guarantee." The company, he wrote, whipped Natives just "for rudeness" and held the children of chiefs as hostages. He wrote how a child accused of a crime was shipped to a remote Russian village near the Arctic Circle to serve out his life as a slave. Davidov saw Native men jump off a cliff into the sea or jab themselves to death with a spear rather than face the dishonor of being whipped by a Russian.[46]

Davidov also described resistance and revenge. He told how Alaska Natives killed all the Russians along the Copper River and nailed their commander to a cross. Then they cut off his penis and forced it into his mouth, saying, "You took away our women—now see if you can do anything with them." Over and over, Davidov saw Kodiak Natives refuse to disclose the location of otters' breeding grounds, telling the guards, "*kulga sokh*," or "I have no ear."[47]

Soon the Russian-American Company faced a shortage of Natives and otters. Older ship captains and experienced furriers had died or returned to Russia, and the otters were disappearing. The Russians had seized the Natives' parkas, food reserves, and kayaks, and many hunters had frozen or starved to death, while others had thrown themselves into the sea, rather than be enslaved, and by 1789 many islands were uninhabited.[48] In 1792 only about six thousand of the original ten thousand Natives remained in the Kodiak Archipelago; by 1806 the population in the Aleutian Islands fell from about six thousand at the time of the Russian invasion of the fur hunters to fifteen hundred.[49]

Meanwhile, Governor Alexander Baranov, a bitter alcoholic, continued to terrorize the islands. With the return of each kayak, he ordered the hunter to sing the "Invocation of Baranov," which tells how he "sent free people out all over the uncharted seas" so that Russia could "become an important place on Mother Earth—yes, important and most fair." With dreams of a glorious empire, valuable otters, and willing Alaskan Natives, the hunter vows never to "transgress the laws of nature or the simple rights of men":

> Oh, rise up in this part of a new world! For Russia is most ambitious—
>   and see! . . .
> The savages—people of all these barbarous clans who at first hurled
> Themselves against us have now, willingly become our friends. . . .
> To discover this new land for the glory of an Empire and its rich
>   inheritance.

Let us go forth again to proclaim
Our good intention of occupying more of America
The savages around, all see it—and they will make peace for what we
    have done.[50]

For two years, no ship arrived from Russia, and the surviving Natives
hoped that they had witnessed the last of the invaders. For fifty years,
Russia had virtually had Alaska to itself, even in the fevered era of colonial
competition for the New World. No European country seriously contested
Russia for dominion over Alaska, Alaska Natives, or the valuable sea otter.[51]
By the 1790s, the sea otter was nearly extinct in the waters of the northern
Pacific, and the Natives and Russians were bitter and emaciated. In 1806
the Russian-American Company itself was at risk: many supply ships had
been lost at sea, and Russians stationed in Sitka were dying of scurvy and
starvation. The response of the Russian-American Company was to pivot
its gaze to California. A Slave Rectangle was born: Alaska–California–
Russia–China.

CHAPTER FOUR

The Undersea People

Ki q'u ke sha nuntaghatl

(Another dark night has come over me).

—QADANALCHEN (Dena'ina, Fort Ross)

THE KASHAYA POMO LIVED on a bluff above Bodega Bay at the place they called "Metini." One day in 1803, while standing on the cliffs at the edge of the Pacific, the tribe saw "something white, sailing in the water"—something they had never seen before. Elder Essie Parrish recalled that the white thing "came closer and closer and unexpectedly it landed, and it proved to be a boat."[1] The Kashaya named the visitors the "Undersea People," for they saw them emerge from the depths of the ocean and rise up on the horizon. The "white people [translated as 'the miracles'] . . . took over the land where the Indians had been living. But the Indians still stayed. . . . Then they put them [the Indians] to work. The women folk too."[2]

Russia had long dreamed of invading California. In Alaska, Russian soldiers and the Alaska Natives now owned by the Russian-American Company were starving. Supply ships coming from Russia were lost at sea and food was running out. In 1803 Boston shipper Joseph Burling O'Cain delivered a shipload of grain to the Russian-American Company in Sitka, Alaska—near fresh otter grounds. O'Cain brokered a deal: he would ferry enslaved Alaska Natives and their kayaks to California and deposit them in the rich coves and inlets of the Spanish province that bordered the Pacific. He would also take along Russian overseers and Native seamstresses. Months later he would retrieve the pelts but leave the Alaska Natives to carry on the hunt. Then O'Cain would sail north to Alaska and split the haul of otter pelts fifty-fifty with the Russians. From Sitka, he would sail on to China and sell the valuable furs in Canton. And on each return trip from California, he would bring back wheat for the hungry invaders.[3] A Pacific Slave Rectangle was born.

The tsar granted the Russian-American Company the right to hold 50 percent of the Alaska Native male population in slavery, each man for a period of five years. The Alaska Native fur hunters would mark the Russian presence in California, block the Spanish empire from moving up the Pacific Coast, and slaughter sea otters to export to China. By now, independent Russian hunters were again under sail, scouting the California coast for otters, and Spain had already ordered their soldiers to "defend us from the atrocities of the Russians, who are about to invade us."[4]

Since 1799 the Russian empire had ruled Alaska through a monopoly that controlled the Native hunters, the land, and one "crop"—the sea otter. It was not going well. Privately owned small ships, or *shitiki*, designed for sailing on Siberian rivers were rushing to Alaska and crashing against the rocky outcroppings of the northern Pacific; the barren and frozen islands provided little food for the bread-loving invaders. And Russia's system of forced labor, which had worked in Siberia, was failing in Alaska, where the revenues from the "harvest" of the little sea otter depended upon Native hunters.

In the decades since Bering's invasion of 1741, the Russians had depopulated thousands of square miles of Alaska. The Native men who fished for salmon or hunted edible sea mammals and the Native women who gathered roots had been taken from their islands in mass deportations; the clans and the hunters were starving. Obsessed with otters, the company could not even feed itself.[5] The otter hunters were dying out.

O'Cain, a New Englander and a shipper, knew that a U.S. ban on the trade in slaves from Africa would take effect in 1808. His deal with the Russians, however, kept Americans involved in the sale and transport of human beings in vessels built, funded, and insured in Massachusetts and New York. California would mark a corner in a new slave passage: from Kodiak Island, it angled south to California and ended in China. Captive and enslaved men and women were again to be carried on American ships. O'Cain's ships were well armed for this Pacific version of a Middle Passage, with eighteen "twelve pounder" and two "six pounder" cannons—

more than a match for anything at the Spanish presidios that guarded the coast.[6]

In October 1803, the ship *O'Cain* sailed from Sitka with the first enslaved people transported into California. Guarded by Cossack soldiers, forty enslaved Alaskan hunters and their kayaks were shipped on the *O'Cain*, sailing past otter nests along British Columbia, where the militant Tlingit would not let them land. The Boston crew and its captive passengers pressed south and reached Trinidad Bay in Northern California, in what is now Humboldt County. Unable to enter the straits into the bay, O'Cain sent the Alaskan hunters in their kayaks to slaughter otters, under armed guard. As he sailed further south along the California coast, he repeated this strategy, exposing only the Alaskans to the tribes and the Spanish soldiers stationed at Franciscan missions.

Once in California, O'Cain abandoned the Alaska Natives to hunt otters in coves or on rocky islands and to fend for themselves. Left with only fishing spears and a scant few pounds of flour, the emaciated Natives faced exposure and starvation on the coast or capture and death at the missions. In the Alaska Natives' first foray, the Spanish captured fifteen Alaskan hunters and killed eleven. Months later O'Cain returned to collect the dried pelts and find the hunters. These men had been seized from their Alaskan islands by privateers, moved one thousand miles across the northern Pacific to Kodiak, conscripted again by the Russian-American Company, and shipped to California to be murdered by the enemy of their enemy. The Alaska Natives were squeezed between two foreign empires, three thousand miles from home.

O'Cain had allowed his most skilled workers to starve.[7] Even so, in 1804 he sailed back to Sitka with eleven hundred valuable pelts that he divided with the Russians, keeping seven hundred otter furs that he had collected in a private deal with Spanish officers. The next year three more American ships—the *Peacock*, the *O'Cain*, and the *Eclipse*, all captained by American skippers who were relatives of O'Cain—sailed from Sitka to California with more slaves of empire.[8]

The otters and the sunshine were found to the south, and Alexander Baranov, the bold governor of the Russian colonies and director of the Russian-American Company, sent Count Nikolai Rezanov, a nobleman and bureaucrat, to select a California base for the captive Alaska Natives and the otter trade. The base would also block the Spaniards moving north, and Baranov hired other Boston shippers for the trade. Early in February 1806, Rezanov sailed through ice floes on two Russian ships—the small

Empress Catherine the Great ordered the first
Russian fur hunters to sail into California waters and
bury copper disks etched with her royal seal along the
Pacific shore, from the fishing village of Trinidad
south to San Diego, bizarrely believing that the
hidden disks would mark the presence of the empire.

(Courtesy of National Park Service, Sitka
National Historical Park, Alaska; SITK 1650.)

brig *Nikolai* and the three-mast *Juno*—to invade California and expand the
size and sweep of the Russian-American Company.

Rezanov was looking for a military and trading site as close as possible
to San Francisco. Sailing south, he copied the strategy of O'Cain and deposited Alaskans to hunt in the unknown estuary of the Columbia River
(now southern Oregon) and in Northern California. He was also seeking
land for settlements in fertile, sun-drenched California soil to end Russia's
desperate dependence on the Spanish for food.

The Russian invasion of California was a rather pitiful show of force.
Catherine the Great ordered the Russians to mark the field of empire by
burying copper disks, chiseled with her royal coat of arms and the proclamation: "Land belonging to Russia." The disks, she said, would be "incon-

trovertible evidence" that California was "subject to the throne."⁹ But the
disks were to be hidden in the earth so that neither the Russian workers
nor the "Native inhabitants" could see them. Meanwhile, Spain, Mexico,
and soon the United States were keen to acquire California's bounties and
sent settlers and militias into the territory. As the Spanish were moving
north into California, planting missions as they went, Meriwether Lewis
and William Clark left from Missouri in 1804 on their renowned expedition to explore the Pacific Northwest—while Russia's vast claim to California was marked by small, hidden metal disks.[10]

Sailing from the north, the brig *Nikolai* wrecked in the fog off the Oregon coast. Quileute Natives seized the Russian sailors and Alaska hunters
and distributed them among several villages to work as slaves.[11] The ship
Juno abandoned them in Oregon and sailed on south with forty soldiers
and sailors and 150 Alaska Natives who found thousands of sea otters. Ap-
proaching the waters near San Francisco, Rezanov saw thousands more
and, as the *Juno* sailed into San Francisco Bay, he forced the Alaska Natives to disembark, climb into their kayaks in unfamiliar rough seas, and
slay the coveted sea mammals. Rezanov was also testing the strength of
the Spanish forts because "Today there is only one unoccupied stretch, so
useful to us and quite necessary." To persuade the priests at Mission Dolores to exchange their wheat and vegetables for his metal tools and pots,
Rezanov became engaged to the besotted teenage daughter of the Mexican commandant of the presidio of San Francisco. Promising to return
for his bride, Rezanov sailed back to Sitka with two thousand sea otter
pelts destined for sale in China. Now was the time, he urged Governor
Baranov, to occupy the entire California coastline north of the mission at
San Francisco.[12]

The invasion exposed the weaknesses of the Russian empire. In 1808
Baranov sent Boston sea captain George Washington Eayrs to California
with "25 kayaks with hunters for joint hunting on distant shore" and ordered O'Cain to deliver Native "wives to mend and sew the new kayaks
and marine clothing." Eayrs only traveled with provisions for the Russian
crew; the Alaska Natives were to bring their own food for the voyage. Eayrs
promised to deliver fresh water but only "on shores where there is none."[13]
Aware of the Alaska Natives' rage at the Russians' sexual assaults, Baranov
asked that Eayrs protect the Indigenous women "against impertinences
and bold propositions of debauchery."[14]

Left for months along the open California coast, many Alaska Natives
died, and O'Cain brought more men on each voyage south. Sailing past
the presidio that guarded San Francisco Bay, he abandoned Alaskan Na-

tives to hunt on the rough barrier islands as far south as San Diego. Whenever he spotted otters near a Franciscan mission, he trained five cannons from the deck of his ship directly on the beach, forcing the Alaskans to dare the Spanish army.[15] While waiting to collect the pelts, O'Cain wintered in the warm Mexican waters of Baja California. Meanwhile, Baranov remained in Sitka to reap the profits: Boston shipper Jonathan Winship sailed with one hundred Native hunters, twelve Native women, three armed Russian supervisors, and seventy skin kayaks and returned to Sitka with 4,820 otter pelts.[16]

Yet Alaska Natives were uniquely mobile slaves taken into captivity with their kayaks; three thousand miles away from the Russian overlords, many simply paddled away in their kayaks, up the rivers and creeks that spill into the ocean in the Pacific Northwest.[17]

The Russian invasion of California was based on an irrational business model: once in California, it was nearly impossible to replace hunters who died on the jagged Farallon Islands or were captured when they were sent ashore in full view of the Spanish garrisons. Why conscript skilled laborers, only to let them perish? Why were the Russians reckless with this unique human asset? This was a time-sensitive invasion searching for just one commodity. Mexico was fighting for independence from Spain, and the Russian Crown's arm's-length distance from the Franciscans was uncertain.

The Russians were not in control. In July of 1806 Spaniards from the presidios seized five of O'Cain's Russian sailors. O'Cain in turn kidnapped Spanish soldiers to trade for the Russian hostages, but he did nothing to rescue the Alaska Natives. As in most systems of unfree labor, the Russians were contemptuous of their skilled Alaskan captives.

And so began a global enterprise in sea mammals and enslaved hunters that crossed oceans and continents and challenged borders. The voyage of the world's finest furs began in California, sailed north to Alaska, and crossed the Bering Sea to a port in Siberia where they were packed onto horses or oxen. At the headwaters of the Lena River, the California pelts were transferred onto barges to float one thousand miles in the spring's high waters to the fur auction in Yakutsk. From there they were carted the last 420 miles to Kiakhta, an inland trading post on the Russian–Mongolian border. Four thousand miles from St. Petersburg and Moscow, furs valued then at 20 to 30 million rubles ($10 million to $15 million today)—from animals slaughtered by enslaved Alaska Natives—were sold each year at this remote trading post, a guarded fort marked only by two wooden posts and a high stockade. Traders at the rough outpost negotiated a price and loaded the furs onto camels or clumsy two-wheeled oxcarts or sleds pulled

Albert Bierstadt, *Seals on the Rocks, Farallon Islands,* ca. 1872. Joseph O'Cain
and Russian ship captains deposited Alaska Natives on the bleak Farallon
Islands to hunt sea otters. After the otters were extinct, the Russians
at Fort Ross ordered the Alaska Natives to hunt seals and sea
lions and survive without food or water until the ships
returned months later to collect the pelts.
Wikimedia Commons.

by reindeer. After fifty days, the long caravans reached the insatiable Chinese merchants in Beijing. Each pelt from this furry sea weasel, three to four feet in length, sold in rubles for what was roughly $3,500 ($70,000 today), compared to American beaver pelts that were going for four dollars apiece.

Between 1803 and 1812, Boston shippers working for the Russian-American Company forced Alaska Native teams to slaughter over twenty-one thousand sea otters—males, fertile females, and small immature pups—whose pelts would warm the throats and wrists of wealthy Chinese merchants.[18] The otter was facing extinction by those who shared its ocean, honored its thirst, and once chose it to be their prey. Like Spain, Russia assumed that expansion into California depended on gathering and maintaining a coerced labor force. In a secret missive to the minister of commerce, Rezanov reported that the Spaniards had designed a "sham system" under a fraudulent god in order to build their supply of slave labor. The Russian-American Company, however, was frankly commercial: "With us, the sole object is the sea otter, and humanity has been forgotten. . . . The Company's overseers are also shareholders. Their object is furs and not Americans [Alaska Natives], whom they will never see again after the expiration of their terms, for whom they have not been responsible."[19]

Ever the mercenary, Rezanov predicted that once the Russians were out of sight of the company, "even worse monstrosities [than in Alaska] can be expected." He blithely assured Empress Catherine that after the Alaskans' "terms" of indenture expired, the Russians would never see them again, for they would escape, following a trail of "defectors." Slave revolts, shrugged Rezanov, were built into Russia's regime. Facing ruthless discipline, abandonment, and starvation in California, many of the indentured Alaska Natives climbed into their kayaks and paddled away.[20]

In the winter of 1807, on the way to his winter vacation in Hawaii, O'Cain deposited 150 Alaska Natives and seventy kayaks on the Farallon Islands, a stark twelve-mile chain of jagged uninhabitable outcroppings. The Alaskans were to kill new herds of the silky otter, live off rainwater, and face the storms and tidal waves of the Pacific.

Despite the armed Spanish guards, American Captain Oliver Kimball, from the brig *Peacock*, ordered the Alaskan hunters to sneak into San Francisco Bay, where thousands of otters still thrived. The Alaskans were to slip in at the narrow strait at the Golden Gate or portage their kayaks across the steep headlands of Marin County. In 1807, after just three months the *Peacock* returned to Sitka with 1,261 pelts. The trade with China was flourishing and, ever greedy, O'Cain ordered the hunters in California to slaughter young otters; half the rapacious "harvest" were yearlings, killed before they could reproduce future generations.

In 1808 Ivan Kuskov, Baranov's senior assistant, sailed into California to find a site for a permanent Russian outpost. He traveled with a crew of 130 Alaska Native men and twenty Alaska Native women. Disregarding the danger of capture by the Spanish, Kuskov ordered the Alaska Natives to plant the tsar's marker "Number 1" on Yurok land near Trinidad Bay, just south of Oregon.[21] On January 8, 1808, Kuskov finally anchored in a shallow rocky inlet now called "Bodega Bay." He returned to Sitka the next year with two thousand pelts.[22] In 1810 Mexico declared its independence from Spain, and Russia decided it was the time to establish a California hub—far enough north not to be under the eye of the Mexicans or the missions, but close enough to San Francisco Bay and the coves along the Pacific to slay the remaining otters.

Kuskov chose a strip of bare bluff on Kashaya Pomo and Miwok land and built a wooden fortress, a sea-faring slave colony two miles long and one mile wide, just fifty miles from the presidio in San Francisco. In November 1811 he returned to Bodega Bay on the *Chiro* with a large crew of armed Russians and eighty more kidnapped Alaska Natives. Bodega Bay was an odd choice. It was twenty miles from the site of the fort, and the Alaskans had to carry all the lumber, supplies, and pelts along a beaten path up and over the cliffs. But the site offered the Russian empire timber, plentiful fresh water, and a secure view from 110 feet above the beach.

"Our Object Is Furs and Not Americans"

In 1812, from atop a sandy bluff, the Kashaya Pomo watched the invaders unload a sailing ship. Over the next few weeks, they saw the invaders build a tall house for the commandant, barracks for soldiers, a jail, a church, and a cooking area. Last, they watched the Russian crew erect a twelve-foot-high redwood palisade, topped by high spikes, and drilled with twenty gun holes. Then the Russians mounted forty-one cannons. The stockade was impregnable. All that was missing was the enemies.

The true purpose of Fort Ross was to preserve and distribute the pelts of otters slaughtered by enslaved Alaska Natives. At the edge of the bluff, the Kashaya Pomo watched Alaska Natives build their communal houses outside the fort in a small village that sprawled toward the sea—exposed to mountain lions, bears, and other tribes beyond the protection of the tall fence. The Russian stockade marked the empire's brief interlude of power in America, between the six thousand to eight thousand years of being Kashaya Pomo land and the waves of settlers, ranchers, and militias, wineries, and tourists that were to follow.

Although Rezanov claimed that these lands were uninhabited, he well knew that he had chosen Indian land already claimed by Spain.[23] On August 30, 1812, the California Native people watched the invaders hoist the Russian flag. The Undersea People named the compound "Fort Ross," a shortened version of Russia or Rossiya.[24]

Twenty-six Russians and 102 Alaska Natives settled at Fort Ross. None was a farmer; none was familiar with the terrain. During the hustle of building the fort, the Russians sent the Alaska Natives out to sea; their slaughter of twelve hundred otters confirmed the choice of site.[25] But for the Pomo people and Alaskan captives, Fort Ross was dangerous: "The Aleuts hunted all day, killing about 100 otters but when we went to the beach . . . to camp for the night, we found [Spanish] soldiers stationed at all the springs who would not allow anyone to take any water. At this, the Aleuts became frightened and started back toward the ship. . . . It was dark, and some wind was blowing and two baidarkas were capsized and the [Native] men, being tired with their day's work, could not save themselves," wrote Russian visitor Vasilii Tarakanov.[26]

The Russians built Fort Ross at Metini, where coastal Miwok and Kashaya Pomo lived on the grass-covered hills, shaded by wild oak; here they gathered in the summer months to fish for salmon and halibut and collect abalone and mussels. In late fall, the clan of about fifteen hundred people moved inland, away from the damp chill of the coast. Their movements followed the ripening of acorns and buckeye, pepperwood nuts, and berries; they speared migrating deer, elk, and birds, and killed small game such as rabbits and quail with stone ball clubs and bows and arrows, and dried the food for the winter months.

The Spanish had not invaded these coastal lands, and the Kashaya Pomo had never been conquered. At first, the Kashaya Pomo welcomed the strange visitors to their seascapes and long hillsides that stretched for forty miles along the coast and crossed four coastal ranges. But they soon learned that the invaders were not "miracles" but armed men who had entered their lands to force them to build their fortress and dig their fields.[27]

The Russians transformed Metini into a multiethnic village, a site of conquest and resistance, negotiation, and interaction.[28] On the cliff by the sea, Metini now included Fort Ross, a Kashaya Pomo encampment at its east, and the Alaska Native communal houses at its west. Metini became a place of bondage.[29] The prosperity of Fort Ross hinged on compulsory Indigenous labor. In its charter, the Russian-American Company allowed kidnapping and ransom, paid for in human beings; it thrived on debt peonage payable in otter furs, debts that bound Alaska Natives to the company. In a census taken in 1820–21, past the peak of the otter hunt, 179 men and eighty-one women lived at Fort Ross: 126 Alaska Natives, fifty-six California Natives, and thirty-eight Russians.[30]

With the Alaska Natives at sea or abandoned on the Farallon Islands, the Russians captured the Kashaya Pomo to build the fort, work in the fields to feed the sailors and the staff, and supply the tsar's starving outposts in Alaska and Siberia. Those Pomo who refused to be "hired" for glass beads were roped together and marched away to plant wheat on the thin coastal soil, land that their ancestors had occupied for over perhaps six thousand years. Wheat soon covered the Pomo hunting grounds, and the Pomo were forced, under the whip, to harvest it by hand, piling chaff onto the dried skin of sea lions and dragging the grain back to be stored inside the stockade.[31] Whenever the Pomo refused to work, during the night twelve to fifteen employees from Ross seized women and men and marched them back to the fort.[32] But unlike the Alaska Natives, the Kashaya Pomo could slip away to their local homes.

The Russians forced the Alaska Natives and the Kashaya Pomo to build their traditional houses outside the protection of the stockade, exposed to the coastal winds, bears, mountain lions, and bobcats.[33] Ivan Kuskov claimed that the California Native chiefs voluntarily ceded the land to Fort Ross that cut straight through a Kashaya Pomo village.[34] The Russians compelled the Pomo to fell trees in the forests where they had always gathered wild foods, where oak trees dropped acorns that held the distillate for tanning hides.[35] After the growing season, the Russians allowed the Pomo and Miwok to return to their villages.

Baron Ferdinand von Wrangel, manager of the Russian-American Company, initially claimed that the Kashaya Pomo and Miwok came to Fort Ross when "they were properly paid or because they needed the work." He conceded that long before the Russians arrived, the Pomo thrived on a varied and full diet; food alone would not induce them to labor in the fields. Now he witnessed the Russian staff at Fort Ross capture the Pomo men and hold them for the planting season: "As many Indians as can be assembled—sometimes as many as 150—are driven together by force and put to hard work in the fields . . . and fed only thin gruel . . . for a period of about a month and a half." Indian fieldworkers, Wrangel reported, had to "reach a state of complete exhaustion" before they were allowed to return to their tribe.

Few California Natives, admitted Wrangel, came to work at the fort "of their own accord," and the "office found itself compelled to search them out in the tundra, fall upon them unexpectedly, tie their hands and drive them like cattle into the colony to work." The Russians entered the villages and seized groups of seventy-five Indian men, women, and children, and marched them over forty miles to harvest the fields, always trying to hide the captives from other Pomo who would try to free them. At the end of the season, the "conscripted laborers" were dismissed to starve. How, wondered Wrangel, "will we make them our friends?"[36]

In its early years, Fort Ross was predominantly a company of men, and one strategy of "friendship," thought Wrangel, would be to encourage a "creole" population among the Russians, Alaska Natives, and Kashaya Pomo. Alaska Native men soon lived with Pomo Kashaya women who also faced constant assault by the Russian soldiers and staff, especially when their Alaska Native spouses were away at sea. Russian goods and Kashaya foods, tools, and clothing were carried between Fort Ross and the tribe; a cross-ethnic population emerged.[37] But powerful castes controlled the fort, and when the Alaska Native men were sent to sea, their Pomo and Kashaya wives "endured terrible privation" and ran back to their tribe.[38]

The Pomo were new and inept farmers on the thin seaside soil, and they suffered for the paltry yield. Concerned about revolts and fearful that hungry Indians would steal from their stores of food, the Russians mounted guards at the warehouses. Pomo who were found inside the fort were imprisoned and, at times, shipped north to Sitka to be punished with harsh labor.[39]

The Kashaya Pomo feared that the Russians wanted to "tame" them. Tribal elder Essie Parrish recalled that the Undersea People "wanted to domesticate [the Indians and] served them some of their own white food. Never having seen white men's food before, they thought that they were being given poison." The Indians, she said, believed that the Russians were evil shamans or bear doctors, and they threw the Russians' food in a ditch and buried it.[40]

The Pomo also survived by dressing in their traditional ways; the men went naked, and the women wore skirts of grass or deerskin so their skin stayed dry. Kashaya Henry James remembered that "cold was a terrible thing," and if a Pomo dressed like the whites he "would die if he got drenched in the rain," yet clothed in a bearskin he "never sickened from the great cold."[41]

California coastal people had no tradition of land ownership, but the Russians claimed that local California Natives had given them their land.[42] In 1817 Captain Leontii Hagemeister, chief officer of the Russian-American Company, produced a treaty written in Russian, in which the local chiefs declared that they "are very much pleased with the occupation of the place by the Russians, that they can now live in security from other Indian chiefs who used to attack them that this novel state of security came only with the establishment of the settlement." Here, it says, the Pomo chiefs also gave the Russians the right to their labor, and they ceded the land around Fort Ross "to the Company for a fortress, buildings, and institutions on sites belonging to Miwok Chief Chu-gu-an." In the document, Chief Chu-gu-an accepts "the obligation to support and assist the Russians." However, only the Russians signed the "treaty."[43]

Russian Lieutenant Vasyli Illyashevich, stationed at Fort Ross, wrote a different history in a letter to his son, saying: "The situation of the Indians is desperate, and in our behavior towards them I find more barbarity than among the Spaniards. This is how it happens: with the approach of harvest time, forty Russians and Aleuts, armed with rifles, go to collect the savages [Pomo]. . . . Year by year in order to escape they withdrew into the interior . . . however many men and women [the Russians] find all have their hands tied and are driven to Ross." Desperately hungry, Natives "who lack the strength to endure the trip become exhausted and are abandoned in the wilds." At night, the three hundred to four hundred Indians held at the fort were locked in sheds: "It is worse than any prison. You see them sitting, emaciated, in a circle around a dying old man, woman, or child. All day, under the supervision of the Russians, they carry sheaves; this lasts until October, when without giving them a blanket or a shirt, they release them, not thinking . . . that they have lost the time for preparing supplies for the winter." The few who come on their own accord have "daughters [who] have been seized by the Russians and are living at the settlement."[44]

Few Russian women came to Fort Ross, but the Russian-American Company continued to ship Alaska Native women to California to sexually serve the officers and staff at Fort Ross and to sew and oil the skin covers for the kayaks.[45] Seeking to document a creole population, Kuskov's census records many Pomo women as the "wife of a Kodiak." Despite multiple rapes, Kuskov saw Pomo women as polygamous, and he recorded many "common law" marriages between Russians and tribal women, unsanctified by the Church.

Kashaya traditions, however, tell of the rape and the frequent suicide of Kashaya Pomo women who married the invaders. A Russian man casually disavowed his Pomo family; as he left for work one day, he warned his wife, "If I find you here at home, I will kill you." The woman told her daughter, "I am going to die today. . . . Your father growled at me so much that I can't go home anymore." As the child grabbed her mother's dress to hold her back, the mother threw herself over the cliff down onto the gravel beach.[46]

During the three decades of the occupation, the Russians held several hundred Alaska Natives in bondage.[47] Rezanov made disingenuous distinctions between the Alaska Natives held at Ross and the California Natives held at the missions. Unlike Russian Orthodox priests, he wrote, Spanish missionaries "completely enslaved their neophytes [converts]. . . . I see only a pure and tidy cattle-yard in which the thrifty master tends them like bulls. The converts derive not the slightest benefit from their work; their hearts are consumed by melancholy and they flee, leaving their wives and children, but they are returned and so must patiently endure their fate. My God!"

With unashamed duplicity, Rezanov wrote, "What is the meaning . . . of a man who can never raise himself and against his will, he must crawl?"[48] He said that "our Americans," meaning Alaska Natives, "are utilized quite freely, their needs are satisfied by nature itself and they can go hunting of their own free will." Indeed, they "have been drenched with a kind of luxury. . . . Each of them seeks every means of getting furs, and when he has bartered something for foppery that he needs, then he is rapturously happy." Rezanov shamelessly declared that when an Alaska Native killed an otter, "his character converges with ours." While the Spanish forced Natives to convert to Catholicism and labor in the fields, he noted, "two thirds of them have died . . . [but] our Russian object is furs and not Americans."[49]

The Islands of the Dead

The seven Farallon Islands are stark outcroppings that lie in the Pacific Ocean, thirty miles west of the Golden Gate Straits, an ancient river delta that separates San Francisco from the Marin Headlands. Lashed by powerful currents and hidden under dense fogs, the Farallones were once a breeding ground, teeming with otters, seals, sea lions, elephant seals, and four hundred species of birds. These cold and bleak sea stacks are surrounded by unique and powerful currents, and here O'Cain abandoned the Alaska Native otter hunters and a few Alaska Native women for months at a time. Captain Vasyli Golovnin observed that "it would be appropriate to call these islands large rocks. . . . There are no trees, soil, or fresh water on them, except rainwater that collects in holes. Timber is found only on the beaches where it is cast by the sea."[50] The local Miwok called the Farallones the "Islands of the Dead."

Guarded by an armed Russian supervisor, the Alaska Natives built dirt shelters on the rocks. Parched with thirst, they searched for rainwater in crevasses and gashes in the rocks. The Farallones are home to the largest colony of seabirds in the United States and still give off a legendary stench from bird excrement.[51] To survive on the rocks, the Alaskan hunters turned to their traditional skills. They smeared seal oil on the bones of sea lions to ignite a hot blaze and burned seal blubber for cooking oil. They ate the small eggs of the murres and gulls, as well as fish and seal meat, for their protein.[52]

Most perilous was the sea itself, for "shivers," or herds, of great white sharks circled the islands to feed on the plentiful sea mammals, and often the sharks mistook the underwater silhouette of the hunters' kayaks for seals.

Four or five times a year, often in the late summer, American ships arrived at the Farallones to carry off hundreds of otter pelts and over fifty tons of dried seal meat that the Alaska Natives had cured. In return, the Russians left a supply of water and some firewood for the hunters and the women, also abandoned on the rocks, who repaired the kayaks and parkas with bone needles and thread drawn from the tendons of the seals.[53]

On one trip the Alaska Natives handed off thirty thousand seal skins to O'Cain's ship the *Albatross;* then, wrote a mariner, the ship "bore away" to the south, dropping another "gang" of Alaska Natives on the Channel Islands off Santa Barbara. When scurvy broke out on the Farallones, the Natives were too weak to hunt or paddle to shore and passed a winter crawling over the rocks to gather gull eggs and eat them raw. It was not until the following summer that a company ship arrived and exchanged the hunters for a fresh group of Alaska Natives.[54]

The otters were soon extinct—"extirpated"—along the California coast, yet from spring through autumn, Boston shippers still left Alaska Natives on the Farallones to hunt the few remaining otters. Stranded sometimes for years at a time, they smoked seal flesh to feed the Russian colony in Sitka. The wheat fields near Ross, however, were never plentiful enough to supply the Russians stationed in Alaska, much less in Moscow and St. Petersburg.[55]

The clash with the Spanish came in the early fall of 1814 in San Pedro in Southern California, when a Russian overseer on the ship *Ilmen* ordered a gang of Alaska Natives to paddle ashore with a few Russian guards. Ordered to climb stealthily onto the beach and up the dunes, enter the mission's corrals, and steal cattle, the Alaskans were quickly surrounded and captured by the Spaniards. While the Russians fled back down to the beach and escaped in the kayaks, the mission soldiers tethered the Alaskans together. For two days they marched the Alaska Natives over ninety-six miles to the mission at Santa Barbara, where they were sentenced to two years to life in prison. The Russians never retrieved the Alaska Natives, and the *Ilmen* sailed back to Fort Ross to procure more hunters.

That year a determined Spanish sergeant ambushed a Russian commandant, Boris Tarasov, and twenty-seven Alaska Native hunters and marched them to the presidio jail in Los Angeles. Tarasov confessed to depositing the "Aleuts" along the coast with orders to collect one thousand otter pelts.[56] This time the Spanish sent the Alaska Native captives to Mexico to be imprisoned with hard labor for three years, enslaved as convict laborers. In 1815 the Spanish seized two more parties of Alaska hunters near Mission San Pedro; when one captive refused the offer of clemency if he agreed to convert to Catholicism, he was beheaded. The soldiers severed the fingers of a second captive who also rejected baptism. When he still refused to convert, the Spaniards cut off both his hands and "cleft his body."[57] At Mission Santa Barbara, Alaskans encountered other fugitives from Fort Ross who had been captured and held in shackles for years.

Meanwhile, the Boston skippers continued to deposit Alaskan hunters along the coast and retrieve more pelts in ever more desolate coves, hoping to find the last remaining otters.[58] In 1815, still at war with Mexico, the Spanish emperor ordered the Russians to leave.

Even in decline, the Russian-American Company relied on unfree Native labor. When teenage employee Zakahar Tchitchinoff arrived from Sitka in 1818 to join his father at Fort Ross, he saw a dozen Aleut women and fifty Aleut men forced from the ship to hunt the sea otter. En route, near Vancouver Island, he saw ten Alaska Natives ordered to go ashore to collect fresh water and he watched the Russians let them drown while they were trying to paddle back to the ship. Tchitchinoff witnessed coastal tribes capture and kill eight "Aleuts" as the captain heard their cries but sailed off.[59] When full crews were captured, the Russians negotiated only their own ransom and left the Alaskans as booty. The Alaska Natives launched one mass escape: they paddled miles up the coast, exhausted, desperate, hiding from Spanish search parties on California's barrier islands, running from two enemies.[60]

Thousands upon thousands of sea otters, however, still nested in the estuaries, marshes, and open waters of San Francisco Bay, and the Russians negotiated for permission to enter the bay by offering Alaska Natives as slaves. While dinners, silks, watches, iron tools, and horses were graciously exchanged between the invading nations, Governor Pablo Vicente de Solá feared that Russians would find such wealth in the fur trade that they would try to remain in California, and he refused to let the Russians hunt south of Fort Ross.

The supply of otters was rapidly depleting, and the *O'Cain* began to cruise ever closer to shore, exposing the Alaskan hunters to the Spanish soldiers. While the Boston crews safely waited in Bodega Bay, Alaska hunters scoured the estuaries around San José at the south end or bottom of the bay, but they were easy targets. After a few days at sea, they needed to beach their kayaks and find fresh drinking water. At Mission Dolores in San Francisco, the Ohlone neophytes, motivated by fear of their own, reported that they had counted 140 kayaks, killed nine Alaska Natives, and caught seven hunting in the bay.[61] The Russians were hurried and desperate. When Alaskan hunters came under fire from the Spanish, Boston Captain William Heath Davis ordered them to continue to hunt in the bay. Despite the loss of Alaskan men, Governor Baranov was extremely pleased with the "yield" of 8,118 otter skins.[62]

American Captain Davis finally accepted the fact that outside the bay, the otter population was gone, and he offered Governor José Argüello three thousand pesos to return all the Alaskan prisoners.[63] In 1817 the Spanish authorities agreed to negotiate, but in fact the Spanish were perfectly happy to use the Alaska Natives for field labor or to serve as translators.

The Alaska Natives were squeezed between two precarious empires. As the otter trade was dying off, the Ohlone were in flight from the Spanish, sailing across San Francisco Bay in reed canoes; the Chumash at Santa Barbara and La Purísima had just torched the mission and escaped into the tules; and Mexico was fighting for independence. The Spanish soldiers were on guard, ready to seize Alaska Natives if they paddled from the Farallones toward the shore. It was easier to flee to the nearby lands of the Pomo and even marry into the tribes. Some just disappeared—paddling east, up the Russian River, or south to the waters of Mexico. We know little of their destiny. Yet the records of Fort Ross reveal that slavery persisted and that the Pomo men who refused to labor in the fields were exiled to the deadly Farallon Islands.

In 1818 the Alaska Natives killed only thirteen otters along the California coast. The silky mammal was extinct. Fearful that the Russians might move further south, the Spanish laid claim to farmlands north and inland from Fort Ross. In 1817 they seized local Kashaya Pomo and sent Indian converts up from Mission Dolores in San Francisco to build Mission San Rafael and Mission Solano in 1824. Both were on Pomo and Miwok land. This time, as the Pomo and Miwok faced the Franciscans' merciless flogging, their tribes rose up and burned Mission Solano.[64]

Displaced by the new missions, the Pomo and Miwok people joined their tribe at the southern edge of Fort Ross. The defunct fort was surrounded by armed and hostile people. In November 1821 Governor José Argüello wrote in his diary, "There is not an otter left from Mission Rosario to Santo Domingo." The Spanish ordered Kuskov to abandon Fort Ross. The two aging Russian heads, Baranov and Kuskov, understood that it was time to leave.[65]

The Russians knew that the little sea otter, *enhydra lutris*, the currency of the Russian empire in the Americas, was no more. There was another concern: the government of Mexico was abolishing slavery. In 1820 the Plan of Iguala abolished slavery, and in 1824 Mexico adopted a constitution that actually freed its enslaved Indian people. Its last slaves were freed in 1829. Slavery, however, survived in the part of Mexico that is now Texas. In turn, the Russians at Fort Ross claimed that freedom would "corrupt [Indians'] morals even more than Mission life."[66] The California Indians, they argued, were incapable of liberty.

For twenty-nine years, the Russians had forced Alaska Natives to poach sea otters in Spanish territory. At the moment of Mexican independence, the presidios of San Francisco, Monterey, and Santa Barbara were compelling captive Alaska Natives to work in the fields with the neophytes until they were ransomed for goods or exchanged for their own imprisoned converts. One type of slavery sat upon another, building a foundation for what was to come.[67]

The otters were gone, and the wheat crop would never become the breadbasket for Alaska and Siberia. Yet ever hopeful, in 1823 the leadership of the Russian-American Company reiterated its right to hold 50 percent of Alaska Natives in bondage both in California and Alaska. A new charter promised that "the islanders, that is, all males eighteen to fifty, shall be obliged to hunt for the Company. Half of the islanders shall be used to perform company duties; they shall be advised of this in the month of January. If American Natives not in 'company service' want to sell furs, they shall have to sell them to the company. Those who are engaged in hunting . . . parties and maintained by the company, shall not have the right to keep any furs for their own use."[68] But no otters were left.

The Return to the Ice Country

In 1824, in an unusual joint revolt, the Pomo Kashaya of Metini, the Chumash at Missions Santa Inez and La Purísima, and a fugitive who had escaped from Fort Ross rose against Spain and Russia.[69] Aware of the risks to the tsar's dream of empire, Wrangel, the chief manager at Fort Ross, sent an urgent dispatch to the company's headquarters in Sitka: "During the past year the Indians rose in the vicinity of Ross, in several of the Spanish missions. The Mission St. Inez was laid level with the ground." The Mexican governor of California blamed Prokhor Yegorov, an Aleut fur hunter who had fled from Fort Ross and joined the resistance at the northern missions.[70] As the Spaniards were leaving California, the Russians reached an accord with the new Mexican government: Fort Ross would deliver gun-powder and rifles to the new rulers of California, and the Mexicans would return Alaskan fugitives who had been held prisoner at the missions.[71]

Death and defeat surrounded Fort Ross. A shaman of the Yakutat Tlingit foretold a "ship of sickness" and blamed the mass deaths on the "disease boats."[72] Ships from across the globe that harbored in Bodega Bay transported diseases to Alaska and California Natives. During three weeks in April 1828, twenty-nine adult Alaska Natives and their creole children died of measles at Fort Ross. In 1833 a mysterious illness incapacitated the entire fort, killing mostly Pomo.

Smallpox entered the Russian empire in the Americas. An epidemic of the pox ravaged Sitka in 1837, killing Alaska Natives, Creoles, and one-half of the population who lived near the Russian garrison. In nearby villages, only the Tlingit children remained alive, and the company sent to Fort Ross for sixty Native men, half the Alaska Natives in California.[73] Sailors carried the pox to Fort Ross and traders brought it to the missions. Fugitives in flight from the Russians and the Spanish spread its deadly pall as far east as the ice-topped volcano Mount Shasta, three hundred miles north-east of San Francisco. Moscow sent only enough vaccine for half the population at Fort Ross, with the serum packed in goose quills that had traveled thousands of miles from Irkutsk in Siberia to Sitka in Alaska and thence to California. By the time it reached Fort Ross, it was inactive or tainted. Three-fifths of the Alaska Natives at Fort Ross perished in 1836, and three thousand converts and two hundred Spaniards perished at the missions. One hundred thousand Indians who lived free, outside the missions, died in the pandemic.[74]

By 1833 only forty-two Alaska Natives remained at Fort Ross.[75] For seventy years the Alaska Natives had been uprooted and displaced over and over again. Now four thousand miles separated them from their home-lands in the Aleutian Islands, and a handful returned on each ship bound for Sitka.[76] With the otters extinct on the coast, Fort Ross's most valuable assets were the Alaska Natives and the three inland ranches along what is now the Russian River; in April 1839 Fort Ross sent only three Alaskans back to Sitka. Two of those men escaped, paddling one thousand nautical miles into Mexico. Following the Indian revolts at the missions, the Franciscan padres refused to return Alaska Natives who had deserted, for they sought their unpaid labor. With their vast homeland at the edge of Fort Ross, only the Pomo and Miwok had a place and a people to which they could return.

The Russians refused to accept that the land of Metini was never theirs, and in 1838 the Russian-American Company decided to sell Fort Ross. It first approached Mexico, but the new nation had no intention of paying squatters for the land they had just won in their war for independence.[77] The Kashaya and Pomo villages, hunting lands, and seed fields predated any concepts of ownership; no document survives that names them as the rightful owners of Fort Ross.

It was time for the Russians to go. The little sea otter, whose numbers were estimated to have once been 150,000 to three hundred thousand, had been reduced to a population of only one thousand to two thousand.[78] So, in 1840 eight Russian families sailed from Fort Ross for Sitka, and the company manager began to collect debts from the laborers. He tried to sell the cattle for slaughter and preserve the meat for "salt beef." After twenty-nine years of occupation, slavery, and ecological annihilation, the Russians abandoned everything that could not fit in the hold of a ship.[79]

The Russians never held title to the land, and no one wanted to buy Fort Ross.[80] Finally, John Sutter, landowner, slaveholder, and slave trader in the Central Valley near Sacramento, purchased the buildings, lumber, and cattle for 20,000 Mexican *piastres*—with a final payment of another 20,000 piastres to be paid in wheat and soap by 1845. However, the wealthy rancher claimed insolvency and never settled in full. Over time, small deliveries of impure soap and moldy grain arrived in Sitka to pay down his debt, but Sutter never paid for the buildings, longboats, or kayaks that together had an estimated worth of about 49,000 rubles. Instead, he sold overpriced grain and parcels of land to California's new settlers—land that had been inhabited by Indigenous tribes since time began.[81]

Pomo elder Essie Parrish remembered that after living at Fort Ross for thirty years, the Alaska Natives returned "to the Ice Country where ice mountains rose from the sea, where the white people drowned and where they didn't listen."[82] The remaining Unangax̂ men started paddling their kayaks north. By the time they reached Haida Gwaii, now northern British Columbia, they were exhausted. They stayed with the local tribe and gave them their songs. The tale is told that the songs are still being kept today. They are waiting for the Unangax̂ to come get them.[83]

"Another Dark Night Has Come over Me"

In his final report, Russian explorer Captain P. N. Golovin made his case to the tsar: it was "unfair to level the charge that the Aleuts are slaves to the [Russian-American] Company. No one deprives them of their belongings; everything they acquire for themselves at sea and on land belongs to them; but since they could not engage in hunting without the assistance of the Company, which furnishes them with everything, naturally they have the obligation to turn over their catch to the Company, which pays them at the established price. . . . One could rather call the Aleuts members of a family of which the [Russian-] American Company is the head." Golovin continued, "By their nature the Aleuts are children, in the full sense of the word, without any thought to their future." The best future for Alaska Natives, he believed, was in "guardianship" by the Russian-American Company.[84]

From the outset, most of the Alaska Natives who had been shipped to Fort Ross knew that they would never return to Alaska. In this eco history, human bondage debased a hunter into unwilling predator and prey; it destroyed an entire species and caused the death of a people who had lived in harmony with their land, animals, other tribes, and spirits. The Russian invasion toppled two conjoined populations: Indigenous Alaska Natives and sea otters, both able to travel vast distances in frigid oceans yet deeply tied to their coastal homes in the icy tidewaters of the North Pacific. These men and women did not choose to move three thousand miles from their ancestral homes to slaughter the little mammal that both guided and embodied them—only so that, in death, its fur would decorate the hemlines of Chinese mandarins and stake a futile claim to California.

Qadanalchen, great-great-grandfather of Dena'ina poet Peter Kalifornsky, was at Fort Ross from 1811 to 1821. Doubting that he would ever return to his village on Cook Inlet, Qadanalchen kept a small bag of soil from his home village and, to ease his sorrow, in a Dena'ina practice he would rub the dirt on the soles of his feet and chant:

> *Ki q'u ke sha nuntaghatl*
> *Qint'a hk'u q'ildu ki*
> *Shesh t'qelani*
> *Shi k'u ki*

> Another dark night has come over me
> We may never be able to return home
> But do your best in life
> That is what I do.[85]

CHAPTER FIVE

Birth of a State

My labor on his farm amounted to $360, I made $5,500 for him in California, he kept my $616 I had saved and sold me for $1,000. In this way clearing $6,676 [*sic*], in clear profit.

—ALVIN COFFEY

The wealth of California is, as it should be, shared by colored as well as white men.

—FREDERICK DOUGLASS

WILLIAM GWIN, U.S. DEMOCRATIC senator from California, decided that George Syer and his wife were too old to continue picking cotton on his Mississippi plantation. So, in 1855 he brought the African American couple to San Francisco to work as his house slaves.[1] Gwin forced the Syers to leave their grown children behind, hostages on his plantation. The Syers—elderly, isolated, and likely illiterate—had no idea that they were now living in a free state; they did not ask Gwin for wages or demand a contract.[2] Two years later, Senator Gwin ran for reelection as a southern sympathizer and lost. He still owned a plantation and two hundred enslaved men, women, and children in Mississippi, so he decided to return to the South. Gwin reckoned that it was not worth the money to transport the aged couple back across the plains. In 1857 he turned the Syers out onto the streets of San Francisco.

Homeless and hungry, the Syers found a neighborhood of free and formerly enslaved Blacks who let the couple know that they had been emancipated the day they crossed into California. The state constitution had set them free. Furthermore, they learned that Gwin should have paid them for their two years of work in California. Backed by their new community, the Syers sued Senator Gwin for holding them in bondage, unpaid, in a free state. In court, the Syers argued the senator had "appropriated their goods"—that is, their bodies and their services—the moment they entered California. They calculated the value of their labor at fifty dollars per month for George and fifty-five dollars per month for his wife (her name is not known)—a higher wage because so few women who could do domestic work had moved west. The Syers sought $2,282 in back pay—or about $64,000 today.

Syer v. Gwin tested whether slavery was legal in California: Could a white resident force Black men and women to work without wages in a free state? Had the couple been white, the law would hold that Senator Gwin had made an "implied promise" to pay them; he would owe them for their work. At the trial, Gwin conceded that he had never given wages to the Syers, but he had provided them with shelter and board, just like parents who do not give wages to their adult children. The Syers, he added, were like family members who are not paid for tasks that they perform out of love or duty, or like relatives who are unpaid but work in anticipation of an inheritance.[3]

The Syers, however, were neither Gwin's children nor his heirs. Nonetheless, an all-white jury decided that the Syers had the wherewithal to know that they were living in a free state. They could have chosen to work for someone else, it said; they could have left Gwin or, indeed, have left the state. Notably, the U.S. district court ruled that men and women transported as slaves into California lacked standing to bring a lawsuit or testify in court against a white man.

Although legally free, the Syers lacked the standing of white people to go to court to claim their rights as free workers. The court said they could have chosen to make a binding contract with their "former master," but instead they worked for him for more than two years "voluntarily as they had formerly done." Without a contract that set their wages, Senator Gwin was free to work them and pay them nothing. Furthermore, he still owned the Syers' bodies, even in California. Should he decide to return with them to Mississippi, their "former relation would revive" and they would have to work for him without pay. Although the court acknowledged that slavery had been outlawed in the state constitution, it let the slavery of African Americans endure in California.[4]

Slaveholders like Senator John Calhoun of South Carolina dreamed that the new West would be an extension of the South: slave labor would stitch California into the fabric of an expanding slave nation and drive the economy. Southern farmers had been bringing enslaved Blacks to California since 1846, because slave labor would make it possible for them to enlarge their landholdings.[5]

A woman named "Mary" was likely the first enslaved Black woman to be brought to California from the South. Since 1846 she had labored as an unpaid servant in her owner's household in San Jose. Mary petitioned the local justice of the peace for "redress"; she sought emancipation under Mexico's ban on slavery and became the first enslaved African American in California to sue for her freedom. Mary prevailed and obtained her release from bondage; she assumed her rightful status as a free person in California.[6]

On January 24, 1848, gold was discovered in California on a streambed near the ranch of John Sutter—a major slaveholder and trader of California Indians. One week later, the United States signed the Treaty of Guadalupe Hidalgo to mark its victory in the war against Mexico; it forced its southerly neighbor to give up the northern half of its land. But neither nation knew that the spoils of war included the wealth that had just been unearthed near Sacramento. At the moment of the discovery of gold, California was still part of Mexico, although by then it was under U.S. military occupation. Oblivious to its new economic value, Mexico ceded 55 percent of its country to the United States, including all of present-day California, Utah, and Nevada, two-thirds of New Mexico, three-quarters of Arizona, and parts of Wyoming and Colorado. In return for this vast swath of Mexico, the United States agreed that Mexico's ban on slavery would endure in these territories.

In 1848 no one had a legal "right" to mine silver or gold on public or tribal lands. California had no legislature and no laws, and white miners created, codified, and enforced their own system of property rights. Land along the rich riverbanks went to the first miner who could post a notice of "discovery and continuous use." There were no true sales or leases of land in the gold country—just "Miners' Codes" that simply said a man could only own one claim. In a sense, it was a very democratic view of land rights:

This illustration, published in London just after the start of the Gold Rush,
depicts two apparently enslaved Black men panning for gold in 1849,
under the control and supervision of white miners. Both Black men
stand in the frigid water as two white men, fully dressed, remain
on the dry shore. In *Illustrated London News*, January 6, 1849.
(Courtesy of *Illustrated London News*.)

the rules were written by the men who worked it. Most miners knew that
soon they would exhaust their twenty-foot claims and move on.[7] Despite
costs to travel west, California was worth the gamble.[8]

Most white miners did not intend to compete with enslaved miners,
and they sought to keep all Blacks from the goldfields. They did not anticipate, however, that over a thousand free African Americans were about to
join the treasure hunt along the riverbanks. Many free Blacks had traveled
west, already schooled in abolitionist struggles; they had not expected to
meet enslaved Blacks who were compelled to dig on behalf of their owners.

California Bound

The discovery of gold transformed California from a Mexican province
into a fantasyland of easy wealth, far from the tempering constraints of

white women. Southern slaveholders believed that here they would be unfettered, far from calls for abolition.

John Sutter had not been looking for gold. He was a cattle rancher and
land swindler. New settlers wanted to build wooden houses. When they
built sawmills along the rivers, they gouged the earth with their picks and
shovels, diverting streams and creating deep cracks in the rocky riverbeds.
In 1848, along the American River, Sutter's carpenter, James Marshall,
tapped into gold nuggets in a five-hundred-mile "mother lode" that lay
along the foothills of the mountains of the Sierra Nevada range.[9]

The discovery of gold amplified the myth of California as an ecology
of limitless abundance and a land without people—the myth inspired buying tools and oxen and paying fees to join wagon trains. In the mass westward migration, white "49ers" were rarely destitute, because it cost about
three years of typical wages to pay for tents, mining tools, and provisions
for the journey. During the next year, 1849, about fifty thousand white people crossed the plains on horseback or in canvas-covered farm wagons—
"prairie schooners"—bound for California. Racing against early snowfalls
in the Sierra Nevada, it took about five months to cross the country. In
1850, one year later, another 140,000 men from all over the world headed
for the western slopes of the Sierra Nevada Mountains. The informal codes
allowed white miners to stake claims of twenty feet of rich riverfront, where
they used sluices and wide pans to sift gold from deposits of silt along
sandy creeks.

By ships, by letters, and in newspapers, word of "Gold!" traveled along
the Pacific Rim to Asia, across the Atlantic to Europe, and down the coast
to Latin America. Veterans marching home from the U.S.–Mexican War
(also known as the "War against Mexico," and in Mexico as the "U.S. Inter-
vention in Mexico"), turned around and headed back west, joining wagon
trains from Missouri, Kentucky, and Tennessee. Mexican traders and defeated soldiers carried fantastic tales. Prospectors arrived from Ireland and
Germany. Thousands of experienced miners came from Chile, Argentina,
Peru, and China.[10] Shopkeepers from Hartford, New Haven, Salem, and
Boston left for California. Unemployed and landless men and farmers
struggling to till worn-out soil in New England succumbed to the manic
rush for gold, certain that their time sifting through the mud in cold rivers
would be temporary. These men would help shape the future of race in
California.

Only about 3 percent of the initial "49ers" were women. Chinese
women, kidnapped from the port cities of Guangdong, were shipped into

California as enslaved prostitutes to service the new unencumbered merchants and miners. For the most part, white women arrived last.[11]

Contending Forces in Early California

After hearing of "Gold!," free and enslaved African Americans collided with white miners in the chaotic foothills of the Sierra Nevada. By the 1850s the South had more money tied up in slaves than it did in land, but gold could refinance the plantation South. California agriculture and cattle might supplement cotton and tobacco—inedible export crops costly in land and fertilizer. All that California lacked was a class of compliant workers.

During the Gold Rush, plantation owners from the South transported about two thousand enslaved African Americans to California for the backbreaking work of sifting pans heavy with river mud to inspect for flakes of gold.[12] Some slave owners scaled the Colorado Rockies or entered California in the brutal heat of Death Valley. Some sailed south from New Orleans or New York, trekked across the jungles of Panama, or rowed along the sweltering Chagres River until they finally reached the Pacific Ocean. There, they waited by the hundreds for ships that would carry them north to San Francisco Bay, forced to pay extra for tickets for Black miners. Others sailed with enslaved men around Cape Horn at the tip of South America.

In 1849 the Louisville *Daily Journal* suggested that "if three to five hundred Georgians immigrated to California, each accompanied by one to five slaves, they could force California to enter the union as a slave state."[13] At first, the *Jackson Mississippian* argued that slavery could not thrive in California's "barren and unproductive country . . . unfit for the general culture of our Southern staples," yet by October 1849 it predicted that "profitable fruits of slave labor" could be made in California.[14] Southern slaveholders had fantasies of enslaved Black men standing up to their waists in the cold rivers, plucking nuggets of gold from the river bottoms, while the slave owners lounged on the shore.[15]

Slave owners pushed westward from Mississippi, Georgia, and Texas. Some sent their sons out ahead with money and enslaved men to add gold to their inheritance of land, jewelry, and human "property." Other young miners traveled with enslaved men to help them quickly strike it rich. Some slaveholders sent groups of enslaved men to work under an overseer. Others transported one or two slaves and worked alongside them in gold digging.[16]

Slaveholders ran ads in southern newspapers seeking partners for wagon trains that would allow enslaved Blacks. One consortium called itself the "Southern Slave Colony," announcing its plan to settle where it would "secure the uninterrupted enjoyment of slave property" and build a utopia of gold and unfettered human bondage. A wagon train called the "Washington County Mining Company" left from Arkansas in 1849 with 123 men and three women; fifteen of those men were from the Cherokee Nation, and five were enslaved Blacks. A year later another group of white southern prospectors set out from the Cherokee Nation in Oklahoma transporting fifteen "negro servants" crossing Pikes Peak, ascending the fourteen-thousand-foot summit in the Colorado Mountains before dropping onto the trail to California.[17]

Within a year, 962 free or enslaved Blacks had arrived in California; about a third were working in the goldfields. Meanwhile, the non-Indigenous population of California grew from eight thousand in 1840 to more than one hundred thousand by the end of 1849.[18] Slave owners now brought gangs of enslaved men to California and angered white miners by registering claims of long stretches of the riverbanks in the names of unfree men. Other slaveholders were disappointed in their finds, but were unwilling or unable to pay the costs of sending the enslaved back to the South. They left many in the mines to make enough money to "buy themselves."

British traveler J. D. Borthwick, an early witness to the Gold Rush, described tense segregation along the riverbeds, but he also heard white miners declare that "a n*****'s dollars were as good as any others" and welcome Blacks into gambling tents.[19] In wayside tents or restaurants, Black miners waited until all the whites left their tables before they were allowed to sit and eat. In San Francisco, neither free nor enslaved Blacks were allowed to share hotel rooms or drink at the same part of a bar as whites.[20]

Wagon trains continued to travel west with enslaved men and women, usually leaving from Independence, Missouri. Slave owners seeking to join the wagons typically chose men skillful with teams of oxen and herds of cattle that needed to water and forage. Bondsmen were often thrust out of the heavy wagons and, like white pioneers who foolishly overloaded their wagons, had to walk across the plains and over the Rocky Mountains to California; each step of the two-thousand-mile journey removed enslaved Blacks further from families left behind.

In 1849 enslaved Blacks crossed feint trails barely visible in the six-foot-tall prairie grass. Through Missouri, Kansas, and Nebraska and across the Rockies at South Pass in Wyoming, they pushed the heavy wagons from behind, across rushing rivers, and coaxed panicked horses and wary cattle up steep riverbanks. They floated wagon beds weighted with tents and months of food across the roaring Snake and Green rivers and trudged onward through Idaho or Utah, the scrub deserts of Nevada, and finally over the eastern slopes of the Sierra into California.

Adam Klippel, a white abolitionist, watched wagon trains pass through St. Joseph, Missouri, with "a considerable number of slaves bound for the 'diggins,' more indeed than I had expected, as I thought the slaveholder would hesitate in taking his so-called 'property' to that distant territory when it is acknowledged on all hands that such 'property' is so extremely liable to become insecure and slippery in California." Klippel counted about three hundred Black men pass through St. Joseph en route to California, and he realized that their "masters" assumed that they had "a 'right' to take their slaves there & keep them there as such."[21]

With the wagons spread apart to avoid each other's dust, enslaved men and women had many opportunities to escape while crossing the plains. But few took the solitary risk of flight, for they, too, depended on the safety of the wagon train. All knew that Native Americans who were watching thousands of strangers cross their lands could ambush, surround, and rain arrows upon the unwelcome wagons. For the first time, many enslaved men were armed, allowed to carry weapons to protect the travelers against bears, panthers, and Indians. The enslaved knew it would be futile to flee in unmarked lands. And slaveholders had powerful leverage against flight—holding Black families hostage on the southern plantations. They saw, too, that their numbers were small compared to the thousands of whites traveling in wagon trains ahead and behind them. On the long journey, enslaved Blacks were forced to face the perils of sudden childbirth, cholera, and rattlesnake bites alongside their owners.[22]

Those held in bondage also dreamed of gold, hoping they could dig in the tailings and buy their way out of slavery. Some had heard that they were traveling to a region where slavery was outlawed, and they hoped to find freedom at the end of the trail. Others trusted their owners to honor contracts to free them. As they swallowed the alkali dust, many imagined that they might flee from California and make their way to Canada or Mexico. Most did not know that a community of free Blacks would be there to receive them in a new land where paths to freedom—safe riverboats and secure houses on the Underground Railroad—had already been charted.

Slaveholders, however, knew they were headed to a free state, and many forced bondsmen to mark indenture "contracts" that "allowed" them to work for their freedom in California. One contract reads: Taylor Barton "owner of slaves . . . set[s] Negro Bob . . . free from bondage to me and all men." But it adds, "Never the less I make this condition that the said Bob agree to remain with me as my slave, faithful and obedient to me until the 25th Day of December next, commonly known as Christmas"—a traditional holiday for manumission.[23] Other owners promised to let the enslaved buy freedom papers for the going price of a human being in the South, but only after serving a period of forced labor.

These sham agreements masked freedom's premise of "employment at will" and disguised the true nature of the journey. A so-called "contract" between slaveholders and enslaved, signed or marked before they left for California, was a cruel hoax predicated on the idea that labor was voluntary and that both parties had equal status. Blacks could not enforce their contracts because in California they were banned from testifying in a court of law; they could not use the contracts as evidence of their freedom. Enslaved men in California's gold country could not openly mine for their own benefit, nor could they quit and find another job, despite the robust market for workers in the West.[24] These bogus agreements fostered a mirage of equality and a false impression that California would enforce the deals. Instead, a contract for bondage could become a marketable commodity in itself that could be bought or sold.

It is impossible to know how many enslaved men and women traveled west in this era. As a free state, California did not record slave status in the census. Yet other records reveal that the state's early courts permitted slavery. In October 1849 farmer Christian Kollar went to court in Sacramento to record his ownership of a Black man who was branded with an "A" on his hip and an "M" on his shoulder, scars from a southern slave market that marked him as human property. California allowed Kollar to prove his ownership of the unnamed man by displaying these brands, letting the cruel evidence define the man's status.[25]

Alvin Coffey was born enslaved in 1822, "an octoroon" (a racial designation for one-eighth Black) raised on his father's plantation in Tennessee. He was sold several times, first by his father and finally to a Dr. Basset in Missouri in 1846 for $600. Three years later, Basset forced Coffey to abandon his wife, Mahalia, and their children in Missouri and travel with him to California. In one of the few overland narratives written by an enslaved man, Coffey described the fearful group of twenty wagons rushing to be out of range of a cholera epidemic spreading through St. Louis and St. Joseph. As the teams pulled the laden wagons across the country, Coffey told how he was further imperiled by his enslaved status. One week out, he witnessed a torturous death on the trail, and he was ordered to bury the infected body.

One by one the oxen in Coffey's train died from thirst and exhaustion, and the white miners crowded into the remaining wagons, forcing the enslaved travelers to walk across the blistering desert toward Black Rock, Nevada. Although the train traveled at night, the cattle perished. Slowly lumbering west, they passed teams of dead oxen rotting in the heat near abandoned wagons still piled high with tools and furniture. Day and night, Coffey walked, driving the oxen. On the mountainous Humboldt Trail, they slid backward on ice "as thick as a dinner plate" and watched wolves trap an ox and eat it while it was still alive. To protect the wagon train from wild animals, poisonous snakes, and Indians, Basset gave Coffey a gun, arming an enslaved Black man. Trekking through miles of poison oak, Basset stopped for Coffey to chop narrow alder trees to feed the starving teams.

When the wagon train finally reached the goldfields, Coffey realized that Basset had not purchased a mining claim along a river. Even before they could set up camp, Basset ordered the men to start to "dry dig" on the mountainside. Until the November snows arrived, each day Coffey carried barrels of mud to the white miners; each night, he carried buckets of water to the oxen. That winter he huddled for warmth in a small tent with ten men, Black and white.

Coffey often slipped away and "dug and dug" for himself; in thirteen months he mined $616 in gold dust to pay for his and his wife's freedom. But Basset refused to hand over the manumission documents. Desperate for his family, Coffey agreed to travel back to the South. On the trail home, Basset fell ill, and Coffey nursed the man who had betrayed him. By 1854 Basset was low in funds, and he let Coffey return to California, where he mined for enough gold to purchase himself, his wife, and their children. In his manumission papers, signed in Missouri on July 24, 1856, his owner agreed to "liberate, emancipate, discharge and set [him] free for his good behavior, good conduct and other good traits in his character too numerous to mention." The freedom papers say he was "born the property of Margaret Cook of Mason County, Kentucky, July 14th, 1822. . . . Sold to the undersigned in 1852. . . . Said Coffey is a bright Mulatto with gray eyes and bushey [*sic*] hair. . . . About five feet ten inches high. Scar on his left cheek." He was freed for the "valid consideration of one thousand dollars," which would be worth over $30,000 today. In all, Coffey spent nearly $7,000 ($212,000 today) to buy himself and his family in the free state of

THE FUGITIVE SLAVE LAW IN OPERATION.

Artist unknown, *Capturing Fugitive
Slaves in California*, 1856.
Blackpast.org.

California. He bitterly recalled, "I made $5,500 for him in California, he kept my $616 I had saved and sold me for $1,000. In this way clearing $6,676 [*sic*], in clear profit."[26]

Slaveholders understood the California codes, and they registered claims for riverfront plots in each of the names of their enslaved men.[27] Enslaved miners who had just walked from Mississippi or Missouri now stood waist-deep in the cold waters of the Sierra Nevada's rivers, sluicing for gold. They carried thousands of pounds of mud up and down their owners' twenty-foot allotments along the steep river gorges. They cooked meals, washed clothes, and handed over any gold they found to their owner. The imperfect federal census of 1850 listed nearly fifteen hundred "Negroes" in the new state; in 1852 California's own census recorded twenty-two hundred. The "49ers" wanted capable cooks and cleaners, and the scarcity of women in the West added to the price of domestic service; soon white men bought and sold Black women and domestic servants as well as miners.

In the "rough and ready" towns of the goldfields, it was impossible to buy food and clothing in a marketplace, take clothes to a laundry, or grow

vegetables in the tent camps. In a state with few women, the "49er" mythology of independence broke down. In California, profits were in ore,
not human beings. By 1850—just a year into the Gold Rush—twenty-five
thousand southern whites reached the gold country with about one thousand enslaved men, making claims and pitching tents along the riverbeds
of the Sierra Nevada.[28]

Southerners in California were not of one mind; once outside the plantation economy, independent southern men joined the call for "free labor"
in order to keep unfree and unpaid workers out of the lucrative goldfields.[29] Walter Colton, the alcalde, or mayor, of Monterey, understood the
hypocrisy: "The causes which exclude slavery from California lie within a
nut-shell. All here are diggers, and free white diggers won't dig with slaves.
They know they must dig themselves; . . . and they won't degrade their
calling by associating it with slave-labor. . . . They have nothing to do with
slavery in the abstract . . . not one in ten cares a button for its abolition . . .
[but] they must themselves swing the pick, and they won't swing it by the
side of negro slaves. That is . . . the upshot of the whole business." Immigrants to California "feel they have got into a new world, where they have
a right to shape and settle things in their own way. They walk over hills
treasured with the precious ores; they fall by streams paved with gold. . . .
All these belong to them; they walk in their midst . . . and partake of their
grandeur. Think you that such men will consent to swing the pick by the
side of slaves? Never."[30] Enslaved African Americans stood out in the global
mélange of the goldfields, in the staging areas where miners waited for
supplies and passage up the rivers, in the diggings and tent camps, and
along the slavery-friendly riverbanks of the American and Feather rivers.

Southern slave owners often worked in groups, supervising their enslaved miners or digging alongside them, building wing dams to divert the
water and expose the riverbed, tying their gold dust in a rag bundle around
their waists to keep it from thieves. But enslaved Blacks often worked alongside low-paid Mexican miners who had been banished from their own diggings by California's backbreaking foreign miners' tax. Side by side, free
and enslaved miners built rock walls to slow the roaring rivers; they rolled
heavy stones through currents four-feet deep. They stretched cloth across
streams of melting snow to trap the gold pouring down from mountain
peaks.[31]

The goldfields of California were also a route to freedom. For free
Blacks and whites, the goldfields offered the chance to work for oneself,
without an employer setting hours and wages or negotiating for pay. For

Blacks, free labor also meant the existential freedom to leave a job. For the enslaved miner, in California he could mine on his own time and find enough gold dust to buy himself, after he sifted through buckets of river mud searching for gold dust for his owner.

As African Americans traveled to the mining country in the Sierra foothills, they saw various regimes of forced labor. They passed Natives tied together by a rope looped around their necks, trudging from their charred villages to ranches in the central valley. Black miners passing through San Francisco saw brothels where young Chinese girls were displayed in cages. In river towns and miners' camps, they saw slave marts and canvas tents where pimps forced Chinese girls to beckon men for sex.[32]

Free African Americans understood that two thousand miles—the wide Mississippi, Missouri, and Colorado rivers, the Rocky Mountains, and the Mojave Desert—stood between them and slave catchers who could seize any Black person as a runaway under the 1850 Fugitive Slave Act. Carrying picks, shovels, and shallow pans, free Blacks from Philadelphia, Baltimore, the western borders of Kentucky, and the plantation South were not only looking for gold but for distance from sheriffs and slave catchers who were fanning across the East Coast.

At first, renowned abolitionist Frederick Douglass feared the Gold Rush would pull other abolitionists and free Blacks away from the cause of freedom building in the East, turning them instead to the American Colonization Society or the Back-to-Africa movement. But in November 1849, he deferred to the popular view: "The wealth of California is, as it should be, shared by colored as well as white men."[33] Douglass realized that over $1.5 billion in gold was headed to banks in New Orleans, New York, and Boston. In California, slavery clashed with paths to freedom, upward mobility, and land ownership.

Once in the goldfields, free Blacks realized that in California, African American men were more valuable than cotton. In July 1849 General Thomas Jefferson Green, a veteran of the Texas Revolution and a former state senator from Texas, arrived at Rose's Bar, a bend along the Yuba River, with fifteen enslaved Black men whom he had bought in the cotton fields as he crossed Texas. Once in the Sierra Nevada Mountains, Green registered a claim in each of their names along one-third of a mile of riverfront.

White miners were angered by southerners like Green who claimed plots on the riverbanks in the names of their enslaved men. They held a mass meeting near Rose's Bar to draft the "Miners' Code" that limited a mining claim to what one man could work entirely by himself: "No slave or negro should own claims or even work the mines."

A delegation of miners left the meeting at the river bend, rode into Green's camp, and told him that he had until the next morning to leave: "It is foolish for you to defy our mining laws. . . . If you want to keep your slaves, you will have to go back to Texas or Arkansas, or by tomorrow morning you will not have one slave left, for the miners will run them out and you will never get them again." That night the enslaved Black miners fled, leaving Green on his own to break camp.[34]

Southerners who came to California found many ways to profit from enslaved Blacks. Thomas Thorne, a northern slaveholder from New Jersey, and his wife, Mary Thorne, a southern slaveholder from North Carolina, calculated the profits they could make by renting out men to work in the goldfields. As they crossed the cotton fields of Texas, the Thornes bought ten enslaved Blacks. Once in California, the Thornes claimed twenty yards of riverfront in the names of each of their slaves. They forced Lewis Caruthers and six other enslaved men to pan for gold, hand over their gold dust, and then build a boardinghouse near the Merced River. Mary Thorne forced enslaved Diana Caruthers and her teenage daughters to cook for local miners at a boardinghouse that became known throughout the diggings for its buttermilk, eggs, turkey, pies, and doughnuts. Miners soon lined up for the Caruthers' meals, and the Thornes thrived.[35]

Miners from the Pacific Rim to Latin America witnessed the brutality that enslaved men endured in Gold Rush country. During the icy winter of 1850 in Calaveras County, Argentine exile Ramón Gil Navarro watched Black men pan for gold while locked in shackles: "By now the twenty Americans who were working near my tent have left, and there are only three or four pairs of Black slaves left who are freezing for their masters. My god! What an impression it makes on me to see slaves in California, slaves chained by Americans, who, more than any other nation in the world, stand for freedom! These poor Negroes can hardly hold their picks they are so cold, and yet they do not move from the place where their masters told them to stay." At times they managed to briefly steal away. Navarro wrote: "Slipping out from under the masters' vigilance, they came over here to heat up a bit. It is such a shame to see human beings, who in every way are just like us, have to drag chains around with them and have owners, as though they were animals." By June, Navarro wrote that Black miners had been replaced by Chinese.[36]

At first, southern slaveholders brought out fewer Black women than

The following curious advertisement—the first
of the sale of a negro in this State—occurs in the
columns of the same paper :—

NEGRO. FOR SALE. On Saturday, the 26th
first, I will sell at Public Auction, a Negro Man,
he having agreed to said sale in preference to being sent
home. I value him at $300, but if any or all of his
Abolition brethren wish to show that they have the first
honorable principle about them, they can have an opportunity of releasing said Negro slave from bondage, by
calling on the subscriber. at the Southern House. previous to that time, and paying $100. I make this great
sacrifice in the value of the property, to satisfy myself
whether they prefer paying a small sum to release him,
or play their old game, and try to steal him. If not redeemed, the sale will take place in front of the Southern
House. 87 J street, at 10 o'clock of said day.
june 17-tdX   B. G. LATHROP.

"NEGRO FOR SALE," advertisement. In the
San Francisco Herald, June 17, 1852.
Newspaper and Microforms Library, Doe Library,
University of California, Berkeley.

they did men, believing that female field hands were unsuited for the hard
physical work of mining or fearing the cost of transporting women and
children across the plains. Yet miners longed for female companionship,
hungered for cooked meals, wanted clean clothes, and craved sex, prompting some slaveholders to transport enslaved women to California and sell
them to white miners and settlers. In 1849 Timothy Dwight Hunt, a Con-
gregationalist minister, witnessed a Rhode Island man buy a Black woman
and her child in Oregon to work as his household servant. He paid $1,900—
two for the price of one.[37] Other slave owners preferred to keep enslaved
mothers and children as hostages in the South, in case their enslaved husbands and fathers tried to flee. Besides, women back on the plantations
would "breed" future slaves.

Slave Labor, Free Labor, and the Alchemy of Gold

In 1848 forty Blacks lived in California; four years later, two thousand
more had arrived. African Americans left Tennessee and Kentucky, Nantucket and New Bedford, Philadelphia and New York, in flight from the
1850 Fugitive Slave Act and the tentacles of plantation slavery that spread
through the global manufacturing, shipping, and sale of southern cotton.

Half of the Blacks who mined along the rushing green rivers in the Sierra Nevada were enslaved.[38]

Along riverbanks, groups of Black and white miners lived and mined together; elsewhere, gangs of white vigilantes robbed Black miners of their gold and tools and drove them from the riverbanks. White miner Benjamin Bowen wrote that white miners near Fort John compelled free Blacks to leave the diggings by diverting streams on their rich claim after they grew "too saucy." Some free Black miners found safety mining with antislavery British miners or northerners. Others moved to remote stretches higher up the mountains. In Amador County, free Blacks shared a distant mining camp with one hundred Chinese miners.[39]

As white miners drove Blacks, Latinos, and Chinese from the crowded rivers, many free African Americans opened restaurants and boardinghouses. Using skills learned on the plantations, they worked as blacksmiths and earned $250 a month (about $8,300 today), cash that could buy their families out of slavery in the South. Black farmers who had hoped to claim land from the vast holdings of the Franciscan missions realized that Mexican grandees and soldiers had taken those lands; others witnessed speculators buy tens of thousands of acres of fields and forests on behalf of Scottish and British land companies overseas.[40]

In Sacramento, Charles Hackett, a free Black man, owned and operated the most popular hotel in California for African Americans. Hackett House was a boardinghouse for Black merchants, Black miners who had been driven from the goldfields, and Black travelers in the city that would be named the state capital in 1854. Hackett House also became a "stop" for runaways on California's Underground Railroad.

George Washington Dennis, an enslaved young man, left a plantation in Mobile, Alabama, with his white owner and slave trader, Green Dennis, who was also his biological father. Traveling with a small party of gamblers, the two sailed out of New Orleans on a ship bound for Panama. At the mouth of the Chagres River, the party rented a small boat, and George rowed through the waterways of the jungles as far as he could. Then, with George carrying his owner's thirty-foot gambling tent, they trekked seventy miles through swamps and reeds, over steep slopes of dense tropical forest, passing the corpses of miners who had died from yellow fever or crocodile attacks and snake bites.

Finally reaching the Pacific Coast of Panama, George and Green Dennis joined hundreds of slaveholders and men in bondage, and they waited to barter for tickets on a steamship to take them four thousand miles north to the port of San Francisco. Banned from transporting slaves into the United States, a ship captain agreed to carry George Dennis for $350 in additional "fees" and simply listed him as "Negro." On the beach and on the ship, the bored gamblers wagered for George. George was won and lost several times before the ship docked in San Francisco Bay. George might have jumped ship at ports along the way, but his owner and father had kept his enslaved mother back on the plantation in Alabama, a hostage for her son's return.

Once in San Francisco, George put together his owner/father's gambling tent on Portsmouth Square and called it the "El Dorado Hotel." Day and night, he swept up coins on the dirt floor that gamblers had dropped during faro and monte games; in three months he bought his freedom from his father, for $1,000, in coins. Still eager for his labor, Green paid his son $250 a month to work as his porter in the thirty-by-one-hundred-foot tent.[41]

In a few months, George Dennis raised $990 to buy his mother from his father. At first, the mother and son team rented a "concession" at the El Dorado where she cooked for the gamblers. Miners and traders paid her Gold Rush prices—twelve dollars for a dozen eggs. With their earnings of over $200 a day, George and his mother set up their own gambling and hotel business and invested in San Francisco real estate. They opened a livery stable and a coal yard and donated profits to California's Underground Railroad and abolition movement.

Across California, free and enslaved Blacks created their own neighborhoods, schools, and churches, living on the edge of freedom. At first paths for Black women entrepreneurs were limited, with little to invest but their bodies. Mary Haley ran a brothel in Sonora. "Priscilla" was a prostitute in Grass Valley.[42]

The California Constitution—A False Promise

Brochures promoting wagon trains or tickets via Panama promoted California as a land of utopian freedom, ecological abundance, and scant population. Three thousand ungovernable miles away from Washington DC, California was becoming wildly rich; both slave and free states hoped that the lucrative newcomer would save the impoverished East in sea-to-sea geopolitics of gold. The states were desperate to admit California as quickly as possible, albeit under their own terms.

Judge Peter H. Burnett, a Democrat from Missouri—soon to be California's first elected governor—observed in 1849 that the discovery of "exhaustless" gold mines had produced "a mixed mass of humans" united in a "feverish drive of fortune making." Having just moved from Oregon, where, as a member of the legislative council, he had tried to ban Blacks from even entering the territory, he now worried that California had "a mixed mass of humans from every part of the wide earth" without "law, order or system."[43] A civic structure was yet to be born.

California's Constitutional Convention met in Monterey in 1849 to write the state into being. Race, not gold, loomed over the forty white and eight Latino delegates who traveled to the former Mexican capital of California. The San Francisco District Council decided that only white men could vote for delegates from the Bay Area.[44] Just seven of the delegates had been born in California.

Struggling white miners sent a delegate to carry the simple message to the Constitutional Convention that "49ers" would not compete with slaves. Sam Brannan, a Mormon delegate and editor of the *Californian*, the first California newspaper, wrote that, although he "dearly loved" the United States, if statehood could not ensure ethnic purity, he begged California to seek an "independent condition" and reject "any degree of slavery, or even the importation of free Blacks. We desire only a white population in California."[45] The conservative *California Star* newspaper agreed: Black workers, enslaved or free, would "drive off to other homes the only class of emigrants California wishes to see: the sober and industrious middle class." If the United States "inflicted" Blacks on California, they would become an "unnecessary moral, intellectual, and social curse upon ourselves and our posterity."[46]

The debate immediately swung from antislavery to anti-Black. The white miners were fearful of competing with teams of unpaid and unfree miners; their cry for "free labor," however, was only for independent free white labor. Moreover, announced a delegate for the miners, any member of this "respectable and intelligent class . . . would leave this country" before he would dig with pick and shovel alongside the African. Other delegates declared that if enslaved Blacks escaped or were emancipated in the goldfields, they would create a large population of "Africans" in California. Enslaved miners, they said, enriched slave owners who did not have to work for gold, giving them an unfair competitive advantage.[47]

Most delegates were in a hurry to return to the goldfields and eager for California to just fulfill the nation's two requirements for statehood: a "sufficiency" of population and a republican form of government.[48] All understood that one way or another, California's admission to the United

States would wipe away the Missouri Compromise of 1820 to admit one free for every enslaved state—the glue that had kept the fractured nation together for thirty years. But there was no slave state to pair with California.

The convention also inherited a national mandate. Mexico abolished the purchase of slaves in 1821 and banned slavery in 1829; the Treaty of Guadalupe Hidalgo of 1848 guaranteed that Mexico's bans would endure in all the lands seized by the United States. But federal legislation that would have banned slavery in the West, the Wilmot Proviso, had failed to pass the Senate. A hard truth lived amid the ruins of that defeat: the U.S. Constitution did not ban slavery. Anything not explicitly excluded in the U.S. Constitution, including the ownership of humans, was left to each state. The Tenth Amendment's promise of states' rights allowed the delegates to declare whether California would be a slave state or a free state. The U.S. Congress, however, had the power to accept or reject California's application to join the union.

The miners' delegates represented men who were white and under age forty. Most miners had only been out west for a few months and chose to identify as laborers rather than farmers or soldiers. The eight Latino delegates spoke for the Californios who insisted that the debates be translated into Spanish. Californios were technically California-born, Spanish-speaking residents, but in effect they were wealthy Mexican ranchers who held hundreds of Indians as unpaid or barely paid peons who fell into debt peonage, legally binding them to the ranchers. Even so, the southern delegates realized that they could not rely on the Mexican ranchers to support Black slavery, because Africans had migrated to Mexico as Spaniards and lived freely south of the border, mainly as soldiers.

A miner who had just arrived from Louisiana summed it up: "The labor of the white man brought into competition with the labor of the Negro is always degraded. There is now a respectable population in the mines; men of talent and education . . . digging there in the pit with spade and pick—do you think they would dig with the African? No sir, they would leave this country first."[49] After just one week, the convention accepted the demand from Irish-born miners' delegate William Shannon, who insisted that gangs of enslaved Blacks should not compete with free white miners. The new constitution should ban slavery. The antislavery sentiment of the miners' delegates foretold a long reign of bigotry. At the same time, it is notable that California's constitution was the first to protect the separate property of married women.

On the rainy morning of November 13, 1849, ballots printed in English and Spanish went forth to male residents of California, who voted 12,061 to 811 in favor of the state constitution.[50] The next year, on September 9, 1850, the state constitution passed both houses of the U.S. Congress and was signed by President Millard Fillmore. The nation's greed for gold and the self-interest of white miners broke the balance of fifteen slave states and fifteen free states. Many slaveholders in Southern California left for Mexico.[51] California, the thirty-first state, entered the union in 1850 with a constitution whose language was copied from the free states of Ohio, Illinois, and Indiana: "Neither slavery nor involuntary servitude, unless for the punishment of crimes, shall ever be tolerated in this state."[52] But of historic significance, "tolerate" is not a legal standard.

After California's constitution was ratified, Frederick Douglass urged free Blacks to travel west to gain distance from the dangerous bigotry in the North and the threat of capture in the South. In California, they could avoid slave catchers who were chasing fugitives and free men alike under cover of the 1850 Fugitive Slave Act. Abolitionists saw that westward migration might even offer Blacks a chance to have the wealth and rights of citizens of a state, though not the nation. Civil rights, it appeared, might be won in the American West rather than in the North.[53] For both enslaved and free Blacks, California appeared to offer a respite from slavery, unemployment, poverty, and fear.

How to Disguise Slavery in a Free State

Slavery survived its ban in California's constitution. The early nuggets of Gold Rush lore were quickly plucked from the rivers.[54] By 1855, seven years after gold was discovered at John Sutter's mill, mining became mechanized and 108 crushing mills were pounding gold from quartz rocks; the next year water-powered hoses—"hydraulic mining"—blasted the hillsides to flush the dirt down to the riverbeds. The iconic prospector wielding only a pan, a pick, and a shovel gave way to industrial mining. Many miners—white and Chinese—now worked for corporate and overseas investors. Others chased new gold strikes further north in California and along the Fraser River in British Columbia. In the foothills of the Sierra Nevada Mountains, small individual claims and deep rivers of gold had become extinct, like the otters at the coast.

Pivoting from prospecting for gold, slave owners rented their enslaved men out to work as servants in new households or as cooks in hotels and restaurants—at times promising that enslaved servants could keep enough money to eventually purchase themselves. Profits from slavery in California now came from the wages the enslaved turned over to their owners—a version of the southern "Sunday system" that allowed enslaved men and women to earn money on the weekends. For slaveholders, "hiring out" in California saved them the cost of transporting south an enslaved person who had spent months or years toiling in a free state. California suddenly offered a frantic and perhaps fleeting chance for the enslaved to free their families. The very presence of free Blacks had revealed the possibility of freedom.[55]

In California, the hiring-out system turned a slave into a commodity that had a value beyond bales of cotton or even nuggets of gold. More money was to be made from renting unfree men and women as miners, drivers, or servants than from gold itself. In 1849, when a slave owner from Alabama faced angry white miners, he pulled his three Black men from the diggings and rented them out for $300 a month. One slave owner from Tennessee wrote home that he was earning $150 a month from a talented cook whom he brought to California only for the purpose of hiring him out.[56] Medic Reuben Knox and his wife, Elizabeth Knox, traveled west with an entourage of enslaved men, women, and a nine-year-old boy, planning to profit from a system where Black bodies had a value beyond nuggets of gold.[57] There was no one to enforce these bogus "contracts," but the manumission or freedom papers from El Dorado, Mariposa, and Butte counties are receipts for the sale of enslaved men and women who worked double time to buy themselves.

Hiring out allowed enslaved Blacks to buy their freedom. In 1851 Peter Brown wrote to his wife from diggings on the Cosumnes River in Northern California that he was paying his owner eighty dollars per month for his freedom, and he had also earned over $300 to purchase their son. Other enslaved miners, he saw, were earning four dollars per day, and all their wages went to their owners. Brown described "immense sums which have been . . . paid to their owners by the colored men who have come here as slaves, and who by a course of honest industry have paid for and obtained their freedom."[58] Yet some enslaved Blacks still dug for gold and carried buckets of mud, unaware that they were free.

Sojourner Subterfuge

How to hold onto enslaved men and women in the free state of California? When slaveholders decided to stay in California, they staked gold claims and bought land. But in order to keep their slaves, they had to figure out how long they could call themselves "temporary residents" or "sojourners." How could they make a convincing case that they "intended" to leave if they had just purchased land and planted crops? Southern slaveholders turned to northern "sojourner" codes that allowed travelers to bring slaves into free states, temporarily. These southern slaveholders, however, were not sightseers or tourists; they were not just passing through.

The surface gold had dried up by 1853 when Thomas Thorne left the mines and opened a boardinghouse and told enslaved Peter Green that he could buy his freedom. In the three years since he had entered California, Green had earned $1,000 mining for himself on his days off. Thorne allowed Green to buy himself, and he recorded the deed in the Mariposa County court: as the "rightful owner of the Negro man Peter Green and entitled to his services as slave, during his life, have this Day . . . released him." Henceforth Green was "free to act for himself, and no longer under bonds as a slave," provided that he "pay me the sum of one thousand dollars . . . or work for and serve me, from the present time until one year from and after the first day of April next [1854]." In agreeing to this contract, the Mariposa justice of the peace had just legalized the purchase and sale of slaves in free California.[59]

CHAPTER SIX

Contending Forces
Enslaved Fugitives in California

IN 1850 A CRUEL bargain allowed California to be admitted to the United States as the thirty-first state and the sixteenth free state. California was a piece of the Compromise of 1850, a deal that the aged Kentucky senator Henry Clay, Sr., had brokered to shelter the American slave trade. The three key elements of Clay's infamous "compromise" were: first, to permit the new territories of New Mexico and Utah to decide for themselves whether to allow or restrict slavery; second, to abolish the slave trade but not slavery itself in the District of Columbia; and third, to pass the Fugitive Slave Act—a dangerous federal mandate to return runaway slaves to their owners.

Henry Bibb fled from slavery in Kentucky to freedom in Canada and wrote to his Black friends in California: "My dear brethren you are standing on a sandy foundation. . . . All the gold in California [might] be the means of losing your liberty."[1]

The Fugitive Slave Act let the country pretend that slavery and freedom could be compatible. That wrenching and impossible dissonance led to the Civil War. In many ways, the Fugitive Slave Act mimicked the capture and sale of free people from Africa: it authorized the federal government to deputize whites as slave catchers—at times against their will—and then set them loose on Black people.[2] Anyone who helped or harbored runaways owed the value of their services to the fugitive's owner. U.S. marshals

$100 REWARD.—The undersigned offers the above reward for the recovery of a NEGRO SLAVE. named MARY HAGER. but generally known and called Mary. She accompanied the subscriber to this country in 1849. and ran away from her in October. 1850 Said slave was 5 feet. 5 inches high. large frame. complexion black. broad fore teeth. and erect carriage It is supposed that she is either in San Francisco or this city. The above reward will be paid for the delivery of the girl to the Sheriff of San Francisco county; or **$150** if she be taken in any other county.
                                    ELIZABETH WARE.
jy2-6*   San Francisco county.

By 1852 ads for the purchase and sale of runaways from slavery began to appear in the San Francisco and Sacramento newspapers. Mary Hager had been transported across the plains by her female owner, Elizabeth Ware, in 1849. Ware posted a reward of $100 for Hager three months after California's Fugitive Slave Act went into effect. In the *Sacramento Daily Union*, July 3, 1852.

Newspaper and Microforms Library, Doe Library, University of California, Berkeley.

were now required to arrest and return a runaway or pay the owner the full value of the enslaved person. If a marshal ignored a claim that a person was a runaway, he faced six months in jail and fines of up to $1,000. Many northern states had passed "sojourner" codes that allowed slaveholders to stay with their bondsmen in free states; the Fugitive Slave Act of 1850 went further and effectively criminalized freedom.

The Fugitive Slave Act let slavery seep into free states. It protected slaveholders who, by 1860, would invest nearly $4 billion in the purchase of four million women, men, and children. Slaveholders and investors intended this new act to expand the empire of cotton into the West.[3] Gold from California flowed to the depleted banks of Boston and New York and triggered a tectonic global migration of people and money. Gold overshadowed the national debate as to whether or not slaveholders should move west.[4] As a state, California would invigorate a nation that lagged far behind Britain in forging an industrial revolution. The Gold Rush had pushed California into a global network of industry and insurance, of shipping and banking. It drove slavery to the molten core of worldwide trade.

The first national fugitive slave clause is in the U.S. Constitution (1788). Article iv states that fugitives from labor, meaning slaves captured in the North, must be returned to the South. The year before, the Northwest Ordinance of 1787 had declared that there would be no slavery in the new territories north of the Ohio River, but fugitive slaves caught in these lands must be returned to their owners. The Northwest Ordinance allowed a slave hunter to capture a runaway in any territory or state just by orally "confirming" that the captive was a runaway slave.[5] With this cover, a slave owner could "pursue and reclaim . . . and arrest a slave" without a warrant. The Fugitive Slave Act of 1850 became the next and most powerful protection for slavery in the country.

Frederick Douglass soon watched a "dismal march" of thousands of fugitives fleeing through upstate New York on their way to freedom in Canada and he urged them to "be resolved to die rather than go back" to a slave state. Douglass saw that the North had also become "a hunting ground for men." The time had passed, he said, where it would be sufficient just to "frown slaveholders down."[6]

How could California undo the freedom that it had just promised in its constitution? In California, rewards for fugitive slaves immediately prompted the kidnapping of free Blacks. Despite the language in the constitution, a runaway could not submit evidence or speak in court or have the right to a jury trial. In California, only the slaveholder could testify.[7] The Fugitive Slave Act laid bare the economic loss of a runaway; ownership of human beings would turn not on morals but on the definition of property and property rights.

Judges who had immigrated to California from the South struggled to align the new state's ban on slavery with the profits slave owners might lose without unpaid workers. A series of court actions exposed the contradiction between the state constitution and the new power of southerners: a Sacramento court ruled in 1851 that the arrest of a runaway was illegal because the state constitution gave the fugitive the right to resist returning to his owner.[8] Another slaveholder, however, was allowed to keep his runaway when a court accepted the claim that the enslaved man owed his owner thousands of dollars in room and board.[9] Despite the freedom clause in California's constitution, its legislature and courts formed a state divided.

In 1849 the "Chivs," short for the Chivalry or southern faction of the California Democratic Party, elected William Gwin as one of the state's first two senators. Gwin owned two hundred enslaved men and women at several plantations in Mississippi.[10] The state's first governor, Democrat

Peter H. Burnett, owned two enslaved men back in Missouri. Burnett announced that Californians had a choice: either admit Blacks "to the full
and free enjoyment of all the privileges guaranteed by the Constitution to
others or exclude them from the State." If California let Blacks settle in
the state, said Governor Burnett, "We will consign them . . . to a subor-
dinate and degraded position, which is in itself but a species of slavery."
Blacks would have no "motives for moral or intellectual improvement, but
must remain in our midst, sensible of their degradation, unhappy themselves, enemies to the institutions and the society whose usages have placed
them there." Because slavery was a "teacher in all the schools of ignorance,
vice, and idleness," Burnett concluded, "the object must be to keep them
out."[11] His vision set the stage for segregation, Indian massacre, and Chinese exclusion.

Governor Burnett had briefly served as a member of Oregon's Legislative Committee and had introduced a measure to make sure that any
"free Negro or mulatto" who did not leave the state would be arrested and
flogged every six months until he left. Oregon was in line with other states.
By the time of the Gold Rush, Kansas, Indiana, and Illinois had banned
Blacks from their states.[12] During the California Constitutional Convention of 1849, southern delegates had nearly banned all people of African
descent from entering or remaining in California. This pernicious vision
resurfaced even before California was admitted into the Union in 1850,
when the legislature passed five acts that coiled slavery around the state's
political foundations. By legalizing forced indenture, the 1850 Act for the
Government and Protection of Indians effectively legalized the kidnap and
sale of Indians.[13]

The new legislature sought a variety of paths to slavery. It wanted to
permit slaveholders to bring enslaved African Americans into the free state
under northern "sojourner" laws, work them in mines and fields, and then
take them back to the plantation South. It debated a Black "migration bill"
that would prohibit "Free Negroes and Persons of Color" from entering
the state, and it would purge all Blacks who had already arrived. African
Americans could be deported as soon as they crossed the state border—an
early exclusion act that would assess fines on all "colored persons" and
stop free, manumitted, or the formerly enslaved from remaining. The
state considered a law to guarantee jail time for anyone who transported
"colored persons," free or enslaved, into California. A "colored person,"
said the legislature, was anyone who was "one-sixth Negro." Finally, the
legislature debated a bill to prohibit "amalgamation"—marriage—between

"colored persons" and whites.[14] Each of these bills failed to pass by only one or two votes.

Causing great danger to both free and enslaved African Americans, the legislature failed to pass an "enacting" law to put California's vague assurance not to "tolerate slavery" into effect. Pro-slavery southerners claimed that California's constitution was just a statement of intent, and it looked to free states in the North for legal ways to preserve slavery.

The new state legislature had to draft civil and criminal procedure acts to create the foundational laws that locked African Americans out of the legal system: no Black, free or enslaved, mulattos, or Indians could testify, present evidence, serve on a jury, or be a witness in any action in which a white person was a party, even if a white person corroborated their testimony. It immediately became impossible for enslaved Blacks to offer proof of when they were brought into the state.[15]

In 1852 southern slave owners brought more enslaved people around Cape Horn, near the southern tip of Chile, than they transported across the Great Plains. Promoting the possibility of slavery in California, the *Charleston Courier* reported that in April a steamer had transported seventy-four enslaved men to California to dig for gold.[16] One southerner reported that "Negro labor" was necessary for fieldwork because poison oak made it impossible for white men to farm in California. A legislator from Virginia unabashedly declared that gold mines could be worked more profitably by slaves.[17] That year, 1,218 citizens of South Carolina and Florida petitioned the California legislature for permission to establish a colony with two thousand slaves through "whose peculiar labor alone our valuable soils may be rendered productive."[18]

The most straightforward path to legalize slavery was either to amend the state constitution or split the state in two and make the southern half a U.S. territory, again open to slavery. Neither option was politically possible. Instead, white southerners in the California State Senate and Assembly passed laws to "tolerate" slavery in California and be more hospitable to rich slaveholders. In May 1850 the *Daily Alta California* reported that it was "well known that slave labor even now is carried on in the rugged declivities of the bold mountains," and that southerners were advising slave owners to remove their "human property . . . beyond the passing gaze of travelers along the road."[19] California's slave owners felt secure advertising the sale of men and women.

The best path to freedom in California for enslaved Blacks was to purchase their freedom, often from a relative. In March 1852 Aleck Long paid

$400 to buy himself from his slaveholding brother who lived in St. Louis, Missouri. The deed, signed in El Dorado County, California, declared that "in consideration of the sum of four hundred dollars . . . have this day liberated, set free, and fully and effectually manumitted, Aleck Long, being as follows: about fifty-seven years old, five feet, ten inches in height, gray hair, dark complexion with a scar on the inside of the left leg above the ankle—The said Aleck Long to enjoy and possess now and from hence forth the full exercise of all rights, benefits and privileges of a free man of color."[20] Aleck Long could never forget to carry that receipt, but he was not allowed to use it in court to prove his freedom.

Voices: Fugitive and Free

Once in California, many enslaved men and women escaped. In 1851, nested in a long column of advertisements in the daily *Sacramento Union* for suction pumps, Havana cigars, and foil-wrapped tobaccos, a notice appeared for a runaway, Samps:

> $100 reward for the delivery of a certain slave named SAMPS. Said boy is 23–25 years old; a light mulatto; spare made; well-favored and about five feet ten or eleven inches high. He was a slave in Alabama and brought to California by me in 1849, and left me on the Mokelumne River, about the 1st of July 1850 and seeking his return to the miners' boarding house seven miles from Jackson Creek in Calaveras County.[21]

When free Blacks arrived in California, they were alarmed to see thousands of enslaved Blacks, and they soon used their abolitionist training to build a West Coast Underground Railroad with secret routes and safe houses to help the enslaved flee. As early as 1850 in San Francisco, Black abolitionist Peter Lester observed that fugitives were "leaving" slavery in California every day.[22]

The *Voice of the Fugitive*, published in Canada by Henry Bibb, who had run away from slavery in Kentucky in 1850, urged men and women in bondage to flee across the border. Each issue also listed Blacks who were leaving for California—some who would lead the fight for civil rights.[23] Bibb wrote in a February 1851 column: "My dear brethren. . . . All the gold in California [might] be the means of losing your liberty."[24] In the first two weeks of October 1851, the Federal Mint received $2,510,000 in California gold.[25] The next year California sent east $45,587,803 in gold—today worth over $1.4 billion.[26]

"Countless slaves, who have escaped or been stolen from their former owners, come to this place of refuge," wrote Swiss traveler Carl Meyer. Yet white miners saw "thousands . . . flock to the gold mines where they perform the most arduous labor, labor which no white man could perform. . . . They work so hard not only to better their own condition but also to obtain the purchase price of their relatives or friends who still languish in the chains of slavery."[27]

Many slaveholders were finding themselves in worse financial shape than when they had left the South. They now were putting their bondsmen up for auction in California. Others tried to sneak them aboard ships sailing back to the South. In 1851 William Donaldson, a Black minister, helped Frank, a twelve-year-old enslaved boy, escape from his owner, John Calloway, in the goldfields. Calloway had brought Frank from Pope County, Missouri, to California in August 1850. Calloway wanted him back and ran ads in the Sacramento newspapers for the return of Frank, a "yellow skin" boy:

> $50 REWARD—Stolen from the undersigned, at Iowa Hill, Placer County, on the 6th inst, by a Negro Preacher—supposed to be connected with a gang of thieves in the vicinity—a small Black Boy, about twelve years old, quick spoken, thick lips, and rather handy; their destination is supposed to be Lower California. Donaldson is thick, heavy set; talks affectionately and kind, and appears to be about forty-five years old. When last heard from they were in the vicinity where the Indian Canon empties in the North Fork of the American River. I will give fifty dollars for the apprehension of the two so that I may get them; or I will liberally reward anyone who may favor me with any information concerning their whereabouts.[28]

As the availability of enslaved Blacks shrank and the organizations of African Americans rose, the Black community rescued and hid the enslaved, and especially enslaved children. With Wells Fargo and Company complicit in collecting the reward, one week later the Sacramento *Daily Union* posted another ad for the runaway boy:

> **LOOK OUT FOR THE THIEVES!**
> Stolen by William Donaldson, colored, and Hall, a small Black boy named Frank, about 12 years old, from me at Iowa Hill on the 6th inst. Donaldson—preacher—carried him to Auburn, Placer County, on the 7th inst., and Hall left there with said boy on the night of the 8th for Mormon Island and was seen in Sacramento on the 12th. Donaldson left for San Francisco on the 9th or 10th [Send bill by Wells, Fargo and Co. for collection].[29]

Frank was hiding in a Black neighborhood in San Francisco, and it took two months for Calloway to track him down. He seized the boy and locked him in a building at the wharf. Black shopkeepers, cooks, and servants quickly hired white attorney Samuel L. Holladay to represent the runaway child. In an affidavit, Frank swore that his master held him against his will and was preparing for their passage back to Missouri.

Frank became California's test of the Fugitive Slave Act. The young boy's attorney demanded a writ of habeas corpus, requiring Calloway to produce Frank in court and then set him free. Frank was going to be allowed to testify. Blacks gathered at the courthouse to hear him say that he had been Calloway's slave in Missouri and to hear Calloway say that, although he had brought his young "servant" to California, he was merely traveling through. Calloway swore that he always intended to claim custody of the boy and return with him to Missouri. But ironically, Calloway could produce no evidence that he in fact "owned" Frank.

The judge ruled that the only question in the case was whether Frank was restrained from his liberty, contrary to California law. Under Missouri law, Frank was a slave, powerless to refuse to travel west with his owner. But a critical distinction emerged: Frank was not a *fugitive* slave because he had not fled *across* state lines. Because he escaped *within* California, he did not fall under the fugitive slave laws. With that, ruled the judge, Calloway was liable under state law for kidnapping the boy.[30]

Then the judge ruled that Frank's testimony stating he had been Calloway's slave in Missouri was inadmissible. As a Black man, Frank was not allowed to testify in court, and if his testimony could not be used in his favor, neither could it be used against him. Frank was free. "Mr. Frank went his way rejoicing amid unbounded applause of his colored brethren," wrote the *San Francisco Herald*.[31] Abolitionists, Black and white, had hidden Frank, paid for his lawyer, and rallied outside the courthouse at the trial. They had created his freedom.[32]

The federal Fugitive Slave Act of 1850 did not work in California because runaways, like Frank, did not cross state borders to flee; they were brought in by their owners and escaped within the state.[33] California sought to fix that loophole, and in 1852 it passed its own Fugitive Slave Act. All enslaved African Americans brought into California before the state constitution of 1849 were now "fugitives from labor" and had to be returned to their owner and removed from the state. With a twelve to ten vote, the California State Senate "grandfathered" the rights of slaveholders who had arrived before California's admission to the Union; in effect, the law legalized slavery in California and suspended the state constitution for three years.[34]

Why did California bother? With about two thousand to three thousand enslaved Africans in the state, fewer than one hundred had escaped. Yet for California to have its own Fugitive Slave Act was a sign of ongoing dominance of southern pro-slavery views. It granted California residents the right to own a human. It acknowledged that California could turn into a western equivalent of a border state with escape routes to freedom in Mexico, Canada, or the wilderness. California was becoming a southern state.

Within two years of statehood, California had assured itself that African American slavery could there endure. An owner could keep an enslaved person if he intended to take him out of California within a year.[35] Anyone "held to labor in any state" who escaped in California could be arrested with just an "oral affidavit," and the owner or his agent could use whatever restraint necessary to take the fugitive back to the South. There were no time limits.[36] The legislature also voted down any amendments that would have strengthened the state's ban on "involuntary servitude." The California State Senate then turned to the section of California's constitution that spelled out property rights and declared that slaves were property.[37]

California's own Fugitive Slave Act was part of a national political struggle for slavery in the West, at just the time that slaveholders in California were losing the critical balance in the state legislature that would give them a veto. Even though the state had upended the balance between free and slave states when it entered the Union, for the time, slavery was secure.[38] Abolitionists sought ways to respond.

Just as the state was joining the union, the national Fugitive Slave Act was ripping the country in two, with "fanatics, free negroes, runaway slaves, amalgamationists [interracial sex or marriage] and abolitionists" in the North, and a defiant "abortive minority" of "miserable secessionists" in the South. Reports of slave revolts traveled west, as did the news that twelve infantry companies had marched into Massachusetts to enforce the Fugitive Slave Act. The *Daily Alta California* grimly predicted that every capture of a runaway in New York would end with the fugitive's return.[39] In 1853 and again in 1854, the California State Senate renewed the Fugitive Slave Act, allowing slaveholders to keep unfree Blacks in the state for two more years.

Slave catching in California became a lucrative occupation.[40] The *Daily Alta California* blamed "free negroes" for standing in the way of the law.[41] Slaveholder Jesse Cooper brought George Mitchell to California in 1849. In 1851 Mitchell escaped and went to work for a doctor in San Jose, and Jesse Cooper returned to the South alone. Back in Tennessee, Cooper saw the high price of the enslaved, and he hired San Jose police officers as private slave catchers.

In 1855 they "repossessed" Mitchell. Tipped off that he was being chased, Mitchell managed to find George Dennis and Mary Ellen Pleasant, who hid him in safe houses.[42] Mitchell hoped to stay hidden until California's Fugitive Slave Act expired. Indeed, in 1855 the law was not renewed, and a San Jose judge set Mitchell free. The national Fugitive Slave Act, however, was still in effect, and Mitchell's former owner turned to the U.S. district court in San Francisco to order his arrest.[43] Mitchell argued that under the state constitution, California did not have the right to pass a fugitive slave law. In any case, it had just expired. The judge agreed and told a crowded and cheering courtroom that any arrests under that act were now void; George Mitchell had been illegally enslaved, and he was legally free.[44]

California was fifteen hundred miles from the closest slave state. To the east were the peaks of the Sierra Nevada Mountains; to the west the Pacific Ocean stretched 840 miles along the coast, and only Indian trails and riverboats connected the goldfields in the Sierra Nevada to the sea. Flight was easy in dark redwood forests, in canoes on rivers that rushed from mining towns down to the ocean, on mail boats flagged down along piers, or on ships bound for Manila, Mexico, Panama, or British Columbia. White miners were more concerned about protecting their claims and hiding their gold dust than they were in capturing fugitive slaves.

California's Underground Railroad

Free Black merchants, teachers, and preachers in San Francisco got the word out that fugitives from slavery were free in California. The community hid runaways in wagons, delivered money for passage to Canada or Mexico, set up safe houses, and paid fees for white lawyers. Free Blacks rescued the enslaved who they found bound in ropes or chains. African American "Black Jack" sailors, ship stewards, and cooks, such as John Pleasant, knew the maritime schedules and routes and when to stow runaways aboard.[45]

Black activists Peter and Nancy Lester came to San Francisco from Philadelphia in 1850. Peter Lester deftly described encouraging Blacks to escape: "I thought when I got here, I would have no anti-slavery work to do, but I find . . . much to do here. . . . Slaveholders are here with their slaves from all the slave States in the Union. We had two in our little domicile last evening. I asked them how much they made a week. '$14' was the reply. We then wished to know who got it. 'Master' of course." Lester added, "When they left, we had them strong in the spirit of freedom."[46]

Free Blacks in California believed that they might free others who could then earn enough money to pay for their families who were still held in the South.[47] Free African American Edwin Morse, age sixteen, landed in San Francisco on June 17, 1850, after 190 days at sea. Suffering from hunger and dysentery, he hired Isadore, who had been brought to California enslaved and had claimed his freedom as soon as California became a free state. Morse paid Isadore eight dollars per day to haul gravel to a creek, where they rinsed it, looking for the heavy gold dust. Isadore used his wages to buy his wife's freedom.[48]

Enslaved in Missouri, Lucy traveled west because her owner, Mr. Brown, promised to free her if she agreed to travel with his son to the goldfields. In Auburn, a remote town in the Sierra Nevada Mountains, the young Brown claimed that Lucy was his slave. Hoping that her freedom papers were lost, he had her arrested and charged as a fugitive. But Lucy had shrewdly given her manumission certificate to a local white lawyer as soon as she had reached California, and she had protected her emancipation and her right to live in California as an "F.W.C.," or "Free Woman of Color."[49]

News of slavery and reports of freedom struggles in California appeared in the Black press across the country. As early as 1850 the *Liberator*, the most widely circulated abolitionist newspaper in the nation, reported that in the Sierra Nevada Mountains, "an old married negro ran away from his master, taking his wife with him. They were pursued, arrested, and brought back to Sonora. . . . The old man cried out that he had induced his wife to run away, and he pleaded with his owner not to whip her. In her place, the owner agreed to whip the elderly man, giving him three hundred and fifty lashes, 'until the blood boiled down his back and filled his shoes.'" A free Black miner heard of the brutal assault; he rescued and then hid the elderly couple on the outskirts of Sacramento.[50] In 1850 the abolitionist weekly *National Era*, published in Washington, DC, reported that although some slaves were transported to California to work "under indenture," many "found it as easy to dig gold for themselves as for others" and left for "'parts unknown' soon after arrival."[51]

Meanwhile, southerners were discovering that the harsh miner's life—sleeping in tents, digging sluices in icy rivers, sifting through mud—fell to them as well as to enslaved Blacks. After a few months, many failed to find gold and bought tickets to sail back to the South, planning to take along their enslaved men and women. Black activists in San Francisco began searching ships bound for New Orleans to find and free the Black passengers forced aboard. Other slaveholders went back to the South after they found enough gold to revive their plantations. Some left their enslaved miners with armed overseers in the goldfields.[52]

Kidnapping free Blacks grew into a profitable business. Judy, an elderly woman in Los Angeles, was "her own mistress," but after the Fugitive Slave Act, she was seized by slave catchers. The Los Angeles county clerk, a man of conscience, ransomed her for $500 and freed her.[53] In May 1852 an unnamed "negro man" was kidnapped in California and rushed to the local magistrate, who then handed him over to a stranger who claimed him as his "property" and "started him to the Atlantic states." The newspapers fretted only that the man was sent into "perpetual bondage" without lawful proof of ownership.[54]

Contending Forces: The Power of Free Blacks

By 1855 a group of experienced Black abolitionists had settled in San Francisco. Many had been leaders in the Colored Conventions movement in the East, the first civil rights drive that annually brought thousands of Blacks together at hundreds of state and national conventions.[55]

James Williams was born into slavery in Maryland in 1825, and when he was thirteen he fled across the state line to Pennsylvania. Taken in by Quakers, he found work driving a wagon and soon used that job as a cover to transport other runaways, moving them from farm to farm. In 1851, hunted by slave catchers, Williams headed for the sunny promise of the goldfields, but vigilantes soon drove him from the riverbanks.[56] Working as a junk dealer and "hod carrier" delivering loads of heavy bricks in Sacramento, he memorized the layout of the raw city. Ever a rover, he used his covered wagon to help fugitives escape.

Williams described his rootless life in one of the few slave narratives written from California. In 1854 he rescued a woman at gunpoint from her owner's house in Sacramento. He said: "In a few days, her master comes . . . bringing an officer, who presented a pistol at me saying . . . you 'must go and get that woman you stole from Mr. Wholeman or I will blow your brains out.'" Williams led him straight to a lawyer who had the "master" jailed for pointing a six-shooter at him. He then fled on a riverboat to San Francisco, where he was beaten up by slaveholders from Missouri. Robbed, broke, and blackmailed, he went on the run, sailing to Guaymas and Mazatlán, in Mexico.

Always in flight from slavery and always a rambler, Williams shipped out on a bark bound for Talcahuano, Chile. But once on board, he witnessed the captain whip the deckhands. Believing his turn for a flogging was assuredly next, Williams incited a mutiny. Fearing that he would be arrested and held on a Chilean chain gang when the ship reached port, he fled again. Williams returned to Sacramento; construction was booming, but the foremen for the city's new levees refused to hire a Black man. This time, Williams stayed, and he led a strike. He won the right for Blacks to work on the city's construction crews. Williams hoped that he could purchase his freedom and end a life on the run. He mined for himself and took domestic jobs, slipping into a growing community of working-class free Black miners, merchants, barbers, ministers, laundresses, tailors, carpenters, bootblacks, minstrels, prostitutes, servants, and men who ran bathhouses.[57]

Contending Forces: The Law

Slaveholder and journalist Jeter T. Thompson boasted to several southern newspapers that slave owners in California "do not feel under any apprehension"; he was never concerned, he said, that California's constitution would interfere with his "arrangements." He wrote that slaveholders in the West were desperate to keep their slaves. When an enslaved man from Arkansas realized that in California he was legally free, he demanded that Thompson give him back wages for his unpaid years of work. In response, Thompson tied him up and called free Blacks over to watch the flogging, writing to the Arkansas press that no one stepped forward to testify against the man's brutal punishment.[58]

By the mid-1850s, white supremacists in California were reading newspapers such as the *Fayetteville Weekly Observer*, which proclaimed: "Slaves command very fine prices, just now, in the South, last week, a family, consisting of eight likely negro men, sold at an average of $1,086, the group bringing $8,551 [about $255,000 today]."[59] Slave owners in California decided the profit was not in the slim pickings of the goldfields but rather in the men and women they had brought into the state or in the kidnap and sale of free Blacks.[60] The state's ban on Blacks' testimony blurred the difference between fugitives and free men and women.

Slavery was the issue that oddly unified diverse parts of the country: southerners dreamed of a global empire founded on cotton, backed by merchant capitalists in New York, shipping interests in Boston, insurance companies from England, fertilizer from Peru, and a labor force of young women working in the mills in Massachusetts and Manchester, England. While enslaved Blacks worked in the fields of the "cotton belt," southerners began talking about annexing Cuba as an agricultural slave state.[61] Many owners who came west with a plan to get rich quickly and return to the South now had more time to profit from their unpaid workers. The *Daily Alta California*, a newspaper read across the West, declared that the state "tolerated slavery . . . in open defiance of the Constitution."[62]

A Dream Distorted

With little but the promise of a state constitution that was never codified into law, free Blacks looked to the East for legal paths to emancipate their unfree brethren and help them run from bondage. Adapting lessons from "freedom suits," they turned to habeas corpus actions to force slaveholders to "produce" captives for the courts. Blacks who had been born free or manumitted often had to sue for wrongful enslavement. Whether born free or manumitted at the death of their owner or the completion of a contract, Blacks often faced slaveholders' claims that they were only residing in free states as "sojourners," enjoying an extended work trip or vacation.

Many Blacks immediately understood that they were free in California, but one effective way for slave owners to hold onto them was to retain their enslaved parents, wives, or children on plantations in the South. Their owners warned the enslaved in California that if they tried to escape, their families would be harmed. Some Blacks brought to California declared they would only mine in return for the freedom of their relatives back in the South.

Slaveholder Charles McDowell left the mining town of Jamestown, California, in May 1853 to return to the South, but rather than pay the travel costs for his enslaved men, McDowell left them in California with a Black overseer, Albert, and his son Samuel. Albert soon wrote to McDowell to say that Samuel had sailed out of San Francisco: he had not "injoyed [sic] himself any," and the "diggings are not near as good as the reports say." Albert could have fled too, but his ties to his wife and children were strong: "I would say unto my wife and children: you have not seen fit to send me, but one letter and I thank you for that one. Be a good woman until I return. . . . If I live I will come home next spring. Do nothing more." In May 1855 Albert wrote again, saying that he had intended to return to the plantation, but his wages compelled him to stay for another year: "I work hard and save my money as you know by what I send home. . . . I will go as you say but I can make 4 or 5 hundred dollars in that time if God gives me Health." Albert enclosed $400 for his owner and $200 toward the purchase of his wife. Over the course of his time in California, he sent $950 back to his owner.[63] Albert's letter depicts the historic irony of these sham promises of freedom obtained through a contract that disavowed its terms and acknowledged his status as human property; the letter exposes the legal fiction that California would honor his freedom.

Often the slaveholder was the only tie enslaved Blacks had to their families. Enslaved Andrew Jackson had been transported from Memphis, Tennessee, to the goldfields in North Yuba City. After his owner died, Jackson tried to negotiate for his family, and he wrote to "Old Mistress," asking for "a bill of sail [sic] as I wish to be as free on my way home." He wrote:

> I take the opportunity of writing you a few lines to know how you
> are and also to know what you will take for me should I return to
> you. I am hear [sic] a free man but I know when I return home I
> am a slave and I would like to know the least money you will take
> for me and if your price is a reasonable one I will come home and

pay for myself as I had rather live in that country than this. . . . I
wish you to be as reasonable as possible on poor Jack.
[Signed,]
Andrew Jackson
P.S. Tell all the Black boys I am doing reasonably well but I would
like very much to return home and see how they are doing. 2 Jun
1852.[64]

Francis Abner, a Black barber, was expelled from the Oregon Territory
in the spring of 1852 and traveled to San Francisco. Barber was a corre-
spondent for the *Liberator* and reported that he was concerned that, like
Oregon, California would soon expel Blacks. He wrote to his friend Frederick Douglass that here the colored citizen "is driven out like a beast in
the forest, made to sacrifice every interest dear to him, and forbidden the
privilege to take the portion of the soil which the government says every
citizen shall enjoy." Indeed, forty more slaves had arrived in San Francisco
just the day before; he wrote, "Soon I look for trouble in this new yet rotten
limb of 'Republican America.'"[65] His comments were prescient; the next
year he wrote to Douglass to say that white miners would not let Blacks
pan for gold next to them on the rivers.[66]

Contending Forces: Freedom on Their Mind

The core risk to fugitives was California's ban on African Americans testifying in court. As fugitives were arrested, held in jails, and tried in California's courtrooms, they needed to establish that they were free people. When
their disillusioned slave owners returned to the South, Blacks needed to
be able to testify that the men who had transported them to the West had
either abandoned them or freed them.[67] The new Black trailblazers took
jobs digging streets and sidewalks, while they built Black churches, schools,
meeting rooms, and the first Civil Rights movement in California.

In June 1849 slaveholder Charles Perkins left his humid Mississippi
plantation for California's gold mines, taking with him Robert Perkins,
Carter Perkins, and Sandy Jones—three of his father's enslaved workers.
(Typically, slaveholders bestowed their own last name on a person they
possessed; often this person was their own biological child, conceived as a
result of rape.)

Not knowing that as soon as they arrived in California they were, in
fact, free, the three mined for Perkins. After three months Charles Perkins

realized he would make more money if he rented the men out, keeping their "wages" for himself while he mined on his own. Within a few weeks, he had had enough of the muck. Disillusioned and tired, Perkins told the men that they had fulfilled their obligations to him and were now free. Charles Perkins returned to the South, and the three Black men returned to the goldfields in Ophir and thrived. But once Charles Perkins was back in Mississippi, he discovered that enslaved men were now selling for $1,000 apiece; he regretted his decision to free the men and decided to get them back.

One night, while Robert Perkins, Carter Perkins, and Sandy Jones slept, slave catchers broke into their mining cabin and tied them up. They loaded the Black men into their own wagon, pulled by their own mule team, and hauled them to a justice of the peace in Sacramento. With the men unable to testify, in April 1852 the justice declared that they were runaways and ordered them to be shipped back to Charles Perkins in the South. Quickly, the Black community raised defense funds to free the three men and launched a movement against the ban on Black testimony. California's own Fugitive Slave Act had barely been in effect for a month.[68]

In a series of trials and appeals, with lawyers funded by the Black community, the three brothers argued that they were free because slavery had been abolished in Mexico since 1829, and California had not passed a law to change that. Chief Justice Hugh Murray of the California Supreme Court heard their last appeal.[69] In the case of *In re Perkins*, Murray ruled that the people of the United States had the right to immigrate to California "with every species of property they had" and enjoy "everything inherent with its use and possession." The body of a slave was property; hence, a slave brought into the free state did not "become *ipso facto* free" because the U.S. Constitution recognized property rights over "this class of persons." The state legislature had not emancipated slaves who were already in California at the time of admission to the United States, and slave owners still had the right to keep the "services" of the enslaved.

Furthermore, the state of California had the jurisdiction to "arrest and restrain runaway slaves" under its general police power. The court turned to recent decisions by U.S. Supreme Court Justice Roger Taney, who had argued that the state had a duty to protect property and a "slave is *property*, and so to be judicially regarded." Justice Murray then declared that the "pernicious" increase of the "free Negro population" in California was a reasonable motive for California passing its own fugitive slave law. Justice Alexander Anderson concurred and, again citing Taney, added that the temporary residence of a slave in free territory was not, per se, manumission. Then Anderson turned to the infamous language in the Constitution that defined a slave as three-fifths of a citizen in determining a state's population. It was this clause, said Anderson, that bound the states of the union together; indeed, he added, slavery defined the "fundamental existence" of the country.[70]

The California Supreme Court ignored the core question facing Perkins: What is the status of an unfree person in a free state? California's ban on slavery was "inert and inoperative," said the court, and its own Fugitive Slave Act was constitutional. In a seven to two decision, the court ordered that the three men be shipped back to Mississippi. The court also decided that California could maintain slavery in order to "obliterate" Blacks from the state. The justices instructed a marshal to load the men onto a ship.[71] "All those who were made free" by California's constitution "are again reduced to slavery" reported the *National Anti-Slavery Standard*, the newspaper of the American Anti-Slavery Society.[72]

En route back to the South, Robert Perkins, Carter Perkins, and Sandy Jones apparently jumped ship in Panama, and we know nothing more. Had they been allowed to testify that first night, Blacks in California would not have faced the dangerous decision that legalized slavery in a free state.[73] *People v. Perkins* gave slaveholders the right to travel with enslaved men and women to California, work them as they wished, and return with them to the South. *In re Perkins* (*People v. Perkins*) opened the western territories to slave labor. The historic *Perkins* decision gave free states the right to define human beings as possessions and the permission to return runaways, now classified as chattel property, to slave owners.

Five years later, in 1857, Roger Taney, then the chief justice of the U.S. Supreme Court, used the arguments of California's *Perkins* ruling in the infamous *Dred Scott* decision to extend slavery across the United States; for many, this ruling was the spark that started the Civil War. Saidiya Hartman, a contemporary historian of slavery, has observed that the Fugitive Slave Act defined slaves as partial humans—part property and part human.[74] As in plantation states, California *criminal law* held slaves in the character of "persons"—human beings capable of moral choice. In California *civil law*, the enslaved became "property" to be bought and sold.[75] And property cannot speak. The following year, the California legislature reauthorized its own Fugitive Slave Act.[76]

The clash over whether California would be a free state or a slave state hinged on the question of who could be heard in court. Robert Smith had

Biddy Mason successfully sued the state of California
for her freedom by arguing that she could
not be held in bondage in a free state.
(Courtesy of Golden State Mutual Life Insurance Company
Records [Collection 1434]. Library Special Collections,
Charles E. Young Research Library, UCLA.)

left his plantation in Hancock, Georgia, and traveled through Mississippi
in 1851 bound for the Mormon settlement in Utah, and he took along a
wedding present: two enslaved women, young Bridget "Biddy" Mason and
Hannah Smith, and their children. Part of the Mormon group of "Mississippi Saints," Biddy and her children walked from Mississippi to Salt Lake
City behind a train of three hundred wagons, herding the sheep and cattle. She served as a midwife on the trail. After three years in Utah, Smith
moved them to a Mormon community in San Bernardino in Southern

California, where he kept Biddy Mason, Hannah Smith, and their children in bondage.

In 1854 Robert Smith began to worry that California might end his "right" to own slaves, and so he planned to move his "patriarchal family"— Biddy, Hannah, and now ten children—to Texas. A free Black woodcutter in Los Angeles, Robert Owens, understood what would happen to the women and children once they were in Texas, and he persuaded a Los Angeles County sheriff to form a posse and take Biddy and the children into protective custody.[77] In turn, slaveholder Smith petitioned for habeas corpus and demanded that the court "produce" Biddy.

By 1856 Bridget "Biddy" Mason had spent five years enslaved in the free state of California, and Judge Benjamin Hayes of the Los Angeles district court decided that she and Hannah were living "in duress and not in possession of their free will." He did not believe Robert Smith's promise that he would free them in Texas. Hayes emancipated Biddy and the children in California because, he said, they were residents of a free state, and as such, they could not "be held in slavery or involuntary servitude," nor could Smith transport them to Texas, where "slavery of Negroes is . . . established by municipal laws."

Once her freedom was assured, Biddy Mason moved to Los Angeles and worked as a nurse and midwife. With her earnings, she bought two parcels of land in downtown Los Angeles. Five years later she sold her land for $200,000 (the price at the time) and became one of the wealthiest Black women in the state. Mason helped found the first African Methodist Episcopal Church in Los Angeles, gave money for Black schools and nursing homes, and took food to Black prisoners in local jails.[78]

In its first five years of statehood, the capture and enslavement of human beings had pitted the ravishing face of California and left permanent pockmarks in its history. Hand in hand, the legislature and the courts had endorsed the forced transport of enslaved Africans, abolished their land and mining rights, ruled that they were property, and blocked civil access to justice.

The journey of enslaved Africans to California, across the plains or the jungles of Panama, was a second "middle passage"—the forced voyage of enslaved Africans to the Americas. The passage to California dispossessed family, tradition, and body. It included the kidnap of grandparents and ancestors, and the sale and purchase of parents and kin. As elsewhere, slavery of African Americans in California operated through interchangeable systems of involuntary labor. As in plantation states, slavery also presumed the right to full sexual access to an enslaved woman—the absolute right to nonconsensual sex, to rape.

The authors of California's Fugitive Slave Act understood that slavery required coerced mobility and immobility, transport, and confinement. California's Fugitive Slave Act spiraled around the national Fugitive Slave Act to reveal the very nature of slavery—the seizure, transfer, sale, and forced labor of a human being. It exposed the economic underpinning of slavery: human beings were a category of property. The value of a person to the property holder could be assessed in currency. Any loss could be assessed as financial damages. In assuring that slavery would endure, the courts turned to barriers against testimony in order to protect miners' and settlers' right to transport and to work human beings against their will.

Frederick Douglass did not believe that the courts would deliver freedom; rather, he had decided, "the only way to make the Fugitive Slave Law a dead letter is to make half a dozen or more dead kidnappers."[79] Despite its own constitution, in the early 1850s California had legalized the traffic in human beings. In the midst of a genocidal war against California's Native Americans, Blacks used this moment of transition to demand freedom and civil rights in the California legislature and courts, in transit, on the riverbeds, and in the new cities of the new state.

CHAPTER SEVEN

Indian Slavery in a Free State

A Deadly Illogic

Why should you ill-treat me? I am a man.

—MOMPET (Pomo), 1850

IN 1837 MEXICAN RANCHERS Prado Masa and José María Amador led a private army of mercenaries sixty miles across brush, sage, and chaparral to the Stanislaus River in the San Joaquin Valley. Just four years before, in 1833, Mexico had disbanded the Franciscan missions, but rather than use the "secularization" law to return the lands to the California tribes, it launched a vast giveaway of 160,000 square miles of the land to wealthy Mexican ranchers and ambitious European settlers who agreed to convert to Catholicism.[1] Amador, the son of a Mexican sergeant at the presidio in San Francisco, received 16,500 acres—half of the grazing land of Mission San José.[2] Now he wanted to remove the Indians who lived on his land. Like many settlers, Amador sought unpaid laborers.

In 1837 José Amador led an expedition of ranchers and soldiers into the San Joaquin Valley, along the river. Amador invited two hundred local Indians to a feast of dried meat and pinole. As his "guests" arrived, his army surrounded them and then divided them into two groups—pagans and Catholic converts. First, his soldiers roped the neophytes—the "mission" or Christian Indians—together and forced them to march: "At every half mile or mile we put six of them on their knees to say their prayers, making them understand they were about to die." Next they shot each one with four arrows, two in front and two from behind. Then Amador turned to the "gentiles" or pagans, Indians who lived "wild," outside the missions. He splashed them with water from his flask, pronounced them baptized Christians, and shot them all in the back.[3] Why had the rancher just slaughtered his new labor force?

The Mexican Era: Expulsion and Enslavement

The earliest invaders to the Americas created the category "Indians" and imposed it on diverse Indigenous people who had never viewed themselves as a race. California "Indians" identified as members of a tribe or clan marked by language and territory, and as shamans, or traders and weavers, or dancers and drummers. Rather than race, Indigenous Californians knew themselves and their neighbors by their history, their kin, and their ancestors. California Natives were people who thrived across geographies and spirits.

After Mexico won independence from Spain in 1821, it was more interested in land than in god. Eager to get California settled and remove local tribes, settlers and soldiers began to seize California Natives who had been left landless by the missions. The new ranchers and settlers first invaded tribal villages that sat beyond the missions' reach, capturing men to work as cowboys, masons to build the haciendas, or fieldworkers to plow the lands, and seizing women to serve as domestics and concubines. In order to convert California into cattle ranches, vineyards, and peach orchards, Mexico adopted the missions' regime of Indian captivity and bondage and imported its own tradition of agrarian peonage. Despite Mexico's antislavery stance, the newest California empire gave ranchers dominion over lands that stretched for miles and allowed them to capture homeless Native Americans.

In 1823 the U.S. Supreme Court decided that Indians could neither own nor hold title to any land within the United States, but they could remain on their ancestral lands with the "right of occupancy." This was a lesser claim than the "right of discovery," a policy of empire that held that land ownership went to the country that discovered it.[4] With this, the U.S. government could claim all Native American lands.

While Mexico was implementing its hold over California, two-term U.S. President Andrew Jackson (1829–37) pushed through the Indian Removal Act of 1830, a vast land swindle in which Indigenous people in Georgia, Tennessee, Alabama, Mississippi, and North Carolina were compelled to trade their homelands for unsettled lands across the Mississippi River. To carve up the rich river land for plantation slavery, the U.S. military overpowered Native Americans and marched five thousand Indians from their homelands. Nearly four thousand displaced Cherokee died on the one-thousand-mile trek to Oklahoma, known as the "Trail of Tears."[5]

U.S. Indian policy was designed to seize Indian lands for cotton and tobacco plantations that could reach the Pacific. The plan reached the highest level of the U.S. government. President James Polk (1845–49) kept a personal slave broker so that he could buy and sell enslaved African Americans from within the White House. Six of the nine members of the U.S. Supreme Court during the 1840s were also slaveholders and issued decisions that allowed Black slavery to spread to Native American lands.[6]

In 1842 Captain Salvador Vallejo hired Mexican soldiers to ride sixty miles north from the Napa Valley to Clear Lake. For over eleven thousand years, Yuki (originally Ukomno'om, meaning "valley people") and Wappo had lived along the banks and on the islands of Clear Lake in Northern California. Its warm waters are on the flyover from Canada, and mallards, grebes, pelicans, blue herons, egrets, and osprey nest along its edge. Around the lake, one thousand ancient volcanic fissures spew warm geysers onto the dry hills. In the nineteenth century, deer, bear, tule elk, and mountain lions hid in the tules and cottonwood along its shoreline. About 350 Habe-matolel Pomo lived in villages by the lake and fished in its waters for large-mouth bass, bluegill, and catfish.

Vallejo wanted to move the Pomo off "his" new land, even though he needed them to tend his livestock and harvest his wheat, and took his mercenaries to Clear Lake. While some of his soldiers pretended to be fur traders seeking to exchange beads for beaver pelts, the others circled the villages along the shore. They rounded up one hundred Indians and marched them into their large *temescal*, or sweat lodge. The soldiers blocked its tunnel-like entrance and transformed the sacred space into a crematorium of the living. Some Pomo escaped the slaughter and leaped into the lake, swimming toward the nearby islands.

Only after Vallejo's band of mercenaries heard the crackling sounds of burning bodies did they depart, but the surviving Pomo attacked Vallejo's men on the route back to his ranch in Napa. As they marched through the forests and along the trails, his army seized three hundred Indian men, women, and children, a diaspora of Native Americans seized for the new rancher.[7]

Manifest Utopia

Early California fieldworkers and ranch hands were stolen people, seized and traded by settlers. Some ranchers forced them to stand through the night as "live fences," tasked with guarding cattle or chasing them in the dark. Others ordered Indians to steal roots and vines from the missions as starter plantings for the vineyards of Napa Valley. Indians captured by rancheros were soon trapped by debt peonage, made to pay for their food and liquor. Logbooks show Indians owing as much as fifty dollars to the ranch owner, yet only earning the equivalent of twelve cents per day—if they were paid at all.[8]

At the cusp of the Spanish invasion in 1769, 310,000 Native Americans lived in California, the highest density of Indigenous people in North America.[9] When the United States invaded California in 1846 at the start of the U.S.–Mexican War, only 150,000 Native people remained. From 1846 to 1873, landowners, vigilantes, and U.S. soldiers slaughtered some sixteen thousand California Natives and seized the survivors of the massacres to labor in bondage.[10] By 1880 the population of California Natives fell to 16,227, as they died from slaughter, hunger, and epidemics of new diseases.[11] These statistics hold the history of searing human bondage and genocide. Government documents, letters, and sparse Native American narratives break through the silence of the horror.

A Deadly Paradox: Settlers and Slavers

In a tragic contradiction, Mexicans, Californios (Spanish-speaking Catholic descendants of early Mexican settlers and Spanish soldiers), and American and European settlers murdered Indigenous people even as they craved their labor to chop brush, channel creeks, build ranch houses, and plow over their tribal lands. California settlers relied on Native Americans who knew the cycles of storms and rains, the spawning of salmon and the running of elk, and who had learned farming skills from their forced toil at the missions. The new ranchers ordered Indian and Mexican vaqueros to steal horses from the missions and the military for the new ranches.[12] Juan Alvarado (1837–42) and Manuel Micheltorena (1842–45), the last Mexican governors of California, were instrumental in the privatization of California, a swift and vast land giveaway before the Americans took over, hoping that settlers in the inland valleys would form an agrarian buffer against the tribes. They gave military rights, judicial authority, and thousands of acres of land to promoters such as John Sutter and his friend John Bidwell. They too wanted laborers.

In 1834 Sutter was in flight from creditors in his native Switzerland. He sailed to New York and, hopping ships, headed west to Missouri, Vancouver, and Hawaii, then north to Alaska. During a one-month stay in Sitka, Sutter saw the profits of the Russian regime of Native slavery. In 1839 Sutter became a Mexican citizen, and Governor Alvarado let him choose nearly eighty square miles where the American River meets the Sacramento River at the base of the fertile Central Valley. Sutter guessed correctly that wagon trains that had just crossed the Sierras would arrive there desperate for supplies and eager for land and laborers.

Sutter's first task was to recruit 150 Mexican and Native men to form a private army at his vast ranch on Nisenan and Miwok land.[13] He dressed his soldiers in bright green and blue uniforms that he bought cheaply from the Russians as they abandoned Fort Ross and used this gaudy military display to enforce his self-styled judicial code. Sutter surrounded his land with a tall palisade, called his ranch "a nation," and named it "New Helvetia," or "New Switzerland."[14]

In 1847 Sutter became the first federal Indian subagent in California. His first duty was to stop hungry Indians from stealing cattle from new ranchers and settlers, and Sutter let the local chiefs know that he had the authority to punish them with an "armed force." With this, the federal government placed the burden of guilt on California Natives for any difficulties in the new territory.[15] That year the *California Star* reported, "We have tidings of an outrage committed by the whites upon a defenseless encampment of Indians, 60 miles north of New Helvetia. . . . The Spaniards, having partaken of their [Indians'] hospitality, commenced making prisoners of men, women, and children, and in securing them, some ten or twelve were killed . . . attempting to escape. Thirty were secured, principally women and children, tied together and driven to the settlements. Young children who were unable to proceed were murdered on the road. In one instance, an infant was taken from its mother, and killed in her presence, and that too, in the most brutal manner."[16]

Sutter thrived from the profits of human trafficking, kidnapping Indians and then leasing or selling them to other ranchers. Some he kept in bondage for his own use; others he held in debt peonage, and a few received a small wage.[17] Claiming he was battling cattle raiders, Sutter's army murdered adult Indians and then seized their orphaned children as "payment for the cost of war." Sutter also purchased Indians from Mexican

Captive Native Californian women, likely Miwok, tan hides at the vast cattle
ranch of physician John Marsh. An early white settler, Marsh was murdered
by three of his Native workers when he refused to give them wages.

(Courtesy of Contra Costa County Historical Society, Martinez, California.)

debtor prisons; others he received as gifts.[18] When wealthy landholders
placed orders for Indians, Sutter sent scouts to scour the foothills, take
captives, and deliver them to his neighbors.

To work his own ranch, Sutter captured more than two thousand Indian men and women from over thirty villages—double the number of enslaved Blacks held at the largest plantations in the U.S. South.[19] By the
1840s most ranches in California held from twenty to several hundred Indians in various forms of peonage. During harvests, Sutter sent his private
army into the hills to capture Nisenan and Pomo Indians in their villages,
and he made agreements with neighbors and nearby ranchers such as Salvador Vallejo not to raid each other's cache of bound Indians.

Sutter closely copied Russia's strategies of unfree labor that he had witnessed in Alaska. He bragged that the Indians at New Helvetia were now
his "subjects . . . on the grounds where they are born and their ancestors

have dwelled."[20] Native Americans trapped on his ranch could only trade at his store and only spend New Helvetia coins—perforated metal disks—strung around their necks. He was his own mint and his own bank, issuing and collecting credit. In the dry and sunny valleys northeast of San Francisco, a fiefdom was born in a modernizing world. Every half hour the bell at New Helvetia tolled the order of the new era.[21]

Sutter advised his neighbors to keep Indians "strictly under fear," and at New Helvetia Indians were flogged, jailed, and executed for disobedience.[22] In one of the few Indigenous depictions of life under Sutter, Nisenan William Joseph recalled that if any Indian failed to work, Sutter's overseers "whipped them with a big whip made of cowhide."[23] Visitor James Clyman reported, "The Capt. Keeps 600 or 800 Indians in a complete state of Slavery. . . . I have had the mortification of seeing them dine [at] 10 or 15 troughs 3 or 4 feet long . . . seated in the broiling sun. All the labourers grate [*sic*] and small ran to the troughs like so many pigs and fed themselves with their hands as long as the trough contained even moisture."[24]

To save on the costs of clothing, Sutter ordered the Indians to "cover their nakedness" with heavy blankets, despite the valley heat. At night, his overseers locked his captives in a fetid chamber and fenced them into high corrals.[25] Heinrich Lienhard, one of Sutter's managers, claimed, "I had to lock the Indian women and men together in a large room to prevent them from returning to their homes in the mountains at night." Nonetheless, "large numbers deserted during the daytime."[26] Sutter was also known for his "harem"—twenty-five Native women and girls, some as young as ten years old, who passed their days in a room next to his office waiting to be summoned. When he tired of a young girl, recounted Lienhard, Sutter expelled her from his fort, to die in the wilderness.[27] Lienhard also declared that Sutter gave him permission to take nineteen Native American "wives" for himself.

Like the Franciscan priests, Sutter built his labor pool through "forced congregation." For thousands of years, California Natives had known when to gather acorns, to burn the fields and regenerate grasses that would attract animals, to catch and smoke salmon, and to let the land rest. Sutter ordered his Indian captives to use his calendar instead for plowing, planting, and harvesting.

Sutter soon discovered that his crops would never yield the same profits as his inventory of Native Americans, so he began buying and selling Indian children, renting them out for one dollar per day, or $700 for extended servitude of two to six months. If any of Sutter's Indians fled, the rancher had to repay him the full purchase price. Mocking California's ban on selling humans, at times Sutter delivered Indians as gifts. In debased irony, once he sent a child to his neighbor, African American merchant and rancher William Leidesdorff, with a note saying, "As this shall never be considered an article of trade [I] make you a present with the Girl."[28]

Without their traditional foods, the Miwok, Yukulme, and Nisenan at Sutter's ranch were dying from starvation. In addition, the Indians were dying from childbirth and assault. In 1858 Indians at Hock Farm, one of Sutter's ranches, demanded wages and freedom—the right to work and shop where they chose. Sutter sent them to his friend, Superintendent of Indian Affairs Thomas Henley, for "federal oversight." Across the lower Central Valley, hundreds of Hock, Yukulme, Sisum, and Ollash were in flight from Sutter's "nation," and Henley sent armed men on horseback to recapture them. His private soldiers executed all the Yalisumni fugitives they could find. Yet settlers believed that Sutter could always replenish their supply of Indian laborers.[29]

The Illogic of Slaughter and Slavery

In the summer of 1846, John Montgomery, the U.S. military commandant for Northern California, sailed into San Francisco on the sloop-of-war USS *Portsmouth* to announce that the United States had seized California from Mexico: the territory was now under U.S. martial law.[30] Montgomery then announced that anyone holding Indians must "release them and permit them to return to their homes unless they can make a legal contract with them." He accused Californians of imprisoning and conscripting Indians "to service, against their will and without any legal contract bill of sale and without a due regard to their rights as freemen, when not under legal contract for service." California Indians, he declared, "must not be regarded in the light of slaves." Indians had the right to choose their own "master or employer." It appeared that Montgomery had just announced that the United States had abolished slavery.

In fact, freedom was contingent. Mexico had released all the "Mission Indians," but Montgomery's twisted decree required all Indians to "obtain employment"; if they "wander[ed] about in an idle and dissolute manner" they faced arrest and punishment "by labor on the public works." Indians who fled from their employers could be bound until they died. In addition, every Indian was required to have an indenture paper ratified by a justice of the peace, but thousands of California Natives were held captive without such a "contract." Montgomery undercut his proclamation that Indians had the freedom to quit an employer.[31] Indians in California who were found guilty of being unemployed or homeless were also to be forced to labor in servitude. Under U.S. military rule, ranchers and settlers had the right to possess California Indians.

In 1846 U.S. Army Captain John Frémont attacked the Wintu with rifles, sabers, knives, and their own tomahawks. Up to one thousand Wintu were "eliminated" in this second massacre of California Indians—hunted down while trying to escape by swimming in rivers swollen by springtime floods. Annihilation traveled up the fertile Sacramento Valley as Frémont's entourage moved north, killing as they went.[32] This early battle marked the start of a genocide that lasted twenty-seven years.

The U.S. military, based at the old Mexican fort in Monterey, announced the protocols that legitimized Indian slavery with the 1847 Ordinance Respecting the Employment of Indians: "Any Indian found beyond the limits of the town or rancho in which he may be employed" who did not have a pass would "be liable to arrest as a horse thief." If an Indian could not produce a certificate to prove he was employed, he was available for sale. Any "employer" who had "claims . . . for wages advanced" was entitled to bind an Indian into debt peonage.[33] Freedom hinged on a shabby piece of paper preserved, against all odds, in the sweat and weather of field labor that could swiftly transform an "employer" into a slaveholder.

Montgomery's decree anticipated the passes for enslaved Blacks under the Fugitive Slave Act of 1850, California's own Fugitive Slave Act of 1852, and the "Geary Act" of 1892 that required all Chinese people to carry photo-identity cards.[34] Any person who "enticed" an Indian away from a "master" faced a fine of five to twenty dollars—a cheap investment in an unpaid worker.[35] Traveler Edwin Bryant watched armed volunteers slaughter adult Indian men, "transfer children" by force, and "impose measures intended to prevent births within the group"—an early form of racial eugenics. Bryant witnessed the "California Battalion" kidnap women and children to fill orders for Indian laborers and deliver them to ranches so distant from their tribes that they could never return. Bondage, deportation, malaria, and measles forged the new settler state.[36] Two decades of slave raiding followed.

From the first invasions, California tribes defied the new settlers. With the birth of California as a state, Mohave Chooksa-homar predicted, "If we let the whites come and live here, they will take your wives. They will put you to work. They will take your children and carry them away and sell them. . . . That is why [we] want to stop them from coming, want them to stay in their own homes."[37] By May 1847 John Sutter was double-dealing as an Indian slaveholder and federal Indian agent, yet he complained that slave raiders, "with little or no cause," were shooting Indian men to "steal away their women and children."[38] That year the Native Americans at Pierson B. Reading's Rancho Buena Ventura rose up, stole his cattle, killed the overseer, and torched his house.[39]

In 1848 the popular *New York Herald* wrote that California Indians "are kept in a kind of slavery and bondage by the rancheros, and often flogged and punished."[40] Charles Stone and Andrew Kelsey, for example, flogged the Indians on their ranch until they were hobbled, injured, and disabled. The ranch owners confiscated bows, arrows, and fishing spears so that the Native people had to depend on them for food. In a grand jury hearing, Hoolampo Pomo Chief Augustine testified that Kelsey carted hundreds of Indians down to the lower valleys, where he "sold them like cattle or other stock."[41] Westward-bound settlers knew they were traveling to a land bountiful in massacred bodies.

In 1849 Pomo workers at Stone and Kelsey's ranch near Clear Lake were ordered to weave long cords. Aware that the ropes were intended to tie them together for a forced march, they planned a revolt. Local Pomo leaders Shuk, Xasis, Ba-Tus, Kra-nas, and Ma-Laxa-Qe-Tu decided to kill their owners. At a signal, the Pomo children who worked inside the ranch house hid Kelsey's weapons; when Stone emerged from the cookhouse with breakfast, as planned, a Pomo man shot him with an arrow. Hearing the struggle, Kelsey came to the door and was stabbed, but he broke loose and dashed across a creek. Waiting for him was a Pomo woman, Da-Pi-Tauo, who shoved a spear through his heart.

Pomo and Wappo leaders knew that they would be hunted for the murder and urged their people to gather corn, slaughter heads of cattle, and escape "to a hiding place . . . wherever else they pleased, as they all had their liberty once more and were free men." Many fled back to Clear Lake, where they hurriedly wove canoes made of rushes and paddled to the islands.[42] But something seismic had taken place that would raise the stakes of slavery for ranchers and Indians, for California—and the United States and the world.

California Gold

On January 24, 1848, thirty-five miles from John Sutter's ranch, carpenter James Marshall was building a water-powered sawmill on the South Fork of the American River when he noticed flakes of gold in a creek. The worth of California forever changed. One week later, on February 2, 1848, American officials claimed victory in the war with Mexico, and the two nations signed the Treaty of Guadalupe Hidalgo. In victory, the United States promised that Indian freedom would endure. As Mexican citizens, California Indians were assured that they "shall be maintained and protected in the free enjoyment of their liberty and property."

Montgomery sailed into San Francisco in a tense interregnum. Three thousand miles from Washington, DC, California was neither a legal territory nor a state, but a landscape stippled with chaotic sites that lacked central authority, and with restless settlers who lacked binding laws—until California voted for a constitution that refused to "tolerate" slavery.

Act for the Government and Protection of Indians, 1850

In early December 1849, as Congress debated whether slavery would be allowed in the new territories, California's eager legislature met in San Jose, nine months before the state was admitted to the Union on September 9, 1850. California upended its new freedom constitution and turned Montgomery's contorted decree into the Act for the Government and Protection of Indians (hereafter the "Indian Act").[43] Southern slaveholders—southern Democrats—pushed the act through in nine days. Many members of the legislature had been ambivalent delegates to California's Constitutional Convention; in less than a year, they erased the freedom promised in the state constitution just as it came into being and created a category of persons who had no ownership of their own bodies, no access to the courts, and no right to their own children.

In this chaotic era of the contending forces of a mass giveaway of Native Americans' lands and human bondage, California's act to "protect" Indians offered options for an unfree Indigenous workforce.[44] California could turn to a long chain of legal sanctions for human bondage. In 1808 Congress had passed the Act Prohibiting the Importation of Slaves, banning the transport of Africans into the country for the purposes of slavery and taking the nation out of the global slave trade, but it did not abolish the sale of human beings *within* the United States. The South compensated for the end of the global slave trade by maintaining the bondage of the offspring of enslaved women already in the United States. In California, however, Indian fertility would be counterproductive to white settlement.

The Indian Act offered access both to Indian bodies and Indian land.[45]

Charles Nahl, *The Attack*, 1850. Native Californians
defend their land against invasion during the Gold Rush.
In "Scenes among the Indians of California," *Hutchings' Illustrated
California Magazine* (April 1859): 443, via Internet Archive.

It was the political scaffolding that allowed settlers to flout both the ban
on slavery in the Treaty of Guadalupe Hidalgo (1848) and the California
constitution of 1849: settlers could now legally remove Native people from
their homelands and seize them as prisoners, child "wards," unfree apprentices, and indentured servants.[46] John Frémont, one of California's first
senators, predicted that massacres would open Indian land to the new settlers and unleash a stream of displaced and available Indigenous people:
"Spanish law clearly and absolutely secured to Indians fixed rights of property in the lands that they occupy." Frémont knew that a "particular provision" would be "necessary to divest them of these rights."[47] Senator John
Weller reminded the state that with "the White man . . . now in the West,"
the Indian must be "crushed . . . humanity may forbid, but the interest of
the white man demands their extinction."[48]

   The Indian Act became that "particular provision" that poured forth
thousands of Indian refugees and war orphans; it was capacious enough to
provide cover to ranchers and householders who would kidnap children

from their parents or seize them from the reservations and military forts. It effectively created a permanent class of unfree refugees who lost dominion over their bodies and labor. The Indian Act invited ranchers to arrest any California Natives found "loitering and strolling about where liquor was sold or leading an immoral life or profligate course of life." When a settler suspected an Indian of these unspecified acts, an officer of the law could arrest and "lease such a vagrant to the highest bidder" within twenty-four hours. Suspicion sufficed, and an "immoral life" was undefined. In less than a day, a free Indian could be seized, leased, or bought at auction. For Indigenous people who could neither read nor write, all that was needed was for them to put a mark on a piece of paper that said they had agreed to be bound.[49]

The Indian Act helped birth the carceral state, for it gave private employers the right to lease convicts. A white rancher or farmer could visit a jail, select an Indian, and pay his fines, bail, and jail costs, and "the Indian shall be compelled to work for the person so bailing until he has discharged or canceled the fine assessed against him." Further, if an Indian could not pay the two-dollar fine for the misdemeanor of vagrancy, "any white" could pay it and have the Indian bound over to him until he completed his term of service or discharged the "loan," which could include costs of food and clothing.

City and county jails became slave marts for Indian prisoners who were to be bound out until they repaid a debt, giving farmers time to get their grain planted and harvested; indeed, child wardship, debt peonage, and involuntary convict labor produced the labor force that launched California wheat. In the new town of Fresno, Native Americans who could not pay their fines for vagrancy or drunkenness were sold at auction.[50]

The Indian Act embraced key elements of slavery: it did not require wages for labor, and it offered no right to terminate an indenture contract. The inability to leave an employer is generally a feature of human bondage.[51] Of great danger, any person who "obtained" an Indian who had been accused of stealing horses or mules could apply up to twenty-five lashes, although, in a parody of scruples, the whipping was only allowed in the presence of a justice of the peace.

A direct path to unfree labor in California was mapped into the act, as well as into California's criminal code, for an Indian could not testify against a white man in court or against anyone who "forcibly conveys an Indian from his home, or compels him to work, or perform any service against his will." Indeed, "in no case shall a white man be convicted of any offense upon the testimony of an Indian." The act, passed in just nine days with little debate, banned Indians from voting, legalized the corporeal punishment of Indians, and established a system of Indian servitude and unfree labor. It was, writes historian Ben Madley, a boon to unfree labor and a foundation of California's genocide.[52]

California was dreaming of a white future.[53] It guaranteed starvation by refusing to grant each Indian one acre of land. It banned Indians from burning grasslands to regenerate their seed fields and attract game. It limited tribal fishing rights. Settlers killed the deer, and their livestock overtook the meadows. As the military killed Native American men (presumably the hunters), women and children wandered into captivity in search of food. The Indian Act was passed by the same legislature that had almost voted to purge all African Americans from the state.[54] After the harvest, some ranchers moved Indians, one hundred or so at a time, to mine for them in the icy goldfields of the Sierras. Other ranchers released them to starve or die from exposure—disposable workers not worth the upkeep until spring.[55] But if Californians sought a pool of unpaid workers, the Indian Act was counterproductive: between 1850 and 1870, the Indigenous population declined, with, for example, the numbers of Indians working in the fields and vineyards of Los Angeles falling from 3,693 to 219.[56]

By 1850 just over four thousand "non-Native women" women lived in California, and white miners and settlers kidnapped thousands of Native women to live with them, to bear their children, and face their abuse.[57] Relationships with Indian women were often temporary, few marriages were recorded, and demeaning slurs marked these interracial bonds.[58]

Suffer the Children

The Indian Act worked hand in hand with the massacres to provide a vast inventory of Indian boys and girls. "Baby hunters" took orders from ranchers, rode into Indian villages, shot down fathers in cold blood, and kidnapped children and sold them far away from their tribe.

From the 1850s to 1870s, from northern Humboldt County down to the high desert east of San Diego, vigilantes slaughtered Indian men, seized the children and women, and deposited them in a county jail for protection. Then, another "trafficker," as they were called at the time, would show up to indenture the children. Slaveholders claimed that they were rescuing orphans.

The new free state had designed a deadly regime.[59] Any Indian child deemed an orphan could be claimed; any white person could go before a local justice of the peace, record the sex and "probable age" of an Indian child, and "keep it." A "master" could sell an indentured Indian child and pass along his "same rights and liabilities." Bondage overruled claims to kinship.[60] It erased collective memory and obliterated many tribal traditions. Along the North Coast, the Yurok built houses of planked redwood; each morning they reentered the world through a round door, daily reborn in a portal that honored a woman's power to give life. In the first year of the Indian Act, John Bidwell—explorer, state senator, and powerful rancher in the Central Valley—wrote, "Here we have not only Indians on our *frontiers*, but *among* us, *around* us, *with* us—hardly a farmhouse—a kitchen without them."[61] The highly touted white household was hardly a place of shelter.

Slavery, the many-headed hydra, slid across the state. In 1852 Mexican grandees Juan Berrellesa (Berryessa family), Ramon Briones, Ramon Mesa, and José María Jacon were arrested in Napa County for kidnapping and selling Indian children in the San Francisco Bay area, but federal agents said that the children were too far from their homelands to ever find their way back, and they released the powerful ranchers.[62]

Even so, news of Indian children's fierce opposition surfaces in court records. Pomo boys La Waiwoi and Kalalo, aged about ten and twelve, had been kidnapped by a child hunter and sold to rancher Ramon Berrellesa, a member of the powerful Bay Area Berryessa clan. In August 1850 Berrellesa rode out with two of his bound Indian men, Mompet and La Komopaw, and the two boys. When they stopped to fix the saddles, Mompet and La Komopaw seized Berrellesa from behind and stabbed him in the throat with his own sword and "pricked him all over his back with his pocketknife." The Indians dragged the dying man into an *arroyo* and tossed in his sword. Then the two Pomo men and two Pomo boys rode to the northern tip of San Francisco Bay, where they built a flimsy little boat. All four were captured within days and spent the summer in prison in Martinez.[63]

At the trial, Mompet testified that just before he killed Berrellesa, he demanded, "Why should you ill-treat me? I am a man." In a world that denied this basic truth, Mompet made it clear that he had to kill the man who had purchased and abused him. The jury agreed: it found Mompet and La Komopaw guilty of manslaughter and fined them one dollar; the men returned to their tribe near Clear Lake. The children, however, were given to a wealthy gold miner with full rights to their labor and earnings.[64]

"Nearly all the children belonging to some of the Indian tribes in the northern part of the State have been stolen," reported the *Daily Alta California*.[65] By 1854 there was no limit on the number of children a white "master" could seize, indenture, and control the earnings of (an Indian boy until he was eighteen or an Indian girl until she was fifteen). Custody included the right to flog an Indian adult or child criminal. The requirement that "employers" had a parent's consent was rarely enforced.

From the Indian Act of 1850 to the Emancipation Proclamation of 1863, approximately ten thousand to twenty thousand Indians were kidnapped, indentured, and delivered into bondage; of those, three thousand to four thousand were children, seized and sold.[66] By 1852 one-third of the Native boys in California were indentured and 65 percent of Native females were bound over before they were fifteen years old. The baptismal records of St. Mary's Catholic Church in Oakland, from 1850 to 1853, list fifty-seven forcibly indentured Indian children whose average age was nine years old.[67]

No more Indian children in Southern California could be found to sell to the ranchers, reported the *Daily Alta California* in 1854. Yet child captives were still being delivered to the Bay Area.[68] María de los Angeles Colos, a Costanoan woman, saw "a wagon filled with Indian children coming from Martinez. Dona____ was in the seat. They were bringing them *como* [like] animals to be bought up by the Spanish Californians." The naked children, she saw, were crying for water.[69]

The Traffic in California Native Women

Single men from all over the world continued to arrive in California and they sought women for love, sex, and domestic labor. John Sutter's records list many white men who held several Indian "wives."[70] Kidnappers began to abduct girls in large groups and sell them with the help of federal Indian agents who simply reported the capture of "twenty or twenty-five" young women from the Mattole Valley.[71] Itinerant slave brokers filled orders from ranchers and homesteaders for Indian women. Newspapers, cartoons, and the law created the image of Native women as promiscuous, slovenly, and backward—instinctually close to nature. Indentured Native American women lost the human right to refuse sexual contact with their owner or captor. No punishment for sexual assault was written into the act to "protect" the Indian; rape was acceptable.[72]

With the massacres ongoing and the Indian Act in place, for the next five years Indigenous women and children were in flight across Northern California, and Robert White, the subagent for Indian Affairs, was desperate to corral them onto the reservations. When private sales of Indians usurped this plan, he began to document the local slave trade: "May 17, 1855: I have just learned that a man named McDonald, with others who live on Cache Creek, has stolen three Indians, a woman and two boys, and started for home with them by a by-road and intends to sell them or trade them for cattle. . . . If you wish me to . . . recover the Indians, let me know."[73] Four months later, White reported that he had been hunting fugitive Indians in Mendocino for twenty days, only to discover that Mexican ranchers had ridden out ahead of him and kidnapped more than twenty young Indigenous Metomas women. Two weeks later, he discovered that most of the women and children had escaped, but white slave hunters had seized thirteen other females and were too far ahead for him to mount a tracking party.[74]

When a cowboy offered mountain traders Pierce and Frank Asbill the option to trade an Indian woman for three saddles, they realized that they would make more money filling orders for Yuki girls than selling buckskin. Soon other ranchers asked them for women from the "Land of the Snows"— the California Sierras—rather than from militant Pit River tribes known for poisoning their owners.[75] The brothers began their trade in the Coastal Range by roping a young Yuki girl who kicked and screamed until they tied her to an alder tree with a dog chain. In 1855 they traded thirty-five young Yuki girls to a Mexican rancher in Red Bluff in exchange for 105 horses. The rancher took the girls away in two creaky wagons, and the Asbills added Mexican horses to their lucrative trade in Indian women and took the profits to buy a vast ranch.[76]

There is no evidence that California Natives practiced sexual assault. There is ample evidence that enraged Indians resisted the sale and rape of Native women and girls. Women from tribes in the Coastal Range or the Siskiyou Mountains or by the rivers near Cottonwood knew where to hide. In May 1852 the *Daily Alta California* reported, "In palliation of the slaughter of the women and children it is stated that the Indians thrust themselves forward as a screen for themselves, and behind their persons, as from a barricade, kept up a fire upon the assailants."[77] Along the Salmon River in the winter of 1854, a gang of white men took up the "habit of forcing" Indian women and shot a Karuk man when he tried to stop them from "ravishing" a girl. Revenge was swift. All knew that bullets had a longer range and capacity for injury than arrows, but California had banned

Indians from owning muskets, pistols, and rifles. Nonetheless, the tribe retaliated, killing four attackers.[78]

The Illusion of Surrender

Many U.S. senators argued that under Spanish and Mexican rule, California Indians had lost all claims to their land. But Senator John Frémont wanted treaties to verify California Indians' surrender of their homelands. In 1851 three federal commissioners traveled the length of California to locate Indian men whom they presumed to be chiefs and enticed them to sign treaties, relinquish their homelands, and move thousands of their people onto reservations. The commissioners were often lost, did not know who the chiefs were, and lacked translators, but they returned to Washington with eighteen treaties.[79] The lead commissioner, Redick McKee, was double-dealing: he had promised these chiefs that "the product of their labor should be their own," but he also assured the senators that the treaties would give settlers cheap Indian workers.[80] U.S. Commissioner of Indian Affairs Luke Lea rejected the plan to "reserve" 11,700 square miles for occupation by 139 tribes, about 7.5 percent of California land.[81]

In fact, neither the state nor the federal government would give any land to California Natives and only offered them titles to "remote lands"—not to exceed one-sixth of the land promised in the treaties. Commissioner Lea objected: these lands were "such as only a half-starved and defenseless people would have consented to receive."[82] In the end, the U.S. Senate blocked all the treaties.

Settlers' demands for servants and ranch hands offset their goal of Indian extinction. In 1852 the first superintendent of Indian Affairs for California, Edward F. Beale, announced that rather than catch Indians "like cattle and making them work and turning them out to starve and die when the work season is over," or hunt them "like wild beasts, lassoed, and torn from homes [and] forced into slavery," he would "invite" California Indians to "assemble" on small "military reservations," whose expenses would be "borne by the surplus produce of Indian labor." To "preserve this unfortunate people from total extinction, and our government from everlasting disgrace," California Natives would live under "a system of discipline and instructions."[83] In 1851 Beale opened the first "reserve" on the barren and steep Tejon Pass next to his own ranch, the largest private landholding in the United States, and the Indian commissioner brought Indigenous people from the reservation to build his Tejon Ranch.[84] Some white settlers let themselves imagine that the reservations would be Christian utopias where Indigenous traditions would vaporize along with land rights; they envisioned self-sufficient detention farms staffed with white teachers and missionaries who would peacefully lead the way to Indian assimilation.

Race, Removal, and Reservations

Spain had hoped to preserve its empire through marriages of Mexican settlers and Native women; their children would establish a permanent Spanish state and a thriving Catholic faith. Meanwhile, "interbreeding" would provide sexual partners for settlers and soldiers and keep the population of laborers high, while the addition of white "blood" would "civilize" the Indians.[85] California had three white men to every white woman in the 1850s, yet settlers remained hostile to "amalgamation" (interracial sex or marriage), and the legislature declared that "all marriages of whites with negroes or mulattoes [were] null and void." But it did not ban sexual assault by white men against Indian women.

Until 1880 the age of consent in California was ten years old; it would have been impossible for a bound ten-year-old girl to charge her owner with assault.[86] Excluded from the courts, young Indian girls became victims of abduction, assault, rape, and murder.[87] After the American takeover, the presence of Indian-Anglo children prompted the derogatory term "halfbreed." As in the South, mixed-race children carried the mark of slavery and the stigma of a conception by rape. Tribal women enslaved by whites involuntarily became cultural brokers; they tried to keep their children safe and still pass on their tribal legacies.[88]

From the beginning, California's reservations were open slave marts. Indian reservations could not "exclude the Whites from entering and occupying the reserves, or even prevent their taking from them Indians, [women], and children," announced the commander of the Department of the Pacific.[89] California Superintendent of Indian Affairs Thomas Henley, in full-dress hypocrisy, reported to Washington that "hundreds of Indians have been stolen and carried into the settlements and sold; in some instances, entire tribes were taken in mass." The slaughter, he said, produced a trade in orphans as "fathers and mothers have been brutally killed when they offered resistance to the taking away of their children." Indian Agent E. A. Stevenson reported that in Mendocino County, whites "seem to have adopted the principle that they [the Indians] belong to them as much as an African slave does to his master."[90]

Captive California Natives, likely Miwok, make bricks for the vast mansion
of rancher and physician John Marsh in Contra Costa County.
(Courtesy of Contra Costa County Historical Society, Martinez, California.)

Chilling reports from Indian agents about slavery at California's reservations landed on the desk of Jefferson Davis, the U.S. Secretary of War
from 1853 to 1857. Davis, however, held ten enslaved Blacks at his cotton
plantation in Mississippi, and in seven years he would ascend to the presidency of the Confederate States of America. Jefferson Davis denied Henley's hypocritical plea to have U.S. soldiers arrest slave traffickers, and he
gave federal immunity to Indian slave catchers in California.[91]

Dreaming of a white state, rancher John Marsh wrote a "booster," or
immigrant recruitment letter, that was published in newspapers across the
country. Marsh depicted a settler utopia in California where an "immense
number of wild, naked, brute Indians . . . grazing together like so many
cattle" would never "stand in the way."[92] Indians were a "race of infants"
and if caught young, they were not "averse to labor." Child captives, he
claimed, did not want to return to a "savage state" and "willingly" became
"serfs [who] submit to flagellation with more humility than the negroes."

All that was needed for their "complete subjugation" was "kindness in the beginning, and a little well-timed severity when manifestly deserved." He reassured the more squeamish settlers that they could "order another Indian to inflict the punishment, which is received without the least sign of resentment." Marsh conceded that without Indian child conscripts in California, "the business of the country could hardly be carried on."[93]

CHAPTER EIGHT

No Further West

Ranches, Reservations, and Slave Labor Camps

There was an old woman . . . still alive when the people came.

She couldn't move because she was stuck in the mud so badly,

and she was singing a song.

—CHERYL SEIDNER, Wiyot Tribal Chair

IN HIS FIRST ADDRESS to the state in 1851, Governor Peter H. Burnett vowed "that a war of extermination will continue to be waged between the two races until the Indian race becomes extinct," and he promised to order the California state militia to join with the U.S. military to drive Indians off their lands.[1] "The white" he added, "to whom time is money, and . . . who labors hard all day . . . cannot sit up all night to watch his property. . . . After being robbed a few times he becomes desperate and resolves upon a war of extermination."[2] The first governor of California had just assured his constituents that the state belonged to "the white."

Congress refused to pass any of the eighteen treaties that granted land to California tribes, and Indian Commissioner Redick McKee predicted a mass slaughter: "As there is now no farther west to which they can be removed, the general government and the people of California appear to have left but one alternative in relation to these remnants of once numerous . . . tribes, viz: extermination or domestication."[3]

"Domestication" involved marching the Indians who survived the massacres to small and remote reservations and transforming them into a submissive slave-labor force. The legislature hoped that "useful" Indians, those trained at the missions, would "resume their former occupation and supply . . . what is so much needed, that labor, without which, it will be long before California can feed herself." If the government could contain the massacres, "the farmer, grazier, and owners of vineyards might derive their accustomed and needed laborers."[4]

These two racial policies—domestication and extinction—worked with stunning synergy to produce a pool of people to enslave. In the fourteen years between 1851 and 1865, the end of the Civil War, the Indigenous population of California declined by another sixty thousand people. To contain the human "remnants," the federal government built five remote reservations and two smaller detention "farms" in areas, remarked Governor Burnett, "where it is not likely any white man would be inclined to settle upon, even if it were not reserved or occupied by Indians."[5]

The Tolowa and Yurok had thrived for thousands of years, near creeks full of salmon and trout, along coastal tide pools lined with clams, where winter seas deliver Dungeness crabs. Under twelve feet of annual rainfall, shadowed by the dense summer fog of North Coast summers, their hunters flushed herds of elk and felled migrating birds during the Pacific Flyway. At the rushing delta where the Klamath River flows into the Pacific, Tolowa and Yurok smoked long strips of salmon on racks of alder wood.

Freedom would come to an end. By 1855 the federal government had built four more reservations in California, including the walled Nome Lackee Reservation in Tehama County. At the Nome Cult Indian Farm in Mendocino County, California Natives were forced to build their own detention center. Here, in 1856 the U.S. military took hundreds of Tolowa prisoners and crammed them into the narrow lighthouse in Crescent City. After a few days, the army marched nearly one thousand captives to the Klamath River Reservation and to Fort Ter-Waw (Terwer) six miles upriver—a vast mass transit camp for twenty-five hundred deportees. When these raw encampments were washed out in a flood, the infantry marched most of the captives 226 miles south to the Round Valley Reservation. The rest of the displaced people trekked sixty miles over the mountains onto Hoopa land along the Trinity River; ten more tribes moved into the new reservation, and the Hoopa became exiles on their own lands.[6] The soldiers banned bows, arrows, and wide skein nets, an order for deliberate starvation. For the past few years, herds of settlers' horses, cattle, sheep, goats, and hogs had destroyed the native oak, clover, berries, and roots, and driven the deer and elk from the lands of these forced labor camps.

As the Indigenous people struggled to stay alive, Indian agents ordered them to convert their open land into fields of wheat and build cabins, barns, and fences, breed horses, and tend cattle. "Insufficiently fed and scantily clothed," reported Special Agent G. Bailey. With nothing to eat on the reservations, agents at Klamath, Tejon, and Nome Lackee sent the survivors of the massacres—many elders, women, and children—into the fields and woods to gather wild foods and fend for themselves. At the Fresno River Farm, Yokuts slaughtered and ate wild horses. By 1858 Wimichi and Nutunutu Yokuts were competing for acorns with the cattle and pigs.[7]

Federal Indian agents at the reservations decided who would live and who would die. They transferred California Natives' ancestral lands to white settlers and oversaw the "removals." They distributed or embezzled federal funds meant for the tribes. Unlike the vast reservations in the East, there was no trade or exchange of Native land in California, and the reservations grew on remote tracts now owned by the federal government.[8]

The U.S. military entered the slave trade in California. In the decade of the 1850s leading up to the Civil War, it sold or simply released Indian captives at the forts and reservations to slave brokers. At Fort Baker along the Van Duzen River, where T'tc~tsa and her mother were detained and sold in 1860 (see the Prologue), soldiers and brokers marketed Indians for $37.50 "a piece"; one trader claimed to have made $15,000 in the autumn of 1860 selling Indians from the military outposts. Troops from the California Volunteers, a state-funded militia, captured Yurok children and sold them directly from the forts. Kidnappers followed the military and, after a massacre, seized women and children to sell or to keep for their own use.[9]

Agent Bailey believed that reservation life would train an Indian to labor for whites; the camps would inhibit his "pig-like urge to wallow in mud" and teach him the joys of "a fixed over a roving life." Unfree labor on the reservation would then lift a Native "out of the slough where he now wallows." Redemption through coerced farm labor was an invocation of the Protestant work ethic and would teach Indians that farming or settled agriculture was a more advanced path to survival than their tradition of following the seasons and traveling to food sources. By 1861, wrote Special Agent for Indian Affairs John Ross Browne, those who survive the reservations "are being exterminated every day."[10] As soldiers were transferred for the final massacres or left for the Civil War, thousands of starving Indians simply wandered off.

Exile

The *San Francisco Weekly National* wrote that the reservations allowed the Indian to procure "abundant food in the shape of acorns, roots, game and fish, without labor," but this natural life had turned him into a "weak degenerate creature." What the Indian needed was a "master, one who can compel him to obey. Leave it all optional with him, and he will labor not, neither will he spin." What he lacked, said the *Weekly*, was a "sufficient white force" willing to "inflict occasional chastisement."[11]

Serranus Clinton Hastings was a member of that white force. Banker, Gold Rush lawyer, and chief justice of the California Supreme Court, Hastings took his savings to buy thousands of acres of ranch land along the Eel River, just south of Round Valley Reservation. Here the starving Yuki, driven from their lands, had resorted to raiding cattle. Hastings claimed that the tribe had slaughtered seventy white settlers and killed his prized stallion. Under California's lax militia orders, volunteers went forth on weekly killing sprees, slaughtering local Indians with legal impunity, paid by the state in wages, food, and ammunition.[12]

Genocide and slavery went hand in hand. In 1859 Justice Hastings hired renowned local Indian fighter Walter S. Jarboe to recruit a state militia and slay the six hundred Yuki who lived on or near his ranch. Jarboe named his crew the "Eel River Rangers" and ordered his men to move along the riverbanks and "kill all the bucks [males] they could find and take the women and children prisoners."[13] Jarboe's Rangers killed Yuki men in groups of sixty at a time and then moved on, once boasting that his militia had killed twenty Indians in less than three minutes. Then he delivered another three hundred emaciated Indians to federal Indian Agent Vincent Geiger to use on his own ranch.[14] That said, white settlers who obtained unpaid Indian workers for small farms or household labor were also often at odds on the issue of genocide and expulsion, even as they turned to kidnap, sale, coercion, and assault to maintain an unfree labor force.[15]

Vigilantes marched California Natives across the western Coastal Range, wrote the San Francisco *Daily Evening Bulletin*, as "the women in the wagons set up that peculiar plaintive cry used by them at their funerals, while the men walked behind the wagons in mournful silence."[16] Indian agents pleaded with Governor John B. Weller (1858–60) to end the slaugh-

ter, but he urged Jarboe to carry on. By the end of this government-sanc-
tioned extermination, the famous "Indian fighter" and his troops had murdered four hundred California Natives, captured six hundred more, and
sold them as "convicts" or "vagrants" to work as unpaid ranch hands. On
April 12, 1860, the legislature wrote Captain Jarboe a check for $9,347.39
for his four months of work, and the governor added a personal note to
thank him for "doing all that was anticipated."[17]

California followed Mexico's plan: open land to wealthy ranchers and
provide them with a ready pool of unfree, unpaid, and landless workers.
Across California, reservations sprang up near white settlements. The U.S.
military offered bounties of 160 acres of land to any militiaman who had
served for fourteen days in the California Indian Wars. Settlers were allowed to freely plunder the lands "reserved" for Indians. Indian agents sent
reports to Congress that farmers near the Nome Lackee Reservation had
"adopted the principle that the Indians belong to them as much as an African slave does to his master. This system of slavery is far more objectionable than that which exists in any other country, as the Indians claim to be
rightful owners of the soil."[18]

Indians who lived at the Round Valley Reservation on a remnant of
Yuki land told of the winter of 1860 when Indian Agent Geiger forced
hundreds of Yuki to carry split rails up and over the Coastal Range for
fences for his ranch. Benjamin Arthur, a Mendocino rancher, testified to
the legislature that "about three hundred died on the reservation, from
the effects of packing them through the mountains in the snow and mud.
. . . They were worked naked, with the exception of deer skin around their
shoulders—some few had pantaloons and coats on; they usually packed fifty
pounds, if able."[19] The aged and infirm, wet and barefoot, were shot for
straggling. Only 277 Yuki reached the Round Valley Reservation.

The line between state militia, U.S. soldiers, and slavers was blurred.[20]
By 1860 the total Indian population of California was down to about thirty
thousand, from over three hundred thousand at the time of the Spanish
invasion.[21] Major newspapers such as the *Daily Alta California* were finally
reporting about the corruption of the Indian agents and exposing the "cruel
outrages" of the employees on the reservations.[22] The *Sacramento Union*
reported that these bleak work farms were never self-supporting and the
Indians were never "civilized"—a goal of the federal plan for Native Americans.[23] In 1868 the *Daily Alta California* wrote that the whole system "has
not taught a solitary red man to live in the fashion of civilization."[24] But it
had created a supply of unfree and unpaid child laborers.

California slavery became national news in the first full year of the American Civil War. In 1861 the *Boston Evening Transcript* quoted the *Humboldt Times* to report that Northern California "is pretty thickly populated with wild Indians, who are now being hunted *for their children.*" Local residents, it said, could order one of the "little fellows" for fifty to one hundred dollars. "The settlers make war for the young ones, so as to take them and sell them; that is to say, they make you a present of a little digger, and you make them a present of a hundred dollars for their trouble in catching him."[25]

Reservations failed to deliver on the promise made by California Superintendent of Indian Affairs Thomas Henley to provide "protection and domestication" to California Natives.[26] As national attention and funds turned toward the Civil War, one reservation after another closed; the Indians who remained were moved to the Round Valley Reservation or to the remote Hoopa Valley Reservation. Pan-Indian communities inevitably grew on Native grounds. While many Indigenous people fled from the "reserves," new massacres emptied entire Native villages, and raiders and traders handily captured thousands of displaced women and children. These refugees were "vagrants" eligible for captivity because they were homeless or on the run.

In July 1863 two white children were murdered near Chico, and local settlers decided that the killers were Indians who were working for wealthy landowner John Bidwell. The military rode into Bidwell's ranch and rounded up 461 Konkow Maidu. Twenty-three U.S. cavalrymen marched the Indians twenty miles a day in the valley heat of the late summer, toward a reservation near Covelo in the conifer forest above the Eel River, finally climbing over a seven-thousand-foot mountain range. Many died from exhaustion, starvation, and dehydration on each day of the march. Eager to finish the drive, in mid-September, the military abandoned 150 Konkow Maidu who were too ill to continue and left them at a desolate mountain camp with food for a month.

The California superintendent of Indian agents witnessed the gruesome trek of one hundred miles: "150 sick Indians . . . scattered along the trail for 50 miles . . . dying at a rate of 2 or 3 a day. They had nothing to eat . . . and the wild hogs were eating them up either before or after they were dead." But he did nothing to intervene. Descendants tell of soldiers shooting their Maidu ancestors who tried to escape, of militiamen taking babies from their mothers and beating children against rocks to hurry them along.[27] They call the march the "Konkow Trail of Tears."[28]

A Legal Apocalypse

Indian slavery became a prosperous and legitimate business. By 1858 three
out of four households in Northern California held at least one Native
American.[29] That year the popular San Francisco *Daily Evening Bulletin*
reported that travelers across California noticed that, at every ranch they
passed, a white man "possessed" an Indian woman.[30]

In 1860 California expanded the trade by updating the Act for the
Government and Protection of Indians: any Native American not already
"under the protection" of a white person could be "put out" to any trade
or "husbandry" for terms that could last twenty years. Any Indian prisoners who had been charged as drunk or vagrant were available for forced
indenture. In other words, Indians of all ages and both sexes could be seized
and sold, whether they were vagrants or fugitives, living freely, or held as
prisoners. The legislature, hoping to dissolve California tribes, added that
Indians could be forced to indenture themselves and perform any work
demanded by an "employer." Almost half of the California Natives now
forcibly indentured or "bound out" were female; three-quarters were under
fourteen years old.[31]

The 1860 revisions dramatically widened the legal path to child slavery. The original 1850 Indian Act required evidence that parents had freely
consented to the indenture of their daughter or son or that no "compul-
sion" had been used to bind over a child. Under the 1860 version, a court
could sign a child's indenture paper without the presence or permission of
a parent or friend. All that was needed was the "consent of the person who
had the care or charge" of the child—that is, whoever had the child in his
possession. A "master" could extend the current indenture of a male until
he reached thirty and a female until she reached twenty-five. At the end of
the indenture, a Native American would receive neither wages nor back
pay.[32] The *Sacramento Union* wrote, "If this does not fill the measure of the
constitutional term 'involuntary slavery,' we shall be thankful if someone
will inform us what is lacking."[33]

Any person in California could legally bind "grown" Indians and children. They could apprentice an Indian "prisoner of war"—any Indian who
had survived a massacre or eviction from his or her homeland. Whites could
bind any Indian who had "no settled habitation or livelihood." A mayor or
even a city recorder could indenture any "vagrant" Indian to the highest
bidder. Homelessness made a California Native available for forced labor.
Any adult Indian could be forced into a ten-year apprenticeship to any
white man. Any Indian male under the age of fourteen could be bound

Camden Family Portrait, ca. 1857–59. An indentured Indian girl was forced
to serve as a nanny; this image is wrongly archived as a "family portrait."

(Camden Family Portrait, circa 1857–1859, courtesy of
Whiskeytown National Recreation Area, WHIS 9066.)

until age twenty-five; any young man bound between age fourteen and
twenty could be held until he reached the age of thirty. California had the
right to disband any tribe that resisted the U.S. military or state militia;
the 1860 law created a pool of vagrants and erased tribal sovereignty. Slave
auctions opened wherever massacres had occurred.[34]

California, as a state, had entered the business of chattel slavery. It had
legalized the purchase or sale of a human being. Any white person who
had an Indian in his "possession" had the right to sell the indenture papers
to a new "guardian."[35] Since an owner could transfer his right of posses-

sion, an Indian became a marketable asset, like any other kind of property. U.S. Army Captain Edward Ord observed that a rancher quickly became a justice of the peace so that he could "buy and keep Indian servants as he may want them, and to punish them at [his] discretion."[36]

The editor of the *Humboldt Times*, Austin Wiley, claimed to oppose Indian indentures but he bought Smoky, an eight-year-old boy, from a trafficker and bound him for a fourteen-year term; Smoky survived on scraps from the table until Wiley shipped him to the Smith River Reservation.[37] Wiley urged slaveholders to quickly legalize their possession of Native women with binding articles of indenture.[38] Ranchers and farmers lost no time filing papers in county courtrooms across Northern California. By November the *Humboldt Times* reported that Indian children in remote areas of the Coastal Range and the inland Siskiyou Mountains were kidnapped and "disposed of"—sold to families in Eureka and Arcata for prices "as may be agreed upon between the high contracting powers."[39] In order to avoid calling these transactions "slave sales," they were recorded as "fees" for the "trouble incurred in obtaining possession of the children."[40]

About half the "indenture holders" in the county were young farmers or ranchers in their twenties and thirties; the other half were town dwellers, mostly unmarried men who wanted female servants or married men with children. Nearly all removed the tribal names of their indentured servants. By the early 1860s, fewer slaveholders in Humboldt County came from the plantation South; thirty came from free states, nineteen came from foreign nations, and nine came from slave states.[41] Rancher Samuel D. Ross from the Mattole Valley in southern Humboldt County boasted, "I have more than a dozen applications, at this time, from citizens of high standing, for young Indians. They want to apprentice them and are willing to pay someone to deliver them for that purpose." Owners of these children, historian Michael Magliari has written, included judges, justices of the peace, constables, and county supervisors.[42]

Slave Marts at the Reservations

Wagons crisscrossed California delivering terrified children. Not one of the handful of indenture papers from Colusa County notes whether the parents of indentured children were alive or dead; not one claims that Native American parents had agreed to the sale of their child. No certificate identifies a child's tribe.[43]

The *Sacramento Daily Union* wrote that the "most disgusting phase of this species of slavery is the concubinage of creatures calling themselves white men" with Indian women.[44] Kidnap and rape at the reservations went unchecked. California in 1860 was an open market for those seeking Indian women and Indian children. Ernestine Ray's grandmother had been a child at Round Valley. She said: "They treated Grandma pretty bad. . . . Mom, she used to cry, 'My poor mother died with scars on her back. They beat her.'"

In the winter the snow made the mountains impassable to horses, and ranchers used Indian men and women as pack mules.[45] Agent John Ross Browne sent reports to Washington, DC, from the Round Valley Reservation: agents and armed vigilantes had gone "into the rancherias in open day . . . and shot the Indians down—weak, harmless, and defenseless women with sucking babes at their breasts; killed or crippled the naked children that were running about."[46] No records indicate that the federal government responded to Browne's report. Besides, Browne set aside his revulsion and bought two Indian children for himself to work at his home in Oakland.

Short and burly Indian Agent Vincent Geiger ran the vast Nome Lackee Reservation as his fiefdom. With unselfconscious greed, Geiger stole the seed and horses that the government had sent for the Indians. He used the reservation's funds to buy a ranch that neighbored the reserve. He then took seventy-two Indians who lived on the reservation and "made them slaves." Using his appointment as an Indian agent, Geiger took in nearly half a million dollars from the state for Indian laborers who were never paid.

When Geiger's mules slipped in the snow in the winter, he substituted the "inmates" and forced them to carry logs on their backs across the mountains and then build his water flumes, hog sheds, a grist mill, a corral, and a cabin. Last, he compelled them to fence themselves in. The logs that were cut for his barn and outbuildings clogged the Noyo River with silt and branches; salmon could no longer swim upriver to spawn, and the tribes lost their source of protein. Meanwhile, Geiger's cattle roamed the reservation, stomping wheat fields and polluting the vegetable gardens.

Indian agents such as Geiger and John Sutter now had the license to steal from the government and the inmates. The *Sacramento Union* reported that Nome Lackee residents trained in agriculture, domestic service, and animal husbandry, barely surviving on federal subsistence, lost even "the semblance of a bond to clothe, feed and protect them." Geiger's youngest captive was twelve; he indentured twenty-six girls for the same lengthy term as the men. The *Union* reported that by 1861, Geiger had abandoned the ill and elderly and claimed the healthiest Indians by virtue of his right as Indian agent and "custodian" of all the teenagers at the reservation.[47] The agents reported to the Department of the Interior that California Indians had lost all "access to their lands"; now there was "no place to which to migrate."[48]

Reports of the kidnap and sale of California Natives seeped from the reservation. In 1858 government inspectors discovered that Geiger was holding a group of Nome Lackee women as his sex slaves.[49] Lieutenant Edward Dillon reported of the situation at the new reservations or "reserves": "It is a common occurrence to have [Indian women] taken by force from the place. About a week ago, some of the rascals came into the yard, broke open a door, and took the [women] that had been locked up by the agent." Rancher William Scott reported that he had "men offer to give me Indian children to send below, if I would get in return for them presents the value of fifty dollars."[50]

With the Civil War underway, word came that General Edwin Vose Sumner was pulling troops from the California reservations in order to deploy them for the Indian Wars.[51] While Geiger seized reservation lands for his own ranch, Indians were living in mud huts.[52] As the Indian commissioner granted white settlers the right to occupy the reservation land, two-thirds of the Indians managed to escape. A journalist sent from the *Independent* to investigate saw "one of the wigwams on fire and heard the Indians crying or howling and making unusual noise . . . tearing their hair and throwing into the flames blankets, old clothes and large quantities of wild oats." The Indians informed him that one of their children had been taken as an indentured servant, and they were treating him as dead because they knew they would never see him again.[53] Geiger had joined a secret secessionist society, the Knights of the Golden Circle, that set fire to the Nome Lackee Reservation in February 1861. Now homeless, the Indian inmates were forced to "apprentice" on Geiger's ranch as newspapers and federal Indian agents began to expose Geiger's embezzlement and brutality.

The U.S. Senate finally abolished California's most decrepit reservations and drove Geiger out of office; in 1863, facing charges for murder, he fled to British Columbia. The Indians at Nome Lackee simply moved away from the reservation and began to farm on small plots of land. Many scattered. Of the two to three thousand Indians held in the first years of Nome Lackee, only two hundred remained. No one was held accountable for the kidnap, sale, and bondage of Indians at Nome Lackee.[54]

Labor and Lust: The Slave Trade in Indian Children

When the Indian Act was renewed in 1860, children who had been held in bondage for years saw their servitude extended. Jesse, a child under age five, was apprenticed in Colusa County because she had not "placed herself" under the protection of another white person. In twenty or so indenture papers preserved from Colusa, only one man claimed to have the permission of the child's mother to indenture a child. In that contract, the child's new owners agreed to pay for his clothing because of the "benefits" they expected to obtain.[55] "Baby hunters" roamed over three hundred miles in the coastal mountains, abducting Indian children who fetched a market price from thirty to two hundred dollars.[56]

In the first year of the Civil War, California straddled its promise of freedom and its loyalty to human bondage. The *Sacramento Daily Union* called the Indian Act of 1860 a "complete system of slavery, without any of the checks and wholesome restraints of slavery."[57] One year later, the *Weekly Humboldt Times* observed, "This [1860] law works beautifully. A few days ago V. E. Geiger . . . had some eighty [Indians] apprenticed to him and proposes to emigrate to Washoe with them as soon as he can cross the mountains. We hear of many others who are having them bound in numbers to suit. What a pity the provisions of this law are not extended to greasers, Kanakas, and Asiatics. It would be convenient, you know, to carry on a farm or mine, when all the hard and dirty work is performed by *apprentices*."[58] Slaves were for sale in nearby San Francisco and Oakland, bought "with the same facility that slaves are in Mississippi," reported the San Francisco *Daily Evening Bulletin*.[59]

Indian Slavery during the Civil War

In the old court library in Eureka are 110 Indian indenture papers documenting the sales of Indians in Humboldt County.[60] The Indians range in age from two to fifty years; almost half are children between ages seven to twelve. Between 1860 and 1863, four were "taken in war [massacres]"; four were "bought" or bestowed as gifts. After they were bound by legal procedures that they could scarcely understand, the children were given Anglo names; their accurate ages are lost. A boy, renamed Perry, was three years old when he was forced into indenture in 1860. George and Kitty were each four. Jane was indentured at age nine, to be held until she was twenty-five; Sarah was sold at age five, Mary at age seven, Kate, age six, Teeny, age eleven, and Ginny, age twenty-seven. Sylvia, indentured at age fourteen, remained in bondage until she reached twenty-nine.[61]

During the Civil War, as high-level public officials bought and sold Indians, California fought on the side of the Union. Colusa County Judge Cornelius J. Diefendorff still ran a public slave mart in his courtroom and marked all the children's documents "supposed orphan." The indenture papers from Colusa in 1861 offer a litany of bondage. Diefendorff signed thirteen male Indians over to John Boggs, giving him the "custody, control, and earnings" of Bill and Nomi, age twenty; Charley and Pico, age eighteen; George, age fourteen; Eddie, age sixteen; Laken, age seventeen; Yousin, age eight; Pike, Pulis, and Peto, age five; and Harry and Luche, age four. Boggs agreed to clothe the children, "provide the necessaries of life," and teach them husbandry. Boggs would go on to become a state senator. In May, he signed Brigham Young, aged about "4 or 8 years," to Amos Roberts and confessed that he "did not know whether the said child has parents living." The boy, he said, had been taken to the jail "from out of the charge of a white person who was arrested on accusation of having kidnapped him with several others." D. P. (Daniel) Dunst, a Colusa physician and state assemblyman, received custody of an unnamed five-year-old girl to perform the duties of his "nurse" and "general house-holder assistant" and to "cheerfully obey" him. Southerner Samuel Wright found Lucy Neal in the jail where an unnamed "white person" had deposited her along with several other Indian children.[62]

Traffickers and "baby hunters" followed the army as it slaughtered Indian warriors, torched tribal villages, and delivered a steady inventory of instant orphans. To keep the children from running away to search for their family or tribe, brokers delivered them to ranches and small towns far from their homelands. During the Civil War, the price for an Indian child rose and the captors became even more ruthless; at Fort Baker, Captain Thomas Ketchum confirmed that as soon as the snow melted, nearby "citizens" would head out to kill the Indian men and "sell the women and children into slavery" for $37.50 per head, totaling, he reckoned, $1,125 profit for ten women and twenty children.[63]

Just Revenge

Driven by starvation, California Natives struck back. After a bitter winter in the Owens Valley in 1861, hungry Indians began to raid nearby cattle ranches. In retaliation, white ranchers raped three young Paiute Shoshone women, including the daughter of the chief. The U.S. military moved in. An order rang forth to "chastise them severely"—the code words for Indian annihilation. It took just over a year, from April 1862 to June 1863, for a company of the California Cavalry to slaughter hundreds of Paiutes and deport one thousand more to the Tejon Reservation north of Los Angeles. The few survivors of the "Owens River War" fled, hoping to make their way back into the eastern slope of the Sierras.[64]

The military met attempts at resistance with the order: "no quarter given."[65] Punishment was swift: in 1861 two Yuki boys in Mendocino County put strychnine into the food of former Indian superintendent Thomas Henley and two other slaveholders. The boys ran off, planning to kill all the ranchers in Round Valley, but Henley discovered the poison and found one of the children; he hanged him from an oak tree for all to see.

In 1863 a Yuki teenager decapitated his master with an ax and fled back to his tribe. The local federal agent could not find the boy, so instead, he seized two random hostages and threatened to execute them if the boy did not surrender. When local whites discovered the young fugitive, they turned him over to U.S. soldiers, who hanged him without a trial. A few months later, settlers at Round Valley Reservation informed the state militia that Indians on the reservation had joined with Yuki to burn the ranches in the mountains, kill all the white ranchers in the valley, and flee. Local settlers captured the leaders, held a mock trial, and lynched them all.[66]

As the Civil War over nationhood and slavery raged on in the East, the brutal facts of Indian child bondage came out from under the euphemism of "indenture"; the *Daily Alta California* ran such headlines as "The Trade in Indian Children" and "The Traffic in Indian Children." Travelers, settlers, and prospectors witnessed men slinging children as young as six years old over mules that carried two to nine at a time; the kidnappers sold the children in San Francisco and at the new ranches bordering the bay. If a "baby hunter" thought that any captive children might escape, he shot them; he knew he could find replacements at the forts and burned villages. Ranchers, once desperate for workers, now casually threatened disobedient Indian children with hanging. The trade in child slaves was out in the open, and there were no consequences.[67]

"There Is No Other Way": The Wiyot Massacre of 1860

The *Humboldt Times* warned in 1858 that "a war of extermination will be waged. . . . Harsh and cruel as the policy of extermination may seem to be—inhuman, indeed, *if* we may call it so, there is no other way."[68]

With the Civil War looming, settlers realized that no fresh troops would arrive to replenish Fort Humboldt. White vigilantes, lawyers, shopkeepers, and journalists took genocide into their own hands; civic leaders continued to keep local tribal people, mainly Wiyot, in their homes working as involuntary servants. Humboldt County Judge Aristides Huestis and Austin Wiley, editor of the *Humboldt Times*, held Indian children in their households, listing them as "prisoners of war."[69]

Civil law gave way. Now unguarded and relentless, twenty-seven vigilantes slaughtered more than two hundred Wintu. Volunteers from the state militia massacred the Yana on Lassen Peak to the east. A white posse tore across the Mattole River and Mad River valleys, killing Nongatl, and moved north to torture captives at the Klamath Reservation. Massacre and slavery emptied the villages.

Three thousand peaceful Wiyot still lived along Humboldt Bay. Dwelling apart from white lumbermen and ranchers, they survived in precarious balance with the settlers in the northern lumber towns. Despite the shadow of captivity, they maintained their traditional culture as they worked in Eureka, selling clams or cleaning houses. The town folk depended on their service.

In the damp February dawn of 1860, the women and children of the Wiyot tribe slept on Tuluwat, an island in Humboldt Bay that is separated from the lumber town of Eureka by a narrow channel of salt marsh and eelgrass. Unaware that a white settler had purchased their island, hundreds of Native American men and women from tribes along the Mad River and Eel River joined the Wiyot in their World Renewal Ceremony, an annual seven-day festival to bring the world into balance. After a day of chanting and dancing, on Sunday, February 26, most of the Wiyot men left the celebration to fish and hunt in order to restock the festival. The women cleaned up the camp and lay down with the babies and children.

No Wiyot knew that local white militia and vigilantes were enraged because the governor had refused to pay them for their work assaulting local tribes. No Wiyot knew that the Humboldt cavalry had resolved to take their anger out on the Indians and "kill every peaceable Indian man, woman, and child in this part of the country."[70]

That night, three killing squads fanned out from the Eel River for a night of manic slaughter. At about four in the morning, one team of five or six white men made their way to the dunes and marshes on Humboldt Bay where they had stashed a small boat. Slowly, so as not to create any noise with the splash of the oars, they rowed out to Tuluwat Island. The men quietly docked their boat and slipped onto the island carrying only hatchets and knives, eager not to wake the sleeping townspeople of Eureka with sounds of gunfire, while other teams of vigilantes invaded two Indian rancherias along the Eel River and Humboldt Bay. The vigilantes crawled onto the beach of the island and began to slay the sleeping mothers and children. Then they slipped back into the rowboat and returned to the mainland. They mounted their horses and rode south to slaughter thirty more Indians at Eagle Prairie, now the lumber town of Rio Dell. It had been an efficient night.

When daylight came, the Wiyot men returned across the narrow slip of water and beheld the corpses of the women and children, some with hatchets still deeply buried in their skulls. They saw babies crawling over piles of women's bodies, some trying to nurse at the breast of dead mothers. Old women and young girls lay dead in a pile. Cheryl Seidner, Wiyot tribal chair, tells the history of the brutal night: "There was an old woman . . . still alive when the people came. She couldn't move because she was stuck in the mud so badly, and she was singing a song."[71] Later that day the Wiyot ferried the dead back to shore.

No one was charged with murder or prosecuted for the slaughter. The Wiyot anticipated the brutality that would follow and destroyed everything they could not carry with them into the captivity that assuredly lay ahead. They split their redwood canoes into pieces and set the fragments adrift. The military detained the Wiyot survivors and held them at Fort Humboldt at the edge of Eureka; others fled across the North Coast. As expected, white residents of Humboldt County rounded up 125 Wiyot along the Mad River.[72] The following year, county judge Huestis ratified the indenture of twenty-nine Wiyot.[73] The massacre of forty-seven women and nine men on Tuluwat Island and nearby villages launched four more years of warfare across Northern California.

By the end of July 1862, the U.S. military had captured seven hundred local Indians and held them in a horse corral at Fort Humboldt, a round trap only eighty feet across. By day, kidnappers arrived at the fort and plucked Indian children to sell; by night, soldiers took Indian women from the corral and raped them. Without food or sanitation, scores of Indians from five tribes quickly died. Soon, soldiers from the fort marched survivors north to the vast Klamath Reservation, where local merchants had stolen the food intended for the reservation. Hungry male captives watched women and children carried away, to be marketed outside the county. Knowing they too were to be sold, and with the reservation too large to be guarded, many inmates of the Klamath Reservation fled to search for their people. Like T'tc~tsa, many Native men chose a life on the run.

In open daylight on March 24, 1862, well-known slave trader George H. Woodman seized several Indian boys and girls and tossed them naked into his wagon. He hid them under blankets dank from the North Coast rains, and drove them south to Ukiah, a valley town midway between San Francisco and the Oregon border.[74] After his deliveries were finished, Woodman hid out in Potter Valley, a strategic base in the tall Coastal Range that blocks cold storms coming off the Pacific Ocean. From here Woodman continued to seize Indian children and sell them in the vineyards springing up across Napa County.

White residents in Mendocino County recognized Woodman's unpainted farm wagon, with its battered bed set low between mud-covered wheels. When he "attend[ed] to biz" or what he called "bringing in quail," he stashed the children in Ukiah. He stopped at the same farmhouse before each delivery, where a housewife would dress the children in old shirts or cover them with rags of calico. Then he loaded the shivering children back into the wagon or tied two or three onto one horse and made his deliveries, sometimes thirty-five or forty more miles down the trail. Woodman priced the children "according to quality." He rightly assumed that within twenty-four hours, local judge William Henry would have granted him guardianship of the children without evidence of parental permission, and he preferred to deliver the children directly to his customers.

Faced with Woodman's brash abuse and exposés of his public sales, in March 1862 the Mendocino County sheriff arrested Woodman and charged him with abducting children. At his trial, eight boys and eight girls huddled in a corner on the courtroom floor as Woodman argued that he was a philanthropist who had rescued one thousand starving Indian children "from the degradations of savage life." He testified that the children, unable to speak on their own behalf, had no other "habitation or means of livelihood" and they "did not desire to place themselves under the care of any other person." Forty white Mendocino residents testified on Woodman's behalf and also took the moment to deny that any of their Indian child servants had been kidnapped. Instead, they claimed, he saved starving children who would otherwise be forced to steal or "be killed like Cioties [coyotes]."[75]

At the trial, however, other witnesses told of Woodman's private shows when he forced his "little brown cubs" to perform like dogs—"Lie down," "Roll over," "Dance"—and then locked the children in his smokehouse. Woodman was found guilty, fined one hundred dollars, and released. The *Marysville Daily Appeal* reported that he was again free to "murder in cold blood all the old ones"—the parents and grandparents—so that he could "safely possess . . . the offspring."[76] The judge annulled Woodman's articles of indenture for each child, but he refused to return them to their relatives, ruling "they would be so much better among the whites." The judge ordered that the children be held in the Ukiah jail until new "guardians" were found. Reports of starvation, cold, and overwork followed these stolen boys and girls who were very visible in the small town.[77]

Few families in Ukiah had not bought a child from Woodman. Some of Woodman's young victims found their way back to the reservations. Some escaped together and hid in the mountains. Most reported that they had been tortured in the households in Ukiah, routinely roped together with horse lariats or whipped with a picket fence. County records show that many died young, suffering from consumption.[78]

Indentured Indian women were regularly abused. Protected by the Indian Act, many white settlers expected sexual access to Native women. Settler Isaac Cox reported that southerners in California purchased young Indian girls and priced them as "fair, middling, inferior, or refuse," but the details of these categories, wrote the *Sacramento Union*, were "unfit to commit to paper."[79] The *Marysville Daily Appeal* reported that unmarried settlers bought young Indian men for sixty dollars to work in the fields and young Indian women for one hundred dollars to satisfy "labor and lust."[80] Virtually no voices of these Native American women emerge in the legal records. In the Mendocino County Court, George Barham, the Indian husband of fifteen-year-old Mary Barham, tried to use his right of "marital privileges," as well as the fact that she was held against her will, to retrieve Mary from her kidnapper, but the judge ruled that under the "Indian Law," the rights of a kidnapper overrode the rights of an Indian husband; he ordered Mary Barham to fulfill the remaining ten years of her involuntary indenture.[81]

The ban on Indian testimony heightened the danger for women and girls. When miners at Buckeye Flat seized two Indian women to sell into prostitution, men from their tribe went to the brothel and demanded their release. The miners killed one of the Native American men and the other was wounded; yet, writes historian Robert Heizer, only Indian evidence could be obtained, and since an Indian's evidence was not allowed against any white man in the state, the miners could not be convicted.[82] In 1861 the San Francisco *Daily Evening Bulletin* reported that "the wives and daughters of the defenseless Diggers are prostituted before the very eyes of their husbands and fathers, they dare not resent the insult, or even complain about the hideous outrage."[83]

Streams of letters and reports from newspapers and agents and officers stationed at the forts exposed the federal government's deliberate silence about the assaults. The San Francisco *Daily Evening Bulletin* condemned the federal commissioner for Indian Affairs for failing to acknowledge the abuse of Indian women or an Indian's "repugnance" at being held on reservations where "his children are taken from him, his wife plucked from his bosom, his daughters prostituted in his very presence, and himself made the unwilling drudge of relentless and unfeeling masters."[84]

Congress also ignored pleas by Indian agents to intervene. But dissent from inside the federal government did not outweigh settlers' insatiable demand for unpaid Indian workers, a demand so great that the *Red Bluff Beacon* proposed that a direct route be built from the town to the Nome Lackee Reservation in order to speed up delivery. Indentured Indians quickly constructed the new road.[85]

The Civil War and Native American Slavery in California

In 1861, just before the outbreak of the Civil War, President Abraham Lincoln appointed fellow Illinois Whig George Hanson as superintending agent for Indian Affairs for Northern California, intending to shame Democrats and slaveholders. Hanson reported that Indian indentures had introduced "actual slavery," and he planned to abolish the "unholy traffic in human blood and souls" by confining all California Indians to reservations, where they would learn to use "modern" tools on lands held for their "sacred use." He ordered police officers to capture "baby hunters" and confiscate—but not release—their captives. Hanson believed that "natural causes" at the reservations would lead to Indians' "extermination . . . to which they are destined."[86]

U.S. troops and local militia still had orders to find and "chastise" any Indians who raided settlers' cattle, and "kidnappers followed the soldiers to seize the children when their parents [were] murdered and sell them to the best advantage." In 1861 Hanson reported that the "creatures" at Nome Lackee were cold and starving; dressed in worn-out blankets, they fled the reservations, only "to be hunted down . . . and brought into slavery."[87]

Hanson's plan of reservations for extinction failed. Lincoln had barely carried the state in 1860 with 32.3 percent of the vote, and early arguments to extend the reach of slavery to California endured. From the moment California entered the United States, pro-slavery factions sought to split the state; the area south of San Francisco would be called the "Terri-

tory of Colorado" and allow slavery. Alternatively, West Coast secessionists, led by former senator William Gwin and former governor John B.
Weller, hoped California would join Oregon and form the "Pacific Republic," unite with southern states, and leave the Union.

Although the shaky coalition fell apart, pro-southern militia units rose
up across the state, where the Los Angeles Mounted Rifles were readying
to fight on behalf of the Confederacy. Californians traveled east to enlist
in the army of the Confederacy, and the governor of California sent arms
to the Mounted Rifles. Local secessionist groups sent stolen gold to the
Confederate Army. Aware that secessionists were the majority in Southern
California, three companies of federal cavalry shipped out in 1861 to sup-
press a pro-slavery revolt. Over the next four years, California sent seventeen thousand men east to the Union Army.

Far from home with no one to fight, U.S. soldiers joined forces with
the California militia to take up arms against Indigenous people. Local
men and vigilantes signed on as military guides in the redwood wilderness.
With this influx of men and arms, vigilantes and Union soldiers profited
from their capture and sale.

Throughout the Civil War, California Democrats opposed emancipation, but the pressures of the war itself, the victory of two Republican
governors, and ultimately a strong vote to reelect Lincoln in 1864 kept the
state in the Union. Forts popped up across the state to mark a federal
presence, but in the absence of major battles, Union soldiers turned their
rifles on California Indians.[88] As Congress began to draw down the reservations, the military rounded up all the Indians in California and, under
guard, marched them to four remote reservations in a mass exodus across
the state.

On January 1, 1863, President Lincoln's Emancipation Proclamation
only freed slaves in Confederate states. This historic act had no effect on
enslaved Blacks or Indians in California, and provided no funds to com-
pensate, transport, sustain, or house African Americans just released from
bondage. The kidnap and sale of Indians went on, and the *Humboldt Times*
headlined "GOOD Haul of Diggers—One White Man Killed—Thirty-
Eight [Males] Killed, Forty [Women] and Children Taken."[89]

After the Emancipation Proclamation, however, California's Republican governor, Leland Stanford, realized that slavery was nearing its end,
and on April 27, 1863, he repealed the section of the Indian Acts of 1850
and 1860 that authorized forced indentures.[90] Yet that year, 4,522 Indian
children were still living in non-Native households in California; the next
year the number rose to 5,987.[91]

The end of the brutal system of legal indenture followed the Emancipation Proclamation by four months. All told, about twenty thousand California Natives had been chained to employers through kidnapping, captivity, involuntary indentures, or forms of human trafficking. With the end of legal indentures and the bloody victories in the "Indian campaigns," most indentured Indians were sent to the Smith River, Round Valley, and Hoopa reservations.[92] Elijah Steele, the superintendent of Indian Affairs for Northern California, continued to compel all "able bodied" Indians to work without wages. Only those who were "actually employed" could receive food. Kidnapping children for forced labor continued.

On December 6, 1865, the U.S. Congress ratified the Thirteenth Amendment and abolished most forms of slavery in the United States and California—not just plantation slavery in the Confederacy. It did not discuss forced indentures, which under the law were defined as contractual—that is, as voluntary. It did not state that Native Americans had the right to abandon their indentures; the commissioner of Indian Affairs announced that whites were still buying Native "children of tender years" from "a degraded class of mountaineers." The commissioner added that unless these children escaped, they rarely lived to grow up.[93] Although the Fourteenth Amendment was written to protect the civil rights of all *people*—not just all *citizens*—in practice, Native Americans in California were left outside the coverage of these core amendments. Fearing Indian claims for civil rights, California passed a law reaffirming that neither an Indian nor any "person having one half or more of Indian blood" could testify against a white person.

By 1879, 1,463 Indian children still lived in white households.[94] California Natives were wandering the state, living off the land and searching for any remaining brethren of their tribes. Some freely joined the new agricultural workforce at pittance wages. Many stole cattle to survive. Others began to forge pan-Indian communities at the reservations or join with survivors they met along the way.

The knot of slaveries that bound California Natives—from contracts, indentures, apprenticeships, and bills of sale to the scourge of whips, lashings, and rape—cast an enduring legacy of racial inequality. Twelve thousand years of ancestral liberty were dashed in 150 years. Violated and dispossessed, Indians began to reconstruct their tribes and their freedom. It would take decades. Today, Native Californians' demand for reparations is the return of the land to its first stewards.

Only the Hoopa lived in a reservation on their own homeland. They call themselves Natinook-wa, "People of the Place Where the Trails Return."

CHAPTER NINE

"Go Do Some Great Thing"

California's First Civil Rights Movement

We are an oppressed people, the subjects of a bitter prejudice,
which we are now seeking to overcome. In appealing to our
oppressors, we desire to do so in a manner that will have weight.

—WILLIAM NEWBY, 1857

IN DECEMBER 1850 SARAH Carroll, a nineteen-year-old prostitute and
free woman of color, appeared at the Sacramento police station to report
a theft. Carroll declared that William Potter had spent the night in her
room, and while she slept, he had taken a key from her skirt pocket, opened
her trunk, and stole one breastpin, one diamond heart, six buttons, one blue
shawl decorated with white flowers, several gold coins, and some gold nuggets worth ten dollars. She said that Potter had hidden her things in his
luggage on board the riverboat *New World*, and she signed her complaint
with an "X." With this, three months after California entered the Union
as a free state, an African American prostitute brought a felony charge of
grand larceny against a client for stealing $700 of her property.

Sacramento police officers located Potter hiding on the *New World*
and arrested him. The state had just banned Blacks from testifying against
whites, and although the census listed Potter as an "FMC"—Free Man of

Color—he shrewdly told the court that he was white. Two days later police released Potter from jail; the local justice of the peace noted, "He is proving himself a white man & none but Colored testimony against him." The police then arrested Sarah Carroll for bringing "false charges" against a white man.[1]

The shadow of slavery fell on free Black people in California who had just put three thousand miles between themselves and slave hunters in the East, only to discover that intrepid white southerners were determined to write loopholes for slavery into state laws and city codes. As free Blacks converged in the West, they took up the gauntlet thrown down by Frederick Douglass: "You've seen how a man was made a slave; you shall see how a slave was made a man."[2] African Americans faced an existential challenge: How could they hold California to account for its promise of freedom? The movement to overturn the ban on Black testimony was that struggle.

In the months after California became a state, the raw legislature had to create a judicial system. It immediately wrote foundational laws that barred free and enslaved African Americans from access to justice—and hence, from access to the freedom promised in the state's new constitution. California's civil and criminal procedures acts stated that no Black person, free or enslaved, no mulattos, and no Indians could testify, present evidence, serve on a jury, or be a witness in any action in which a white person was a party, even if a white person corroborated their testimony. It was thus impossible for free Black people to prove that they were in fact free. New laws and legal decisions ensured that the liberty delivered in the new constitution only applied to Black men and women who arrived *after* statehood; without the right to testify and enter evidence, they had no way to offer proof as to when they were brought into the state.[3]

Freed Black people could not use their manumission papers. In 1852 James Washington Finley brought thirty-six-year-old Plim Jackson and forty-year-old Sampson Gleaves to the Santa Clara Valley from Missouri and recorded them as his slaves in the 1852 California census. On November 14, 1854, Finley signed a receipt stating that the two men owed him no further service. Finley waited three years after he arrived in California to manumit the men. Protecting this document was critical because Finley and Jackson could not testify in court that they were free.[4] The path to freedom was blocked by the courtroom door.

The national Fugitive Slave Act of 1850 was part of the national "compromise" to admit California as a free state. It covered territories as well as states. Now no Black person had the right to testify or the right to a defense: "In no trial or hearing . . . shall the testimony of the alleged fugitive be admitted into evidence." It followed that alleged fugitives did not have the right to a jury trial.[5]

"What? Discouraged? Go Do Some Great Thing"

In 1850 Mifflin Wistar Gibbs sailed for California. Gibbs was born in 1823 as a free child of color in Pennsylvania and raised in Philadelphia, a city of abolitionists. He was indentured as a boy to a doctor and drove his buggy through the streets of Philadelphia and, once, to a nearby plantation on the Maryland shore. There, for the first time, Gibbs saw rows of enslaved Black field hands assaulted by "drivers with scourging whip in hand." Jolted to learn that wealthy Philadelphians were the absentee owners of plantations that were "stocked with slaves," Gibbs took a job driving the horse-drawn omnibus so that he could transport fugitives to safe houses.[6]

On May 14, 1838, Gibbs was at the grand opening of the abolitionist Pennsylvania Hall; three days later he witnessed a mob set fire to the splendid new meeting hall while firefighters stood by watching it burn to the ground. The *Liberator*, the influential abolitionist newspaper, presciently wrote, "A fire has in fact been kindled that will never go out."[7]

Gibbs feared that flame. He was at the wharf in Pennsylvania when Frederick Douglass welcomed Joseph Cinqué, leader of the 1839 mutiny aboard the slave ship *Amistad*. Gibbs felt inspired as "two giants locked in each other's embrace. . . . One by indomitable will was making slavery odious by his matchless and eloquent arraignment; the other had . . . written his protest with the blood of his captors." He opened the box at the Philadelphia headquarters of the Anti-Slavery Society in March 1849 that contained enslaved Henry Brown, who had shipped himself from Virginia to freedom in the wooden crate.[8]

In 1849 Douglass invited Gibbs to move to Rochester, New York, to study the "curriculum" of abolition. Rochester, wrote Gibbs, "proved to be my pathway to California." When gold was discovered, Gibbs wanted to head west. Yet Douglass demanded that he first spend a summer on the speaking circuit with him and British abolitionist Julia Griffiths in western New York state. But in a "cold and heartless" winter, churches and halls closed against them. Annoyed at Gibbs's early pessimism, Griffiths charged him to leave for California: "What? Discouraged? Go do some great thing."[9]

Gibbs bought a steerage ticket on the steamer *New York* and sailed two thousand miles down the Atlantic to the mouth of the Chagres River on the

Caribbean coast of Panama.[10] He hired a Native boatman with a dugout canoe, and they paddled thirty miles up the shallow waters to a village where he transferred to a burro and rode through jungles of rotting vegetation. In humid and decaying Panama City, Gibbs waited with restless miners finally to sail north to San Francisco on the steamship *Golden Gate*.[11] With the last ten cents in his pocket, he found a place to sleep in a Black-owned boardinghouse, where he met African American miners who had been driven out of the goldfields.

Gibbs decided to seek a job in construction in the new hotels, stables, and houses in the boomtown. White carpenters knew that a Black man would work for less pay, and at every construction site they threatened to strike if Gibbs was hired. Penniless and unemployed, he began to work on the streets as a bootblack.

San Francisco in 1850 had a small African American neighborhood, and here Gibbs encountered Peter and Nancy Lester, whom he had met at the National Anti-Slavery Society Convention in Philadelphia. The Lesters had moved west to escape the soldiers and dogs who were snaring both free and enslaved African Americans under the Fugitive Slave Act. Now they were in a state that made it impossible for Black people to find work and deemed "all marriages of whites with negroes or mulattoes . . . to be null and void."[12] "Blacks," wrote Peter Lester to the *Liberator*, had "migrated" to the shores of the Pacific only to "meet with one continuous series of outrages, injustices and unmitigated wrongs, unparalleled in the history of nations." With their freedom at risk, without the right to testify, they could not enter into evidence birth certificates, manumission papers, or contracts that proved that they were free.[13]

Unable to find jobs, in 1851 Gibbs and Lester opened the Emporium for Fine Boots and Shoes; in the boom time of the Gold Rush, it became one of the largest shoe stores in the West. Immediately the city of San Francisco billed each man three dollars for the "poll tax," despite the fact that it did not allow Blacks to vote. Lester wrote, "White men in California are willing to pay taxes because the government gives them every privilege—from the right to rob a negro up to that of being Governor of the State," but Black men "feel the flagrant injustice of compelling 'colored men' to pay a special tax for the enjoyment of a special privilege, and then break their heads if they attempt to exercise it."[14]

Invoking the refrain "no taxation without representation," in an act of passive resistance the two men ran an announcement in the *Daily Alta California* saying that even if the tax collector "lugged off twenty or thirty dollars' worth of goods in 'payment,'" they would not pay the tax but would use "all moral means to secure legal claim to all the rights and privileges of American citizens." Police officers took the men up on their ultimatum and seized all the shoes from the store and put them up for auction. As the bidding opened in the street in front of their shop, Gibbs's and Lester's white friends wound through the crowd urging shoppers to give the shoes a "terrible letting alone." No one bid; the auction ended, and the two men took their goods back into their store. Gibbs wrote to the *Liberator,* "We will never willingly pay three dollars as poll tax as long as we remain disfranchised, oath-denied, outlawed colored Americans." Although a poll tax would endure through the Jim Crow era as a southern tactic for voter suppression, after the auction, wrote Gibbs, in San Francisco the tax "relapsed into innocuous desuetude."[15]

In 1851 two white men entered the boot emporium and attacked Peter Lester. Gibbs recalled: "With vile epithets, using a heavy cane, again and again [they] assaulted my partner, who was compelled to tamely submit, for had he raised his hand he would have been shot, and no redress. *I would not have been allowed to attest to the 'deep damnation.'*" He feared that as a Black man, he would have been shot if he protected his partner. Further, he was not allowed to testify against these men, and Gibbs felt "ostracized, assaulted without redress, disenfranchised and denied [his] oath in a court of justice."[16]

Lester understood the growing racial inequity Blacks faced in California and wrote: "There are many who, ever since this unjust enactment, have taken every opportunity to wrong us, both civilly and criminally, and . . . they remain sheltered under these unjust statutes." A pro-slavery minority, wrote Lester, had created a "political complexion more resembling a country under the servile and humiliating circumstances of slavery than as one of the sovereign and independent States of a free and enlightened people."[17]

A coalition of free Black people rose in their first year in California. In 1851 Gibbs and Lester joined Jonas Townsend, a teacher and editor of the *New York Hyperion,* and William Newby ("Nubia"), a journalist who wrote for Frederick Douglass's paper, to write to the *Daily Alta California* to denounce the racism. In what Gibbs called "the first pronouncement of the colored people from the state," they declared that California's codes produced the "circumstances of slavery," and they announced they would use "all moral means to secure legal claim to all the rights and privileges of American citizens."[18] Together the four men founded the first Black news-

Mifflin Wistar Gibbs, ca. 1870.
Schomburg Center for Research in Black Culture, New York
Public Library, via National Humanities Center
Resource Toolbox: The Making of African
American Identity, vol. 1, 1500–1860.

paper in the West, to create a Black voice in the press. Within a year the *Mirror of the Times* had thirty correspondents and subscription agents.[19]

Black dissent created waves that "would go on and on to beat against the rock and make sandy shores," wrote Gibbs. This surge would crumble that rock to build a new state where "a man's a man for all that." In *Shadow and Light* (1902), one of the first Black memoirs of California, Gibbs wrote, "What would I have others do to me? . . . That whites lack the pulsations of a common humanity . . . [that] never ceased to trouble them."[20]

In the early 1850s, to escape the Fugitive Slave Act or pan for gold, nearly two thousand free Blacks were bound for California. James Brown and Mary Ellen Pleasant, like Lester and Gibbs, had led abolitionist rallies in the East and rescued runaways from slavery. Most rushed up to the rivers of gold in the foothills of the Sierra Nevada Mountains; nine hundred free African American men and women stayed in San Francisco and Sacramento, counting on freedom and jobs.[21] Banned from owning property in the East, they hoped to claim mission or Native lands, have their own farms, and purchase families out of slavery in the South.

Enslaved and free Blacks watched California flout its ban on slavery. Free Black merchants, drovers, bricklayers, and cooks feared the new private armies and discovered that it was risky to quit a job or travel. They watched the state legalize forced indentures and entrapment and snare African Americans, Native Americans, and Chinese migrants.

At the same time, enslaved Blacks brought to California by their owners did not know they had been transported to a free state; to protect their freedom, they had to be able to prove that they had entered California after the state passed its freedom constitution. The California constitution had declared that the new state would never "tolerate" slavery, but when southerners met in the first legislature to design California's judicial system, they copied codes in slave states: "Any persons having one-half or more of negro blood, shall not be witnesses in an action or proceeding, to which a white person is a party."

Gibbs exclaimed that this law put a Black woman in a particularly precarious situation: free or enslaved, if she was raped by a white man she would need to testify on her own behalf, for it was unlikely that a white witness would have been present to corroborate the assault.[22] The state codes trapped enslaved men and women, blocking them from a way to protect their freedom.

The first California legislature replicated bans on Black testimony in free states. In northern states, such as New Jersey, a Black woman was deemed "incompetent" to testify that a white man was the father of her child; blackness created a presumption of slavery and, hence, of incompetence to testify. In New York, enslaved Blacks could not serve as witnesses; emancipated Blacks could only testify about assaults they had suffered before they obtained their freedom. They could not testify against a white kidnapper. Indiana, Iowa, and Ohio had joined southern states to prohibit "Negros or mulattos" from testifying against a white person. In Maryland and the District of Columbia, that injunction was waived if a "mulatto" was born of a white mother.[23]

Abolitionist Senator Charles Sumner warned Congress that these bans on Black testimony included "a license to commit, in the presence of any number of persons of that description, all imaginable crimes" and left a Black person "absolutely without legal protection of any kind, the victim of lawless outrage."[24] California absorbed these codes and wrote them into law. African Americans in California, regardless of their legal status, were threatened with kidnap and sale.

In 1851, early in statehood, as Gibbs, William Newby, William Hall, a prosperous Black miner and barber, and Jonas Townsend watched police officers and private slave hunters discover and arrest fugitives, they launched the Franchise League in San Francisco. The four experienced leaders saw that abolition hinged on access to the courts, and they circulated petitions to the new legislature demanding the right for Blacks to testify.[25] The legislature, however, copied the "gag rule" of the U.S. Congress—a total ban on even debating slavery on the floor of the House—and refused to receive the petitions. One member moved to "burn them."[26] The politics of abolition in California were homegrown and defined by an expanding core of Black activists and writers. At the center was abolitionist Mifflin Wister Gibbs.[27]

Black Migration, Black Truths

In 1848 only forty African Americans lived in California, working as servants or sailors.[28] After gold was discovered, southerners traveled west, often taking one or two enslaved men to work at the mines. In 1850 slaveholders from Virginia, Missouri, Kentucky, and Tennessee brought about two hundred enslaved men and women to slave-friendly Gold Rush counties. Southern slave owners, like African Americans, knew that California's "intolerance" to slavery was deliberately tepid and vague, and they were ready to gamble on the southern sympathies of the new state legislature. Suddenly California had more enslaved African Americans than any state or territory west of Texas.[29] By 1852 southerners had transported about fifteen hundred enslaved African Americans to the new state; although without state tax or property records, that figure is an estimate.[30] Few enslaved people fled *to* California—it was far away.

By 1855 five thousand Blacks had come to California.[31] Driven from the goldfields, in the bachelor society of the Gold Rush they took jobs cooking and serving meals or tending guests at a boardinghouse; many earned eleven dollars per week.[32] By 1860, after California's first decade as a state, free Blacks were only 1 percent of the growing population.[33]

At first few Black women crossed the country, unwilling to bring children to an unknown land where 92 percent of the population was white men. Nonetheless, they overcame their reluctance when they heard that free Black women in the South were earning about one to two dollars a week as servants, in New York, six to seven dollars a week, and in California, thirteen dollars a week plus board.[34] In 1850 only nine Black women lived in the new state; by 1860, 1,259 had settled throughout California.[35]

In Sacramento, the teeming departure point for the goldfields, tens of thousands of miners—white and Black, enslaved and free—met immigrants from China, Mexico, Chile, and Argentina in crowded rooming houses and tent camps; they competed for sifting pans, shovels, buckets, and ropes, waiting for a mule or a seat in a wagon to the mountains. But competition, race hatred, and violence settled in along the riverbanks, in the boardinghouses and "eating houses." From the steamboats into San Francisco up to the riverbanks of the Sierra Nevada Mountains, free Blacks shared the news with enslaved Blacks that in California all African Americans were legally free.

Racial equilibrium fell apart when the miners came down from the mountains. Black residents in San Francisco lived in segregated neighborhoods and, like Gibbs, were banned from the coveted jobs building new houses, hotels, restaurants, churches, and roads. Sacramento and San Francisco were interracial, raw, and chaotic workingmen's towns. Gambling houses, saloons, and brothels abounded. The wealth coming down from the goldfields did not remain to build California. In the first two years of the Gold Rush, $80 million worth of gold dust ($2.2 billion today) flowed down the mountains, passing through on the way to banks in the East.[36]

Unfreedom

The ban on testimony was the legal linchpin that made it possible to kidnap, conscript, and sell free African Americans.[37] Free men and women including Mifflin Wistar Gibbs, Peter Lester, and Nancy Lester launched petition drives and organized rallies. They rescued runaways and paid for white attorneys. In the new churches, schools, and clubs, Blacks' calls for the right to testify stitched together a community that was scattered throughout the new towns.

The right to bear witness contradicted debasing portrayals of African Americans as subservient, hypersexual, or brutish, images that marked them through their working or sexual bodies. It challenged notions that African

Americans were voiceless or that their words only marked their comic charm.[38] This right would topple disinformation.

Many free Black émigrés to California arrived able to read and write. Many had attended schools run since the 1780s by Quakers or by abolitionist and manumission societies, and arrived with skills in geography and math.[39] Most could spell their names and sign petitions.

Yet bans on Black testimony diminished the humanity of African Americans.[40] They were deemed not "oath-worthy"—that is, not Christians and thus, not fearful of divine wrath if they lied; they were judged as being organically unable to distinguish truth from falsehood.[41] In the California courtroom, the oath "to tell the truth so help me god" was recognized as a sign that god had granted the ability to tell the truth. It affirmed that the law held them to be credible, with the intellect to reason. Permitting Black men and women to be "sworn in" would establish their right to speak on their own behalf. "Swearing in" publicly and before god would establish Black people's human ability to talk and to talk back. It would undo the assumption that enslaved people had no will of their own.[42] Testimony was proof of civic belonging.

Southerners in California knew that the way to build an all-white state was to copy laws from states that had closed their courts to testimony, evidence, and lawsuits by African Americans. Governor Peter H. Burnett claimed that "any time a slave testified, an owner suffered." If free Blacks were allowed to testify in California, he said, all whites would surely lose. Before the Civil War, free Blacks could not testify in Maryland, Virginia, Tennessee, Illinois, New Jersey, Indiana, Iowa, and Ohio. In 1849 Burnett pleaded with the legislature to copy these states and also keep in place the ban on testimony by Indians and Chinese immigrants.[43]

In 1854 George Hall, a white miner, was charged with assaulting and robbing a Chinese man along the Bear River. Ling Sing heard shouts and ran to help, but Hall had already shot and killed the man. Based on Ling Sing's testimony, Hall was sentenced to hang. Immediately, the chief justice of California's Supreme Court, Hugh Murray, overturned the ruling. *People v. Hall* hinged on the testimony of the only witness, Ling Sing, a Chinese man.

In contorted reasoning, Murray held that long ago "Asiatics" had crossed the Bering Strait, migrated south, and descended into American Indians; the Chinese were therefore Indians, Indians could not testify in court, and hence, neither could the Chinese. The chief justice claimed that archeologists insisted that "Indian, Negro, Black and White, are generic terms, designating race. That, therefore, Chinese and all other people not white, are included in the prohibition from being witnesses against Whites." He said there was an "impassible difference" between "us" and "people marked as inferior"—that is, people who differed from "us in language, opinions, color, and physical conformation." He went on, "In the days of Columbus all shores washed by the Chinese were called the Indies, therefore all Asiatics were Indians." All people who "were not of white blood did not have the right to swear away the life of a citizen" nor participate in "administering the affairs of our government." Based on "the similarity of features and physical conformation," wrote Murray, Christopher Columbus "gave to the Islanders the name of Indians, which appellation was universally adopted, and extended to the Aboriginals of the New World, as well as of Asia." Indeed, it was better to release a convicted murder than to tamper with white supremacy. Judge Murray excluded the Chinese witness.[44]

With that, the court effectively divided California into two discrete peoples with two discrete legal standings: white and not white.[45] It created a civic identity that differentiated Californians by race and then determined their access to justice.[46]

Freedom Fighters: Freedom to Speak

Black testimony meant something different in California than it did in the plantation South. A white southern slaveholder had an economic interest in keeping a valuable worker out of prison. Why go to court? A slaveholder had the right to use brute force on his human property; he could demand information, force a confession, and impose any punishment he might wish—and still enjoy the uninterrupted labors of his unpaid worker. California lacked even the legal guardrail of plantation slavery. For example, when a group of enslaved men in Mississippi was charged with murdering their owner in 1856, the judge ruled that no slave could testify honestly when he was "always under a superior, controlling his actions and his will." How could he "act or speak voluntarily if he was surrounded by those whom he was bound by law to obey?"[47] California, by contrast, wrote the scaffolding for slavery into law; its ban on a Black person testifying against a white person turned the courts into surrogate slaveholders.

Led by seasoned Black abolitionists, African American political organizations emerged in California's first year of statehood and fueled the energies of resistance. In 1851 they had launched the Franchise League in San Francisco to circulate the "Petition to the California Legislature to

Overturn the Ban on Blacks and Mulatto Persons Testifying and Giving Evidence against White Persons, So That Colored Persons Are No Longer Denied the Protection of Law in the Enjoyment of the Rights of Property and Personal Security; and the Vicious and Unprincipled Take Advantage of This Disability." This early and prescient civil rights drive demanded that free Blacks have the right to testify in court.[48] A miner, Daniel Blue, formerly enslaved in Kentucky, founded the St. Andrews African Methodist Episcopal Church, the first African American church west of the Rockies, and held the first service in his basement.[49] Other Black newcomers launched the social, religious, and civic organizations in California that had sustained them in the East. William Newby, William Hall, Jonas Townsend, and Mifflin Wistar Gibbs turned to a tactic that was practiced in the East.

In his opening address to the state, Peter H. Burnett, the popular first governor of California, asked the new legislature to create an all-white state because "no race of men, under the precise circumstances of this class in our state, could ever hope to advance a single step in knowledge or virtue."[50] African Americans had hoped for fair play in the West. But unlike Ohio and Indiana, California had not freed any enslaved men or women when it entered the union. Yet the new state needed laborers. Builders needed more carpenters and masons, and some free Blacks found construction jobs in cities that seemed to spring up from nowhere. Both unpaid slave labor and a free Black working class were threats to whites. Meanwhile, California was suffering from drought. White miners were purging Latinos and Chinese from parched and unyielding riverbeds.

In 1852 California copied the most ruthless federal law in U.S. history and passed its own Fugitive Slave Act. This act closed a loophole and made it legal to capture runaways who fled from *inside* the state rather than by crossing a state line. Slave catchers seized both free as well as enslaved Blacks in California. With a total ban on Black testimony and evidence, free Blacks were unable to support their rightful free status.[51]

The need was urgent. Sailors, ministers, and brothel owners formed a West Coast Underground Railroad that ran from San Diego to Vancouver, British Columbia, carrying fugitive slaves to safe houses in churches, hotels, ranches, and homes. Along this artery, Black runaways were offered refuge as well as lawyers who could document their free status and right to liberty under the state constitution and the terms of its admission to the United States.[52] They filed cases demanding to be heard in court.

California's legislature copied the U.S. House of Representatives' "gag rule" of 1836 that banned all debate about slavery and straight out rejected the petitions. For the next eight years, it refused to receive 130,000 abolitionist petitions to Congress into the congressional record.[53] Within two years of statehood, California's legislators refused even to enter petitions into its own records. The state legislature revealed California's intention to preserve slavery.

If the California constitution "would not tolerate" slavery, the Black Franchise League "would not tolerate" the gag order. It barraged the legislature with petitions to repeal the law that founded California's judicial system, the "Act Concerning Crimes and Punishments," which denied "to all such colored persons the protection of law in the enjoyment of the rights of property and personal security." The league argued that the "vicious and unprincipled" were taking "advantage of this disability [to] prey upon those rights with impunity."[54]

The petitions were delivered to the legislature in March 1852, just as it was passing California's own Fugitive Slave Act. These first waves of petitions, held in the state archives in Sacramento, carry the signatures of hundreds of African Americans—from Black ranchers in the foothills of the Sierra Nevada Mountains, shopkeepers in Sacramento, and lodging house owners in San Francisco.[55] Teachers and ministers took up the pen to record their names across the state. One outraged legislator moved to throw the petitions out the window; another moved to burn them.[56] The California State Assembly voted not to "receive" petitions from "such a source."[57] The "memorials" from "colored persons praying for an amendment" to the Civil Practices Act were defeated, fifty-three to zero.[58]

Many free African Americans—like many impoverished whites and immigrants—had believed California's promise of freedom. Violence spewed against Blacks in the Sierra Nevada Mountains, against Chinese miners in segregated gold digs, and against Natives all across the state. The petitions became a stress test of the new state constitution, of the nascent democracy rising along the Pacific Coast, and of the hypocrisies that attended the birth of the state.

Civic Death

Black miners and field hands at remote ranches and goldfields, in tent camps in the Sierra Nevada, and in fishing towns along the Pacific lived on a knife-edge of capture, far from the determined organizations rising up in the new cities in the early 1850s.[59]

In 1849 slaveholder Wood Tucker brought his bondsman, Stephen

Spencer Hill, with him from Arkansas to the goldfields in Tuolumne County, where he had heard that the Stanislaus River carried flakes of gold down from stern granite peaks. But Tucker found no gold. In 1853 he decided to return to the South. Before leaving, he allowed Hill to purchase his freedom and signed Hill's manumission papers. Hill stayed on in the mountains and claimed 160 acres of rolling green land for a ranch in the Tuolumne River watershed. He built a cabin, farmed, and grazed cattle. That same year, with improbable luck, Hill unearthed a nine-ounce gold nugget and used his fortune to invest in wagons, and he hauled heavy farm harvests throughout the county. Hill's ranch matured into one of the most prosperous in the county, worth about $4,000.

Owen Rozier, a slave catcher, had his eye on Hill's land. In 1854 Rozier squatted on Hill's ranch and announced, true or not, that he was an agent for Hill's former owner and that Hill was a fugitive slave. Rozier seized Hill and carted him to the jail in Sonora in one of Hill's own wagons. Then Rozier moved into Hill's cabin as the Black rancher languished in a jail cell, his freedom papers having disappeared from his cabin. Rozier decided to sell Hill back into slavery in the South and carted him to Stockton, where he chained him in a boat soon bound for San Francisco. As the two men waited for the ship to sail, Hill's friends got Rozier drunk, cut the chains, and allowed Hill to flee. Hill was not permitted to testify in court that he was a free man and a legal property owner. The court supported Rozier's claim to the land, and Hill lost his ranch, reduced to "grubbing" in the Sierra Nevada.[60]

The First Civil Rights Movement in California: The Colored Conventions

California's Fugitive Slave Act put every African American in the state—enslaved or free—at risk of capture. Initially, early Black activists, ministers, and journalists turned to the strategies that had worked over three decades in New England, New York, and Pennsylvania.

In the early years of the Gold Rush, Mary Ellen Pleasant, trained by Black abolitionists around Nantucket, arrived in California with a $15,000 inheritance from her late husband, formerly enslaved abolitionist and contractor James Smith. Pleasant invested these funds in banks, laundries, brothels, and rooming houses, all "safe houses" on California's loosely structured Underground Railroad.[61] She helped fund the Athenaeum, a two-story house with a saloon on the ground floor and a library that held

Mary Ellen Pleasant, California abolitionist.
(Courtesy of Everett Collection, Inc.,
Newark, New Jersey.)

eight hundred volumes and an assembly hall upstairs. Here Black merchants discussed issues of the day with the Black working class of San Francisco. And here five Black men—teachers, merchants, and preachers—launched the plan for the first Colored Convention in California.[62]

In 1855 the Franchise League published a bold notice in the *Sacramento Daily Union*, a newspaper with a statewide readership, and copied it in the Black press. Addressed to "The Colored Citizens of California," the "card," a racial reveille, announced that a mass civil protest would convene in Sacramento on November 20, 1855, at 10 a.m.: "Your state and condition in California is one of social and political degradation, . . . Since you have left your peaceful friends and homes in the Atlantic States and migrated to the shores of the Pacific . . . you have met with one continued series of outrages, injustices, and unmitigated wrongs unparalleled in the history of nations. You are denied the right to become owners of the soil. . . . You are compelled to labor and toil without any security that you shall obtain your just earnings as an inheritance for yourself or your children." The card stated that California, "which should be to us as the rivers of water in a dry place, like the shadow of a great rock in the weary land, where the wretched should find sympathy and the weak protection, spurn[s] us with contempt and den[ies] us common humanity."[63]

"In the view of these wrongs which are so unjustly imposed upon us," the leaders called for a gathering to design the way "to obtain our inalienable rights and privileges in California."[64] So, in 1855, 1856, and 1857 three large statewide Colored Conventions met to protest the ban on testimony. The Colored Conventions pulled together a Black community that was diffused across a state; organizers hoped it would outshine the sun.

The 1850 national Fugitive Slave Act, California's entry ticket into the United States, shaped the drive for freedom in the new state. Facing a unique geographical and legal trap, free and enslaved Blacks needed to testify when their owners decided to return to the South and insisted they return with them; at times, to save the costs of passage, the owners freed their bondsmen in California.[65] Blacks, born free or enslaved, needed to prove that they had purchased themselves, or that they had worked unpaid with the promise of eventual manumission—ransom for their working bodies.

Blacks in California shaped the national tradition of Colored Conventions to this unique threat.[66] Colored Conventions had begun in 1830 when the American Society of Free Persons of Colour met in Philadelphia. For the rest of the nineteenth century, Colored Conventions offered African Americans venues in which to gather, plan, debate, and put forth national or statewide demands—to end slavery and to have the right to own land and to send their children to public schools. They were well covered in local newspapers. Their calls for assembly, unity, and action reverberated in their new churches and the Black press.[67] In the African American Methodist Episcopal Church and Black-owned newspapers, voices emerged unfiltered by the words of white reporters, as the Colored Conventions galvanized Black activism in a hostile state. The California Colored Conventions tapped into the legacy of the convention movement in order to plan how Blacks could protect their freedom in an unfree state.

In late November 1855, forty-nine elected Black delegates traveled from eleven distant counties to meet at the African Methodist Episcopal Church that sat a few blocks from the state capitol in Sacramento where

California's own Fugitive Slave Law was passed.[68] California had no railroads yet, and delegates boarded riverboats or wagons or rode horses or mules, taking days to reach Sacramento in order to challenge the ban on Black testimony.[69]

The strategy of the California Colored Conventions was to create a defiant communal voice—through the convention itself, through the movement it would spawn, and through a challenge only to one law.[70] William H. Yates, chair of the convention, was a hopeful warrior for racial uplift. Born enslaved, Yates had a job as a custodian at the U.S. Supreme Court. There he witnessed historic debates and also earned enough money to buy himself, his wife, and their two children out of slavery. Known to be active on the Underground Railroad in Washington, DC, Yates was expelled from the city and in 1849 fled to California, where he found work as a steward on a luxury steamer that plied the waters of San Francisco Bay and carried white patrons, fugitive slaves, and Black news.

Differences over Black identity, Black rights, and Black entitlement surfaced in the opening hours of the first Colored Convention in California. Some delegates' rousing calls for racial justice bounced against others' demands for political inclusion based on their financial worth, assessed by acreage, buildings, and taxes.[71] William Newby declared that Blacks were entitled to testify because "our social, moral, religious, intellectual and financial condition . . . compare[s] favorably with any class in the community." Another speaker echoed Newby: he cited Blacks' equivalent financial worth compared to white settlers and boasted that four thousand free Blacks in California held $2,413,000 of capital; they had earned the right to testify.[72]

Delegate William Harden reminded the convention that these tallies of savings and property did not include the "immense sums which have been, from time to time, paid to their owners by the colored men who have come here as slaves, and who, by a course of honest industry, have paid for and obtained their freedom." Reverend John Jamison Moore, born enslaved and the first teacher at the first Black school in San Francisco, spoke against the popular and debasing images of the "primitive" Black; African Americans in California, he declared, were now "fit" for freedom. Reverend Moore preached, "Do not let those who deny us the possession of intellect and soul [see us fail] . . . because we cannot govern our passions. Let us . . . work for moral regeneration. We are Americans—colored Yankees."[73]

The delegates found consensus in demands "for the security of life and property," and after three days they voted to collect twenty thousand signatures to prove that Blacks' right to testify was popular with whites as well as African Americans. Delegates agreed to raise enough money to print five thousand copies of the proceedings and fund the Black newspaper the *Mirror of the Times*.[74]

The convention encouraged Black residents across California to enroll their children in public school: "You call upon us to pay enormous taxes to support Government, at the same time you deny us the protections you extend to others; the security of life and property. . . . You receive our money to educate your children, and then refuse to admit our children into the common schools."[75]

Blacks intended to claim their rights as citizens. Over the next two years, the delegates delivered eight thousand separate petitions to the legislature demanding the repeal of the ban on Blacks' testimony. That said, the first convention never referred to California's genocide of Native Americans, assaults on Chinese and Latino miners, or slavery's commonalities across races. The petitions compared the righteousness of Black testimony to that of Chinese migrants who followed an "idolatrous religion." The convention recalled that the "exclusion of the testimony of the descendants of Africans, in the United States, commenced as incident to slavery, and should be discontinued with it."[76]

Demands for the abolition of slavery were more direct at the second California Colored Convention, which met the next year. James Hubbard rose to denounce all "the laws which sustain her slave pens and prisons, her auction blocks, and the selling of human beings, the branding of men and the scourging of women, the separation of man and wife, parents and children. I hate them." William Newby said the petitions were humiliating: why petition white legislators when "they have the power. We know it. They know it. We appeal to them as whites to use their power beneficently towards us." The convention adjourned unhappily with a commitment to circulate another one thousand separate petitions against the ban on Black testimony.[77]

One year later, in 1857, the U.S. Supreme Court ruled against Dred Scott, an enslaved African American man whose owners had taken him from Missouri and leased him in the free territory of Wisconsin. Scott escaped in Wisconsin, was recaptured, and sued for his freedom. He argued that he had lived for four years where slavery was banned. Justice Roger Taney ruled that Black people "are not included, and were not intended to be included, under the word 'citizens' in the Constitution." Dred

Scott was not a citizen, and hence not a legal person. Scott and his wife, Harriet, remained the property of their owner, and property cannot be taken without due process of law. He was a fugitive; nowhere in the country would he be free. Slaveholders, he added, now had the right to take enslaved men and women into the territories. Finally, Taney included the territories under the 1850 Fugitive Slave Law.[78] The ruling was a dire omen for Blacks in California.

In the late spring of 1858, Mary Ellen Pleasant traveled east from California to central Canada to meet with John Brown, a white abolitionist, at a secret gathering in a large settlement of runaway slaves in Chatham, Ontario. Brown divulged his plan to form a separate nation of formerly enslaved people in the Appalachian Mountains. He would seize weapons from the arms manufactory and storage armory at Harpers Ferry, Virginia, and distribute them to local Blacks who would unleash a slave revolt.[79] Rumors endure that Pleasant gave Brown a vast sum (some histories say $10,000; some $30,000) toward the ill-conceived and failed uprising of 1859. She returned to California wondering if Brown's strategy of revolt would work in the West.[80]

Was California freedom land? An angry and collective voice rose when sixty-one delegates met at the African Methodist Episcopal Church in 1857.[81] William Newby, now editor of the *Mirror of the Times*, was indignant, and he opened the third Colored Convention by disputing the language in its platform that declared that Black people "loved the country." Newby also refused to swear that he would "protect [the United States] against foreign invasion." Aware that he was verging on treason, he vowed to welcome any army that "provided liberty to me and my people in bondage." He insisted that the convention reject any reference to progress in a country that had just extended slavery to Texas, Kansas, and Nebraska. Clearly, he concluded, "they hate us."

The Judiciary Committee in the state legislature received the petitions from the 1857 Colored Convention in the early spring of 1858. And there the petitions died.[82] The struggle had been exhausting and expensive, and the leaders were disheartened. Jonas Townsend (the businessman who, with Mifflin Wistar Gibbs and other Black leaders in California, had founded the *Mirror of the Times*), wondered, "What are we doing to advance the cause of our rights at present? We have settled down into a state of indifference and lethargy . . . while the enemy is making great inroads upon us, and forging chains to bind us to the course of policy that must . . . prove our ruin in this State."[83]

Yet the gatherings, newspapers, petitions, court cases, and perilous escapes affirmed that a righteous spirit propelled Black Californians. It then challenged them all, as it had urged a dejected and pessimistic Gibbs years before, to "go do some great thing."

CHAPTER TEN

"A Change Has Come over the Spirit of Our Dreams"

The Negros have reared a nation.

—CALIFORNIA COLORED CONVENTION, 1865

IN 1855 BLACK ABOLITIONIST William Newby wrote to Frederick Douglass from California, saying, "A change has come over the spirit of our dreams."[1] After the successful first Colored Convention, with new Black churches, schools, and Black-owned shops, and a growing number of Black families, Newby was hopeful. Was Newby's observation a celebration? Or was it an admonition to African Americans to redouble their efforts against slavery in a free state?

In the early years of the Gold Rush, several thousand enslaved Black men lined the creeks and riverbeds in the rolling foothills of the Sierra Nevada, carrying buckets of heavy mud, clearing shrubs and boulders from riverbanks, and cooking meals for their owners. The federal Fugitive Slave Act of 1850 was working well, so in 1855 California let its own Fugitive Slave Law lapse. Slaveholders who had crossed the country with enslaved African Americans still had that federal law at their back.

"Sing! For the Pride of the Tyrants Is Broken"

In 1857 Mississippi slave owner Charles V. Stovall crossed the plains with enslaved eighteen-year-old Archy Lee and a small herd of cattle. Lee cooked for the wagon train and drove the oxen that pulled the heavy loads. He walked most of the two thousand miles across the plains to California, prodding the thirsty animals. Left behind on the plantation were Lee's mother, his two brothers, and a sister. Stovall had inherited this "property." He would hold Lee's family hostage to ensure that he would return to Mississippi. Once the tattered wagon party reached California, Stovall needed to pasture his emaciated animals and hastened to buy land in the Sierra Nevada Mountains.

That October, Stovall made his way down the mountains into Sacramento with Lee. Desperate for cash, he decided to open a school and he rented a classroom. Then he placed an ad in the *Sacramento Age* seeking students whose families would pay five dollars per month, in advance.[2] But another school had opened the year before, and after two months, his scheme failed, and Stovall was broke. He decided to "hire out" Lee for thirty dollars a month and keep the wages for himself. Stovall moved with Lee to Sacramento, just as a small group of Black abolitionists was arriving to plan the 1857 Colored Convention.

That October, Lee met Charles Hackett and Charles Parker, members of the Executive Committee of the Colored Convention, who lost no time letting him know that he had been transported to a free state. Stovall realized that he could lose his human property and stream of income. Barely a year after his wagon train had left the South, in early January 1858 he informed Lee that they would be returning to Mississippi. But Lee now knew he was a free Black man. And he refused to leave California.

Hackett and Parker helped Lee escape and hid him at Hackett House, their hotel in the center of Sacramento's tight Black community and a safe "stop" on California's Underground Railroad network.[3] When Stovall could not find Lee, he hired slave catchers who easily found the fugitive at the hotel and persuaded the sheriff to arrest him.

Lee spent the next eight months between captivity and escape, as a political movement to free him spread from Sacramento to San Francisco.[4] The Executive Committee and a coalition of free Blacks were raising money for attorneys to represent fugitive slaves in California. Many had attended the Colored Conventions and monitored Lee's plight. What was at stake was the right of a Black person to remain in the free state.[5] Lee quickly fled, was found, and arrested again; each time Black leaders filed a writ of habeas corpus that required the state to "produce" him and stop Stovall from taking him back to Mississippi. Lee, they argued, could not be a "fugitive from service" in California because he was a free man.[6]

Stovall needed to persuade the county court that he was a "sojourner" visiting the state for his health, just a traveler passing through California with his slave, and he took the stand to assert that his ownership of Lee was legally binding. Stovall claimed that even though he had purchased a pasture and ranch in the Sierra Nevada, and even though he had placed a newspaper advertisement for a school in Sacramento, he was not a California resident and had no intention of remaining in California.

Lee's legal hurdles were high: to escape the shadow of the Fugitive Slave Act, he had to prove that he had not crossed into California as a runaway from slavery. He also had to face the decision in the *Perkins* case that an enslaved man who had been transported onto free soil was not automatically free. Even more daunting, Lee faced the recent *Dred Scott* decision in which the U.S. Supreme Court had ruled that residing in a free state did not automatically emancipate a slave; enslaved men and women were property and under the Fifth Amendment any law that deprived a slave owner of that property was unconstitutional. In turn, Lee's lawyers argued that none of those protections applied: Lee had not fled *to* California; his owner had deliberately brought Lee into the free state.[7] Lee's case, like most of the freedom cases in California, hinged on the claim that Lee was no longer a slave, and hence he could not be a runaway slave.

Did a Black man—officially free under the state constitution—have the right to remain in California, unbound from the white man who had brought him there? Did he have the right to remain in California if his owner was returning to his southern home state?

Stovall's lawyers reminded the court that nothing in the U.S. Constitution banned slavery. It could exist anywhere in the United States. Lee's enslaved status moved with him, wherever he traveled or dwelled. In addition, the federal Fugitive Slave Act of 1850 provided for the "reclamation" of fugitives.[8] Both the Bill of Rights and the *Dred Scott* decision guaranteed the right to property and, as a slave, Lee was Stovall's property. Besides, insisted Stovall's lawyer, the ban on slavery in California's constitution was "inoperative" because the legislature had failed to pass an "enabling law" to enforce it. And so, because Lee was not permitted to testify to his free status, he spent most of 1858 in and out of jails and courtrooms.

Newspaper reports of Lee's flights, captures, and trials brought together a working coalition of free and formerly enslaved Blacks. Mary Ellen Pleasant and other donors raised money to hire white abolitionist lawyers Joseph Wynand and Edwin Crocker. Their first task was to invoke writs of habeas corpus (produce the body) to keep him in California and prevent Stovall from taking him back to Mississippi. Their next was to convince the court that an enslaved man automatically became free once he entered California. Wynand and Crocker argued that "the master's control over a slave" ended in California, where any slave "becomes virtually free." Further, Stovall's activities were not those of a traveler or businessman "passing through," a "sojourner" who was entitled to keep his enslaved servant.[9] Once Stovall bought the ranch in the Sierra Nevada Mountains, under California law he became a landowner rather than a tourist or traveling salesman. Stovall had also advertised his plan to open a school—further evidence that he was a resident who intended to remain.

At first, Lee's lawyers prevailed. The California constitution did not permit either a citizen of the state—or a visitor of *any duration*—to hold a person against his or her consent. Lee had to be freed.[10]

But Stovall had another court and another judge waiting and poised for his appeal: California Supreme Court Judge Peter H. Burnett—slaveholder in Tennessee, real estate agent for John Sutter, and the former California governor who had tried to ban all African Americans from California. Burnett immediately ordered the marshals to lock Lee in manacles and return him to his cell "for his own protection," while he adjourned to consider his final ruling. A concerned Black crowd followed Lee to the jail.

For nearly a year, Lee had faced inconsistent rulings. Although usually bound in chains, he managed to break free and he escaped three times. Then Lee waited in jail for three weeks for Judge Burnett to issue his ruling. Burnett conceded that the "mode of expression in the Constitution [is] that every inhabitant of the state should be free." But he turned his eyes toward California's natural beauty and remarked on its sunny climate; he predicted that many travelers would soon come to California "for health and pleasure." Southern travelers, he observed, were "accustomed" to journey with their enslaved servants whom they viewed as "part of the family," and he ruled that the court should not prevent slave owners from enjoying the sights of the Golden State by denying them the help of their "domestics." Besides, wrote Burnett, Lee's owner was just a young man who might not have understood that the state constitution was "in effect."[11] With that, he overrode the lower court and handed Lee back to Stovall. Stovall whisked him away in heavy chains.

Where did Stovall take Archy Lee? Stovall had last been seen leading Lee from the courthouse by his chains. There were rumors. One was that Stovall was hiding Lee on his ranch in Carson Valley. Another was that Stovall had sailed with him down the Sacramento River. Some heard they were both on a Wells Fargo stagecoach, headed for the East. The outraged and invigorated Black community formed the Committee of One Hundred to raise money for attorneys and to offer rewards to find and retrieve Lee. Ultimately it was reporters who located him in the jail in the river town of Stockton, penned up until Stovall could book them passage on a ship back to New Orleans.

Lee's appeals had been put before all the likely judges. His supporters turned to James Riker, a ship steward, past delegate to a Colored Convention, and, notably, a low-level African American city commissioner. Riker used his authority to issue a warrant to arrest Stovall and charged him with kidnapping Lee. Riker attached a writ of habeas corpus ordering Stovall to "produce" Lee. Stovall refused.

By 1858 Black men who had been delegates to the three Colored Conventions were working as cooks, waiters, and deckhands on the small steamboats that delivered mail and food to lumber and fishing towns up and down the coast. These free "Black Jacks," or sailors, were the eyes and ears of Black neighborhoods. James Pleasant, the husband of Mary Ellen Pleasant, was the cook on board a steamship bound for New Orleans. It is likely James Pleasant let it be known to Mary Ellen Pleasant that early on March 5, 1858, the ship *Orizaba* was to leave from the Vallejo Street dock in San Francisco and sail toward a secret rendezvous in the middle of San Francisco Bay. That morning, two police officers quietly boarded the ship, as George Dennis and Mary Ellen Pleasant followed in a tugboat that they "rented" from the San Francisco police for $3,050—a costly bribe—to follow the *Orizaba* and be ready to retrieve Archy Lee. In the choppy waters of San Francisco Bay, all were scanning the waves for a little rowboat that would deliver Lee to the steamship. This time, however, the police were enforcing the order of a Black city commissioner, and they carried a warrant for the arrest of Charles Stovall.

Lee had spent the damp night in a little boat, concealed in a hidden cove of Angel Island, just inside the Golden Gate. Under the armed watch of Stovall and four of his mates, at dawn they forced Lee to crouch down in the bottom of the rowboat that was headed for the rendezvous with the steamship *Orizaba*, waiting in the bay. Lee believed he was on his way to be shipped back to the South.[12] In no time the San Francisco police officers spotted the little boat; Stovall was standing with Lee still crouched in the hull. The police waited until the rowboat slid alongside the *Orizaba*. As Stovall and his friends were lifting Lee onto the ladder to climb aboard the ship, the police seized the Black man. Yells arose on the ship as the police took Lee into custody—yet again for his own "protection." Stovall drew his pistol, but the police seized him and took both men back to the Market Street wharf in the police tugboat. A cheering crowd met the freedom party at the dock.[13]

Archy Lee was again on trial in San Francisco. The straightforward legal issue was still whether Lee was a free man or an enslaved man. As ever, freedom hinged on the right of a Black man to testify against a white man. Stovall argued, before yet another judge, that the writ that took Lee from the *Orizaba* had been signed by a Black man—albeit one who held a city office—a man who could not even testify against a white man; the order was invalid. Besides, argued Stovall's lawyers, Lee was still enslaved and, under the federal Fugitive Slave Act, his owner was entitled to capture him.

Crowds gathered outside the courthouse demanding that Lee be allowed to speak in court. First to testify on Lee's behalf were his white employers from Sacramento. They confirmed that Stovall had owned Lee in Mississippi, but they had hired Lee and paid him directly; he had been a true employee, not a slave rented from Stovall.

Lee's lawyer saved his most potent evidence for the end: he held up the ad in the *Sacramento Age* in which Stovall promoted his school and asked for a tuition of five dollars per month, to be paid in advance.[14] The ad proved that Stovall had planned all along to remain in California. He was not a traveler; he was a California resident, and as such, he could not keep a slave.

P r i v a t e   S c h o o l
FOR BOYS AND GIRLS
BY
C. A. STOVALL
K street near 7th. To commence on Monday, the
12th of October, 1857
Terms—$5 per month, in advance

This time the judge permitted Lee to testify, and the voice of a Black defendant speaking out against a white accuser was heard in a California courtroom. Lee was sworn in and testified under oath. He had been a defendant in several trials; now he was on a witness stand able to assert that he was a free man. All along Stovall had claimed that Lee was his slave from Mississippi, but in the end he could produce no evidence that he or his father owned Lee. After all the strenuous litigation, Stovall lacked the document to support the claim that Lee was a runaway slave. The judge ruled that if Lee was not a slave, then he could not be a fugitive slave.[15] He released Lee.

The victory was bittersweet; Archy Lee's freedom did not hinge on a freedom provision in the state constitution nor his bold escapes nor his righteous determination; his freedom was delivered by experienced Black leaders and aggressive civil rights lawyers who won for him the right to testify on his own behalf.

Suddenly the judge, the arresting officers, and the spectators in the full courtroom realized that Stovall faced perjury charges and jail time for testifying that he rightfully possessed Lee. As the trial ended, Stovall quickly left the courtroom, slipped down to the docks, and boarded a ferry to the middle of San Francisco Bay that took him to a mail steamer back to the South—alone. Lee was free at last. He walked out of the courtroom into a jubilant Black crowd and jumped into a buggy that delivered him to the safe home of Mary Ellen Pleasant.[16]

Lee's victory, however, had not produced a seismic change in the civil rights of free or enslaved Blacks in California. Fracture lines in the free Black community that had surfaced at the Colored Conventions now cracked open. A few men on the Executive Committee feared that they would face conspiracy charges for having helped Lee escape from jail over the past year and published a "card," or notice, stating that it was "an un-qualified falsehood" that they "had counseled . . . to rescue the boy Archy." The signers said they were "a law-loving and law-abiding class of persons" and boasted that even in the face of "innumerable wrongs [perpetrated upon us] . . . [we] always quietly submitted to the unjust enactments that have been imposed on us."[17]

"We Have Practical Slavery in Our Midst"

In January 1858 Democratic governor John B. Weller declared that al-though California had "decided that slavery should not exist in this state," it could not "impair the constitutional rights" of other states—a classic states' rights argument. The South had more money invested in human beings than in land, and abolition would "lessen the value of a neighbor's property." Other states, said Weller, had the sovereign right to "enjoy" slavery, and California had a legal obligation not to trespass on this right. Weller concluded, "Disunion is inevitable."[18]

In 1858 the legislature tried again to reprise the "Migration Acts." One would ban the entry of African Americans into California, and the other would ban the entry of Chinese. One state senator claimed that the Committee of One Hundred, forged by free Blacks to free Archy Lee, was proof that emancipation made Black men "insolent and defiant." If Blacks arrived in California "in sufficient numbers, [they] would become danger- ous."[19] Governor Burnett declared that more and more enslaved African Americans had been brought to California bound to service for a limited period as hirelings: "We have . . . practical slavery in our midst. That this class is rapidly increasing in our state is very certain."[20]

The fallout from Lee's victory was a surge of white purity legislation. California tried again to pass acts for "racial restriction," or white purity, identical to migration laws in Maryland, Virginia, Delaware, and Geor- gia, where codes required free or freed African Americans to be expelled, imprisoned, or sold if they did not leave. Despite the profits in hiring low-paid free Blacks, many states were deporting them. Without Black testimony, the courts could exclude all their manumission papers or free- dom documents. California's state legislature nearly passed a law to ban manumission altogether.[21]

In 1858 California sought to fortify its support for slavery. The State Assembly wanted to copy the system of slave passes from the South and proposed the Negro Immigration Act. This exclusion act said that any African American already in California, free or enslaved, would have to register for a pass by October 1, 1858. Assemblyman Isaac Allen, the bill's author, declared that since a free Black man could neither vote nor testify in court, he was not "socially or politically" the equal of a white man. In- deed, a free Black, "by nature indolent in a state of freedom becomes ready prey to vice." Freedom generated "a constant source of disquiet" in Black people. A class of white men with "false Philanthropy," said Allen, had fostered the "ignorant pride of the free negro, so that he becomes insolent and defiant, and if in sufficient numbers, would become dangerous, as ev- idenced by recent occurrences"—referring to the liberation of Archy Lee.

The racial trope of a dangerous, angry Black person seeped through the 1858 proposals. If the Negro Immigration Act passed, all Blacks in California would have had to carry a pass to prove that they had arrived before October 1858; otherwise, they would have been auctioned off for forced labor for a period of six months and then expelled from the state. African Americans living in the East or South could not join their families in California. African Americans living in California could not reenter if they left. If a white person brought an enslaved person into California with the intention of freeing him in the state, he could be charged with a misdemeanor.[22] Any resident of California who had "purchased the services" of (as opposed to having hired) a Black person could claim ownership and then pay the state of California for that person's removal at the end of a period of forced indenture. With this fee, the state itself would become a profiteer in the slave trade. The Negro Migration Act passed the California State Assembly by an overwhelming vote of forty-five to eight; it was only defeated when the California State Senate sought to exempt Blacks, free or enslaved, who were already in the state from being expelled.[23]

In the midst of California's Indian genocide, the migration bill would legalize ethnic cleansing. But where would the state send its Black residents? Would there be reservations for African American deportees? Would Blacks have to pay for their own deportation? What if they refused to go? Or to pay? Would an employer be held liable if he employed a colored person?[24]

And who, in fact, was "colored"? The San Francisco School Board willingly contributed a definition of race: anyone who was one-eighth or more Negro could not attend public schools with white children, and it expelled Nancy and Peter Lester's daughter.[25]

Mifflin Wistar Gibbs felt a "disheartening consciousness that while our existence was tolerated, we were powerless."[26] As Archy Lee hid in the home of Mary Ellen Pleasant, hundreds of African Americans met to celebrate at the African Methodist Episcopal Zion Church in San Francisco. They sang "The Year of Archy Lee Is Come." In protest hymnody, the Black community voiced its place in California:

> Sound the glad tidings o'er land and sea.
> Our people have triumphed and Archy is free.
> Sing! For the Pride of the tyrants is broken; . . .
> How vain was their boasting—their plans so long broken.
> Archy's free—and Stovall is brought to the dust.[27]

They took up a collection to pay Lee's triumphant, persistent lawyers. Then, most agreed, the time had come to leave California.[28]

Exodus

In Vancouver, British Columbia, James Douglas, the mestizo, or "Métis," governor, had been closely following the legislature's assaults on Blacks in California and thought that it might force the state to secede.[29] Meanwhile, Douglas watched miners from all over the world stampede through Vancouver to the new Gold Rush on the Fraser River. Along with the British home government, the governor wanted to keep the tiny colony of Vancouver from falling into the hands of American miners who were "hankering in their minds after annexation to the United States."[30] British Columbia had only five hundred subjects, and Douglas wanted to populate the colony with families and farmers, merchants and small manufacturers who would vote to remain British—settlers who wanted land and suffrage and were not loyal to the United States. This was his moment to dilute the vote.

Two nights after Archy Lee was freed, Jeremiah Nagle, captain of the steamship *Commodore*, which plied the waters between San Francisco and Victoria, and friend of Governor Douglas, showed up at the jubilation at the African Methodist Episcopal Church in San Francisco. Nagle brought an irresistible invitation from Douglas and a map of Vancouver. He unrolled the map and announced Douglas's offer to the wary crowd. Douglas, said Nagle, welcomed all African Americans in California to British Columbia. Black Californians, he promised, would have the right to vote and to send their children to integrated public schools. They were welcome to join the Church of England. Shrewdly, the governor offered each Black émigré twenty-acre plots of undeveloped land at a rough price of about five dollars an acre.[31] Finally, Nagle also reminded the African American crowd—Blacks who had come to celebrate the freedom of Archy Lee—that they would never again fear bondage; Britain had outlawed the slave trade in the empire in 1807 and had abolished slavery altogether in 1833.

Since 1849 about six thousand free and enslaved Blacks had crossed the plains or the jungles of Panama to make a home in California. Now, a decade later, many anticipated the Civil War that was to come, and they feared that southern Democrats would try to pull the state from the union.

It was time to be on the move again—in flight from California, the Fugitive Slave Law, and the pending Migration Law. The gates of education were closing against Black children, and the state wanted new laws to ban Blacks from owning land, voting, and testifying. Within days of hearing Douglas's offer, hundreds of African American residents of California sold or packed what property they could and began to say farewell to the Black friends, ministers, merchants, ranchers, and teachers who remained behind.[32]

On the morning of April 20, 1858, four days after Archy Lee's release, African American leaders and residents of San Francisco met at the wharf to watch the first émigrés sail from California. Each traveler paid fifteen dollars for a one-way ticket and then boarded the steamship *Commodore*, an unseaworthy old ship, to sail 950 miles north to British Columbia.[33] Mifflin Wistar Gibbs and Archy Lee were on that boat. All told, there were thirty-five African American seekers, free and enslaved. They carried what they needed for their new futures: cash, lumber, and carpentry tools. Gibbs packed merchandise for a new emporium. Ironically, California was purging Blacks from the state.

The first group of Black settlers on the *Commodore* made landfall in Victoria five days later, along with impatient miners bound for the Fraser River, who were scrambling for tools and to wagons or mules to carry them to the new gold strike. The emigrants from California called themselves the "Black Pioneer Club," rented a room from a local carpenter, and on that hopeful if daunting Sabbath night, they prayed.[34]

Over the next two weeks, about eight hundred more African American refugees joined the mass exodus from California to British Columbia. Many, wrote Douglas, came to earn enough money to purchase their enslaved family members.[35]

African Americans abandoned their new homes and churches in California. The enslaved Blacks headed north, following a trail of safe houses and ranches. Some trekked on foot, aware that they were surrounded by the U.S. military and vigilantes who were slaughtering Indians and kidnapping Native women and children. "All this puts one in mind of the Pilgrims . . . when those adventurers embarked for their new homes across the seas," wrote the San Francisco *Daily Evening Bulletin*. "When the colored people get their 'poet,' he will no doubt sing of these scenes which are passing around us almost unheeded, and the day when colored people fled persecution in California may yet be celebrated in story."[36]

Before the next group of Blacks sailed from San Francisco, they published "A Declaration of the Sense of the Colored People Seventy-Five Years after the Declaration of Independence." In the midst of a mass exodus, the Black exiles declared independence from the United States: "Whereas we are fully convinced that the continued aim of the spirit and policy of

our Mother County is to oppress, degrade, and entrap us. We have therefore determined to seek an asylum in the land of strangers, from the oppression, prejudice, and relentless persecution that have pursued us for
more than two centuries in this, our mother country." They had lost friend-
ships and land; they had been compelled to abandon "ties" that "bind mankind to the places of their nativity." With this, they marked the assaults
they faced, and they bitterly pointed to their exclusion from nationhood.
Then they agreed to work for an antislavery future: "We pledge our self to
this cause and will make every effort to redeem our race from the yoke of
American oppression." In farewell, "after the toil and hardships that have
wrung our sweat and tears for centuries," they cast their lots "in that land
where bleeding humanity finds a balm . . . where slavery has laid aside its
weapons, and the colored American is unshackled."[37] Six years before the
Thirteenth Amendment, they declared independence from the United
States and freed themselves.

In 1858 Sylvia Stark, born into slavery in Missouri, was living in the
foothills of the Sierra Nevada. As she watched the trials of Archy Lee unfold, she feared that she would not be allowed to testify that her father,
Howard, had purchased the family's freedom. The Fugitive Slave Act could
return her family to bondage.

Sylvia Stark and her children decided to sail from the San Francisco
wharf to Steilacoom, near the border of British Columbia. Louis Stark had
gone on ahead, joining a historic cattle drive of Black California ranchers
who drove their cattle one thousand miles to British Columbia. In this
risky venture, they slowly moved their cattle north through Oregon, where
for fourteen years Blacks had been banned from entering the state. African
Americans likely knew that free Blacks would be put up "publicly for hire"
to any white person who swore to remove them from the territory. In
1857, the year before the exodus, 89 percent of the white residents of Oregon had voted for a constitution that would exclude Black and mixed-race
people from the state.[38] The Stark family reunited at the border town and
continued together to Victoria—abandoning the California ranch they once
believed could be their freedom home.[39]

By the late summer of 1858, several hundred African Americans—
about one-eighth of the free Black community of six thousand—had fled
from California to British Columbia. Mifflin Wistar Gibbs and Peter
Lester opened a new emporium in Vancouver, selling supplies to Black
settlers and to the new miners, and they prospered. Many Black émigrés
from California settled on Salt Spring Island just off the coast of Vancou-

ver. Here the Starks bought Indian land from the government and moved onto the traditional hunting lands of the Cowichan and Chemainus First People.

After the swift exodus from San Francisco, Archy Lee settled in Victoria, British Columbia, and took a job making pickets for fences.[40] Mifflin Wistar Gibbs prospered as a merchant and railroad magnate, and in 1866 he was elected to the Victoria City Council, becoming the second Black official elected in Canada. After the war, Gibbs returned to the United States and studied law at Oberlin College in Ohio. He settled in Little Rock, Arkansas, and in 1873 was elected as a municipal judge, the first Black to be elected as a judge in the United States.[41]

Freedom: The Right to Speak Truth to Power

Many African American men in California enlisted in the Union Army. Once the Civil War began, Blacks again gathered signatures and signed petitions asking California to repeal the ban on Black testimony—in civil actions by persons of "one-half or more of Negro blood" and in criminal actions by persons of "one-eighth or more" of "Negro ancestry." This time the petition excluded the Chinese—those of a race "having an idolatrous religion." But this time, they reminded the legislature that the slave trade in Africans had ended in 1808; Blacks in California had been born in the United States. And all were legally free. The ban on testimony by "descendants of Africans" began "incident to slavery"; now, as Americans, they demanded it should end.[42]

In 1860 power was shifting in the West; the new Republican Party won control of the state legislature with a tepid call for "the complete withdrawal of support of slavery by the federal government, without disturbing that institution as it exists in the present slave states." The next year, however, twenty-four California Republicans joined fifty-four Democrats to require the state to comply with the Fugitive Slave Act and to allow slavery to endure in existing slave states and the District of Columbia. Governor Leland Stanford argued that "the settlement among us of an inferior race is to be discouraged by every legitimate means" and damned "the fanatical spirit of abolition" because, he said, it would inexorably lead to the slaughter of white men.[43]

In 1862, the second year of the Civil War, the ban on Black testimony lapsed, although Stanford and his successor, Frederick Low, continued to support the drive to purge Blacks from the state. In 1862 the Republican-controlled California State Senate cast only one vote to approve emancipation and arm southern Blacks who were fleeing to the Union Army.[44]

As the blood-soaked war dragged on, across the country abolitionists were pushing Republicans to define the Civil War as a struggle against slavery rather than a struggle against secession. The Black *Pacific Appeal* wrote that slavery still "had its fangs" in the Democratic Party in California and "women-whippers . . . Northern demagogues and Eastern doughboys" still endorsed slavery.[45] In 1862 the California State Senate voted fifteen to thirteen to keep the ban on Black testimony. The San Francisco *Morning Call*, a Republican paper, asked, "Is the antipathy to color so rooted" that it produced this "shameful vote?"[46]

The new year, 1863, began with the Emancipation Proclamation, but even the Republican members of the state legislature endorsed it only as a "military necessity." Black journalist Peter Anderson wrote in the *Pacific Appeal*: "The day is not far distant when we shall enjoy all the rights of free men." But if the state continued to deny African Americans the right to testify, all white Californians were "aiders and abettors of Slavery."[47] Only in the midst of the Civil War did the state repeal the law that barred African Americans from testifying in court against a white person. The legislature continued the ban on testimony by all "Mongolians, Chinese, Indians, or persons of one-half or more of Indian blood."[48]

The California Colored Conventions had brought together hundreds of African Americans who had come to California, free and enslaved. This first Civil Rights movement in California protested the ban on Black testimony, votes, the right to hold property, and school integration. Blacks published their minutes, hymns, and sermons and three newspapers—the *Mirror of the Times*, the *Pacific Appeal*, and the *Elevator*—and gathered eight thousand signatures that testified to the antislavery struggle in California and the right of an African American in California to be a witness.[49] "Witness": an observation, a person, a religious moment, a legal transaction, a right.

With the end of the Civil War, some Black Americans returned from British Columbia to search for their free but scattered families. Blacks in California tried to find their relatives in the South, but many had been violently dispersed by slave sales, flight into the Union Army, or the chaotic displacements of a war fought mainly in the South. Like Jews looking for their families after the Holocaust or families wandering through hospitals after the terrorist attacks of 9/11, in June 1865 George Dennis posted an ad in the Black California newspapers the *Elevator* and the *Anglo African*, looking for his lost brothers:

Information Wanted
OF ANDREW DENNIS AND RICHARD DEN-
NIS, generally called Dick. When last heard
from, some six years ago, they resided in Cowiche
County, Georgia.

It is supposed they joined the Union army.

Their mother, brother, George W. Dennis, and
Sister, Cordelia, are residing in San Francisco, and
Wish information respecting them.

Direct to P. A. BELL, office of the Elevator.

Anglo African will please copy six months,
and send bill to this office.[50]

Redress

Ninety-two years before Rosa Parks refused to give up her seat in the "whites only" section of a public bus in Montgomery, Alabama, there was Charlotte Brown.

On April 17, 1863, Charlotte Brown, a nineteen-year-old free Black woman, took a seat in a tram reserved for white people. For four months, the Omnibus Railroad Company had been running new horse-pulled trams along tracks that linked neighborhoods on the steep hills of San Francisco. In the early evening, just after the streetlamps were lit, testified Brown, "I started from home for the purpose of visiting my physician on Howard St. On going down Filbert, one of the cars came along and the driver hailed me by giving me a signal of raising his hand. I returned the signal, the car stopped, and I got in."[51]

Brown chose a seat midway in the nearly empty tram and traveled for a few blocks. On that spring evening, only three other riders were in the car, which could hold forty passengers. She remembered: "Between Union and Greene, the conductor went around to collect tickets and when he came to me, I handed him my ticket and he refused to take it." She told the conductor that she had been "in the habit of riding ever since the cars had been running," and had bought her ticket on the way home from church the Sunday before. She said that the man replied, "'Colored persons are not allowed to ride' and I would have to get out."

Brown objected to his order. She said, "I had a great ways to go and I was later than I ought to be," and she refused to get off the tram. Suddenly, the conductor "pulled the strap" and the driver stopped the tram. Brown again refused to leave her seat. At each stop, the conductor ordered her off, and at each stop she remained, reminding the conductor that the "car was a public conveyance." She ignored his command to "step off" and repeated, "Positively I would not get out." At the corner of Pacific and Jackson streets, she reported, the conductor "took hold of me. I then asked him if he intended to put me out and he said 'yes.'" Again, the conductor "took hold of me, by the left arm. . . . I made no resistance as he had taken me by the arm. I knew it was of no use to resist. . . . He kept hold of me until I was out of the car, holding on to me until I struck the walk." Bruised and humiliated, Brown turned to the conductor and made a historic statement: "I said I would seek redress."[52]

In November 1863, in the middle of the Civil War, Brown sued the Omnibus Railroad Company for $200 in the Twelfth Circuit Court, and a jury trial followed. The conductor testified that, indeed, he had allowed her to board the car. Brown had draped her face in a long mourning veil to hide her race; the conductor did not realize that she was Black until a white female complained about sharing the car with a colored woman. Omnibus Railroad's superintendent summed up the company's policy: "If any colored persons got on the car, and objections were made to them, to ask them to go off civil, and if they did not, put them off." Judge Samuel Cowles instructed the jury that the company could only exclude a passenger who "misbehaved." Was Brown's act of civil disobedience "misbehavior"?[53]

When the jury returned with its verdict, the foreman announced that they had ruled in favor of Brown. A Black woman, they decided, had the right to take public transportation, and they awarded her six cents—the cost of her ticket; they denied her demand for damages. Then Judge Cowles made a historic ruling: "Those white folks who are so fastidious that they cannot ride in a car 25 or 20 feet long when a negro is in it . . . must go on foot or in his own carriage."[54] The San Francisco *Daily Evening Bulletin* reported that the trams would only stay integrated until the company built separate cars for Black riders.[55]

Today, in a thin file in the vaults of the California Historical Society, there is a scrap of brown paper with a note written in thick black pencil by Charlotte Brown's father, James Brown. James Brown had been enslaved. His wife, seamstress Charlotte Brown, Sr., had purchased his freedom in Maryland just before they crossed the country to California. In San Francisco, James Brown bought a stable and used the profits to help publish the first African American newspaper in California, *Mirror of the Times*.[56]

In 1863, three months after the city celebrated the Emancipation Proclamation and a few days after his daughter's verdict, Brown jotted down, "I purchased that ticket on the Friday before the conductor of same car, No 4. Paid [one] dollar got 1/4 back and three tickets."[57] As a journalist and experienced abolitionist, Brown was likely aware that this torn piece of paper would become part of a court record, evidence that Charlotte had a legal ticket.

Five years before the country promised equal protection under the law and guaranteed access to the courts in the Fourteenth Amendment, Charlotte Brown and her father decided that she would again ride the tram to challenge the law against integration on the new San Francisco Omnibus. He bought two tickets: "Rode without objection," he noted. He bought two more tickets; again Charlotte boarded a tram and again she was thrown off. This time Charlotte Brown sued for $5,000 and testified on her own behalf: "Twice the cars started and I rode without objection." She stated that although no white passenger complained, "the conductor of car No. 3 objected and forced [me from] that car."[58]

In October 1864, Judge Orville C. Pratt of the Twelfth District Court ruled that the tram company had no grounds to refuse to transport Charlotte Brown: she did not have a contagious disease, was not "shockingly filthy," and had not refused to pay the fare. Then Pratt talked about slavery in California: "It has been quite too long tolerated by the dominant race to see with indifference the Negro or mulatto treated as a brute, insulted, wronged, enslaved, made to wear a yoke, to tremble before white men, to serve him as a tool, to hold property and life at his will, to surrender to him his intellect and conscience, and to seal his lips and belie his thought through dread of the white man's power."[59]

In order to avoid further damages, the Omnibus Railroad Company notified Charlotte Brown that it had rescinded its order to "exclude colored persons from their cars." In 1866 she accepted a settlement for $500, and the judge denied Omnibus a retrial.[60] The *San Jose Mercury* pointed to the hypocrisy of "the person who would object to riding in the same car with a respectable, well-dressed woman, and yet who would not object to having that woman as a servant in their families, to cook their food, or to fondle and take care of their children."[61]

Charlotte Brown prevailed because she used her right to testify about the injustice shown to her by a tram company.[62] As with other civil rights victories, this battle had to be fought over and over again. In 1866 Mary Ellen Pleasant brought a lawsuit against the North Beach and Mission

"'The Effect of Judge Pratt's decision.' Poor Charlotte Brown. . . . She said that her sensitive feelings were hurt to the amount of $5,000 by being led out of the car by the conductor, and a jury only gave her $500. . . . Judge Pratt is very partial to n****** . . . the darker the complexion the better. . . . You Charlotte are a real n*****, are you not, Charlotte? You did not use burnd cork for the purpose of gaining your point, did you?" wrote the San Francisco *Daily Evening Bulletin*, November 14, 1863.
In Quintard Taylor and Shirley Moore,
African American Women Confront the West 1600–2000
(Norman: University of Oklahoma Press), 81.

Railroad Company for refusing to pick her up, and she finally won her case in the California Supreme Court. Segregation on the streetcars was now illegal in California.[63]

Contested Freedom

In 1868 the California legislature refused to ratify the Fourteenth Amendment; it feared the racial equality foretold by the victory of the North in

Edward West Parker, the first African
American to vote in California.
Safero.org.

the Civil War, Charlotte Brown's legal triumph, and the possibility of Black
and Chinese suffrage. The Fourteenth Amendment prohibited states from
depriving any *person*—not just any citizen—of due process and equal protection under the law. Two years later the Civil Rights Act of 1870 banned
racial discrimination in taxes and in the courts that targeted specific groups,
such as the poll tax or the Foreign Miners' Tax. California bowed to the
Fourteenth Amendment, and in 1872 finally removed all bans on testimony by African Americans, Native Americans, and Chinese Americans.

The Democratic state supreme court managed to defer the protection for another year.[64]

Edward West Parker was born into slavery in Virginia and escaped to San Francisco during the Civil War. He opened a boot-making business on Third Street and thrived. In October 1865, at the end of the Civil War, Parker traveled to Sacramento for the fourth California State Convention of Colored Citizens.

Abolition in California had been won on the battlefields. The delegates resolved that Blacks now had "a new love for the American Union" and "rejoice[d] in the 'overthrow of slavery [and] the freedom of our race.'" They had "saved the government from destruction and sacrificed hundreds and thousands of their lives." California's constitution, they recalled, "decreed that no bondsman ever should be held by legal enactment within her limits"—that is, it banned slavery in the state. After 250 years of bondage, the delegates to the fourth California Colored Convention declared, "Negros have reared a nation." As citizens, the Black people of California, legally free under the Thirteenth Amendment, demanded that the union and the state grant Black people the "right of elective franchise"—the vote.[65]

The Republicans in the California legislature refused to support the Fifteenth Amendment until it was already ratified and part of the U.S. Constitution in 1870. Although the right to vote was the law of the land, California waited until 1962 to ratify the Fifteenth Amendment to the U.S. Constitution.[66] On April 15, 1870, Edward West Parker, Sr., age fifty-four, registered to vote, the first day African American men were allowed at the polls in California.[67]

CHAPTER ELEVEN

The Importation
of Females in Bulk

A green mansion is a place of filth and shame

Of lost chastity and lost virtue

Most repulsive is it to kiss the customers on the lips

And let them fondle every part of my body

I hesitate, I resist

All the more ashamed, beyond words.

I must by all means leave this troupe of flowers and rouge

Find a nice man and follow him as his woman.

—ANONYMOUS, *Songs of Gold Mountain: Cantonese Rhymes from San Francisco Chinatown*

IN 1886, IN GUANGZHOU (Canton), a port city on the southern coast of China, a broker paid 1,205 yuan ($524 today) to purchase Xin Jin, a little girl eight to ten years old. To avoid being arrested for buying a child, he handed the money to the girl and she, in turn, presented it to her father. The price included her steamship ticket to San Francisco. The broker then handed Xin Jin a contract, likely one that she was unable to read, but she marked it with an "X." With her "X," Xin Jin promised to "prostitute my body for the term of four and one-half years and receive no wages. If, in that time, I am sick one day, two weeks shall be added to my time; and if more than one day, my term of prostitution shall continue an additional month. But if I run away from the custody of my keeper, then I am to be held as a slave for life." Xin Jin also agreed that if she were to become ill with one of "the four loathsome diseases," her "procurer" had the right to return her. Illness included her days of menstruation. In fact, Xin Jin would probably die from syphilis or abuse before her contract expired.[1] Often Chinese girls marked their contracts with a thumbprint, sometimes in blood.

Almost forty years after California banned slavery in its constitution, Xin Jin was shipped to San Francisco to begin her life as an enslaved prostitute. Xin Jin had become a *baak haak chai*—a "wife of one hundred men"—or, more cynically, a *lougeui*—"a woman always holding her legs up."[2]

In 1849 sailing vessels carried the news to the shores of South America, Australia, and East Asia that gold had been discovered in California. Ship captains altered their routes to pick up adventurous Chinese men who had rushed to the port cities in southern China and paid $1,900 to $3,600 in today's money for tickets to sail to California—in the same ships that carried more and more girls like Xin Jin, conscripted to sexually service the miners.[3]

In the nineteenth century, the Chinese called these young migrant women "go-away girls." During eras of war and famine, destitute families sold young girls to brokers; at times they resorted to infanticide. In the city of Chaozhou, baskets were fastened to the city wall where impoverished families could deposit a newborn girl; anyone could take her and, as she grew up, work her as they liked.[4] Local traffickers working for Chinese merchants in San Francisco lured, snatched, or purchased girls off the streets of Canton for the California market, posting the prices they would pay for female children. During these dire years, families with as many as eight or ten children might depend for their survival on the sale of one prostituted girl.[5]

These girls were *mui tsai*—prostitutes, bond servants, or concubines—oftentimes translated as "little sister" or, in the census, "daughter." In this system of selling Chinese girls, impoverished parents sold a girl who would move to her husband's or owner's house, often to be overworked by her mother-in-law and sexually available to her master and his sons. During the Taiping Rebellion (1850–64)—a civil war over political turf and millennial visions of the future—millions of Chinese died or were starving, and by

1867 hundreds of thousands of refugees were moving across the country-side, creating another pool of vulnerable women and girls. Twenty thousand kidnapped women were marked for sale.

Before a kidnapped girl in China could board a ship bound for San Francisco, the American consulate in Hong Kong had to attest to her character as neither "lewd nor debouched [*sic*]." In 1879 U.S. Consul General David H. Bailey in Hong Kong personally took ten to fifteen dollars (about $390 today) for each woman he accepted. Then he stamped her arms and sent her on to the harbormaster, who questioned her again and permitted the broker to purchase her ticket. During the 1860s and 1870s, Chinese syndicates in the port towns of China held as many as eight hundred girls from ages two to sixteen years old at any one time, ready to ship to the United States.[6]

Kidnapped girls were held at the docks in Canton or in dank boarding-houses at the ports until they became human cargo to be shipped steerage class for a thirty-day passage across the Pacific.[7] In 1869 the San Francisco *Daily Evening Bulletin* reported that every steamer from China carried slave girls by the hundreds.[8] Between 1860 and 1874 the Pacific Mail Steamship Company carried some 125,000 Chinese migrants across the Pacific, receiving a revenue of $5.8 million just from steerage fares.[9] On board the largest steamships ever built, agents for the shipping company rehearsed the girls in how to answer U.S. customs inspectors about their prospects in America.[10]

Once under sail, many girls bound for California leaped overboard when they were brought up from the hold to be washed down. Others jumped off the deck into the choppy water as soon as the ship docked in San Francisco. Others died from contagion spread on board or by assault by guards, sailors, and other male passengers. Despite the contracts that limited their years of servitude in California, Chinese girls would never have the freedom or funds to board that ship to return home.

The *San Francisco Chronicle* called the trade "the importation of females in bulk" because each steamer arrived with "consignments of women, destined to be placed in the 'markets.'"[11] At the dock, porters carried some of the Chinese girls off the ships in heavily padded crates, billed as freight. Other girls walked down the gangplank guarded by the ship's captain, who handed them over to their new owner. Sometimes a trader was waiting in a "brothel wagon" that was surrounded by men trying to grab the women who were being carted to slave "dens." Here they would be sold to brothels in Chinatown.

Wagonloads of Chinese women leave the dock in San Francisco, exposing
the vulnerability of the enslaved prostitutes and the collusion of the San
Francisco Police, Chinese merchants, and Chinese working-class men.

In "Arrival of Shipload of Chinese Women at San Francisco Leaving
from the Dock in Express Wagons," *Frank Leslie's Illustrated
Newspaper*, April 10, 1869, via Internet Archive.

Rumors of the profits in Chinese girls matched rumors of the profits
in gold. During the 1850s and 1860s, Chinese girls were taken by criminal
syndicates who auctioned them on the docks of San Francisco. Under the
watch of corrupt police officers, a Chinese trafficker was paid about forty
dollars (about $1,250 today) for each girl he delivered and fifty dollars for
the cost of her ocean passage.[12] Girls who did not get sold at the piers were
taken to warehouses or slave dens where they were displayed for sale, naked.

Earnings from the sex trade helped create California's first class of
Chinese elite merchants who formed six *huiguan*, or Chinese Six Companies, societies from the same locale or clan.[13] The powerful companies
provided loans, ship tickets, housing, and jobs; they paid off customs inspectors and dock workers. Operating outside a legal system that banned

Chinese testimony, they provided protection and settled disputes. The companies ran the urban brothels.

As the merchants sought respectability over time, in the 1870s two syndicates of organized crime, the Suey Sing Tong and the Hip Yee Tong, were competing for control of the trade in women in San Francisco. At the height of its reign of terror, the Hip Yee Tong imported six thousand Chinese prostitutes, or almost 90 percent of the Chinese women in California. The tong charged a pimp a forty-dollar fee for each girl's protection and ten dollars for a kickback to the San Francisco Police. In the twenty years between 1852 and 1873, the Hip Yee Tong made over $5 million in today's value from the flesh trade in Chinese girls and women. If a girl escaped, Hip Yee hired "hatchet men" to find her and either return her to her owner or execute her.[14]

The selling of Chinese girls was open and brazen. After being locked belowdecks for a grueling sea voyage and passing through demeaning customs' inspections, the girls were taken to the "Queen's Room," an apartment on Dupont Street, a well-known slave market. Here traders sought to calm terrified naked girls by promising that now they would meet husbands.[15] The unfree girls wore layers of clothing, with coats and undergarments lined with opium; they had become opportune mules in the drug trade.

Like slave markets in the U.S. South, in the Queen's Room and other dens, slave dealers, speculators, brothel keepers, individual men, and "highbinders" mauled and inspected the girls and then made their bids. Girls designated for rural towns would climb into wagons with strangers for a ride that could be hundreds of miles along the twisting Coastal Range to new cities or into the raw Gold Rush camps in the foothills of the Sierra Nevada. Some landed in hidden coves up and down the Pacific Coast and were handed off to brokers or new owners waiting on the deserted beaches. Others still were sent up the coast on mail boats to the Chinatown in Eureka, a Northern California logging town on Humboldt Bay, where they would service woodcutters who had come west to fell the giant redwood trees for the construction boom in the new cities.

There are two stories of Chinese migration to California: the man's story and the woman's story. Adult male Chinese laborers have been called "coolies," "indentured," "impressed," "contract laborers," "trafficked," "bound," "involuntary," "unfree," or "enslaved." To some, the men's labor was part of a global vision of Chinese American unity—for commerce or conversion. Others, like Presbyterian minister William Speer, imagined a population of low-paid diligent workers. A few sought to adapt the "coolie" system that was supplying voluntary Chinese laborers through five-year contracts to work on the sugar plantations in the Caribbean at a sparse wage of fifty dollars per year, only to find themselves in debt, facing fines and imprisonment at forced labor.

American terms for Chinese laborers, then and now, muddy the image of their work. In a few decades, California slid from a post-medieval world of monasteries and encampments to a swirling state where agriculture, mining, commerce, and industry swiftly grew amid distinct ecologies, national identities, and class expectations—usually with deeply inaccurate assumptions of racial difference. Here expectations about Chinese laborers slipped between dreams for an economic ecology of an unpaid workforce, an unbalanced population of men and women, and dissimilar traditions of gender. In the new Chinatowns, where families lived above restaurants and shops, where Confucian, Daoist, and Buddhist shared temples, where Chinese opera and gambling dens thrived, the lives of Chinese migrants outgrew the early expectations. Labels that described Chinese immigrants in California imploded. Chinese women were unfree, indentured, impressed, or trafficked; sojourners and settlers; Chinese and Chinese American. The lived history of Chinese women in California defeats stereotypes about Asian American docility and endurance.

Framed by the California Indian genocide (1850–63) that slaughtered a potential workforce, and the Civil War (1861–65) that seemingly brought chattel slavery to an end, the new state turned to unpaid or low-paid Chinese immigrants. In the midst of struggles for freedom in an era of invasion and expansion—Indians on the run from forced indentures, African Americans on the run from the Fugitive Slave Acts—in 1852 the new California State Senate barely rejected two pieces of legislation that would have legalized "coolie" labor, five- or ten-year "contracts" at a lowly wage of fifty dollars per year.[16]

By the end of the Gold Rush, Chinese migrants were working for new mining cartels, lugging heavy hydraulic hoses to wash away gravel riverbeds to expose the ore and quartz beneath the surface. Although white settlers referred to Chinese men as "coolies"—a Hindi term from the British empire for day laborers or slaves—in California they were free to work for wages and quit when they wanted, as long as they paid their debt to the merchants who financed their transport and tools.

Few if any coolies arrived in California. Few Chinese men were captured and transported to work on the railroad. Indeed, on June 29, 1867, two thousand Chinese laborers on the Central Pacific Railroad went on strike. The Chinese men working on the railroad were one of the most visible signs that Chinese men were wage laborers.[17]

On May 10, 1869, ten thousand free Chinese railroad workers finished the Transcontinental Railroad and came down from the Sierras. They had been recruited and transported to blast tunnels through the Sierra Nevada and lay track on the western end of the line, from California to Utah. For several years they had lived in ice caves, blasting the frozen ground, granite walls, and forty-foot snowdrifts of the Sierra Nevada, readying the "beds" for the iron wheels that would cross under its peaks.

When the railroad was finished, most of the Chinese men stayed in California. Still in debt for their journey to California, they opened brothels in shacks and railroad cars and started restaurants and shops in the Sierra Mountains, in Sacramento, Marysville, Stockton, and San Francisco. They built gambling tents and laundered miners' mud-caked shirts. The powerful Chinese Six Companies made a deal with the Pacific Mail Steamship Company not to allow a Chinese man to sail home unless they stamped his ticket to prove that he had paid all his debts. That stamp alone cost the miner between twenty-five and fifty dollars, to be paid to the company that was likely the underwriter for his transportation, tent, and tools.[18]

Importing the Moral Evil

Enslaved Chinese girls arrived alongside their free Chinese countrymen: merchants and miners, laborers and railroad workers, and soon, actors, opera singers, and Buddhist and Taoist priests. All would build Chinatowns— segregated enclaves in the new towns of California. And they sought Chinese women. A decade after the Thirteenth Amendment abolished slavery, the California census often listed a single Chinese man residing with several "daughters."

California hoped to purge foreign competitors in the goldfields. In 1850 the state's first legislature passed an exorbitant foreign miners' tax that forced miners from Mexico, Chile, Argentina, and China to pay the state a monthly fee—an impossible tax that floated between three and twenty dollars per month (about $400 today).[19] Anti-Chinese sentiment drenched the state; vigilantes brandishing revolvers and whips rode along the creeks, rounding up and assaulting miners from Latin America and China, demanding the tax. Most Chileans and other Latin American miners returned home.[20]

By the end of the 1850s, $15 billion worth of gold in today's money had been mined in California. The ore, however, was untaxed, a staggering giveaway of finite resources removed from Native land. Instead, funding for the new state fell on Chinese miners who paid an astounding $58 million in the Foreign Miners' Tax. Between 1852 and 1870, this tax produced one-fourth to one-half of the state's revenue.[21]

The image of the exotic, willing, and hypersexual young "Oriental" girl and "coolie" man provoked U.S. Supreme Court Chief Justice Roger Taney to rule that California could expel Chinese miners because they "were likely to produce physical or moral evil among its citizens."[22] In a state that had just vowed to "tolerate . . . neither slavery nor involuntary servitude," white, Latino, and Chinese men eagerly bought sexual services of enslaved Chinese prostitutes.

In 1866, just after the Civil War and the passage of the Thirteenth Amendment, Republicans in California passed the Act for the Suppression of Chinese Houses of Ill-Fame. The true target of the law was not slaveholders but enslaved women who could now be arrested and face six months in county jail as public nuisances for living in a brothel.[23] If a landlord was convicted of leasing a building for use as a brothel, he only had to forfeit that month's rent. A tenant found guilty of using a building for a Chinese brothel could be fined three times the value of the property. Any man who frequented a Chinese brothel could face jail time or fines—although this part of the law was rarely enforced.[24]

The enslaved Chinese prostitutes—not their owners or customers— became criminals. The San Francisco Police announced that they would arrest Chinese prostitutes until the "worst alleys" were cleared and mass detentions began.[25] In 1866 and 1867 alone, Judge Alfred Rix charged fifteen brothel owners and madams with running houses of Chinese prostitution. Surprisingly, Rix decided that the law unjustly favored prostitutes and brothel owners of "Caucasian origin" who, he said, were "protected in the prosecution of their wretched business at the expense of another."[26] San Francisco's Committee on Health declared that these Chinese roundups would not improve urban sanitation but would cause a "wholesale slaughter of Chinese prostitutes . . . guilty of no crime greater than those following the same business as those with white skins."[27]

Some Chinese prostitutes sought arrest as a way to escape the "cribs" and be returned to China. Others hired former state attorney general Frank Pixley, who accused the mayor and police of targeting the women for their race rather than for the danger they posed to public health. Pixley

argued that American, German, French, and Spanish prostitutes "flaunt
their full-blossomed vice" yet remained free. He demanded individual jury
trials for each Chinese woman he represented.[28]

Despite the hypocrisy, the sale of sex with Chinese girls and women
fed the roiling tide of ethnic cleansing in the streets, legislature, and courts.
Most towns forbade Chinese merchants from owning land, so they invested in females instead. In 1860, long after the peak of the Gold Rush,
six hundred of the 681 Chinese women in San Francisco were captives in
the sex trade. In rural towns, almost all of the Chinese women were prostitutes. For example, one hundred Chinese women lived in the mountain
town of Nevada City; the census listed ninety-four of them as "daughters,"
or prostitutes.[29] Nonetheless, the brothels supplied the only available Chinese women; Chinese men knew that without these Chinese women, there
would be few children, a small number of Chinese families, and a thin
lineage.

As part of attempts to brand Chinese migrants as eternally foreign,
Chinese men were marked as diseased, immoral, and perverse—addicted
to opium and willing to work for low wages. California wrote these divi-
sive images of inferiority into law; in 1855 it assessed a fifty-dollar fee on
each Chinese immigrant who was unable to become a "citizen of California" and ordered shipmasters to post $500 bonds for each Chinese passen-
ger. Although the U.S. Supreme Court ruled that these fees trespassed on
federal authority over immigration, it endorsed California's desire to "prevent and remove the evil"—the "evil" of dirt, suffering, disease, abuse, and
being enslaved.[30]

Schools, churches, and the halls of justice closed their doors to enslaved Chinese girls. Few could read and write. The bodies of Chinese
girls became urban combat zones. Their Chinese owners and customers—
miners, laborers, bankers, ship captains, and sailors—bribed the San Francisco police to ignore the prostitutes, while Protestant ministers and white
merchants pressured the city to move the caged shanties away from tourists and shoppers. Marking the girls as signs of urban "degradations and
vice," rather than as evidence of slavery, businessmen and city councilmen
demanded that Chinese pimps hide the captive Chinese girls from white
women and children who passed by on streetcars.[31] During the Civil War
to end slavery, Chinese merchants and pimps paid from $200 to $500 to
buy a Chinese girl who would pass her life in a so-called "green mansion,"
or Chinese brothel—a place of filth and shame.[32]

As early as 1854, San Franciscans were able to witness the police round

Chinese girls, kidnapped from the southern coast of Guangdong,
were carted to Gold Rush towns in the foothills of the Sierras,
where they were sold to miners and new ranchers in slave dens.
(Peter Palmquist Collection, Courtesy of the Beinecke Rare Book
and Manuscript Library, Yale University Library, New Haven.)

up Chinese prostitutes. Within a decade, by 1865 the police chief was urging public health authorities to "herd" Chinese women beyond the town
limits where they would not "offend public decency."[33] The county jail was
quickly overcrowded with Chinese girls, and the police stashed them in the
old firehouse and the holding cell beneath City Hall, where there was not
enough floor space for each woman to lie down. Disease spread through
their forced confinement.[34]

The Burlingame Treaty of 1868 tightened the status of the enslaved
girls. The treaty granted "most favored nation" status to the United States
and China. Now, even the poorest Chinese migrant had the right to go
to court, file a lawsuit, and enjoy equal protection under the Constitution.
Written to promote trade between the two countries, the treaty made it a

penal offense for a citizen of the United States to force a Chinese subject—male or female—to move without her consent. However, by allowing an unfettered flow of migrants from China, the treaty increased the transport and sale of enslaved girls and women.

On January 9, 1863, two years into the Civil War, the Transcontinental Railroad broke ground on Front Street in Sacramento. With numbers rising from about twenty Chinese railroad workers in 1864 to about fifteen thousand at its completion in 1869, free Chinese laborers changed the demographics of Chinese people in the American West.[35] After Chinese railroad workers came down from the mountains, their distinctive broad-brim hats appeared in the vast orchards, citrus groves, and vegetable fields. Paid below-subsistence wages and living in tents, the Chinese worked in "squat" labor and spent their free time at the opera, in gambling dens, visiting temples, and going to brothels.[36] Brokers sold Chinese prostitutes in Marysville, Rocklin, Tacoma, and Los Angeles.

In 1870 about 60 percent of the 3,536 Chinese women in California were prostitutes. The Democratic Party, Workingmen's Party, and Anti-Coolie leagues—often in concert—turned to the Thirteenth Amendment as a way to ban Chinese prostitution and, hence, to ban thousands of new Chinese immigrants. For three decades the abolition of slavery became a rationale for roundups and pogroms in more than two hundred new towns across the West.

The blame for slavery in California now fell on the Chinese. In 1869 a placard appeared on the brick walls of San Francisco's Chinatown: "Chen Ha is searching for his sister, Ah Shau"; she had been kidnapped in China when bandits overran their village and took her to Macau, where for two days she resisted all efforts to "dishonor" her. Once broken in, she was shipped to San Francisco. Chen Ha pleaded with his countrymen to find his sister, for "who that has a sister would endure the thought of her being taken to a brothel?" Reverend A. W. Loomis reprinted the card in the *Overland Monthly* as evidence of "the Chinese sin." Chen Ha finally located his sister in a locked brothel in San Francisco and sued for her release, but his long effort to "return her to virtue" was for naught when the court handed her back to her procurer. The money to be made from Chen Ha's sister was worth the costs of litigation.[37]

"This form of bondage," wrote the San Francisco *Daily Evening Bulletin*, did not end with the Civil War. In 1873, in the dangerous "Slaughterhouse Cases," the U.S. Supreme Court gutted the protections of the Burlingame Treaty and the Thirteenth and Fourteenth amendments. The court held that the Fourteenth Amendment only protected formerly enslaved Blacks—not Chinese immigrants; states could choose to ignore its protections for "all persons."[38] California was free to override the antislavery protections won in the Civil War. In 1874 the courts upheld the Chinese merchants' right to possess the girls, and police returned runaway prostitutes to their "rightful owner."[39] Sometimes the girls fled, only to become trapped in shirt-waist factories, early sweatshops that often served as a front for a brothel or slave den.[40]

The nation wrote its contempt for Chinese women into the Page Act of 1875, the country's first ban on immigrants. Prompted by journalists' hype of enslaved and diseased Chinese women, the act banned the entry and "importation" of "lewd and debauched . . . Mongolian women . . . for the purposes of prostitution." The act said that "a country that had only recently fought a great Civil War to rid itself of slavery should not allow itself to be inundated with the Chinese." Chinese "polygamy and prostitution and so-called coolie labor . . . were the work of a slave-like, inferior people." Alluding to slave contracts marked by illiterate Chinese girls, the Page Act prevented anyone who came for a fixed "term of service" from entering the United States.[41] California followed with a series of "Passenger Acts" and "Anti-Kidnapping Acts" that imposed extra fees on ships' captains who transported the captive girls.[42]

The Page Act only targeted women. Chinese men could still enter the United States, but Chinese women could only legally come as spouses through "family migration."[43] Of the 320,000 Chinese people who had entered the United States between 1850 and 1880, fewer than 5 percent were unfree prostitutes.[44] How would the act's ban on Chinese women override the market for sex slaves? For the Chinese, California remained a bachelor society that coiled racism around homophobic stereotypes of short Chinese men with long braids, dressed in silk gowns.[45]

Up through 1877, the Hip Yee Tong bribed City Hall to keep investigators out of Chinatown. That year, the city of San Francisco hired a special police force to extort fees from prostitutes, brothel owners, and men searching for runaway girls. Each Chinese prostitute paid fifty cents a week to the "Chinatown Specials," the other name for this special police force.[46] In small towns, placards promised reward money for runaway Chinese women.[47] When the legislature sought to allow the commissioner of immigration to prevent these "lewd and debauched" women from coming ashore, Hip Yee and the Chinese merchants simply paid larger bribes to U.S. consular offices in China or to customs officials in San Francisco.[48] If a sheriff or police officer found a runaway, her madam or pimp paid reward money for her return.

The Market in Chinese Women

Brokers, pimps, and Chinese merchants marketed enslaved Chinese women as passive, eternally prepubescent, and hypererotic. During the long era of forced prostitution, the American middle classes were importing Asian objects—costly or cheaply reproduced objects such as fans, screens, porcelains, and silks—with a tempting aura of luxury and decadence that could be owned and consumed. The Chinese woman was also a desirable object, available for investment, invasion, and sale. In the myth-making that was the American origin story, the United States, and California in particular, represented the dynamic, adult, expansive, energetic, and masculine West, and China was the static, childlike, and feminine East—a fable that never fit the era's fearful myth of Chinese "hordes" invading the Pacific Coast. White missionaries in California lamented the "traffic in women": if the "inferior" Chinese race "mingled" with the "superior" white race, moral degeneration would follow. Christian "godliness" affirmed ethnic purity and rumors that Chinese girls were bringing in leprosy.[49]

The price of mui tsai was climbing. During these decades, a procurer paid a mother in China ninety-eight dollars for her daughter and sold the unnamed girl in San Francisco for $1,950. For the next two years the girl brought in $290 per month; when he sold her for $2,100, he had taken in a gross income of $9,600 on the use of her body, or $203,687 in modern value.[50] In despair, many girls were tempted, and some were forced, to take opium to make them compliant; then the pimps used the girls' insurmountable drug debts to increase the duration of their service—sometimes unto death.[51]

Chinese prostitutes, wrote the *Sacramento Daily Union*, were "compelled by their degraded owners to submit to every pollution dictated by corrupt minds."[52] The girls were displayed in locked cages or exhibited behind barred windows facing commercial Jackson Street or Dupont Street in San Francisco. When a girl enticed a customer, her owner or madam—typically a merchant's wife—accepted the payment, drew the curtains, and unlocked the pen only long enough for a girl to service her customers, who might be white, Black, Mexican, or Chinese. The enslaved Chinese woman was only dangerous in the imagination. The highest price for sex was seventy-five cents—about half of a day's wages for a white laborer in

The popularized image of selling Chinese babies displaced
the vexed reality of the sale of Chinese women and girls
that endured after the Page Act of 1875, the Chinese
Exclusion Act of 1882, and the Geary Act of 1892.
This caption reads that the peddler "sells babies
as he would vegetables." Illustration in "Strange
Adventures of a Woman Missionary in China,"
San Francisco Call, February 6, 1898.
Center for Bibliographical Studies and Research,
University of California, Riverside.

San Francisco. A "lookee" pitched to the popular belief that a Chinese
woman's vaginal opening was horizontal rather than vertical. It cost between a dime and a quarter. (This titillating legend was "set to rest" for
"students of nature" by a journalist who undertook firsthand research
to determine that the "conformation is identical" in white and Chinese
women.)[53]

Leen Hoo died in the cellar of a brothel on Jackson Street in 1856
from an accidental overdose of mercury, an ineffective treatment for syphilis. The next year, when a Chinese prostitute in the mining town of Hor-
nitos refused to service a customer, her owner shot her.[54] Sing Ho, a young

A Chinese prostitute empties night waste in the
streets of Chinatown, San Francisco,
overseen by her owner.

Photo by Arnold Genthe. Library of Congress Prints and
Photographs Division, Washington, DC.

prostitute, escaped, jumped into a well, and drowned near the row of brothels on Jackson Street, in San Francisco. For whites who wanted to go slum-
ming, a lurid drug and sex tourism trade flourished in Chinatown. The
timid or prurient turned to guidebooks and street maps. Tour guides, often
off-duty detectives or police officers, offered sightseers "protection" as
they led them to restaurants, temples, and the Chinese theater. For a small
fee, the guide would break down a phony door in a Chinese slum and even
arrange for a visit to opium dens.[55] The emerging middle-class tourist was
a safe and salacious spectator to a cruel underworld of drugs, filth, and pornographic sets.[56]

Chinese madams, working for Chinese merchants, displayed young Chinese prostitutes in caged brothels on Jackson Street in downtown San Francisco. At times a girl was forced to display herself naked; other times she wore a turquoise ribbon or collar to signify her status as an available prostitute.
(Peter Palmquist Collection, Courtesy of the Beinecke Rare Book and Manuscript Library, Yale University Library, New Haven.)

**CHEONG SUE
CHINATOWN GUIDE**
Explains Chinese Rarities and Many Curiosities
                                        Visits the Opium Joints
   Parties wishing to see the sights in Chinatown will find me a capable and most reliable guide. By calling in person or sending postal to my address you will avoid imposition by irresponsible and incompetent people. Also takes visitors to Restaurants, Theaters, and Joss Houses. Send orders by Messenger or Postal
901 DUPONT ST   SAN FRANCISCO[57]

   The haze of opium wound around the enslaved girls, tethering together the white and Chinese communities without the taint of human bondage. In the Treaty of Nanking of 1842, a victorious Britain sought to balance its demand for Chinese tea and silk by forcing China to buy opium, a commodity grown in India, a British colony. In the mid-nineteenth century, opium, marketed under the name "laudanum" and sold as "a tincture" or medicinal extract, was a legal drug in the United States, advertised as an antidepressant in women's magazines. Yet the blame for this addiction fell on the Chinese. San Francisco's Board of Supervisors reported that Chinatown had twenty-six opium dens with 320 beds, for both white and Chinese addicts. White journalist Iza Hardy was taken to visit an opium den by a police guide, and she described a small, cramped space, "unlit, unventilated, very like the steerage cabin of an emigrant steamer, equally evil-odorous." Hardy even offered a recipe: "Take a pinch of the dark jelly-like substance on a wire and melt it over the lamp, then smear it over the aperture in the pipe, and draw it with great deep breaths into the lungs."[58] The titillating image was meant to mark the Chinese as passive and foul-smelling, lacking self-control of mind and body.

Journalist Eleanor Caldwell described Chinese men as "unhumanized beings, lolling in pale and imbecile torpor, or glaringly, gauntly resentful." What surprised tourists in these lairs littered with mattresses, rugs, and pipes were white women, drugged out and "asleep" on filthy coverlets and pillows. Another white visitor, E. W. Wood, came upon "the sons and daughters of the wealthiest and most refined families . . . laying on the filthiest covered bunks alongside cracked and broken layouts, smoking and sleeping their lives away."[59] For the Chinese prostitutes, however, opium offered a respite from pain and a path to debt slavery.

In 1860, 583 enslaved Chinese prostitutes lived in San Francisco—85 percent of the known female Chinese population in that city. Outside of San Francisco, nearly all the Chinese women were prostitutes. The few Chinese women who managed to survive their "contract" worked as domestic servants, cooks, laborers, seamstresses, and actors in the popular Chinese theaters. In 1870, only 137 of the Chinese women in San Francisco were housewives.[60]

Driven Out "in a Dignified Manner"

By the end of the 1850s, millions of dollars in California gold had traveled east, yet many of the miners—white, Latino, and Chinese—were broke. They abandoned their claims and drifted into San Francisco and Sacramento, and with their last monies sought out prostitutes—mostly Chinese,

When journalists and police raided opium dens in Chinatown,
they often discovered white women lying on beds or pallets,
smoking opium pipes and intoxicated by the powerful drug.
In I. W. Taber, "Album of Views of California and the West, Canada, and China."
BANC PIC 1999.055:05—fALB San Francisco's Chinatown, Bancroft Library,
University of California, Berkeley, via Online Archive of California.

Chilean, and white. In 1859 the chief of the San Francisco Police pleaded
with city officials to regulate this local trade of over five hundred Chinese
prostitutes and six hundred prostitutes of "other nationalities," if only "to
limit the injury done by it to society"—that is, the spread of syphilis, the
"loathsome disease." The city finally forced many brothels to move away
from the commercial thoroughfares of San Francisco or to close down.
Pimps and tongs shipped Chinese prostitutes to rural towns.[61] By banning
the legal immigration of Chinese women for work or for family, the Page
Act had encouraged the ongoing sexual slavery of hundreds more girls.

On Saturday, April 30, 1876, the town doctor in the coal and copper
town of Antioch announced that seven young "sons of respectable citizens"

were under his treatment for syphilis after having visited a Chinese house of prostitution.[62] The boys' fathers had taken their sons to a brothel to initiate them into sex. The *Antioch Ledger* reported that when the "respectable" parents heard their boys were infected with syphilis, forty residents marched to Antioch's Chinatown, built along the flood banks of the Sacramento River. They pounded on the doors of the "Chinese dens" or "green mansions"—wooden shacks along the riverbank—and warned each Chinese woman to leave town by three o'clock that afternoon "or trouble would ensue."[63]

The notion of impure Chinese female bodies infecting the bodies of white American boys provided a powerful mirror of the broader ethnic and racial "cleansing" that was taking place in California. No one in the press or pulpit raised the concern about the inevitable contagion that passed to white wives from white husbands who had taken their sons to a ritual and racialized sexual initiation.

The Chinese women of Antioch wrapped their clothing and bedding in scarves and baskets. They trudged to the pier, ahead of a growing mob. Rather than wait for the next steamer bound for San Francisco, the frightened group of about thirty women climbed aboard a fishing boat and set sail up the San Joaquin River toward Stockton. Also on board was the local Chinese contractor who likely owned several of the women. Likely many Chinese women had fled from the brothels in San Francisco and now faced a terrifying return to sexual slavery. Besides, some of the Chinese women who were forced to board the little boat were not in fact prostitutes. The town of 620 residents congratulated itself on driving out the Chinese prostitutes "in a dignified manner." The local newspaper reported that as the boat sailed off, the townspeople watched from the dock, grimly pleased.

The next afternoon, Sunday, May 1, word flew through Antioch that the Chinese women had turned the boat around and were back. The people of Antioch decided not to "disturb the serenity of the Sabbath." But at eight o'clock that evening Chinatown was ablaze. The fire department declined "to stay the progress of the fire fiend."[64] As the white townspeople of Antioch watched from the streets, all but two of the Chinese shops and houses by the water collapsed into ash.

Chased by vigilantes and flames, the remaining Chinese fled and paid twenty-five cents each for a ticket to board the next steamer bound for San Francisco. The local *Antioch Ledger* cheered, "Antioch is now free from this disreputable class."[65] The presence of the Chinese prostitutes had confirmed the infidelity of married Christian men, and their sons' infection with syphilis exposed the unspoken risk to the white wives. At the time, the facts of syphilis were tainted. In 1878, for instance, the *Medico-Literary Journal* warned that if Chinese nannies raised white children, or cooked, cleaned, and laundered in white homes, syphilis would spread to the entire household.[66] The cure was to round up and drive out Chinese women.[67]

Like other California towns, Antioch had passed a batch of racial codes to ensure the segregation, harassment, and, ultimately, expulsion of Chinese residents. Chinese people were forbidden to own land in the town. Ordinance Thirty-Three imposed a fine of one hundred dollars on any person caught watching an opium smoker, an amount equal to two months' salary for most white men. Antioch had passed a curfew requiring Chinese men to be off the streets by sunset or a town officer could cut off his "queue" or long braid, a style that harkened back to the Qing emperor and signaled a proud and shared Chinese masculine identity. It could be cut off—a symbol of castration. In the Western imagination, the queue was feminine, and also implied vulnerabilty.[68]

Purging the Body Politic

The sentiment against Chinese women was embedded in the racial purity sentiments of the era.[69] The presumption that Chinese women were "debauched" was tangled in sentiments that facilitated the massacres of Native Americans by marking them on a racial ladder as savage or not-yet civilized. On a rung up were the "semicivilized" Chinese—peoples of a once-great nation, stifled by centuries of despotism.[70] As California entered the national rush toward progress, industry, and Christianity, the Chinese— represented as passive and atrophied in a decaying past—were thought to be holding it back, unsuited to thrive on an equal basis in the aggressive West.

Terms such as "Yellow Peril," "Mongolian idiot," or "Asian cholera" (and more recently, "Asian flu" and the deadly "Chinese flu") used the body to designate the Chinese as dangerous and contaminating.[71] National identity seeped into racial identity. Defined through skin color, the "yellow race" was deemed incapable and unworthy of assimilation. Physical markers of difference—size, hairiness, eye shape, skin color, and body size—became cultural as well as physical markers of difference.

Defined by disease and bondage, the Chinese woman carried a scar that signified she was politically unworthy.[72] The 1875 Page Act turned to physiology and gender to subjugate the Chinese prostitute. At a time when white men and women transmitted the same venereal infections, the enslaved Chinese prostitute, like the women in Antioch, became propaganda for the surveillance and expulsion of all Chinese migrants.

The Chinese man could also be expelled. Equally troublesome, he could choose to leave with his dollars. Or he could send his wages home, removed from the U.S. economy. While forbidden by many towns to own land, the Chinese accumulated money and sent a constant stream of wages back to their villages and family in China. These funds repaid their loans and preserved their patriarchal roles as husband and father. In the short term, these "remittances," carried by trusted shippers or "water ghosts," bound migrants to their families and forestalled the destitution that would cause the further sale of sisters and daughters.

The Chinese were demeaned "sojourners"—people who moved back and forth. But their American funds, often used to buy land in China, never came back. Segregated into Chinatowns, degraded by stereotypes, and banned from holding many jobs, "sojourners" were reluctant to assimilate, averse to joining communities from which they were in actuality banned.[73] Few Chinese prostitutes, however, would return to China; few could send money home.

Perhaps the deepest source of racism stemmed not from perceptions of difference but from the sharp awareness of the commonality of lives of dirt, hunger, and disappointed dreams of working-class Chinese and whites. In the dire depressions of the 1870s, millions of white men and women across the country were living in tenements similar to the "Chinese dens" mocked and derided in editorials and cartoons. Immigrants from Ireland and Eastern Europe had arrived in a rapidly industrializing United States. The new "night shift" was pulling men and women from their homes and sending them into mills and factories. In California, the working-class household teetered precariously in a frontier culture. Perhaps white Californians deplored the Chinese because their lives looked so much like their own.

Meanwhile, the enslaved Chinese prostitute sat at the crossroads of profit, migration, criminality, and sexuality. A local San Francisco doctor wrote that the Chinese prostitute willfully distributed "germs of death to another better race."[74] Venereal disease was equated with race; pathology was equated with difference.[75] Health officials claimed that Chinese women did not exhibit traditional signs of contagion and inspected their naked bodies and "organs," starting with the eyes, and then probed "beneath the skin."

White women living in rural towns seized on the image of the Chinese prostitute to deflect from their own limited status and heighten their own condition as virtuous females. At the same time, widespread demands to end the slavery of Chinese women rose from an urgency to free women from captivity, serial rape, and exposure to disease.

Across the country, white women were leaving farms and kitchens to work in shops and mills; they were demanding increased pay, an eight-hour day, urban sanitation, and the vote. Sympathy for Chinese prostitutes arose from white women in the new industrial working class, some of whom were likely members of the first American working-class and interracial organization, the Knights of Labor. Meanwhile, California labor leaders blamed the high rate of unemployment in the 1870s on low-paid Chinese immigrants. On July 23, 1877, thousands of unemployed white farmhands, miners, mechanics, and shopkeepers gathered in front of San Francisco City Hall to support the Great Railroad Strike in the East. In a night of jubilant arson, and backed by the Democratic Party, six thousand men began to burn Chinatown and torch the docks of the Pacific Mail Steamship Company, the shipping firm that had transported Chinese men and women to California.

By early autumn, thousands of unemployed men had formed a workers' party under the banner of "anti-coolie" clubs. Denis Kearney, a young Irish American, led meetings of hundreds of unemployed men on vacant lots in front of the mansions of key industrialists Charles Crocker, Leland Stanford, and Mark Hopkins, who had imported Chinese workers to build the Transcontinental Railroad. Kearney always ended his speeches with the rousing chant: "The Chinese must go!"[76]

As Kearney's men raged against Chinese immigrants, white men continued to pay for sex with enslaved Chinese girls. But the trade in Chinese sexual labor was changing. Over time, pimps and madams had died or moved back to China, and some girls moved into fancy Chinese brothels marketed as private clubs furnished with Chinese silk, porcelain vases, and heavy mahogany. Meanwhile, aging prostitutes were relegated to the "cribs" or shacks where sex cost twenty-five to fifty cents.[77]

Whites were encouraged to assume the worst of Chinese immigrants. One member of Congress warned, "all Chinamen look alike, all dress alike, all have the same kind of eyes" and pressed the federal government to require each Chinese immigrant to provide three identical photos to match their face upon their arrival.[78] In the era of eugenics and phrenology, photographs were thought to identify criminal inclinations.[79] By the

Likely an advertisement or "card" of a young Chinese prostitute from
Humboldt County in Northern California, photographed in an unusual
studio portrait, 1886. Her languorous "Odalisque" pose and her exposed legs
are atypical for a photograph of an immigrant woman. Who posed her?
Who paid for this photo? Was it taken to advertise her? Why is she posed
with chrysanthemums, a Chinese image of purity? Was she reclaiming
innocence, or had her owner inserted the flowers to suggest her virginity?
Why would an impoverished girl have bound feet? She would
soon be purged from Humboldt County.

(Peter Palmquist Collection, Courtesy of the Beinecke Rare Book
and Manuscript Library, Yale University Library, New Haven.)

1870s Chinese immigrants feared that their photo-identity records, which
looked like prison mug shots, could be used against them. With the opening of Chinese photographic studios in San Francisco and access to inexpensive cameras, the Chinese took control of their own depiction. Like
everyone else, they learned to produce their own photographs, pose for
inexpensive studio shots, and mail their own images to their families in
China. Photographs of enslaved Chinese girls also appeared on "cards" or
advertisements.

In the summer of 1876, a special joint committee of the U.S. Congress followed a California State Senate investigation and arrived in San Francisco to examine Chinese immigration and enjoy three months in the fashionable Palace Hotel, away from the stagnant humidity of Washington, DC. The committee focused on syphilis—Chinese women's "pestilence" was a threat "to our own race." One-third of the dozens of witnesses were police officers. The committee also subpoenaed eighteen Chinese men, mostly merchants. Several doctors testified about syphilis in Chinese prostitutes and the threat to the morality and health of white laborers. One after the next declared that the willingness of Chinese men to accept low wages reduced the already pitiful wages of white domestic servants and factory girls. In fact, they even argued that these low wages had driven white women into prostitution.[80] No Chinese woman was allowed to testify before either committee.[81]

Chinese prostitutes, the doctors testified, threatened both white "boys of a tender age" and men who "come here without their families. Families are the center of all that is elevating in mankind."[82] Chinese prostitutes were threatening the white family that was emerging in the West.[83] And the slave labor of Chinese women "induces our laborers . . . to live like vermin."[84]

Dr. Hugh Huger Toland of the San Francisco Board of Health dominated the national press when he testified that he was seeing cases of a particularly virulent strain of syphilis in white boys as young as five who, he claimed, contracted it from Chinese prostitutes.[85] If the city would remove Chinese prostitutes entirely, Toland insisted, prosperity would come to the city's white working class and unemployed poor. Chinese women's bodies slid into one image of "the most abject and satanic conception of human slavery and the source of contamination and hereditary diseases."[86]

Physicians knew that they could do little to cure contagious diseases. The science of epidemiology awaited Louis Pasteur's germ theory in the 1880s.[87] For now, medical "diagnoses" intensified the lurid threat of the Chinese prostitute.[88] The Chinese female, believed to be racially disposed to immorality and "hygienic lassitude," was more diseased than other residents of California. By shifting the terms for racial difference from skin color to medical pathology, physicians reframed the science of contagion, and hence, the "science" of race and perils of integration.

Without medical care, nearly all prostitutes, white and Chinese, became ill after a short time in the trade. California adopted the flawed model of the English Contagious Diseases Acts of the 1860s that imprisoned infected prostitutes in public "lock hospitals." In many towns, a Chinese prostitute who was hopelessly diseased was cast into the streets or locked in a room with one cup of water, a bowl of rice, and left to die. Most Chinese prostitutes in California died after four years in the trade.[89]

Demands for medical inspections of prostitutes, however, appeared to endorse commercial interracial sex. Organizations dedicated to women's rights condemned urban codes that singled out prostitutes, both white and Chinese, while ignoring the men who spread "contamination" as they enjoyed the "vice." Yet for many California men, the enslaved Chinese prostitutes were still a prop for their bachelor lifestyle and fantasies of frontier freedom, especially the freedom from marriage. From the Gold Rush years to the anti-immigrant purges of the 1880s, few police officers or judges acknowledged that California's constitution and the Thirteenth Amendment that banned slavery should apply to enslaved Chinese prostitutes.

CHAPTER TWELVE

"She Had Stolen Nothing from Him but Herself"

Chinese Women and the Body Politic

This affidavit . . . is made for the purpose of identifying me in case I should be kidnapped or in case any criminal charge should be brought against me and by reason of the fact that my husband, Charlie Jones, is now in jail charged with a criminal offense and I fear that his enemies may try to do away with me, either by bringing some fictitious charge against me or by kidnapping and imprisoning me.

—YOKE LEEN, 1910

IN 1871 IN THE small lumber town of Eureka, Qui Com vanished from the home of her owner, merchant Mun Ching, and married a countryman. When Mun Ching learned of the wedding, he convinced the local police to arrest Qui Com for grand larceny, claiming that she owed him $300 for her passage from China and for three years of her "service"—debt peonage. Mun Ching searched for the girl in lumber and fishing villages along the coast and at last found her in Arcata, on the far shore of Humboldt

Bay, where he had her arrested for the outstanding "debt." In an innovative reading of the Thirteenth Amendment, the court granted Qui Com her freedom because "she had stolen nothing from him but herself."[1]

The Thirteenth Amendment abolishing slavery should have freed the Chinese prostitutes held in bondage in California. In 1988 in the case of *United States* v. *Kozminski*, the Supreme Court finally made it clear that "involuntary servitude" was a kind of slavery and, hence, forbidden by the Thirteenth Amendment. The case involved two mentally challenged men who were forced to labor seven days a week, seventeen hours a day, on a work farm. The Thirteenth Amendment, it said, was intended not only to abolish the chattel slavery of African Americans but also to ban other forms of compulsory labor such as peonage, debt slavery, or indentured servitude.[2]

California, however, has long believed in its own exceptionalism, and freedom from slavery went against many of the state's long-range ambitions for itself. California's systems of slavery endured after the Civil War. Even as it adhered to the law that ended the slavery of African Americans, the roots of sex slavery were so deeply burrowed in its history that removing them was a struggle in the streets, the courts, and along icy trails in the mountains.[3]

Qui Com was not alone. During the 1870s Chinese prostitutes fought against their bondage in a series of daring encounters with police, their own countrymen, pimps and madams, and the merciless tongs that imported them and sold them to locked brothels. When one sixteen-year-old Chinese prostitute refused to perform sex acts, her owner starved her, whipped her, and threatened to kill her. After several weeks of watching this torture, the other girls helped her escape to the safety of the Mission Home.[4]

The Presbyterian Church was chagrined by its failure in the 1860s to convert Chinese in Hong Kong and Canton and turned its attention to offering refuge to runaway Chinese prostitutes in California. The Church opened the Occidental Mission Home for Girls in 1874 to take in Chinese women and child prostitutes who were "refugees from a slavery worse than death."[5] Donaldina Cameron, a determined six-foot, one-inch white missionary, appealed to female missionaries' own resentment at their lower status as women and disgust with male immorality. The Salvation Army, the Society for the Restoration of Fallen Women, the San Francisco Ladies' Protection and Relief Society, and the Mission Home were part of a white, middle-class women's reform movement in the West that agreed that the price of sanctuary was conversion to Christianity. The promise of housing, education, food, and protection adhered to these women's visions of purification and redemption.[6] In order to rescue tainted Chinese women, the missions needed to rescue the men—that is to say, close the bars and brothels that profited from male vice. Dramatic rescues from the "slave dens" would expose men's promiscuity and marital infidelity, while white female sympathy would rehabilitate the "fallen girls."[7]

Tung Chee Ah Ho, a twenty-three-year-old prostitute, was held in a locked brothel in San Francisco. She remembered: "I was the second wife of a man in China and have one child there. I came to California induced to leave home by a woman who promised to find work for me in Singapore, but she brought me to Hong Kong instead, and placed me in *Tan Kaw*, a place where women are kept for sale. . . . I did not know that I was sold until I was put on board the steamer. The price paid for me in China was $270."

Tung Chee Ah Ho was sold down a chain of brokers who "forced me to receive the money and pay it over." One day Tung Chee Ah Ho was standing outside the brothel waiting to board a carriage that would transfer her to a brothel in a rural town, and she began to scream. In 1873, after four months of sexual bondage, she escaped to the Mission Home. A Chinese cigar maker who was standing nearby came to her rescue and took her to the Chinese Mission House. When the police arrested her owner they found her contract, in which she became "indebted to her mistress for passage . . . and for an advance of $630." In return, "[Tung Chee] Ah Ho distinctly agree[d] to give her body to Mr. Yee Kwan for service as a prostitute for a term of four years. . . . Ah Ho shall receive no wages. . . . If Ah Ho shall be sick at any time for more than ten days, she shall make up by an extra month of service for ten days' sickness."[8]

Protestant missions became stops on an Underground Railroad in California for enslaved Chinese prostitutes. At these safe houses, the girls lived behind barred or wired windows, were fed bland food, and dressed in plain cotton shifts. Their days were spent in stiff routines of cooking, sewing, and prayer. After a time, they earned a small wage for piecework or domestic service, but few found other employment.[9] Eventually, the missions could no longer house all the runaway Chinese girls and became way stations to a Christian marriage.

For some fugitive girls, Cameron's Mission Home and Methodist Mission House were welcoming and caring; for others, the confined regimen added to their shame and reminded them that they had been contaminated. The first goal was for each new inmate to spend a year learning the gospel and then return to China to spread god's word. Second-best was to marry her to a Chinese man, preferably a convert, who paid the mission sixty dollars for her upkeep and for arranging the match.[10] Many of the new "husbands," however, appear in the census as "Chinese keeper of brothel" or "keeps house of ill-fame." Some already had wives in China but planned never to return. By 1880, 50 percent of Chinese women in San Francisco were listed in the census as "married"; most of these wives were former prostitutes who had been bought from a brothel or a mission for a "bride price"—legal covers for prostituting the girls again.[11]

Between 1874 and 1889 the Presbyterian mission sheltered 261 girls, but after seventeen years of ministering to hundreds of fugitive prostitutes, it had only converted 167 women.[12] What was the legal status of enslaved Chinese prostitutes under the Thirteenth Amendment? Donaldina Cameron found lawyers to challenge the women's "contracts" and help the girls sue for their freedom. Despite abuse, isolation, and distance from home, other enslaved Chinese women managed to break out of locked brothels, bribed police to look the other way, and fled to rural Chinatowns hundreds of miles from San Francisco.

During the 1870s the ratio of Chinese females to males in California fell from seventy-eight women per one thousand men to forty-eight women per one thousand men. As the Page Law intended, this figure was low enough to risk the future of Chinese America. The Chinese women trapped in the brothels grew sick, grew old, and died; the number of rescues and runaways fell. Only a few lived to finish their "indenture" contracts.

The Transcontinental Railroad was finished in May 1869, and thirteen thousand Chinese men, free laborers who were invited and brokered to work in California, were quickly unemployed. European investors were abandoning their big American projects, in particular the railroads, and a massive stock market crash ignited the historic economic "Panic of 1873." In the midst of a terrifying economic downturn with thousands of unemployed white laborers, the Chinese were working in plain view. Many blamed the national depression, unemployment, and destitution on the ethnic composition of the new working class. Cartoons appeared in *Harper's Magazine* depicting Chinese immigrants as strikebreakers who reduced the living standards of the white family. The economic depressions of the 1870s spurred anti-Chinese hatred. The end of Reconstruction—post–Civil War moves toward racial equality—allowed assaults on Chinese migrants. In California the 1870s marked a rise in deportations and aggressive anti-Chinese codes and legislation.

The Knights of Labor—the first mass interracial labor organization—

gave way in the West to the leadership of Denis Kearney, who drove unemployment tensions into an anti-Chinese mania. In twenty years, from
1870 to 1890, San Francisco grew from a town of 149,000 to 298,000, and
Los Angeles grew from a village of 5,728 to a city of 50,395. The desperate
years of unemployment brought a churning fear of foreigners. Irish immigrants arrived in the United States enraged at British injustice and despotic seizure of their land; now they were unemployed and turned their
anger on the Chinese.

Thousands of unemployed white workers ignored the fact that they
shared poverty and class commonalities with Chinese migrants, and they
followed Kearney. Unemployed Irish workers in California likely did not
know that it was Chinese railroad workers who had launched the first strike
for an eight-hour day in 1867. Trapped in snowbound tent camps high
in the cold peaks in the Sierras, the Chinese had demanded that investor
Charles Crocker give them equal pay with whites while they worked in ice
tunnels deep within the Sierra Nevada.

Americans' fears of the "Yellow Peril"—an invasion by "Chinese
hordes"—fell on the Chinese male migrants and female prostitutes. Cartoons and editorials depicted Chinese men as small, hardworking, and docile.[13] But the skilled Chinese railroad workers had completed the death-
defying labor of dynamiting tunnels through the solid ice and granite of
the Sierra Nevada. This historic feat had nothing to do with feminized
stereotypes of Chinese men dressed in richly colored silk robes wearing
a "queue," or long braid—womanly images in a racialized economy that
sought to pay them less.[14]

After the Page Act limited the migration of Chinese women, Chinese
prostitutes became more valuable. Tainted as sexually willing and stigma-
tized as already debased, they were sold again and again.[15]

The Body Politic and the Case of
the Twenty-Two Lewd Maidens

The ship *Japan* docked in San Francisco's harbor in August 1874 after thirty
days at sea, carrying 589 Chinese passengers; eighty-nine were women,
twenty-two of whom were traveling alone. When the California commissioner of immigration boarded the ship, he marked all the unaccompanied
women as "suspicious" because they had traveled without husbands or
children. He detained them and then ordered the captain of the *Japan* to
return them to China.

The commissioner had the right to decide on the spot if any "foreigners" on the ship were "lunatics, idiotic, deaf, dumb, blind, crippled, infirm, paupers likely to become a public charge, convicted criminals, or lewd and debauched women." He ordered the captain of the *Japan* to pay him $500 for each of the twenty-two Chinese "maidens" before he would allow them to disembark. He claimed his fee to indemnify San Francisco against liability for housing the "lewd and debauched women" was $2,250 ($11,000 today). When the captain refused to pay, the commissioner announced that these unaccompanied women were likely to "become convicted criminals," and he held them in a tiny anteroom at the dock. Then they waited for purchasers to appear with bonds or bribes.

Ah Fook and Ah Fung, two sisters aboard the *Japan*, spent a month in detention, trapped by California's 1870 Act to Prevent the Kidnapping and Importation of Mongolian, Chinese, and Japanese Females for Criminal and Demoralizing Purposes.[16] For the preceding four years, the only Asian women who had been allowed to land had to prove they had traveled "voluntarily" and had "correct habits and good character." Ah Fook and Ah Fung said that they were going to join Ah Fook's husband and find work as seamstresses. Several white passengers, however, claimed that the sisters had been shipped to California against their will. Other passengers swore that they could tell that the women were prostitutes by the width of their silk sleeves and the gaudy colors and rich embroidery of their dresses.

California argued it had "states' rights" to block Ah Fook and Ah Fung and bring an end to Chinese slavery. This argument, however, collided with the federal government's constitutional right to control immigration and the Burlingame Treaty's (1868) protections of the "inherent and inalienable right" of any Chinese migrant "to change his home and allegiance."

At issue in the women's four-day hearing was the state's assumption that all Chinese females were "lewd and debauched" and that they carried a "pestilential immorality." How to prove that all of the twenty-two Chinese women traveling alone aboard the ship *Japan* were lewd? This erotic dilemma overtook the state's need to prove that they were unfree. Judge Robert F. Morrison opted for judicial voyeurism; he said that there would be "no indelicacy or impropriety in gazing down their sleeves" in an open courtroom as long as the exposure was in the service of discovering the women's immigration status. The Chinese women's white lawyer "performed the operation" and announced that they were all wearing some sort of "undergarment of gaudy colors." Judge Morrison was satisfied; this proved, he said, that the twenty-two Chinese women were in fact "lewd."

Women's clothing and underwear became evidence of criminality: What width of sleeves signified that a woman was a prostitute? What floral print established her livelihood? And what did colorful underwear prove? California, said Judge Morrison, had a right to preserve its "well-being and safety," and he ruled against the women. To assure men's innocence, women's underwear became a standard for legal entry. The twenty-two lewd women were to be deported.

Prosperous Chinese merchants—bankers, shopkeepers, herbalists—understood that their lucrative investment in the sex trade was at risk, and they appealed the ruling. The California Supreme Court soon upheld the lower court's decision to expel the women; California law, it said, had the right to ban all "elements dangerous to the health and moral well-being of the country." The "elements" were the women themselves.[17]

Even with so many forces aligned against her, Ah Fong appealed her case to the U.S. circuit court. What began as California's corrupt demand for landing fees evolved into a case about human trafficking, civil rights, and the Fourteenth Amendment. The judges were at odds and issued a tangle of decisions. Judge Stephen Field was more troubled about migration than morality and wanted to protect the federal government's authority to decide immigration cases. Field ruled that California's Act to Prevent the Kidnapping and Importation of Mongolian, Chinese, and Japanese Females for Criminal and Demoralizing Purposes was too sweeping: "It is hardly possible to conceive a statute more skillfully framed, to place in the hands of a single man the power to prevent entirely vessels engaged in a foreign trade, say with China, from carrying passengers, or to compel them to submit to systematic extortion of the grossest kind."

Of lasting impact, Justice Field then turned to the capacious Fourteenth Amendment, which grants civil rights to all persons living in the United States. He ruled that by only targeting immigrants who arrived by sea (in this case, Chinese women), California had singled out just one group of immigrants and had thus violated their right to equal protection under the law.

California's ban on Chinese immigrants was a holdover from the era when states sought to "exclud[e] free negroes from their limits," and it had inserted racial profiling into U.S. immigration policy. Explained Field, "I have little respect for that discriminating virtue which is shocked when a frail child of China is landed on our shores, and yet allows the . . . painted harlot of other countries to parade our streets." He observed that "the commissioner has but to go aboard a vessel filled with passengers ignorant of our language and our laws . . . and without trial or hearing or evidence, but from the external appearances of persons with whose former habits he is unfamiliar, to point with his finger . . . and say to the [ship's] master, 'These are idiots, these are paupers, these are convicted criminals, these are lewd women, and these others are debauched women.'" Any commissioner could say, "I have the power to commute all this for you—for any sum I may choose to take in cash. I am open to an offer; for you must remember that twenty per cent of all I can get out of you goes into my own pocket, and the remainder into the treasury of California." Justice Field ordered the commissioner to release all the women.

Immigration law, human bondage, and race crossed paths in Judge Ogden Hoffman's dissent. He conceded that the United States had indeed abolished slavery, but it had not abolished states' rights. As a state, California had the right to exclude citizens of other countries "whose presence might seem to threaten the security of property in slaves."[18] He ruled that the shipment of the prostitutes was protected international commerce. California's Act for the Suppression of Chinese Houses of Ill-Fame, added Hoffman, violated the Fourteenth Amendment's equal protection rights of traffickers, the Hip Yee tong, and the Pacific Mail Steamship Company. The act deprived both the Hip Yee Tong and the steamship company of an economic opportunity. The steamship company that transported the maidens and the merchants who owned them had the right to decide the women's destiny. Had he been in the majority, said Hoffman, he would have released Ah Fung to her owner.[19] Judge Hoffman would have preferred to give a private company and a gang of human traffickers the same rights to equal protection as other people, and he would have protected a global slave trade in women.

Chy Lung, one of the Chinese women who had traveled on the *Japan*, was now facing sexual slavery or deportation; the twenty-two women held for deportation collectively appealed the decision in her name. In 1876, for the first time a Chinese person, indeed a Chinese woman, appeared before the U.S. Supreme Court. In *Chy Lung v. Freeman*, the court said that California had given despotic powers to a petty official who could create "systematic extortion of the grossest kind. . . . Whether a young woman's manners . . . justified the commissioner in calling her lewd may be made to depend on the sum she will pay for the privilege of landing."[20]

With that, a Chinese woman, Chy Lung, expanded the scope of the Fourteenth Amendment: the U.S. Supreme Court insisted that the Fourteenth Amendment not only "declares that no state shall make or enforce any law which abridges the privileges or immunities of citizens of the United States," but it also says that "no state shall deprive 'any *person*' of life, liberty, or property without due process of the laws." For emphasis, it repeated: "equality of *privilege* is the constitutional right of all citizens, equality of *protection* is the constitutional right of all *persons*." The court insisted that only the federal government, not a state, could impose restrictions that would limit Chinese immigration.[21]

The twenty-two "maidens" established that the Fourteenth Amendment covers immigrants—not just U.S. citizens—and proved that California's immigration ban violated the Constitution. The Supreme Court allowed each of the "twenty-two maidens" to decide for herself whether to return to China or remain in the United States, and then released the Chinese women.[22] We don't know what became of them, or if in the end they were truly free. Although the "Case of the Twenty-Two Chinese Maidens" brought an end to California's nativist act, it helped spawn decades of dire national anti-immigrant laws.

Had the Page Act passed before 1875, it would have prevented the entry of 90 percent of the Chinese women then living in the United States; it likely would have stopped the twenty-two maidens before they set sail. This early immigration law closed the gate on Chinese women entering the United States for the next thirty-five years. The immigration of almost all Chinese women into the United States remained illegal until 1911.

Why target Chinese women in the West when there were so few? By preventing the entry of wives, daughters, single women, and enslaved prostitutes, the Page Act limited the growth of a Chinese population in the United States. Chinese women who managed to receive a U.S. consul's certificate to land often faced expensive habeas corpus hearings in San Francisco, and brokers and pimps added the cost of these legal bills to the girls' already enormous "debt."

By 1870 only about two thousand Chinese women in San Francisco were prostitutes—or 60 percent of all Chinese women who lived in California.[23] Slave brokers had to find new ways to smuggle Chinese girls. Some prostitutes were imported to work as concubines, high-end courtesans to service prosperous Chinese merchants in San Francisco; unknown numbers were sold to "parlor houses" to provide sex to wealthy tourists and white businessmen. But most were still sold into ragged brothels or forced to work out of shacks, inevitably contracting syphilis and left to die alone.[24] During the annual Midwinter Fair in San Francisco's Golden Gate Park, tong boss and shoe manufacturer Fong Ching imported one hundred women to work as prostitutes, passing them off as acrobats and actors; afterward, he sold them to brothels in a mass sale for $50,000 (over $1.2 million today). Other girls were smuggled into the country dressed as boys or hidden in padded crates with bills of landing marked as dishes.[25]

Fugitive Slaves: Chinese Women

A Chinese woman who fled from the locked brothels took tremendous risks. Gangsters hired by the merchants or by the Hip Yee Tong would track her in an alley or along a mountain trail. The tong hired "hatchet men" to find her and return her to her owner or execute her; the missions were not safe from the tongs, and a Chinese woman had no place to run.[26] If she fled to a police station, she was returned to her owner. She found no refuge in the Thirteenth Amendment; at times her "husband" turned to the courts for help, claiming that she had absconded with his clothing, money, or jewelry.

Although the historical footprints of most runaways have faded, some tracks can still be followed. A series of telegrams tells the story of two runaway Chinese prostitutes, Gan Que and Wah How. In the cold spring of 1874, they escaped from their owners, and a group of Chinese men sought to capture them as they fled in the snow. Trying to track them down, the men telegraphed each other with demands for money to pay for clues or bribes to police officers or fees to local attorneys for false marriage certificates.

But Gan Que and Wah How remained on the run, at times traveling by stage, other times hiking between mountain towns in the snow-covered foothills of the Sierra—Nevada City, Downieville, Auburn, and Marysville. These telegrams detail a desperate flight to freedom and urgent pursuit by slaveholders. We do not hear the women's voices, but we can glimpse them through the men's cryptic and urgent telegrams. From the spring through fall of 1874, their owners often sent several in one day.

DID THE GIRL WAH HOW NO COME HERE LAST MONTH. I THINK SHE IS KIDNAPED [*sic*]. ANS IF SHE WAS. *Yuk Fong, Virginia City, Nev., to Luk Chung, March 20, 1874, 1:30 p.m.*

SHE HAS NOT COME HERE YET. HAVE NEVER HEARD ANYONE SPEAK OF HER BEFORE. IF I DO I WILL TELE-

GRAPH. *Luk Chung, Downieville, Calif., to Yuk Fong, Virginia City, Nev., March 30, 1874.*

YOUR WOMAN SHE GO COLUSA. YOU WANT HER GO THERE. *Fong Sing, Tie Yuen, Oroville, Calif., to Lem Lun, June 12, 1874, 9:55 a.m.*

TELL HER TO WAIT FOR ME TO COME AND IF SHE WANTS TO GO I WILL LET HER. DON'T CARE. ANSWER. *Kaw Chung, Downieville, Calif., to Fook Sing, Wadsworth, Nev., July 26, 1874.*

WOMAN WENT TO VIRGINIA TOWN WITH HOW AH SING. YOU BETTER COME HERE AND TALK TO THE COMPANY. KEEP QUIET. I KNOW ALL ABOUT IT. IT IS ALL RIGHT. *Ah Tri, Auburn, Calif., to Ah Tom, August 2, 1874, 11:05 a.m.*

GUM SING AND WOMAN ARRESTED. HERE TOMORROW. SEND SIXTY DOLLARS. *Tie Yuen Company, Nevada [City], Calif., to Fook Sing, Downieville, Calif., August 3, 1874, 1 p.m.*

BRING WOMAN UP RIGHT AWAY WILL PAY THREE HUNDRED DOLLARS. ANSWER. *Sing Lung, Ah Yik to Tie Yuen, Fook Sing, Marysville, Calif., August 13, 1874.*

THE WOMAN IS IN JAIL HERE NOW. SEND ONE HUNDRED DOLLARS TODAY BY TELEGRAPH FOR EXPENSE TO TAKE THE WOMAN UP TO NEVADA [CITY] YOU NO SEND MONEY SHE NO GO. FOOK SING HE STOP NEVADA. YOU NO GOT MONEY, ANSWER. *Eing Goon to Sing Lung, Marysville, Calif., October 5, 1874, 4:20 p.m.*

SEND ONE HUNDRED DOLLARS. WE HAVE WOMAN. *Ah Tien, Ah Heing Store, to Fook Sing, Nevada (City), Calif., October 6, 1874, 8:50 p.m.*

KEM SING WITH OFFICER GO DOWNIEVILLE TODAY. HIDE WOMAN. *E. Barry to Ah Wan, Nevada (City), Calif., October 8, 1874, 10:45 p.m.*

WHEN YOU COMING TO PAY. IF NOT IN FEW DAYS
WILL SEND OFFICER AFTER YOU. *Tie Yuen to Hong Hi Wien,
Nevada* (City), *Calif., October 13, 1874, 1:30 p.m.*

GIM SING AND GAN QUE IN JAIL. SEND MONEY
QUICKLY. *Yuen Store to Fook Sing, Nevada* (City), *Calif., November 6, 1874, 4:20 p.m.*

YOUR WOMAN GO TO SAN FRANCISCO TONIGHT
WITH LEE HUNG. SING HOE GO BACK TO CHINA.
YOU WANT TO LET HER GO ANSWER QUICK.
[Sender unknown][27]

For a brief interlude in the summer and fall of 1874, Gan Que and
Wah How braved the mountains and the unknown, evading capture and a
return to men who claimed them. Ultimately, both women were seized by
the police and shipped back to San Francisco.

By 1880 the number of Chinese enslaved prostitutes declined by 50
percent. The Page Act, disease, and infertility from assault and inept abortions reduced the number of Chinese women. The fate of Chinatowns and
the future of Chinese America were at risk.[28]

With fewer Chinese women, the price of sex with Chinese girls soared,
and the Hip Yee Tong and brothels became even more brutal as they tried
to keep them from fleeing or from being kidnapped by other pimps. The
Page Act failed to close the market for Chinese women. Some madams
posed as mothers of multiple daughters; some claimed that they were marriage brokers; others posed as managers of sewing factories. In 1880 the
police made no arrests for running houses of prostitution but 547 arrests
for street "pimping"—perhaps because the brothel owners were funding
the police squads in Chinatown. The local patrols also profited from the
girls who paid for protection.[29]

In 1882 the U.S. Congress passed the Chinese Exclusion Act, the first
immigration law to ban a people by race.[30] The Exclusion Act banned the
entry of any Chinese woman who was born outside the United States,
even if she was married to a Chinese man "domiciled" in the country.[31]
Chinese laborers who were already in the country faced prison or deportation, but unlike merchants, they could no longer return to China and then
reenter the United States with their families. Chinese wives could not join
their husbands in the United States; no longer could a Chinese woman,
free or enslaved, become a U.S. citizen through marriage.

Chinese women were blamed for their bodies; Chinese men were blamed for their work. To justify the wave of deportations, city officials again diagnosed Chinatowns as dangerous and diseased. Crime squads raided the brothels, and vigilantes torched Chinese homes, shops, restaurants, and brothels, despite the popularity of Chinatowns and the familiarity across races who worked side by side in service jobs, restaurants, and brothels.[32]

San Francisco and rural towns embedded brutality in the city codes. In 1882 Ah Lin, age thirteen, was arrested at a locked brothel in San Francisco, along with her madam and the other child prostitutes. Ah Lin testified that in her village in China, her mother had sold her to an American broker when she was eight years old. Since her arrival on the docks of San Francisco, she had been sold to four different brothels and trafficked between mountain towns. Ah Lin did not know her original price, but her last two owners had paid $700 and $800 for her, in turn. The madam claimed she was Ah Lin's mother—indeed, the mother of all the other teenage girls in the brothel. U.S. Circuit Judge Lorenzo Sawyer freed Ah Lin and delivered her to the Chinese Mission House. But in a cruel and arbitrary decision, he released the younger girls onto the streets, inevitably to be seized or sold to new owners.[33] The madam was not held to account.

Sexual Congress: The Eugenics Movement

The last decades of the nineteenth century saw interracial sex as a threat to white purity and, hence, to white dominance. In 1880 the California legislature passed an anti-miscegenation act and banned interracial sex and interracial marriage. The U.S. Supreme Court upheld these state laws: because the anti-miscegenation laws applied equally to whites and non-whites, they did not violate the Fourteenth Amendment. The early Spanish and Russian invaders had encouraged interracial marriage and interracial sex as a strategy of conquest, to dilute Indigenous lineage. At the same time Black civil rights leader W. E. B. Du Bois denounced anti-miscegenation acts because he believed that biological "amalgamation" would help solve "the race problem."[34]

Still, everywhere were Chinese children born into brothels or born into Chinese merchants' families. According to the Constitution, they were also born into American citizenship. The growing number of children conceived in unions between Chinese women and white settlers fueled fears that these biracial children marked an end of white identity and "racial purity." Yet Chinese brothels were dens of rape that produced significant numbers of interracial children. Popular medical pamphleteer Dr. Arthur B. Stout feared that "by commingling with the Eastern Asiatics, we are creating degenerate hybrids," and he yearned for a West "only populated by a superior white race." Rather than through military invasion, the "yellow horde," he feared, would overtake the country through interracial sex.[35]

The Page Act of 1875 and the Chinese Exclusion Act of 1882 deprived Chinese babies born in the United States of their constitutional right to American citizenship—a preview of the federal government's 2019 attempts to undermine "birthright citizenship." The laws gave Chinese men two options: sail back to China to marry, start a family, and then try to return; or purchase and marry an enslaved prostitute already in the United States.[36]

Driven Out: The *Pai Hua*

In the last two decades of the nineteenth century, over two hundred violent anti-Chinese purges blew across the state. Nearly all of the Chinese prostitutes who were living in rural towns had fled from brothels in San Francisco and now faced the threat of being returned to sexual slavery.[37] In the terrifying firestorms the Chinese call "*pai hua*," or "the driven out," the Chinese were violently gathered up, marched out of towns or driven out in carts, or shipped out on mail boats or rafts rushing down California rivers. They trekked out, often under armed guard, along the railroad tracks they had built. They were loaded onto railroad cars, forced onto logging rafts, or killed. In the 1880s Chinatowns in Penryn, Rocklin, Grass Valley, Walnut Grove, and Dutch Flat were burned to the ground.[38]

On the night of Lunar New Year 1885, the Chinese in Eureka were told they had to pack up and leave town before sunup. Vigilantes scoured the town for any remaining Chinese person. They found "China Mary," a prostitute with no legal first or last name, in the county hospital suffering from syphilis. The mob decided to ignore her.

At dawn, teams of armed vigilantes marched the Chinese to a cold warehouse at the docks. Two mui tsai from Eureka—by now a label for an enslaved or unwilling prostitute—trekked to the wharf. One was twenty-three years old, the other fourteen.[39] Wives of Chinese merchants trudged on painfully bound feet. All weekend, three hundred refugees waited in a warehouse to board two ships bound for San Francisco; the women feared they would be recaptured by the pimps and madams who owned their contracts.

Finally, on Sunday night, the tide carried the two small ships across the shoals of Humboldt Bay, and the steamships docked in San Francisco early on Monday morning: the enslaved women were back in the city of their captivity. Nonetheless, on that afternoon, many of the Chinese who had been driven from Eureka gathered at one of the Chinese Six Companies who invited the mayor and members of the press. The Chinese consul in San Francisco, Colonel Fred A. Bee, made a historic announcement: "We intend to seek redress in the courts. Somebody will have to pay for the injury done to these refugees." In the 1880s the anti-Chinese attacks in California had provoked anti-American riots in Canton, which destroyed American hospitals and Christian missions. China had just paid the United States $700,000 in today's money in "full liquidation." Now, said Bee, it was America's turn to pay the Chinese.[40]

In 1886 two Chinese prostitutes bravely joined fifty Chinese men from Eureka to file *Wing Hing v. The City of Eureka*, likely the first lawsuit for reparations in the United States and the first lawsuit to demand reparations for having been driven out by a mob. The Chinese from Eureka collectively sought $75,245 for the town's "carelessness or negligence" for their property that was "removed, carried away, and destroyed." What turns *Wing Hing* into a historic reparations case rather than a simple demand for damages was that the Chinese also sued for $37,670 for having been made the "victims of mob violence"; the city had neglected its legal duty. Together, the insistent plaintiffs sought over $112,000 for being the targets of a race riot and for suffering racial brutality; they sued as a group because the violence perpetrated against them treated them as a group. The enslaved Chinese prostitutes were members of that group.

The Chinese lost *Wing Hing v. The City of Eureka*. The court held that because the Chinese did not pay taxes on land—land, they were reminded, they were not allowed to own—they had lost nothing "of value." Although they had been forced to leave behind furniture, dairy cows, mining equipment, and fishing boats, the judge ruled that their property counted for nothing because personal belongings do not appear on tax rolls. Although it failed, *Wing Hing v. The City of Eureka* signaled a pugnacious and litigious Chinese response that put other rural towns on notice that future purges would be costly.[41]

In 1886, over six brutal weeks, Chinese residents of Crescent City at the far northwestern corner of the state were forced onto small mail boats. When the boats were full, vigilantes took the few remaining Chinese women and their children in a wagon up to the redwood forest and dumped them out by the Smith River. Up in the Sierra Nevada, the railroad town of Truckee now feared a lawsuit and expelled one thousand Chinese wood-cutters. The editor of the local *Truckee Republican* headlined the strategy "Starve Them Out," and then gloated as Truckee burned its Chinatown to the ground. All that remained was the opium den, safely built of brick; the opium den was on whites residents' side of the Truckee River.

Across California, cities and counties passed local codes to make it impossible for Chinese women to survive. The regulations slammed the doors on women seeking to escape from the sex trade to take jobs as seam-stresses, shopkeepers, proprietors, or cannery workers. Many Chinese prostitutes also worked in laundries during the day, making extra money for their owners or occasionally for themselves. A special "tax" forced Chi-nese launderers to pay fifteen dollars per month to wash clothes and bed-ding and prohibited them from delivering clean clothes in a wagon, making them carry their heavy loads on foot. When an 1880 code banned "wash-houses" in wooden buildings, the prostitutes saw many Chinese laundries burn to the ground. In San Francisco, Chinese prostitutes were not allowed to ride in buggies. The city passed "Cubic Air Ordinances" that limited the number of Chinese people permitted to live in one room. In effect, the codes created a ban on being poor, which drove Chinese women back into the brothels.

Traditionally, Chinese bodies were interred in segregated cemeteries until it was assumed that the flesh had fallen off—about eight years after burial. Then, the bones were exhumed and shipped back to China on "death ships" for ritual burial in a home village. But the corpses of Chinese pros-titutes, presumably contaminated, had to be burned immediately; their re-mains and their spirits stayed in California.[42]

The Chinese Exclusion Act of 1882 removed immigration decisions from the courts and assigned them to lowly port inspectors, leaving Chi-nese women without a path to appeal. Naturalization, a legal fiction that one can be reborn as an American, came to an end for Chinese immigrants. Even a Chinese woman who had U.S. citizenship by birth or by naturaliza-tion could not testify or sit on a jury. Judge Lorenzo Sawyer added more restrictions for Chinese immigrants. When Ah Quan, the wife of a laborer, sought to enter the United States, he ruled that after her marriage to a Chinese laborer she acquired her husband's status as an unwelcome mi-grant, and she was shipped back to China.[43]

As fewer girls slipped through immigration, their value rose. The See Yup Company, one of the largest merchant associations, hired gangsters to

Despite anti-Chinese immigration laws, the slave dens, or *bagnios*, endured in San Francisco through the 1880s and 1890s.
(Peter Palmquist Collection, Courtesy of the Beinecke Rare Book and Manuscript Library, Yale University Library, New Haven.)

raid the high-end brothels and demand "tribute" in jewelry, silk dresses, and girls. As a warning to the madams not to report extortion, "high binders," or Chinese gangsters, raped the prostitutes, murdered the guards at the brothels, and assaulted servants and cooks. The only witnesses were Chinese women and men who were banned from testifying in court against white or Chinese assailants.[44]

"In Case I Should Be Kidnapped"

After the Chinese Exclusion acts and the routs, raids, and expulsions, only 2,100 Chinese women and children lived in San Francisco.[45] Three decades after the passage of the Thirteenth Amendment, most were still enslaved; half of the two thousand Chinese women who lived in the United States were still held "in bondage" of some sort. In addition to the sex

trade, Chinese merchant families "leased" young mui tsai to work as servants and nannies. After the Exclusion Act of 1882, a one-year-old Chinese
baby girl cost one hundred dollars; a girl of fourteen cost $1,200. The girls
were raised as servants in a brothel and typically assaulted. In September
1892 red posters appeared on the walls of Chinatowns across the country.
Every ten years the 1882 Exclusion Law was to be renewed. Its first reprise, the Geary Act of 1892, went one step further: it required all Chinese people living in the United States to carry certificates of residence—
photo-identity cards.[46] The Chinese called it the "Dog Tag Law"; under the
Geary Act, the mui tsai were questioned, photographed, and registered.
Then they were returned to their owners.

In 1892 and 1893 posters on buildings and barns urged the Chinese
in the United States to rise up in the country's largest civil disobedience
up to that time. Backed by the imperial Qing dynasty, a staggering 107,000
of the 110,000 Chinese immigrants refused to register for an identity card—
the first federal internal U.S. passport. The certificate hearkened back to
passes for plantation slaves and paseos at the Franciscan missions.

Some enslaved Chinese prostitutes, however, thought that the certificate might provide legal cover for themselves and their children. In March
of 1893 forty runaway prostitutes and their five children showed up at the
Chinese consulate in San Francisco; they were examined, measured, photographed, and issued identity cards.[47] Captive girls were taken off ships
and delivered to judges bribed by the owners, who signed their cards knowing that they had entered the United States as unfree migrants. When the
girls were sent to other cities, their residence certificates were sold from
vendor to vendor—with or without the girl. The Geary Act provoked a new
wave of purges, and Chinese prostitutes were, once again, returned to San
Francisco, where they faced double jeopardy as slaves and immigrants.[48]

To protect a profitable "asset"—now selling for $500 to $5,000—
procurers declared that the public registration sites were "promiscuous,"
a term for public spaces shared by men and women. Madams and pimps
feared that the prostitutes would flee when they left the brothels to register for the cards and "invited" the Internal Revenue officers to meet the
girls at the brothels. The "Dog Tag Law" became another way to locate and
arrest runaway Chinese prostitutes.

The county jails were full and filthy with Chinese immigrants; the
state penitentiary of San Quentin Prison was overflowing the detainees.
Neither the state nor the federal government had the will to pay the thousands of dollars to confine, feed, prosecute, try, and deport each Chinese

migrant who refused to register.[49] May 5, 1893, the national deadline to register for the certificate of residence, came and went.

The next morning, three thousand miles from California, on busy Mott Street in New York, two brave Chinese laborers and one laundryman stepped out of a crowd and, as planned, were arrested for failing to carry a certificate. Although the three men had been in the country for thirteen years, the court ordered them to be deported. In this deliberate test of the 1892 law and with lawyers funded by the Chinese merchants, they immediately appealed the decision to the U.S. Supreme Court.

Fue Yue Ting v. United States raised a series of constitutional questions that shaped the destiny of the enslaved prostitutes and, indeed, all Chinese women and men in the United States. These questions endure: What was the legal status of long-term residents? Did the Geary Act violate the Fourteenth Amendment's ban against taking someone's liberty without due process? Were immigrants entitled to jury trials before deportation— what the Chinese called "transportation for life"? Did deportation violate the Eighth Amendment's ban on cruel and unusual punishment? What would happen to the women who had been forcibly brought into the country illegally? And who would fund the legal defense for an illegally enslaved Chinese prostitute?

The U.S. Supreme Court took only five days to rule on the *Fue Yue Ting* case. Before a stunned crowd, the court announced that if the country had the power to exclude any person or race that it wished, it also had the power to deport any person or race that it wished. Of gravest danger, the court gave Congress the power to decide who was a "person" under the Fourteenth Amendment. Over one hundred thousand migrants had refused to register for identity cards; the boycott lasted nearly a year but collapsed when China stopped funding the lawyers, publicity, and organization of the boycott. China abandoned its overseas migrants in return for a trade treaty with the United States.[50]

For some Chinese women held in sexual bondage, the identity cards were tickets to freedom. When the kidnapped women met the registrars, they could finally declare that they had not traveled "voluntarily" and demand to be returned to China. Others managed to use the certificates, real and counterfeit, as immigration documents and escape the "green mansions." Still, the easiest way out of the locked brothel was to marry; whether the men were true husbands or traffickers remains unclear. In 1897, nearly fifty years after California's slave trade in Chinese girls began, a girl from age nine to twelve years had a market value in San Francisco of $150 to

$500. A girl from age twelve to sixteen sold for $500 to $1,500, and girls over sixteen—the most desired age—had a purchase price of up to $3,500.[51]

During the 1890s, alarm over the American economy deepened; efforts at expansion into Samoa, Hawaii, and the Philippines fell short, and Californians rushed to close the borders.[52] In 1893 the market in wheat collapsed and California's new agricultural economy tumbled. In an urgent America first vision, a new wave of race hatred and hate crimes surged and produced the harsh exclusion acts of the 1890s.

In 1900 twenty-five hundred Chinese women lived in San Francisco— fifteen hundred of whom were prostitutes. The Protestant missions continued to rescue girls tortured by their pimps, who propped open the girls' eyes and dragged them by the hair and burned them with red-hot irons. The pimps tried to force their way into the rescue missions and retake the runaway girls.[53] Now if a girl escaped and was retrieved during her four years of "service" she became a slave for life.[54] The Hip Yee Tong lost control of the trade to the powerful Chinese Six Companies who still owned the urban brothels and purchased the goodwill of the police.[55]

On January 17, 1894, missionary Annie Houseworth rescued young Tien Fuh Wu, who had been sold by her father to a procurer on a riverboat headed to Ningbo, a coastal city south of the Yangtze River Delta. He slipped her into the United States with the performers for the Midwinter Fair in San Francisco; still a child, she was delivered to the "Peking," a brothel, to work as a servant. Whenever customers came, the brothelkeeper hid the child under a bed and pushed a trunk in front to block her from view. In debt, her owner sold Tien Fuh Wu to a gambling den; seemingly too young for the sex trade, she cared for the owner's baby and washed diapers. When the baby cried, its mother singed Tien Fuh Wu's arm with red-hot fire tongs or dripped hot candle wax on her arms. With tragic irony, these punishments left scars that would identify Tien Fuh Wu as a child slave and soon lead to her rescue. Tien Fuh Wu escaped to the Methodist Mission and survived to become the lifelong companion and translator for missionary Donaldina Cameron. Tien Fuh Wu long remembered the smell of her own burning flesh.[56]

At 5:12 a.m. on the morning of April 18, 1906, the city of San Francisco trembled as a legendary earthquake roiled the town. Flimsy buildings in Chinatown collapsed or burned in the fires, spreading the natural disaster. Roads buckled from the heat. U.S. soldiers entered Chinatown and rescued three hundred Asian women from the brothels and discovered a hidden trade in Japanese girls, offered as Chinese. After San Francisco barred the homeless Chinese from the relief camps, Chinese brothels opened in the grand old houses in nearby Oakland, in the shadow of the new state university campus in Berkeley built on land seized from the Ohlone.[57] In these posh East Bay brothels, iron bars and wire nets marked off the "cribs" on the ground floor, while shops and theaters flourished above.

The five-story brick Chinese Mission Home at 930 Sacramento Street withstood the powerful first shock of the earthquake, and missionary Donaldina Cameron rescued all sixty fugitive girls who were in hiding at the safe house, among them a newborn baby and her young mother. For days Cameron roamed the rubble of Chinatown in search of other Chinese girls and sent them on a ferry to a makeshift shelter in Oakland, a barn on the grounds of a seminary. Yet even with the city in ruins, the organized labor movement took the moment to ban any union member from working on a building site that had been cleared of rubble by Chinese workers.

The fires that consumed San Francisco also devoured immigration files, building permits, police and court records, and the internal documents of the Chinese Six Companies. With that sinkhole of lost documents, white lawyers and notaries created false papers, and Chinese migrants sailed again to California. In that brief era, "paper" relatives, mainly young Chinese men, traveled with counterfeit certificates of residence and claimed past residence or parents in the United States. Loopholes in the immigration bills for family reunification created families with sham husbands, brothers, and parents. In 1910 the federal government opened Angel Island Detention Center inside the Golden Gate Straits of San Francisco Bay, where Chinese women, "paper wives," were interrogated and held, sometimes for up to two years, until they could establish that they were meeting a husband.

As San Francisco's Chinatown was rebuilt from the seismic devastation, the trade in women spread across San Francisco Bay to Oakland, up the Sacramento River Delta, and south to Palo Alto. San Francisco's City Council failed to permanently move Chinatown outside the city limits when the heads of the Chinese Six Companies reminded them that here the Chinese owned the Chinatown's land and were entitled to return. Chinatown would be rebuilt in the center of the city, right where it had stood since the 1850s. Determined to overcome the neighborhood's lure as a pornographic grid of gambling halls, opium dens, and brothels, Chinatown would rise as a commercial and tourist destination. Reinventing the image of Chinatown, the merchants set to rebuild with pagoda rooflines and curved tile awnings copied from a model of a Chinese village and the

Angel Island Detention Center in San Francisco Bay, where Chinese women,
behind bars with their children, were detained and repeatedly interrogated.
(Courtesy California Historical Society, San Francisco, CHS2009.091.)

Forbidden City in Beijing that had been created for the 1893 Chicago's
World Fair.[58] A colorful *paifang*, a painted archway, marked the border of
Chinatown on Grant Avenue.

As San Francisco recovered from the quake, its brothels returned. The
"Queen's Room"—the original slave mart on Dupont Street—was restored,
and kidnappers, brokers, procurers, pimps, and madams again bought and
sold women. Two to six girls were now displayed naked, calling to men
from a window that opened into the streets or alleys.[59]

The cusp of the twentieth century saw new terms of procurement. In
1898 brokers in China distributed coaching books to provide kidnapped
girls with answers to a standardized set of eighty-one immigration questions they would likely hear on the docks in California. Each new girl was
warned that she would be tortured by her California owner if she failed to
pass the exam.[60]

The Qing dynasty collapsed in 1911–12, just as the United States
slammed the door on new immigrants from China. Under the new Republic of China, the transport of Chinese women and girls to the United

Four Chinese women, dressed as boys in long overcoats and soft hats, were
seized and smuggled into San Francisco on the steamship *Nippon Maru* in 1912.
The girls had been drugged in Hong Kong and lured aboard the ship. They
were stowed in the coal bunkers in the hull of the ship, fed only small quantities
of rice, and then confined at the immigration station at Angel Island.

In the *San Francisco Chronicle*, November 27, 1912.

States waned. Enslaved prostitutes who were deported from the United States
returned to a changing country with a ban on foot binding and the promise of education and political equality for women.[61] In the early twentieth
century, Chinese women shopkeepers, vendors, and merchants' wives found
the freedom of the streets of San Francisco.

In that chaotic mix, the Chinese Six Companies took control of the
sex trade from the Hip Yee Tong. When California passed the Red-Light
Abatement Act in 1914, San Francisco closed Chinese "bordellos" and
moved the prostitutes to the even greater dangers of the street.[62] The
women who escaped slavery found work in sweatshops and the sewing
trades, and earned, like their Eastern European counterparts, thirty cents
per dozen slippers.[63]

Despite the roundups, the burned-out brothels, and fears of forced
prostitution, many Chinese women in California refused to submit to their
purchase and sale. In 1910 Yoke Leen climbed the steps of the courthouse

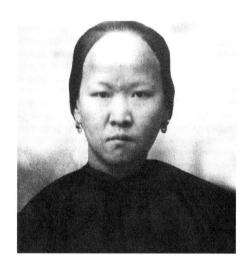

Yoke Leen.
(Courtesy Tuolumne County Museum,
Sonora, California.)

in the mountain town of Sonora and demanded that her deposition be taken and preserved in the county records in case anyone tried to claim her. Yoke Leen swore that she was a native-born American citizen, that she was a free woman, and that no man could ever own her again:

> I reside in the City of Sonora, State of California, and am of the age of 36 years. That I am a native of the State of California, having been born in San Francisco. . . . That I am about five feet tall and weigh 110 pounds. That I have a scar on my face on the right side of the nose near the right eye and also a large scar on the right side of the mouth, also a small raised scar at the base of the index finger of the right hand and a small scar on the right hand about an inch below the wrist at the base of the thumb. . . .
>
> This affidavit with the annexed photograph is made for the purpose of identifying me in case I should be kidnapped or in case any criminal charge should be brought against me and by reason of the fact that my husband, Charlie Jones, is now in jail charged with a criminal offense and I fear that his enemies may try to do away with me, either by bringing some fictitious charge against me or by kidnapping and imprisoning me. The annexed signature is my name written in English and also in Chinese.
> Signed,
> Yoke Leen,
> 21 February 1910.[64]

CHAPTER THIRTEEN

"Except as a Punishment
for Crime"

The Birth of the Modern Carceral State

In 1849 CALIFORNIA HAD no state laws and collected no taxes. During the first six years of the Gold Rush, four thousand new residents were murdered in California; twelve hundred mostly white and Latino men were killed in San Francisco alone.[1] And the mass Indian genocide went on. The *Daily Alta California* complained, "Without money . . . we have no police, no organization for preventing and extinguishing fires, no jail, no courts for the proper trial and punishment of offenders."[2] Wealthy ranchers and vigilantes served up justice with fists, guns, and ropes. Under U.S. rule, Indigenous people lost the judicial protection of Mexican citizenship. Ranchers invented their own judicial codes and built their own pens on their new estates to jail their own prisoners and compel them to construct fences and breed cattle. Due process was inconvenient.

Gold dust and nuggets went to banks in the East and overseas, never remaining in San Francisco to pay for a new city or found a new system of justice. There were no sheriffs, police, or miners in the goldfields who were willing to protect the Mexican and Chilean miners when vigilantes stole their nuggets or gold dust, smashed their tools, or lynched them. Latinos knew that they were on their own. When a white miner broke into the cabin of a young Mexican woman, she stabbed him to death. She was seized by a white mob that chanted, "Give her a fair trial and hang her." The mob hanged her in Downieville.[3]

San Francisco was crude and makeshift. The bay seeped into the town with the tides and flooded the streets; the drinking water was putrid. Sanitation was nonexistent. With few houses in the haphazard port city, new immigrants lived in tents on the chilly hills where ocean winds tore through the straits of the Golden Gate. Wealthy residents had wildly prospered from Mexico's corrupt distribution of mission lands and paid no taxes to build the state. No other large city in the United States came into being as suddenly as San Francisco. Yet the city was growing: the population of San Francisco was one thousand in January 1848 and twenty-five thousand in December 1849.[4] Meanwhile, no one was designing a municipal government. No one knew how to adjudicate crime and punish wrongdoers. The solution was to arrest wrongdoers and put them to work.

"We Can Get Away with It"

In the summer of 1849, the Hounds, a white paramilitary group of veterans from the U.S.–Mexican War, swaggered into the lawless breach with the motto, "We can get away with it." After meeting in a large tent near the City Hotel, they adjourned to "hound" Chileans out of California and steal whatever they might get from residents of San Francisco. Wearing old uniforms scrounged up from the war, the Hounds paraded around the city plaza on Sunday afternoons, brandishing clubs and loaded pistols. They vowed to rid California of anyone who spoke Spanish; they robbed Latino miners, burst into brothels in the Chilean neighborhood, and raped the prostitutes. Witnesses saw the Hounds shear off the ears of a Black man and then rip out the tongue of a Mexican man who dared confront them. The Hounds elbowed into taverns with revolvers raised, demanding free liquor and food and seized the customers' money and jewels. They robbed the new stores and destroyed furniture that had been carried overland from the East.[5] In the summer of 1849, the Hounds demanded that the city pay them for protection against "foreigners."[6] Chilean miner Vincent Pérez Rosales wrote in his diary that the city was "young, vicious and shameless."[7]

So it was that in 1851 over two hundred white merchants, clerks, and workers rose at a mass meeting in Portsmouth Square to form the San Francisco Committee of Vigilance. Led by future city councilman Sam Brannan, the members of the committee organized themselves into a self-appointed force of "special constables." Poet Stephen John Hartnett named it a "gentleman's lynching club."[8] Wealthy merchants donated rifles, and the Committee of Vigilance managed to round up twenty of the Hounds and, in a grand display, marched their captives to the harbor and threw the Hounds down the hatches of the U.S. ship *Warren*. With no judicial system or secure prison, an impromptu court with a self-appointed judge was called to order and sentenced the leaders of the Hounds to serve ten years in prison at hard labor. A system of convict labor was in place.

In the goldfields, bands of white miners called themselves "tribunals" and rushed to deliver impromptu justice to men accused of murder, gambling debts, violations of water rights or land claims, theft of shovels and axes, and, worst of all, stealing gold dust. It was not uncommon to hang Natives for petty pilfering from the tent camps.[9] A Committee of Vigilance of six thousand men held its own trials for the assaults on the Chileans. Sentences included whipping and the deportation of Irish Catholics. On May 22, 1856, the San Francisco Committee of Vigilance lynched James P. Casey and Charles Cora on Sacramento Street.[10]

Profits from Punishment

California was unready for statehood. Helter-skelter, the state lacked any infrastructure to finance or build schools, hospitals, or sewage systems. Roads were remnants of ancient Indian trails, and municipal offices took over decrepit Franciscan missions. There were crimes and there were cruelties, but there were no prisons.

Led by southern plantation owners and a motley assortment of merchants and miners, the new legislature wrestled to write a vision of white justice into law and retrofit vigilante deeds into codes. California began to look at unpaid convicts for a labor force to build public works projects. But as yet, there was no pool of prisoners.

California's first legislature delivered an organized system of mass punishment and penal slavery. Convict labor would pay for itself; it would also generate profit by leasing prisoners to new businesses. In the first contract, the state offered to build a penitentiary, pay for food, guards, clothing, and medical care for the prisoners, and pay the lessee $10,000 per month and allow him to work the prisoners for his own profit. But first, convicts had to build San Quentin Prison.[11]

Convict labor offered legal cover, wrapped in virtue, to deliver an unpaid workforce in a state that would not "tolerate" slavery. Most new towns had only one or two rudimentary cells, often in the basement of the court-house or even a school. As refined theories of confinement, retribution, and criminal rehabilitation were taking hold in the East, California was build-ing rickety jails—a wooden cabin, an iron door, and a lock—and sending prisoners out to build the state. From the 1850s forward, legions of shack-led prisoners shuffled up and down the state carving roadbeds. They broke granite boulders for government buildings, paved sidewalks, and laid pipes for sewers and canals. Then they built their own windowless prison. By propagating the mass incarceration of Native Americans, Blacks, immi-grants, and poor people, the state of California became a high-density slaveholder and prolific slave broker for the cities, the state, and private farms and factories.

White settlers sought cooks and launderers, and ranchers sought field hands and cowboys for their vast land grants. The settlers began to kidnap Native prisoners from local jails—legally available for forced labor under the 1850 Act for the Government and Protection of Indians. Urban gangs such as the Los Angeles Rangers, notorious vigilantes, became efficient em-ployment agencies. They raided the jails and then "leased" Native Amer-ican prisoners to businessmen and ranchers who agreed to provide food and shelter and guard the convicts in cattle pens. Money for the use of these early prison laborers was handed to a warden as a bribe or it was sent to the state treasury as "rent" for a human being. In Stockton, Sacramento, and San Francisco, merchants rented convicts from the town jails and locked them at night in abandoned ships or "hulks." California had be-come a slave trader.

The California penal system was built on the assumption that certain groups of people were inherently deficient, aggressive, undeveloped, and destined to a life of crime. In the 1850s state prisoners were likely Black, Indian, Chinese, foreign, and expendable. Arrested for violating the har-mony and moral codes of the new towns, they were quickly charged and "proven" guilty by white courts.[12]

Convicts helped fuel California's breakneck growth in agriculture and manufacturing; their involuntary labor readied an economic colossus. From virtually the moment of statehood in 1850, private businesses built financial empires by leasing or just appropriating unpaid prisoners, sell-ing their products, and subcontracting their services, while California tax-payers provided food, cells, and surveillance; the prison-as-business model gave legitimacy to the young marriage of human bondage and merchant capitalism.

By 1851 San Francisco had grown from a Spanish fort and cow town built for the trade in cattle hides, which were drenched, stretched, and dried for boots or saddles. The rough-hewn waterfront boomtown was now a thriving commercial and residential hub of thirty-four thousand people.[13] Construction quickly drove the city into a $30,000 debt (almost $1 million today). The only place to incarcerate thieves, murderers, and rapists was in the basement of the old City Hall. The cheapest way to handle a prisoner was to hang him.[14] "Away with all mock sentimentality and false mercy," wrote the *Daily Alta California* in 1851; the city purchased iron to forge balls and chains for the prisoners who built San Francisco "in conditions akin to slavery."[15]

The Eighth Amendment bans cruel and unusual punishments that violate "standards of decency that mark the progress of a maturing society."[16] Did the founders anticipate the blistering pain endured by men and boys chained together, dragging iron links soldered to shackles about their ankles? Was this medieval contraption a fair punishment for crimes such as pickpocketing or petty theft? Regardless, the noisy clatter and drag of the heavy metal was another way to generate money for the impoverished state.

Rarely did the punishment fit the crime. Ankle chains rattled as convicts crushed granite to pave the streets of Gold Rush San Francisco; shuttles screamed as prisoners stood silent, working for twelve hours at looms in a jute mill inside San Quentin Prison; sitting behind rows of industrial sewing machines at the Richard J. Donovan Correctional Facility in the Ojai Desert, convicts clipped "Made in Honduras" labels off cotton T-shirts as armed guards patrolled from a mezzanine overhead.

From 1850 to the present, California's penal system has been an organized grid of forced labor sites. Crime paid—to the state of California, private factories, and the prison industry itself. When an insatiable need for labor arose in California, prisons begat prisons in an unending and profitable system of coerced labor. In cruel symmetry, crime and punishment also reproduced notions of white order and ethnic disorder.

The Thirteenth Amendment that abolished slavery contained a crucial concession: "except as a punishment for crime." That exception would move California from the widening periphery of a global economy toward its powerful center. Each empire that reigned over California added bricks to build a carceral state. On April 25, 1851, the legislature passed a law to allow private "lessees" to run a prison system for the new state.[17]

The Slave State and the Carceral State

Prison walls in California were never just ramparts to confine the guilty within and protect the innocent beyond. From the military presidios at the Spanish missions to contemporary for-profit prisons and immigrant detention centers, unpaid convict labor has been an intractable workaround to the pledge of freedom in the Treaty of Guadalupe Hidalgo, to the California constitution, and, in particular, to the Thirteenth Amendment—overriding its clause "except as a punishment for crime." The slave state and the carceral state were attached at the head of the mythical hydra. California's prisoners were compelled to build farms, dams, industries, and penitentiaries where once there were none. The mission system was a closed "penal colony, the dystopia from which it was practically impossible for the Indians to escape," says historian Rosaura Sánchez; the missions forged the first systems of mass incarceration in California, adds scholar Ben Madley.[18]

Because the Franciscan missions needed Native penitents in the fields, the Spanish padres and soldiers delivered punishment based on degrees of pain rather than length of confinement. After Mexico seized California from Spain and disbanded the missions, it allowed ranchers to punish Native American fieldworkers and cattle hands with ruthless techniques of torture and retribution that it had evolved over centuries of peonage. Stockades, chains, and whips embedded with pointed nails delivered obedience, fear, and hard labor. With statehood, California copied Pennsylvania's and New York's extreme models of punishment and incarceration because, plainly, the new state was not going to build itself. California needed prisoners to lay its roads, dig its ditches, and erect its dams.

Presidios and Penal Villages

Under Spanish rule, four presidios served as the first prisons and supplied the first prison guards (*carceleros*) who had been conscripted from Mexican prisons. Their first duty was to seize local Indians to build the churches and dormitories, and then turn to whips and shackles so that they would continue to labor in the hot fields and cultivate the crops for the twenty-one Catholic compounds that stippled the region. California Natives who refused were locked into stockades and made to beg for water. In full view of tribal members, the soldiers shackled runaways into weighted and rigid wooden boots and returned them to plow the fields.[19] In 1810 a fifth presidio was built at Mission Sonoma under Mexican rule, to serve as a military buffer against Russian encroachment around Fort Ross. As the headquarters of the Mexican army in California, it had a military and carceral role in the conquest and shape of California. The soldiers at the presidios worked as farmers and carpenters and served as agents who used punishment to deliver involuntary and unpaid labor; they also hunted for runaway Indians.[20] One of the first structures in Los Angeles was a jail soon filled with members of the proud and resistant Tongva (Gabrielino) tribe.

Under Mexican rule, makeshift jails on new ranches sprawled into crude penal villages crowded with Native convicts.[21] In January 1836 the Los Angeles Ayuntamiento—the City Council—required all Natives to work or face arrest. Indian convicts served on chain gangs, sweeping horse manure and sewage from the roads and carrying rotting animal and human carcasses to dumps outside the city.[22] These foul and unpaid urban jobs were early bricks in building the carceral state.

Floating Capital

California wanted a real state penitentiary, a statement edifice. But its new towns had no money and no large empty buildings to donate. Lumber was at a premium, and carpenters were leaving for the goldfields.

Meanwhile, ships delivering goods and passengers were anchored in San Francisco's harbor. Sea captains, porters, stewards, and kitchen staff disembarked with severe cases of "gold fever"; they abandoned their ships to head for the goldfields. Left behind were hundreds of cargo and passenger ships; a dense forest of masts bobbed over hulls that were rotting from saltwater and becoming dangerous obstructions to harbor traffic. Scavengers dismantled them plank by plank and recycled them for saloons, warehouses, and boardinghouses. Aspiring merchants towed the "rush ships" (named after the Gold Rush) to the wharfs and converted them into floating shops.[23] Why not prisons?[24] Towns on the Sacramento Delta towed the abandoned vessels up the river, where workmen repurposed the decaying hulls into floating jails.

In August 1849 Councilman Sam Brannan purchased the hulk *Euphemia* for $3,500 to house criminals arrested in San Francisco. Brannan stripped off its iron, beams, and sails and transformed it into a "floating brig." Then he billed the city $5,357.55 plus his "costs" for removing the fixtures and lumber and sold the materials to the city for the jail; he paid himself from the state treasury. Meanwhile, Brannan and other members

The prison brig *Euphemia* was docked
beside the Apollo Saloon, a bar at the wharf
of San Francisco.

In Frank Soulé, John H. Gihon, and Jim Nisbet, *The Annals of San
Francisco: Containing a Summary of the History of California, and a
Complete History of Its Great City* (New York: D. Appleton, 1855).

of the town council had cheaply bought up empty lots on the valuable
waterfront and built wharves to rent back to the city. Here he anchored his
floating prison *Euphemia* between two reclaimed vessels, a hotel ship, and
a saloon ship. Then he filled the ship with minor offenders: Peter Orius
had stolen a few bottles of claret from a local wine shop; John C. Allen was
serving ten days for disorderly conduct.[25]

Brannan retrofitted the hulks of the *Euphemia* and *Waban* into racially
segregated jails and rented them to San Francisco. The city had the hulls

The *La Grange* was the Sacramento County Prison from 1850 until
it sank in the 1861–62 flood. The brig was built onto a rotting
ship and moored on the Sacramento River in 1860.
(Courtesy of the California History Room, California State Library, Sacramento.)

towed around the bay, as prisoners, mostly Latino, constructed government
buildings. To some city residents, the brigs looked like leaky slave ships.[26]
Rotting hulls made for porous prisons. Dozens of prisoners escaped from
the *Euphemia* and *Waban* in the first year, cutting their chains, bribing a
guard, or just walking away from the stench, the cold, and the cruel labor
of the prison hulk. Newspapers called for a more secure facility.[27]

The Birth of the Prison Industrial Complex

California's legislature mandated that a new penitentiary contain "the het-
erogeneous elements composing the population." On April 25, 1851, California passed "An Act Providing for Securing of State Prison Convicts,"
creating a system to lease convict laborers to a private subcontractor who
would provide for their housing, food, and discipline while the government
took a cut. It put the project out for bidding.

James Madison Estell, a veteran of the U.S.–Mexican War and California soldier, and Mariano Guadalupe Vallejo, state senator and rancher,
won the contract to build California's first penitentiary, with a low-ball bid

of $100,000, but Vallejo withdrew when the legislature refused to locate the state capital on his vast ranch in Sonoma Valley. California's former governor John McDougal had served as the superintendent of the ruthless Indiana state prison and bought Vallejo's share of the new prisoner leasing scheme.[28]

Estell was a southern slaveholder who had traveled overland from his native Kentucky with fifteen enslaved men. Ambitious, crooked, and inept, he had just bankrupted an express mail business by dumping letters on the prairie.[29] Estell decided to build and run the penitentiary himself, and he persuaded the state to choose land on Point San Quentin, an empty peninsula that jutted into the northern end of San Francisco Bay. In July 1852 the state bought twenty acres for $10,000 and deeded them to Estell. The seller threw in another sixteen acres, rich in clay and next to the prison site, for Estell's own brick factory.[30] Estell had just won for himself a granite quarry for massive building stones and a clay mine, ideal for bricks.

Then the legislature gave Estell ownership of the prisoners, $100,000 for their labor and for construction materials, and, finally, a lease on the land and the as-yet-unbuilt prison. As important as land, clay, and granite was the steady supply of unpaid convicts housed next to Estell's building site. As the building contractor, Estell had full use of the convicts' labor to build the penitentiary and his own private enterprises. He leased another quarry on Angel Island and sublet it to his own prison fund. Then he forced the prisoners to crush stone, all under the supervision and salary of the San Francisco sheriff's office.

Estell had promised that the new prison would be "inhabitable and operational" in nine months. Now, with contract in hand, he lobbied for more time and for another $800,000.[31] He designed a prison that was $700,000 over budget and awarded the contract to a silent partner—himself. The *Sacramento Daily Union* estimated that the deal would add more than $1 million to the state debt and would give Estell another $15,000 per month.[32] Estell understood the overlapping interests of government and industry. He cannily tapped into California's tolerance for unpaid work, evidenced by the Act for the Government and Protection of Indians, which passed at the same time. Estell was speculating on the value of unfree human beings in this early California experiment in the prison industry. It did not take long before the *Daily Alta California* named the project the "State Prison Swindle."[33]

Immediately, journalists and residents were concerned that the state's most violent prisoners would be jailed on a neck of land surrounded by water on only three sides. Either Alcatraz Island or Angel Island in San Francisco Bay would have been more secure, and rumors flew that Estell also owned the land. Either way, Estell had bought himself a working estate on San Francisco Bay, and his first goal was to collect prisoners. He then bought the leaky *Waban* from San Francisco. When seventeen of his first thirty-four prisoners easily escaped, he hired a crew to retrofit the putrid hull so it could contain fifty men in cell blocks built into the hold.[34]

Estell expanded his own enterprise zone. In 1851 California took over the management of the old presidios and all the local jails in San Diego, Los Angeles, Santa Barbara, San Jose, and San Francisco and rebranded them as state prisons.[35] Governor John McDougal then directed city jails from across the state to ship 150 prisoners to his business partner, Estell, who locked them up in the hold of the *Waban*, four to eight to a cell. The governor also ordered the convicts to pay rent to Estell for their housing. No receipts mark the transfer of these men, nor how convicts, working without wages, could pay. Estell enlarged his floating prison.

Five female and 145 male prisoners were locked in the dank rows of eight-foot-square cells below deck, surviving in an abyss of fear, breathing a miasma of decomposing human waste. Every night the guards locked the men in their compartments. The stench of urine, feces, and sweat was so putrid that the guards refused to sleep on the ship or even go below until the hatch was unlocked and lower decks were aired out. When it rained, often from November through March, the convicts stayed below, day after day.

On December 18, 1851, a tugboat towed the *Waban* to Angel Island, six miles from Point San Quentin, and the inmates began to quarry stone from immense granite outcroppings and boulders that backed onto the narrow beach and to break rocks to construct their own prison.[36] But rather than use the boulders to build San Quentin, Estell sold them as paving stones to San Francisco for streets and sewage troughs.[37]

Meanwhile, the convicts found it easy to escape from the ship or run from the quarry. As a means of ridding themselves of the more dangerous criminals, guards arranged for prisoners to escape from the *Waban* or construction sites.

The prisoners on the *Waban* rose up, broke out, and organized revolts on the reeking dungeon ship. In 1851 they locked the guards in the ship's staterooms and rushed down the gangplank. The next year, twelve convicts were brought onto the deck struggling with the heavy iron shackles on their legs, but despite the weight of the cables, they tied up two guards, seized their revolvers, and jumped into a longboat. The fugitives sailed along the bay, and one by one they jumped off at remote beaches and made their way inland. Over the next couple of weeks, some fled along the Sacramento River Delta still chained to one another; others were found hiding out at ranches. Most were recaptured. Soon three other convicts whom Estell had rented out to build a house in San Francisco used the carpentry tools to cut their chains. They crawled under the construction site and escaped into the city.[38]

The legislature was still waiting for the penitentiary. But Estell and McDougal concocted a plan to turn the new penitentiary into a profitable enterprise. Former governor McDougal persuaded the legislature to give the partners a raise and issue a ten-year bond for $137,000 (over $4.5 million today) to finally build the state prison. Estell persuaded the legislature to grant them unlimited use of the prisoners' labor and permission to lease the convicts to construction firms. The state also allowed Estell and Mc-Dougal to keep the prisoners' wages. The partners turned to construction on public works, and the state of California became their large-scale client.

To launder the state funds and disguise his ownership of the prison, Estell formed a shell company, the San Francisco Manufacturing Company, and sold shares to his friends; his sole proprietorship of an unlimited stock in human beings morphed into a business venture, held in common by reputable investors. Estell's first job for the prisoners from the *Waban* was to build himself a brick factory with the clay at San Quentin. In the midst of San Francisco's first construction boom, he sold bricks across the city. Then he sold the prisoners' food and prisons' construction tools to settlers and miners heading north.[39] He pocketed the money allocated for prison uniforms and instead marked the men as convicts by shaving their heads.[40] It was rumored that for $200 he sold prisoners the right to escape.[41] If California's carceral state was born in the presidios at the Franciscan missions, it grew in the stone quarries along the bay and in the ruthless hold of the *Waban*.[42]

San Quentin by the Bay

In 1852 male guards and five female prisoners—mainly Mexican and Chilean—moved ashore to California's first state penitentiary. A couple of the women were sent to live in the overseer's house so administrators could "visit" them, and Estell pocketed the fees for their "service."[43]

The state's first for-profit prison was soon jammed with six hundred men trying to survive under a regime hatched by a powerful southern Democrat who had been reared in the playbook of plantation slavery. Estell worked the prisoners so efficiently that the city and the state began to compete with each other for Estell's convicts. When newspapers began to expose the layers of corruption, the legislature tried to buy back Estell's contracts. But Democratic governor John Bigler was Estell's friend and stood by him. Estell quickly took the opportunity to demand another $100,000 in state bonds, another $50,000 for machinery, and another $70,000 in "interest."[44] Estell had called their bluff.

San Quentin opened its heavy wooden gates in 1854. The top three floors of the gothic fortress held forty-eight cells—five feet eleven inches wide by nine feet ten inches long. Although Estell said they were designed for "contemplative" punishment of solitary confinement, each chamber was immediately jammed with four prisoners. The cells had no ventilation, light, or sanitation. "As you know," reported a concerned physician to the legislature, "the men when locked up are literally piled one upon another; this fills the room with animal heat and impure air."[45] Nationally, prisons were trying out methods of discipline and control—isolation, abuse, and forced prayer—and as state legislatures debated theories of retribution or reform, Estell turned to the model of Sing Sing Prison in New York. Sing Sing profited by selling products made by convicts in on-site factories and by selling the prisoners' labor itself. At Sing Sing, factory owners supplied the raw materials, and the prison provided the workforce, housing, and guards. Working silently and under the lash, convicts at Sing Sing became "living machines" whose unpaid labor made contractors very rich. Sing Sing had become a profitable factory that made and sold furniture, carpets, tapestry, shoes, bedding, cigars, and cut stone.

San Quentin copied from regimes at state penitentiaries in New York, Connecticut, New Hampshire, Ohio, and Michigan that used unpaid convict labor. These states had built their prisons near quarries, clay pits, forests, and railroad crossings and invited citizens and private firms to work their felons without pay to make wagons, barrels, iron goods, bricks, hoes, and rakes.[46] Many penitentiaries across the country were then open to the public, and tens of thousands of visitors came each year. To a Christian public committed to moral surveillance, the new prisons appeared completely transparent. Some prisons, such as Auburn State Prison in New York, were designed with concealed passages, so tourists could wander into prison workshops and observe prisoners silently and somberly repaying their debt to society. Meanwhile, prisoners at these model penitentiaries were forbidden from speaking, looking, or making any gestures toward the visitors. Prison guards were strictly instructed to never discipline inmates in front of the tourists. In the rare diary of a convict, Austin Reed tells how he was never allowed to make eye contact with visitors and never allowed to have his hands in his pants or coat when visitors were in the prison.[47]

Estell was eager to conscript more convicts, and he converted the mess hall into cells, which were immediately overcrowded. Uncovered pails served as toilets or "night buckets." At lockup, prisoners were sealed in 148 cells behind iron doors with only a "Judas hole"—a twelve-by-four-inch slit to admit air and a tin plate for meals. On the first floor, male prisoners slept in a "congregate" room, "like so many brute animals in a corral," wrote one visitor. Fourteen-year-old boys—usually first-time offenders—slept alongside hardened older criminals and all too often endured the terror and reality of rape.[48] Each morning the prisoners left their cells in work gangs to chop wood to fuel Estell's brick kiln, labor on roads, or hoe and harvest at local farms. All the profit of their labor went to Estell.

Estell continued to cut costs. He refused to hire more guards, whose food and pay came from his own pocket. He used the state's money to upgrade his private quarry with a guardhouse, cookhouse, and blacksmith shop. The state still gave him funds to operate the *Waban*, where another 250 men slept in the crowded hull. The guards would only sleep ashore. During the day, convicts from the *Waban*, shackled to one another, graded the steep streets of San Francisco or pushed carts filled with heavy clay through clouds of dirt and dust, returning at sundown to sleep in the hold of the ship.[49] To further expand his crews, Estell preyed upon petty offenders. From 1851 to 1880, two-thirds of San Quentin's inmates were held for minor crimes against property.

Before Estell reluctantly used the state funds to build the prison wall, hundreds of convicts simply walked out when they were marching to their meals.[50] Some fled by just wandering off into the chaparral of Marin County; during nights of dense fog, others fled south, hiding for months in the redwood forest on Mount Tamalpais and stealing food from nearby ranches.[51]

San Quentin's prisoners built escape into the prison's wall. In laying the bricks, they deliberately did not line up the sides squarely and used mortar from the nearby beach that was saturated with saltwater. With just a few swift strikes, it crumbled easily. The prisoners also left stones loose. More than once, they pulled them out, crawled through the holes, and ran to the unguarded shore.[52]

Newspapers dashed out stories of mass escapes. In 1852 eighty-three

San Quentin Prison gate.
Bancroft Library, University of California, Berkeley, via Online Archive of California.

prisoners escaped, killing several guards on their way out. Seventy-five men broke out in 1854, the year that San Quentin fully opened, and the *Alta California* predicted a mass escape, warning "the consequences of three hundred wretches being at large in the community are too horrible to contemplate." San Quentin, it cautioned, "will challenge comparison for the wretchedness of its system and the inefficiency of its conduct with the worst in the Union."[53]

Six hundred and sixty-four escapes from San Quentin occurred between 1854 to 1864. Estell frequently failed to pay the twenty guards at the prison and the sentries at the brig, so they turned their anger against the prisoners. On an early June afternoon in 1859, a handful of guards at San Quentin opened the massive gate to let in a work crew of two hundred Mexican and Native convicts who had been working at Estell's brickyard.[54] As the heavy gate swung open, a group of fifty white prisoners inside the yard seized the gatekeeper and a few guards and then locked the gate from the outside. Using the guards as shields, they rushed up the road and made their escape.

Most of the guards were now locked inside the compound. The sentries, stationed high on the wall, remained frozen, terrified that they might shoot the hostages. Trapped inside the prison and impotent in their rage, the guards turned a cannon and their rifles on the 250 Mexican and Indian men, who fell to their knees and made the sign of the cross, believing they must prepare to die.

Punishment

The new penal system was held together by a policy of deliberate sadism. For a bonus of twenty-five dollars per month, a designated "flogger" wandered through the workshops of San Quentin and whipped prisoners who were working slowly.[55] At night, "convicts under punishment" were chained to the wall of their cells. Prisoners who worked on the roads were punished for "disobedience" by being forced to wear "cross-irons"—chains that were attached to their heavy picks, crisscrossed the body, and locked their wrists to their ankles. California's roads were built by prisoners painfully hobbled and bent over.

San Quentin grew alongside the anti-flogging movement. The U.S. Navy banned whipping as a form of discipline in 1850, yet the next year, the captain of the guards and the warden of San Quentin administered 220 lashes between them, whipping prisoners on the buttocks for trivial offenses such as talking at meals.

Inmate James Hudson received fifty lashes for "general inattention to his duties as a cook." Leonard Tufts was dealt 150 lashes, accused of having planned a mass revolt. Convicts endured thirty lashes for insubordination, ten for lying, and thirty for "indulging in the most disgusting propensities"—presumably, masturbation or gay sex.[56] Painful tight scars, muscle wounds, and bleeding organs did not keep the men out of Estell's workforce. California did not abolish floggings as a form of prison punishment until 1880.[57]

In 1856 the Board of Prison Directors discovered that the warden had introduced the "shower bath." With this torture, guards shoved a convict laborer under an overturned wooden barrel and poured ice water over his naked body to simulate drowning—an early form of waterboarding.[58]

Fears of ethnic "disorder" appear in the punishments meted out to the population of racially mixed inmates. In 1855 three hundred of the 526 San Quentin convicts were "foreigners" who lived in racially segregated cell blocks and joined racially segregated riots. The prison housed 158 Chinese prisoners in isolation. It was the Latino and Native American prisoners who were the favored targets of the guards.[59]

"Negro Convict Showered to Death." Illustration
in *Harper's Magazine*, December 18, 1858.
(Courtesy of New York Public Library.)

Convict Slavery and the Early Prison Industrial Complex

By the mid-1850s Estell faced accusations of profiteering. Newspapers
in 1856 accused him of shipping two Black prisoners to New Orleans to
be sold as slaves. As prisoners starved, Estell was denounced for selling the
prison's food on the outside. He skimmed large sums of money that the
state had allocated for medical care, warm clothing, and new cell blocks.
Inmates were herded into crowded buildings designed for one-eighth of
its population. Petty criminals shared cells with murderers and violent

repeat offenders. No one supervised the guards. But Estell had partnered with the governor; he kept the putrid prison brigs and rented them back to the state—that is, back to himself.

Dozens of prisoners who were missing from roll call would later be found at Estell's own construction sites dotted around San Francisco Bay. Others bought pardons from the warden and just walked out. A damning string of escapes and mass revolts prompted the legislature to cancel Estell's contract time and time again.[60] In 1852–53 Estell was elected to the California State Senate, and he knew how to spread his profits around the capital. For the first five years of the life of San Quentin, the state not only renewed his contract but agreed to pay him another $10,000 per month. It specified that as a contractor, Estell had the right to work for his personal profit, setting a precedent that would endure for nearly two hundred years.[61] Time and time again the state renewed his contracts, for there was no one else who could get the job done.[62]

The legislature struggled with how to both keep Estell's profitable regime and corral his flagrant abuses. A delegation of legislators visited the prison and held a roll call of four hundred prisoners, and as each man came forward, the officials saw raw sores on the prisoners' bodies from being chained to the walls and observed scars from over one hundred lashes. From the window the legislators watched prisoners stumbling barefoot across the yard. In 1856 the legislature heard rumors that Estell had murdered a "wench" in Missouri and that he encouraged "licentious behavior" between the guards, prisoners, and the few female convicts. Yet it was the public's fear of escapes and mass revolts that prompted the state to try to fire Estell. Reluctant to lose the profitable contractor, however, the state blamed the local Marin County Grand Jury for failing to contain San Quentin's abuses.[63]

Escapes, revolts, and violent manhunts continued. In 1862 the prisoners were starving and took axes and tools from the workshops and started a riot. While some stormed the armory, two to three hundred others rushed out the heavy front gate, taking the warden as a hostage and holding him in front, as a human shield. Three months later, three hundred convict laborers escaped with their next hostage, the lieutenant governor of California, John Chellis. Chellis was too heavy to keep up with prisoners on the run, and they let him return to his quarters, where he slept through the dramatic night while the fugitives fled through the sloughs and lagoons at the edge of San Francisco Bay. Hunted by schooners on the dark sea and by mounted guards on land, the posse squeezed the fugitives into surrender just four miles from San Quentin. At the end of a long pursuit, twenty escapees remained at large and twenty-nine were killed.[64] The legislature reported, "We are of the opinion that a larger number of prisoners has been killed in attempted revolts in the State Prison of California than in all the other states aggregated."[65]

Estell finally lost control of San Quentin. In one year, from 1855 to 1856, the prison's costs rose from $58,000 to $411,000—for bricks, mortar, and the upkeep of the convicts; the state budget bore the costs for Estell's own projects.[66]

Chain Gangs Once More

The Anti-Vagrancy Act, or "Greaser Act," of 1855 defined vagrants as "all persons who are commonly known as 'Greasers' or who are the issue of Spanish and Indian blood . . . and who go armed and are not peaceable and quiet persons." The Anti-Vagrancy Act created a new pool of convict laborers to build San Francisco, and the police began to arrest Mexicans and "debtors"—beggars, prostitutes, drunkards, and vagrants. With that, the law criminalized homelessness, and vast numbers of poor people were swept up and sentenced to hard labor.[67] Yet again, chain gangs paved the streets, usually in front of the homes of city officials.[68] Without the food and shelter of a jail, the men were barefoot and cold, surviving on bread and water. Lacking tools, they carved out the streets of San Francisco with their bare hands.[69]

Like the penitentiaries in the East, the chain gangs were humiliating street theater.[70] San Franciscans gawked at convicts shackled with four-foot chains of heavy iron, one end strapped around their waist and the other fastened to a ring at their ankle.[71] Lightly guarded, the first gang soon discovered that the lock was only fastened by a small screw, and many escaped.

As the Gold Rush came to an end, thousands of miners and migrants arrived in the cities needing jobs; but, instead, in 1858 San Francisco hired a chain gang to build sewers and level fields for new houses. Sentences at hard labor served an insolvent city looking for unpaid workers: in 1857 Michael Butler spent sixty days on the chain gang for the crime of being homeless. Samuel T. Davis, an African American, was sentenced to 180 days on the chain gang for petty larceny; Michael Gifflin, a white man, was sentenced to forty days for stealing flour and sugar; George Rowe stole cards from a printer's office and faced thirty-five days of hard labor.

Desperate for even more laborers, San Francisco rented a chain gang from Sacramento.[72]

In California, poverty became a gateway crime, punishable by unpaid labor on a chain gang. In Marysville, the chain gang served as an orphanage for homeless boys and provided a ready supply of unpaid child labor.[73] Historian Ruth Wilson Gilmore calls the poor a "surplus population"— people who are idle until the need for their labor arises again, and then the prison rates climb.[74] Prisoners resented becoming spectacles trudging through the streets, attached to a ball and chain; urged on by the *San Francisco Sun*, in November 1858 the convicts on San Francisco's chain gang launched a three-day hunger strike.[75] Yet city officials defended these "street jails" as visual warnings to young boys.[76]

Slavery Out of Sight

James Estell died at his home in San Francisco in 1859. The state took control of San Quentin and built on Estell's legacy; at taxpayers' expense, it enlarged the private factories inside the gates. Lit only by gas, a village of slave factories grew inside the dark prison where prisoners worked on-site for thirty to seventy-four cents a day, making cabinets and furniture, rolling cigars, and producing high-end saddles, boots, and shoes.[77]

At the start of the Civil War, Mexicans represented 16 percent of California's prison population, six times higher than their presence in the state as a whole.[78] In 1862 the San Francisco *Daily Evening Bulletin* tallied the makeup of the San Quentin population: 258 "Americans" and 333 "Foreigners."[79] War veterans and white European immigrants were out of work, and the legislature heard complaints that convict labor took up jobs, reduced wages, and exposed war heroes to destitution.

During the era of abolition and the Civil War, San Quentin made efforts to conceal the unpaid laborers, who were locked in chains, working bent over, scared, and hungry. California's young labor movement took notice. In 1862 local cigar makers protested competition from unpaid prisoners who hand-rolled cheap cigars. Four years later, toward the end of the Civil War, skilled trade workers demanded that the state ban all unfree and unpaid convict workers who were undercutting their own struggles for less grueling hours and higher pay. Yet the small movement against unfree labor failed.[80]

Meanwhile, the convicts suffered. San Quentin's walls were wet and rain-sodden; there was little drinkable water at the prison. Nearly one-third of the prisoners were barefoot, and others wore rough burlap or gunny sacks, or pieces of woolen blankets tied around their feet. The state decided that the way to protect citizens from frequent prison breaks was to make convicts conspicuous, and the warden finally outfitted the prisoners in black-and-white striped uniforms. Four hundred new cells were added for solitary confinement, but several prisoners slept in each cell. By 1873 the prison's growth had doubled and San Quentin held 931 convicts. One-half of San Quentin's prisoners worked for private contractors, received no pay, and generated nearly $300,000 ($6 million today) per year in income for the state.[81]

In 1874, as the state headed into economic collapse, the legislature easily rejected pleas from a weak labor movement to ban convict labor. The California Supreme Court went further and allowed private "tenants" or manufacturers to oversee prison workers; more contract work money poured into the factories of San Quentin. By 1876 the California Manufacturing Association, a factory founded by Estell, occupied the entire second floor of the penitentiary; a shoe factory rented the long upper floor, including the prison library.[82]

An organized racial caste system seeped into the prison. By 1874, 168 Chinese convicts slept packed together in the wagon factory—a fifty-eight-by-thirty-nine-foot room in the cold basement of the prison.[83] The unpaid work of Chinese convicts further angered the young labor movement that was growing in response to the depression of the early 1870s. Invigorated by the statewide purges of Chinese migrants and the rants against Chinese workers, the unions depicted both Chinese convict workers and Chinese immigrants as enslaved "coolies." Across California, shoppers demanded that products such as cigars be made by "white hands only."

The prison's renowned corruption finally prompted a series of state inquiries: it found that women prisoners were compelled to "visit" the guards, and guards were selling protection by taking prisoners' "gate" or discharge pay of three to five dollars. As months of investigations went on, the inmate witnesses disappeared. But as a result, in 1879 California became the first state in the union to ban the leasing of convicts *unless* it was to produce products or to work on construction projects that were for the benefit of the state.[84]

The legislature, again responding to the white working class, raised the cost of hiring "skilled convict labor" and doubled the cost of hiring a prisoner to a minimum of a dollar a day; but in turn, San Quentin labeled all prisoners "unskilled," saying they had never completed a union apprenticeship.[85]

The racial demographics at San Quentin never represented the state. In 1882 the U.S. Congress passed the Chinese Exclusion Act, and by the next year, of 1,103 convicts working at the prison, 243 were Chinese men, 137 were Mexican—that is, one-third of the convict laborers at San Quentin were Chinese or Mexican. At the peak of the anti-Chinese roundups in 1885–86, a California penal commission concluded that the Chinese "have driven many of the white race from avenues of employment and have introduced to the youth of the State some of the most debasing Asiatic vices, while members of the race form a large part of our criminal population."[86] The suffering of convicts working inside San Quentin had little impact on the job opportunities for free white men.[87]

The painful period of unemployment from 1873–78 gave rise to two organizations of workers—the Knights of Labor, the first national labor organization in the United States, soon to be displaced by the American Federation of Labor. Building a political front called the "Workingmen's Party of California," and led by anti-Chinese leader Denis Kearney, labor organizations envisaged a specter of unpaid convicts working on modern machinery.[88] The free white working man, claimed the Knights, was squeezed between "Chinamen on one side and convict labor on the other."[89] The party won enough seats in the 1878 election to draft a new constitution that deprived Chinese men of the right to vote and declared that after January 1, 1882, "the labor of convicts shall not be let out by contract to any person, co-partnership, company, or corporation, and the legislature shall, by law, provide for the working of convicts for the benefit of the state."[90] The deal lasted less than a year.

The state's solution to overcrowded cells was to force convicts to build another penitentiary.[91] In a Möbius strip of corruption and brutal labor, California purchased land at the desolate and hot edge of the Sacramento River Valley, on the tribal lands of the Nisenan people. The site for Folsom Prison was about one hundred miles due east of San Quentin, and hundreds of its prisoners were sent to do the backbreaking work of carving granite to build the new prison and a grand hydroelectric dam on the rushing American River. Under the blazing sun and the constant threat of torture, the involuntary and unpaid laborers from San Quentin quarried and transported hundreds of granite blocks, weighing twelve tons each. When the construction of the dam was finished in 1880, the state gave the land and the dam to the Natoma Electric Company.[92]

To build California's first utility companies and deliver electricity to the industrializing state, the new prison, built to house "incorrigibles," gave a private firm over half a million days, or one-quarter of a million dollars' worth, of unpaid labor. In 1895 the Folsom Water and Power Company threw the switch that sent electrical power to Sacramento.[93] Folsom prisoners—whipped and abused—were responsible for the electric illumination of the state's new homes and buildings.[94]

Starting in the 1870s, federal troops withdrew from the South. In a racial free-for-all, Mississippi, Georgia, and Alabama arrested thousands of formerly enslaved men and leased the new convicts to plantation owners to rebuild a cotton empire and lay tracks for the new railroads. Convicts also worked on levees, laid railroad tracks, and slept in shacks or former slave quarters at run-down plantations across the South. Thousands of men, once enslaved, were now shackled into chain gangs to chop turpentine trees, pick cotton, and mine coal. California planned to adopt that shape-shifting form of slavery. With immigrants from China, Eastern Europe, India, Ireland, and the South arriving in the West, however, California finally had a large working class; at the end of the nineteenth century, California's prison industry was a losing investment.[95]

San Quentin State Prison, a fearsome granite structure perched at the edge of the salt marshes, adapted to the economic dreams of the twentieth century. When compared to the total number of workers in industry, the number of convict laborers seems small, but in California their concentration in a few industries—boots and shoes, brick-making, furniture, farming, and burlap bags—was vital to the new state. Looking backward over the nineteenth century, a few systems of convict labor quickly dominated. One was the "contract system" in which the contractor supplied the raw material, bore the risk of profit and loss, and supervised the laboring prisoners, while their care and custody remained with the state—a profitable skimming. San Quentin also had a piecework scheme where prison guards supervised the forced labor. Facing objections from labor organizations and small businesses, San Quentin's wares were sold with the stipulation that only the prison or the state could use the shoes, desks, and doors for itself.

With an eye for unpaid labor for the state, convict labor would construct public works—from roads to hydroelectric dams. In all these systems, free labor had to compete with unpaid convict labor, and private manufacturers who employed free workers faced competition from the state system that enjoyed the profits from unpaid workers whose costs would not match the barest wage. In 1861 prisoners earned between thirty and seventy-five cents a day and then had their costs deducted.[96]

Coerced convict laborers created a rock-crushing industry that built the roads, bridges, forestry camps, and state parks for twentieth-century automobiles and tourism, and for prisons. Involuntary convict labor produced California's twentieth-century prosperity that was based on trucks delivering lettuce and strawberries, and automobiles carrying tourists along its highways to the waterfalls of Yosemite, the orange groves of Pasadena, and the redwood and fern forests of the North Coast.[97]

CHAPTER FOURTEEN

A Fortress Economy

DONALD LOWRIE, AN UNEMPLOYED bookkeeper, stenographer, and some-time journalist, traveled a hard road to San Quentin. At some point in 1901 he had not eaten for three days. "Breadless" and "living rough," he wandered the streets of San Francisco. In a trance of fatigue and hunger, he passed an open window, partly concealed by a rosebush. Lowrie had never committed a crime before but, now desperate, he climbed in the window, wandered through the house, and tiptoed upstairs. In the quiet, he heard a ticking sound; he grabbed what he could—a diamond watch and a purse that held three twenty-dollar gold pieces and some silver coins.[1] That night he ate in a café, bought a twenty-five-cent cigar, and went into a pawn shop to hock the stolen goods—detached from his culpability.

Within an hour, the pawnbroker informed the police of this unlikely owner of a diamond watch. The police found Lowrie as he was stepping into a cheap boardinghouse and slapped on handcuffs. Lowrie was sentenced to fifteen years in jail and loaded onto a ferry bound for San Quentin Prison. That afternoon he was processed, photographed, and given a mattress in a cold cell that held six men.

Lowrie's first job at San Quentin was to empty the night buckets. After four days, the warden summoned the new prisoner and issued him a blunt pair of scissors. Prisoner 19093 entered a dimly lit cavern where, he recalled, he "traversed several long aisles, with whirring belts, roaring machinery and acne-faced men all about us and stopped at the far end of the mill—at loom 201." Surrounding him were hundreds of sweating men working in their undershirts, inhaling air heavy with dust, heat, and threads.

The Jute Mill: A Gulag on the Bay

Donald Lowrie had been sent to the jute mill, a factory that was built inside San Quentin, where unpaid prisoners stood at machines carding long jute fibers and spinning them into rough thread. The men fed the threads into one of the hundreds of looms that wove them into burlap. As Lowrie watched prisoners bend over industrial sewing machines, stitching the rough material into tall bags, he noticed other prisoners slumped against the damp walls.

Lowrie joined the eighteen hundred convicts working in the jute mill and entered San Quentin's world of the "lowest of the low"; the mill workers were fed the coarsest food and slept "penned up like dogs." He was warned that if he did not complete his daily quota of cloth or bags, he would be hung by his wrists to the wall of a stone cell, dangling for hours in chains or leather straps, his arms painfully stretched overhead. If he did not complete his weekly quota, on Saturday night he would be sent to the "hole" to stay until Monday.

Standing at loom 201, Lowrie was a figure in a global chain of a particular kind of slavery that began in India on jute plantations. Here the coarse plant was harvested by "coolies"—a Hindi euphemism for enslaved men adopted from Britain's proud post-slavery era. In 1880 Indians were hand-sewing twenty-five million jute bags in workshops across the subcontinent. Drivers carted the bags to Calcutta and loaded them onto ships in the Bay of Bengal bound for San Francisco. From there the bags were shipped to the new "wheat barons" in California.

Governor George Perkins (1880–83) wanted California to reap these revenues and make its own jute sacks, which held loose kernels of wheat.[2] Wheat had saved California during the long depression in the 1870s; now farmers used rustic sacks to ship grain for export. California had no grain elevators stationed along railroad tracks, and farmers carried the sacks across gangways to send along riverways in flatboats, barges, and steamboats.

Perkins decided that behind the wall at San Quentin, prisoners would build a jute mill and then weave the bags; the warden would sell them to California farmers. Standing in his way was the 1879 amendment to the state constitution: California was the first U.S. state to abolish convict labor and outlaw renting prisoners or prison "manufactories." The only exception was if the goods they produced were useful or profitable to the state.[3] Perkins had found a way for convicts to pay for their own imprisonment and also bring "hard cash" into the public treasury. Besides, he said, "productive labor" would teach "habits of industry to unfortunate members."[4]

San Quentin again became a site of involuntary prison labor, this time in a global industry for the profit of the state, prison, and farmers.[5] And just like that, the 1879 constitution that had banned involuntary and unpaid prison labor was handily set aside.

The public immediately objected. In August of 1881 the *Daily Alta California* said a jute mill was "illegal, un-businesslike, unsafe and justifying severe censure." Lowrie's torture as punishment for a torn piece of cloth disrupts the logic of crime and punishment. Who was to benefit from his vengeful discipline? The directors at San Quentin had a secret plan to create for themselves "a system of great remuneration."[6] The Knights of Labor jumped aboard: the jute mill was "nothing but a scheme by which individuals would be enabled to use the capital and slaves of the state to compete with enterprising capitalists and honest mechanics."[7] The state would buy the jute; the looms and the convicts at San Quentin were free for the taking.

On May 1, 1882, twenty-five looms began to roar at the steam-driven mill. The jute mill had been built by prisoners, yet still cost the state $300,000. This prison within a prison just needed to find convicts, and that year the state doubled San Quentin's population to three thousand men. From the first, conditions at the mill were life-threatening. Prison records show numerous cases of tuberculosis, byssinosis, and brown lung disease from air "charged with fine particles of dust, fatal to the weak lunged convicts." Prisoners lost fingers and limbs in the whirling machines.[8]

The revenue from the first run of bags cut the costs of running San Quentin in half, and warden James Ames shut down all the other factories inside the prison and sent those convict laborers into the jute mill. New fields of wheat and burlap bags, dreamed Ames, would expand California's agricultural economy. Indeed, convicts turned California's pioneer crop into a national commodity. The legislature approved: no white industries were at risk; the only ones suffering were a few Chinese businessmen who owned a small jute mill in Oakland.[9] For the next twenty years, the price of grain fell about 60 percent. During the financial crisis of 1873, amid rising railroad fees for shipping crops and national moves to reduce paper money, farmers, backed by the Grange or Patrons of Husbandry movement, turned to the state. One source of help was in unpaid prison labor: San Quentin bought the looms from the foundry James F. Low and Company in Monifieth, on the east coast of Scotland, and then sold the essential jute bags to California farmers at under cost; they hid the profits from buying and shipping fibers from India, and, as important, they disguised the low costs for the "keeping" of the prisoners.[10]

The jute mill, San Quentin Prison, 1919.
(Courtesy of the Anne T. Kent California Room,
Marin County Free Library, San Rafael, California.)

The true costs rebounded to the convicts. One day a tear showed up in Donald Lowrie's burlap—a flaw in his work, not in the fiber. He remembered: "Well, they said I made bad cloth, and I promised to do better, but it was the fourth time this month. When the mill shut, they took me down to the dungeon and into one of the dark cells. There was an old mattress on the floor, and they told me to lay down on it, and they put the 'jacket' on me. It held my arms so I couldn't move them, but that wasn't enough. They turned me over on my stomach and laced me up. R—put his foot in the middle of my back so as to pull the ropes up tight, and when I hollered, he laughed and said, 'You'll make bad cloth, will you? We'll teach you how to make it good.' . . . For half an hour or so I didn't suffer much, but gradually I began to feel smother[ed]. . . . I got scared and began to holler, but that only made my heart hurt. Pretty soon my arms and hands began to tingle." When Lowrie heard the clang of the lockup bell, he realized that he had only been laced into the full-body jacket for two hours; he faced twenty-two hours more. But the straitjacket, he was told, was a

Donald Lowrie, a prisoner at San Quentin,
described the "punishing torture" of having
his hands tied behind him as his body fell
forward over a metal bar or he was hung from
"bull rings," causing panic and agony.

In Griffith J. Griffith, *Crime and Criminals* (Los Angeles:
California Prison Reform League, 1910), via Internet Archive.

reprieve from the "straps" that paralyzed prisoners working at the jute
mill.

Lowrie slipped into a state of constant terror of dying from the tor-
menting punishment. Fifteen years after the passage of the Thirteenth
Amendment, in 1881 San Quentin adopted the Pennsylvania or Quaker
"associate silent system," which banned convicts from talking to each other
at the loom, at meals, or while marching across the yard. The prison had

three times as many prisoners as looms, and the remaining men and a few women stood for twelve hours, afraid to talk or slouch against the factory wall. Lowrie faced torture over and over again. He described a clinching panic when the guard tied his hands behind his back, his body fell forward over a metal bar, and the guard left.[11]

Prisoners understood that their punishment was almost always worse than the violence for which they were incarcerated. The torture impressed on inmates their loss of mobility and safety. Days of forced silence and time in solitary became an existential condition of incarceration for the jute mill workers. Brutality was a reminder of the prison's capricious power. Like modern "enhanced interrogation techniques," the discipline for Lowrie's inevitable mistakes at the loom terrorized his mind as well as his body.

Torture was embedded in California's systems of convict labor—at times, an effective prod to force a reluctant confession, but generally an ineffective system of punishment. San Quentin had a variety of punitive instruments that punished not only the errant convict but the other prisoners who were forced to witness or hear screams coming from the dungeon.

Historically, all regimes of California slavery have turned to torture. Generally, torture is used on those who lack civil status or civil protection—children, prisoners, and the enslaved—those who are not fully accepted as human and presumed to be guilty of something. Torture is a shared experience of slavery and incarceration that erases identity—beyond a shaved head, an assigned number that replaces a name, and a striped uniform instead of street clothes. When Lowrie first walked through the heavy gates, he was more curious than fearful about what was to come, but he soon understood that he was totally dependent on the disposition of his torturer and the power of his jailers.[12]

As a convict laborer, Lowrie was an unfree man with undetermined rights. Once autonomous with the civil privileges of whiteness and adulthood, now he was destitute and suddenly and forcibly reliant on San Quentin. No longer able to make choices that represented his free will, in San Quentin he absorbed the status of a child and a slave.

By 1907, while Lowrie was standing at a loom or stationed against a wall, the subsidies of convict labor sailed across the world. The Prison Board argued that the jute mill prevented idleness and taught important skills—skills, noted the press, that were useless outside San Quentin. As Lowrie calculated the penitentiary's profits and losses, he came to believe that the jute mill existed only to compel prisoners to labor.

Lowrie found ways to survive. And after eight years, he began to write, smuggling out short stories and hundreds of pages of notes, compelling readers to become "eye-witnesses" to the crime of convict labor; by writing, he reentered the world of civic recognition mocking the threat of convict invisibility. He figured out that for a sack of tobacco, a fellow convict would help him finish twenty yards of jute, or for five cents, do an hour of his work.[13] Finally transferred from his job in the mill, Lowrie chose isolation. When at last he stepped into the daylight, he walked directly to the offices of the San Francisco *Daily Evening Bulletin* to write *My Life in Prison*, his story as a victim and as a witness to the carceral state.[14]

Prisoner Colonel Griffith J. Griffith was a coal baron. Convinced that his wife was conspiring with the pope to poison him, in 1903 Griffith took his wife and son to a hotel in the beach town of Santa Monica. Here Griffith held a Bible in one hand and a pistol in the other. He forced his wife to kneel at his feet and shot her in the eye. The judge diagnosed Griffith with "alcoholic medical insanity," an early insanity plea, and sentenced the wealthy philanthropist to two years in San Quentin.

Griffith thought he had the stamina and nerves, the education and curiosity, to survive in San Quentin. He expected he would face hard labor and likely torture. But he was daunted by the surveillance at the jute mill: "I found myself one of some eight hundred prisoners, under direct custody of a dozen guards, in a building . . . 1,000 feet long." Through the grimy glass roof, he could see armed guards stationed along the prison wall, ready to fire. He was also frightened of the other prisoners. To avoid charges of enslavement, San Quentin paid each convict ten cents a day, but when Griffith's mates realized that he had "more than my share of the good things in life," they targeted him with spinning bullet-shaped shuttles.

After Griffith endured a full year of forced silence, he decided to ingratiate himself, first by selling tobacco to his fellow convicts and then by reading newspapers aloud to them at night, creating a covert camaraderie. In 1906, the year of the fateful San Francisco earthquake, Griffith read out the news that San Francisco was ravaged, enraging the guards by challenging the prison's sadistic hold on information. Blindsided, the officers struck back, beating Griffith on his feet with lead walking sticks. They forced him to submit to a deadly "bombshell cathartic" administered with a thirty-two-inch rubber hose that was attached to gallons of water. Afterward, the guards forced him to watch as they built a bonfire in the yard and burned his books and photographs.

For two years Griffith kept a hidden diary. He wrote of the "ordinary" tortures—how guards mixed young boys with older prisoners and then

watched the child rapes. He wrote how the guards forced a confession from
"Boston Blackie," a prisoner nicknamed after the hero of a pulp crime
novel, who had been falsely accused of smuggling opium into the prison;
the guards forced Blackie to admit to the crime by tying him into a straitjacket for 140 hours. The straitjacket compressed Blackie's organs and severed his arm from his body: "His life was at the mercy of the officials who
dictated his testimony. Every convict is equally helpless, and this helplessness is the fundamental fact that must not be forgotten."[15] Griffith saw the
"Humming Bird" applied to a prisoner: chained at his wrist and with his
feet in a metal tub, he was zapped with electricity until his muscles spasmed.
People choked, fainted, and, often, died from strangulation.[16]

As the aging looms deteriorated, Griffith watched prisoners beaten
for producing flawed cloth. He saw a guard choke a prisoner to death for
not obeying a work order, but the convict spoke only Italian and could not
understand the instruction.[17] Helpless to protest, Griffith kept his secret
notes, always alert to the "125 guards, each a walking arsenal" of Gatling
guns, Winchesters, double-barreled loaded shotguns, rapid-fire revolvers,
and twelve thousand rounds of ammunition. Griffith believed that "only
one hopelessly insane would dream of resistance; . . . even to plot of escape
is proof of despair run mad."[18] For the production of what was a cheap
burlap bag, San Quentin brutalized the prisoners to the point where they
were worthless as laborers. But more men were always available.

In January 1896 the legislature canceled the mill workers' ten-cent
daily "wage" and announced they were already paid with their "board"—
spoiled soup, rancid meat, and cold chunks of fat and rotten beans. That
year the prisoners who worked in the bakery reported to the Board of
Trustees that a latrine was leaking urine and fecal matter into the bread
dough, and the trustees finally paid a visit to the prison. When word
reached the convicts that this meeting was taking place, hundreds gathered in the yard and declared a strike. The warden was angered that the
protest over contaminated food had erupted in the presence of the trustees. He ordered a lockdown and canceled all the strikers' "good time," or
early release.[19]

One year later, on the morning of Thursday, May 27, 1897, the trustees returned to San Quentin. This time 720 men—about half the prison's
population—marched into the mill and took their positions at the looms.
But as the machines started to whirl, the convicts stood still, making no
motion to start work. In this early sit-down strike, the "jute mill gang," as
they were later called, remained silent, as required, but they ignored the

An early form of waterboarding, the "water cure"
was a form of punishment at San Quentin that
duplicated strangulation and drowning.
In Griffith J. Griffith, *Crime and Criminals* (Los Angeles:
Prison Reform League, 1910), 284, via Internet Archive.

guards' order to start work. The machines growled into the silent air. And then, as one, on cue, the convicts began to howl—an open, communal, organized guttural wail, different from the familiar screams of agony at the hands of torture.

The trustees hid in the warden's office and offered "safe conduct passes" to the strike committee to come voice their complaints. The strike leaders marched to meet a trembling warden, W. E. Hale. They said that they spoke on behalf of white, Black, and Chinese convicts, American and foreign-born prisoners, men who spoke different languages. Fearful that the strikers would destroy the looms, Hale promised to fire the cooks and charge the baker with graft for using flour thick with maggots and for encouraging kitchen workers to commit "unmentionable acts" upon the bread dough. But Hale refused to charge the cook with assault. In the midst of the negotiations, the piercing lockup bell screeched, and armed guards marched four hundred strikers into their cells and crammed seventy others into solitary "holes" in the dark dungeon below.

At six o'clock, the prisoners again began to howl and bang on the doors of their cells. Throughout the night, each time the "watch" called out the hourly "All is well," the prisoners howled. Watching reporters, neighbors, and prisoners' families gather on a hillside outside the gate, Warden Hale feared that the foul conditions at the mill would be exposed to public scrutiny. He ordered the guards to silence the prisoners. Several prisoners pulled loose bricks from their cells and hurled them at the guards. The strikers remained in lockdown.

On day two, the strikers resumed their chant, and Hale ordered the guards to wheel out the fire hoses. One by one, the prisoners were taken out of their cells, stripped naked, and locked back in. The guards put the hoses up to the "Judas holes" and, moving from one cell to another, they forced water through the small openings, pummeling the prisoners, knocking the naked men around their cells, and pounding them against the walls. The guards made the strikers stay naked and wet for a week.[20]

What finally became clear to California taxpayers was that while they paid for the guards, rank meals, and crumbling cells, the profits from the labor of California's convicts were sent abroad.[21] In the autumn of 1897, the San Francisco *Daily Evening Bulletin* published "The Paradise of the Pacific," a ruthless exposé of the jute mill, and revealed that the machinery, spindles, and building itself were owned by a British syndicate.[22] A global syndicate had invested $1 million ($1 billion today) to buy jute in Calcutta, corner the market, drive up the price, and reap the profits of California's convict workers. By law, those profits belonged to the state. The state was held hostage. In effect, wrote the *Bulletin*, the deal levied a $1 million tariff on California taxpayers and gave a $1 million subsidy to California farmers, handing them bags just above cost.[23] For now, the mill was prospering.

The farmers, ironically, were not. The relentless production of a single crop had exhausted California's soil. Ready to profit from the invention of the refrigerated railroad car and from hiring low-paid Chinese, Japanese, Sikh, and Eastern European fieldworkers, farmers abandoned wheat and planted peach and plum orchards.

In April 1951 the jute mill at San Quentin Prison, then exporting hundreds of thousands of orders for Korea, burned to the ground, a darkened emblem of the history of California slavery. Most people suspected arson. The jute mill was never rebuilt.[24]

A Separate Sphere

From the first, the California legislature assumed there would be a women's building in the penitentiary, with segregated labor and separate meals. The state's goal was neither to protect nor rehabilitate "fallen women," as female prisoners were called, but to make sure that they avoided sexual contact with male prisoners. Nonetheless, when the five women who had been held on the *Waban* came ashore, they saw that Estell had not built a "female department."

No more women were imprisoned at San Quentin until 1879. From 1880 through 1910, only 231 women out of approximately 16,630 prisoners (1.4 percent) appear in the San Quentin Prison register. Only forty-six females were sentenced for "violent crimes"—murder, assault, and robbery—while twenty-five were Black, Mexican, or Chinese. Several women "poisoners" were convicted of killing men, usually with arsenic, available as rat poison. Few were held for prostitution, for at the time it was not a crime in itself and, besides, male customers were reluctant to report crimes associated with their purchase of sex.[25]

In the early twentieth century, criminality was often explained by pseudo-biology notions—reductive race-based explanations that arose along with eugenics and phrenology—that claimed the shape of the skull, length of ear lobes, and size of lips were predictors of delinquency, theft, and assault. Misappropriating Charles Darwin's theory of evolution, sociologists analyzed the origins of criminal behavior and concluded that females were naturally followers or passive criminals. As evidence, they compared the immobile female ovule or egg to the active sperm. Other pseudoscientists tried to correlate women's arrest records for shoplifting with their monthly menstrual cycles, times of "irritability" and "anxiety" that entitled women to leniency in sentencing. In 1924 Sigmund Freud suggested that menstruation reminded women of their biological inferiority and caused them to seek revenge.[26]

Nonetheless, women in the reform movements of the Progressive Era took note of their imprisoned sisters whose labor was involuntary and unpaid. Hester Griffith, president of the Los Angeles Women's Christian Temperance Union, visited the women's "chamber" in 1907, where she witnessed green moss and mold on dank walls. She saw an "army of gigantic rats" scurry across the floor and invade the women's pantry.

The female prisoners were thought to be controlled and debased by their bodily functions: still forced to use buckets, each morning their job was to scoop sewage from forty night pails that hung from the ceiling and

Clara Newton, age twenty and listed as "Mulatto," was sentenced in February 1910 to a term of three and a half years for "abduction." Erma Le Dou was paroled in July 1920, returned to San Quentin in 1933, transferred to Tehachapi Women's Prison, and sentenced to life imprisonment for murder in 1933. Maria Sanchez, age twenty-nine and listed as "Dark Complexion," was sentenced to eight and a half years for "assault by means likely to produce bodily injury" in Mariposa County.

All BANC PIC 1988.046, from John E. Hoyle's Papers Relating to San Quentin Prisons, 1894–, Bancroft Library, University of California, Berkeley.

dump the fetid contents into a vat that was drilled into the floor of the laundry; from there the sewage flowed under their dining room, and the stench seeped up through the floorboards. They shared one bathroom that remained locked. The women's only source of clean water was a tap in the prison laundry, down a dark flight of stairs and across the yard. Twice a week, in all weather, the women prisoners carried water up and down stairs to scrub the walls and floors.

Female convicts at San Quentin in the early twentieth century worked in a small factory in a pit, behind sealed windows. Here they shared two broken-down sewing machines and stitched eighty to one hundred suits of men's underwear each week. Unlike the segregated men's rows, wrote Griffith, in the women's pit all "colors and classes" were "penned in together." In return for her labor, every Monday afternoon a female convict received a sack of tobacco and a package of cigarette papers. The women were never allowed outdoors, and they told Griffith of their anger at standing at their cell windows watching the men work in the garden. Only after Griffith's diary was published, with its lurid observations and a graphic appendix of crimes against female prisoners, did the female convicts receive designated funding.[27]

Women prisoners were prostituted to the male guards and male prisoners. For amusement, an infamous prison matron and cadre of abusive male guards ordered the female convicts to dance and kick up their legs. If a woman prisoner refused, she was thrown into a dungeon, given bottles of urine instead of water, or strapped into a straitjacket and made to swallow castor oil. The female prisoners never knew what might provoke brutal punishment from the guards. "What is right today is wrong tomorrow. One does not know until, in the matron's own phrase, she 'lands' on one," reported Hester Griffith.[28] When the female prisoners complained to the warden about sanitation, they were stripped by a male guard and locked into a lower dungeon that was reserved for those who dared to raise their voice.

Women who did not complete their assigned "stitching" were punished in ways that were "too degrading" to print, wrote Griffith. Some died from tuberculosis and intestinal diseases. At the end of their sentences, San Quentin released many female convicts directly into a nearby insane asylum.[29]

Eugenics Experiments: A Body of Science

At 10:03 a.m. on May 11, 1928, on the top floor of the prison in a sky-colored and robin's-egg blue room that held two gallows, chief surgeon

Dr. Leo L. Stanley watched the death by hanging of Clarence "Buck" Kelly, who had murdered four people in a grisly two-day drunken spree. Buck Kelly's body dropped through a trap door. The prison's "scavenger crew" cut Kelly from the ropes and carried his body to a modern autopsy room built over the women's "pit." Eight minutes later Stanley removed Kelly's testicles and immediately transplanted them into an aging prisoner. When Kelly's family received his body for burial, they discovered that his testicles were missing. His mother sued Stanley for $50,000 for mutilating her son's dead body. She also demanded Stanley's resignation.[30]

From the 1920s through the 1940s, San Quentin was a site for pseudo-medical sexual and genetic research on convicts' bodies. Stanley was attempting to replicate the work of a fringe set of Paris-based scientists who were doing eugenic experiments on monkeys, a sham science of evolution and reproduction intended to improve the human species. Stanley had a better pool of specimens than monkeys: male prisoners were his involuntary subjects for research on "gland therapy"—testicular transplants. During an era of horrific experiments on racial minorities in prisons, hospitals, and work camps, these implants, he claimed, would cure skin problems, poor eyesight, loose teeth, dementia, impotence, and the "moral perversion of old age." Stanley argued that every murderer had an overdeveloped thyroid and every forger had underdeveloped pituitary glands.

Stanley also sought volunteers from the convicts, promising them that testicular implants taken from dead bodies would offer them sexual vigor and relief from the depression of prison life. The court cleared Stanley of the charge of mutilating Kelly's body, holding that his experiments regenerated "the health of the whole society." It accepted Stanley's claim that young, healthy testicles could repress criminal instincts and curb the reproduction of the "unfit."[31] Testicles of dead convicts, it agreed, served as repayment of the costs borne by imprisonment at San Quentin. Insofar as his theories addressed women, Stanley placed the blame for criminality on indulgent mothers.[32]

In 1909 California passed a sterilization law that allowed state prisons and mental institutions to sterilize those convicts labeled "unfit," "feeble-minded," or suffering from a mental disease that could allegedly be transmitted to descendants.[33] With this law at his back, Stanley decided that 20 percent of all inmates qualified for sterilization, which, he said, "when given its chance, will do much to stamp out crime."[34]

Stanley also believed that sterilization could rid the world of homosexuality, a birth defect that he could surgically correct. After men came back from World War I, California amended the sterilization law to include all those "suffering from perversion."[35] In 1917 Stanley examined Maurice, a young boy who had been arrested for acts of sodomy and burglary. Stanley wrote that Maurice was "a pretty boy. That sly air of innocence and delicate manner is peculiar to the homosexual." But he was also a "pervert, malingerer, moron, and homosexual."[36] And San Quentin was an opportune place for this involuntary experiment.

White heterosexual men were the intended beneficiaries of this research. According to inmate records, by 1936, 115 of 136 of Stanley's transplant subjects were white; eleven were Mexican; none was Black. Although he also argued that "comingling" of "whites, Negroes, and Indians" was sordid, he indulged in the myth of Black male virility and gladly implanted testicles from executed young Black murderers into impotent elderly white prisoners.[37] When Stanley ran out of human testicles, he injected a "slurry" of ground-up testicles from male goats, boars, deer, and sheep into the groin of a prisoner. "Comingling" species of humans and animals was a different matter.

Stanley blurred the lines between physician, researcher, and despot. The doctor delivered testicles to desperate prisoners through coercion, threats of punishment, or, most easily, the promise of sexual prowess ever after. He boasted that in 1931 alone he performed 520 "implantations," and that by 1940 he had sterilized about six hundred prisoners.[38] By 1940 over ten thousand testicular implantations had taken place at San Quentin Prison.[39] Leo Stanley retired from his medical practice at San Quentin in 1951 to become a physician on cruise ships.

Paving the Way

On September 27, 1908, the "Model T" automobile made its debut at the Ford Motor Company plant on Piquette Avenue in Detroit, Michigan. The next year California passed its first highway bond of $18 million and sent prisoners out to lay 3,052 miles of new roads. Unpaid, underpaid, and coerced labor once again transformed the landscape of California. Automobile clubs and rural counties turned to prison labor to pave the way— so long as convict construction workers slept in remote road camps.

From 1915 to 1923 felons chopped through virgin redwood forests and climbed summits of the Coastal Range with shovel and ax to carve what became Highway 101. Convicts erected suspension bridges in the searing summer heat and risked their lives to build roads along the edge of the Eel

An Indian section gang works on the Atchison, Topeka,
and Santa Fe Railroad track in El Cajon, California, 1943.
Photo by Jack Delano. Library of Congress Prints and Photographs Division, Washington, DC.

River and over Tuolumne Pass into Yosemite Valley. If they received a daily wage, it was at most two dollars and fifty cents, but from this, the state deducted the costs of their food, medicine, and transportation to the camps. Felons working on the road also had to pay the salaries of their guards and the costs of running the camps. In addition, they were forced to "donate" toward a $200 fund for the capture of each escaped prisoner.[40] They cost the state little.

During the Great Depression of the 1930s, California prisons were overcrowded with hungry and unemployed men and women from Dust Bowl states who hitchhiked, drove, or road in railroad boxcars, hoping to find fieldwork in California. Some committed minor crimes.

With Californians desperately looking for work, the state passed another series of laws that declared that prison industries could only manufacture and sell goods to the state. In 1935 Congress idled prison industries altogether when it approved the Ashurst-Sumners Act, which banned all products made by convicts from interstate commerce.[41] Yet from 1933 to the early 1940s, under President Franklin D. Roosevelt's New Deal, the public depended on convicts building roads, laying railroad tracks, and clearing trails in forests.

Look for the Prison Label

In 1996 California businessman Pierre Sleiman signed a contract with California's Joint Venture Program to build a vast twenty-eight-thousand-square-foot factory within the walls of the Richard Donovan State Correctional Facility at Otay Mesa, a bare mile and a half from the Mexican border.[42] There in the desert, under two guard towers, behind five barbed-wire fences, four identification checkpoints, and a fifty-thousand-volt electric fence, hundreds of convicts dressed in blue uniforms worked at Sleiman's factory, sewing T-shirts to be sold under the label "C. M. T. Blues." With a joint venture contract from the state, Sleiman had at his disposal an entire workforce of inmates whom he designated as "trainees"; as such they did not receive overtime. Sleiman also got a discount of 25 percent on workers' compensation withholding taxes, and he wrote no checks for health insurance or sick leave.

Ever ambitious, Sleiman decided to rent the entire prison from the state for less than one-fifth of what he would have had to pay for factory space and a workforce anywhere on the commercial market outside the prison walls. Since his T-shirts were framed as a joint venture with the state, he received a 10 percent break on his state business taxes. And because his factory sat within a state prison, California paid the armed overseers who watched the convicts on the shop floor as they toiled at sewing machines in a factory circled by rows of fences.

Pierre Sleiman owned two other garment factories—one in Mexico with two hundred employees and another in Honduras with twelve hundred employees who were each paid a dollar seventy-five an hour. Unlike sweatshops in East Lost Angeles or *maquiladoras* across the Mexican border in Tijuana, the Otay T-shirt factory in the California desert was rimmed by a fourteen-foot coiled razor wire fence; three to four prisoners shared small cells designed for solitary confinement.[43]

Sleiman understood that workers at his C. M. T. Blues prison factory could neither refuse to work nor could they quit. The penitentiary promised the hundreds of men who worked for Sleiman that they would be granted "good time"—time toward parole—if they obeyed him. Lured by the possibility of early release, some prisoners accepted jobs at C. M. T. Blues. Facing boredom and routine violence in the cell blocks, many convicts felt that they had no real choice but to sign on. Like undocumented sweatshop workers, convicts could not organize for their rights or join a union. They were well aware that state health and safety codes did not apply to them and that inspectors were banned from entering factories built inside the walls of California's prison factories.[44] Neither Sleiman nor the prison issued face masks to protect the men from inhaling a white fog of fine filament and microscopic dust particles that swirled in the hall and infiltrated their eyes, throats, sinuses, and lungs.

In the summer of 1999, Charles Irvin and Sherwood Fleming, two convicted murderers, were serving time at Donovan. Both men sued Sleiman, C. M. T. Blues, the warden of Donovan Correctional Facility, and California's Department of Corrections for operating an illegal sweatshop behind bars. Irvin and Fleming insisted that they were private employees who were not paid minimum wage or paid on time.

One day, the two inmates managed to make a furtive telephone to a television reporter at Los Angeles station KGTV and quickly described how C. M. T. Blues was violating wage and safety regulations. They reported that in addition to sewing T-shirts, they were ordered to snip off the "C. M. T." and "Made in Honduras" labels and replace them with the new "No Fear" brand and a "Made in USA" tag, adding consumer fraud to their charges against C. M. T. Blues. Sleiman "fired" Irvin and Fleming, and prison guards handcuffed the two men and marched them off the factory floor and into solitary confinement.

In response to the two men's claims about the T-shirt factory, the state of California charged them with being members of a "conspiracy to mastermind a sabotage effort to discredit and . . . put out of business a California Joint Venture Project." The warden at Donovan ordered that each man be held in solitary for forty-five days for "impugning the credibility of the C. M. T. Blues Joint Venture Program when they contacted the news media"; furthermore, the warden declared that they were "a threat to the safety and security of the institution." The state transferred the two men to separate prisons, where they were kept away from telephones and a chance to reach the press.

In January 2003 Irvin and Fleming won their lawsuit against prison labor as a "taxpayer waste action." C. M. T. Blues was ordered to pay them back wages of $841,000.[45] In a landmark case backed by UNITE—the Union of Needletrades, Industrial and Textile Employees—the California Court of Appeals held that since California had used its right to take a percentage of the inmates' wages to defray the expenses of their room and board, as a private sector manufacturer C. M. T. Blues was required to pay "prevailing wages" to inmates—what they would earn if they worked outside the prison. The verdict also included a historic injunction: henceforth all California prison contractors had to inform prisoners of their rights under state and federal labor law to a "prevailing wage" or "comparable pay."

Three years later Sleiman shut down C. M. T. Blues and with his son opened Go Green Agriculture, a hydroponic nursery that grew vegetables in water inside climate-controlled greenhouses—a technique adapted from indoor marijuana "grows." Ten years later, in 2013, President Barack Obama honored the father-son team at the White House as "Champions of Change."[46]

In 2009 female inmates were required to "demanufacture," or recycle, computers for Dell Technologies at the federal penitentiary at Atwater, California. Forced to work in an exposed mezzanine, their first task was to open the old computer casings with screwdrivers; if the screws were stripped, they used hammers: "When the operation began," testified Prisoner "D," most of the women would raise the cathode ray tubes over their heads and "slam them down on the metal table and keep slamming on the table until the glass broke away from whatever they were trying to remove."[47] Once they could reach inside the computers, the prisoners removed and stacked the tubes that contained both lead and cadmium.

Often the thin tubes broke, causing explosions of black dust that would "poof up in the air." Layers of the dust covered the floor and coated the women's shoes and prison uniforms. The inmates ate lunch in their uniforms and wore them back to their cells; the dust traveled to other prisoners along the corridors, through open doors, and into the laundry. The black dust stuck to their skin; one prisoner described how she could see it clinging to the hairs on her arms. Despite steel-toed boots and work gloves, the fine dust entered the bodies of the female convicts at Atwater Prison.

The prison, the state, and a series of federal agencies knew the dangers that the convict laborers faced at Atwater. Four years earlier, in March 2005, Leroy Smith, the health and safety manager at Atwater, began a campaign to get the Environmental Protection Agency (EPA), Dell Technologies, the Bureau of Prisons, the Occupational Safety and Health Administration (OSHA), the Department of Justice, a special counsel to the president of the United States, and UNICOR, the corporate manager of the prison, to look into the prison's practice of "demanufacturing" computers.

Smith became a whistleblower. The EPA and OSHA determined that each computer held five to seven pounds of lead, enough to cause convul-

sions, coma, and death. The lead exposure affected fetuses and young children. Cadmium, noted OSHA, causes lung cancer, kidney damage, and
bone disease. Mercury in computers causes brain damage. All these metals
are designated "permanent pollutants," says Dr. Richard Lipsey, a forensic
toxicologist. After the prisoners, guards, and nurses at Atwater Prison displayed symptoms of contamination, UNICOR insisted that each prisoner
sign an affidavit declaring that she had a clean bill of health.

Smith, however, along with courageous prisoners, persevered. The
story made national news, and the prison guards' union filed claims and
grievances against UNICOR—a powerful enemy; in 2005 UNICOR managed 106 factories at 73 prisons with almost twenty thousand prison laborers, including seven "e-waste" prison recycling facilities. The prisoners
believed that UNICOR had opened the recycling facility at Atwater "knowing the dangers of processing CRTs [cathode-ray tubes] and other waste
and having us inmates doing it in such a hazardous way that a lot of us
have been poisoned, injured by lacerations, and God only knows what the
long-term effects are going to be on us."

In 2009 to 2010, nine women who had worked on the computers at
Atwater joined women at five other prisons nationwide and jointly sued
the prisons' landlord—the U.S. government. Guards, nurses, and cooks at
Atwater, as well as their spouses and children, joined the legal challenges.
The path to environmental justice for involuntary convict laborers was
unclear. Years of hearings came and went, and the work proceeded. Dell
Technologies conceded that the Electronic Industry Code of Conduct prohibited the use of "indentured labor," but it said nothing about the use of
prison labor.

Meanwhile, the female convicts who refused to dismantle toxic elec-
tronics were sent to solitary confinement.[48] When Dell Technologies finally
heard from angry customers, it resolved the complaints by ending its contract with UNICOR. During the year of the Atwater protest, UNICOR
launched a major public relations campaign but continued its e-waste recycling program that provided $8 to 10 million in revenue per year.[49]

The fortress economy—prisons, penitentiaries, and detention centers—
has fulfilled the business model of San Quentin's first contractor, James
Estell: first, take advantage of prisoners' unpaid labor, and second, reap
profits from owning and running the prison itself. Today, high profits
mainly come from building prisons, managing prisons, and warehousing
prisoners.[50] Estell profited not only from the labor of prisoners but from San
Quentin itself, the brick factory, and prison ships—and from selling crushed

stones and renting construction tools. Anticipating a future UNICOR, he was an early subcontractor who employed guards and cooks, supplied clothing, food, and equipment, and then rented it all back to himself. Estell used state funds to build and run San Quentin, paid himself for its expenses, and hired himself as the uber contractor. His greatest profit was setting himself up as a dummy owner of San Quentin Prison and then leasing it to the state of California.[51]

"Rape Is Never the Sentence for a Crime"

In addition to using the working bodies of convicts, prisons also controlled convicts' sexual and reproductive bodies. Prison rape is hidden from the outside world, but behind the walls, it is obscenely public. Sexual assault in prisons exposes the instability of the meaning of legal personhood and the antislavery provisions of the Thirteenth Amendment.[52]

Prisoners' complaints of fear, fatigue, and hunger are hard to track, but statistics of sexual assaults appear in government reports. In 2003 the Department of Justice estimated that it would cost $12 billion to eliminate rape in prison, and Congress refused to fund the Prison Rape Elimination Act it had just passed.[53] In 2012 the Contra Costa County detention facility in Martinez, California, reported that 11 percent of its inmates suffered sexual abuse inside the prison. San Francisco County Jail #3 reported 10 percent of its inmates were sexually assaulted while incarcerated in the prison. California paid $15,156,020 to settle thirty-six cases of sexual harassment in 2011 to 2012, but the state refused to report the specific nature of the crimes and the identities of the perpetrators.[54]

In 2005 Alexis Giraldo, a male-to-female transgender person with the physical appearance of a woman, was arrested for violating parole. Despite the "intake" recommendation that Giraldo be placed in a facility with a transgender population, she was sent to a male unit at Folsom Prison. Within a week, an inmate who worked as a clerk transferred her to his own cell. He raped her daily, and after two weeks sold her to another inmate who also raped her, again daily. Both inmates told fellow prisoners that they owned her.

Giraldo desperately sought a transfer to a women's prison or transgender unit, but at all levels, Folsom's staff ignored her pleas. The prison correctional counselor told her to be "tough and strong" and returned her to her cell. Fearing for her safety, she begged again to be moved to another prison. It was not until her male cellmate attacked her with a box cutter

Alexis Geraldo photographed at the Superior Court
of California at San Francisco, July 20, 2007.
In the *Orange County Register*, July 21, 2007. (Courtesy AP Photo/Jeff Chiu.)

that she was placed in a segregated unit, one designated for psychologically troubled inmates. Giraldo was terrified that she would be released back into the male prison population.

In 2007 Giraldo sued the state of California, the California Department of Corrections, and thirteen staff members of Folsom Prison for negligence, for abandoning its "duty to care," and for violating the Constitution's ban on cruel and unusual punishment. Giraldo named the guards, a prison psychologist, a medical officer, and the inmates who claimed that they owned her. A year and a half had passed since she had been jailed for parole violation. Geraldo knew that her case would become moot if she were to be paroled again and asked for a trial within ninety days. Instead, the California Department of Corrections advanced her parole date, and in July 2007 released her. Because Giraldo was no longer a prisoner, the Court of Appeals dismissed all charges against Folsom, except her claim that the prison was negligent.[55] It held that Folsom's duty to protect prisoners from "foreseeable harm," including sexual abuse, only referred to assault by other prisoners. In 2012 Geraldo settled the case for $10,000, for the charge of emotional distress.[56]

In 2007, 41 percent of transgender inmates reported that they had been raped while serving time in a California prison.[57] In 2011, 50 percent of transgender convicts reported that they had been sexually assaulted inside prison. They all told of their struggles to obtain their hormonal medications. Transgender convicts still seek safe assignment to prisons and cells.[58]

The Thirteenth Amendment states: "Neither slavery nor involuntary servitude, except as a punishment for crime whereof the party shall have been duly convicted, shall exist within the United States, or any place subject to their jurisdiction." Forced labor, sadistic torture, illegal confinement, irrational transfers, and being used for medical experiments violate the amendment's ban on slavery, "except as a punishment for crime." The Thirteenth Amendment, the "Freedom Amendment," has a legal loophole that sanctions another form of human bondage.[59]

CHAPTER FIFTEEN

Native American
Boarding Schools

"Things We Should Remember
and Things We Should Forget"

Leticia Nichols will not work out this year. For some reason she objects very strongly to being sent out.

—HARWOOD HALL

FRANCES MORONGO, A TRIBAL elder, remembers that when she was a young girl she was taken from her family on the San Manuel Indian Reservation to the Sherman Institute, a boarding school for Indian children in Riverside, California. Morongo did not know where she was or how to find her way home. Homesick and ill, she was admitted to the school's hospital. From her second-floor window she saw a large arrowhead carved into the south side of the San Bernardino Mountains, and she believed that it pointed her way home. In the night, Frances Morongo escaped from the Sherman Institute. She walked twenty miles across the desert to return to her home at the reservation, tucked into the base of the mountain range. Perhaps, she thought, the large arrowhead marked the way for children fleeing from captivity at the school.[1]

A Curriculum for Captivity

The Thirteenth Amendment (1865) that abolished slavery in the United States did not free the four thousand Native children in California who were held in human bondage, legally trapped until their "indentures" expired.[2] In 1867, two years later, the U.S. Congress passed the Anti-Peonage Act, which banned "the holding of any person to service or labor under the system known as peonage" and "any attempt" to demand "the voluntary or involuntary" labor of anyone as payment for a debt.[3]

Nonetheless, a decade later, 1,463 Indian children were still in the possession of white ranchers and farmers who kept the children as unfree workers until their bonds expired.[4] About six thousand to eight thousand Indian women were also held as concubines by white "heads of household" who owned their "contracts." From San Diego to Los Angeles to Eureka, Native American children were trapped for another fifteen years.[5]

In the first decades of the twentieth century, California's new farmers, ranchers, and rural households wanted low-paid workers. Indian boarding schools became the next broker to deliver Indian captives—children who were living with their kin on reservations. In a system called "outing" programs, the California boarding schools taught Indian children menial tasks and tried to instill habits of obedience to whites. Then they sent the children on long assignments to perform menial work at ranches, farms, households, and hotels—unpaid. The racial ideology that had evolved from the Franciscan missions to the state prisons reached into Indian schools and reservations. These young students, initiates in the carceral state, would involuntarily serve in jobs that would not threaten the emerging white working class.[6]

In 1868 President Ulysses S. Grant announced an "Indian Peace Policy," designed to end the massacres and remove corrupt Indian agents from the reservations. He declared that the federal government had the right to seize tribal lands and move Indians to reservations where they would learn "civilizing" skills. In place of Indian agents, he would hire missionaries to teach California Natives to farm, read and write, wear "Euro-American" clothes, and "embrace Christianity."[7] The "Peace Plan" became the template for a new system of displacement, forced assimilation, and unpaid Indian labor; its racial shadow fell over education and economics, parenting and private property.

Across the country, the Jim Crow era of the 1880s spawned new ways to "segregate and confine" Indians, distribute their lands to white settlers, and deliver a controlled workforce. The Dawes Severalty Act of 1887 was a mass giveaway of tribal territories, delivered under the pretense of promoting private Indian land ownership. Its purpose was to bring an end to the communal life of Native Americans' extended families and villages; the Dawes Act subdivided tribal lands into separate "allotments" and gave these plots to Indian individuals or "heads of families," leaving the rest of the country for homesteaders.[8] As white settlers in California took advantage of the bargain distribution of Indian land, their demand for labor grew. Like sedimented rock, Indian boarding schools would separate tribal families, sustain a white land grab, and provide unpaid workers to the new owners.

With easy symmetry, the economic and educational blueprint of the "Peace Plan" perpetuated Indian relocation and bondage. In 1902 Commissioner of Indian Affairs William Atkinson Jones wrote that the Dawes Act had initially been the "outgrowth of the policy of the Government in dealing with wild bands of marauding savages who . . . roamed over large sections of the United States. It was a matter of segregating and confining them . . . upon limited areas . . . where they could either be under definite surveillance or exterminated as a race."[9]

The industrial Indian boarding school emerged as a new type of reservation that would transform Indian children into a pool of unpaid laborers.[10] In the last decades of the nineteenth century, mandatory boarding schools began to supply California settlers with controlled and involuntary Indian field and domestic child workers. For sixty years, twelve "off-reservation" regimented schools would instruct California Indian children in the values of Christianity, teach them to submit to hard labor, and train a rural workforce.[11] Congress only required that the schools be economically self-sufficient and teach Indian children "Christian" values of hard labor.[12] J. D. C. Atkins, another commissioner of Indian Affairs, believed that Indian education and private property went hand-in-hand: "The Government has entered upon the great work of educating and citizenizing the Indians and establishing them upon homesteads."[13] "Citizenizing" was a word wrapped in a camouflage of care, indoctrination, and human bondage.

Captain Richard Henry Pratt was a member of the 10th U.S. Cavalry and served in the Great Plains during the Indian Wars. He participated in the military campaign at the massacre of the Cheyenne on the Washita River in Oklahoma and fought in the Red River War of 1874 against the last free-roaming tribes on the southern Great Plains.

Pratt evolved a tactic to assure Indian erasure: "All the Indian there is in the race should be dead. Kill the Indian . . . and save the man." Better than a loaded musket, an Indian boarding school would teach his Cheyenne, Kiowa, Comanche, and Arapahoe prisoners the blessings of "acquisitive Capitalism" and "lift up the race."[14] Toward that end, in 1879 he opened the first "off-reservation" boarding school in an abandoned military barracks in Pennsylvania.[15]

As the influential director and founder of the United States Indian Industrial School in Carlisle, Pennsylvania, also known as the Carlisle School, Pratt proselytized the merits of his solution to the "Indian problem."[16] Pratt claimed that the Indian was "born a blank, like the rest of us. Left in the surroundings of savagery, he grows to possess a savage language, superstition, and life." "Natives," promised Pratt, had the capacity to learn, and boarding schools could erase "Indian savagery." He sent scouts to round up children from the reservations, for Indians, "the original inhabitants, from whom we were wresting so much, should be admitted to the very best opportunities to prove their worth."[17]

Pratt refined these "best opportunities" in 1883 at the posh Mohonk Mountain House, a 259-bedroom resort in the Catskill Mountains in upstate New York. Here he gathered missionaries, military officers, philanthropists, congressional committees, and representatives of the Bureau of Indian Affairs for the first annual meeting of the influential "Friends of the Indian." Guided by the tenets of evangelical Protestantism, they designed policies to "upgrade" Indians from "savagism" to civilization and from paganism to Christianity. George Manypenny, former director of the Bureau of Indian Affairs, announced an allied attack on tribal identity: the Indian needed to learn to say "I" instead of "we," "me" instead of "us," and "mine" instead of "ours." Compulsory residential education would teach the doctrine of "possessive individualism" so that an Indian child would never want to return to the reservation.[18] But it was hard for lonely and impoverished children to learn the rewards of ownership and self-sufficiency at boarding schools that undermined their Native American traditions of communal trust and shared land stewardship.[19]

Secretary of the Interior Carl Schurz believed that by converting the day schools on the reservations into boarding schools in remote areas, the government would help to erase Indian identity: "Boarding schools are required [because] it is just as necessary to teach Indian children how to live as how to read and write." In 1886 the federal Indian school superintendent went further: "Only by complete isolation of the Indian child from his antecedents can he be satisfactorily educated."[20] Commissioner of Indian

Affairs William Atkinson Jones joined in, accusing the day schools of de-luding Indian children with wrongheaded ideas about their likely futures: "The fallacious idea of 'bringing the Indian into civilization and keeping him there'" had become "too prominent," he wrote in 1904.[21]

With these racial directives in mind, a dozen Indian boarding schools were built across California early in the twentieth century with the mandate to "rescue" Indian children and educate them far from home. Congress had made education compulsory for all Native American children in 1891. With few public or church schools on reservations, the law ensured that many Indian children would have to enter boarding schools. With that, a coalition of missionaries, private entrepreneurs, and the federal government opened over three hundred Indian boarding schools across the country.

Indian Removal: "Taking Children by Force"

In the early years, the California Indian boarding schools hunted for chil-dren who were descendants of "Mission Indians," presuming that the Cath-olic priests had trained them in a life of routine, confinement, and hard work, and had efficiently eradicated tribal identity. The core of the new plan was to assimilate Indian children through unpaid labor.[22] With pittance wages paid to the boarding school, the scheme would fulfill a congressio-nal mandate that Indian boarding schools be economically self-sufficient.[23] White female teachers, often missionaries from the cities, joined the front line in this compulsory "civilizing" of Indian children.

In 1892 the Bureau of Indian Affairs opened the Perris Indian School in the desert southeast of Los Angeles, the first "off-reservation" Indian boarding school in California. Here founder Harwood Hall offered ranch-ers, farmers, and homesteaders a ready pool of unpaid Indian child labor-ers. In exchange for room and board, the Perris "outing students" attended classes during the week, learned English, and were taught rudimentary industrial skills; on weekends they worked full-time at nearby farms and households. The cost of their meals was deducted from their meager pay-checks. It was a year-round curriculum.[24]

A decade later, in 1902, booster Frank Miller, owner of the Glenwood Hotel in the citrus town of Riverside, approached Hall; he was seeking female students from Perris School to work as maids at his hotel. At first, Riverside residents and farmers in the heart of the orange and lemon groves had despaired at the loss of lucrative land for a vast Indian school with hundreds of students. But Hall had promised the new town a steady stream of child workers—unpaid and compliant—and Riverside had allowed the school to be built.[25]

In 1902 Hall opened the Sherman Institute with students as young as four and as old as twenty. A Sherman education, boasted Hall, would prepare Indian children for a life of marginalized labor, "civilizing" them as they baled hay, harvested beets, and scrubbed floors. To attract tourists to the town of Riverside, he designed the school to resemble a Franciscan mission.[26]

As in all the Indian boarding schools in California, the children at the Sherman Institute had been seized from their families and from their tribes. In 1907 the commissioner of Indian Affairs allowed local police officers to use force if parents refused to surrender their children.[27] There were precedents. At the Fort Hall Agency School in northern Idaho, the school supervisor reported that he had been compelled "to choke a so-called Chief into subjection" in order to take his children, and he acknowledged that he had "taken a number of school children by force."[28] In California, eager Indian agents or boarding school officers often arrived on the reservations without alerting tribal parents that they would be coming to take their children. Warned by other parents, frantic mothers and father often slipped into the woods, hid their sons and daughters in bushes, rolled them into rugs, or buried them in the sand with breathing straws or tubular weeds, hiding with their children until "recruiting" season was over.[29] At times, entire villages refused to send their children to the schools. When Joseppa, a Pomo mother, refused to let her son Billie go away to school, government agents took him while she was at work.[30] Removing Indian children from their parents had the full force of the federal government, which ordered local Indian offices in 1893 to "withhold rations, clothing, and other annuities from Indian parents or guardians who refused or neglected to send and keep their children in school a reasonable amount of the year."[31] Federal funding depended on school enrollment, and children at the boarding schools became legal wards of the state, to be deployed as it wished.

Racial segregation in California schools reinforced the boarding schools. At the time, many towns in California, such as Covelo near the Round Valley Reservation, banned Indian children from public schools. In 1915 only Indians who owned their land allotments and paid property taxes could send their children to public school. Meanwhile, the state deliberately situated the Indian boarding schools far from Native American population centers. Children from Humboldt County were sent to Chemawa Indian School near Salem, Oregon.

To get to the Sherman Institute from Round Valley, for example, Nom-laki Eugene Jamison rode sixty miles in a wagon from his home to the town of Ukiah, boarded a train to Sausalito, and from there got on a ferry to San Francisco; upon arrival in the city, he found another train to deliver him to Riverside—six hundred miles from the reservation.[32]

Once young conscripts arrived at the boarding schools, they were sorted by degrees of "Indianness," and their intake documents identified them as "digger," "half-breed," or "full-blood, half-degree-, 1/4 degree." From a student's first day, Sherman, like the other California boarding schools, launched its attack on signs of Indian identity. Upon arrival, new children were made to strip off their own clothes; then the girls were dressed in cotton shifts and the boys in scratchy military uniforms. The school gave the children new "white" first names and surnames, because, as Pratt mockingly asserted, doing so would help identify them when they inherited property. Equally painful, students at the schools had to ignore their siblings or face confinement.[33]

Commissioner of Indian Affairs William Atkinson Jones insisted that "in keeping with the advancement they are making in civilization," the boarding schools must cut Indian children's long hair. Indian men from many California tribes only cut their hair at a funeral to signify loss and to accept that the hair growing in its place reflected a new beginning. School commenced with a shameful initiation, signaling the loss that was to come. Indian foods were also banned, and students learned to use knives, forks, and spoons.[34]

Harwood Hall hoped that a cold dormitory and cropped hair would Americanize Sherman students. More crushing was the rule that forbade the children from speaking their Indian languages. In 1887 J. D. C. Atkins, then the commissioner of Indian Affairs, forced all the schools on Indian reservations to teach only in English. Former boarding school students across the country told of being whipped, swatted with a ruler, or having their mouth washed with lye when caught speaking their Native language. Most of the Indian boarding schools had some sort of jail, and speaking their own language landed the children in lockup. Resourceful students nonetheless took the risk and found secret places in the school or nearby fields to talk to each other in their own tongue.[35] Viola Martinez (Paiute), sent to the Sherman Institute from Arizona, recalled, "I made up my mind I was not going to forget my language. . . . I remember they had tall palm trees at Sherman. . . . My cousin and I would climb up where we couldn't be . . . heard." When the teachers heard Martinez speaking Paiute, they

Sober, uniformed students at the Sherman Institute, 1905.
Not all of this class lived to grow up.
Sherman Indian School Museum, via Calisphere, University of California.

forced her to scrub the showers and toilet bowls; to her lifelong regret, she lost her language.[36]

The boarding school classroom itself defiled Indian ways of knowing. Rather than learning by gathering knowledge from the elders and from their dreams, the children memorized texts written in English. Nationally, about one-third of the 357 known Indian boarding schools were run by Christian denominations; many were Catholic, and a rudimentary ability to read and write marked a child as civilized and on the path to Christianity.[37]

Often the schools barred Native children from returning to their homes, fearing they would be drawn back into the spiritual and communal experience of the tribes and might forget Christianity and the white ways of agriculture and industry. When children at the Greenville School in the Sierra Mountains returned after the summer break, they were ordered to quit the Indian dances they enjoyed during their visits home. Greenville denounced the dances as "subterfuges to cover degrading acts and disguise immoral purpose."

If children refused to put on their white "citizens' clothing" when they

returned to school, Greenville withheld their food, and if they became "ob-
streperous," the teachers locked them in the guardhouse "at hard labor
with shorn locks." The school insisted that it had the right to scrub off
Maidu children's body paint because the tradition retarded the school's
civilizing effect and, it claimed, led to eye infections.[38] In fact, wrote Jones
to the superintendent at the Round Valley Reservation, body paint "causes
the majority of the cases of blindness among the Indians of the United
States"; he added that "students who do not comply should not be fed"
and employees who did not enforce the rules should be fired.[39]

   Greenville Indian Industrial School had a history of runaway female
students. On December 5, 1916, several girls had been "strapped" with a
leather paddle for not getting up and dressed on time. All were homesick.
That winter night, after dinner, Mollie Lowry (age eleven), Elweza Stone-
coal (age thirteen), Edith Buckskin (age fourteen), Rosa James (age fifteen),
and Katherine Dick (age fifteen) fled into the woods with just sweaters for
warmth. Mollie was found frozen on the ground; Edith died from exposure, frostbite, and infections from the subsequent amputations of her feet
and lower legs. The school doctor reported that the girls were "of defective
mind" and they often appeared "demented"—conclusions not supported
by the girls' academic records or the testimony of the other children. The
investigators never explored the school's history of captivity, malnutrition,
and abuse, but turned the girls on each other, finally deciding that the only
true culprit was one of the dead girls who organized the escape. In this
early instance of missing Indian girls, the commissioner for the Bureau of
Indian Affairs found the school blameless of abuse and negligence.[40]

Outing

In 1907 Harwood Hall began to send unpaid child workers from the Sherman Institute "out" to farm, inaugurating the infamous "outing" system
in California. In the shatter zone of bondage, the boarding schools copied
the genteelly named program designed by Richard Henry Pratt for the
Carlisle School. Under this bogus intern scheme, Indian boarding schools
sent their students to live and work "out" from the campus. At white farms,
hotels, and households the children would study how to harvest a field of
beets or scrub a kitchen floor.[41]

   The outing programs were intended to impose middle-class ways of
learning. They turned to military models to supervise, segregate, and discipline the students, taught them 180 English words a year, and compelled

the ones who remained on campus to attend weekly Christian Sunday services.[42] Sherman students were to learn basic industrial skills, forget their traditional hunting and fishing practices, and abandon their spirits and gods. At the same time, the outing program itself would profit from their labor. Rather than assimilate Indian children into some vague destination in mainstream America, the outing programs inducted them into the lowest tier of the emerging working class.[43]

To arrange the lease of Indian children for these unpaid jobs, the schools hired "outing matrons" to match students with "patrons" and make sure the children dutifully embraced white systems of labor and behavior.[44] By 1909 Hall was conscripting Native American teenagers whose indentures had expired. Children were plucked from forts and reservations in Pennsylvania and the Southwest. Within a few years, Indian children were being shuttled between boarding schools and job postings across the country, at times thousands of miles from home.

Deliberately isolated, California's Indian boarding schools were often located on old military forts that had been built during the wars of genocide and the Civil War. The Hoopa Indian Boarding School was built in barracks at Fort Gaston, along the western bank of the Trinity River in northwestern California. The school was at the site of a bloody defeat of the Hoopa on Christmas night 1863, when the tribe tried to take several log buildings at the fort. The Hoopa Indian School was built on the ruins of the night of 1863.[45] Fort Bidwell Indian School opened in the remote northeast corner of the state in 1898 at a military base that was built to thwart joint attacks on the U.S. Army by tribes from northeastern California, southern Oregon, and western Nevada who were trying to protect their lands from ranchers, settlers, and soldiers.

Some Native Americans still refer to the schools as "Death by Civilization."[46] Like the Franciscan missions and the Indian reservations, the California boarding schools were spaces of incarceration and forced labor. Estelle Reel, superintendent of Indian schools from 1898 to 1910, wrote, "The Indian child must be placed in school before the habits of barbarous life have become fixed and there he must be kept until contact with our life has taught him to abandon his savage ways and walk in the path of Christian civilization."[47] A Chemehuevi elder from the Mohave Desert remembered how priests and nuns at the St. Boniface Indian Industrial School, built into the rugged San Gorgonio Pass, north of Los Angeles, "stole" his language by forbidding him to speak in his Chemehuevi tongue.[48]

Separated from their kin and culture, children at the California board-

At many Indian boarding schools, photographers took before-and-after pictures, first when the children were admitted wearing tribal garments and long hair, and then when their braids were cut and they were dressed in uniforms. Photographers used tinted lenses to suggest that these children had whiter complexions, suggesting a successful racial as well as cultural assimilation.
Smithsonian National Anthropological Archives.

ing schools learned to plow and mow, cook, sew, and launder, and enter the lowest tier of an industrializing state.[49] Enforcing what historian Beth Piatote (Ni:mi:pu: [Nez Perce]) calls "disciplinary paternalism" and historian Laura Wexler calls "tender violence," the schools sought to assimilate the children by disrupting spiritual relationships with land and labor that they had learned from their tribe and from their elders.[50] In a Darwinian vision, Pratt, the director of the Carlisle School, believed that removal and education would "render Indians indistinguishable from whites," and then their homelands and families would "fade and disappear." Pratt declared, "In Indian civilization I am a Baptist because I believe in immersing the Indians in our civilization and when we get them under, holding them there until they are thoroughly soaked."[51]

With the advent of outing programs, the California boarding schools, like the reservations, became at best employment agencies or, more likely,

Corner School laundry, where teenage girls
were trained for domestic servitude, ca. 1910.
(Courtesy of Sherman California Indian Museum.)

slave marts that matched white settlers with unpaid child workers who,
Hall promised, were "accustomed to taking orders."[52] Such labor would
inculcate young Indians with the qualities needed for racial "uplift"—thrift
and a willingness to work long days while they lived in tents or shoddy
quarters. The Sherman Institute's version of Indian "uplift" quickly took
shape as a new iteration of human bondage.[53] Within a year from opening
their doors, most of the Indian boarding schools in California were offering up a reliable stream of "compliant" young workers who could be ordered to dig ditches, pick fruit, or scrub kitchens.[54]

In 1890 over twelve thousand children—half the Indian children in
California—were enrolled in schools of some sort where an army of Christian schoolteachers tried to win the final battle against the Indians.[55] What
the schools did not anticipate was that once the students were literate, they
would use their skills to post letters home, albeit in English, and let their

parents know that they were sick, tired, sad, and always hungry. From these letters many Indian parents learned of the schools' contempt for their children, the horrors of physical and sexual abuse, and the forced conversion to Christianity; they struggled to get their children back.[56] Yet it was the Indian agents who decided if a family home was suitable for a child's return, even for the summer months.

The United States' commitment to the schools appeared in dollars. Congressional monies for Indian education swiftly rose: in 1877, $20,000; in 1880, $75,000; in 1890, $1,364,568; and in 1900, $2,936,080 (or $91 million today).[57] On a per-student basis, however, the larger California boarding schools received little federal funding. In 1908, for example, 550 students were enrolled at Sherman and occupied thirty-four buildings, yet the school received $157 from the federal government per year for each student.[58] By the first decade of the twentieth century, "student laborers" at Sherman began to receive some token wages—in 1907 young domestic workers earned twelve dollars per month—but their "wages" were sent directly to the school, usually after expenses for housing and food were deducted. By adding the students' paltry pay to the government's funding, Sherman was double-dipping; still, the students went unpaid. Some worked a staggering number of long days and nights, some for weekends only, some for a straight month at a time. Often the students had to fight to receive their slim pay.[59]

For students who worked fifty-two hours a week in the fields or lived full-time in remote households, education was not the point of their forced stay at Sherman. The superintendents of Sherman required students to be in school only eighty days a year.[60] The school "assigned" hundreds of its boys, at times under threat, to work on ranches all across Southern California. Student Hugh Bell's work records show that he typically put in eighty-four hours a week as a migrant farmworker.[61]

Don Talayesva was a teenager working at the Hopi Boarding School in Keams Canyon, Arizona, in 1906 when the principal transferred him to Sherman, along with his other "brightest" Hopi children. Talayesva boarded a train, riding six hundred miles from his village on a high mesa on the Hopi Reservation in Arizona. He rode across the lands conquered by Spain, Mexico, and the United States—the home of the Hualapai, Mohave, Chemehuevi, Cahuilla, Tongva, and Kumeyaay—to the citrus capital, Riverside. After only a few months at Sherman, Talayesva got his first outing assignment and trekked fifteen miles in the high desert to work at Fontana Farms, one of the largest agricultural operations in North Amer-

ica. Fontana Farms was owned by the same developer who had pushed
Harwood Hall to move the Sherman school to Riverside.

The Sherman students built Fontana into a company town. Between
1908 and 1929, 347 boys from Sherman raised hogs at Fontana Farms—
heaping trash into the feeding pits, shoveling pig manure, and herding
pigs onto train cars. In the winter they set smudge pots to warm the citrus
groves and then picked, sorted, and packed lemons and oranges. Talayesva
and the other Sherman outing students slept with the Mexican migrant
workers in shacks, divided by race; they received the same wages as the
lowest-paid Mexican migrant workers, but their pay was sent directly to
the school. When not tending to the hogs or harvesting oranges, Sherman students wrote letters to the school pleading for their earnings. Those
monies, however, were often applied against the boys' medical bills for tuberculosis that they had caught in packed migrant workers' camps.[62] After
Talayesva completed a season at Fontana, Sherman moved him to harvest
cantaloupes in California's Imperial Valley. The next season the school sent
him to work at a dairy farm in San Bernardino, fifteen miles northwest of
Riverside, and then back to Fontana Farms for the rest of the summer.
During his two years as a Sherman Institute student, Talayesva journeyed
over fifteen hundred miles for work.

Talayesva returned to Hopi deeply conflicted: "I could talk like a gentleman, read, write, and cipher. I could name all the states in the Union
with their capitals, repeat the names of all the books in the Bible, quote a
hundred verses of Scripture, sing more than two dozen Christian hymns
and patriotic songs, debate, shout football yells, swing my partners in square
dances, bake bread, sew well enough to make a pair of trousers and tell
'dirty' Dutchman stories by the hour. It was important that I had learned
how to get along with white men and earn money by helping them."

Yet his assimilation troubled him. He reflected: "My death experience
[from pneumonia] had taught me that I had a Hopi Spirit Guide whom I
must follow if I wished to live. I wanted to become a real Hopi again, to
sing the good old *Katcina* songs, and to feel free to make love without fear
of sin or a rawhide."[63]

In 1915, 205 male Sherman students were sent "out" to cut and bale
hay, dig potatoes and irrigation ditches, and pick fruit. Others went to work
as janitors and housekeepers at a hotel. Some earned less than one dollar
per day and then saw the cost of their "board" or meals deducted. Most,
however, were still paid only in room and board.[64] Hall did not negotiate
on behalf of his students and told one rancher to just "take the young man

and pay him whatever he is worth."[65] Sherman easily found jobs for its students in the service of a rapidly industrializing state. The Salt Lake Rail Road Company, the Riverside Power Company, the Trust Company, and the San Jacinto Land Company would take child workers from Sherman's outing program.

From daybreak to sunset, Sherman boys also worked at nearby farms, harvesting oranges in the hot sun. At night they slept out near the orchards, in barns or tents maintained by the Riverside Orange Company. Sherman's reach grew, and children arrived from all over the Southwest to crisscross the country for outing jobs. Navaho boys from Sherman were driven across the plains to Kansas to harvest beets and top the stalks in the high plains, in ten unpaid hours a day of broiling-hot, stooped labor.[66] From Riverside to Kansas, Native American students learned "sedentary farming"—where the same crops are planted on the same piece of land— which was considered a more "civilized" agricultural system than their traditional practices of following the migration of deer, salmon, grouse, and ducks, the bursting seeds and ripe berries, all food customs that required mobility.[67]

Under the supervision of Methodist missionaries and the YWCA, Sherman required all tribal children to obey their "patron" and attend his church.[68] In 1924 the school took their wages, deducted the costs of their transportation and meals, then delivered three-fourths of their remaining pay to the school superintendent, who only allowed them to draw from their thin accounts on the third Friday of each month—after providing a written document justifying how they planned to spend their money.[69] A group of male students, some of whom were orphans, pressed hay for two months on a ranch in the hot, dry fields of Brawley. Their "employer" refused to pay the boys, claiming that he had health issues and had fallen into debt. The California State Division of Labor Statistics and Law Enforcement allowed the rancher to defer paying the boys who wrote letter after letter to Sherman demanding that the school retrieve their pay. One year later the California Labor Commission sent each boy twenty dollars, his sum total.[70]

Living for and between Others: Native American Female Students

While the California boarding schools sought to train tribal boys to tend orchards and dig trenches, they aimed to transform Native girls into "civilized women."[71] Harwood Hall believed that Native American girls were more pliable than Native American boys; learning to do domestic work in white households or hotels would make them valuable assets. He sent girls who were between ten and twelve years of age out to serve as "nurses" or nannies to small children. Older girls cleaned, did laundry, and washed dishes, and the oldest cooked for the "outing families," all effectively unpaid.[72] Most lived and worked at their "employers'" houses year-round.[73]

During the first decade of the twentieth century, the Sherman Institute rented girls, ages ten to thirteen, for a dollar a month to sew, iron, cook, and learn "what home means."[74] White families were allowed to loan the Indian girls to other households for weeks or months. Young Mary Barker reported that she was shipped from family to family, but the Sherman Institute failed to supervise any of her "assignments."[75]

In fact, Hall gave families and farmers license to treat the children as they wished. He sent two boys to a rancher with a note assuring him that the boys "are accustomed to taking orders and will come to you with that understanding—not only in work, but in general conduct as well." Hall made the rancher's power quite clear: "I am sure that such cannot be objectionable, as it will only make their services more valuable to you."[76] Hall was more concerned with pleasing the homeowners than caring for the Native American girls, and he switched them from house to house to mollify angry employers.[77]

"For Some Reason She Objects Very Strongly to Being Sent Out": Resistance and Resilience

Outing matrons knowingly sent girls into households where they were sexually vulnerable. At the Round Valley Indian School, Superintendent George Patrick reported that it was impossible to protect "young and half-grown girls" when they worked as domestic servants.[78] Many Kwatsáan (Quechen) girls were sent from Sherman to work in urban Los Angeles. Like other girls from the reservation at Fort Yuma (where California, Arizona, and Mexico meet near the Colorado River), when Eve Arvaez wanted to visit her family, she paid her own ten- to twenty-dollar fare and traveled for ten hours. A man in her outing household made Eve pregnant, and her family demanded that the father of the baby pay her twenty-five dollars per month until the child was one year old.[79]

Outing matrons at Sherman put the responsibility on the girls to control their sexual urges and beware of "insults" by young "bucks"—male

Indian students who lived in the fields.[80] Sherman's school newspaper published articles aimed at Indian girls, with headlines such as "Living for Others" and the portentous "Things We Should Remember and Things We Should Forget." Nonetheless, teenage girls from the boarding schools, isolated and overworked, sought less restrictive lives. The girls sent to households in Los Angeles slipped out to make friends and find romance. One matron at the Sherman Institute reported in 1917 that Emma Willis "got out and ran away from outing several times" and "visited a Mexican dive in Corona."[81]

Refusal

Lorenzia Nicholas from Sherman refused to return to an abusive outing household. "Lorenzia Nicholas will not work out this year," Harwood Hall tactfully informed the Bakewell family, adding, "For some reason she objects very strongly to being sent out."[82]

Other outing girls just refused to obey their bosses or fulfill their daunting tasks. Mrs. Charles Martin wrote from Glendora, a small town forty miles from the school, to complain about a Sherman outing girl who had recently begun working for her as a full-time domestic servant. She wrote: "When she first came I took considerable pains in showing her the things I expected of her, but after two weeks it is necessary for me to do over almost everything she does." Among other daily tasks, Martin had ordered her to clean tables, sweep the floors, wash dishes, launder and organize clothes, and care for her infant. She added: "The lack of progress in her understanding discourages me and I find I cannot even depend on her to keep an eye on my year-old baby and therefore she is no benefit to me whatsoever."[83]

When Harwood Hall interviewed a potential employer, he sought no information about corporal punishment or sexual safety. Boarding school girls also faced physical abuse at the schools. Martha Manuel Chacon (Serrano) washed underwear at St. Boniface Indian Industrial School; once, when she decided to wash a load of dirty blue jeans instead, a matron whipped her with a leather belt.[84]

Although the children were hundreds of miles from their homelands, many fled.[85] While the girls in the schools' outing programs slept indoors, the boys who worked in citrus groves or open fields baling hay would typically sleep in the fields, and many found it easy to just run away. When Indian students managed to flee from fields or kitchens, the schools often turned to the local police. In 1918 Horace Anderson (Konkow) fled from Sherman and was returned. He ran away again the next year and was found a month later hundreds of miles to the north in Stockton, arrested on charges of burglary—stealing a coat. He was released on the condition he return to the school.[86] Often the police did not bring the children back.

In 1929, however, student Martin Fisher walked away from a job as a ranch hand near Corona, just south of Riverside. The Sherman Institute notified the police, who found Fisher hiding at a nearby ranch and held the boy behind bars at the Riverside County Jail until the school's superintendent retrieved him and took him back to the school. Desperately unhappy and abused, boys ran away time and time again.[87]

Parents tried to reclaim or protect their children and wrote to the distant schools demanding they return their children. Occasionally parents came to the schools, often from hundreds of miles away, to try to retrieve their kidnapped child or object to their hungry child's meager diet or and their reports of malnutrition. Parents were concerned about the overwork and the thin uniforms issued to their children.[88] When parents tried to rescue their children from the Round Valley Indian School, the director refused to let them go; without the boys, the school would have no firewood or fresh vegetables, and without the girls, the teachers' clothes would remain unwashed, un-ironed, and un-mended. Some students who did make their way home wrote to Sherman demanding wages for their work.[89] Others who remained at the schools managed to hold on to Indigenous food and spiritual practices; they fished or went into the fields to hunt for their food and cook it in outdoor firepits.

At times, frustration and rage blazed among boarding school students, especially in their teenage years. In 1883 and again in 1910, students torched the Round Valley Indian School. In 1914 the Indians at the Round Valley Reservation were angry that they were forced to build a school with lumber that had been set aside for their families' houses; that year the school burned to the ground.[90] A grand jury was convened to investigate the fire, and thirty children submitted affidavits, stating that for minor acts of naughtiness or disobedience, boys were stripped and whipped with heavy straps and held in a "dark, dismal, and dirty dungeon."[91] The boys who set the 1914 fire at Round Valley Indian School were banished from the reservations. Some were sent to the Sherman Institute, hundreds of miles to the south, and others were shipped across the country, to the Carlisle School in Pennsylvania.[92] The Round Valley residential school was never rebuilt. Other boarding schools were also set ablaze; Paiute and Modoc children torched the Fort Bidwell Indian School in the early 1900s and again in 1930.

Resilience

By the 1920s national visions that the schools would deliver Indian assimilation withered. The federal government tired of the expenses of training and housing Indian children. Many of the schools were unfunded and crumbling. In 1928 the Meriam Report sponsored by the Rockefeller Foundation (officially "The Problem of Indian Administration") exposed the abuses, including starvation, overcrowding, and racial segregation at boarding schools across the country. It also exposed the fact that only the outing programs and student labor kept the schools open. At the cusp of the Great Depression, compelled by law to educated Native American children, public schools finally began to appear on the reservations in California, closer to home.[93]

The carceral nature of the California boarding schools and their military style of control and punishments lasted until 1929, when Commissioner of Indian Affairs Charles Burke banned "flogging"; but he granted school principals full authority to punish the children in all other ways, and abuse endured. During the Great Depression, most of the Indian boarding schools were unfunded, and by 1935 they subsisted only on student labor; the children were compelled to work longer and harder. A Bureau of Indian Affairs employee reported that the Indian schools had become "penal institutions—where little children [are] sentenced to hard labor for a term of years for the crime of being born to their mothers."[94] Historian David Wallace Adams observed, "They were coming for the children."[95]

Those who believed in assimilation thought that if California Natives adapted well to bondage, they would be welcomed into white American society. Instead, the California boarding schools absorbed the nation's low expectations for Indian children and tried to train them to submit. They readied the children to enter a racially segregated world of low-paid labor, doomed to remain at the bottom. Parents at the Hoopa Reservation had "a strong feeling that the Indian school is not as efficient as the local public schools. They want to study the same as the white children and they feel that because the Indian school does not pattern after the local white school, they are not being educated."[96] For the most part, the effects of servitude, camouflaged as education, were disastrous. Historian K. Tsianina Lomawaima explains that federal boarding schools never intended to train Indian youth "to assimilate into the American melting pot." Instead, forced labor was meant to teach Native children to adopt the work discipline of the Protestant ethic and learn to accept their place in society as a marginal class.[97]

Alumnae, descendants, and scholars dispute the impact of the Indian boarding schools. The very rudimentary and out-of-date industrial skills the boys learned were usually roads to economic futility. Those few who were taught true mechanical skills had the best hope of economic security. When Joe Blackwater (Pima) entered Sherman at age thirteen, he refused to join the summer outing program until the school sent him to work in the printing office of the local newspaper, the *Riverside Enterprise;* as an adult, he returned to Sherman to work in the school's print shop. Other graduates also found jobs as part of Sherman's workforce. Galen Townsend (Paiute) from Fort Bidwell returned as an assistant carpenter. Sherman alumna Laura Premo (Shoshone) came back as an outing matron.

Some Indian children who grew up in the California outing system learned to find their way in the white world of employment and migration, traveling thousands of miles for jobs.[98] And although Indigenous children were introduced into the cold realities of wage labor and the capitalist marketplace, at times their jobs made it possible for their kin in Northern California to keep their land allotments.[99] For some, the Indian boarding schools became singular spaces of inter-tribal knowledge, friendship, and, at times, romance.

On balance, some Native American parents believed that the boarding schools united survivors of many tribes, and like the missions, forged new bases of community, spirituality, and survival. Forced contact between people of different tribes gave rise to a pan-Indian collective voice that honored the food, ritual, language, clothing, spiritual, and family traditions of diverse tribes. The schools gave Indian children a chance at literacy. Many outing girls sent into domestic service in the sprawling new Los Angeles found their way and often found one another and became the vanguard of communities of urban Indians who were, as historian Philip Deloria has observed, both modern and Indigenous.[100] Yet the assaults upon Indigenous children's bodies and minds seep into issues that California tribes face today as they work to preserve Native identities, land, and water rights, and argue for Native American human rights. They hold California and the federal government accountable for past misdeeds and current assaults.[101]

Some boarding school alumni, such as renowned author Zitkála-Šá (Lakota for "Red Bird"), used their skills honed at a boarding school to promote Indian rights. Some became prosperous professionals, attorneys, physicians, and musicians and advocated for Native Americans through organizations such as the Society of American Indians, which thrived from 1911 to 1923, during the peak of the outing programs. In the 1950s and 1960s, activists who came of age at the Bureau of Indian Affairs' boarding schools formed the National Indian Youth Conference and organized to pursue financial support for tribes and Indians' "inherent sovereign rights," including rights to "full participation and consent" in the domestic, land, and legal matters of Indigenous people. Some boarding school alumnae became advocates for Indian education, including survival courses, tribally controlled schools and school boards, and tribal colleges.[102]

The outing system in the California boarding schools endured for over seventy years. In 1909–10, the Sherman Institute sent eighty-six children out to work. Between 1910 and 1918, its first outing matron placed fifteen hundred Sherman students and found slots for students from remote reservations in hopeless and effectively unpaid jobs in the boom towns of Riverside and Los Angeles.[103] The outing programs' role of supplying unpaid workers shifted after the exposés of neglect in the 1928 Meriam Report. Six years later, the 1934 Indian Reorganization Act led to the closing of most California Indian boarding schools. Sinking under the costs of teachers' salaries and crumbling schoolhouses and dormitories, and reports from alumnae and exposés in newspapers and radio about abuse and escapes, the boarding schools closed. Schools such as the Round Valley Indian School that had lasted for forty years eventually competed with the public schools, where the state, not students' "wages," paid the nine cents per day tuition.

It was not until 1978 that "autonomous" Indian adults had the legal right to make decisions about their children. Influenced by the American Indian Movement (AIM) and the Red Power and Indian Rights movements, the U.S. Congress passed the Indian Child Welfare Act. With that, Indian families finally had the right to reject involuntary foster care, forced adoption, and the coercion to send their children to Indian boarding schools. That law also gave tribal governments authority over children who lived on reservations.[104] The tribal people of California understood that the struggle for their labor and their minds was a struggle for their homelands; education coiled the state's demands for conversion and assimilation.

The Indian boarding schools were the next chapter in the serial theft of Native children for slave labor. The last "Great Indian War" was waged against the children.

CHAPTER SIXTEEN

"We Are the Jury"

Modern Sex and Labor Trafficking

I viewed a prostitute like Julia Roberts in *Pretty Woman*—a fierce
independent woman. I believed that image up until the moment
that my trafficker said, "This is how prostitutes are made."

—ELLE SNOW, 2018

CALIFORNIA IS A SHIMMERING hologram: tilt it one way, we see images of
free-spirited prosperity, tolerant indolence, awe of the natural environment, and diverse residents. Tilt it another way, and we see the ravenous
hydra twisting through a landscape of slavery and profit. We see Indigenous Guatemalan women selling long-stem roses by the off-ramps of old
Highway 99 as it winds along the spine of the state; we see Latina women
changing the sheets in stylish conference hotels and Latino men waving
leaf blowers on suburban lawns. Korean men stand watch at the entrances
of pop-up nail salons where young women give inexpensive pedicures while
others perform sex acts in a room just behind the row of massage chairs;
their fees are paid to the owner.[1] Historian and activist Kevin Bales calls
these neighbors the "slaves next door."[2]

Today's hydra finds sustenance within California's jagged fault lines of
poverty, displacement, and racial inequality, while tourists eat fusion noo-
dles and visit Universal Studios. Slavery has turned California into a hall

of mirrors with distorted representations of its intertwined realities. San Francisco, Los Angeles, and San Diego are three of the ten worst sites of child sex trafficking in the United States, because California is porous.[3] Twenty-seven commercial airports and eight hundred miles of coastline offer access to cargo tankers, private jets, and small fishing boats; to the south the state presses against the Mexican border, a gateway to Latin America. Human traffickers rightly assess the state as low-risk, high-yield, and profitable.[4]

California has the most reported cases of human trafficking in the United States. Two-thirds of its 1,656 victims in 2019 were women and girls who were prey to sex traffickers; 90 percent of them were between ages fifteen to seventeen.[5] Over 165 years after the Thirteenth Amendment and two hundred years after the defeat of the former Confederacy, California is still a slave state. Here, *de jure* and *de facto*, in law and in reality, trafficked workers have become the personal property of an "employer" who buys, sells, rents, and even gifts human beings—an "employer" who controls the sexual and laboring bodies of the women, men, and children detained in involuntary labor. The owner takes 100 percent of the fruits and profits of the slave's labor.

Unlike plantation or chattel slavery, modern human slavery in California is not a lifetime status bestowed at birth, but it may last for years, until a trafficked sex slave or fieldworker escapes or is rescued. At times modern human slavery only ends with death. This head of the hydra has forged its own twisted power. Today, California thrives on evolving systems of bound and unfree labor, visible at detention centers and airports and in the fields.

U.S. and international laws classify victims of labor trafficking as people recruited, transported, or held through force or fraud for the purpose of slavery, unpaid labor, or debt bondage.[6] Many are migrants, lured in their home countries or recruited at the California border by human smugglers who offer sham jobs and fake visas; trafficking, forced transport, sexual assault, and torture are never far behind. During the presidency of Donald Trump, family separations at the southern border and ruthless bans on refugees allowed migrants to be trafficked from detention centers, afraid to turn to the guards or to ICE. One-third of those captives are children. "America First," "white power," and anti-immigrant codes feed the deathless snake.

People held in captivity or on the run do not stop to write. Their stories surface once they are safe, and tell of rescues triggered by a neighbor who reports something incongruous, something that doesn't make sense: Why are there so many male visitors next door? Why do toddlers at the park have a child for a nanny?

A captive girl rescues herself when she reads a help-line number on a toilet door at a rest stop and frantically finds a moment to dial; her frightened voice is retained in a 9-1-1 audiotape. Men and women who have escaped human trafficking have found ways to tell their histories of modern slave labor in California's farms, sweatshops, or the sex trade. Their histories of captivity echo the harrowing accounts of fugitives from the Franciscan missions, of Alaska Natives who paddled away, of Black miners who ran from the gold diggings, of fugitives from the fields, factories, mines, and brothels of two centuries ago.

A Slave Triangle in the Marijuana Grows

Humboldt, Mendocino, and Trinity counties in Northern California form the Emerald Triangle in the vast northwestern corner of the state, renowned since the 1960s as the nation's epicenter of marijuana "grows."[7] Here layers of fog slice the coastal mountains and brown inland hills. Salt air from the Pacific Ocean and 175 days of rain each year create a perfect ecosystem for the cultivation of "Humboldt Gold," known for its potency and flavor as the finest cannabis in the country. The Klamath, Mattole, Salmon, Eel, Trinity, and Mad rivers flow through the Emerald Triangle and irrigate the crop with an estimated market value of $3.1 billion in 2019 and $5.6 billion in 2020.[8] Like wines pressed from the grapes of Napa Valley vineyards a hundred miles to the south, Humboldt is a globally coveted "brand," a tourist draw for trademark "California Dreaming."

California has the largest sales of legal marijuana in the world. After the state voted in 1996 to legalize medicinal cannabis, it became the leading cash crop in the state—triple the value of vegetables and five times the value of the grapes used in California wines. The following year, 1997, marijuana generated $26.1 billion in revenue to local growers.[9] The profits spiked in 2016, when Californians passed Proposition 64, a voter initiative to legalize and regulate recreational cannabis, which is now under the state government's Bureau of Cannabis Control.[10] Nationally, cannabis brings in more revenue than corn.[11] The legalization of cannabis oils, creams, medications, and "edibles" has swollen its profitability. It is not hard to grow. "It's not called weed for nothing," one illegal grower commented to me about the prolific psychogenic bush.[12]

The costs of legalization have been high; discouraged growers found it expensive to meet state standards and obtain local licenses, and now illegal "grows" thrive alongside the taxed and regulated plots. In 2019 the *Los Angeles Times* estimated that California took in $8.7 billion in illegal sales of pot.[13] Yet no one knows its true and staggering value because even in states where it is "legal," possession of marijuana is still a federal crime.

Who grows, trims, and extracts the oils from all this pot?[14] Human trafficking in marijuana has been an illegal industry within an illegal industry; it is hard to trace. Still, professional organizations in the cannabis industry suggest that only 4 percent of the revenue goes to the fieldworkers and trimmers.[15] The California legislature issues bill after bill defining chemical standards for cannabis and setting sales taxes, ready to protect Humboldt County's "appellation" or place brand—akin to France and Champagne. Modern California growers cultivate hybrids and premium strains in a long menu of options of calibrated effects and potency, but the state legislature has done nothing to protect the wages, health, and safety of the fieldworkers who produce this crop. Facing the risks of the Covid-19 epidemic and the epic wildfires that raged through California in 2020, the state designated field laborers as "essential workers," whether they grow fruits, vegetables, or cannabis for medical marijuana.[16] County sheriffs in these underfunded counties are loath to drive hundreds of miles for what are now minor offenses in well-guarded grows.

Ninety percent of California fieldworkers are born in Central America, and more than half enter the United States undocumented—without visas.[17] In 2020 a federal "H-2A" visa for a temporary agricultural worker cost an employer ten dollars. But typically, the farmer docked a migrant's wages anywhere from $2,000 to $5,000 or "advanced" the costs for this immigration document, creating a formidable debt. Trafficked farmworkers in the Central Valley owe their broker for rides to a physician and visits to a clinic. Such fees turn into debt bondage; when legal migrants overstay their visas, they find themselves in the vulnerable world of undocumented workers. About one-third are trafficked.[18]

In the early 1970s, César Chávez and Dolores Huerta of the United Farm Workers of America led long strikes in California's fields and vineyards and compelled the state to grant agricultural workers the right to join a union. Yet fifty years later, farmworkers have no limit on hours in the sun or protection from lethal pesticides. Farmers can hire children as young as twelve in industrial agriculture and legal marijuana grows.[19] Because their very existence is hidden from view, trafficked farmworkers have no real protection under labor law.

Since the 1960s, California growers have concealed marijuana plots in national forests and on remote Indian reservations—protected federal lands that cannot be seized in an arrest. Hoopa and Yurok tribes along the Eel, Trinity, and Klamath rivers resent the diversion of their water to the cannabis grows that contaminate rivers on the reservations.[20] The fertilizer used for marijuana has so enriched the sandy river bottoms that salmon can no longer swim to their spawning areas, now overgrown with weeds and algae. The tribes are starving. In 2016, when Hoopa elders asked the Humboldt County sheriff to remove the grows from their sacred and life-sustaining river lands, it was undocumented fieldworkers who faced the police.[21]

The Emerald Triangle is hungry for workers. Ten thousand rugged square miles lie between the sunny mountains of the Coastal Range and the foothills of the Siskiyou Mountains, from the mouth of the Klamath River through the redwood forests and purple madrone trees of Humboldt, Mendocino, and Trinity counties. In the month of October, drug dealers cruise up and down Highway 101 through dairy and mill towns, past tourist stops, tattoo parlors, and roadside pull-offs, recruiting workers for the cannabis harvest. Teenage runaways, often destitute and homeless, hope to find easy wages working the grows.

Led in part by AIDS activists who saw merciful pain relief in cannabis, the legalization of "medical" marijuana in California exempted patients and caregivers from criminal prosecution. After the state legalized the sale of recreational marijuana in 2018, tourists flocked in to buy marijuana, and the trade grew until legalization in states across the country undercut the local market.

As marijuana developed into agribusiness, its needs for planters, harvesters, and trimmers proliferated. In the same way that cotton and tobacco stimulated regimes for slave labor in the eighteenth century, cannabis drew traffickers to provide agricultural workers to tend the valuable plants with grow lights, organic fertilizers, and calibrated irrigation drips in vast fields or sheds the size of football stadiums. To deter thieves at the harvest, fieldworkers trapped in the hills are the first to face armed robbers, animal traps, and cages of rattlesnakes. In a drought-stricken state, growers divert water from creeks and rivers, and other plant and animal species are dying of thirst, while fertilizers and insecticides have eradicated deer and rabbits who nibble on the plants or drink from the waste runoff. These chemicals foul the rivers and kill salmon, steelhead, and trout. Rodenticides and industrial toxins poison the food chains. Hikers routinely come upon the carcasses of rodents, bears, and mountain lions poisoned by the toxins that are also inhaled and handled by both trafficked and free farmworkers. Because these fieldworkers are largely undocumented or fearful of law enforcement, no court will hear their appeals for medical help following their prolonged inhalation and exposure.

Green Gold

Few migrant workers who hold legal visas choose to travel to the remote hills of Northern California to tend the new "green gold"; instead, traffickers seize men and women at the Mexican border to work in the trade. International drug cartels kidnap men and women from Asia and Latin America. Thousands of Hmong, a Laotian hill people who fought alongside the Central Intelligence Agency during the Vietnam War, joined the flight of the U.S. military in its retreat in 1973. Skilled in opium cultivation, many moved to the Emerald Triangle. Hmong, Russian, Bulgarian, and Mexican drug cartels such as Sinaloa and Jalisco Nueva Generación have overtaken many independent farmers in the Emerald Triangle.[22]

In 2020 reports from the U.S. Forest Service revealed that Mexican cartels were transporting kidnapped men across the California border to work at remote and guarded cannabis sites. The cartels also lured or seized men in Vietnam and Eastern Europe, gave them fake passports or purchased forged visas, and then flew the undocumented or uninformed workers to California. Other brokers for cartels kidnap migrants and refugees as they make the journey from Latin America through Guatemala and Mexico to the California border. *Coyotes*, or traffickers, seize their passports or identity papers—real or fake—and take their money and phones before driving them into the mountains.

The legalization of recreational marijuana did not bring an end to human trafficking in the cannabis industry. Confronted with daunting new taxes and high costs of obtaining permits, fewer than one-fourth of the cannabis growers in Humboldt County have legal permits. Most marijuana fields and sheds remain tucked away on unmarked dirt roads. For the most part, the fieldworkers transported to Northern California to plant, tend, and harvest cannabis do not speak English.

The first sign that a U.S. resident has been trafficked in the Emerald Triangle typically comes through a missing person report filed with the county sheriff. Humboldt County has the highest number of people reported missing of any county in California, and Sheriff William Honsal calls it "modern slavery." He explained, "This is an illegal industry, and it requires a lot of workers. If they can bring in free [unpaid] labor through human trafficking, they'll do that." Honsal says that every year he gets telephone calls from desperate parents who report a missing son or daughter, and he finds many of these young people have been forced into slave labor, locked behind multiple gates in remote areas of the rural county: "Females have been drugged and raped and held against their will; . . . that has happened."[23]

From late May to early November, free and trafficked workers appear in the Emerald Triangle. If a trafficked migrant tries to leave before the end of the harvest, the boss, or *jefe*, often threatens to murder the worker's family back home. Because trafficked migrants are not U.S. citizens and do not hold temporary farmworker H-2A visas—or, indeed, any visas at all—they are naturally afraid to talk to law enforcement or disclose the identity of their "employers." During a cannabis raid along the northern Klamath River in 2015, none of the dozen Latino workers even knew which state they were in.[24]

At the end of the growing season, unpaid and cast-off migrants often gather homeless, country-less, and penniless in inland towns such as Weaverville on the highway that bisects the Emerald Triangle or in railroad towns such as Dunsmuir along the eastern spine of the state. Most are from Mexico; many are from the cartel-led state of Michoacán in the western part of the country.[25] A trucker who delivers fertilizer and propane and a contractor who builds large drying sheds have both said that the numbers of trafficked Latino, Vietnamese, and Hmong workers for this lucrative crop are underreported.[26] Most trafficked fieldworkers in California spend four to five years in bondage, and if they are found or freed they get nothing more than the fare for a bus ride home.[27]

By mid-autumn, the sticky cannabis buds are ripe, and thousands of young women from overseas or American students on a gap year or summer break stand by the side of Highway 101, their faces turned toward the oncoming trucks and cars, hoping to be offered work clipping cannabis buds from the stalks. Standing along the freeway, they make "scissor" motions with their fingers to show that they are looking to "trim." They hop into trucks with strangers to be driven several hours on unmarked dirt roads into the hills. Sometimes they are blindfolded, so they know neither their route nor destination. These seasonal "trimmigants" sleep in tent camps or cabins and clip the cannabis buds in cavernous drying barns or farm kitchens. Many are lured by the promise of fifty to one hundred dollars an hour, in cash, off the books. Until the era of decriminalization, all trimmigants were illegal workers; even now no one knows their real numbers.[28]

An ad in Craigslist posted during the harvest in October 2020 sought trimmers ready for "prolonged standing, some bending, stooping, and stretching. . . . Lifting up to 50 pounds and push/pull up to 100 pounds. . . . Eye-hand coordination and manual dexterity sufficient enough to operate manicuring tools [scissors]. . . . An ability to identify cannabis varieties using visual and olfactory senses is highly desirable. . . . Work is performed at a busy outdoor and indoor cannabis facility, . . . exposed to the natural elements. Workers should be prepared for . . . sun exposure and allergies. Work may include dealing with difficult people and/or law enforcement."[29]

Music and drugs keep the boring task moving as trimmers work behind chain-link fences and locked gates, often with no phone service, no wages, and, most terrifying of all, no transportation off the mountains at the end of the season.[30] Here the border between labor trafficking and sex trafficking is porous. Sexual assaults by overseers are frequent; sometimes the girls are proffered to fieldworkers as an incentive.

Sheriff Honsal says that human trafficking is the county's fourth-most underreported crime, ranked right after child abuse, rape, and spousal abuse: "People have been straight up kidnapped, put in the back of trucks or vans with blindfolds on and forced up to the mountains to trim." Growers lure female trimmers by the promise of harvest wages of $300 a day. In 2018 two English women came to the county having heard it was the "work/play" destination of the world, but after two weeks they found themselves caught on a mountain, stun-gunned if they didn't take off their clothes and dance into the evening.[31] If they refused, they risked being cast out with neither transportation nor money, in a wilderness of logging roads winding through miles of redwood and spruce forest.[32] Honsal concedes that law enforcement knows that "more girls go in than come out."[33] Where are the bodies?

Abolition in Modern Times

Thousands of migrants who come to California in search of political sanctuary are held captive by a coyote whom they have paid to transport them across the border. They stumble through the Mojave Desert carrying plastic water jugs stuffed with cloves of garlic, a concoction to repel rattlesnakes. Others crawl through well-established tunnels from Tijuana on the Mexican side of the border into the suburbs of San Diego. Many discover that they have handed thousands of dollars for safe transit to a recruiter (or *el reclutador*) as "a down payment," but soon discover they have only paid to ride on the wheel bed of a truck that may deliver them to a trafficker. With the promise of wages of several thousand dollars a month, they may have leveraged their family farm in Guatemala or Honduras, only to find that there are no wages and no jobs for them in California; they realize that they have been trapped into debt bondage that may last indefinitely.

Each week, freighters arrive in California ports carrying human cargo—men, women, and children as young as ten or eleven years old. Trafficked workers climb from container ships, crawl under the lid of a popped trunk of a car, or walk down passenger ramps into Los Angeles International Airport bearing falsified passports or work visas provided by crime syndicates.[34] They have been seized or lured by brokers operating the streets of Thailand, the Philippine Islands, Malaysia, or Eastern Europe, middlemen who have promised them jobs as welders, fieldworkers, nannies, and manicurists.

In the late 1980s, slave brokers began to canvas the slums of Bangkok and rural villages in Thailand to "recruit" workers for California's growing garment trade. In 1995 such a broker sought out Rotchana Cheunchujit, a twenty-four-year-old garment worker, and he tempted her to leave her farm with the promise of an eight-hour workday, money to help her children—aged two and three—who were to be left behind, and $4,800 to repay her "loan" for her airplane ticket and visa.[35]

At the airport in Bangkok, the broker draped jewelry around Cheunchujit's neck so she would look like a wealthy tourist, and he boarded the flight with her. As soon as they passed through the immigration checkpoints at Los Angeles International Airport, he took her passport, money, and the jewelry. Cheunchujit and seventy-one other Thai migrants were driven in vans to El Monte, an industrial suburb about twelve miles outside of Los Angeles. There they were locked in a compound of decrepit townhouses with boarded-up windows, all surrounded by a spiked fence topped with thick razor ribbon. Private armed security guards patrolled the area. Behind the plywood façade they found hundreds of other Thai migrants who sewed for seventeen to twenty-two hours a day. At the end of their workdays, they would sleep by their sewing machines or under blankets heaped on a concrete floor, sprawled next to eight other workers. When one worker was caught attempting to escape from the sweatshop, a guard shaved his head and told him that if he tried another time, he would never see his family again. His coworkers told him that the owners had circulated his photograph—a cautionary tale.

"When I first came, I didn't realize I was a victim," Cheunchujit recalled. "After almost a year, I realized, well, I can't leave. I can't go anywhere. I can't say anything."[36] Some of her fellow workers had been locked in the compound for years, sinking deeper into debt as they "bought" food from a make-shift *cantina*, or commissary, in a garage inside the fence. Their letters home were censored or destroyed, and no news of their plight reached the outside world. Meanwhile they stitched garments marketed under the brand names Anchor Blue, B.U.M., High Sierra, CLEO, and Tomato Inc., sold in Filene's Basement and Macy's department stores across the country.[37]

After seven years, one woman escaped; fearing that the traffickers would make good on their threat to kill her family at home, she hid in the Thai community in Los Angeles. There she drew a map that showed where the guards were posted, and she penciled a letter to the police and passed the map and note to a friend, describing the entrapment and conditions, and adding, "Please be careful. *Very Dangerous.* Please bring much manpower. Don't forget to be careful."[38]

Early one morning in August 1995, local police and federal and state agents launched a coordinated raid and eluded the guards. They intercepted trucks being loaded with vast quantities of finished garments—priceless evidence—and then entered the El Monte compound and arrested the eight Chinese and Thai owners.

However, when the police came upon seventy-two captive garment workers, rather than free them, they shackled them together and bused them to the Immigration and Naturalization Detention Center in Los Angeles County. Accused of having entered the country illegally many years before, the traumatized and destitute Thai prisoners were unable to post bail for nine days. The Thai Community Development Center in Los Angeles and other national and Los Angeles–based Asian American advocacy groups staged sit-ins until the seventy-two El Monte workers were released and granted "S," or "snitch," visas, the slang term for migrants testifying against drug traffickers (an immigration loophole). Seven of the nine owners of the sweatshop were found guilty of conspiracy and "imposing involuntary servitude" and sentenced to serve up to seven years in prison. Two others evaded arrest and escaped to Thailand.

The "Case of the El Monte Garment Workers" in Los Angeles was the first legal victory over modern-day slavery in the United States. The Thai El Monte sweatshop workers forced the foreign factory owners, manufacturers, and American retailers to pay over $4 million in settlements for having profited from seven years of their enslaved labor. The civil action

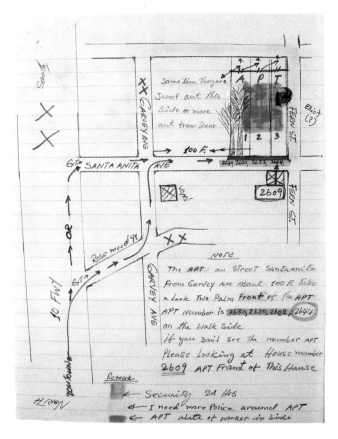

A woman who managed to escape the El Monte sweatshop
after being held for seven years drew this map for the
police to locate the guards and the captured workers, 1995.

State of California, Department of Industrial Relations,
Division of Labor Standards Enforcement. Smithsonian
Museum of American History, Washington, DC.

of the El Monte workers ignited the anti-trafficking movement in the
United States and led to the first Victims of Trafficking and Violence Protection Act of 2000; the new law also covered undocumented migrants.[39]

Victims of labor trafficking work and live invisibly among us. Shyima
El-Sayed Hassan (Shyima Hall) was born in 1989. She was the seventh of
eleven children born into a poor and abusive family in a small town outside
of Alexandria, Egypt. There, several families and eleven children shared
two rooms and slept on the floor. In desperation, Shyima's father had sold

Rescue and detention of trafficked garment workers.
(Courtesy Rick Meyer. Copyright © 2017. *Los Angeles Times.* Used with Permission.)

her eldest sister, Zahra, to Abel Nasser Eid Youssef and Amal Admed Ewis-Abd El Motelib, to work on their estate. Not long after, the pair accused Zahra of stealing thirty dollars and returned her to her parents, telling them, "You can't pay back what your girl stole, so you can either provide us with someone else or we'll call the police."[40]

To pay her elder sister's thirty-dollar theft, her parents delivered eight-year-old Shyima. The only child among seven other servants on the estate, she washed dishes and cared for the family's five children. In the year 2000, the Egyptian government accused Youssef of fraud, and he quickly fled with his family to Irvine, in Southern California. He claimed that the child had not yet paid off the family's debt and compelled Shyima's father to sign a contract as a ten-year child *khadamah*, meaning she was indentured as a maidservant.[41] One of Youssef's employees flew the frightened child to California, persuading immigration authorities that he was transporting her for adoption.

For two years, Shyima rose every morning at five o'clock in the morn-

Shyima Hall.
In Yasmin Aslam, "The Call: End Human Trafficking,"
MSNBC.com, September 16, 2008. (Courtesy AP Photo/Ric Francis.)

ing and cooked and cleaned for the next twenty hours. She got the children ready for school and washed the family's clothes. Once a day she was allowed to eat—scraps from the family's meals. "The Mom" and "The Dad," as she was taught to address them, slapped her and called her stupid. She recalled, "I slept in a tiny windowless storage room in the three-car garage, with no heat and no light." When Egyptian guests visited the family, the couple locked her in the pantry, and if she let anyone see her, they beat her. Day after day the "parents" told her, "You're nothing, nobody. You're lucky to be here. No one else would want you." After the terrorist attacks of September 11, 2001, things became worse. The frightened Middle Eastern family rarely left the house. They ordered Shyima to keep her eyes lowered, never answer a knock on the door, and always smile.

A neighbor, however, noticed an undernourished young girl caring for other children and realized that she was not going to school. In 2002, when Shyima was twelve years old, "someone, a wonderful someone," she recalls, "someone—maybe a mom who had seen me at the park with the children . . . made a phone call." That anonymous "someone" had reported Youssef to Child Protective Services. "The Mom" and "The Dad" were arrested and charged with harboring an illegal alien, obtaining labor by threats of physical restraint, and transnational labor trafficking. Shyima testified at their trial: "Wasn't I a human being? I slept in the garage . . . and waited on them hand and foot, even when I was sick. . . . I was nothing when I was with them."

"The Dad" was sentenced to three years in prison, "The Mom" to twenty-one months, "equal to the time I'd been held against my will," said Shyima. In addition, "They were ordered to pay me $76,137 . . . equivalent to what they would have paid me if I'd earned a minimum wage for the estimated number of hours I 'worked' for them after I came to the United States."[42] As she watched the police handcuff her captors, she remembered, "The Dad just stood there, but The Mom began to scream." Afterward, Shyima was placed with three different foster families, including Chuck and Jenny Hall, who adopted her. However, the Halls had access to her bank account and stole all of the restitution funds she received for the time she served as a slave.[43]

Shyima Hall shattered the silence of human trafficking with the publication of *Hidden Girl: The True Story of a Modern-Day Child Slave*, a memoir written for young adults. In it she writes: "A child might not remember the details of a bad dream, but the feeling of terror the dream brings can remain for a life-time. That's how the day I was sold into slavery is for me."[44] The modern-day slave in Southern California became an advocate for victims and testifies as an expert for the U.S. Court of Appeals for the Ninth Circuit.[45] She is a fierce survivor. And she is not alone.

"This Is How Prostitutes Are Made"

Elle Snow was eighteen when she was trafficked into the world of sexual slavery. (Elle Snow is a name she invented to protect herself.)[46]

Snow stands six feet one inch tall, with long hair, dyed black, and muscular arms each etched with a thick black tattoo—a devil on one, an angel on the other. She is wary and intensely alert. Snow says that as a tall white woman, she does not fit the image of a target. She grew up in the fishing port of Eureka on the Humboldt County coast of Northern California, outside the local pot culture, outside the world of loggers, and outside the circles of backpackers who hike in the forests of ancient redwoods, the thousand-year-old trees that catch the fog and slice the sunshine along ridges that slope down to the sea.

"I grew up a tough, crazy girl," says Snow. In 2003 she was distressed over a broken romance and living with her mother and fourteen-year-old sister. She had just been promoted to manager at Sbarro's pizza restaurant in Eureka's shopping mall, on Highway 101 at the south edge of town. For a few weeks, she had noticed that a handsome Black man had been showing up, seemingly wherever she happened to be. He stood out in the white fishing town; his hair, worn in short cornrows, was woven with bright beads, and he drove a red Jaguar XF, a car conspicuous among the surfers' vans and the growers' dirt-splattered pickup trucks. One night, as she was leaving a club, Snow saw him waiting. He beckoned her to come over. Although she did not like his demanding attitude, she was curious and walked to him. He introduced himself as David Bernard Anderson, and they went to a party.

Anderson, then twenty-nine, came across as "a very attractive, very charismatic, very smooth individual," remembers Snow. But she fretted, "This guy maybe was a 'player'—the worst thing a guy could be—juggling multiple girlfriends." After the party Anderson called Snow every day, sometimes twice a day, drawing her out. She confided to him that when she was a little girl, a "pastor uncle" had molested her. Anderson pressed her: What did her uncle "look like? What did he wear? How did he smell?" He urged her to tell him more about her childhood and listened as she described her chaotic home, her father who had abandoned the family, and her fears for her teenage sister. He told her that it was "therapy" for her to relive these experiences and share her secrets with him. Although she was flattered, she began to realize that she didn't know a lot about Anderson.

Anderson continued to collect her intimate information. After a month of long telephone calls, he urged Snow to let him take her away from the "drama" at her home. She agreed to spend a weekend with him at his apartment in Sacramento, about 290 miles south of Eureka. Snow remembers the first night there as "Hennessey, talk, and romance."

The mood changed when Anderson's alleged cousin came into the bedroom in the middle of the night and showed her his gun. The next morning, Snow recalls, "I woke up and David was standing over me, trying to jolt me awake." She was naked. "I couldn't get up from the floor." Her clothes, purse, credit cards, and phone were gone. Wordlessly, Anderson handed her a pair of six-inch stiletto heels and "hideous, nasty clothes. I was supposed to put them on and go walk the street—the 'track' a couple of blocks away; I needed to go make money." Gone was the caring tone of the phone calls as he ordered her to get dressed. She remembers that he told her that "I was going to walk on Stockton Boulevard, and I was going to have sex with men for money." He said that he was a pimp and that Snow "was going to be his prostitute."

Before that time Snow had thought that a prostitute was the free-spirited Vivian, portrayed by Julia Roberts in *Pretty Woman* (1990)—"a fierce, independent woman." She remembers, "I believed that image until I couldn't get up from the floor, the moment that my trafficker said, 'This is how prostitutes are made.'"

Anderson told her that she was in a Sacramento ghetto filled with pimps, but he assured her that he was "a nice one." Then, she says, "he started threatening me. Telling me he was going to hurt me, beat me up if I didn't put on the clothes and get out there." But "I literally couldn't move. I'm from Humboldt County. I never heard of these things before."

Over the next two days, Anderson told Snow that she had to pay back what he had spent for gas and renting a car to pick her up. He said that from now on, he would "decide [her] reality"; he added, "I have this guy out in front of your house and he sees your sister. This is going to happen to your sister, too."

Anderson's threats went on for a couple more days until he conceded that "I looked good enough that I don't have to be on the streets." He would "let" her work at a "cat house," a brothel in Walnut Creek, an affluent suburb across the bay from San Francisco. He added that she "could [also] work off the Internet, which was just on the rise with trafficking," and told her that she would post ads for herself on pornography sites that sell sexual "meet-ups" and charge by the act or by the hour.

Anderson drove Snow to Walnut Creek, about an hour away, for her "interview," and she prayed for the car to crash. She thought: "Something's got to happen. Something's going to stop this. This isn't going to happen." Nonetheless, a madam, who called herself Leilani, was waiting in her car outside her brothel, A-1 Pleasures, to inspect Snow. Anderson told Snow that if she let Leilani know that she had been abducted, he would dump her in the Russian River and "make good" on the threats to her younger sister. When he insisted that she had to trust him, she says, "That's when my mind went 'there's no reason here.'"

Snow's first customer reminded her of her predatory uncle, down to his clothes. Terrified, she was convinced that Anderson had reproduced the details she had confided to him of her childhood. "Traffickers" she explains, "look for women who were previously sexually abused and then reinstate that trauma and shame when they say, 'This is what you are. You're a prostitute now.' I crossed over into 'the matrix.' *That's* the real world. *This* is a fabrication." Among Snow's customers, or "tricks," were men who claimed to be doctors, lawyers, and professional men. She recalls a police officer who casually tossed his badge on the dresser.

Snow was always under surveillance: "I wasn't left alone for a second," she says. Whenever Anderson went outside, his "cousin" was standing by. "I didn't have anyone to call. I had nowhere to go and now no one's going to want anything to do with me," she remembers. Her new world was "everywhere—people, hotels, the Internet." Now when Anderson also told her that she had been abandoned by her family and friends, she believed him.

Barely literate, Anderson forced Snow to compose advertisements touting her sexual prowess and post her fees on websites such as Cityvibe, Backpage, and Craigslist.[47] In this online buffet of sex, she realized, trafficked women and girls are less protected by law than are the websites themselves.

For the next eight months, Snow worked at the brothel during the day and at hotels during the evening, "on call." Whenever she asked when "this would end," Anderson beat her or choked her. When she fought back, he warned her that he would shave her head. Once he told her that she could leave, but added, "You are not taking your hair with you because I made your hair"—that is, he had paid for it to be dyed.

Anderson sold sex with Snow by the half-hour. She explained: "You get to rent someone's body for $100 for a half an hour. A lot of people can afford that. They can save up for that." She recalls that all of the women she met at the brothel were taught to tell the same story to their upscale customers: "We were sexually liberated college students. Absolutely that is the industry standard. I said I was studying to be a lawyer." About 30 percent of her earnings at the brothel went to Leilani and every other penny went to Anderson.

This Is How a Pimp Is Made

Before these eight cruel months, Elle Snow thought human trafficking was about "some girl from Russia who was forced over here to work as a nanny." As her months in captivity went on, she wondered how a pimp was made. Anderson, explained Snow, had studied a "curriculum" and followed playbooks on how to become a sex trafficker and how to break a woman down. *The Pimp Game: Instructional Guide*, written by adult filmmaker Mickey Royal, taught Anderson to calibrate a rhythm of tenderness and shaming, praise and threat, and sleep deprivation.[48]

The Pimp Game trains a trafficker to "do things to and for his ho [whore] that her priest, children, etc. can't do. He can take the pain away. How? Simple, by taking her away from the pain. Show her the fantasy that comes with you"—physical, financial, and emotional protection. "A ho is always searching. . . . A pat on the back and social acceptance is worth its weight in gold to a ho." Most important, a pimp must not do anything without receiving sex. In addition, "A pimp must become a warden who sets traps and awaits his victims."[49] *Pimpology: The 48 Laws of the Game* teaches a trafficker to "tear someone's ego down to nothing." Then, "show them that it's your program that takes them from darkness to hope, . . . even if the weakness you rescue them from is one you created."[50]

As Snow's months in captivity went on, Anderson sensed that soon she would try to escape, and he became ruthless. As they drove around Southern California, he forced her to listen to rapper Too $hort's (Todd Anthony Shaw) song "Fifty Cent Pimp" and to hip-hop music that encourages pimping and male brutality; more than once, he threatened to "bust open her head."

This Is How a Freedom Fighter Is Made

Snow says, "I'm not easy to break. I argue, and I never stop. I was screaming. I was telling him to die. I was making him acknowledge what he was doing." At times she became desperate: "I just want this all to be gone. I want this world to stop. Why hasn't the world stopped? I want it to stop."

Snow tried to escape three times. The first time was when Anderson wanted her to post an ad selling a seventeen-year-old girl on the website Backpage. This demand, she said, "shocked me . . . so I ran. After about a week of being gone, I decided I was going to make some money. I felt I needed to get something out of this. So, I advertised, and I went back to work. Cause I ran with nothing." She recalled her despair: "At one point I was standing over a balcony. The employees at the hotel were laughing at me; they looked at me like I was the scum of the earth. It would be so much easier if I was just gone." But Anderson found her, took her, and worked her from the street. In each car she pleaded with the "customer" to drive her to a police station. All refused.

Snow realized she had to flee again and she began to hide her tips in the zippered lining of a rolling suitcase. One day in a hotel in Southern California, Anderson left the room to buy cigarettes. Barefoot, wearing only shorts and a shirt, Snow grabbed her cash and ran down the stairs toward the back door of the building. When she saw his car pull into the parking lot, she dashed back inside. She ducked below the registration desk and slipped into the hotel office, where she crouched down and watched her freedom unfold on the security monitor. She saw Anderson return with cigarettes. Minutes later, she saw him rush out with both of their suitcases. Only then did Elle call a friend to pick her up. Next, she called the Orange County Police Department.

After Anderson's conviction, Snow moved to Portland, Oregon, where she lived for ten years until the Humboldt County district attorney's office found her to ask for her help. Anderson had been arrested again, for rape of a minor, false imprisonment, and human trafficking, the first such charge in Humboldt County. The district attorney wanted her to return to California to testify on behalf of a sixteen-year-old victim. Pained by memories of Anderson's threats to her sister, Snow agreed. Snow joined three other women whom Anderson had previously trapped to testify against him. He was found guilty and sentenced to ten years in prison, and served three. Within months of his early release in 2019, Anderson was again arrested and sentenced to five years in prison for kidnap and rape of a minor with the intent to prostitute her. When a detective searched his apartment, she found his library of pimp instruction manuals.

Game Over

Sexual slavery, the modern head of the hydra, keeps changing its face. After 9/11, immigration restrictions created a rise in homegrown trafficking. "With the rise of the internet," says Snow, "it's gone wildfire." The hidden or "dark web" has offered traffickers infinite customers and business tools. "Why," insists Snow, "should a pimp still sit at a public intersection watching a girl?"

Snow sees a crucial difference between labor trafficking and sex trafficking: "Getting raped every day is not the same thing as working in a field. You can't get pregnant from labor trafficking."[51] Both forms of modern human slavery are underreported and demand different solutions. She believes that the public has "overfocused" on the victims of human trafficking and has failed to address its roots. After David Anderson's trial and sentencing in Humboldt County, in 2016 she launched Game Over, an organization to teach local police officers, rape counselors, teachers, attorneys, high school students, and the Humboldt County Board of Supervisors how to spot it.

This "It's Game Over" tattoo is in stark contrast to barcode tattoos that still mark the ownership and sale of a human being. This is the logo for the not-for-profit Game Over founded by Elle Snow to combat sex trafficking in Northern California.
Soroptimists International of Eureka, California.

Snow urges physicians and parents to learn the language of tattoos—the "stuff that could be other stuff." Sex traffickers brand their victims, says Snow, "just like owners of plantation slaves used to do when they would put a slash on the bottom part of a runaway slave's left eye." Trafficked girls are marked with tattooed dollar bills, dollar signs, and bar codes, with diamonds and crowns because a pimp calls himself the "king" and "promises a young girl that she will be his queen."

Snow makes the invisible visible. She has told police that a man's T-shirt printed with the graphic "CEO" signals a trafficker, and has urged law enforcement to be alert to an older man accompanying a frightened teenage girl and to notice young girls with prepaid credit cards and burner phones. She has told police officers to look for Western Union receipts, for that is how she sent her tip money home. In 2018 Snow joined the legal team that shut down backpage.com, the largest marketplace for buying and selling sex on the internet.[52] This blackout spawned the paired Stop Enabling Sex Traffickers Act and Fight Online Sex Trafficking Act.[53]

In 2018 the California legislature explicitly defined modern human trafficking as a form of slavery; it expanded its pimping and pandering laws to make it a crime to deprive someone of their liberty with the intent to obtain forced labor or service. The state that had legalized slavery finally dragged its criminal code into compliance with the Thirteenth Amendment. The new codes also define child pornography and child sexual exploitation as human trafficking and identify transporting a person without consent as a form of kidnapping. Even if a trafficker is mistaken about the age of his captive, he could face fifteen years to life in prison and fines up to $1 million under the Californians Against Sexual Exploitation Act.[54] Prosecutors or victims can take websites to court if they post ads for sex trafficking.[55]

Human traffickers are protected by silence, according to Snow, but now "we need to start talking about these things." This includes "men amongst men. Because this is where the demand is. If the jury doesn't understand what is going on in front of them, then the traffickers are not going to get convicted. Because we are the jury."

Epilogue
To Witness

T'TC~TSA, A WAILAKI GIRL, was kidnapped, sold, confined, and raped, then she fled and was recaptured, in endless repetition. At age ninety-one, free and seeking to record the history of her bondage, she decided to tell her story of forty years of serial enslavement. She said: "If you could only know the truth of [how] the Indian has been treated since the first white man came into his part of the country it would make an ordinary man shake and shudder. I would like to tell you the whole story. I am afraid it would not be allowed to be put in print."[1]

California was conceived in slavery. California nurtured slavery in regimes that sunder its true history from its myths and marketing. For each regime there were witnesses. This narrative of 250 years of slavery in California is a gathering of witnesses whose reporting dramatically reveals the conceit that California's people and natural resources were there for the taking—otters, streams and rivers, gold nuggets, and redwood forests, Native Americans, refugees, and destitute immigrants. These witnesses tell how California was a come-hither state that, to invaders, enslavers, and entrepreneurs, promised souls to be saved and convicts to be worked; unpaid and unfree field hands to plant wheat and trim cannabis; unpaid and unfree women, children, and migrants to wash dirty clothes, tan hides, and forage for food and tend the sick. All the paths to human bondage in California—kidnap, forced transport, abuse, and sale—were witnessed. Indians routed from their villages and African Americans, Native Americans, and migrants from Asia and Latin America who were sold, worked, and raped in California were seen.

No convict laborer who recycles the lead in computers or victim of modern human trafficking who lists herself on Craigslist believes that California is a post-slavery or post-racial state. Yet throughout its centuries of human bondage, witnesses believed that California had a more perfect future. The witnesses told, recorded, reported, or chanted their tales of human bondage, and they demanded the right to testify. They had freedom on their mind.

In 1849 California passed a constitution that said, "Neither slavery, nor involuntary servitude, unless for the punishment of crimes, shall ever be tolerated in this State." "Tolerate" is not a legal standard. But the U.S. Congress required California to include this declaration as a condition of statehood. Eager to bring an end to the military occupation that was marking California as property of the United States and also guarantee ownership of the newfound gold, delegates to the California Constitutional Convention wrote this tepid promise into law.

The enslaved knew that California did not abolish slavery. They saw that the free state did not liberate those who had been brought across the plains or shipped across the Pacific in steerage class. Their status remained unchanged by any formal declaration that repudiated slavery. California's constitution did not ban southern slaveholders from bringing more plantation slaves into the state. It did not interfere when California Indians stood in the living room of a justice of the peace who stamped their forced indenture contracts.

Slavery in California was supposed to end more than once. When the 1848 Treaty of Guadalupe Hidalgo carved away 55 percent of Mexico to create the U.S. West, it also declared that Native Americans were to remain free. At the end of the Civil War in 1865, the country adopted the Thirteenth Amendment to the U.S. Constitution: "Neither slavery nor involuntary servitude, except as a punishment for crime whereof the party shall have been duly convicted, shall exist within the United States, or any place subject to their jurisdiction." California grudgingly signed the amendment twelve days *after* it became the law of the land.[2]

Three years later, in July 1868, the nation ratified the Fourteenth Amendment and gave any person living in the United States the right to equal protection under the law. California refused to sign on for nearly one hundred years, and only in 1959 did it acknowledge the new law; over the next three decades a handful of Confederate states followed. The Fifteenth Amendment, the third and last of the Reconstruction Amendments after the Civil War, said that the "right of citizens of the United States to

vote shall not be denied or abridged by the United States or by any State on
account of race, color, or previous condition of servitude." Its support was a
precondition for Virginia, Mississippi, Texas, and Georgia to rejoin the union
and thus was ratified in 1870. And once again, California refused to sign
until 1962, when the Civil Rights movement shamed it into compliance—
ninety-two years after it had been ratified.[3] By then its signature was merely
symbolic.

California as a slave state is not the California that most people know
now. Yet its unbroken history of holding humans in bondage was known
by the stolen people. This history of slavery takes us to where we are now.

After California passed its freedom constitution in 1849, southern
plantation owners transported more and more enslaved African Americans
across the plains, to dig ditches and shovel mud during the Gold Rush. But
many of the enslaved escaped from the creek beds in the Sierras and hid
in riverboats heading down to the coast. Archy Lee and James Williams,
African Americans who had been born into slavery, met free Blacks in
churches, in shops, and along the riverbanks. Hundreds of enslaved Blacks
fled along a West Coast Underground Railroad—a chain of safe houses,
hotels, steamships, and hidden paths. Today, victims of modern sex trafficking wait for a quick moment to flee from locked hotel rooms or gated
brothels. They flag down a car to flee or find a burner phone to call for
rescue or dial 9-1-1. Then, like Elle Snow, they tell other victims, juries,
and the police the story of months as a sex-trafficked teenager or a trapped
garment worker.

During the 1850s Native American women and children who had been
sold to ranchers as concubines, nannies, or field hands fled on foot, trekking for hundreds of miles along ancestral trails, living on seeds and acorns,
attempting to reunite with their families and tribes. Chinese prostitutes
escaped from the caged brothels of San Francisco and crossed the snowy
foothills of the Sierras on foot to safety in new Chinatowns scattered
across California.

The witnesses also tell a serial testimony of slave revolts in California.
Three years after Father Junípero Serra crawled over the sand dunes in
1769 with Spanish priests and soldiers and launched California's first slave
regime at Mission San Diego de Alcalá, the Kumeyaay swept down the canyons into the Franciscan compound. They burned the church and barracks
to the ground and killed the senior priest. Then they freed hundreds of
their tribe who were held captive by the padres.

In the decade of the 1850s, a thousand convicts at San Quentin Prison

were daily made to stand in rigid silence for twelve-hour shifts at the looms
of a private mill built inside the penitentiary. On Thursday, May 27, 1897,
more than one hundred years before the historic prison riots of Attica, convict laborers turned off the steam that fed the shuttles, and one thousand
prison workers at San Quentin went on strike, challenging the carceral
state that was built on their unpaid and involuntary labor. On his first day
out of San Quentin, Donald Lowrie went to the office of the San Francisco *Daily Evening Bulletin* to write the memoir of his years in the jute
mill in the prison by the bay.

A State of Redress

From the moment the Kumeyaay swept down to Mission San Diego de
Alcalá in 1775, the enslaved in California have called for justice that compensates and makes amends. In late 2021 California became the first state
in the union to launch a task force to study the consequences of slavery and
systemic racism. Several members of the reparations task force are scholars, lawyers, and activists who are descendants of slaves.[4]

The hurdles are many. How to repair the decades of genocide that
created thousands of refugees available to enslave, "vagrants" like T'tc~tsa?
A palimpsest of different forms of slavery and harm requires different forms
of restitution. With the diversity of slaveries in California, there is no single legal path to restoration or repair. Yet there are many sorts of acts that
constitute reparations. (And many that are too late.) Should they only go to
direct descendants of the enslaved? To racial communities long impacted
by the cruel deprivations of slavery? Reparations may include education
and scholarships, economic opportunities, new protections of voting rights,
safe housing, and environmental restoration of toxic and impoverished
urban sites. They may include police and prison reform. California Native
Americans seek land restitution and removal of dams that send their water
to agribusinesses. Still, all forms of reparations depend on witnesses, evidence, and history. The enslaved were witnesses; they were surrounded by
witnesses. Witnessing is a source of knowledge.

To establish amends, reparations first seek recovery of forgotten truths
and established facts. California's courts, newspapers, and legislature sought
to silence the evidence of slavery—the brutality, losses, and soul destruction that are the conditions of human bondage. The stolen people, dis-
tanced from the law and erased from history, nonetheless undid the deep
silences of slavery. Brutalized by slavers and banished from the courts and

legislature, they refused to endorse the fiction of a free state. Where they could, they told their truths. The stories of their quests for freedom found cracks in history's silences; their stories arose in wiry growths that pushed up through the sealing mortar of political denial. The modern demand for reparations cuts through swaths of academic forgetting.

Since undoing history is impossible, what constitutes amends? California is grappling with inevitable questions: What constitutes reparations to descendants of the enslaved? Who is entitled? How much would it cost? Who is liable? The state? The federal government? The many who profited? What does it cost to repair a state that indeed "tolerated" slavery? South African author Achmat Dangor writes that his people "want to forgive . . . we don't want to forget."[5]

Although those who lived in freedom in California often looked away, slavery was visible and on display. Here people in bondage found ways to warn one another of dangers; they beckoned their communities and rewrote the utopian tale of Gold Mountain, El Dorado, Haight-Ashbury, the Emerald Triangle, Silicon Valley, and Napa Valley. The ancestors, the Californians who were shackled and sold, told this history in letters and lawsuits, in diaries and documents, in demands for the legal right to tell their truths. Their poetry and songs tell dangerous truths. Enslaver and enslaved understood that the right to testify is not only a demand for truth but a call for freedom.

Justice That Repairs

There is, as yet, no consolation or reckoning to close this study of the stolen people in California. There are living descendants—living victims and living heirs—their story is not over. They ask: What's the verdict? Is there a punishment adequate to the crime of human bondage? Is there a remedy? Is there revenge when most of the perpetrators are dead? Instead, the descendants insist on change. And they seek amends.

The descendants of the enslaved have been stricken in different ways, and they want different recompense. For modern California Natives, Alaska Natives, and Chinese immigrants, their stolen ancestors not only live in memory. Their bondage, assaults, forced transport, and unpaid wages are empirical lineage. The enslaved and their descendants seek compensation. Opportunities lost over generations cannot be restored, but the descendants want these opportunities now—in the return of land, sexual safety, free college education, and the vote. Reparations may mean electricity on

Indian reservations, vaccines delivered in rural library vans, and work visas so migrant laborers don't get trafficked at the border.

Corrina Gould (Ohlone/Lisjan) has said that "all of California is 'Stolen land.' . . . We are landless Indians in our own territory." California Natives have seen their traditional lands covered by golf courses, universities, and freeways, and their green rivers diverted by hydroelectric dams. For Gould, "The only compensation for land is land." Reparations must include the return of soil and waterways, sites tied to beliefs of the sacred unity of humans and spaces. Only Indian stewardship will repair the devastation and offer stewardship of Indian homelands.[6]

Reparations require a collective reckoning and valuation of the magnitude of what has been taken. Estimates run to trillions of dollars. Still, in 2015 the Kashaya Pomo insisted that California return seven hundred acres of land in the fertile wine country, the lands of Metini on the cliffs over Bodega Bay where Russian fur traders captured their tribal members to build a slave colony for the devastation of otters. In 2019 the Weott persuaded the city of Eureka in Humboldt County to return two hundred acres of Tuluwat Island, their spiritual homeland and the site of slaughter and mass kidnap 144 years ago. Although the U.S. Congress rejected every treaty that would return the land to California's Indigenous people, today 45,864,800 acres of federally owned land in California (nearly half the state) is undeveloped. There is land that could be returned to the tribes.[7]

Toppling statues of Junípero Serra or John Sutter or removing the name of Serranus Clinton Hastings—the slaveholder and rancher who masterminded a slaughter of the Yuki people—from the University of California Hastings College of the Law acknowledges a forgotten history of human bondage in California and undoes mythologies that justify long-held claims for wealth and power. June 19—Juneteenth—is the annual holiday that celebrates the proclamation that emancipated enslaved African Americans. On Juneteenth 2020, crowds toppled a thirty-foot statue of mission priest and slaveholder Junípero Serra, whose shadow had loomed over a neighborhood park in San Francisco. Three days earlier, a cohesive protest led by Black Lives Matter convinced the city of Sacramento to remove a statue of iconic slaveholder and Gold Rush hero John Sutter from the eponymous Sutter Medical Center. There are still twenty-four Sutter Health acute-care hospitals, two hundred Sutter Health clinics, several streets in downtown San Francisco and the state capital Sacramento, and many elementary and middle schools that are named for the man who enslaved three thousand California Native men, women, and children.[8] How to put a price on the pain of a Native American teenager who is walking to class and passes the daunting figure of a man who sold an ancestor? Removing such monuments acknowledges a truth, evidence for reparations and a foundation for repair.

For some, statements of regret create a form of reparation. An apology cannot undo the harm, but it does accept that an atrocity occurred. Starting in 2009, hundreds of years after the fact, statements of remorse for the slavery of California Natives and African Americans were uttered throughout California by those who did not perpetrate the violence. Today, statements of contrition flow from university presidents and state officials who built prestigious institutions of higher learning on Yurok, Ohlone, and Miwok land. Even a staged or ambivalent apology is a collective admission—and then is accepted as evidence and acknowledgment—that a grievous wrong was committed. An apology offers context to demands for equity, suffrage, and access to justice.[9]

In 2019 California governor Gavin Newsom apologized for the "war of extermination" that Peter H. Burnett, the first governor of California, launched against all California Natives in 1851. Newsom then convened a Truth and Healing Council.[10] Many Costanoan/Ohlone Indians, however, oppose this council because, they say, Californians are not ready to "listen with their hearts so that they can understand and help carry the burden. . . . To have a healthy relationship, it takes two healthy parties." California "still turns the missions into tourist attractions and uses the state parks for monetary gain." Tribal Chair Valentin Lopez adds that the state has not even restored Native names to sacred sites.[11] For the Ohlone, an apology without redress is premature, even hypocritical. A true apology goes beyond contrition. It is a pledge of self-correction. It is a promise to fix a problem. It is a call and response.

California Natives seek a "land acknowledgment," a formal recognition of Native Americans as the traditional stewards of the land. Recent land acknowledgments, often at public talks or celebrations, testify to the enduring relationship between Indigenous people and their time-honored territories; they also thank a tribe for letting people study or work on land that was stolen, paved, and built over. A land acknowledgment does not exist in the past tense; it recognizes that there is still an unpaid debt.[12] While some call land acknowledgments "alibis for theft" that do not return property or pay for stolen territory, they offer prestigious evidence of theft.[13]

California slavery was costly; it created debts. Kidnapped Alaska Natives shipped to California for the otter hunt missed the long summers when salmon spawn in the creeks, and the people starved. During the anti-Chinese roundups of the 1880s, enslaved girls who had fled from caged brothels were again on the run, driven from friends and the sanctuary of Chinatowns and their new jobs in shops or kitchens. Enslaved prostitutes joined other Chinese immigrants who were forced to leave behind homes, farms, fishing boats, and vegetables still rooted in the gardens. Together they were marched out of town or loaded onto railroads; within days their white neighbors raided their shops for intricately carved mahogany furniture, costly silk fans, and delicate porcelain vases.[14] In the 1886 case *Wing Hing v. The City of Eureka*, two enslaved prostitutes joined fifty other Chinese residents from Eureka and sued the city, both for damages and for over $130,000 for being driven out by a mob. This was the first lawsuit for reparations in California.[15]

How to run a tab on the costs of human bondage? Where to begin to pay down the crushing debt? How to pay down the future? To whom? To direct descendants of the enslaved or to the populations who suffered the racial legacy of human bondage in lasting segregated neighborhoods, underfunded schools, and polluted neighborhoods? Ta-Nehisi Coates explains, "What I'm talking about is more than recompense for past injustices—more than a handout, a payoff, hush money, or a reluctant bribe." Coates seeks "a national reckoning that would lead to spiritual renewal. Reparations would mean a revolution of the American consciousness, a reconciling of our self-image as the great democratizer with the facts of our history."[16]

A vow to witness, acknowledge, and speak the history of slavery in California is a painful first step. The histories of generations of California's Indigenous children appear in the logs of the Indian boarding schools, in letters demanding pay for children's field labor. History appears on their unnamed graves. During its first annual "National Sorry Day" on May 26, 1998, the federal government of Australia apologized for the "Stolen Generations"—Aboriginal children seized from their families and sent to missions or reform schools that would try to inculcate them with European values and work habits. Civil rights groups gave out "Sorry Books"—blank journals in which Indigenous people recorded their feelings about their lost childhoods. But the government never fulfilled the Human Rights Commission's call for financial restitution.[17] Aboriginal leader Noel Pearson wrote: "Black fellas will get the words, the white fellas keep the money."[18]

Can history reverse the effect of injustice? Does history point to the fact that loss is real and financial equality is fair, that payment for damages means that the state has taken responsibility for harm?[19] "Justice that re-pairs" compensates not only for past injuries, lost education, and unpaid labor, but also for current inequities that flowed from slavery.[20]

History is a kind of reparation; it assumes that truth is a condition of restitution. Can witnesses to a history of slavery also be hopeful? Telling the truth of California marks a closure to silence. Telling the truth of California testifies to a resistant tradition, a foundation on which to build. In 1858 Black abolitionists in San Francisco pulled Archy Lee, a fugitive from slavery, out of a rowboat that was ferrying him to a ship bound for New Orleans and they set him free. Stories of the Chinese ancestors who hid runaway girls and free Blacks who signed eight thousand petitions for the right to testify may be helpful to today's young descendants of the enslaved who are crafting their own calls for justice.

The California Task Force on Reparations does not see its work as a "reckoning"—a moral calculation of slavery that points to forgiveness—because human bondage is not an event that occurred in the past.[21] It sees slavery in California as a sustained structure of economic, gender, and racial power. It cannot be peeled away on its own. California's Truth and Reconciliation Commission for Native Americans opened by acknowl-edging the Act for the Government and Protection of Indians of 1850 that sanctioned kidnap and forced indenture.

History cannot write checks to descendants and affected communi-ties. Across the nation, that task has been kicked between Congress, state legislatures, and the courts that, from the birth of the state, mutually legal-ized and sanctioned slavery. Financial reparations must overcome the legal barrier of owners long-dead and institutions defunct and the legal prece-dent of "sovereign immunity"—a government cannot be sued without its own consent for wrongs committed in its name. But history can lead to honesty and repair. After scores of witnesses, the U.S. Congress granted $20,000 each to Americans of Japanese descent, most from California, who were detained in "Internment Camps" during World War II. In 2015 Congress authorized payments of up to $10,000 per day for the fifty-two people taken hostage in Iran in 1979, the nation's largest reparations pro-gram ever, but those funds were never delivered.[22]

Demands for financial reparations recalibrate economic equations with facts; these demands erase dangerous stereotypes, such as nineteenth-cen-tury images of diseased Chinese prostitutes that have been reborn in recent anti-Asian assaults based on the falsehood that Covid-19 is the "Chinese flu." History has aided the return of sacred regalia and human bones to California tribes. Descendants of the captive Sugpiaq, Dena'ina, and Tlingit Alaska Natives have joined the Kashaya Pomo to build a trail from Fort Ross on the cliffs over Bodega Bay down to the sea, to tell visitors and schoolchildren that the imposing tourist site is a rebuilt plantation on a damaged ecosystem. The trail also marks the creation of an intertribal community. Yurok Jack Norton says that although the past has been "destroyed in whole or in part," to know the history, he adds, is "to live more graciously upon this land."[23]

As I close this book, the country is facing an existential debate about facts, truth, and accountability. Commissions, hearings, and criminal trials will rely on the voices of those who were deceived, those who resisted, those who witnessed. This history of the enslaved in California does not calculate a total sum of evil; hopefully, it makes the invisible visible. The voices of the men and women held in human bondage have smuggled out shards of the evidence of slavery to be pieced together.

The distance between the voices in this book and my own is great. Yet together they insist that we recognize California as a dystopia that grew outside the national myth of progress. The voices of the enslaved insist that many of us are travelers, not owners of the land; they insist that for 250 years, the enslaved in California cried forth in bondage and demanded their freedom. That demand is, as ever, hopeful.

As T'tc~tsa, a captive Indian girl who fled to freedom, explained, "That's [the] reason I tell it. That's history."[24]

Acknowledgments

IN WRITING *THE BEADWORKERS*, recalls Beth Piatote (Ni:mi:pu: Nez Perce), there were times when "I faced the entire ocean of words and I feared the undertow would pull me under, like an eagle who is dragged into the current of a river, talons locked on the back of a salmon." But, she adds, later "I would learn another word, and I would hold it just as close." For me, these other words were the surprises, wisdom, observations, letters, testimonies, freedom papers, and encouragement that made this book possible, and I am deeply grateful. During the research, writing, and editing of *California, a Slave State*, voices from the archives encouraged me to find their words of forceful resilience and revolt in this history of human bondage and the long pursuit of freedom in California. They also encouraged me to tell this story now—in the time of taking down statues of Junípero Serra and John Sutter; of examining the role of detention centers, prisons, and the carceral state; of understanding the political life of contagion; of discovering the unmarked graves of children at Indian boarding schools; of Black Lives Matter; of movements to end labor trafficking and sex trafficking; and of telling truths.

I thank my formidable editor, Deborah Hofmann Asimov, who helped me develop, synthesize, and edit this vexed history, and encouraged me to tell it boldly. The late historian and editor Jeffrey Escoffier helped me conceptualize how human bondage shaped California's legal and economic history. Jeffrey listened out loud. Historian Edward Blum urged me to tell this history of unfree labor in a straightforward voice. I thank the scholars, activists, colleagues, librarians, curators, government officials, and tribal leaders who listened, observed, corrected, taught, startled, supplemented, disabused, and/or invited me to think aloud with them.

Special Investigator Kaila Baxley, Humboldt County Sheriff William Honsal, scholars Joshua S. Meisel and Lynette Mullen, and human trafficking survivor Elle Snow shaped my understanding of modern labor and sex trafficking in Humboldt County. It was an honor to work with Lawrence-Minh Davis of the Smithsonian Asian American Program; student activist Diego Liebman Galvez; historians Connie Young-Yu and Shelley Fisher Fishkin; and colleagues in the Eureka Chinatown Project and the Chinese Railroad Workers Project who helped me explore how public history is a form of reparations.

Pier Gabrielle Foreman, James Casey, and John Ernest helped me understand the formidable presence of free and enslaved African Americans in California and explore how African American voices traveled in the Black press, slave narratives, and the Colored Conventions movement.

Legal scholars Anita Allen, Kathy Krieger, Davis Yee, Tony Platt, and Peter Panuthos patiently explained, sometimes over and over again, how basic tort and trespass cases that arose from expulsion, detention, and human bondage were foundational demands for reparations.

Skilled research assistance, shared curiosity, and perseverance made it possible for me to locate and give voice to enslaved Indigenous Californians, African Americans, Chinese Americans, convict laborers, and victims and survivors of human trafficking, and I'd like to thank: Steven Cohen, Clay Colman, Leonie Coolen, Samantha de Vera, Darlea Dominelli, Rachel Gearhart, Joellen Lippett, Cory Ridgeway, Arline Wilson, Yan Miao Xie, and Joo Lee Yung.

This book was made possible by research and travel grants from the Library of Congress; the A. Bartlett Giamatti Fellowship, Beinecke Library, Yale University; the University of Delaware; a Fulbright senior scholarship, the University of Utrecht; the Center for International Studies; the University of Exeter; the University of Graz; and the Vielberth Fellowship, University of Regensburg, and Johannes Gutenberg University, Mainz.

During my fellowship at the Beinecke Library, George Miles and Matthew Mason deposited forgotten diaries, photographs, and watercolors that depicted the forced transport of the enslaved and the long history of slavery in California, and they helped me make sense of the impact of visual images on the history and ideology of human bondage in the American West. During my fellowship, Miles placed a large book of Louis Choris's watercolors of the Russian invasion of Alaska and California on my desk and said, "Your book should start here."

Throughout, colleagues, friends, and family accompanied me on this journey, read version after version, and let me think aloud: thanks to Susan Bernardin, Roger Blacklow, Judy Braun, Sophia Panuthos Buell, Edie Butler, Krista Comer, Jenn Dodenhoff, Robert Levine, Joellen Lippett, Peter Lippett, Ben Madley, Linda Morris, Marianne Noble, the late Peter Palmquist, Peter Panuthos, Carla Peterson, Johanna Pfaelzer, Alvina Quintana, Carol Rudisell, Shirley Samuels, Karen Sánchez-Eppler, Lyman Tower Sargent, Karolyn Smardz-Frost, the late Kevin Starr, James Stewart, Laura Wexler, and Steve Zeltzer. Tony Platt's generous brilliance on the history of race in California and Mike Magliari's precise notion of how terminology needs to be particularized for California were invaluable to my analysis.

Martha Macri (Cherokee) and Beth Piatote (Ni:mi:pu: Nez Perce) helped me consider choices for transcription of Native American oral narratives and the complexities of written dialect.

I am grateful to my international hosts in American Studies for creating spaces for me to share my work and develop the global and empire implications of this history: Udo Hebel and Birgit Bauridl, University of Regensburg; Nassim Balestrini, University of Graz; Jaap Verheul, University of Utrecht; Hans Bak, Radboud University, Nijmegen; Damian Pargas, Leiden University; Kristopher Allerfeldt, Jamie Hampson, and Tim Cooper, University of Exeter, Cornwall; Pia Wiegmink, University of Mainz; and Helena Oberzaucher, University of Vienna.

I thank my undergraduate students, graduate students, and colleagues in the departments of English, Asian Studies, and Women and Gender Studies at the University of Delaware; in American Studies and Gender Studies at the University of Utrecht; in American Studies at the University of Graz; in American Studies at the University of Regensburg; and in Heritage Studies at the University of Exeter, Cornwall.

For the opportunity to take this story to many audiences, even as it evolved, thank you to: National Public Radio stations, C-SPAN, Public Broadcasting Stations, Comcast, Pacifica Radio San Francisco/KPFA, China Television Global Network, Voice of America, and PBS/CCBS. It was a privilege to work with Ric Burns and Li-Shin Yu, directors of PBS's *The Chinese Exclusion Act*.

I am honored by the respect for the purport of this book by Alaska Native archivists at the Aleutian Pribilof Islands Association, the Alutiiq Museum, Fort Ross Conservancy, Sitka National Historical Park, and the Smithsonian Arctic Studies Center. At the University of Fairbanks's Rare Book Room I found documents and listened to hitherto unheard waxed cylinders containing early oral histories of Alaska Natives. Particular thanks to Réne Azzara (Dena'ina), Aron Crowell, Aaron Leggett (Dena'ina), Millie McKeown (Unangax̂), Lauren Peters (Agdaagu Unangax̂), and Douglas Veltre, who guided me through local Indigenous archives of the Russian invasion of Alaska, the maritime and spiritual traditions of Indigenous Alaska Natives, the nature of Russian captivity, bondage, and revolt, and the role of Fort Ross as a site of human captivity and marine devastation, and who believe in the truths of stories, dreams, and oral history.

I completed this book during the Covid pandemic and the raging California wildfires of 2020 and 2021. Libraries, government archives, museums, and historical societies where I had identified or already explored archival and historical materials quickly closed. However, the generosity and determination of librarians and archivists made it possible for me to continue to document this history so that the enslaved, the enslavers, and the freedom fighters could tell their own stories. During a brief lull in the fire in Shasta County, even as a family member was on the fire line, Glendee Ane Osborne, the only archivist remaining at the Whiskeytown National Recreation Area, opened the library to retrieve a significant photograph.

Like all my research, the archival epicenter of this book is Bancroft Library, University of California, Berkeley, and its generous, brilliant, and curious librarians. Thank you to the ACLU of Northern California; Alameda County Historical Society, Oakland; British Museum, London; Butte County Historical Association,

Oroville; California African American Museum, Los Angeles; California Historical Society, San Francisco; California Museum, Sacramento; California State Archives, Sacramento; California State Library, Sacramento; Chinese Historical Society of America Museum, San Francisco; Chinese Historical Society of Southern California, Los Angeles; Clarke Historical Museum, Eureka; Colored Conventions Project; Contra Costa County Historical Society, Martinez; El Dorado County Historical Museum, Placerville; Ethnic Studies Library, University of California, Berkeley; Ethnic Studies Library, University of California, Los Angeles; Franciscan Monastery Archives, Catholic University of America, Washington, DC; Gilder Lehrman Center for the Study of Slavery, Resistance, and Abolition, Yale University, New Haven; History San Jose; Humboldt County Historical Society, Eureka; Humboldt Institute for Interdisciplinary Marijuana Research, Cal Poly Humboldt, Arcata; Humboldt Room, Cal Poly Humboldt, Arcata; International Slavery Museum, Liverpool; Amador County Historical Society, Jackson; Kelley House Museum, Mendocino; Kings County Historical Society, Hanford; Library of Congress, Washington, DC; Los Angeles Public Library; Magnes Collection of Jewish Life and Art, Berkeley; Marin County Historical Society; Meriam Library at California State University, Chico; Moffitt Library, University of California, Berkeley; Morris Library, University of Delaware, Newark; Museum of the African Diaspora, San Francisco; Sacramento Historical Society; San Diego Historical Society; San Francisco Public Library; Schlesinger Library of NY Public Library; Shasta County Libraries; Sierra County Historical Society, Sierra City; Smithsonian Asian Pacific American Center; Smithsonian Museum of American History, Washington, DC; Tuolumne County Library, Sonora; University of California Santa Barbara Library; University of Exeter Library, United Kingdom; U.S. National Archives and Records Administration, Washington, DC, College Park, MD, and San Bruno; Viejas Band of Kumeyaay History (website); and Wells Fargo History Museum, San Francisco.

My agent, Don Fehr, at Trident Media Group, and my editor, Adina Berk, at Yale University Press, with the team of Ash Lago and Laura Hensley, brought expertise, patience, and perseverance. Thank you for your support and guidance.

I thank and honor my daughters, Johanna Pfaelzer and Sophia Panuthos Buell, and my stepson, Jon Panuthos, for their wit, wisdom, and care. Most of all, thank you to my husband, Peter Panuthos, who read, listened, and accompanied me on this journey into dark and hidden places in a state I thought I knew well. I cherish your brilliance, hope, patience, and love.

Notes

Prologue

1. I am grateful to Professor Martha Macri (Cherokee), University of California, Davis, and Professor Beth Piatote (Ni:mi:pu: [Nez Perce]), University of California, Berkeley, for discussing with me how to reproduce a transcription of a creolized Native American slave narrative. They encouraged me to insert modern English vocabulary and verb tenses in order to avoid the estrangement and oftentimes comic reading of "dialect."

2. U.S. War Department, *The War of the Rebellion: A Compilation of the Official Records of the Union and Confederate Armies* (Washington, DC: Government Print Office, 1897), ser. I, vol. 50, chap. 62, pt. 1, "Operations on the Pacific Coast," January 1, 1861–June 30, 1865, 18–19; Calif. Stat., ch. 133 (April 22, 1850); Frank Essene, *Round Valley* (New York: Kraus, 1976), 89, argues that T'tc~tsa was three-fourths Lassik and one-fourth Wintun. Benjamin Madley, *An American Genocide: The United States and the California Indian Catastrophe, 1846–1873* (New Haven: Yale University Press, 2016), 12, dates the California genocide from the U.S. takeover in 1846 until 1873, the end of the Modoc War and last organized military assault on a California tribe.

3. Lucy Young [T'tc~tsa] with Edith V. A. Murphey, "Out of the Past: A True Indian Story Told by Lucy Young, of Round Valley Indian Reservation," *California Historical Quarterly* 20, no. 4 (December 1941): 349–64. All quotations by T'tc~tsa are from this publication. See also Erik Krabbe Smith, "Lucy Young or T'tc~tsa: Indian/White Relations in Northwest California, 1846–1944" (master's thesis, University of California, Santa Cruz, 1990). According to Professor Martha Macri (Cherokee), director emerita, Native American Language Center, University of California, Davis, T'tc~tsa would be pronounced guttural "Zikza" in Wailaki. Wailaki is no longer a living language. Lynwood Carranco and Estle Beard, *Genocide and Vendetta: The Round Valley Wars of Northern California* (Norman: University of Oklahoma Press, 1981),

20. T'tc~tsa's father was Alder Point Wailaki and her mother was Lassik. Edith Van Allen Murphey recorded Young's oral history as part of a New Deal work relief project from the State Emergency Relief Administration (SERA) arranged by Alfred Kroeber. Frank Essene, a graduate student, hired T'tc~tsa (whose owner changed her name to Lucy Young) to serve as an ethnographic informant. Unlike the WPA slave narratives, California Native Americans interviewed other California Native Americans and then anthropologists transcribed the histories. See also Edith Van Allen Murphey, *Indian Uses of Native Plants* (Ukiah, CA: Mendocino County Historical Society, 1987); Victor Golla, *California Indian Languages* (Berkeley: University of California Press, 2011), 80–82. T'tc~tsa delivered her narrative in English to Murphey. T'tc~tsa spoke a creolized version of English inflected by her native Wailaki Athabascan syntax that may reveal the communal and dependent story of the men and women in her kin, clan, and tribe. Other details of T'tc~tsa's biography are also drawn from Frank Essene, "Round Valley: Culture Element Distributions," *University of California Anthropological Records* 8, no. 1 (1942): xxi, i–viii, 1–97; "Lucy and Sam Young and Soldier Basin," SolarArch, http://wordpress.solararch.org/wp-content/uploads/2021/02/b03_lucy_and_sam_young_overview.pdf. Fort Seward was a new and temporary military outpost built three miles from Alderpoint. See also Madley, *American Genocide*, 3.

4. Fort Seward, a military fort in southern Humboldt County, opened in September 1861, the month before the military rout of the Wailaki village at Alder Point. It was decommissioned a year later, in 1862, but the site remained open for further assaults on Northern California tribes; "Fort Wiki," http://www.fortwiki.com. On June 24, 1862, T'tc~tsa was among the "36 bucks, 50 [women], and 26 children [moved] from Fort Seward to Fort Baker" in a chronology established by Smith, "Lucy Young or T'tc~tsa," 140–41.

5. U.S. War Department, "Operations on the Pacific Coast."

6. Act for the Government and Protection of Indians, Calif. Stat., ch. 133 (April 22, 1850), which granted employers the right to obtain children and keep them until they reached eighteen years old for men, and fifteen years old for women. Under the amendments of 1860, Native American children could be acquired "for the purpose of employment or training." Men could be held until they were forty years old and women until they were thirty-seven, without parental approval.

7. Calif. Const. of 1849, http://www.dircost.unito.it/cs/pdf/18490000_UsaCalifornia_eng.pdf.

8. "Indian Affairs Report of 1861," cited in Owen C. Coy, *The Humboldt Bay Region, 1850–1875* (Eureka: Humboldt County Historical Society, 1929), 167.

9. Richard H. Dillon, "Costs of the Modoc War," *California Historical Society Quarterly* 28, no. 2 (June 1949): 161–64. Benjamin Madley dates the California genocide from the U.S. takeover in 1846 until 1873, the end of the Modoc War and the last organized military assault on a California tribe: Madley,

American Genocide, 12. See Louis Herman Heller, *Portrait of the Family of Kientpoos or "Jack," Imprisoned Modoc Leader*, Beinecke Rare Book and Manuscript Library, Yale University Library, New Haven.

10. Carranco and Beard, *Genocide and Vendetta*, 59, 60, 135nn27–28. See David Rich Lewis, *Neither Wolf nor Dog: American Indians, Environment, and Agrarian Change* (New York: Oxford University Press, 1994); Madley, *American Genocide*, 277.

11. Madley, *American Genocide*, 109, cites thirty-five to one hundred dollars. Stacey L. Smith, *Freedom's Frontier: California and the Struggle over Unfree Labor, Emancipation, and Reconstruction* (Chapel Hill: University of North Carolina Press, 2015), 21, 147, 148–49, cites sales of women for three horses, or for cash from forty-five to one hundred dollars.

12. Captain C. D. Douglas, commander of Fort Wright, Second Infantry, California Volunteers, to Lieutenant Colonel R. C. Drum, assistant adjutant-general, Department of the Pacific, February 8, 1863, in U.S. War Department, *War of the Rebellion*, 18–19, 306–7. Essene, *Round Valley*, 89.

13. Erik Krabbe Smith surveys other anthropologists who interviewed T'tc~tsa. See Smith, "Lucy Young or T'tc~tsa," passim.

14. Douglas to Drum, February 8, 1863, in U.S. War Department, *War of the Rebellion*, 18–19, 306–7.

15. T'tc~tsa and Murphey, "Out of the Past," 358. See also Smith, "Lucy Young or T'tc~tsa."

16. T'tc~tsa and Murphey, "Out of the Past," 357–58.

17. For the interwoven and current history of the local impact of anthropologists, see Tony Platt, *Grave Matters, Excavating California's Buried Past* (Berkeley: Heyday, 2011).

18. Essene, *Round Valley*, n484, n1578.

19. Murphey was likely collecting legends for the New Deal Federal Writers' Project, part of the Works Project Administration. Description of material gathered on the Federal Writers' Project San Francisco, 1936, Federal Writers' Project of California records, 1930–1942, funded under the Depression-era Federal Writers' Project, San Francisco State University: Labor Archives and Research Center, http://www.oac.cdlib.org/findaid/ark:/13030/kt2h4n f1np. On the friendship of T'tc~tsa and Murphey, see Smith, "Lucy Young or T'tc~tsa," passim.

20. Golla, *California Indian Languages*, 80–82.

21. Penelope M. Kelsey, "Legible Natives: Making Native Women Visible in the Literary Arts," *Legacy* 34, no. 1 (2017): 198.

22. To read slave narratives well, critic John Ernest suggests that we listen for the political conditions of a "telling," conditions that may obscure our access to the inner life of an enslaved person. He urges us to hear political dreams alongside fears of self-revelation. Ernest asks us to read for the many versions of the self. See John Ernest, "Introduction," in *The Oxford Handbook of*

The African American Slave Narrative, ed. Ernest (New York: Oxford University Press, 2014), 3–20.

23. Frederick Douglass, "The Nature of Slavery: Extract from a Lecture on Slavery, Rochester, December 1, 1850," in *My Bondage and My Freedom* (New York: Miller, Orton, and Mulligan, 1855), 429.

24. T'tc~tsa does not intend to provoke sympathy. Saidiya Hartman asks if sympathy in fact conceals "our inability to feel." Reading the history of slavery can provide an emotional surrogate for our own pain or racism. Sympathy, she suggests, can offer a secret mask of cruelty: see Saidiya Hartman, *Scenes of Subjection: Terror, Slavery, and Self-Making in Nineteenth Century America* (Oxford: Oxford University Press, 1997), 4.

25. T'tc~tsa and Murphey, "Out of the Past," 350–51.

26. T'tc~tsa and Murphey, "Out of the Past," 349–64. See also William Bauer, Jr., *California through Native Eyes: Reclaiming History* (Seattle: University of Washington Press, 2016), 24.

27. T'tc~tsa and Murphey, "Out of the Past," 349–64.

Introduction

1. Thadeus Greenson, "'Extremely Disturbing': Two Men Suspected of Enslaving Runaway Teen Face Federal Pot Charges," *Times-Standard* (Eureka), July 26, 2013. See also *United States of America v. Ryan Alan Balletto*, CR No. 13-515 CRB, U.S. District Court, N.D. California, San Francisco Division, August 6, 2013.

2. Frederick Douglass, "The Nature of Slavery: Extract from a Lecture on Slavery, Rochester, December 1, 1850," in *My Bondage and My Freedom* (New York: Miller, Orton, and Mulligan, 1855), 429. Karl Kerényi, *The Gods of the Greeks* (1951; repr., New York: Grove, 1980), 182ff.

3. "California Now Has the World's Fifth-Largest Economy," CBS News, May 4, 2018.

4. Garci Rodriguez de Montalvo, *Las Sergas de Esplandián* (1510). Calafia has also been linked to "Khalifa," the leader of the Muslim people who ruled Spain between 757 and 1492. Robert Petersen, "California, Calafia, Khalif: The Origin of the Name 'California,'" KCET Departures, December 15, 2015, https://www.kcet.org/shows/departures/california-calafia-khalif-the -origin-of-the-name-california.

5. Walter Johnson, s.v. "Slavery," in *Keywords for American Cultural Studies*, ed. Bruce Burgett and Glenn Hendler (New York: New York University Press, 2014), 224; Andrés Reséndez, *The Other Slavery: The Uncovered Story of Indian Enslavement in America* (Boston: Mariner, 2017), 317–21; Kevin Bales and Ron Soodalter, *The Slave Next Door: Human Trafficking and Slavery in America Today* (Berkeley: University of California Press, 2009); Marisa Fuentes, *Dispossessed Lives: Enslaved Women, Violence, and the Archive* (Philadelphia: University of Pennsylvania Press, 2016).

6. Reséndez, *Other Slavery*.

7. John Bouvier, s.v. "slave" and "death," in *Law Dictionary*, 1st ed. (Philadelphia, 1839). See Jeannine Marie DeLombard, *In the Shadow of the Gallows: Race, Crime, and American Civic Identity* (Philadelphia: University of Pennsylvania Press, 2012), 60.

8. DeLombard, *In the Shadow of the Gallows*, 60, 64. Saidiya Hartman, *Scenes of Subjection: Terror, Slavery, and Self-Making in Nineteenth-Century America* (New York: Oxford University Press, 1997), 126.

9. Walter Johnson, "Slavery," in *Keywords for American Cultural Studies*, ed. Bruce Burgett and Glenn Hendler (New York: New York University Press, 2014), 224–25.

10. Stacey L. Smith, *Freedom's Frontier: California and the Struggle over Unfree Labor, Emancipation, and Reconstruction* (Durham: University of North Carolina Press, 2013), 2.

11. Reséndez, *Other Slavery*, 305–6.

12. Douglass, "Nature of Slavery," 429–31. Elizabeth Swanson and James Brewer Stewart aptly summarize the evolution of slavery as a form of "labor substitution" and delineate the many forms of "slavery by another name." Elizabeth Swanson and James Brewer Stewart, "Introduction: Getting beyond Chattel Slavery," in *Human Bondage and Abolition: New Histories of Past and Present Slaveries: Slaveries since Emancipation* (Cambridge: Cambridge University Press, 2018), 1–40.

13. Iyko Day, "Being or Nothingness: Indigeneity, Antiblackness, and Settler Colonial Critique," *Critical Ethnic Studies* 1, no. 2 (Fall 2015): 104–5. This analysis turns on the classic definitions of settler colonialism put forth by Patrick Wolfe that speaks to its irreversible nature: see Patrick Wolfe, *Settler Colonialism and the Transformation of Anthropology: The Politics and Poetics of an Ethnographic Event* (London: Cassell, 1998); and "Settler Colonialism and the Elimination of the Native," *Journal of Genocide Research* 8, no. 4 (2006): 387–409. It also speaks to Lorenzo Veracini, *Settler Colonialism: A Theoretical Overview* (New York: Palgrave-Macmillan, 2010); and Walter Hixon's insertion of the American West in *American Settler Colonialism: A History* (New York: Palgrave-MacMillan, 2013). Critical to my analysis is the work of Roxanne Dunbar-Ortiz, *Not "A Nation of Immigrants": Settler Colonialism, White Supremacy, and a History of Erasure and Exclusion* (New York: Beacon, 2021); J. Kēhaulani Kauanui, who has argued for the enduring presence of Indigenous peoples who "exist, resist, and persist" and the ways in which indigeneity "holds out against" settler colonialism, in "'A Structure, Not an Event': Settler Colonialism and Enduring Indigeneity," *Emergent Critical Analytics for Alternative Humanities* 5, no. 1 (2016), https://doi.org/10.25158/L5.1.7; and Gerald Horne, who discusses compelling early links between settler colonialism and slavery in *The Apocalypse of Settler Colonialism: The Roots of Slavery, White Supremacy, and Capitalism in Seventeenth-Century North America and the Caribbean* (New York: Monthly Review, 2018). I also have been influenced

by Lisa Lowe's original links between colonialism, global trade, and African slavery in *The Intimacies of Four Continents* (Durham, NC: Duke University Press, 2015).

14. Benjamin Madley, *An American Genocide: The United States and the California Indian Catastrophe, 1846–1873* (New Haven: Yale University Press, 2016), 347, cites conflicting estimates of the decline in the population of California Indians. The figures for 1860 fall between 17,798 and 35,000, down from the generally accepted number of 300,000 to 310,000 at the moment of the Spanish invasion in 1769.

15. This discussion of meanings and the debate between intention and consequences of the term "genocide" is influenced in particular by Michael F. Magliari, "Free Soil, Unfree Labor: Cave Johnson Couts and the Binding of Indian Workers in California, 1850–1867," *Pacific Historical Review* 73, no. 3 (August 2004): 349–90; and Madley, *American Genocide*, 4–5, who argues persuasively for the importance of going past previous terms such as "liquidating, military casualties, and social homicide which fail to capture the full meaning of genocidal events." See Madley, *American Genocide*, 6 and 3–8, in particular, for a discussion of the historiography of the term. I am indebted to Michael Magliari for his nuanced and extraordinarily relevant discussions of terminology surrounding genocide in a series of book reviews that speak to the implications of the term, in particular, his review of Madley's *An American Genocide*, in *Ethnohistory* 64, no. 2 (2017): 341–42; Magliari's review of Robert Aquinas McNally's *The Modoc War: A Story of Genocide at the Dawn of the Gilded Age*, in *The Journal of Military History* 82, no. 2 (April 2018): 630–32; and Magliari's influential review of Gary Clayton Anderson's *Ethnic Cleansing and the American Indian: The Crime That Should Haunt America*, "Naming the Crime: Genocide, Extermination, or Ethnic Cleansing?," in *H-AmIndian* (December 2016), https://www.h-net.org/reviews/showrev.php?id=46891. Historian Andrés Reséndez estimates that between 2.5 and 5 million Indigenous people were enslaved in the Americas from the time of Columbus to the end of the nineteenth century, a figure that includes Native Americans in the United States: see Andrés Reséndez, *The Other Slavery: The Uncovered Story of Indian Enslavement in the Americas* (New York: Houghton Mifflin, 2017), app. I, 5, 324.

16. Madley, *American Genocide*, 347.

17. Robert F. Heizer and Alan F. Almquist, *The Other Californians: Prejudice and Discrimination under Spain, Mexico, and the United States to 1920* (Berkeley: University of California Press, 1971), 27.

18. Douglass, "Nature of Slavery," 429–31. These overlaid yet distinct definitions influenced the argument and organization of this book. In addition to Walter Johnson, Kevin Bales, Andrés Reséndez, and Marissa Fuentes, this book builds upon the foundational work of Edward E. Baptist, who turns to testimonies, archival records, and newspapers to document the role of plan-

tation slavery in the development of modern capitalism: see Edward E. Baptist, *The Half Has Never Been Told: Slavery and the Making of American Capitalism* (New York: Basic, 2014). Although I trace a more resistant history, I turn to Orlando Patterson for a comparatist methodology across geography and chronology to introduce the concept of "social death"—a definition that arises from the recruitment, domination, and, in his view, ultimate consequence of alienation or death: see Orlando Patterson, *Slavery and Social Death* (Cambridge, MA: Harvard University Press, 2018); and Saidiya Hartman, who describes the "afterlife of slavery" to consider the imprint of slavery and explain the endurance of racial violence. As I seek to retrieve and restore the histories of slavery found in California's archives that point to its transcendent violence, particularly regarding enslaved women, Hartman traces its footprints in the political and social life of Black America where slavery persists "not because of an antiquarian obsession with bygone days or the burden of a too-long memory, but because black lives are still imperiled . . . by a racial calculus and a political arithmetic that were entrenched centuries ago." In this book, the afterlife of slavery is not only the modern poverty, premature death, and incarceration that Hartman cites, but the national ideological permission and legal prescriptions for more slavery: see Saidiya Hartman, *Lose Your Mother: A Journey along the Atlantic Slave Route* (New York: Farrar, Straus and Giroux, 2007). I build on the methodology that shapes the essays in Edward E. Baptist and Stephanie M. H. Camp, eds., *New Studies in the History of American Slavery* (Athens: University of Georgia Press, 2006), in particular the essays by Jennifer Morgan and Stephanie Camp that particularize the lived history and gendered forms of resistance of enslaved African American women. I am deeply grateful to the astute discussion regarding definitions of slavery led by Adam Rothman on the H-Net web page about slavery, H-Slavery, https://networks.h-net.org/node/11465/pages/74727/defining-slavery, in particular the contributions by Marcy Tanter, Trish Roberts-Miller, David E. Paterson, Paul Finkelman, David Brion Davis, and Manisha Sinha during the years 2005–6. James Brewer Stewart and Elizabeth Swanson describe the evolution of slavery as a form of "labor substitution, whether recast as convicts, indentured or contract involuntary migrant laborers, debt peons, delineating the many forms of 'slavery by another name'"; see James Brewer Stewart and Elizabeth Swanson, "Old and New Abolitionists: Symmetries of Past with Present," introduction to *Human Bondage and Abolition: New Histories of Past and Present Slaveries* (Cambridge: Cambridge University Press, 2018).

19. "Squawmen" was traditionally a derogatory term for white men who lived with Indian women, and after the 1850 Act for the Government and Protection of Indians, it morphed in California into a common reference for white Indian slave traders.

20. U.S. Const. art. I, §9, cl. 8.

21. U.S. Const. amend. IX and X (ratified December 15, 1791).

22. U.S. Const., art. I, sec. 2, 9; art. 4, sec. 2. See DeLombard, *In the Shadow of the Gallows*, 328: "It is the three-fifths clause's reference to 'Indians' that, arguably, makes race specific" in art. I and IV.

23. DeLombard, *In the Shadow of the Gallows*, 57.

24. DeLombard, *In the Shadow of the Gallows*, 78.

25. "Human Trafficking," California Victim Compensation Board, https://victims .ca.gov/for-victims/victims-of-human-trafficking/.

26. Kamala Harris, *The State of Human Trafficking in California* (Sacramento: California Department of Justice, 2012), 4. Shoshana Walter, "In Secretive Marijuana Industry, Whispers of Abuse and Trafficking," Reveal, September 8, 2016, https://revealnews.org/article/in-secretive-marijuana-industry-whispers -of-abuse-and-trafficking/.

27. Bales and Soodalter, *Slave Next Door;* Kevin Bales, *Disposable People: New Slavery in the Global Economy* (Berkeley: University of California Press, 2012). Sally Lieber, a California State Assembly member, asserted in signing the California Trafficking Victims Protection Act, AB 22, of 2005: "The problem of human trafficking has reached into neighborhoods throughout California." California Alliance to Combat Trafficking and Slavery Task Force, "Human Trafficking: Final Report," State of California Department of Justice, https://oag.ca.gov/sites/all/files/agweb/pdfs/publications/Human_Trafficking _Final_Report.pdf.-

28. Valerie Alvord, "Toxic River Becomes Path to USA," *USA Today*, May 11, 2000. Laris Karklis, Ann Gerhart, Joe Fox, Armand Emamdjomeh, and Kevin Schaul, "Borderline," *Washington Post*, October 17, 2018; Jenna Krajeski, "The Hypocrisy of Trump's Anti-Trafficking Argument for a Border Wall," *New Yorker*, February 5, 2019.

29. Sue Dremann, "Hidden in Plain Sight," *Palo Alto Weekly*, May 8, 2015.

30. Bales and Soodalter, *Slave Next Door;* Bales, *Disposable People*.

31. "California," National Human Trafficking Hotline, https://humantrafficking hotline.org/state/california; Kristina Davis, "Experts Are Skeptical That a Trump Border Wall Would Reduce Human Trafficking," *Los Angeles Times*, February 17, 2019; Sebastien Malo, "Is the Super Bowl Really the U.S.'s Biggest Sex Trafficking Magnet?," Reuters, February 1, 2018; Aaron Cline Hanbury, "The Facts behind the Super Bowl Sex Trafficking Epidemic, and What You Can Do about It," Relevant, February 4, 2016, https://relevant magazine.com/current/facts-behind-super-bowl-sex-trafficking-epidemic/; Phillip W. Martin, "Nail Salons and Human Trafficking," Huffington Post, December 6, 2017, https://www.huffpost.com/entry/nail-salons-and-human -tra_b_669076.

32. "Attorney General Becerra: Court Allows Prosecution in Sex Trafficking Backpage.com Case to Proceed," State of California Department of Justice, press release, August 23, 2017.

33. David Blight, "The Civil War Lies on Us Like a Sleeping Dragon," *Guardian*, August 20, 2017.

34. "Old Russian Cemetery," Fort Ross Conservancy, https://www.fortross.org/cemetery.

35. William Wells Brown, "A Lecture Delivered before the Female Anti-Slavery Society of Salem at Lyceum Hall, Nov. 14, 1847," in *Four Fugitive Slave Narratives*, ed. Larry Gara (Reading, MA: Addison-Wesley, 1969), 81–82.

36. Eric Gardner, *Black Print Unbound: The Christian Recorder, African American Literature, and Periodical Culture* (New York: Oxford University Press, 2015), 84, 91.

37. Saidiya Hartman, quoted in Danielle Spratt, "Surrogacy and Empire in *The Man Plant* and Eighteenth-Century Vernacular Medical Texts," in *The Routledge Companion to Humanism and Literature*, ed. Michael Bryson (New York: Routledge, 2022), 242; John Ernest, "Introduction," in *The Oxford Handbook of the African American Slave Narrative*, ed. Ernest (New York: Oxford University Press, 2016), 4–5.

38. Douglass, "Nature of Slavery," 433.

39. Lucy Young [T'tc~tsa] with Edith V. A. Murphey, "Out of the Past: A True Indian Story Told by Lucy Young, of Round Valley Indian Reservation," *California Historical Quarterly* 20, no. 4 (December 1941): 358.

Chapter One. Wikamee

Epigraph: Constance Dubois, "Diegueño Myths and Their Connections with the Mohave," *Proceedings of the 15th International Congress of Americanists* 2 (1907): 129, cited in Richard L. Carrico, *Strangers in a Stolen Land: Indians of San Diego County from Pre-History to the New Deal* (San Diego: Sunbelt, 2008), 1.

1. Florence C. Shipek, *Pushed into the Rocks: Southern California Indian Land Tenure, 1769–1986* (Lincoln: University of Nebraska Press, 1988), 25.

2. Herbert Eugene Bolton, *Fray Juan Crespí: Missionary Explorer on the Pacific Coast, 1769–1774* (Berkeley: University of California Press, 1927), 4.

3. Geralyn Marie Hoffman and Lynn H. Gamble, *A Teacher's Guide to Historical and Contemporary Kumeyaay Culture* (San Diego: Institute for Regional Studies of the Californias, San Diego State University, 2006), 71.

4. The journal of Juan Crespí, *A Description of Distant Roads: Original Journals of the First Expedition into California, 1769–1770*, trans. and ed. Alan K. Brown (San Diego: San Diego State University Press, 2001), uniquely was not edited or censored by Serra. Crespí was a diligent botanist. See the following Indigenous websites: "Kumeyaay History," Kumeyaay Information Village and History, http://www.kumeyaay.info/history/; and Kumeyaay, http://www.kumeyaay.

5. "Junípero Serra to Fr. Juan Andrés," February 10, 1770, in *Writings of Junípero*

Serra, vol. 1, ed. Antonine Tibesar (Washington, DC: Academy of American Franciscan History, 1956), 153.

6.   Junípero Serra, "On the Road to San Diego: Junípero Serra's Baja California Diary," trans. and ed. Rose Marie Beebe and Robert Senkewicz, *Journal of San Diego History* 59, no. 4 (Fall 2013): 1–52.

7.   Bolton, *Fray Juan Crespí*, 4.

8.   "Junípero Serra to Fr. Juan Andrés," in Tibesar, *Writings of Junípero Serra*, 1:135, 137.

9.   While I view the chain of California missions as a string of theological plantations of conversion and surveillance, forced labor camps designed to recruit and brutally confine field laborers and mark the northern edge of its empire against encroachments by Russia, England, and France, Benjamin Madley appropriately sees the missions as early systems of mass incarceration. See Benjamin Madley, "California's First Mass Incarceration System: Franciscan Missions, California Indians, and Penal Servitude, 1769–1836," *Pacific Historical Review* 88, no. 1 (Winter 2019): 14–47. Rosaura Sánchez describes the California mission system as "a penal colony, the dystopia from which it was practically impossible for the Indians to escape": see Rosaura Sánchez, *Telling Identities: The Californio Testimonios* (Minneapolis: University of Minnesota Press, 1995), 51.

10.   "*Nuevo México*" in Spanish; "*Yootó Hahoodzo*" in Navajo. See Paul W. Mapp, *The Elusive West, and the Contest for Empire, 1713–1763*, Omohundro Institute of Early American History and Culture (Chapel Hill: University of North Carolina Press, 2011), 64.

11.   Economic historian Marie Christine Duggan argues that under Spanish reign, "Mission Indians" were not slaves because they were not property, did not have a price, and did not yield a profit, but worked mainly for consumption and subsistence: see Marie Christine Duggan, "Beyond Slavery: The Institutional Status of Mission Indians," in *Franciscans and American Indians in Pan Borderlands Perspective: Adaptation, Negotiation, and Resistance*, ed. Jeffrey Burns and Timothy Johnson (Oceanside, CA: American Academy of Franciscan History, 2017), 238–45.

12.   Preeminent historian Lisbeth Haas traces the musical, aesthetic, spiritual, and philosophical endurance of tribal cultures of California, particularly of Chumash and Luiseño people, that continued hundreds of years of tribal consciousness even under the most tortuous situations, formed the spiritual and ideological basis for rebels and fugitives, and selectively absorbed Catholicism into ancestral practices, allowing diverse philosophical, artistic, and spiritual traditions to endure. In particular, while I do not reiterate the elaborate tapestry of Haas's *Saints and Citizens, Indigenous Histories of Colonial Missions and Mexican California* (Berkeley: University of California Press, 2014), her work has influenced my understanding of how, facing confinement and brutality, both converts and "gentiles" maintained contact, family, and culture

that foster and explain the nature of tribal rebellions. See also Elias Castillo, *A Cross of Thorns: The Enslavement of California's Indians by the Spanish Missions* (Fresno, CA: Craven Street, 2015), 123.

13. Florence C. Shipek, "California Indian Reactions to the Franciscans," *Americas* 41, no. 4 (April 1985): 483. In Edward D. Castillo, ed., *Native American Perspectives on the Hispanic Colonization of Alta California* (New York: Garland, 1991), 26:483–84.

14. Bolton, *Fray Juan Crespí*, 15, quoted in Michael Connolly Miskwish, *Kumeyaay: A History Book* (El Cajon, CA: Sycuan, 2007), 49. "Jayme to Fr. Raphael Verger," in *Lands of Promise and Despair: Chronicles of Early California, 1535–1846*, ed. Rose Marie Beebe and Robert M. Senkewicz (Berkeley: Heyday, 2001), 155–61.

15. "Jayme to Fr. Raphael Verger," in Beebe and Senkewicz, *Lands of Promise and Despair*, 155–61.

16. "Jayme to Fr. Raphael Verger," in Beebe and Senkewicz, *Lands of Promise and Despair*, 155–61.

17. Castillo, *Cross of Thorns*, 72–73.

18. Steven W. Hackel, *Children of Coyote, Missionaries of Saint Francis: Indian-Spanish Relations in Colonial California, 1769–1850* (Chapel Hill: University of North Carolina Press, 2005), 46.

19. George Harwood Phillips, *Chiefs and Challengers: Indian Resistance and Cooperation in Southern California, 1769–1906* (1975; repr., Norman: University of Oklahoma Press, 2014), 28.

20. Sherburne F. Cook, *The Conflict between the California Indian and White Civilization* (Berkeley: University of California Press, 1976), 18.

21. Lisbeth Haas, *Conquests and Historical Identities in California, 1769–1936* (Berkeley: University of California Press, 1996), 13; Andrés Reséndez, *The Other Slavery: The Uncovered Story of Indian Enslavement in America* (Boston: Houghton Mifflin, 2016), 7; Hackel, *Children of Coyote*, 2ff.

22. Castillo, *Cross of Thorns*, 167–69; Robert H. Jackson and Edward D. Castillo, *Indians, Franciscans, and Spanish Colonization: The Impact of the Mission System on California Indians* (Albuquerque: University of New Mexico Press, 1996), passim; "Mexican Secularization Act of 1833," Wikipedia, https://en.wikipedia.org/wiki/Mexican_secularization_act_of_1833; Cook, *Conflict*, 91; Kent G. Lightfoot, *Indians, Missionaries, and Merchants: The Legacy of Colonial Encounters on the California Frontiers* (Berkeley: University of California Press, 2006), 102; James Sandos, *Converting California: Indians and Franciscans in the Missions* (New Haven: Yale University Press, 2004), 51.

23. For important discussions of California Indigenous/Spanish relations, see Iris H. W. Engstrand, "Seekers of the 'Northern Mystery': European Exploration of California and the Pacific," in *Contested Eden: California before the Gold Rush*, ed. Ramón Gutiérrez and Richard Orsi (San Francisco: University of California Press, 1997), 78–104; Henry R. Wagner, *Spanish Voyages to the*

Northwest Coast of America in the Sixteenth Century (Mansfield Centre, CT: Martino, 2008); Hackel, *Children of Coyote*, 27–42; Phillips, *Chiefs and Challengers*, 33.

24. Michael Connolly Miskwish, "Kumeyaay: Spanish Contact," Kumeyaay, https://www.kumeyaay.com/kumeyaay-spanish-contact.html. See Michael Connolly Miskwish, *Kumeyaay: A History Textbook*, vol. 1, *Precontact to 1893* (El Cajon, CA: Sycuan, 2006); Castillo, *Cross of Thorns*, 9, 72.

25. James J. Rawls, *Indians of California: The Changing Image* (Norman: University of Oklahoma Press, 1984), 14–16.

26. Phillips, *Chiefs and Challengers*, 28, quoted in Richard Steven Street, *Beasts of the Field: A Narrative History of California Farmworkers, 1769–1913* (Stanford: Stanford University Press, 2004), 22; "Antonio Bucareli," in Tibesar, *Writings of Junípero Serra*, 1:363; Sandos, *Converting California*, 53; Edward D. Castillo, "Gender Status Decline, Resistance, and Accommodation among Female Neophytes in the Mission of California: A San Gabriel Case Study," *American Indian Culture and Research Journal* 18, no. 1 (1994): 67–93; Tibesar, *Writings of Junípero Serra*, 1:368; letter from Serra to Colonel and Governor don Felipe de Neve, in Rose Marie Beebe and Robert M. Senkewicz, *Junípero Serra: California, Indians, and the Transformation of a Missionary* (Norman: University of Oklahoma Press, 2015), 366–67; Cook, *Conflict*, 102.

27. Zephyrin Engelhardt, *The Franciscans in California* (Harbor Springs, MI: Holy Childhood Indian School, 1897), 269; Street, *Beasts of the Field*, 22–24; "Antonio Bucareli," in Tibesar, *Writings of Junípero Serra*, 1:363; Sandos, *Converting California*, 53. See Castillo, "Gender Status Decline"; Tibesar, *Writings of Junípero Serra*, 1:368.

28. Tibesar, *Writings of Junípero Serra*, 1:353.

29. Hackel, *Children of Coyote*, 2; Maynard J. Geiger and Clement W. Meighan, *As the Padres Saw Them: Californian Indian Life and Customs as Reported by the Franciscan Missionaries, 1813–1815* (Santa Barbara: Santa Barbara Mission Archive Library; Glendale, CA: A. H. Clark, 1976), 81–82; Sandos, *Converting California*, 8.

30. For discussions of the impact of the Spanish empire in the formation of the mission system, see Castillo, *Cross of Thorns*, 7–22.

31. "Serra to Neve," January 7, 1780, in Tibesar, *Writings of Junípero Serra*, 3:411–15.

32. "Jayme to Verger I," in Beebe and Senkewicz, *Lands of Promise and Despair*, 156. For discussions of motivations to enter the missions, see Julia Costello, ed., *Documentary Evidence for the Spanish Missions of Alta California* (New York: Garland, 1992), 167–69; Jackson and Castillo, *Indians, Franciscans, and Spanish Colonization*, 75ff; Castillo, *Cross of Thorns*, 119.

33. "Jayme to Verger I," in Beebe and Senkewicz, *Lands of Promise and Despair*, 156.

34. "Jayme to Fr. Raphael Verger," in Beebe and Senkewicz, *Lands of Promise and Despair*, 156.

35. Sandos, *Converting California*, 56.
36. "Jayme to Fr. Raphael Verger," in Beebe and Senkewicz, *Lands of Promise and Despair*, 156–60.
37. Castillo, *Cross of Thorns*, 77; Tibesar, *Writings of Junípero Serra*, 3:368.
38. "Junípero Serra to Antonio Bucareli," in Tibesar, *Writings of Junípero Serra*, 1:363.
39. See Sandos, *Converting California*, 24–27.
40. "Serra to Fr. Raphael Verger," August 8, 1772, in Tibesar, *Writings of Junípero Serra*, 1:259. See Tibesar, *Writings of Junípero Serra*, 1:777, 779; Tibesar, *Writings of Junípero Serra*, 3:159, 305, 334.
41. Geiger and Meighan, *As the Padres Saw Them*, 81–82; "Jayme to Fr. Raphael Verger," in Beebe and Senkewicz, *Lands of Promise and Despair*, 156–60; Cook, *Conflict*, 61–63; Lightfoot, *Indians, Missionaries, and Merchants*, 90; Castillo, *Cross of Thorns*, 1, 38–39ff.
42. Tibesar, *Writings of Junípero Serra*, 1:363.
43. "Serra to Fr. Bucareli," in Tibesar, *Writings of Junípero Serra*, 1:363.
44. Antonia I. Castañeda, "Sexual Violence in the Politics and Policies of Conquest: Amerindian Women and the Spanish Conquest of Alta California," in *Sexual Violence in Conflict Zones*, ed. Elizabeth D. Heineman (Philadelphia: University of Pennsylvania Press, 2011), 23–25; Albert L. Hurtado, "Sexuality in California's Franciscan Missions; Cultural Perceptions and Sad Realities," *California History* 71, no. 3 (Fall 1992): 370–85. For a significant and well-documented discussion of the imposition of Catholic regulations on tribal sexual, marital, and family customs, see Hurtado, "Sexuality in California's Franciscan Missions," 375–79.
45. Beebe and Senkewicz, *Junípero Serra*, 364.
46. Beebe and Senkewicz, *Junípero Serra*, 368.
47. Beebe and Senkewicz, *Junípero Serra*, 348–49; Phillips, *Chiefs and Challengers*, 28; Miskwish, *Kumeyaay*, 15–16.
48. Tibesar, *Writings of Junípero Serra*, 3:369.
49. Beebe and Senkewicz, *Lands of Promise and Despair*, 104–5.
50. Cook, *Conflict*, 116–21.
51. Jean-François de Galaup La Pérouse, *Life in a California Mission: Monterey in 1786*, ed. Malcolm Margolin, illus. Linda Gonsalves Yamane (Berkeley: Heyday, 1989), 80–81, 85, 89. See Malcolm Margolin, *The Ohlone Way: Indian Life in the San Francisco–Monterey Bay Area* (Berkeley: Heyday, 1978), 162.
52. La Pérouse, *Life in a California Mission*, 91.
53. Jackie Teran, "The Violent Legacies of the California Missions: Mapping the Origins of Native Women's Mass Incarceration," *American Indian Culture and Research Journal* 40, no. 1 (2016): 22–23.
54. Teran, "Violent Legacies of the California Missions," 22–23, also citing Sherene Razack, *Race, Space, and the Law: Unmapping a White Settler Society* (Toronto: Between the Lines, 2002), 12.
55. Fernando Librado, *Breath of the Sun: Life in Early California as Told by a Chu-*

mash Indian, Fernando Librado, to John P. Harrington, ed. Travis Hudson (Ventura, CA: Ventura County Historical Society, 1979), 53.

56.   Hugo Reid, "A Scotch Paisano: Hugo Reid's Life in California, 1832–1852, Derived from His Correspondence," ed. Susanna Bryant Dakin (Berkeley: University of California Press, 1939), 225–26, 476, 497–98.

57.   Beebe and Senkewicz, *Junípero Serra*, 328.

58.   Castañeda, "Sexual Violence," 24–25; Hurtado, "Sexuality in California's Franciscan Missions," 375.

59.   La Pérouse, *Life in a California Mission*, quoted in Shipek, *Pushed into the Rocks*, 6; and Castillo, *Cross of Thorns*, 113.

60.   Lorenzo Asisara, oral history taken between 1818 and 1820, in Edward D. Castillo, "An Indian Account of the Decline and Collapse of Mexico's Hegemony over the Missionized Indians of California," *American Indian Quarterly* 13, no. 4 (1989): 397–98; and in "The Native Response to the Colonization of Alta California," in Castillo, *Native American Perspectives*, 424. Ramón A. Gutiérrez, *When Jesus Came, the Corn Mothers Went Away: Marriage: Sexuality, and Power in New Mexico, 1500–1846* (Stanford: Stanford University Press, 1991); Lightfoot, *Indians, Missionaries, and Merchants*, 89.

61.   Geiger and Meighan, *As the Padres Saw Them*, 65.

62.   I am indebted to the outstanding social histories and cultural anthropologies of Hurtado, "Sexuality in California's Franciscan Missions," 370–85, esp. 371–74. See Cook, *Conflict*; and Robert F. Heizer and M. A. Whipple, eds., *California Indians: A Source Book* (Berkeley: University of California Press, 1972).

63.   Hurtado, "Sexuality in California's Franciscan Missions," 379.

64.   Ibram X. Kendi, *Stamped from the Beginning: The Definitive History of Racist Ideas in America* (New York: Nation, 2016), argues that stereotypes and racist representations justified the many histories of slavery in California.

65.   La Pérouse, *Life in a California Mission*, 111.

66.   Francis F. Guest, *Fermín Francisco de Lasuén: A Biography* (Washington, DC: American Academy of Franciscan History, 1973), 207, cited in Hurtado, "Sexuality in California's Franciscan Missions," 374. Geiger and Meighan, *As the Padres Saw Them*, 65.

67.   José Señán, *The Ventureño Confesionario of José Señán*, ed. Madison S. Beeler, trans. Bernardo García (Berkeley: University of California Press, 1967), uniquely contains a translation into one of the dialects of the Chumash language. Sandos, *Converting California*, 97–98.

68.   Geiger and Meighan, *As the Padres Saw Them*, 125–26.

69.   Sandos, *Converting California*, 97. See James Sandos, "Levantamiento! The 1824 Chumash Uprising Reconsidered," *Southern California Quarterly* 67, no. 2 (Summer 1985): 109–33; and Señán, *Ventureño Confesionario*.

70.   Señán, *Ventureño Confesionario*, esp. 33–63.

71.   Señán, *Ventureño Confesionario*, 63.

72. Juan Cortés, *The Doctrina and Confesionario of Juan Cortés*, comp. and ed. Harry Kelsey (Altadena, CA: Howling Coyote, 1979), 112–23.

73. Sandos, *Converting California*, 51–52.

74. Cortés, *Doctrina and Confesionario*, 123.

75. Bolton, *Fray Juan Crespí*, 171.

76. Sandos, *Converting California*, 25; Hurtado, "Sexuality in California's Franciscan Missions," 376–77.

77. See Sandos, *Converting California*, 24–27.

78. Sandos, *Converting California*, 25; Hurtado, "Sexuality in California's Franciscan Missions," 376–77. See Sandra Hollimon, "Chumash Gender Identity," Gender Identity and Society Roles, December 13, 2014, https://nwc genderid.wordpress.com/2014/12/13/chumash-gender-identity/; Luhui White-bear (Coastal Band of the Chumash Nation), *Unsettled Records and the Restoration of Cultural Memories in Indigenous California* (unpublished manuscript, Western Historians Association, 2021).

79. These statistics are drawn from different sources, and some may overlap. La Pérouse, *Life in a California Mission*, 89; Carey McWilliams, *Southern California Country: An Island on the Land* (New York: Duell, Sloan, and Pearce, 1946), chap. 2, passim; Cook, *Conflict*, 15–22.

80. Sandos, *Converting California*, 52, 167.

81. Sandos, *Converting California*, 102; James A. Sandos, "Between Crucifix and Lance: Indian-White Relations in California, 1769–1848," in *Contested Eden: California before the Gold Rush*, ed. Ramón A. Gutiérrez and Richard J. Orsi (San Francisco: University of California Press, 1997), 201, 216, 224n17; Edward D. Castillo, "Neophyte Resistance and Accommodation in the Missions of Alta California," *The Spanish Missionary Heritage of the United States* (1993): 60–75. Reid, *Indians of Los Angeles County*, 87; Castillo, *Documentary Evidence, Native American Perspectives*, 274; Fermín Francisco de Lasuén, *Writings of Fermín Francisco de Lasuén*, vol. 2, trans. and ed. Finbar Kenneally (Washington, DC: Academy of American Franciscan History, 1965), 210; Guadalupe Vallejo, "Ranch and Mission Days in Alta California, Part I and II," *Century Magazine* 41 (December 1890): 186.

82. Geiger and Meighan, *As the Padres Saw Them*, 63, 71.

83. Cook, *Conflict*, 15–22.

84. Hackel, *Children of Coyote*, 95–96, 101–6.

85. Modern cultural anthropologists and medical historians have identified the European strain as distinct from infections present before contact. Cook, *Conflict*, 24–30.

86. Geiger and Meighan, *As the Padres Saw Them*, 105.

87. See James Sandos's astute discussion of the origins and spread of syphilis in California Indians at the missions in *Converting California*, in particular chap. 8, "Syphilis, Gonorrhea, and Other Diseases." Castillo, *Cross of Thorns*, passim.

88. Mariano Payéras, *Writings of Mariano Payéras*, quoted in Castillo, *Cross of Thorns*, 154–57.

89. Hackel, *Children of Coyote*, 17–26.

90. Randall Milliken, *A Time of Little Choice: The Disintegration of Tribal Culture in the San Francisco Bay Area, 1769–1810* (Menlo Park, CA: Ballena, 1995), 90.

91. Dubois, "Diegueño Myths," 129, cited in Carrico, *Strangers in a Stolen Land*, 1.

92. Geiger and Meighan, *As the Padres Saw Them*, 58–59.

93. Josep M. Fradera and Christopher Schmidt-Nowara, "Introduction," in *Slavery and Antislavery in Spain's Atlantic Empire*, ed. Fradera and Schmidt-Nowara (New York: Berghahn, 2013), 7, 9.

94. Reséndez, *Other Slavery*, 4, 5. The review of slavery in the New World in this chapter, and throughout this history, begins with the three foundational texts of Robin Blackburn: *The Making of New World Slavery: From the Baroque to the Modern, 1492–1800* (London: Verso, 2010), which makes profound links between empire and slavery; *The American Crucible: Slavery, Emancipation and Human Rights* (London: Verso, 2011), which charts the global trajectory of abolition; and *The Overthrow of Colonial Slavery: 1776–1848* (London: Verso, 1988), which marks the overthrow of slaveries in the mid-nineteenth century. Blackburn has made possible our analysis of the economic networks that impacted each other to engender enduring yet multiple systems of human bondage. By 1767 the Jesuits had been expelled from Spain under the Bourbon reforms. The Crown was jealous of their wealth, power, and autonomy, and eager to reassert itself in Mexico and claim the revenues from the vast Jesuit estates. James Lockhart and Stuart B. Schwartz, *Early Latin America: A History of Colonial Spanish America and Brazil* (New York: Cambridge University Press, 1983), 350; Mapp, *Elusive West*, 252.

95. Thinley Kalsang Bhutia, s.v. "Haitian Revolution," in *Encyclopedia Britannica*, https://www.britannica.com/topic/Haitian-Revolution.

96. Mapp, *Elusive West*, 84–85.

Chapter Two. "The Flame of Their Fury"

Epigraph 1: Miroslava Chávez-García, *Negotiating Conquest: Gender and Power in California, 1770s to 1880s* (Tucson: University of Arizona Press, 2006), 10. Epigraph 2: Antonia L. Castañeda, "Sexual Violence in the Politics and Policies of Conquest: Amerindian Women and the Spanish Conquest in California," in *Sexual Violence in Conflict Zones*, ed. Elizabeth D. Heineman (Philadelphia: University of Pennsylvania Press, 2011), 23.

1. Lisbeth Haas, *Saints and Citizens: Indigenous Histories, Colonial Missions and Mexican California* (Berkeley: University of California Press, 2014), 2. See Gustavo Adolpho Flores Santis, "Native American Response and Resistance to Spanish Conquest in the San Francisco Bay Area, 1769–1846" (master's thesis, San Jose State University, 2014).

2. Leanne Hinton, *Flutes of Fire: Essays on California Indian Languages* (Berkeley: Heyday, 1994), 14, 21. For an effective map of the language families and tribal affinities, see Haas, *Saints and Citizens*, 3.

3. Maynard J. Geiger and Clement W. Meighan, *As the Padres Saw Them: Californian Indian Life and Customs as Reported by the Franciscan Missionaries, 1813–1815* (Santa Barbara: Santa Barbara Mission Archive Library; Glendale, CA: A. H. Clark, 1976), 58–59. See Santis, "Native American Response."

4. See Elias Castillo, *A Cross of Thorns: The Enslavement of California's Indians by the Spanish Missions* (Fresno, CA: Craven Street, 2015), 72; Antonine Tibesar, ed., *Writings of Junípero Serra* (Washington, DC: Academy of American Franciscan History, 1956), 1:368.

5. Cited in Castillo, *Cross of Thorns*, 173; Sherburne F. Cook, *The Conflict between the California Indian and White Civilization* (Berkeley: University of California Press, 1976), 66; and Richard L. Carrico, "Sociopolitical Aspects of the 1775 Revolt at Mission San Diego de Alcalá," *Journal of San Diego History* 43, no. 3 (July 1997): 777–80.

6. Michael Connolly Miskwish, *Kumeyaay: A History Textbook*, vol. 1, *Precontact to 1893* (El Cajon, CA: Sycuan, 2006), 51; George Harwood Phillips, *Chiefs and Challengers: Indian Resistance and Cooperation in Southern California, 1769–1906* (1975; repr., Norman: University of Oklahoma Press, 2014), 33; Carrico, "Sociopolitical Aspects."

7. James Sandos, *Converting California: Indians and Franciscans in the Missions* (New Haven: Yale University Press, 2004), 59; Tibesar, *Writings of Junípero Serra*, 2:449–58.

8. "Fr. Vincent Fuster to Junípero Serra," in Tibesar, *Writings of Junípero Serra*, 2:451.

9. Francisco Palóu, *Historical Memoirs of New California*, vol. 1, ed. and trans. Herbert E. Bolton (New York: Russell and Russell, 1926), 62.

10. Steven W. Hackel, *Children of Coyote, Missionaries of Saint Francis: Indian-Spanish Relations in Colonial California, 1769–1850* (Chapel Hill: University of North Carolina Press, 2005), 22.

11. "Fr. Vincent Fuster to Junípero Serra," in Tibesar, *Writings of Junípero Serra*, 2:449.

12. The history of the revolt is based on: "Fr. Junípero Serra to Fr. Vincent Fuster," *Writings of Junípero Serra*, 2:449–54, repr. in Rose Marie Beebe and Robert M. Senkewicz, eds., *Lands of Promise and Despair: Chronicles of Early California, 1535–1846* (Berkeley: Heyday, 2001), 186–92; Richard L. Carrico, *Strangers in a Stolen Land: Indians of San Diego County from Pre-History to the New Deal* (San Diego: Sunbelt, 2008); Carrico, "Sociopolitical Aspects"; Castillo, *Cross of Thorns*; Hubert Howe Bancroft, *History of California*, vol. 1, *1542–1800* (Santa Barbara: Wallace Hebbered, 1963).

13. Beebe and Senkewicz, *Lands of Promise and Despair*, 191.

14. Francisco Ortega, *Expediente y Investigacion*, November 13, 1775, in Beebe

and Senkewicz, *Lands of Promise and Despair,* 62; Sandos, *Converting California,* 64.

15. Carrico, "Sociopolitical Aspects."

16. From the Diary of Fernando Rivera y Moncada, quoted in Castillo, *Cross of Thorns,* 79.

17. Cook, *Conflict,* 53–54.

18. Tibesar, *Writings of Junípero Serra,* 1:341; Castillo, *Cross of Thorns,* 173, for various translations of this quote.

19. Haas, *Saints and Citizens,* 5.

20. Tibesar, *Writings of Junípero Serra,* 2:407. See Castillo, *Cross of Thorns,* 72.

21. Carrico, "Sociopolitical Aspects."

22. Randy Leffingwell, *California Missions and Presidios: The History and Beauty of the Spanish Missions* (Stillwater, MN: Voyageur, 2005), 68.

23. Phillips, *Chiefs and Challengers,* 28.

24. James Sandos, "Junípero Serra's Canonization and the Historical Record," from an interview with Carolbeth Laird in *Native American Perspectives on the Hispanic Colonization of Alta California,* ed. Edward D. Castillo (New York: Garland, 1991), 464–65.

25. Gloria E. Miranda, "Racial and Cultural Dimensions of 'Gente de Razón' Status in Spanish and Mexican California," *Southern California Quarterly* 70, no. 3 (Fall 1988): 265–78.

26. Antonio María Osio, *The History of Alta California: A Memoir of Mexican California,* trans. Rose Marie Beebe and Robert M. Senkewicz (Madison: University of Wisconsin Press, 1996), 55.

27. Douglas Monroy, *Among Strangers: The Making of Mexican Culture in Frontier California* (Berkeley: University of California Press, 1990), 40–41.

28. Hackel, *Children of Coyote,* 264.

29. See James Sandos, "Toypurina's Revolt: Religious Conflict at Mission San Gabriel in 1785," *Boletín: The Journal of the California Mission Studies Association* 24, no. 2 (2007): 4–14; Castillo, *Cross of Thorns,* 161–66; Robert F. Heizer, *Handbook of North American Indians* (Washington, DC: Smithsonian Institution, 1978), 8:538–49; Thomas Workman Temple II, "Toypurina: The Witch and the Indian Uprising at San Gabriel," *Masterkey for Indian Lore and History* 32, no. 5 (1958): 136–52; Haas, *Saints and Citizens,* 54–55; Antonia I. Castañeda, "Engendering the History of Alta California, 1769–1848: Gender, Sexuality, and the Family," *California History* 76, no. 2/3 (1997): 235–37; Hackel, *Children of Coyote,* 262–68.

30. Laura M. Furlan, *Indigenous Cities: Urban Indian Fiction and the Histories of Relocation* (Omaha: University of Nebraska Press, 2017), 41–42.

31. Santis, "Native American Response," cites Argüello correspondence, June 28, 1797, Archives of California, Provincial State Papers, XVI 90.

32. Testimony signed by José Argüello and other Spanish soldiers, from "Letters of José Maria Fernandez" and the 1797 "Military Interrogation of San Francisco Indians," in Beebe and Senkewicz, *Lands of Promise and Despair,* 262–69.

See also Hackel, *Children of Coyote*, 123; Randall Milliken, *A Time of Little Choice: The Disintegration of Tribal Culture in the San Francisco Bay Area, 1769–1810* (Menlo Park, CA: Ballena, 1995).

33. Edward D. Castillo, trans. and ed., "The Assassination of Padre Andrés Quintana by the Indians of the Mission Santa Cruz in 1812: The Narrative of Lorenzo Asisara," in Castillo, *Native American Perspectives*, 117–25. For historical debates about the oral history, see Doyce B. Nunis, Jr., and Edward D. Castillo, "California Mission Indians: Two Perspectives," *California History* 70, no. 2 (Summer 1991): 206–15.

34. Castillo, *Cross of Thorns*; Beebe and Senkewicz, *Junípero Serra*, 104–5.

35. Natale Zappia, "Captivity and Economic Landscapes in California and the Far West, 1769–1850," in *Linking the Histories of Slavery: North America and Its Borderlands*, ed. Bonnie Martin and James F. Brooks (Santa Fe: School for Advanced Research Press, 2015), 132–33. For a discussion of the links between the tribes of Southern California and the trade in hides and horses between the unfree and free Mohave and other California Natives who lived to the east of the mission chain, see Zappia, "Captivity and Economic Landscapes," 134–35.

36. Hackel, *Children of Coyote*, 91–92.

37. The horse facilitated Indians' own traffic in Native Californians along the Old Spanish Trail that ran from the Pacific Coast east to the Colorado River. By the 1830s Ute and Mohave kidnapped and sold Indian women and children to the new rancheros. See Zappia, "Captivity and Economic Landscapes," 136–39, for the raiding and slave trading of Paiute.

38. Within this vast bibliography, see Robin Blackburn, *The Making of New World Slavery: From the Baroque to the Modern, 1492–1800* (New York: Verso, 1997); Greg Grandin, *The Empire of Necessity: Slavery, Freedom, and Deception in the New World* (New York: Macmillan, 2014); Andrés Reséndez, *The Other Slavery: The Uncovered Story of Indian Enslavement in America* (Boston: Houghton Mifflin, 2016). See also Kris Manjapra, "When Will Britain Face Up to Its Crimes against Humanity?," *Guardian*, March 29, 2018.

39. Marie Christine Duggan, "With and without an Empire: Financing for California Mission before and after 1810," *Pacific Historical Review* 85, no. 1 (February 2016): 27–28.

40. Wallace McKeehan, "Plan of Iguala and Treaty of Cordova," Sons of De-Witt Colony Texas, http://www.sonsofdewittcolony.org/iguala.htm.

41. My analysis is influenced by Evelyn Nakano Glenn's discussion of settler colonialism in "Settler Colonialism as Structure: A Framework for Comparative Studies of U.S. Race and Gender Formation," *Sociology of Race and Ethnicity* 1, no. 1 (2015): 54–74.

42. Stephen W. Silliman, "Theoretical Perspectives on Labor and Colonialism: Reconsidering the California Missions," *Journal of Anthropological Archaeology* 20, no. 4 (December 2001): 379–407.

43. Geiger and Meighan, *As the Padres Saw Them*, 48.

44. Maynard Geiger, "Fray Antonio Ripoll's Description of the Chumash Revolt at Santa Barbara in 1824," *Southern California Quarterly* 52, no. 4 (December 1970): 345–64.

45. Travis Hudson, "The Chumash Revolt of 1824: Another Native Account from the Notes of John P. Harrington," *Journal of California and Great Basin Anthropology* 2, no. 1 (Summer 1980): 123–26.

46. Haas, *Saints and Citizens*, 120–25.

47. Sandos, *Converting California*, 119.

48. Dee Travis Hudson, "Chumash Canoes of Mission Santa Barbara: The Revolt of 1824," *Journal of California Anthropology* 3, no. 2 (Winter 1976): 4–15.

49. Hudson, "Chumash Canoes," 123–26.

50. James Sandos, "Levantamiento! The 1824 Chumash Uprising Reconsidered," *Southern California Quarterly* 67, no. 2 (Summer 1985): 109–33.

51. Sandos, "Levantamiento!," 109–33.

52. For discussion of Estanislao and this phase of the revolt, see Jack Holterman, "The Revolt of Estanislao," *Indian Historian* 3, no. 1 (1970): 43–54; Sandos, *Converting California*, 170–72; Castillo, *Cross of Thorns*; Thorne B. Gray, *The Stanislaus Indian Wars: The Last of the California Northern Yokuts* (Modesto, CA: McHenry Museum, 1993); James D. Adams, *Estanislao—Warrior, Man of God* (La Crescenta, CA: Abedus, 2006). See also Cook, *Conflict*, 64; Kent G. Lightfoot, *Indians, Missionaries, and Merchants: The Legacy of Colonial Encounters on the California Frontiers* (Berkeley: University of California Press, 2006), 89.

53. Haas, *Saints and Citizens*, 129.

54. Haas, *Saints and Citizens*, 131.

55. The pass, where the Chumash would rebuild their culture in the safety of a mountain canyon, was renamed "Walker Pass."

56. In the enumeration by the California legislature of 1850 as part of admission to the Union, no Indians were counted in the area now called "Walker Pass"; apparently, none of the Chumash from the coastal missions survived.

57. Haas, *Saints and Citizens*, 141.

58. "Pablo de la Portola to José Figueroa, January 23, 1835," quoted in Haas, *Saints and Citizens*, 159.

59. Haas, *Saints and Citizens*, 142.

60. Dorothy Krell, ed., *The California Missions: A Pictorial History* (Menlo Park, CA: Sunset, 1979), 316; Antumi Toasije, "The Africanity of Spain: Identity and Problematization," *Journal of Black Studies* 39, no. 3 (January 2009): 348–55.

61. Eric Wolf, *Sons of the Shaking Earth* (Chicago: University of Chicago Press, 1959); *Europe and the People without History* (Berkeley: University of California Press, 1982).

62. Haas, *Saints and Citizens*, 177–84.

63. Haas, *Saints and Citizens*, 8–10.

64. Haas, *Saints and Citizens*, 140–46.

Chapter Three. A Slave Rectangle in the Pacific

Epigraph: "Ukut Skuunat" (These Schoolers), as sung by Mary Peterson and Jennie Zeeder, from *Generations: An Alutiiq Music Collection*, by Stephen Blanchett, Alutiiq Museum and Archeological Repository, Kodiak, AK (2007), CD. Courtesy of the Alutiiq Museum and Archeological Repository.

1. Aron Crowell and April Laktonen, "Súgucihpet 'Our Way of Living,'" in *Looking Both Ways: Heritage and Identity of the Alutiiq People*, ed. Aron L. Crowell, Amy F. Steffian, and Gordon Pullar (Fairbanks: University of Alaska Press, 2001), 25, 144–49, 163.

2. Kaj Birket-Smith, *The Chugach Eskimo* (København: Nationalmuseets Publikationsfond, 1953). Also see Crowell, Steffian, and Pullar, *Looking Both Ways*, 144–49.

3. Dylan Matthews, "What It's Like to Hunt Sea Otters," Vox, May 2, 2014, https://vox.com/2014/5/2/5671548/i-hunt-otters-ama.

4. Crowell, Steffian, and Pullar, *Looking Both Ways*, 163–65.

5. Aron Crowell, "Russians in Alaska, 1784: Foundations of Colonial Society at Three Saints Harbor, Kodiak Island," *Kroeber Anthropological Society Papers* 81 (1997): 14.

6. Andrei V. Grinev, "The Plans for Russian Expansion in the New World and the North Pacific in the Eighteenth and Nineteenth Centuries," in "The North-West Pacific in the 18th and 19th Centuries," special issue, *European Journal of American Studies* 5, no. 2 (2010): 1.

7. F. A. Golder, *Bering's Voyage: An Account of the Efforts of the Russians to Determine the Relation of Asia to America* (New York: American Geographical Society, 1972), 90; Barbara Boyle Torrey, *Slaves of the Harvest: The Story of the Pribilof Aleuts* (Alaska: Tanandgusix Corporation, 1978), 26–29.

8. "Historic Range of Sea Otters," fig. 1 in "The Effects of Sea Otter Reintroduction," Sea Grant Alaska, https://seagrant.uaf.edu/nosb/papers/2011/juneau-otters.php.

9. John A. Love, *Sea Otters* (Golden, CO: Fulcrum, 1992), 9–16.

10. John R. Bockstoce, *Furs and Frontiers in the Far North: The Contest among Native and Foreign Nations for the Bering Strait Fur Trade* (New Haven: Yale University Press, 2010), 71–72; P. A. Tikhmenev, *A History of the Russian-American Company*, trans. and ed. Richard A. Pierce and Alton S. Donnelly (Seattle: University of Washington Press, 1978), 144; James R. Gibson, "Russian Dependence upon the Natives of Alaska," in *Russia's American Colony*, ed. S. Frederick Starr (Durham, NC: Duke University Press, 1987), 80.

11. Ilya Vinkovetsky, *Russian America: An Overseas Colony of a Continental Empire, 1804–1867* (New York: Oxford University Press, 2014), 29, 31; Gavril Ivanovich Davidov, *Two Voyages to Russian America, 1802–1807*, trans. Colin Bearne, ed. Richard A. Pierce (Kingston, ON: Alaska Limestone, 1977), 82; R. G. Liāpunova, *Essays on the Ethnography of the Aleuts: At the End of the Eighteenth and the First Half of the Nineteenth Century*, trans. Jerry Shelest, ed.

William B. Workman and Lydia T. Black (Fairbanks: University of Alaska Press, 1996), 108.

12. Owen Matthews, *Glorious Misadventures: Nikolai Rezanov and the Dream of a Russian America* (London: Bloomsbury, 2013), 233.

13. "*Promyshlenniki*": translated, a man who leaves his own country to engage in trade in foreign lands; a fur trapper. Liãpunova, *Essays on the Ethnography of the Aleuts*, 108; Vinkovetsky, *Russian America*, 29.

14. For a discussion of the various Cossack roles and descendant and immigrant communities, see "Fur trade," Northwest Power and Conservation Council, https://www.nwcouncil.org/reports/columbia-river-history/furtrade.

15. Liãpunova, *Essays on the Ethnography of the Aleuts*, 108.

16. David Igler, *The Great Ocean: Pacific Worlds from Captain Cook to the Gold Rush* (New York: Oxford University Press, 2013), 106.

17. Chris Alexie, "Knowledge of Native Elders: Larry and Martha Matfay" (unpublished manuscript, H90–06–24, University of Alaska, Anchorage).

18. Torrey, *Slaves of the Harvest*, 13.

19. Allen P. McCartney and Douglas W. Veltre, "Aleutian Island Prehistory: Living in Insular Extremes," in "Arctic Archaeology," special issue, *World Archaeology* 30, no. 3 (February 1999): 503–15.

20. Michael J. Oleksa, *Alaskan Missionary Spirituality* (New York: Paulist, 1987), 3.

21. Hubert Howe Bancroft, *The Native Races, 1882–86* (San Francisco: History Company, 1886).

22. Daniel Merkur, "Becoming Half Hidden: Shamanism and Initiation among the Inuit" (PhD thesis, University of Stockholm, 1985; Stockholm: Almqvist and Wiksell, 1985); I. Kleivan and B. Sonne, *Eskimos: Greenland and Canada, Iconography of Religions*, section 8, "Arctic Peoples," fascicle 2 (Leiden: Brill, 1985).

23. See Lydia T. Black, *Russians in Alaska: 1732–1867* (Fairbanks: University of Alaska Press, 2004), for a discussion of discrepancies in various census figures, including who would be counted and what defined an "able-bodied man." Black estimates that pre-contact, there were approximately ten thousand Natives in the Aleutian Island Archipelago, and about ten thousand Natives on the Kodiak Archipelago. Black, *Russians in Alaska*, 128–29.

24. Vasilii N. Berkh, *A Chronological History of the Discovery of the Aleutian Islands or the Exploits of Russian Merchants*, trans. Dmitri Krenov, ed. Richard A. Pierce (Kingston, ON: Limestone, 1974), 32.

25. Berkh, *Chronological History*, 34; Torrey, *Slaves of the Harvest*, 32–35; Hubert Howe Bancroft, *History of Alaska, 1730–1918* (San Francisco: A. L. Bancroft, 1981), 120–21; S. B. Okun, *The Russian-American Company*, trans. Carl Ginsburg, ed. B. D. Grekov (Cambridge, MA: Harvard University Press, 1951), passim.

26. Berkh, *Chronological History*, 24, 26–29; Torrey, *Slaves of the Harvest*, 31.

27. See Black, *Russians in Alaska*.

28. "The Afognak-Alutiiq People, Our History and Culture," Afognak, https://www.afognak.com/wp-content/uploads/2012/06/The-Afognak-Alutiiq-People....pdf; *Finding Refuge*, first aired October 3, 2015, on PBS. Also quoted in Heinrich J. Holmberg, *Holmberg's Ethnographic Sketches*, trans. Fritz Jaensch, ed. Marvin W. Falk (Fairbanks, AK: Limestone, 1985), 59.

29. *Finding Refuge.*

30. Okun, *Russian-American Company*, 194n4. See Native testimony in "Five Reports from 1789–90 Concerning Treatment of Aleuts," trans. Antoinette Shalkop, Yudin Collection, Box 11:23, Manuscript Division, Library of Congress, Washington, DC.

31. Tikhmenev, *History of the Russian-American Company*, 16–17; Basil Dmytryshyn, E. A. P. Crownhart-Vaughan, and Thomas Vaughan, eds. and trans., *Russian Penetration of the North Pacific Ocean, 1700–1797: A Documentary Record* (Portland: Oregon Historical Society Press, 1988), 310; Black, *Russians in Alaska*, 132.

32. Quoted in Black, *Russians in America*, 126.

33. Okun, *Russian-American Company*, 10, 27, 270.

34. "Five Reports from 1789–90."

35. "Ukut Skuunat" ("These Schooners"), from *Generations: An Alutiiq Music Collection*. Courtesy of the Alutiiq Museum and Archeological Repository.

36. Lauren Peters (Agdaagux̂ Tribe, Unangax̂), "Kuskov, an Alaska Native Perspective," Fort Ross Conservancy, https://www.fortross.org/ivan_kuskov.htm; Black, *Russians in Alaska*, 121.

37. Hector Chevigny, s.v. "Aleksandri Andrevich Baranov," in *Encyclopedia Arctica*, vol. 15, *Biographies* (1947–51), https://collections.dartmouth.edu/arctica-beta/html/EA15-07.html.

38. Black, *Russians in Alaska*, 133.

39. "Five Reports from 1789–90."

40. "A History of the Russian Orthodox Church in Alaska," s.v. "Russian Orthodox," AlaskaWeb, http://alaskaweb.org/religion/russortho.html.

41. Okun, *Russian-American Company*, 196; Vinkovetsky, *Russian America*, 166.

42. P. A. Tikhmenev, "Supplements," *Historical Survey of the Formation of the Russian-American Company*, pt. 1–2 (St. Petersburg, 1863), 98.

43. Torrey, *Slaves of the Harvest*, 37.

44. The term "peon" is used here to refer to low-level menial or agricultural workers held in various forms of compulsory servitude. In eighteenth- and nineteenth-century Russia, it could be used interchangeably with "slave," "bondman," "thrall," "serf," "bondservant," "bondslave," and "bondsman." The laborer may have received a wage, perhaps "in kind" for food. A peon had little control over conditions of employment. It also referred to forced or unfree laborers. During the colonial eras of Mexico and the Caribbean islands, peonage was common and referred to Native people forced to work for Spanish planters and mine operators. Bondage may have been incurred debt.

45. I am deeply grateful for the many conversations with Lauren Peters (Agdaaguŵ Tribe, Unangaŵ) and Rene Azzara (Dena'ina) for discussions on unraveling the history, categories, and vocabulary of the slavery of Alaska Natives and the history of Native Americans at Fort Ross. See Andrei V. Grinev, "The Kaiury: The Slaves of Russian America," trans. Richard L. Bland, *Alaska History* 15, no. 2 (2000): 1–18; Vinkovetsky, *Russian America*, 75–76; Okun, *Russian-American Company*, 193, with slightly different definitions of categories; Igler, *Great Ocean*, 76. See also Leland Donald, *Aboriginal Slavery on the Northwest Coast of North America* (Berkeley: University California Press, 1997); Robert Ruby and John A. Brown, *Indian Slavery in the Pacific Northwest* (Spokane, WA: Arthur Clark, 1993). "Shelikhov-Golikov Company's promyshlenniki seized a number of Koniags' [from Kodiak] slaves as booty. Promyshlenniki called these slaves *kaiuri*, a term used locally in Kamchatka to denote servants." Winston Sarafian, "Economic Foundations of Russian America" (Kennan Institute for Advanced Russian Studies, the Wilson Center, 1979), 19.
46. Davidov, *Two Voyages to Russian America*, 106–11, 116, 164–65, 193–97.
47. Davidov, *Two Voyages to Russian America*, 188–89, 163, 171.
48. "Five Reports from 1789–90."
49. Black, *Russians in Alaska*, 128–29. The population figures are difficult for historians to compute, as initial censuses were based only on able-bodied men who were often at sea. See Black, *Russians in Alaska*, 127–28, for a thorough summary of the contested number and the facts of hunters at sea, many forced deportations and assignments to unpopulated islands, unregistered births, causes of death, and renaming.
50. Alexander Baranov, "The Spirit of Russian Hunters Devised: The 'Song of Baranov,'" repr. in *Overland Monthly and Out West* 66, no. 6 (December 1915): 522–23.
51. James R. Gibson, "Russian Expansion in Siberia and America," *Geographical Review* 70, no. 2 (April 1980): 34.

Chapter Four. The Undersea People

Epigraph: Peter Kalifornsky, *A Dena'ina Legacy: The Collected Writings of Peter Kalifornsky (K'tl'egh'i sukdu)*, ed. J. M. Kari and A. Boraas (Fairbanks: Alaska Native Language Center, University of Alaska Fairbanks, 1991), 253.

1. Essie Parrish, "Living Conditions Improving for Sonoma County Indians," *Press Democrat* (Santa Rosa, CA), August 9, 1970.
2. Hannah Ballard, "Ethnicity and Chronology at Metini, Fort Ross State Historic Park, California," *Kroeber Anthropological Society Papers* 81 (1997): 121. The history of "Fort Ross" as a fort hinges on reconstruction, focusing on the stockade, the cannons, and the commander's housing and granary. These reconstructions have not included the buildings that were forced to lie out-

side the stockade. Native historians and anthropologists are looking at the cemetery and have been instrumental in the representation of the lives of Alaska Natives and California Natives. The role of the forced labor of the Alaska Natives, Pomo, Kashaya, and Miwok people, their interrelationships, and their cultural practices are currently being revised by the descendants of the Native workers, their partners, spouses, and children. E. Breck Parkman discusses early efforts at a respectful and fulsome history in "A Fort by Any Other Name: Interpretation and Semantics at Colony Ross" (paper presented at the Annual Meetings of the Alaska Anthropological Association, March 1992, Fairbanks, AK); this is ongoing through insistent input and collaboration of Pomo, Kashaya, Coastal Miwok, and Alaska Native leaders, activists, and historians. Current investigations are ongoing regarding the funding and influence of contemporary Russian investors and will be published as they are completed.

3. Kenneth N. Owens, "Frontiersman for the Tsar: Tmofei Tarakanov and the Expansion of Russian America," *Montana: The Magazine of Western History* 56, no. 3 (Autumn 2006): 1–21; John Polich, "Joseph Burling O'Cain in Spanish California," *Southern California Quarterly* 65, no. 1. (1983): 95–106.

4. Allan Temko, "Russians in California," *American Heritage* 11, no. 3 (April 1960), https://www.americanheritage.com/russians-california; Owen Matthews, *Glorious Misadventures: Nikolai Rezanov and the Dream of a Russian America* (London: Bloomsbury, 2013).

5. Andrei Val'terovich Grinëv, *Russian Colonization of Alaska: Preconditions, Discovery, and Initial Development, 1741–1799*, trans. Richard L. Bland (Lincoln: University of Nebraska Press, 2018), 221–28.

6. Polich, "Joseph Burling O'Cain," 102.

7. Elton Engstrom and Allan Engstrom, *Alexander Baranov and a Pacific Empire* (self-published, 2004), 160–61.

8. Andrei V. Grinëv, "The Dynamics of Fleet Composition of the Russian-American Company (1799–1867)," trans. Richard Bland, *Journal of the West* 57, no. 2 (Spring 2018): 16–17.

9. "Shelikhov to Gov. General Pil of Irkutsk," "General Pil to Empress Catharine," 1890, in *The Russian-American Company*, trans. S. B. Okun, ed. Carl Ginsburg and B. D. Grekov (Cambridge, MA: Harvard University Press, 1951), 118.

10. I. V. Iakobi, "Instructions, Lieutenant-General I. V. Iakobi, Governor-General of Siberia, to Samoilov and Delarov, June 21, 1787 (Secret)," in *A History of the Russian-American Company*, vol. 2, trans. P. A. Tikhmenev, ed. Dmitri Krenov, Richard A. Pierce, and Alton S. Donnelly (Kingston, ON: Limestone, 1979), 17–18.

11. "A Report from the Board of Directors of the RAC," 1811. See the documents collected in James Gibson and Alexei A. Istomin, *Russian California, 1806–1860: A History in Documents* (London: Hakluyt Society, 2014), 1:288, doc. 21.

12. P. A. Tikhmenev, "Supplements," *Historical Survey of the Formation of the Russian-American Company*, pt. 2 (St. Petersburg, 1863), 267. Hunt Janin and Ursula Carlson, *The Californios: A History, 1769–1890* (Jefferson, NC: McFarland, 2017), 74–75.

13. "A Contract between Governor Baranov and Captain Eayrs for Joint Sea Otter Hunting on the Coast of California," May 25, 1808, in Gibson and Istomin, *Russian California*, doc. 21, 1:288; doc. 9, 1:249–51.

14. "Contract between Governor Baranov and Captain Eayrs."

15. Adele Ogden, *The California Sea Otter Trade, 1784–1848* (Berkeley: University of California Press, 1941), 46–47. In his expedition diary, *The Diary of Captain Argüello: The Last Spanish Expedition in California, October 17—November 17, 1821*, trans. Vivian Fischer (Berkeley: Friends of Bancroft Library, University of California, 1992).

16. E. W. Giesecke, "Discovery of Humboldt Bay, California 1806: In 1806 from the Ship O'Cain, Jonathan Winship, Commander: An Episode in a Bostonian-Russian Contract Voyage of the Early American China Trade" (unpublished paper, Fort Ross Conservancy Library, 1997).

17. Engstrom and Engstrom, *Alexander Baranov and a Pacific Empire*, 162.

18. Nikolai Rezanov, "Report," in Gibson and Istomin, *Russian California*, doc. 3, 1:220.

19. Gibson and Istomin, *Russian California*, 1:68–72n93; Gibson and Istomin, *Russian California*, 1:12; Nikolai Rezanov, "A Report from Imperial Chamberlain Rezanov . . . ," Gibson and Istomin, *Russian California*, doc. 3, 1:227.

20. Rezanov, "Report," 1:220.

21. Okun, *Russian-American Company*, 119. For the origins of Fort Ross, see also E. O. Essig, "The Russian Settlement at Ross," *California Historical Quarterly Journal* 12, no. 3 (September 1933): 191–209.

22. Ogden, *California Sea Otter Trade*, 5.

23. Nikolai Rezanov, "Report," in Gibson and Istomin, *Russian California*, doc. 3, 1:214; Ballard, "Ethnicity and Chronology at Metini," 121.

24. Ballard, "Ethnicity and Chronology at Metini," 131.

25. My interpretation has been deeply influenced by the work of David Igler, *The Great Ocean: Pacific Worlds from Captain Cook to the Gold Rush* (New York: Oxford University Press, 2013), esp. 3–15.

26. Vasilii Petrovovich Tarakanov, "Statement," in Gibson and Istomin, *Russian California*, 2:5.

27. Otis Parrish, *The First People* (Fort Ross, CA: Fort Ross Interpretive Association, 1998).

28. Sara Lynae Gonzalez, "Creating Trails from Traditions: The Kashaya Pomo Interpretive Trail at Fort Ross State Historic Park" (PhD diss., University of California, Berkeley, 2011), 5–12.

29. bell hooks has observed that "margins" are often "sites of radical possibility," a place at once of activism and return: bell hooks, *Yearning: Race, Gender, and Cultural Politics* (Boston: South End, 1990), 149.

30. From Alexie A. Istomin, *The Indians at the Ross Settlement, According to the Censuses by Kuskov, 1820 and 1821* (Fort Ross, CA: Fort Ross Interpretive Association, 1992), 10–11, cited in Gonzalez, "Creating Trails from Traditions," 124–25.

31. Kent G. Lightfoot, *Indians, Missionaries, and Merchants: The Legacy of Colonial Encounters on the California Frontiers* (Berkeley: University of California Press, 2006), 172.

32. In 1861, the first year of the American Civil War, Captain P. N. Golovin reported to the tsar that it was "unfair to level the charge that the Aleuts are slaves to the company. No one deprives them of their belongings; everything they acquire for themselves at sea and on land belongs to them; but since they could not engage in hunting without the assistance of the Company, which furnishes them with everything, naturally they have the obligation to turn over their catch to the Company, which pays them at the established price. . . . One could rather call the Aleuts members of a family of which the American Company is the head. As head, or solicitous guardian, the Company . . . constantly adheres to the improvement of the lives of the Natives, and responsible as well for the supervising their moral and intellectual development. . . . And on the other hand, by their nature, the Aleuts are children, in the full sense of the word, without any thought to their future." Their future was in the safe "guardianship" of the Russian-American Company that made sure that "furbearing animals have not yet been exterminated around the Aleutian Islands."

33. A. B. Duhaut-Cilly, "View of Fort Ross," 1828, Colonial Voyage, https://www.colonialvoyage.com/es/view-of-fort-ross-1828-a-b-duhaut-cilly-fort-ross-state-historic-park-photo-archives-no-copyright-5/.

34. Stephen Watrous, "Ivan Kuskov: 'Steadfast Zeal for the Common Welfare,'" *Californians* (March–April 1992): 12. For an admiring and well-drawn overview of Kuskov's role in early Fort Ross, see Ballard, "Ethnicity and Chronology at Metini," 131.

35. Lightfoot, *Indians, Missionaries, and Merchants*, 169, 172–74.

36. Ferdinand von Wrangel, "A Report from Governor Wrangel . . . About an Inspection of Ross Counter," in Gibson and Istomin, *Russian California*, doc. 290, April 10, 1834, 2:269. Glenn J. Farris, *The Day of the Tall Strangers*, in "Recognizing Indian Folk History as Real History: A Fort Ross Example," in "The California Indians," special issue, *American Indian Quarterly* 13, no. 4 (Autumn 1989): 471–80.

37. See Kent G. Lightfoot, Thomas A. Wake, Ann M. Schiff, "Native Responses to the Russian Mercantile Colony of Fort Ross, Northern California," *Journal of Field Archaeology* 20, no. 2 (January 1993): 169. The registers of 1820 list no Russian women, although diaries refer to visits. Of the women living with Russian men, all were Kashaya Pomo or Miwok. There were seventeen "common law wives" living with Aleut men, likely Kashaya Pomo, and perhaps with husbands at sea or held hostage. There were twenty Kodiak, Aleut,

and "Creole" women. About half the women at Fort Ross were Alaskan Natives, and the other half were Pomo or Miwok. Okun, *Russian-American Company*, 144n50; Watrous, "Ivan Kuskov," 15.

38. Comment by Kiril Khlebnikov from Antoinette Martinez, "View from the Ridge: The Kashaya Pomo in a Russian-American Company Context," *Kroeber Anthropological Society Papers* 81 (1997): 143, 146.

39. See Glenn J. Farris, "The Age of Russian Imperialism in the North Pacific," *Kroeber Anthropological Society Papers* 81 (1997): 190.

40. Lightfoot, *Indians, Missionaries, and Merchants*, 162.

41. Lightfoot, *Indians, Missionaries, and Merchants*, 162.

42. Okun, *Russian-American Company*, 125; Lightfoot, *Indians, Missionaries, and Merchants*, 158.

43. Okun, *Russian-American Company*, 128–29n22; Archives of the Chancery of the Ministry of Foreign Affairs, Moscow, 1823, File no. 3646, 1, 24; Watrous, "Ivan Kuskov," 14; Otto von Kotzebue, *A Voyage of Discovery, Into the South Sea and Bering Straits* (Amsterdam: Israel, 1967), 2:121–22.

44. Vasyli Illyashevich to his son, "The Settlement of Ross," in Gibson and Istomin, *Russian California*, doc. 492, 2:564–65.

45. Istomin, *Indians at the Ross Settlement*, 4.

46. Lightfoot, *Indians, Missionaries, and Merchants*, 165.

47. Daniel F. Murley, "Interpretation of Culture Contact at Colony Ross," *Proceedings of the Society for California Archaeology* 18 (papers presented at the annual meeting of the Society for California Archaeology, 2005), 212.

48. Nikolaĭ Petrovich Rezanov, *The Rezanov Voyage to Nueva California in 1806* (Fairfield, WA: Ye Galleon, 1988), n.p.

49. Rezanov, *Rezanov Voyage*.

50. Vasyli Golovnin, "Excerpts from a Journal of a Visit to Alta California and New Albion during the Round-the-World Voyage of the Sloop *Kamchatka*, 1817–19," in Gibson and Istomin, *Russian California*, doc. 48, 1:358.

51. For a discussion of the biodiversity of the Farallones, see Greater Farallones Association, http://farallones.org. A live webcam is available through at "Farallon Islands Live Webcam," California Academy of Sciences, https://www.calacademy.org/webcams/farallones/.

52. Danny Sedevic, "A History of the Farallon Islands," Farallones Marine Sanctuary Association, https://www.farallones.org.

53. Ogden, *California Sea Otter Trade*, 49. P. N. Golovin, *The End of Russian America: Captain P. N. Golovin's Last Report, 1862*, trans. Basil Dmytryshyn and E. A. P. Crownhart-Vaughan (Portland: Oregon Historical Society, 1979), 162, 166; Kiril T. Khlebnikov, *Notes on Russian America*, pt. 1, trans. Serge LeComte and Marina Ramsay, ed. Richard Pierce (Kingston, ON: Limestone, 1994), 222; Lightfoot, *Indians, Missionaries, and Merchants*, 124.

54. Zakahar Tchitchinoff, *Adventures in California of Zakahar Tchitchinoff, 1818–1828* (Los Angeles: Gen Dawson, 1956), 4–7.

55. Tchitchinoff, *Adventures in California*, xi.

56. Ogden, *California Sea Otter Trade*, 62n67.

57. Ogden, *California Sea Otter Trade*, 63n70.

58. "Manager Kuskov to Governor Hagemeister about the Il'mena Island Affair," July 15, 1818, in Gibson and Istomin, *Russian California*, 1:336–37.

59. Tchitchinoff, *Adventures in California*, 1, 2–3.

60. "The Testimony of Partovshchik Kylaya about the Spanish Seizure and Captivity of a Russian Hunting Party," May 1819, in Gibson and Istomin, *Russian California*, Document 57, 1:406–8, 1:135–36.

61. Antonio María Osio, "Historia de California 1815–1848" (original manuscript in the Bancroft Library, University of California, Berkeley), translation in Ogden, *California Sea Otter Trade*, 56n40. William Dane Phelps, "Solid Men of Boston in the Northwest" (manuscript, 1870s, Hubert Howe Bancroft Collection, CD ROM, BANC CPF 209, Bancroft Library, University of California, Berkeley), http://www.oac.cdlib.org/search?group=Items;idT=Ucb 112375054.

62. Ogden, *California Sea Otter Trade*, 56n40.

63. Ogden, *California Sea Otter Trade*, 56.

64. Athanasius Schaefer, "San Francisco Solano: Sonoma Mission," http://www .athanasius.com/camission/sonoma.htm.

65. See Khlebnikov's biography of Baranov, *The Khlebnikov Archive: Unpublished Journal (1800–1837) and Travel Notes (1820, 1822, and 1824)*, ed. L. A. Shur, trans. John Bisk (Fairbanks: University of Alaska Press, 1990); P. A. Tikhmenev, *A History of the Russian-American Company*, trans. and ed. Richard A. Pierce and Alton S. Donnelly (Seattle: University of Washington Press, 1978).

66. Peter Kostromitinov or Paul Shelikov, "Brief Remarks on the Indians of Ross, 1834–5," in Gibson and Istomin, *Russian California*, doc. 306, 2:284–91.

67. Murley, "Interpretation," 214; Khlebnikov, *Khlebnikov Archive*, 91; Khlebnikov, *Notes on Russian America*, 12; Ogden, *California Sea Otter Trade*, 61–63; Lightfoot, *Indians, Missionaries, and Merchants*, 126.

68. Khlebnikov, *Notes on Russian America*, 84–85.

69. Diane Spencer Pritchard, "The Good, the Bad, and the Ugly: Russian-America Company Employees of Fort Ross," *Californians* 8 (March–April 1991): 44–46; Okun, *Russian-American Company*, 144.

70. See Farris, *Day of the Tall Strangers*, 15; and Okun, *Russian-American Company*, 144n52, for slightly different translations of Wrangel.

71. Farris, *Day of the Tall Strangers*, 15; Okun, *Russian-American Company*, 144n52.

72. Igler, *Great Ocean*, 46.

73. Gibson and Istomin, *Russian California*, 2:542.

74. Gibson and Istomin, *Russian California*, 1:83n3; 134–35.

75. Okun, *Russian-American Company*, 140.

76. Okun, *Russian-American Company*, 142.

77. Gibson and Istomin, *Russian California*, 1:161–62.

78. M. L. Riedman and J. A. Estes, "The Sea Otter (Enhydra Lutris): Behavior, Ecology, and Natural History," *U. S. Fish and Wildlife Service, Biological Report* 90, no. 14 (1990): 1–126.

79. Alexander Rotchev, "A New Eldorado in California," 1849 (doc. 32), in *California through Russian Eyes, 1806–1848*, vol. 2, ed. and trans. James R. Gibson (Norman: University of Oklahoma Press, 2013), 459–63.

80. See the documents collected in Gibson and Istomin, *Russian California*, reports 427 to 492, 2:467–565.

81. Gibson and Istomin, *Russian California*, doc. 481, 2:545.

82. Lightfoot, *Indians, Missionaries, and Merchants*, 169, 172–73.

83. Lauren Peters (Agdaagux̂ tribe, Unangax̂), "Kuskov, an Alaska Native Perspective," Fort Ross Conservancy, https://www.fortross.org/ivan_kuskov.htm.

84. Samuel N. Dicken, *End of Russian America: Captain P. N. Golovin's Last Report, 1862* (Oregon Historical Society, 1974), 162, 166.

85. Dena'ina Poet Peter Kalifornsky's great-great-grandfather, Qadanalchen, composed this song while he was at Fort Ross, sometime between 1811 and 1821. Kalifornsky, *Dena'ina Legacy*, 253. See also Glenn Farris, "Life at Fort Ross as the Indians Saw It: Stories from the Kashaya," Fort Ross Conservancy Library, 1992, http://www.fortross.org/lib/41/life-at-fort-ross-as-the-indians-saw-it-stories-from-the-kashaya.pdf.

Chapter Five. Birth of a State

Epigraph 1: Jeannette Molson and Eual D. Blansett, Jr., *The Torturous Road to Freedom: The Life of Alvin Aaron Coffey* (self-published, 2010), n.p.
Epigraph 2: Frederick Douglass, *North Star,* November 30, 1849.

1. This chapter is indebted to the foundational work on Blacks in the West by Quintard Taylor, *In Search of the Racial Frontier: African Americans in the American West 1528–1990* (New York: Norton, 1998); and *Seeking El Dorado: African Americans in California* (Seattle: University of Seattle Press, 2001); and Quintard Taylor and Shirley Ann Wilson Moore, *African American Women Confront the West 1600–2000* (Norman: University of Oklahoma Press, 2003). California became a state on September 9, 1850, and elected John C. Frémont, Free Soil Democrat, and William Gwin as its first two senators. By a random draw of straws, Frémont won the shorter senate term. In Washington, he supported bills that would lock in Mexican land grants, including his own, and prevent foreign miners from owning gold claims. His term lasted 175 days, to March 3, 1851, and he lost reelection to pro-slavery John B. Weller. Although known as an abolitionist and officer in the Union Army, upon his arrival in California, Frémont participated in brutal Indian massacres. For this role, see Benjamin Madley, *An American Genocide: The United States and the California Indian Catastrophe, 1846–1873* (New Haven: Yale University Press, 2016), 42–69.

2. Edward E. Baptist, "'Stol and Fetched Here': Enslaved Migration, Ex-Slave

Narratives and Vernacular History," in *New Studies in the History of American Slavery*, ed. Edward E. Baptist and Stephanie M. H. Camp (Athens: University of Georgia Press, 2006), 244–48. Rereading the WPA narratives and focusing on migrations to Texas, Baptist describes the forced migrations of people compelled to travel with their owners during eras of territorial expansion to the Old Southwest.

3. *Syer v. Gwin*, 2 Cal. Dist. Ct. 55 (1857).

4. *Syer v. Gwin*, 2 Cal. Dist. Ct. 55 (1857); Henry J. Labatt, *Reports of Cases Determined in the District Courts of the State of California* (San Francisco: Bancroft; Whitton, Towne, 1857), 55–57; 56 *District Court Reports; Marysville Daily Herald*, October 21, 1857; "Services by Slaves Brought into a Free State," *Daily Evening Bulletin* (San Francisco), December 21, 1857. See Leonard L. Richards, *The California Gold Rush and the Coming of the Civil War* (New York: Alfred A. Knopf, 2007), for the role of Gwin and the origins of southern control of the legislature. See also Gerald Stanley, "Senator William Gwin: Moderate or Racist?," *California Historical Quarterly* 50, no. 3 (September 1971): 243–55.

5. William J. Cooper, *Jefferson Davis, American* (New York: Knopf Doubleday, 2000), 257.

6. Rudolph Lapp, *Blacks in Gold Rush California* (New Haven: Yale University Press, 1995), 8–9, citing San Jose, California Archives, and Bancroft Library, University of California, Berkeley.

7. Andrea G. McDowell, "From Commons to Claims: Property Rights in the California Gold Rush," *Yale Journal of Law and the Humanities* 14, no. 1 (January 2002) 1–72. McDowell cites General Persifor F. Smith, who wrote on April 19 that he could not even find a copy of the laws of the United States in California. See California and New Mexico, Cong. Doc. Ser. 573, S. Exec. Doc. No. 18, H. Exec. Doc. No. 17, 31st Cong., 1st sess. (1850), 698.

8. Charles J. Hughes, "The Evolution of Mining Law," *Twenty-Fourth Annual Meeting of the American Bar Association* (1901): 332–34.

9. Robert V. Hine and John Mack Faragher, *The American West: A New Interpretive History* (New Haven: Yale University Press, 2000), 235–38.

10. H. W. Brands, *The Age of Gold: The California Gold Rush and the New American Dream* (New York: Anchor, 2002), 48–53.

11. Susan L. Johnson, *Roaring Camp: The Social World of the California Gold Rush* (New York: Norton, 2000), 280, 313.

12. "Gold Rush and Shattered Dreams," ACLU of Northern California, https://www.aclunc.org/sites/goldchains/explore/gold-rush.html.

13. *Louisville (Kentucky) Daily Journal*, May 9, 1849.

14. Cited in Stillson, *Spreading the Word*, 34; *Jackson Mississippian*, October 26, 1849, quoted in Richard T. Stillson, *Spreading the Word: A History of Information in the California Gold Rush* (Lincoln: University Nebraska Press, 2006), 34.

15. Stillson, *Spreading the Word*, 34n25.

16. Stacey L. Smith, *Freedom's Frontier: California and the Struggle over Unfree Labor, Emancipation, and Reconstruction* (Chapel Hill: University of North Carolina Press, 2013), 41.

17. Ralph Bieber, ed., *Southern Trails of California in 1849* (Glendale, CA: Arthur H. Clark, 1937), 334.

18. Eugene Berwanger, "The Black Law Question in Ante-Bellum California," *Journal of the West* 6, no. 2 (April 1967): 205–20. See Jacob Stover, "The Jacob Y. Stover Narrative: History of the Sacramento Mining Company of 1849," ed. John Walton Caughey, *Pacific Historical Review* 6, no. 2 (June 1937): 177, for description of free Black vintners at Pokomongo, or "Negro Ranch."

19. John David Borthwick, *Three Years in California (1851–1854)* (Edinburgh: W. Blackwood, 1857), 163–64, 215.

20. Borthwick, *Three Years in California*, 164–65.

21. Paul Finkelman, "The Law of Slavery and Freedom in California," *California Western Law Review* 17 (1981): 440.

22. For a description of transporting enslaved Blacks across the plains, see J. Watt Gibson, *Recollections of a Pioneer* (St. Joseph, MO: Nelson-Hanne, 1912).

23. B. Gordon Wheeler, *Black California: The History of African Americans in the Golden State* (New York: Hippocrene, 1992), 62; E. F. Taylor et al., "California Free Papers," *Journal of Negro History* 3, no. 1 (January 1918): 47–48.

24. See Eric Foner, "The Idea of Free Labor in Nineteenth Century America," preface to *Free Soil, Free Labor, Free Men: The Ideology of the Republican Party before the Civil War* (New York: Oxford University Press, 1995), ix–xxxix.

25. Foner, "Idea of Free Labor," ix–xxxix.

26. Molson and Blansett, *Torturous Road to Freedom*. See also Jeannette Molson, "Alvin Aaron Coffey, Sr.," Black Past, https://www.blackpast.org/african-american-history/coffey-alvin-aaron-1822–1902/. There are a few copies of California manumission papers extant in museums and county and state archives. "Alvin Coffey's manumission papers," El Dorado County Record Book, 1852, A545, El Dorado County Historical Museum. See also Alex Long's deed of manumission, executed in El Dorado County on March 2, 1852, three years after California entered the union as a free state. Long, "free of any claims of servitude," was fifty-seven years old; he spent his final years in a mental institution.

27. Lapp, *Blacks in Gold Rush California*, 31.

28. Smith, *Freedom's Frontier*, 41. See her note in chap. 1, 74, 75.

29. Johnson, *Roaring Camp*, 188–93.

30. Walter Colton was editor of the *American Spectator*, appointed *alcalde* of Monterey, launched the state's first newspaper, the *Californian*, and built Colton Hall, where California's Constitutional Convention was held. Walter Colton, *Three Years in California* (New York: A. S. Barnes, 1850), 374–75.

31. Daniel B. Woods, *Sixteen Months at the Gold Diggings* (New York: Harper and Brothers, 1851), 155.

32. Among the vast literature on free and wage labor, I was particularly influenced by the classic essays: Foner, "Idea of Free Labor," xxiv; Sean Wilentz, "The Rise of the American Working Class, 1776–1877"; and Alice Kessler-Harris, "A New Agenda for American Labor History: A Gendered Analysis and the Question of Class," in *Perspectives on American Labor History, The Problems of Synthesis*, ed. J. Carroll Moody and Alice Kessler Harris (DeKalb: Northern Illinois University Press, 1989), 55–79, 217–34.

33. Frederick Douglass, *North Star*, November 30, 1849.

34. Allen B. Sherman and Edwin A. Sherman, "Sherman Was There: The Recollections of Major Edwin A. Sherman," *California Historical Society Quarterly* 23, no. 4 (December 1944): 350–52; Lapp, *Blacks in Gold Rush California*, 76; Smith, *Freedom's Frontier*, 47–48, 86; Berwanger, "Black Law Question," 207.

35. Delilah Beasley, *The Negro Trail Blazers of California*, repr. of author's ed. (1919; repr., New York: MacMillan, 1997), 84.

36. Rámon Gil Navarro, *The Gold Rush Diary of Rámon Gil Navarro*, ed. and trans. Maria del Carmen Ferreyra and David S. Reher (Lincoln: University of Nebraska Press, 2000), 94, 126.

37. *Liberator*, June 29, 1849.

38. Lapp, *Blacks in Gold Rush California*, 49.

39. Lapp, *Blacks in Gold Rush California*, 59, 64n37, quoted in James Hutchings' Diary, Bancroft Library, University of California, Berkeley.

40. Paul W. Gates, *Land Policies in Kern County* (Bakersfield, CA: Kern County Historical Society, 1978).

41. Nancy J. Olmsted, "The Golden Era, 1848–1853," Found SF, http://www.foundsf.org/index.php?title=The_Golden_Era,_1848-1853. See Elizabeth Parker and James Abajian, *A Walking Tour of the Black Presence in San Francisco during the Nineteenth Century* (San Francisco: San Francisco African American Historical and Cultural Society, 1974).

42. Sylvia Roberts, *Mining for Freedom: Black History Meets the California Gold Rush* (Bloomington, IN: iUniverse, 2008), 100.

43. Quoted in Carey McWilliams, *California: The Great Exception* (Berkeley: University of California Press, 1949), 42. See Dr. Gayle Olson-Raymer, "History 383," GOR History, http://users.humboldt.edu/ogayle/hist383/GoldRush.html.

44. Berwanger, "Black Law Question," 209.

45. *The Californian*, March 18, 1848. See Taylor, *In Search of the Racial Frontier*, 77–80; Berwanger, "Black Law Question," n110, from San Francisco *Californian*, March 5, 1849; *California Star*, March 25, 1848.

46. *California Star*, March 25, 1848.

47. John Ross Browne, *Report of the Debates in the Convention of California, on the Formation of the State Constitution, in September and October 1849* (Washington, DC: J. T. Towers, 1850), 144, 333.

48. *Daily Alta California*, October 15, 1850.

49. Browne, *Report of the Debates*, 144, 333.
50. Browne, *Report of the Debates*, app., xxi–xxii.
51. William Henry Ellison, "The Movement for State Division in California, 1849–1860," *Southwestern Historical Quarterly* 17, no. 2 (1913): 112.
52. Kevin Starr, *California: A History* (New York: Modern Library, 2007), 95–99.
53. J. W. C. Pennington, George Downing, Charles Lenox Remond, Henry Bibb et al., "Great Anti-Colonization Mass Meeting of the Colored Citizens of New York," *National Anti-Slavery Standard*, May 3, 1849.
54. Hine and Faragher, *American West*, 238.
55. Edlie L. Wong, *Neither Fugitive nor Free: Atlantic Slavery, Freedom Suits, and the Legal Culture of Travel* (New York: New York University Press, 2009). For previous interpretation of James Williams, see also Smith, *Freedom's Frontier*, 55–65. See Ira Berlin, *Many Thousands Gone: The First Two Centuries of Slavery in North America* (Cambridge, MA: Harvard University Press, 1998), 52–53, 236–37, 282–83.
56. Johnson, *Roaring Camp*, 190; Smith, *Freedom's Frontier*, 52–54.
57. Reuben Knox, *A Medic Fortyniner: Life and Letters of Reuben Knox*, ed. Charles W. Turner (Verona, VA: McClure, 1974), 69. See Smith, *Freedom's Frontier*, 42, 45.
58. "Peter Brown to Mrs. Ally Brown," St. Genevieve City, MO, December 1, 1851, P. Brown, Amoureux-Bolduc Papers, Missouri Historical Society, St. Louis, cited in Taylor, *In Search of the Racial Frontier*, 18. Taylor, *In Search of the Racial Frontier*, 84.
59. Johnson, *Roaring Camp*, 69, 115, 190; Beasley, *Negro Trail Blazers*, 84. Also quoted in Robert F. Heizer and Alan F. Almquist, *The Other Californians: Prejudice and Discrimination under Spain, Mexico, and the United States to 1920* (Berkeley: University of California Press, 1977), 126.

Chapter Six. Contending Forces

1. *Voice of the Fugitive*, February 12, 1851.
2. David Brion Davis, *The Problem of Slavery in the Age of Emancipation* (New York: Vintage, 2015), 252.
3. For an astute analysis of the global implications of Henry Clay's proposals, see Steven Hahn, *A Nation without Borders: The United States and Its World in an Age of Civil Wars, 1830–1910* (New York: Viking, 2016), 150–52. Henry Louis Gates, Jr., "Slavery, by the Numbers," The Root, February 10, 2014, https://www.theroot.com/slavery-by-the-numbers-1790874492; Jenny Bourne, "Slavery in the United States," EH.Net Encyclopedia, ed. Robert Whaplers, March 26, 2008, https://eh.net/encyclopedia/slavery-in-the-united-states/, provides a clear survey of the debates about the economics of slavery put forward by preeminent scholars and argues strongly for the profitability of slavery, generally at least a 10 percent return on an investment.

4. See Hahn, *Nation without Borders*, 146–52; Manisha Sinha, *The Slave's Cause: A History of Abolition* (New Haven: Yale University Press, 2016), 490–99.

5. An Ordinance for the Government of the Territory of the United States North-West of the River Ohio; the Northwest Ordinance was passed on July 13, 1787, Article VI.

6. David W. Blight, *Frederick Douglass: Prophet of Freedom* (New York: Simon and Schuster, 2018), 234–36, 240–43, traces Douglass's fear and rage at the Fugitive Slave Act and a shift in his thinking about "righteous violence."

7. Statutes of California (1852), 67–68; Fugitive Slave Act of 1850 § 4, 5, 6, 7. Gary Gallagher, "Taking Stock of the Nation," in *America on the Eve of the Civil War*, ed. Edward L. Ayers and Carolyn R. Martin (Charlottesville: University of Virginia Press, 2010), 21; "Fugitive Slave Act 1850," National Center for Public Policy Research, http://www.nationalcenter.org/FugitiveSlave Act.html. The national Fugitive Slave Act of 1850 explicitly extended to territories as well as states. No Black person had the right to testify or the right to a defense: "In no trial or hearing . . . shall the testimony of the alleged fugitive be admitted into evidence" (Fugitive Slave Act of 1850 § 6). It followed that alleged fugitives did not have the right to a jury trial.

8. Benjamin Hayes, "Scrap Book, I," 28, in Hon. Benjamin Hayes Papers, BANC MSS C-B 82, Bancroft Library, University of California, Berkeley; Rudolph M. Lapp, *Blacks in Gold Rush California* (New Haven: Yale University Press, 1995), 135. For cases, also see *San Francisco Herald*, April 1 and 2, 1851.

9. Lapp, *Blacks in Gold Rush California*, 134.

10. See Leonard L. Richards, *The California Gold Rush, and the Coming of the Civil War* (New York: Alfred A. Knopf, 2007), for the role of Gwin and the origins of southern control of the legislature.

11. Peter Burnett, "First Annual Message of the Governor of the State of California," *Daily Alta California*, December 26, 1849.

12. Lucile Eaves, *A History of California Labor Legislation* (Berkeley: University of California Press, 1910), 89.

13. Donna R. Mooney, "The Search for a Legal Presumption of Employment Duration or Custom of Arbitrary Dismissal in California, 1848–1872," *Berkeley Journal of Employment and Labor Law* 21, no. 2 (2000): 7–8, 51. For recent discussions, see Benjamin Madley, *An American Genocide: The United States and the California Indian Catastrophe, 1846–1873* (New Haven: Yale University Press, 2016); Andrés Reséndez, *The Other Slavery: The Uncovered Story of Indian Enslavement in America* (New York: Houghton Mifflin Harcourt, 2016).

14. *Journal of the House of the State of California* (1850): 1223, 1232; *Journal of the Senate of the State of California* (1850): 337, 357.

15. Saidiya Hartman, *Scenes of Subjection: Terror, Slavery, and Self-Making in Nineteenth-Century America* (New York: Oxford University Press, 1997), 7–8.

Also quoted in Edlie L. Wong, *Neither Fugitive nor Free: Atlantic Slavery, Freedom Suits, and the Legal Culture of Travel* (New York: New York University Press, 2009), 4.

16. Eaves, *History of California Labor Legislation*, 91; see also *San Francisco Herald*, April 16, 1852. See also the *Pacific Appeal*, April 23, 1852, n29.

17. Eaves, *History of California Labor Legislation*, 91; *Pacific Appeal*, March 12 and April 23, 1852.

18. Eaves, *History of California Labor Legislation*, 92; *Daily Eve Picayune*, February 11, 1852, n32.

19. "What Does It Mean?" *Daily Alta California*, May 4, 1850.

20. E. F. Taylor et al. "California Free Papers," *Journal of Negro History* 3, no. 1 (January 1918): 46. This was signed "*S. A. Grantham, his heirs, and Executors . . . forever.*"

21. *Sacramento Daily Union*, October 30, 1851.

22. Cited in Lapp, *Blacks in Gold Rush California*, 137. *Pennsylvania Freeman*, December 5, 1850.

23. *Voice of the Fugitive*, December 3, 1851.

24. *Voice of the Fugitive*, February 12, 1851.

25. *California Gazette*, November 29, 1851.

26. "American Experience: The Gold Rush," aired November 6, 2006, on PBS, http://www.pbs.org/wgbh/americanexperience/films/goldrush/.

27. Carl Meyer, *Bound for Sacramento: Travel-Pictures of a Returned Wanderer*, trans. Ruth Frey Axe (Claremont, CA: Saunders Studio, 1938), 144.

28. In nineteenth-century journalism, "inst" refers to the current month.

29. *Sacramento Daily Union*, July 6 and July 10, 1855.

30. *Weekly Pacific News*, April 4 and April 15, 1851.

31. *Daily Alta California*, March 31, April 1, and April 2, 1851; *Weekly Public News* (San Francisco), April 1, 1851; "J. B. Pierce to William Lloyd Garrison," published in the *Liberator*, May 9, 1851; *San Francisco Herald*, April 1, 1851; Lapp, *Blacks in Gold Rush California*, 138–39; Stacey L. Smith, *Freedom's Frontier: California and the Struggle over Unfree Labor, Emancipation, and Reconstruction* (Chapel Hill: University of North Carolina Press, 2015), 66–67.

32. *Daily Alta California*, March 31, April 1, and April 2, 1851; *Weekly Public News* (San Francisco), April 1, 1851; "J. B. Pierce to William Lloyd Garrison," in Lapp, *Blacks in Gold Rush California*, 138–39; Smith, *Freedom's Frontier*, 66–67.

33. *Daily Alta California*, December 1, 1850; "Fugitive Slave Act 1850." The national Fugitive Slave Act of 1850 applied to territories as well as states. Congress voted down pleas that the language permit trial by jury and reinstate habeas corpus. It allowed masters, upon "satisfactory proof being made," to "take and remove such fugitives from service or labor [back] to the state or territory from which such persons may have escaped or fled" (Fugitive Slave Act of 1850 § 4). If a slave escaped from a federal marshal who was pursuing him, the marshal was liable for the full value of the slave (Fugitive Slave Act

of 1850 § 5). Now a slave owner had the right to "pursue and reclaim . . . and arrest a slave" without a warrant. Indeed, all that was needed was an affidavit by a master that he had the authority to claim a person's "service or labor." No Black person had the right to testify or the right to a defense—"In no trial or hearing . . . shall the testimony of the alleged fugitive be admitted into evidence." And it followed that an alleged fugitive did not have the right to a jury trial (Fugitive Slave Act of 1850 § 6). And most precarious, any person who hindered a slave owner or his agent "from arresting a fugitive slave, or any person who aided or assisted" a fugitive slave or "harbored or concealed" a fugitive slave could be fined up to $1,000 and imprisoned for up to six months (Fugitive Slave Act of 1850 § 7) in a state or territory and pay civil damages to the slaveholder for $1,000 for each slave arrested.

34. "An Act Respecting Fugitives from Labor and Slaves Brought to This State Prior to Her Admission into the Union." *Statutes of California* (1852), 77. Eaves, *History of California Labor Legislation*, 94.

35. *Sacramento Weekly Union*, April 15, 1852.

36. Laws of the State of California (1852), ch. 33, 67; "An Act Respecting Fugitives from Labor, and Slaves Brought to This State Prior to Her Admission into the Union," *Daily Alta California*, June 14, 1852.

37. *California Senate Journal* (1852): 277; *San Francisco Herald*, February 8, 1852; *Sacramento Union*, April 9, 1852.

38. Jeffrey Rogers Hummel and Barry R. Weingast, "The Fugitive Slave Act of 1850: Symbolic Gesture or Rational Guarantee," *SSRN Electronic Journal* (January 2006): 1–40.

39. *Daily Alta California*, December 1, 14, 25, and 31, 1850.

40. Fugitive Slave Act of 1850 § 10.

41. *Daily Alta California*, December 1, 1850.

42. "Fugitive Slave Case," *Daily Alta California*, April 22, 1855; Lynn M. Hudson, *The Making of "Mammy Pleasant": A Black Entrepreneur in Nineteenth-Century San Francisco* (Urbana: University of Illinois Press, 2003), 37n96. Mary Ellen Pleasant's papers are at the Bancroft Library, University of California, Berkeley, among other places.

43. Lapp, *Blacks in Gold Rush California*, 147.

44. *Daily Alta California*, April 7, 22, and 23, 1855; *Sacramento Daily Union*, April 25, 1855; Hudson, *Making of "Mammy Pleasant."* Delilah Beasley, quoting the California legislative reports, wrote of several such cases: "Daniel Rodgers came across the plains with his master from Little Rock, Arkansas, worked in the mines in Sonora, California, during the day for his master and at night for himself, earning and paying his master $1,100 for his freedom. Soon afterward the master returned with him to Little Rock and sold him. A number of the leading white gentlemen of Little Rock raised a sum of money, paid for his freedom, and set him free. William Pollock and his wife from North Carolina came to California with their master who settled at Cold Springs,

Coloma, California. He paid $1,000 for himself and $800, for his wife. The money was earned by washing for the miners at night and making doughnuts. They removed to Placerville, California, and afterward earned their living as caterers. In 1849 a slaveholder brought his slave to California. Not wishing to take the Negro back to his native State, Alabama, he concluded to sell him by auction. An advertisement was put in the papers, the boy was purchased for $1,000, by Caleb T. Fay, a strong abolitionist, who gave the boy his freedom. A Mississippi slaveholder brought several slaves from that State and promised to give them their freedom in two years. They all ran away save one, Charles Bates, when they learned that they were already free. The owner, finding mining did not pay, started east, taking Charles with him. On the Isthmus of Panama, Charles was persuaded to leave his master. He returned to California and to Stockton with his true friend. On the street one day he was recognized by a party who had lent money to Charles's master. The debtor got out an attachment for the former slave as chattel property, and according to the state law, the Negro was put up and sold at auction. A number of anti-slavery men bought the boy for $750 and gave him his freedom." *California Reports*, 1:424–42, 6. See Delilah L. Beasley, "Slavery in California," *Journal of Negro History* 3, no. 1 (January 1918): 33–44.

45. H. Robert Baker, "The Fugitive Slave Clause and the Antebellum Constitution," *Law and History Review* 30, no. 4 (2012): 1163. Congress voted down pleas that the language permit trial by jury and reinstate habeas corpus.

46. Peter Lester, "Letter from California," *Pennsylvania Freeman*, December 5, 1850. Written from San Francisco, October 13, 1850; biographical information also from "Peter Lester to William Still," November 30, 1859, published in *Weekly Anglo-African* (New York), May 12, 1860. Lapp, *Blacks in Gold Rush California*, 137 and n28.

47. Wong, *Neither Fugitive nor Free*. For previous interpretation of James Williams, see also Smith, *Freedom's Frontier*, 55–65. See Ira Berlin, *Many Thousands Gone: The First Two Centuries of Slavery in North America* (Cambridge, MA: Belknap Press of Harvard University Press, 2000), 52–53, 236–37, 282–83.

48. Edwin Franklin Morse, *The Story of a Gold Miner: Reminiscences of Edwin Franklin Morse* (dictated to his daughter, Mary Phipps Morse), *California Historical Society Quarterly* 6, no. 3 (September 1927): 223.

49. Lapp, *Blacks in Gold Rush California*, 140.

50. *Liberator*, August 30, 1850; *New York Journal of Commerce*, 1850. See also Lapp, *Blacks in Gold Rush California*, 136. For discussion of the Underground Railroad in the West outside of California, see William Loren Katz, *The Black West: A Documentary and Pictorial History* (New York: Anchor, 1973), 97–106. Thomas D. Morris, "Slaves and Rules of Evidence in Criminal Trials," in *Slavery and the Law*, ed. Paul Finkelman (Lanham, MD: Rowman and Littlefield, 2001), 211.

51. *National Era*, July 11, 1850.

52. Frederick Law Olmsted, *Journey and Explorations in the Cotton Kingdom: A Traveler's Observations on Cotton and Slavery in the American Slave States* (London: Sampson Low, 1861), 136.

53. Eaves, *History of California Labor Legislation*, 98n49; Hayes, "Scrap Book, I," no. 28.

54. "A Kidnapping Case," *California Christian Advocate*, May 20, 1852.

55. See the Colored Conventions Project, www.coloredconventions.org.

56. See James Williams, *Fugitive Slave in the Gold Rush: Life and Adventures of James Williams* (Lincoln: University of Nebraska Press, 2002), 26–28.

57. Williams, *Fugitive Slave in the Gold Rush*; Wong, *Neither Fugitive nor Free*; Smith, *Freedom's Frontier*, 55–65. For an important compendium of information on particular free and enslaved Blacks in California in the 1850s, see Guy Washington, "California Pioneers of African Descent," *National Park Service*, December 2010, available at the library of the California Historical Society, San Francisco.

58. *National Era*, May 2, 1850, quoting a letter from Jeter T. Thompson published in the *Cherokee Advocate*.

59. "High Price of Negroes," *Fayetteville Weekly Observer*, December 15, 1856.

60. Walter Johnson, "Taking Stock of the Nation," in *America on the Eve of the Civil War*, ed. Edward L. Ayers and Carolyn R. Martin (Charlottesville: University of Virginia Press, 2010), 17–18.

61. Johnson, "Taking Stock of the Nation," 18.

62. "Slavery Propagandists," *Daily Alta California*, March 1, 1852.

63. "Albert McDowell to Charles McDowell and Mrs. McDowell," April 25, 1853; July 13, 1854; May 13, 1855, BANC 93/59c, Bancroft Library, University of California, Berkeley.

64. "Andrew Jackson to Sarah Trigg," October 19, 1851, Wyles MSS 75, Slave Documents Folder 32 Jackson, A. 1 ALS, October 19, 1851 (misidentified 1837 and 1851), William Wyles Manuscript Collection, University of California at Santa Barbara.

65. "Francis Abner to Frederick Douglass," November 13, 1851, Frederick Douglass Papers, Black Abolitionist Papers, University of Michigan, Ann Arbor, 7715.

66. "Francis Abner to Frederick Douglass," April 17, 1852, Black Abolitionist Papers, University of Michigan, Ann Arbor, 12790, 7696.

67. Mifflin Wistar Gibbs, *Shadow and Light: An Autobiography with Reminiscences of the Last and Present Century* (Washington, DC, 1902), 46–47.

68. Rudolph M. Lapp, "Slavery and the Fugitive Slave in California," in *Blacks in Gold Rush California*, 126–57.

69. *In re Perkins* 2 Cal. 424 (Cal. 1852) and *In re Perkins*, 2 Cal. 438 (1852). See also *Dred Scott v. Sandford*, 60 U.S. 393 (1857).

70. *In re Perkins*, 2 Cal. 438 (1852). For a discussion of Justice Anderson's concurrence, see Eaves, *History of California Labor Legislation*, 97.

71. *In re Perkins*, Cal. 424, 455 (1852) (Anderson, J. concurring). Paul Finkelman, "The Law of Slavery and Freedom in California," *California Western Law Review* 17 (1981): 444.

72. *In re Perkins;* George Henry Tinkham, *A History of Stockton from Its Organization Up to the Present Time* (San Francisco: W. M. Hinton, 1880), 128; Harry L. Wells, Frank T. Gilbert, and W. L. Chambers, *History of Butte County, California in Two Volumes* (San Francisco, 1882), 199; *Sacramento Daily Union*, June 15, 1852; *San Francisco Herald*, June 19, 1852; *San Francisco Herald*, June 12, 1852; *New York Times*, September 1, 1852.

73. Finkelman, "Slavery and Freedom," 444; *In re Perkins*, Cal. 424, 455 (1852) (Anderson, J. concurring); Tinkham, *History of Stockton*, 128; Wells, Gilbert, and Chambers, *History of Butte County*, 119.

74. Wong, *Neither Fugitive nor Free*, quoting Hartman, *Scenes of Subjection*, 7–8.

75. Wong, *Neither Fugitive nor Free*, 4, quoting James Kent, *Commentaries on American Law, 1826–1830*, 11th ed., ed. George F. Comstock (Boston: Little, Brown, 1866), 2:285–88n56.

76. Baker, "Fugitive Slave Clause," 1134–36, addresses Paul Finkelman's argument that the Fugitive Slave Act of 1793 exposed that a slaveholder held decisive political influence. Baker challenges this view of judicial supremacy and turns to a broader field of local courts and state legislatures that involved local compromises and the evolution of constitutional views on slavery.

77. Monroe Lee Billington and Roger D. Hardaway, eds., *African Americans on the Western Frontier* (Boulder: University Press of Colorado, 2001), 20.

78. State of California, County of Los Angeles, In the matter of Hanna et al., "California Free Papers," *Journal of Negro History* 3, no. 1 (January 1918): 47–48; Shirley Anne Wilson Moore, "We Feel the Want of Protection," in *Taming the Elephant: Politics, Government, and Law in Pioneer California*, ed. John F. Burns and Richard J. Orsi (Berkeley: University of California Press, 2003), 109; Eaves, *History of California Labor Legislation*, 9; Hayes, "Scrap Book, I," 519 Jean Kinney Williams, *Bridget "Biddy" Mason: From Slave to Businesswoman* (Minneapolis: Compass Point, 2006).

79. Quoted in James Oliver Horton and Lois E. Horton, *Slavery and the Making of America* (New York: Oxford University Press), 193.

Chapter Seven. Indian Slavery in a Free State

Epigraph: *People v. La Komopaw and Mompet*, Contra Costa County (June 1850).

1. Sherburne F. Cook, "Expeditions to the Interior of California: Central Valley, 1820–1840," *UC Anthropological Records* 20, no. 5 (1962): 197–98, 151–214. See also Manuel P. Servín, "The Secularization of the California Missions: A Reappraisal," *Southern California Quarterly* 47, no. 2 (June 1965): 133–49; and "Decree for the Secularisation of the Missions of the Californias" (1833).

2. Chapters 7, 8, and 9 have been influenced by the presentations and conversations at the "Indigenous Enslavement and Incarceration in North America International" conference, Gilder Lehrman Center, Yale University, New Haven, November 15–16, 2013. I am particularly grateful to the papers and discussions with the Honorable Justice Murray Sinclair, chair of the Truth and Reconciliation Commission of Canada; Dennis Banks, founder of the American Indian Movement; and Howard Sapers, correctional investigator for Canada; and the presentations and foundational research of David W. Blight, Ned Blackhawk, Lisa Brooks, Christina DeLucia, Robbie Ethridge, John Mack Faragher, Margaret Jacobs, Tsianina Lomawaima, Tiya Miles, Khalil Gibran Muhammad, Beth Piatote, Rachel Purvis, Debbie Reese, and Fay Yarbrough.

3. Cook, "Expeditions to the Interior of California," 197–98, 151–214. Cook suggests that while true, aspects of Amador's narrative, recalled in his later years, may be somewhat exaggerated: "I suspect that our friend Amador murdered a number of Christian Indians on his own initiative and concocted this tale of 'justice' to cover his tracks"; Cook, "Expeditions to the Interior of California," 209. See also Gregorio Mora-Torres, trans. and ed., *Californio Voices: The Oral Memoirs of José María Amador and Lorenzo Asisara* (Denton: University of North Texas Press, 2005).

4. *Johnson v. McIntosh*, 21 U.S. (8 Wheat.) 543 (1823), which held that a European power gains radical title (also known as sovereignty) to the land it discovers. As a corollary, the "discovering" power gains the exclusive right to extinguish the "right of occupancy" of the Indigenous occupants, which otherwise survived the assumption of sovereignty.

5. "The Treaty of New Echota and the Trail of Tears," NC Department of Natural and Cultural Resources, https://www.ncdcr.gov/blog/2015/12/29/the -treaty-of-new-echota-and-the-trail-of-tears.

6. David Blight, "Expansion and Slavery: Legacies of the Mexican War and the Compromise of 1850," video lecture, Yale University, New Haven, 2008.

7. By turning attention to the labor of California Indians, Albert L. Hurtado addresses the paradox of genocide and slavery, particularly in "California Indians and the Workaday West: Labor, Assimilation, and Survival," *California History* 69, no. 1 (Spring 1990): 2–11.

8. Richard Steven Street, *Beasts of the Field: A Narrative History of California Farmworkers, 1769–1913* (Stanford, CA: Stanford University Press, 2004), 99, 101, 110, 141–42.

9. See Benjamin Madley, *An American Genocide: The United States and the California Indian Catastrophe, 1846–1873* (New Haven: Yale University Press, 2016), 230 and passim, for well-documented population figures for California Natives and detailed impacts of the genocides and forced removal.

10. "Early Statehood: Slavery," Texas State Library and Archives Commission, https://www.tsl.texas.gov/treasures/earlystate/slavery-01.html.

11. Madley, *American Genocide*, 3, 36; Sherburne Cook, *The Conflict between the California Indian and White Civilization*, vol. 3, *The American Invasion, 1848–1870* (Berkeley: University of California Press, 1943), 3; James J. Rawls, *Indians of California: The Changing Image* (Norman: University of Oklahoma Press, 1984), 6, 171; Tomás Almaguer, *Racial Fault Lines: The Historical Origins of White Supremacy in California* (Berkeley: University of California Press, 1994), 109; Walter L. Hixson, *American Settler Colonialism: A History* (New York: Palgrave-MacMillan, 2013), 123. These numbers are never identical between scholars, and I have relied on respected scholars in the field who turn to these statistics.

12. For scholarly discussions, I have turned to the foundational work of Tomás Almaguer, *Racial Fault Lines*. Benjamin Madley, "'Unholy Traffic in Human Blood and Souls': Systems of California Indian Servitude under U.S. Rule," *Pacific Historical Review* 83, no. 4 (November 2014): 626–67; Michael Magliari, "Free Soil, Unfree Labor: Cave Johnson Couts and the Binding of Indian Workers in California, 1850–1867," *Pacific Historical Review* 73, no. 3 (August 2004): 349–90; Howard Lamar, "From Bondage to Contract: Ethnic Labor in the American West, 1660–1890," in *The Countryside in the Age of Capitalist Transformation: Essays in the Social History of Rural America*, ed. Steven Hahn and Jonathan Prude (Chapel Hill: University of North Carolina Press, 1985), 293–324; Cook, *Conflict*, 48–62; Robert F. Heizer and Alan F. Almquist, *The Other Californians: Prejudice and Discrimination under Spain, Mexico, and the United States to 1920* (Berkeley: University of California Press, 1971); Stacey L. Smith, *Freedom's Frontier: California and the Struggle over Unfree Labor, Emancipation, and Reconstruction* (Chapel Hill: University of North Carolina Press, 2013).

13. Albert L. Hurtado, *John Sutter: A Life on the North American Frontier* (Norman: University of Oklahoma Press, 2006), 48–49.

14. Hurtado, *John Sutter*, 76; George Harwood Phillips, *Indians and Indian Agents: The Origins of the Reservation System in California, 1849–1852* (Norman: University of Oklahoma Press, 1997), 32–33; Michael Gillis and Michael Magliari, *John Bidwell and California: The Life and Writings of a Pioneer, 1841–1900* (Spokane, WA: Arthur Clarke, 2003).

15. Albert Hurtado, *Indian Survival on the California Frontier* (New Haven: Yale University Press, 1988), 90–91.

16. "The Indians Again," *California Star*, July 24, 1847.

17. Hurtado, "California Indians and the Workaday West," 5.

18. George Harwood Phillips, *Indians and Intruders in Central California, 1769–1849* (Norman: University of Oklahoma Press, 1993), 119.

19. Thomas L. Scott, "9 of the Biggest Slave Owners in American History," *Atlanta Black Star*, December 23, 2014.

20. "Sutter to Henley," February 9, 1856, quoted in Street, *Beasts of the Field*, 143.

21. Hurtado, *John Sutter*, 76; Hurtado, *Indian Survival*, 57.

22. Cited in Hurtado, "California Indians and the Workaday West," from Sutter to Pierson B. Reading, May 11, 1845. Reading Collection, California Room, State Library, Sacramento.
23. Hurtado, *John Sutter*, 80.
24. James Clyman and Charles L. Camp, "James Clyman: His Diaries and Reminiscences," *California Historical Society Quarterly* 5, no. 2 (June 1926): 129.
25. Hurtado, *Indian Survival*, 58.
26. Hurtado, *John Sutter*, 65.
27. Hurtado, *John Sutter*, 78; Hurtado, *Indian Survival*, 63.
28. Hurtado, *Indian Survival*, 60, 61.
29. Hurtado, *Indian Survival*, 60, 61, 62; Hixson, *American Settler Colonialism*, 25.
30. John Drake Sloat commanded the Pacific Squadron that landed in Monterey and raised the flag at the Customs House. On July 7, 1846, Sloat proclaimed that California was part of the United States. Montgomery raised the U.S. flag in San Francisco, then Yerba Buena two days later.
31. John B. Montgomery, commandant of the Northern Department of California, "The Indians," *Californian* (Monterey), November 7, 1846.
32. Madley, *American Genocide*, 42–49 and passim.
33. "An Ordinance Respecting the Employment of Indians," *Californian*, January–March 1847. See also Madley, *American Genocide*, 147, 580n4. In 1836 California's Mexican governor, Chico, ordered that "every Indian found away from his residence without license from the alcalde . . . or missionary, should be arrested and sentenced to labor on the public works."
34. An Act to Prohibit the Coming of Chinese Persons into the United States (1892), 27, Stat. 25.
35. John B. Montgomery, "Proclamation to the Inhabitants of the Northern District of California," in "Apprenticing Indians," *Sacramento Daily Union*, July 31, 1860.
36. Edwin Bryant, *What I Saw in California: Being the Journal of a Tour, by the Emigrant Route . . . in the Years 1846, 1847* (New York: D. Appleton, 1848).
37. Helen Carpenter, *Ukiah Republican Press*, April 2, 1897; Linda Pitelka, "Mendocino: Race Relations in a Northern California County, 1850–1949" (PhD diss., University of Massachusetts, Amherst, 1994), 294, 296–97, 302, 303; "Dept. of the Interior Office of Indian Affairs, Washington January 13, 1902," repr. in Lynette Mullen, NorCal History Blog, https://lynette707.wordpress.com/?s=Dept.+of+the+Interior+Office+of+Indian+Affairs%2C+Washington+January+13%2C+1902.
38. "George W. Harrison to Capt. Dupont, Sonoma, March 17, 1847," in *The Destruction of California Indians; a Collection of Documents . . .* , ed. Robert F. Heizer (Santa Barbara: Peregrine Smith, 1974), 6.
39. "Pierson Reading to Phillip Green," February 7, 1844, quoted in Hurtado, *Indian Survival*, 75.
40. *New York Herald*, August 19, 1848.

41. "Grand Jury Presentment on Kidnapping," December 13, 1852, Contra Costa County Historical Society.

42. Madley, *American Genocide*, 107–14; Lyman L. Palmer, *History of Napa and Lake Counties, California* (San Francisco: Slocum, Bowen, 1881), 2:34, 50; William Ralganal Benson, "The Stone and Kelsey 'Massacre' on the Shores of Clear Lake in 1849: The Indian Viewpoint," *California Historical Society Quarterly* 11, no. 3 (September 1932): 266–73.

43. *The Statutes of California: Passed at the First Session of the Legislature, Begun the 15th Day of Dec. 1849, and Ended the 22d Day of April 1850, at the City of Pueblo de San José* (San Jose: J. Winchester, 1850), 408, chap. 133. For significant historical discussions of the act, see Magliari, "Free Soil, Unfree Labor," 349–58; Rawls, *Indians of California*, 86–108; Madley, *American Genocide*, 157–60; Hurtado, *Indian Survival*, 128–32.

44. Magliari, "Free Soil, Unfree Labor," 349–90.

45. This view counters that of much settler colonial analysis—for example, Patrick Wolfe, "Settler Colonialism and the Elimination of the Native," *Journal of Genocide Research* 8, no. 4 (December 2006): 388, 393, who argues that "territory is settler colonialism's specific, irreducible element," and that in California, settler colonialism was not simply a "land centered project."

46. For the ways in which this very early expression of American California's slave policy was in continuity with traditions in Hispanic California and in Latin America from the sixteenth century on, from *encomienda to hacienda*, of forcing Indians to obtain service and remain with their employers, thereby divesting them of access to live in and defend their homelands, see Rawls, *Indians of California*, 85. Discussions of this act can be found in Hurtado, *Indian Survival*, 129–31.

47. "Senator John Frémont to President Millard Fillmore," September 16, 1850, cited in Paula Giese, "California Indian Treaties—they exist (sort of)," January 23, 1997, Beaded Lizard Books, http://www.kstrom.net/isk/maps/ca/caltreaties.html.

48. Senator John B. Weller, cited in George E. Anderson, W. H. Ellison, and Robert F. Heizer, *Treaty Making and Treaty Rejection by the Federal Government in California, 1850–1852* (Socorro, NM: Ballena, 1978), 96.

49. Street, *Beasts of the Field*, 119.

50. Street, *Beasts of the Field*, 126; *Napa Register*, December 20, 1858.

51. Magliari, "Free Soil, Unfree Labor," 353; Madley, *American Genocide*, 158–59; Cook, *Conflict*, 48–49; Rawls, *Indians of California*, 86; Street, *Beasts of the Field*, 122.

52. Madley, *American Genocide*, 158, 160.

53. Evelyn Nakano Glenn, "Settler Colonialism as Structure: A Framework for Comparative Studies of U.S. Race and Gender Formation," *Sociology of Race and Ethnicity* 1, no. 1 (2015): 58–59.

54. Michel Foucault, *"Society Must Be Defended": Lectures at the College de France,*

1975–76, trans. David Macey, ed. Mauro Bertani and Allesandro Fontana (New York: Picador, 2003), 255–59.

55. Rawls, *Indians of California*, 121–26; Hubert Howe Bancroft, *The Works of Hubert Howe Bancroft*, vol. 24, *History of California* (San Francisco, 1890), 478.

56. Madley's term "disposable labor" aptly points to self-serving systems of agricultural labor that avoided notions of mutual dependency, employment, or contract. Madley, "Unholy Traffic in Human Blood and Souls," 628ff; Andrew Shaler, "Indigenous Peoples and the California Gold Rush: Labour, Violence and Contention in the Formation of a Settler Colonial State," *Postcolonial Studies* 23, no. 1 (2020): 79–98.

57. "California," in U.S. Department of Commerce, Bureau of Census, *The Seventh Census of the United States, 1850* (Washington, DC: Government Printing Office, 1853), 2.census.gov/prod2/decennial/documents/1850a-01.pdf.

58. "Squawmen" was also a racist nineteenth-century term that denoted non-Indian men married or cohabiting with American Indian women. These men were sometimes the targets of racial violence.

59. Anna Mae Duane, "'All Boys Are Bound to Someone': Reimagining Freedom in the History of Child Slavery," in *Human Bondage and Abolition: New Histories of Past and Present Slaveries*, ed. Elizabeth Swanson and James Brewer Stewart (Cambridge: Cambridge University Press, 2018), 173–89.

60. *Sacramento Daily Bee*, July 21, 1857.

61. John Bidwell to Joseph W. McCorkle, December 20, 1851, quoted in Gillis and Magliari, *John Bidwell and California*, 293–94, cited in Michael Magliari, "Free State Slavery: Bound Indian Labor and Slave Trafficking in California's Sacramento Valley, 1850–1864," *Pacific Historical Review* 81, no. 2 (May 2012): 157.

62. "Grand Jury Presentment on Kidnapping," December 13, 1852, Contra Costa County Historical Society.

63. *People v. La Komopaw and Mompet*, Contra Costa County (June 1850); J. P. Munro-Fraser, *History of Contra Costa County, California* (Los Angeles: Historical Record Company, 1926), 341; Aimee L. Arrigoni, "None of Which Requires a War to Be Defeated: Indian People of Contra Costa, 1850–1870" (master's thesis, California State University, Hayward, 2004), 67; Nilda Rego, *Days Gone by in Contra Costa County, California* (Pleasant Hill: Contra Costa County Historical Society, 1998).

64. *People v. La Komopaw and Mompet*; Munro-Fraser, *History of Contra Costa County*, 341; Arrigoni, "None of Which Requires a War to Be Defeated," 67; Rego, *Days Gone By*, 40.

65. *Daily Alta California*, October 2, 1854.

66. Hixson, *American Settler Colonialism*, 125; Cook, *Conflict*, 314–15. See also Robert F. Heizer, "Indian Servitude in California," in *Handbook of North American Indians* (Washington, DC: Smithsonian, 1978), 4:415.

67. Baptismal Register, Indian baptisms, 1850–1853, St. Mary's Church, Oakland,

CA, reproduced in Arrigoni, "None of Which Requires a War to Be Defeated," 78–80 and 90.

68. *Daily Alta California*, October 7, 1854.

69. Randall Milliken, "California Indians of the Mission San José Outreach Area," *Far Western Anthropological Research Group* (2002): 67; Arrigoni, "None of Which Requires a War to Be Defeated," 85.

70. Madley, *American Genocide*, 55–56.

71. From the *Placer Times*, quoted in *Humboldt Times*, May 5, 1855.

72. Sarah Deer, "Relocation Revisited: Sex Trafficking of Native Women in the United States," *William Mitchell Law Review* 36, no. 2, Faculty Scholarship Paper 157 (2010): 641–42.

73. "Robert White to T. J. Henley," May 15, 1855, cited in Robert F. Heizer, *The Destruction of California Indians* (Santa Barbara: Peregrine Smith, 1974), 226–27, 6:2.

74. "Robert White to T. J. Henley," August 9, 1855, cited in Heizer, *Destruction of California Indians*, 227, 6:3, 6:4.

75. Lynwood Carranco and Estle Beard, *Genocide and Vendetta: The Round Valley Wars of Northern California* (Norman: University of Oklahoma Press, 1981), 172.

76. Frank Asbill and Argle Shawley, *The Last of the West* (New York: Carlton, 1975), 34–35, 43; Pitelka, "Mendocino"; Carranco and Beard, *Genocide and Vendetta*, 172–73; Ray Raphael, *Little White Father: Redick McKee on the California Frontier* (Eureka: Humboldt County Historical Society, 1993), 7.

77. *Daily Alta California*, May 4, 1852.

78. *Daily Alta California*, January 27, 1855.

79. Robert F. Heizer, *The Eighteen Unratified Treaties of 1851–1852 between the California Indians and the United States Government* (Berkeley: Archaeological Research Facility, Department of Anthropology, University of California, 1972), 3–4.

80. From the notes taken during the treaty expedition by John McKee, Redick McKee's son, *Minutes Kept by John McKee*, 33rd Cong., Spec. sess., Senate Exec. Doc. No. 4. Serial No. 688 (Washington, DC: GPO, 1853), 137. Also see the discussion in Raphael, *Little White Father*, 41.

81. Heizer, *Eighteen Unratified Treaties*, 19.

82. Report of the Commissioner of Indian Affairs, repr. in *New York Times*, December 8, 1851.

83. See "Report of the Special Committee to Inquire into the Treaties Made by the United States Indian Commissioners in California," *California State Senate Journal* (1852), 600–604. Larisa K. Miller, "The Secret Treaties with California's Indians," *Prologue* 45 (Fall/Winter 2013): 38–39; Hurtado, *Indian Survival*, 136–41; Heizer, *Eighteen Unratified Treaties*, 22.

84. Executive Documents, 33rd Cong., Spec. sess. (1854), doc. 4, 373–74. See Rawls, *Indians of California*, 148–51. See E. F. Beale to Luke Lea, commis-

sioner of Indian Affairs, Washington, DC, November 22, 1852. S, Doc 57; 32nd Cong. 2 Sess. (1853), cited in Madley, *American Genocide*, 646n85; Heizer, *Handbook of North American Indians*, 110; John Ross Browne, "The Coast Rangers: A Chronicle of Events in California, Part 2: The Indian Reservations," *Harper's New Monthly Magazine* 23 (August 1861): 306–7. "R. N. Woods to Beale," January 13, 1853, *Sacramento Daily Union*, April 7, 1862.

85. In support of this perspective, see, for example, Cook, *Conflict*, 258.

86. "Ages of Consent in the United States: History of California Laws," Wikipedia, https://en.wikipedia.org/wiki/Ages_of_consent_in_the_United_States #History_of_California_laws.

87. Wolfe, "Settler Colonialism," 388. Cal. Compiled Laws of California, Calif. Stat., ch. 35 § 3 (1850). Hrishi Karthikeyan and Gabriel Chin, "Preserving Racial Identity: Population Patterns and the Application of Anti-Miscegenation Statutes to Asian Americans, 1910–1950," *Asian American Law Journal* 9 (2002): 1–40; Madley, *American Genocide*, 162.

88. Barbara Voss, "Domesticating Imperialism: Sexual Politics and the Archaeology of Empire," *American Anthropologist* 110, no. 2 (July 2008): 191–92, 199.

89. Major General John Wool, commander of the Pacific Department, to U.S. Senators D.C. Broderick and Wm. Gwin, January 28, 1857, 2, 4, Interior Department Appointment Papers, Held-Poage Library, Ukiah, CA. U.S. Senate, Hearings before the Committee on Indian Affairs, 6.

90. Thomas J. Henley to General George Mannypenny, commissioner of Indian Affairs, April 14, 1856, NARA M234 RG 75, Reel 35:312; and E. A. Stevenson to Thomas J. Henley, July 31, 1856, in U.S. Office of Indian Affairs, *Annual Report of the Commissioner of Indian Affairs, 1856* (Washington, DC: Government Printing Office, 1856), 251, cited in Madley, *American Genocide*, 162.

91. Deborah A. Miranda, *Bad Indians: A Tribal Memoir* (Berkeley: Heyday, 2013), 45–46.

92. Arrigoni, "None of Which Requires a War to Be Defeated," 10.

93. John Marsh, "Letter of Dr. John Marsh to Hon. Lewis Cass," *California Historical Society Quarterly* 22, no. 4 (December 1943): 315–22, repr. in "A Scrap of History," *Contra Costa Gazette*, December 21, 1867.

Chapter Eight. No Further West

Epigraph: "Cheryl Seidner and the Wiyot Tribe in Eureka, CA," interview, Paul E. Nelson, December 23, 2015, https://www.paulenelson.com/2015/12 /23/cheryl-seidner-the-wiyot-tribe-in-eureka-ca.

1. Peter Burnett, "Message to the California Legislature," *California State Senate Journal*, January 7, 1851.

2. Thomas Knight, "Statement of Early Events in California, 1879," 15–16, Bancroft Library, University of California, Berkeley, Adjutant General's Office, Old Files Division, Document No. H155/R133, 1853, cited in Robert F.

Heizer, ed., *The Destruction of California Indians* (Lincoln: University of Nebraska Press, 1993), 246–48.

3. G. W. Barbour, Redick McKee, and O. M. Wozencraft, "To the People of California," *Daily Alta California*, January 14, 1851.

4. California Legislature, *Journal of the Senate*, 3rd sess. (1852): 579–601. See James J. Rawls, *Indians of California: The Changing Image* (Norman: University of Oklahoma Press, 1984), 141–53.

5. Burnett, "Message to the California Legislature."

6. Loren Bommelyn, "Test-ch'as (The Tidal Wave)," in *Surviving through the Days, Translations of Native California Stories and Songs, A California Indian Reader*, ed. Herbert W. Luthin (Berkeley: University of California Press, 2002), 67. David G. Lewis, "Klamath River Reservation and White Privilege, 1856," Quartux, April 23, 2017, https://ndnhistoryresearch.com/2017/04/23/klamath-river-reservation-and-white-privilege-1856.

7. There are as yet few found records by California Natives who lived on reservations. I am indebted to Albert L. Hurtado, *Indian Survival on the California Frontier* (New Haven: Yale University Press, 1988), esp. 150–56, for his rigorous collection and analysis of government correspondence on California reservations. See also Edward D. Castillo, "California Indian History," State of California Native American Heritage Commission, http://nahc.ca.gov/resources/california-indian-history/.

8. Sherburne F. Cook, *The Conflict between the California Indian and White Civilization* (Berkeley: University of California Press, 1976), 256. See Rawls, *Indians of California*, 144–57, for an excellent survey of the data and legislative debates.

9. Lucy Young [T'tc~tsa] with Edith V. A. Murphey, "Out of the Past: A True Indian Story Told by Lucy Young, of Round Valley Indian Reservation," *California Historical Quarterly* 20, no. 4 (December 1941): 349–64. Lynwood Carranco and Estle Beard, *Genocide and Vendetta: The Round Valley Wars of Northern California* (Norman: University of Oklahoma Press, 1981), 109–10.

10. John Ross Browne, "The Coast Rangers: A Chronicle of Events in California, Part 2: the Indian Reservations," *Harper's New Monthly Magazine* 23 (August 1861): 315.

11. Cited in Tomás Almaguer, *Racial Fault Lines: The Historical Origins of White Supremacy in California* (Berkeley: University of California Press, 1994), 115n31.

12. See Brendan Lindsay, *Murder State: California's Native American Genocide, 1846–1873* (Lincoln: University of Nebraska Press, 2012), 200–210, for a detailed description of the relationship between Hastings, "Jarboe's Rangers," the Mendocino community, and the willing dispersal of funds by the state of California.

13. Carranco and Beard, *Genocide and Vendetta*, 89.

14. Carranco and Beard, *Genocide and Vendetta*, 88–97.

15. Michael F. Magliari, "Masters, Apprentices, and Kidnappers: Indian Servitude

and Slave Trafficking in Humboldt County, California, 1860–1863," *California History* 97, no. 2 (2020): 3.

16. *Daily Evening Bulletin* (San Francisco), September 22, 1857.

17. William B. Secrest, *When the Great Spirit Died: The Destruction of the California Indians, 1850–1860* (Sanger, CA: Word Dancer, 2003), 288–305; Benjamin Madley, *An American Genocide: The United States and the California Indian Catastrophe, 1846–1873* (New Haven: Yale University Press, 2016), 279–82; Carranco and Beard, *Genocide and Vendetta*, 94–98.

18. E. A. Stevenson, agent for the Nome Lackee Reservation, House Doc. 1, 34th Cong., 3rd sess. (1856), 802. This chapter is indebted to the book-length, detailed, and compelling view of the genocidal wars in Northern California, in Humboldt, Shasta, Del Norte (Trinity), and Shasta, in Madley, *American Genocide*, esp. chap. 7, "Perfecting the Killing Machine," 231–88, in which Madley provides multiple accounts, diaries, military logbooks of expenditures, and extensive government correspondence to expose the evolution of the wars of extinction. Madley persuasively argues for the deliberate genocidal intentions of federal and state policy.

19. Benjamin Arthur, deposition, February 28, 1860, *Majority and Minority Reports of the Special Joint Committee on the Mendocino War* (Sacramento, 1860), 51.

20. Madley, *American Genocide*, 332. See also Lindsay, *Murder State*, 201–9; Robert F. Heizer, "Indian Servitude in California," in *Handbook of North American Indians*, vol. 4, *History of Indian-White Relations*, ed. William C. Sturtevant and Wilcomb E. Washburn (Washington, DC: Smithsonian, 1988), 404–16; Heizer, *Handbook of North American Indians*, 8:309; Cook, *Conflict*, 315.

21. See Madley, *American Genocide*, 347, who cites various and conflicting estimates of the decline in the population of California Indians. The figures for 1860 fall between 17,798 and 35,000, down from the generally accepted number of 300,000 to 310,000 at the moment of the Spanish invasion in 1769. Walter L. Hixson, *American Settler Colonialism: A History* (New York: Palgrave-MacMillan, 2013), 123n4.

22. Quoted in Rawls, *Indians of California*, 154.

23. *Sacramento Union*, July 2, 1860. For an assessment of the *Daily Alta California*, see Lindsay, *Murder State*, 326.

24. *Daily Alta California*, June 18, 1868.

25. "Enslaving the California Indians," *Humboldt Times*, October 5, 1861, cited in Magliari, "Masters, Apprentices, and Kidnappers," 13.

26. Quoted in Rawls, *Indians of California*, 154.

27. Frank H. Baumgardner, *Killing for Land in Early California: Indian Blood at Round Valley, 1856–1863* (New York: Algora, 2005), 12; Dorothy Hill, *The Indians of Chico Rancheria* (Sacramento: State of California Resources Agency, 1978).

28. Leland Fulwider, interview by Les Lincoln, June 22, 1990, in William Bauer, Jr., Round Valley Oral History Project, 1860, www.roundvalleyproject.com;

William Bauer, Jr., *We Were All Like Migrant Workers Here: Work, Community, and Memory on California's Round Valley Reservation, 1850–1941* (Chapel Hill: University of North Carolina Press, 2012), 50.

29. "California," in U.S. Department of Commerce, Bureau of Census, *Seventh Census of the United States, 1850* (Washington, DC: Government Printing Office, 1853), 2.census.gov/prod2/decennial/documents/1850a-01.pdf.

30. *Daily Evening Bulletin* (San Francisco), January 2, 1858.

31. *The Statutes of the State of California Passed at the Fourteenth Session of the Legislature, 1863, Begun on Monday, the Fifth Day of January, and Ended on Monday, the Twenty-Seventh Day of April* (Sacramento, 1863), 743. See also Magliari, "Masters, Apprentices, and Kidnappers," 8.

32. "Laws of California," *Sacramento Union*, July 31, 1860.

33. *Sacramento Union*, July 31, February 4, 1860, and January 30, 1861. See Richard Steven Street, *Beasts of the Field: A Narrative History of California Farmworkers, 1769–1913* (Stanford: Stanford University Press, 2004), 704n32.

34. *Sacramento Daily Union*, February 4, 1861; Benjamin Davis Wilson, *The Indians of Southern California in 1852* (San Marino, CA: Huntington Library, 1952).

35. *The Statutes of California Passed at the First Session of the Legislature, 1849–1850* (San Jose, CA; J. Winchester, 1850), 408. For a discussion of the additions to the 1850 Indian Act, see Michael F. Magliari, "Free Soil, Unfree Labor: Cave Johnson Couts and the Binding of Indian Workers in California, 1850–1867," *Pacific Historical* Review 73, no. 3 (August 2004): 352–57.

36. From Edward O. C. Ord, *The City of the Angels and the City of the Saints, or, A Trip to Los Angeles and San Bernardino in 1856*, ed. Neal Harlow (San Marino: Huntington Library, 1978), 32, quoted in Patrick Wolfe, "Settler Colonialism and the Elimination of the Native," *Journal of Genocide Research* 8, no. 4 (December 2006): 358.

37. Magliari, "Masters, Apprentices, and Kidnappers," 6.

38. "Need to Remove Indians from Humboldt Bay," *Humboldt Times*, March 28, April 11 and 21, and June 30, 1860.

39. *Humboldt Times*, November 10, 1860.

40. *Humboldt Times*, December 22, 1860.

41. Magliari, "Masters, Apprentices, and Kidnappers," 8–9.

42. *Humboldt Times*, March 9, 1861, quoted in Magliari, "Masters, Apprentices, and Kidnappers," 8, 9, 11.

43. Indian Indenture Papers, Archives Colusa County Court House, Colusa, CA. I am very grateful to the clerk and the recorder, office of Colusa County, for assistance in locating these documents.

44. *Sacramento Daily Union*, July 31, 1860.

45. Ernestine Ray, interview by Les Lincoln, April 1990, Round Valley Oral History Project, quoted in Bauer, *We Were All Like Migrant Workers Here*, 50.

46. Browne, "Coast Rangers," 306–7.

47. *Sacramento Union*, February 4, 1861.

48. *Official Report on Indian Affairs Commission William P. Dole Report to Sec. of the Interior* (Washington, DC: Government Printing Office, 1862). *Daily Evening Bulletin* (San Francisco), December 17, 1862.

49. *Sacramento Daily Union*, December 17, 1864, and August 6, 1858; *Red Bluff Independent*, October 23, 1863; *Red Bluff Beacon*, June 2, 1858.

50. Carranco and Beard, *Genocide and Vendetta*, 61, 68.

51. "Indian Affairs in the Northern District the Reservation System," *Daily Evening Bulletin* (San Francisco), July 27, 1861. See Stacey L. Smith, *Freedom's Frontier: California and the Struggle over Unfree Labor, Emancipation, and Reconstruction* (Chapel Hill: University of North Carolina Press, 2015), nn28–29 and 185: this removal was "brot [*sic*] about by Lynch law" and other Indians living in bondage were "shot down at their work." *Humboldt Times*, April 11, 1863.

52. Donald Lindsay Hislop, *The Nome Lackee Indian Reservation, 1854–1870* (Chico: Association for Northern California Records and Research, Occasional Publication Number 4, 1978), 50.

53. *Independent*, January 18, 1861; Hislop, *Nome Lackee Indian Reservation*, 50–55.

54. *Sacramento Daily Union*, July 21, 1860, January 30, 1864, and January 2, 1865; *Marysville Daily Appeal*, December 10, 1863. See also "A History of American Indians in California: Historic Sites, Nome Lackee Indian Reservation," *Five Views: An Ethnic Historic Site Survey for California*, https://www.nps.gov/parkhistory/online_books/5views/5views1h55.htm; Hislop, *Nome Lackee Indian Reservation*, 56.

55. I am indebted to the Colusa County Clerk recorder for locating and reproducing the extant indenture papers.

56. See also the original discussion of Colusa County in Michael F. Magliari, "Free State Slavery: Bound Indian Labor and Slave Trafficking in California's Sacramento Valley, 1850–1864," *Pacific Historical Review* 81, no. 2. (May 2012): 155–92.

57. "Servitude: Work for the New Indian Agent," *Sacramento Daily Union*, February 4, 1861.

58. "Apprenticing Indians," *Humboldt Times*, February 23, 1861.

59. "Grand Jury Presentment on Kidnapping," December 13, 1852, Contra Costa County Historical Society. See also *Daily Evening Bulletin* (San Francisco), January 2, 1858.

60. Magliari, "Masters, Apprentices, and Kidnappers," 5ff, discusses the archival finds and losses of indenture records in California, and the two caches of documents available from Humboldt County and Colusa County. For copies of the documents from Humboldt County, see Robert F. Heizer and Alan F. Almquist, *The Other Californians: Prejudice and Discrimination under Spain, Mexico, and the United States to 1920* (Berkeley: University of California Press, 1977), 53.

61. See *Sonoma Democrat*, October 24, 1861; Office of Indian Affairs, Department of the Interior, *Report of the Commissioner of Indian Affairs for the Year 1862*, no. 63 (Washington, DC: Government Printing Office, 1863), 315. See also Mary Siler Anderson, *Backwoods Chronicle: A History of Southern Humboldt 1850–1920* (Redway, CA: SoHumCo, 2006); Hon. George M. Hanson, Superintending Agent of Indian Affairs for Northern California, *Report Commander of Indian Affairs (for 1862)* (1863), 315.

62. Colusa County California Indian indenture contracts, Colusa County Court Archives. In possession of the author.

63. "Col. Francis Lippitt to Major R. D. Drum," assistant adjutant-general, Department of the Pacific, February 12, 1862, in Scott, *War of the Rebellion*, 1:50:1, 803; and "Capt. Thomas Ketchum, to Lieut. John Hanna, Jr.," acting assistant adjutant-general, April 3, 1862, in *War of the Rebellion*, 1:50:1, 982, quoted in Benjamin Madley, "'Unholy Traffic in Human Blood and Souls': Systems of California Indian Servitude under U.S. Rule," *Pacific Historical Review* 83, no. 4 (November 2014): 655. See Madley, *American Genocide*, 157–89, for modifications of the laws defining Indian testimony.

64. Madley, *American Genocide*, 313–15. For the origins of the California Volunteers as, according to Madley, "a killing machine," in the California Cavalry, whose express intent was the extermination of Mattole, Yurok, and other Indian people in Humboldt County, see also Madley, *American Genocide*, 301–2.

65. Madley, *American Genocide*, 302.

66. *Humboldt Times*, July 20, 1861; *Mendocino Herald*, April 10, 1863; Bauer, *We Were All Like Migrant Workers Here*, 51. See also Heizer and Almquist, *Other Californians*, 53; Smith, *Freedom's Frontier*, 185.

67. "Traffic in Indian Children," *Daily Alta California*, May 10, 1862.

68. *Humboldt Times*, October 2, 1858.

69. *Humboldt Times*, March 19, 1859.

70. Madley, *American Genocide*, 282n124.

71. "Cheryl Seidner and the Wiyot Tribe in Eureka, CA." See also Robert N. Scott, *War of the Rebellion: Official Records of the Union and Confederate Armies* (Pasadena, CA: Broadfoot, 1985), 20, cited in Ray Raphael and Freeman House, *Two Peoples, One Place* (Eureka, CA: Humboldt Historical Society, 2007), 178–79.

72. *Humboldt Times*, March 3, April 14 and 21, May 26, 1860; Carranco and Beard, *Genocide and Vendetta*, 128–30.

73. Magliari, "Masters, Apprentices, and Kidnappers," 18.

74. Helen Carpenter, "Among the Diggers of Thirty Years Ago," pt. 2, *Overland Monthly and Out West Magazine* 21 (1893): 389.

75. *The People v. G. H. Woodman and B. W. Pickett*, 106 (March 26, 1862; March 28, 1862; April 1, 1862; April 5, 1862). *James S. Siddons on Behalf of Named Indian Children Henry, Henry, Moses, Sam, William, Peter, Peter, John, Sara, Kate, Kate, Jane, Betsy, Harriett, Harriett, and Lucy v. G. H. Woodman*, April 5,

1862, California State Archives, Mendocino County; "The Trade in Indian Children," *Daily Alta California*, June 21, 1862.

76. *Marysville Daily Appeal*, May 1862.

77. *Daily Evening Bulletin* (San Francisco), March 27, 1861, 3; *California Farmer and Journal of Useful Sciences* 17, no. 6 (May 2, 1862); *Sacramento Daily Union*, June 20, 1862; "Traffic in Indian Children," *Daily Alta California*, May 10, 1862; *Siddons v. Woodman*, 106 (1862), California State Archives, Sacramento.

78. "Selling Indian Children," *Sacramento Daily Union*, October 8, 1862; *Daily Alta California*, April 9, May 10, and October 5, 1862; *Sacramento Daily Union*, March 13, 1863; Carpenter, "Among the Diggers of Thirty Years Ago," 389–99. "A Singular Correspondence," *Marysville Daily Appeal*, June 18, 1862.

79. *Sacramento Union*, July 31, 1860.

80. *Marysville Daily Appeal*, December 6, 1861. See Smith, *Freedom's Frontier*, 156–58, for a summary of local efforts to banish traffickers.

81. Smith, *Freedom's Frontier*, 160.

82. Heizer, *Destruction of California Indians*, 14.

83. Heizer, *Destruction of California Indians*, 14, 278.

84. "D. C. Buell to Capt. C. S. Lovell, l," Gaston, CA, cited in San Francisco *Evening Bulletin*, July 13, 1861.

85. Cited in Lindsay, *Murder State*, 325.

86. "A Plea for the Indians," *Daily Evening Bulletin* (San Francisco), June 11, 1861. See Smith, *Freedom's Frontier*, 186n32.

87. Office of Indian Affairs, Department of the Interior, *Annual Report of the Commissioner of Indian Affairs to the Secretary of the Interior* (Washington, DC: Government Printing Office, 1861), 150–51, http://images.library.wisc.edu /History/Efacs/CommRep/AnnRep61/reference/history.annrep61.i0013.pdf.

88. Amid the extensive literature on Civil War history, see Leonard L. Richards, *The California Gold Rush and the Coming of the Civil War* (New York: Vintage, 2007); Richard Hurley, *California and the Civil War* (Charleston, SC: History, 2017); *Michael DiLeo and Eleanor Smith, Two Californias: The Myths and Realities of a State Divided against Itself* (Covelo, CA: Island, 1983); Kevin Starr, *California: A History* (New York: Modern Library, 2007).

89. "Good Haul of Diggers," *Humboldt Times*, April 11, 1863.

90. Calif. Stat. ch. 45 (1863): An Act for the Repeal of Section Three of an Act for the Government and Protection of Indians, passed May 22, 1850, and Section One of an Amendment thereof, passed April Eighteenth, 1860. Chap. 1, 475, 743.

91. Smith, *Freedom's Frontier*, 190–91; Bauer, *We Were All Like Migrant Workers Here*, 68–69; Lindsay, *Murder State*, 267.

92. Michael Magliari, "Masters, Apprentices, and Kidnappers," 3.

93. Office of Indian Affairs, U.S. Department of Interior, *Report on Indian Affairs for 1867* (Washington, DC: Government Printing Office, 1868), quoted in Rawls, *Indians of California*, 104–5.

94. Brendan Lindsay drew upon the annual and biennial reports of the superintendent of public instruction of the state of California, *Journals of the Senate and Assembly of the State of California, 1864–1880*, to compile these statistics, noting that based on incomplete and sporadic data from school districts, these number should be considered conservative. Lindsay, *Murder State*, 267; Smith, *Freedom's Frontier*, 190–91; Bauer, *We Were All Like Migrant Workers Here*, 68–69.

Chapter Nine. "Go Do Some Great Thing"

Epigraph: Mifflin Wistar Gibbs, *Shadow and Light: An Autobiography with Reminiscences of the Last and Present Century* (Washington, DC, 1902), 31, 36.

1. *People v. W. H. Potter* (December 12, 1850), State of California, Sacramento County.
2. Frederick Douglass, *Narrative of the Life of Frederick Douglass, An American Slave* (Boston: Anti-Slavery Office, 1845), 41. © 2005 the Antislavery Literature Project.
3. Saidiya Hartman, *Scenes of Subjection: Terror, Slavery, and Self-Making in Nineteenth-Century America* (New York: Oxford University Press, 1997). Also quoted in Edlie L. Wong, *Neither Fugitive nor Free: Atlantic Slavery, Freedom Suits, and the Legal Culture of Travel* (New York: New York University Press, 2009), 4.
4. Certificates of Manumission, History San Jose, 1997–297–1 and 1997–214–35. Roxanne L. Nilan, "Two Years a Slave in the Santa Clara Valley: Sampson Gleaves and Plim Jackson," History San Jose, https://historysanjose.org/two-years-a-slave-in-the-santa-clara-valley-sampson-gleaves-and-plim-jackson/.
5. Fugitive Slave Act of 1850 § 6.
6. Gibbs, *Shadow and Light*, 21.
7. "Burning of Pennsylvania Hall," *Liberator*, repr. from *Maine Advocate of Freedom*, June 15, 1838.
8. Gibbs, *Shadow and Light*, 26.
9. Gibbs, *Shadow and Light*, 33, 36.
10. "The Forty-Niners," in *California as I Saw It: First-Person Narratives of California's Early Years, 1849 to 1900*, Library of Congress Digital Collections, https://www.loc.gov/collections/california-first-person-narratives/articles-and-essays/early-california-history/forty-niners/.
11. Frederick Douglass, *North Star*, November 30, 1849; Henry Simpson, *The Emigrant's Guide to The Gold Mines* (New York: Joyce, 1848), 27.
12. Compiled Laws of California, Calif. Stat., ch. 35 § 3 (1850).
13. "Signed Lester and Gibbs," *Liberator*, July 3, 1857; Calif. Const. of 1849, ch. 3, §394.
14. "Signed Lester and Gibbs"; Gibbs, *Shadow and Light*, 47. See James A. Fisher, "The Struggle for Negro Testimony in California, 1851–1863," *Southern Cal-*

ifornia Quarterly 51, no. 4 (December 1969): 313–24; *California Journal of the Assembly* (1852): 395.

15. "Signed Lester and Gibbs"; Gibbs, *Shadow and Light*, 47, 51.

16. Gibbs, *Shadow and Light*, 46.

17. Peter Anderson et al., "The Mirror of the Times," *Black Abolitionist Papers Editorial*, Black Abolitionist Papers, University of Michigan, Ann Arbor, 8431, 25626, 25627, 25628.

18. Gibbs, *Shadow and Light*, 47.

19. Howard Holman Bell, *A Survey of the Negro Convention Movement, 1830–1861* (New York: Arno, 1969), 203.

20. Gibbs, *Shadow and Light*, 48.

21. See Stacey Smith's careful "Appendix" in *Freedom's Frontier: California and the Struggle over Unfree Labor, Emancipation, and Reconstruction* (Chapel Hill: University of North Carolina Press, 2013), 237, with thoughtful estimates of African American "masters and slaves." Quintard Taylor, *In Search of the Racial Frontier: African Americans in the American West, 1528–1990* (New York: W. W. Norton, 1998), 78, has overall higher estimates.

22. Rudolph M. Lapp, *Blacks in Gold Rush California* (New Haven: Yale University Press, 1995), 5–16.

23. Jean Pfaelzer, "None but Colored Testimony against Him: The California Colored Convention of 1855 and the Origins of the First Civil Rights Movement in California," in *The Colored Convention Movement: Black Organizing in the 19th Century*, ed. Pier Gabrielle Foreman, Jim Casey, Sarah Patterson (Chapel Hill: University of North Carolina Press, 2021), 330–48.

24. Alfred Avins, "The Right to Be a Witness and the Fourteenth Amendment," *Missouri Law Review* 31, no. 4 (Fall 1966): 471–504.

25. "William Hall," *Pacific Appeal*, August 23, 1863. In the East, Hall and Gibbs had worked closely with abolitionists Dr. J. McCune Smith, Reverend Theodore Wright, and Reverend Alexander Crumwell to organize petition drives demanding that free Blacks have the right to testify.

26. *California Journal of the Assembly* (1853). See *California Legislature*, 4th sess. (March 12, 1853); *Sacramento Daily Union*, March 15, 1853; *California Journal of the Assembly* (1854): 259–61. The 1853 petition, suggested Assemblyman George Carhart, should be thrown out the window, or, alternatively, proposed his colleague A.G. McCandless, burned.

27. *Minutes of the State Convention of Colored Citizens of Pennsylvania*, convened at Harrisburg (December 13–14, 1848).

28. Donna R. Mooney, "The Search for a Legal Presumption of Employment Duration or Custom of Arbitrary Dismissal in California, 1848–1872," *Berkeley Journal of Employment and Labor Law* 21, no. 2 (2000): 633–76; Lapp, *Blacks in Gold Rush California*, 1, 8, 25.

29. Taylor, *In Search of the Racial Frontier*, 78.

30. Forty-three enslaved African Americans came from Virginia, and twenty-

seven each from Missouri, Kentucky, and Tennessee. Howard H. Bell, ed., *Minutes of Negro State Colored Convention, California, 1855*, cited in Bell, *Survey of the Negro Convention Movement*, 137, 203. Regarding the debate over the political equivalency of the moves to Africa and California, Bell argues, "There was no tendency in 1858 for the established abolitionist leaders to favor emigration under any circumstances"; Bell, *Survey of the Negro Convention Movement*, 214.

31. Without census, school, and tax records, absolute numbers are unavailable. Bell, *Minutes of Negro State Colored Convention*, cited in Bell, *Survey*, 137. See Bell, *Survey*, 214 for the debate over the political equivalency of the moves to Africa and California.

32. Lynn M. Hudson, *The Making of "Mammy Pleasant": A Black Entrepreneur in Nineteenth-Century San Francisco* (Urbana: University of Illinois Press, 2003), 32.

33. Michael R. Haines and Inter-University Consortium for Political and Social Research, *Historical, Demographic, Economic, and Social Data: The United States, 1790–1970* (Ann Arbor, MI: Inter-University Consortium for Political and Social Research, 1997); Erin Bradford, *Free African American Population in the U.S.: 1790–1860* (University of Virginia Library: Geostat Historical Census Browser, 2008).

34. For a reliable biography of Mary Ellen Pleasant and an astute analysis of the opportunities for Black women in this liminal state, see Hudson, *Making of "Mammy Pleasant,"* 32–33.

35. Lawrence B. De Graff, Kevin Mulroy, and Quintard Taylor, eds., *Seeking El Dorado: African Americans in California* (Seattle: University of Washington Press, 2001), 103.

36. J. S. Holliday, *Rush for Riches: Gold Fever and the Making of California* (Berkeley: University of California Press, 1999), 90.

37. I am grateful to Jeannine DeLombard, "'Eye-Witness to the Cruelty': Southern Violence and Northern Testimony in Frederick Douglass's 1845 *Narrative,*" *American Literature* 73, no. 2 (2001): 245–75, for marking and mapping the crucial shifts from witnessing to testifying, from seeing to speaking, in the passage from slave to activist.

38. Thomas D. Morris, "Slaves and Rules of Evidence in Criminal Trials," in *Slavery and the Law,* ed. Paul Finkelman (Lanham, MD: Rowman and Littlefield, 2001), 211.

39. For example, literacy was taught at the Pennsylvania Society for Promoting the Abolition of Slavery and at the African Free School founded by the New York Manumission Society. Paul J. Polgar, "'To Raise Them to an Equal Participation': Early National Abolitionism, Gradual Emancipation, and the Promise of African American Citizenship," *Journal of the Early Republic* 31, no. 2 (Summer 2011): 229–58.

40. Hartman, *Scenes of Subjection,* 7–8.

41. Morris, "Slaves and Rules of Evidence," 212.

42. *State v. Ben*, 8 N.C. (1 Hawks) 434 (1821), cited in Morris, "Slaves and Rules of Evidence," 233n29.

43. Morris, "Slaves and Rules of Evidence," 211; Pfaelzer, "None but Colored Testimony against Him," 330–48.

44. *People v. Hall*, 4 Cal. Rep. 339 (1854).

45. See Jean Pfaelzer, *Driven Out: The Forgotten War against Chinese Americans* (New York: Random House, 2007), 39–40, 173, 246; D. Michael Bottoms, *An Aristocracy of Color: Race and Reconstruction in California and the West, 1850–1890* (Norman: University of Oklahoma Press, 2013), 14–17.

46. *People v. Hall.*

47. Morris, "Slaves and Rules of Evidence," 227.

48. California State Archives, Sacramento, 1852. "William Hall," *Pacific Appeal*, August 23, 1863.

49. Asal Ehsanipour, "How the Founder of California's First Black Church Fought Its Last Known Slavery Case," *California Report Magazine*, May 10, 2020.

50. Peter H. Burnett, Inaugural Address, *Journals of Legislature* (1851).

51. An Act Respecting Fugitives from Labor and Slaves Brought into This State Prior to Her Admission to the Union (April 15, 1852), Ch 33, SC, at 67–69. See Stacey Smith's fulsome discussion of the pressures and drafting of this act, in particular, chap. 2, "Planting Slavery on Free Soil," in *Freedom's Frontier*, 47–79.

52. For a discussion of how Black communities in California forged organizations and communities that embodied the legacy of the East, see Lawrence B. De Graaf and Quintard Taylor, "Introduction: California in African American History," in *Seeking El Dorado*, 3–17. Eric Gardner, *Unexpected Places: Relocating Nineteenth-Century African American Literature* (Jackson: University Press of Mississippi, 2011), has shattered the North/South divide of U.S. slavery studies by turning to vast and often hitherto unknown archives, to extend our sense of where African Americans moved, organized, suffered, and wrote in a variety of forms and genres. His influence has reformed my thinking in the very assumption of slavery in California and the American West.

53. Ira Berlin, *Slaves without Masters: The Free Negro in the Antebellum South* (New York: Pantheon, 1974), 36–37. See Rudolph M. Lapp, "Negro Rights Activities in Gold Rush California," The Museum of the City of San Francisco, http://www.sfmuseum.net/hist6/blackrights.html.

54. "To the Honorable the Legislature of the State of California," March 10, 1852, California State Archives, Sacramento. See also "William Hall," *Pacific Appeal*, August 23, 1863; Hudson, *Making of "Mammy Pleasant,"* 36nn88 and 89.

55. For a history of the state capital, see Daniel Visnich, "California State Capitol: A Cast-Iron Classic Taken for Granite," United States Capitol Historical Society, https://uschs.org/explore/historical-articles/california-state-capitol -cast-iron-dome/.

56. *California Journal of the Assembly* (1853). See California Legislature, 4th sess., Assembly, March 12 (1853); *Sacramento Daily Union*, March 15, 1853; *California Journal of the Assembly* (1854): 259–61.

57. *Pacific Appeal*, September 13, 1862. Thousands of these petitions are at the California State Archives, Sacramento.

58. *California Journal of the Assembly, Legislature of the State of California* (1853); *California Legislature* (March 12, 1853); *Sacramento Daily Union*, March 15, 1853; *California Journal of the Assembly* (1854): 259–61. See also from Theodore H. Hittell, *History of California* (San Francisco: N. J. Stone, 1853), 2:111. These nascent if futile activities marked a powerful difference between political opportunities for enslaved Blacks, enslaved Native Americans, and free and enslaved Chinese immigrants. Evelyn Nakano Glenn, "Settler Colonialism as Structure: A Framework for Comparative Studies of U.S. Race and Gender Formation," *Sociology of Race and Ethnicity* 1, no. 1 (2015): 54–74; Patrick Wolfe, "Settler Colonialism and the Elimination of the Native," *Journal of Genocide Research* 8, no. 4 (2006): 387–409; Orlando Patterson, *Slavery and Social Death: A Comparative Study* (Cambridge, MA: Harvard University Press, 1985); Lorenzo Veracini, *Settler Colonialism: A Theoretical Overview* (New York: Palgrave-MacMillan, 2010). The bold petitions are now inside the metal vaults of the California State Archives, Sacramento.

59. James Brewer Stewart and Elizabeth Swanson, "Introduction: Getting beyond Chattel Slavery," and James Sidbury, "Slavery and Civic Death: Making Sense of Modern Slavery in Historical Context," hold that the enslaved are invariably suffering from civic death. The practices of enforcing "civic death" as Sidbury defines it are also part of the definition of slavery. In *Human Bondage and Abolition: New Histories of the Past and Present Slaveries*, ed. Elizabeth Swanson and James Brewer Stewart (Cambridge: Cambridge University Press, 2018), 1–37.

60. *Wood Tucker v. Stephen Hill, et al.* County Court, Tuolumne County, petition for writ of injunction filed by O. R. Rozier on behalf of Wood Tucker (August 12, 1854); *Daily Alta California*, September 1, 1854, April 9, 1858; Carlo De Ferrari, ed., *Gold Spring Diary: The Journal of John Jolly and Including a Brief History of Stephen Spencer Hill Fugitive from Labor* (Sonora, CA: Tuolumne Historical Society, 1966), 125–42. See also Lapp, *Blacks in Gold Rush California*, 140–41; *Daily Alta California*, April 9, 1858, 1, quoting *Sonora Herald*, August 1854.

61. Hudson, *Making of "Mammy Pleasant,"* 33; Susheel Bibbs, "Mary Ellen Pleasant: Mother of Civil Rights in California," *Historic Nantucket* 44, no. 1 (Spring 1995): 11.

62. Hudson, *Making of "Mammy Pleasant,"* 36.

63. "The Convention of 1855," *Pacific Appeal*, April 12, 1862; Delilah Beasley, *The Negro Trail Blazers of California* (1919; repr., New York: MacMillan, 1997), 55.

64. "The Convention of 1855"; De Ferrari, *Gold Spring Diary*, 125–42; *Wood*

Tucker v. Stephen Hill, et al.; Daily Alta California, September 1, 1854, April 9, 1858. See also Lapp, *Blacks in Gold Rush California*, 140–41.

65. Gibbs, *Shadow and Light*, 46–47.

66. Pfaelzer, "None but Colored Testimony against Him," 330–48.

67. American Society for Free Persons of Colour, "Constitution of the American Society of Free Persons of Colour, . . . also, the Proceedings of the Convention with Their Address to Free Persons of Colour in the United States," Colored Conventions Project, http://coloredconventions.org/items/show/70.

68. Herbert G. Ruffin II, "The Conventions of Colored Citizens of the State of California (1855–1865)," Blackpast, February 4, 2009, https://www.black past.org/african-american-history/conventions-colored-citizens-state-cali fornia-1855-1865/.

69. See the Colored Conventions Project for national archival history of the Colored Convention movement in the United States, http://coloredconventions .org. Pfaelzer, "None but Colored Testimony against Him." This chapter draws in particular from the works of Howard H. Bell, including *Survey of the Negro Convention Movement;* "Free Negroes of the North 1830–1835: A Study in National Cooperation," *Journal of Negro Education* 26, no. 4 (1957): 447; *Minutes and Proceedings of the National Negro Convention;* "National Negro Conventions of the Middle 1840s: Moral Suasion vs. Political Action," *Journal of Negro History* 42, no. 4 (1957): 247; "Some Reform Interests of the Negro during the 1850s as Reflected in State Conventions," *Phylon* 21, no. 2 (1960): 173–81. Philip Sheldon Foner and George Elizur Walker, eds., *Proceedings of the Black State Conventions: 1840–1865*, 2 vols. (Philadelphia: Temple University Press, 1979). Eric Gardner, "Early African American Print Culture and the American West," chap. 4 in *Early African American Print Culture*, ed. Lara L. Cohen and Jordan A. Stein (Philadelphia: University of Pennsylvania Press, 2012). Bella Gross, *Clarion Call: The History and Development of the Negro People's Convention Movement in the United States from 1817 to 1840* (New York, 1947); see also Gross, "The First National Negro Convention," *Journal of Negro History* 31, no. 4 (1946): 435; Gross, "Negro Conventions and the Problem of Black Leadership," *Journal of Black Studies* 2, no. 1 (1971): 29–44; Gross, *They Who Would Be Free: Blacks' Search for Freedom, 1830–1861* (New York: Atheneum, 1974). Patrick Rael, *Black Identity and Black Protest in the Antebellum North* (Chapel Hill: University of North Carolina Press, 2001). Derrick Spires, "Imagining State of Fellow Citizens: Early African American Politics of Publicity in the Black State Conventions," in *Early African American Print Culture*, ed. Lara L. Cohen and Jordan A. Stein (Philadelphia: University of Pennsylvania Press, 2012), 274–89.

70. For extensive and accessible documents, records, minutes, biographies, maps, menus, and debates, see the Colored Conventions Project (www.colored convtions.org), a vast digital humanities project sponsored by the University of Delaware. I am deeply grateful to the director and founder, Professor Ga-

brielle Foreman; Carol A. Rudisell, head of Reference and Instructional Services, University of Delaware Library; James Casey; and current and former graduate students Clay Colman and Samantha deVera. *Proceedings of the First State Convention of the Colored Citizens of the State of California* (Sacramento: Democratic State Journal Print, 1855), 16. See Bell, *Minutes of Negro State Colored Convention*, 3. See also *Proceedings of the Second Annual Convention of the Colored Citizens of the State of California* (San Francisco: J. H. Udell and W. Randall, 1856); *Proceedings of the State Convention of Colored Citizens* (San Francisco: Printed at the Office of the *Elevator*, 1865); John Ernest, *A Nation within a Nation: Organizing African American Communities before the Civil War* (Chicago: Ivan R. Dee, 2011); John Ernest, *Liberation Historiography: African American Writers and the Challenges of History, 1794–1861* (Chapel Hill: University of North Carolina Press, 2004); Jane H. Pease and William H. Pease, "Negro Conventions and the Problem of Black Leadership," *Journal of Black Studies* 2, no. 1 (1971): 29–44. See also Ruffin, "Conventions of Colored Citizens."

71. All of the quotations are found at "Digital Records," The Colored Conventions Project, https://omeka.coloredconventions.org/items/show/265. *Proceedings of the First State Convention of the Colored Citizens of the State of California* (Sacramento: Democratic State Journal Print, 1855), 16. See also *Proceedings of the Second Annual Convention; Proceedings of the State Convention of Colored Citizens*; Ernest, *Nation within a Nation*; Ernest, *Liberation Historiography*; Noel, "Jeremiah B. Sanderson," 151–58; Pease and Pease, "Negro Conventions and the Problem of Black Leadership," 29–44. See also Ruffin, "Conventions of Colored Citizens."

72. Bell, *Minutes and Proceedings*, 5. In 1851 Douglass changed the title of his Rochester-based newspaper, the *North Star*, to *Frederick Douglass' Paper*.

73. Lapp, *Blacks in Gold Rush California*, 167.

74. David Lewis, "Second Annual Convention of the Colored Citizens of the State of California," in *Proceedings of the Black State Convention, 1840–1865*, ed. Philip S. Foner and George E. Walker (Philadelphia: Temple University Press, 1980), 155. Also quoted in Gardner, *Unexpected Places*, 3. See Gardner for a foundational discussion of the political impact of African American print culture. *Proceedings of the First State Convention of the Colored Citizens of the State of California. Held at Sacramento Nov. 20th 21st, and 22d, in the Colored Methodist Church* [sic] (Sacramento: Democratic State Journal Print, 1855), http://coloredconventions.org/items/show/265.

75. Ernest, *Liberation Historiography*, 223, reminds us to consider how the oration and the widely dispersed minutes of the Colored Conventions contributed to the possibility of re-envisioning and transforming the present. See also Carter G. Woodson, ed., *The Mind of the Negro as Reflected in Letters Written during the Crisis, 1800–1860* (Westport, CT: Greenwood, 1969), 654, quoted in David Brion Davis, *The Problem of Slavery in the Age of Emancipation* (New York: Knopf, 2014), 193.

76. Frances Kaplan, "Petition for Legal Recognition of Black Californians," ca. 1852–1862, MS 169A, California Historical Society, San Francisco.
77. *Proceedings of the Second Annual Convention of the Colored Citizens*, 42–43.
78. *Dred Scott v. Sanford* 60 U.S. 393 (1856).
79. Charles M. Christian and Sari Bennett, *Black Saga: The African American Experience: A Chronology* (New York: Civitas, 1999), 165.
80. Beasley, *Negro Trail Blazers*, 56.
81. Beasley, *Negro Trail Blazers; Proceedings of the California State Convention of Colored Citizens* (San Francisco: Printed at the office of *The Elevator*, 1865), https://omeka.coloredconventions.org/items/show/267.
82. *Sacramento Daily Union*, February 2, 1858.
83. Philip Montesano, *Some Aspects of the Free Negro Question in San Francisco, 1849–1870* (San Francisco: R and E Research, 1973), 41; *Mirror of the Times*, December 12, 1857.

Chapter Ten. "A Change Has Come over the Spirit of Our Dreams"

Epigraph: *Proceedings of the California State Convention of Colored Citizens* (San Francisco: Printed at the office of the *Elevator*, 1865), n.p.
1. "William Newby ('Nubia') to Frederick Douglass," *Frederick Douglass Paper*, June 1, 1855.
2. *Sacramento Age*, October 1857.
3. William Burg, *Sacramento's K Street: Where the City Was Born* (Charleston, SC: History, 2012), n.p.
4. Delilah Beasley, *The Negro Trail Blazers of California* (1919; repr., New York: MacMillan, 1997), 78.
5. "Case of 'Archy,'" *Sacramento Daily Union*, January 9, 1858.
6. Beasley, *Negro Trail Blazers*, 78.
7. *Dred Scott v. Sandford*, 60 U.S. 393 (1857).
8. 31st U.S. Congress, An act to amend, and supplementary to, the act entitled "An Act Respecting Fugitives from Justice, and Persons Escaping from the Service of Their Masters," approved February 12, 1793, Pub. L.31–60. 9 Stat. 462.
9. *Ex Parte Archy*, 9 Cal. 147 (1858).
10. *Matter of Archy*, 9 Cal. 147 (1858).
11. *Matter of Archy*, 9 Cal. 147 (1858), *supra* note 60, at 167. Paul Finkelman, "The Law of Slavery and Freedom in California," *California Western Law Review* 17 (1981): 437, 461.
12. Beasley, *Negro Trail Blazers*, 82–83.
13. Lynn M. Hudson, *The Making of "Mammy Pleasant": A Black Entrepreneur in Nineteenth-Century San Francisco* (Urbana: University of Illinois Press, 2008), 38.
14. *Sacramento Age*, October 1857. See also Rudolph Lapp, *Archy Lee: A California Fugitive Slave Case* (San Francisco: Book Club of California, 1969), 10.

15. Edlie Wong points out that for Blacks to sue for *wrongful* enslavement, they had to assent to the idea that there was *rightful* bondage: Edlie Wong, *Neither Fugitive nor Free: Atlantic Slavery, Freed Suits, and the Legal Culture of Travel* (New York: New York University Press, 2009), 7.

16. While he was in jail, age nineteen, Archy gave a reporter the history of his slave status—an enslaved man whose ownership became an object of dispute between Stovall relatives. Born in Pike County, Mississippi, explained Archy, he was "last" in the possession of Charles Stovall. The fight over Archy's ownership began one night when he was working at Charles Stovall's mill in Choctaw country. One night, a Stovall cousin tried to seize Archy by forcing his slave, Smiley, to entice Archy to run away. When Archy refused to flee, Carroll Stovall and Smiley seized him, and Archy drew a knife and stabbed Smiley twice in the left breast. The next morning, the manager at the mill hid Archy in some bushes until dark, when he spirited Archy to nearby Middletown and delivered him to Charles Stovall. Charles Stovall drove Archy in a buggy to a friend's plantation in Cape Girardeau, Missouri, where he hid Archy, apparently as he prepared for the overland journey. From Missouri, Archy was transported again, this time ferried across the Mississippi River into Tennessee. There, Charles Stovall claimed him and, with two Stovall brothers, the men began their trek across the plains to California. Thus, as Archy made clear to the *Alta California*, he was never a fugitive—either from Mississippi or from Missouri. "Archy's Story," *Sacramento Daily Union*, April 2, 1858.

17. See *Ex Parte Archy*, 9 Cal. 147, 171; *In the Matter of Archy on Habeas Corpus: Supreme Court of California* 9 Ca. 147; January Term (1858), Cal. LEXIS 83. California Supreme Court, *In Re the Petition by Stovall, Claimant, for the Body of Archy, His Alleged Slave* (1858), 1–22; *Sacramento Daily Union*, January 9, 12, 27, 28, February 6, 11, 12, 13, 16, 18, March 18, 20, 24, and April 2, 15, 17, 1858; *Daily Evening Bulletin* (San Francisco), January 19, February 13, 24, and March 5, 6, 1858; *Daily Alta California*, February 14, March 18, 19, 20, 22, and April 14, 1858; Petition and Affidavit of C. A. Stovall January 8, 1858; *Charles Stovall v. Archy a Slave*, March 17, 1858; Affidavit of C. A. Stovall, March 29, 1858; *C. A. Stovall v. Archy a Slave*, Affidavit of E. H. Bake and E. R. Doyle, March 29, 1858; Subpoena for Archy's Witness (Freeman and Doyle), March 9, 1858; Affidavit of S. J. Noble, March 29, 1858, includes Stovall's advertisement; "Brief for Respondent and Statement of Facts," April 1858; "Unsigned and Undated Notes Believed to Be Those of US Commissioner on Application of Fugitive Slave Act in the Case," April 1858, all California State Archives.

18. John B. Weller, Inaugural Address, January 8, 1858, Governors' Gallery, https://governors.library.ca.gov/addresses/05-Weller.html.

19. Ira Berlin, *Slaves without Masters: The Free Negro in the Antebellum South* (New York: Pantheon, 1974), 94–95, 139, 144–45. See also Alfred Avins, "The Right

to Be a Witness and the Fourteenth Amendment," *Missouri Law Review* 31, no. 4 (Fall 1966), https://scholarship.law.missouri.edu/cgi/viewcontent.cgi?article=1954&context=mlr.

20.   California Assembly Bill 385, Report Committee on Federal Relations (April 21, 1858); *Sacramento Daily Union*, March 27, 1858; Rudolph M. Lapp, *Blacks in Gold Rush California* (New Haven: Yale University Press, 1995), 239–40. Lucile Eaves, *A History of California Labor Legislation* (Berkeley: University of California Press, 1910), 99–103; William E. Franklin, "The Archy Case: The California Supreme Court Refuses to Free a Slave," *Pacific Historical Review* 32, no. 2 (May 1963): 137–54; *Daily Evening Bulletin* (San Francisco), March 27 and April 15, 1858. See also Eugene H. Berwanger, *The Frontier against Slavery: Western Anti-Negro Prejudice and the Slavery Extension Controversy* (Urbana: University of Illinois Press, 2002), 76 and 66–68, for a thorough and well-documented discussion of the anti-Black immigration initiatives in the California Constitution Convention and early legislature.

21.   Berlin, *Slaves without Masters*, 94–95, 139, 144–45. See also Avins, "Right to Be a Witness."

22.   Act to Restrict and Prevent the Immigrations to and Residence in this State of Negroes and Mulattoes," AB 395 (1858).

23.   California Assembly Bill 385, Report Committee on Federal Relations (April 21, 1858); *Sacramento Daily Union*, March 27, 1858.

24.   *Journal of the Ninth Session of the Assembly of the State of California*, 9 (1858): 623; *Quarterly of the CA Historical Society* IX (1930): 281ff.

25.   *Daily Evening Bulletin* (San Francisco), October 30, 1857; Robin W. Winks, *Blacks in Canada: A History* (Montreal: McGill-Queen's University Press, 1992), 272n3; F. W. Howay, "The Negro Immigration into Vancouver Island in 1858," *British Columbia Historical Quarterly* 3 (April 1939): 104.

26.   Mifflin Wistar Gibbs, *Shadow and Light: An Autobiography with Reminiscences of the Last and Present Century* (Washington, DC, 1902), 63.

27.   Philip S. Foner, *History of Black Americans*, vol. 3, *From the Compromise of 1850 to the End of the Civil War* (Westport, CT: Greenwood, 1983), 94–95.

28.   The Mexican government welcomed Black runaways as a way to weaken the institution of slavery in Texas and deter further territorial assaults by the United States. Not all Mexican government officials agreed; so many enslaved African Americans attempted to escape that Mexico's congress passed a law to promote capturing American runaways to stifle the trend, and to counter Mexico's encouragement of fugitivity. Despite the escape of at least three thousand slaves to Mexico by 1851, slavery as an institution was not threatened, and it continued to be as important in Texas as it was to the rest of the United States. Andrew Waters, *I Was Born in Slavery: Personal Accounts of Slavery in Texas* (Winston-Salem, NC: John F. Blair, 2003), x, 5–6; Randolph B. Campbell, *An Empire for Slavery: The Peculiar Institution in Texas, 1821–1865* (Baton Rouge: Louisiana State University Press, 1989), 62–64;

W. Sherman Savage, *Blacks in the West* (Westport, CT: Greenwood, 1976), 145; Ron Wilkins, "Mexico Welcomed Fugitive Slaves and African American Job-Seekers: New Perspectives on the Immigration Debate," *San Francisco Bay View*, May 4, 2006; *Sacramento Daily Union*, April 16, 1858.

29. Peggy Cartwright, *Black Pioneers in Gold Rush Days* (Victoria, BC: Manning, 1993), 4.

30. Cartwright, *Black Pioneers in Gold Rush Days*, 4.

31. Crawford Kilian, *Go Do Some Great Thing: The Black Pioneers of British Columbia* (Burnaby, BC: Commodore, 2008), 34.

32. Gibbs, *Shadow and Light*, 15–45; Winks, *Blacks in Canada*, 273.

33. Kilian, *Go Do Some Great Thing*, 30.

34. Kilian, *Go Do Some Great Thing*, 30–34.

35. Julie H. Ferguson, *James Douglas: Father of British Columbia* (Toronto: Dundurn, 2009), 151.

36. *Daily Evening Bulletin* (San Francisco), May 12, 1858.

37. *Daily Evening Bulletin* (San Francisco), May 12, 1858.

38. Or. U.S. Const. art. I, § 35 (1857): "No free negro, or mulatto, not residing in this State at the time of the adoption of this Constitution, shall come, reside, or be within this State, or hold any real estate, or make any contracts, or maintain any suit therein; and the Legislative Assembly shall provide by penal laws, for the removal, by public officers, of all such negroes, and mulattoes, and for their effectual exclusion from the State, and for the punishment of persons who shall bring them into the state, or employ, or harbor them."

39. Their flight to safety, crossing the plains and later traveling north from Placer County to settle on Salt Spring Island, British Columbia, takes the African American slave narrative into new geographies. See "From Slavery to Freedom: The History of the Stark Family" in *Gulf Islands Driftwood*, November 7, 1979, available at Salt Spring Island Archives, https://www.saltspring archives.com/driftwood/stark.pdf. See also "Salt Spring Island's Cultural History," Salt Spring Island Archives, https://www.saltspringarchives.com/multi cultural/index.htm.

40. *Sacramento Union*, June 2, 1858.

41. *Sacramento Union*, June 2, 1858.

42. In 1861, at the start of the Civil War, the California legislature reiterated that any expansion of rights for witnesses "shall not be held to impair or in any way affect the existing provision of law by which persons of Indian or Negro Blood are excluded from being witnesses." Calif. Stat. ch. 467 (1861): 521; Petition against Prohibition of Black Witnesses in California to the California State Legislature, Petitions to the State Assembly, February 20, 1862, California State Archives, Sacramento, Black Abolitionist Papers, University of Michigan, Ann Arbor, 6901. See also Philip Montesano, *Some Aspects of the Free Negro Question in San Francisco, 1849–1870* (San Francisco:

R and E Research, 1973), 35; Gibbs, *Shadow and Light*, 47; Rudolph M. Lapp, "Negro Rights Activities in Gold Rush California," *California Historical Society Quarterly* 45, no. 1 (1966): 8; Beasley, *Negro Trail Blazers*, 54.

43. For an astute summary of the ambivalence of the political leadership of California on the issue of slavery, see Gerald Stanley, "Civil War Politics in California," *Southern California Quarterly* 64, no. 2 (Summer 1982): 115–32. Gerald Stanley, "Slavery and the Origins of the Republican Party in California," *Southern California Quarterly* 60, no. 1 (1978): 1–16.

44. Stanley, "Civil War Politics in California"; Stanley, "Slavery and the Origins of the Republican Party."

45. *Pacific Appeal*, May 17, 1862.

46. *Morning Call*, April 25, 1862; *Pacific Appeal*, May 3, 1862.

47. "'Subscriber' to Peter Anderson," *Pacific Appeal*, March 14, 1863.

48. Quoted in Stanley, "Civil War Politics," 122. See the discussion of the Perkins Bill introduced by Richard F. Perkins, in Shirley Ann Wilson Moore, "'We Feel the Want of Protection': The Politics of Law and Race in California," *California History* 81, no. 3–4 (2003): 96–125. John Haskell Kemble, ed., "Andrew Wilson's 'Jottings on Civil War California,'" *California Historical Society Quarterly* 32, no. 4 (December 1953): 308.

49. For an astute discussion of the development of the early Black press, see Eric Gardner, *Unexpected Places: Relocating Nineteenth-Century African American Literature* (Jackson: University of Mississippi Press, 2009), in particular, "The Black West: Northern California and Beyond, 1865–1877," 92–132.

50. *Elevator*, July 21, 1865.

51. "Prejudice," *Pacific Appeal*, March 14, 1863; November 21, 1863; March 19, 1864. See Quintard Taylor, *In Search of the Racial Frontier: African Americans in the American West, 1528–1990* (New York: W. W. Norton, 1999), 93. See also Barbara Y. Welke, "Rights of Passage: Gendered-Rights Consciousness and the Quest for Freedom, San Francisco, California," in *African American Women Confront the West, 1600–2000*, ed. Quintard Taylor and Shirley Ann Wilson Moore (Norman: University of Oklahoma Press, 2003), 80–86, for an astute discussion of Charlotte Brown and the public and private dichotomies of male and female transportation.

52. 12th Circuit Court, City and County of San Francisco, *Charlotte Brown v. The Omnibus Railroad Company* (1863), Evidence of Plaintiff; Amended Answer; Evidence of Defendant Thomas S. Dennison; Evidence of Mr. Gardner, Superintendent of Omnibus Railroad Co; 12th Circuit Court, City and County of San Francisco, *Charlotte Brown v. The Omnibus Railroad Company* (1863).

53. *Daily Alta California*, November 14, 1863.

54. "Charlotte Brown," n.d., California Historical Society, San Francisco. See "Brown, Charlotte L. Plaintiff's Statement," *Brown v. Omnibus Railroad Company*, District Court of the 12th Judicial District, April 17, 1864; James Brown,

"Trial Statement from Brown vs. Omnibus Railroad Company," May 6, 1863, Black Abolitionist Papers, University of Michigan, Ann Arbor, 6905.

55. *Daily Evening Bulletin* (San Francisco), November 14, 1863.

56. Jonas H. Townsend and William Newby served as the first coeditors of *Mirror of the Times.* Albert S. Broussard, "Civil Rights, Racial Protest, and Anti-Slavery Activism in San Francisco, 1850–1865," *National Maritime Museum* (1999): 1–50.

57. James Brown scrap in the California Historical Society, MS228A 1964.

58. *Charlotte Brown v. The Omnibus Railroad Company* (1863); *Pacific Appeal,* March 14, November 21, 1863, March 19, 1864; Taylor, *In Search of the Racial Frontier,* 93.

59. Quoted in "San Francisco's Own Rosa Parks," *SFGate,* April 5, 2012.

60. *Elevator,* April 7, 1865.

61. Repr. in the *Pacific Appeal,* May 23, 1863. See *Pacific Appeal,* November 21, 1863; March 19, 1864.

62. *Brown v. Omnibus Railroad Company; Marysville Daily Appeal,* January 19, 1866.

63. *Pleasant v. North Beach and Mission Railroad Company* (June 20, 1867), California State Archives, Sacramento; *Pacific Appeal,* May 24, 1862, and March 4, 1863.

64. Moore, "We Feel the Want of Protection," 119–20.

65. *Proceedings of the California State Convention of Colored Citizens.*

66. Broussard, "Civil Rights, Racial Protest," 1–50; Brainerd Dyer, "One Hundred Years of Negro Suffrage," *Pacific Historical Review* 41 (February 1968): 1–20.

67. The Great Registrar of Voters, California, "Statement Regarding 1870 Voter Registration of Edward West Parker Sr.," Safero, http://www.safero.org /family/EdParkerRegistrionLetter.html.

Chapter Eleven. The Importation of Females in Bulk

Epigraph: Marlon K. Hom, *Songs of Gold Mountain: Cantonese Rhymes from San Francisco Chinatown* (Berkeley: University of California Press, 1987), 319.

1. I am indebted to the work on Chinese prostitution in the nineteenth century by Lucie Cheng Hirata, "Free, Indentured, Enslaved: Chinese Prostitutes in Nineteenth-Century America," in *History of Women in the United States: Historical Articles on Women's Lives and Activities,* ed. Nancy F. Cott (Munich: K. G. Saur, 1993), 9:123–49; Nayan Shah, *Contagious Divides: Epidemics and Race in San Francisco's Chinatown* (Berkeley: University of California Press, 2001); Benson Tong, *Unsubmissive Women: Chinese Prostitutes in Nineteenth-Century San Francisco* (Norman: University of Oklahoma Press, 1994); Herbert Asbury, *The Barbary Coast: An Informal History of the San Francisco Underworld* (New York: Pocket, 1933); Margit Stange, *Personal Property: Wives, White Slaves, and the Market in Women* (Baltimore: Johns Hopkins University

Press, 1998); Helen Fletcher Collins, "An Historical Local Commerce: Pros-
titution," *Pacifica: Magazine of the Northcoast* (May 1972): n.p.; George Anthony
Peffer, *If They Don't Bring Their Women Here: Chinese Female Immigration before
Exclusion* (Urbana: University of Illinois Press, 1999).

2. Hom, *Songs of Gold Mountain,* 309.

3. June Mei, "Socioeconomic Origins of Emigration: Guangdong to Califor-
    nia, 1850–1882," *Modern China* 5, no. 4 (October 1979): 488.

4. From "Confessions of a Chinese Slave-Dealer," transcribed by Helen Grey,
    in Judy Yung, *Unbound Voices: A Documentary History of Chinese Women in San
    Francisco* (Berkeley: University of California Press, 1999), 153.

5. D. Chen, *Zhong-guo fu-nu sheng-huo-shi* (Shanghai: Shang-wu, 1928), 296,
    cited in Hirata, "Free, Indentured, Enslaved," 125.

6. Mary Roberts Coolidge, *Chinese Immigration* (New York: Holt, 1909), 419.

7. *West Coast Signal,* January 1, 1875.

8. "Letter from China," *Daily Evening Bulletin* (San Francisco), July 21, 1869;
    West Coast Signal, January 1, 1875.

9. Gordon H. Chang, *Ghosts of Gold Mountain: The Epic Story of the Chinese Who
    Built the Transcontinental Railroad* (New York: Houghton Mifflin Harcourt,
    2019), 28. Sucheng Chan, ed., *Entry Denied: Exclusion and the Chinese Com-
    munity in America, 1882–1943* (Philadelphia: Temple University Press, 1991),
    94–146.

10. Charles Frederick Holder, "Chinese Slavery in America," *North American
    Review* 165, no. 490 (September 1897): 292.

11. *San Francisco Chronicle,* December 5, 1869.

12. Holder, "Chinese Slavery in America," 292n22; Elizabeth Sinn, *Pacific Cross-
    ing: California Gold, Chinese Migration, and the Making of Hong Kong* (Hong
    Kong: Hong Kong University Press, 2013), 99.

13. Him Mark Lai, *Becoming Chinese American: A History of Communities and In-
    stitutions* (Walnut Creek, CA: AltaMira, 2004), 46–74.

14. Jacqueline Baker Barnhart, "Working Women: Prostitution in San Francisco
    from the Gold Rush to 1900" (PhD diss., University of California, Santa Cruz,
    1976), 123; Tong, *Unsubmissive Women,* 12.

15. Dupont Street is now known as Grant Avenue and runs through the heart of
    modern Chinatown.

16. Mae Ngai, *The Chinese Question: The Gold Rushes and Global Politics* (New York:
    Norton, 2021), 83, image #6, image #7; Smith, *Freedom's Frontier,* 99–100.

17. William Gow, "The Chinese Railroad Workers in United States History
    Textbooks: A Historical Genealogy," in *The Chinese and the Iron Road,* ed.
    Gordon H. Chang and Shelley Fisher Fishkin (Stanford: Stanford Univer-
    sity Press, 2019), 240. Jean Pfaelzer, "'STRIKE!' The Chinese Railroad Work-
    ers' Strike of 1867: Beyond Memory" (forthcoming).

18. *Inter Ocean,* September 4, 1874; *Daily Evening Bulletin* (San Francisco), Jan-
    uary 19, 1884.

19. Turning to a 1790 federal law that held that only "free white persons" could be naturalized, the tax was soon changed to apply only to those not ever eligible for citizenship, i.e., Latinos and Chinese. *Californios*, specifically Mexicans who remained in the new U.S. territory for a year, would automatically become American citizens, although Gwin's Act of 1852 would strip them of much of their land. Hirata, "Free, Indentured, Enslaved," 130; Robert F. Heizer and Alan F. Almquist, *The Other Californians: Prejudice and Discrimination under Spain, Mexico, and the United States to 1920*, 2nd ed. (Berkeley: University of California Press, 1977).

20. Jean Pfaelzer, *Driven Out: The Forgotten War against Chinese Americans* (New York: Random House, 2007), 3–48.

21. Pfaelzer, *Driven Out*, 3–46; J. S. Holliday, *Rush for Riches: Gold Fever and the Making of California* (Oakland: Oakland Museum of California; Berkeley: University of California Press, 1999), 152.

22. Chief Justice Roger Taney alleged Chinese immigrant women's threat of "moral evil" when he ruled that California could bar Chinese miners because "the people of the States of this Union reserved to themselves the power of expelling from their borders any person, or class of persons, whom it might deem dangerous to its peace, or likely to produce physical or moral evil among its citizens." *Smith v. Turner* (1849); similarly in *Holmes v. Jennison* (1840).

23. See Stacey L. Smith, *Freedom's Frontier: California and the Struggle over Unfree Labor, Emancipation, and Reconstruction* (Chapel Hill: University of North Carolina Press, 2015), 202; *Sacramento Daily Union*, March 20, 1866.

24. An Act for the Suppression of Chinese Houses of Ill Fame, Calif. Stat. (1865–66), ch. DV, 641–42.

25. *Sacramento Daily Union*, February 9, 1866; *Daily Evening Bulletin* (San Francisco), February 23, 1866; *Daily Alta California*, April 5, 1866.

26. *Daily Alta California*, December 22, 1867.

27. *Salt Lake Daily Telegraph*, May 4, 1866.

28. Smith, *Freedom's Frontier*, 204, citing *California Police Gazette*, September 8, 1866; *Golden Era*, June 3, 1866; *Sacramento Daily Union*, June 1, 1866; *Daily Evening Bulletin* (San Francisco), June 1, 1866.

29. Chang, *Ghosts of Gold Mountain*, 176, 178.

30. *Lin Sing v. Washburn*, 20 Cal. 534, 554–55, 575 (1862); Najia Aarim-Heriot, *Chinese Immigrants, African Americans, and Racial Anxiety in the United States, 1848–82* (Urbana: University of Illinois Press, 2003), 72.

31. Shah, *Contagious Divides*, 81.

32. See *San Francisco Chronicle*, December 5, 1869.

33. "San Francisco Board of Health," *SF Municipal Report* (1864–65), 139, quoted in Shah, *Contagious Divides*, 81.

34. *Daily Evening Bulletin* (San Francisco), April 11, April 13, and May 4, 1866; *Daily Alta California*, May 1, 1866.

35. See Gordon H. Chang, "The Chinese and the Stanfords: Nineteenth-Century

America's Fraught Relationship with the China Men," in *Chinese and the Iron Road: Building the Transcontinental Railroad*, ed. Gordon H. Chang and Shelley Fisher Fishkin (Stanford: Stanford University Press, 2019), 86–102.

36. Carey McWilliams, *Factories in the Field: The Story of Migratory Farm Labor in California* (Berkeley: University of California Press, 1966), 67–72, 79.

37. A. W. Loomis, "Chinese Women in California," *Overland Monthly and Out West Magazine* 2, no. 4 (April 1869): 345–51.

38. *Daily Evening Bulletin* (San Francisco), January 28, 1874. *Slaughter-House Cases*, 83 U.S. 36 (1873). See Ronald Labbé and Jonathan Lurie, *The Slaughterhouse Cases: Regulation, Reconstruction, and the Fourteenth Amendment* (Lawrence: University Press of Kansas, 2003).

39. *Daily Evening Bulletin* (San Francisco), January 28, 1874.

40. *Daily Evening Bulletin* (San Francisco), February 1, 1879.

41. Major studies of the anti-Chinese legislation include Mae M. Ngai, *Impossible Subjects: Illegal Aliens and the Making of Modern America* (Princeton, NJ: Princeton University Press, 2004); Erika Lee, *The Making of Asian America: A History* (New York: Simon and Schuster, 2015); Nayan Shah, *Contagious Divides: Epidemics and Race in San Francisco's Chinatown* (Berkeley: University of California Press, 2001); George Anthony Peffer, *If They Don't Bring Their Women Here: Chinese Female Immigration before Exclusion* (Urbana: University of Illinois Press, 1999). Nancy Cott, "Marriage and Women's Citizenship in the United States, 1830–1934," *American Historical Review* 103, no. 5 (December 1999): 1457.

42. Kerry Abrams, "Polygamy, Prostitution, and the Federalization of Immigration Law," *Columbia Law Review* 105, no. 3 (April 2005): 668–90.

43. Anna Pegler-Gordon, *In Sight of America: Photography and the Development of U.S. Immigration Policy* (Berkeley: University of California Press, 2009), 30n31. See Eithne Luibhéid, *Entry Denied: Controlling Sexuality at the Border* (Minneapolis: University of Minnesota Press, 2002), 31–54.

44. Sucheng Chan, "Chinese Livelihood in Rural California: The Impact of Economic Change, 1860–1880," in *Working People of California*, ed. Daniel A. Cornford (Berkeley: University of California Press, 1991), 57; Ronald Takaki, *Strangers from a Different Shore* (New York: Little, Brown, 1998), xxx; Chang, *Ghosts of Gold Mountain*, 44–45.

45. 43rd Congress. Sess. II. Ch. 141 (1875), chap. 141, An Act Supplementary to the Acts in Relation to Immigration.

46. A California Senate report cited in Hirata, "Free, Indentured, Enslaved," 140.

47. Lucie Cheng Hirata, "Chinese Immigrant Women in Nineteenth-Century California," in *Women of America: A History*, ed. Carol Ruth Berkin and Mary Beth Norton (Boston: Houghton Mifflin, 1979), 227–33.

48. See *U.S. Industrial Commission Report*, vol. 15 (Washington, DC: Government Printing Office, 1901), 762.

49. Arthur B. Stout, "Impurity of Race, as a Cause of Decay," *First Biennial Report of the State Board of Health of California for the Years 1870 and 1871* (Sacramento: D. W. Gelwicks, 1871), 71.

50. Hirata, "Free, Indentured, Enslaved," 135.

51. *California Senate, Chinese Immigration* (Sacramento: State Office, 1878), 99, 213, 164–66. See Jean Pfaelzer, *Muted Mutinies* (forthcoming). As the British sought to withdraw from the kidnap and sale and shipment of Chinese men bound for the cane fields of Cuba and the guano islands off Peru, the trade moved up the peninsula to Portuguese-held Macao—a port, like Guantanamo, held by a foreign nation to the rage and shame of China. As enslaved men were shipped to Cuba and Peru, enslaved girls were shipped to Hong Kong from this Portuguese jumping-off point.

52. *Sacramento Daily Union*, March 20, 1866; *Daily Evening Bulletin* (San Francisco), March 18 and 21, 1866.

53. Asbury, *Barbary Coast*, 5. For wages, see "Pauperism, Crime, and Wages," in *Statistics of the United States (including mortality, property, &c.) in 1860: Compiled from the Original Returns and Being the Final Exhibit of the Eighth Census* (Washington, DC: Secretary of the Interior, United States Census Office, 1990), 512.

54. *Daily Evening Bulletin* (San Francisco), August 13, 1856. Other examples can be found in *Daily Alta California*, August 25, 1856.

55. Barbara Berglund, "Chinatown's Tourist Terrain: Representation and Racialization in Nineteenth-Century San Francisco," *American Studies* 46, no. 2 (Summer 2005): 8–9, 13.

56. See Stephanie Foote, *Regional Fictions: Culture and Identity in Nineteenth-Century American Literature* (Madison: University of Wisconsin Press, 2001), 124–53.

57. "Tour Guide Business Card, San Francisco Chinatown," Flickr, live.static flickr.com/2094/1617459619_64b3165bf6_z.jpg" class="main-photo" alt= "Tour Guide Business Card, San Francisco Chinatown."

58. Barbara Berglund, *Making San Francisco American: Cultural Frontiers in the Urban West, 1846–1906* (Lawrence: University Press of Kansas, 2007), 53.

59. Berglund, *Making San Francisco American*, 53–60.

60. Tong, *Unsubmissive Women*, 94, 96–97; Yong Chen, *Chinese San Francisco, 1850–1943: A Trans-Pacific Community* (Stanford, CA: Stanford University Press, 2000), 56.

61. *Daily Evening Bulletin* (San Francisco), February 7, 1859.

62. The 1880 census lists 620 total residents for Antioch, CA.

63. "The term Green Mansion was originally used to refer to the grand buildings where kings and nobles lived. Over time, it became a term used to describe the grand places of dwelling of the best courtesans before eventually being loosely used to refer to brothels." "Mirage of a Chinese Garden," Hanfugirl, February 13, 2019, https://hanfugirl.blog/2019/02/13/mirage-of-a -chinese-garden.

64. J. P. Munro-Fraser, *History of Contra Costa County, California* (San Francisco: W. A. Slocum, 1882), 495. *San Francisco Chronicle*, May 2, 1876; *Daily Alta California*, February 26, 1886; *Public Opinion*, May 6, 1876; *Sacramento Daily Record*, May 2, 1876.

65. Contemporary newspapers that reported on the Chinese women include the *Antioch Ledger, San Francisco Chronicle, Daily Alta California, Public Opinion, Weekly Antioch Ledger, Humboldt Times, California Census Index, Sacramento Union*, and *Sacramento Daily Record*.

66. *Medico-Literary Journal* (1878), vol. 5, cited in Susan Craddock, "Embodying Place: Pathologizing Chinese and Chinatown in Nineteenth-Century San Francisco," *Antipode* 31, no. 4 (1999): 363.

67. Pfaelzer, *Driven Out*, 99.

68. Earl Hohlmayer, "Chinese Were Treated as Lesser Human Beings," *Antioch Daily Ledger*, April 2, 1990. Other journalists and local historians of Antioch writing in the *Daily Ledger* who have contributed to this chapter include contemporary series by Paul Allen, Elizabeth Rimbault, and Nilda Rego.

69. Pfaelzer, *Driven Out*, 89–120.

70. John Kuo Wei Tchen, s.v. "Asian," in *Keywords for American Cultural Studies*, ed. Bruce Burgett and Glenn Hendler (New York: New York University Press, 2014), 26–29.

71. Tchen, "Asian."

72. Mai M. Ngai, *Impossible Subjects: Illegal Aliens and the Making of Modern America* (Princeton, NJ: Princeton University Press, 2004), 6–7, 23.

73. Erika Lee, *At America's Gates: Chinese Immigrants during the Exclusion Era, 1882–1943* (Chapel Hill: University of North Carolina Press, 2003), 120–23.

74. M. P. Sawtelle, "The Plague Spot," *Medico-Literary Journal* 1, no. 4 (December 1868): 10–12, quoted in Shah, *Contagious Divides*, 107.

75. John D'Emilio and Estelle Freedman, *Intimate Matters: A History of Sexuality in America* (New York: Harper and Row, 1988), 146–48, 204.

76. Pfaelzer, *Driven Out*, 77–78.

77. Holder, "Chinese Slavery in America," 292–93; Hirata, "Free, Indentured, Enslaved," 133.

78. Pegler-Gordon, *In Sight of America*, 23–25; Lee, *At America's Gates*.

79. Pegler-Gordon, *In Sight of America*, 25, 27–29, 38.

80. "Chinese Immigration: Its Social, Moral, and Political Effect," in *The Report to the California State Senate of the California Special Committee on Chinese Immigration in 1876* (Sacramento: State Office, F. P. Thompson, Supt. State Printing, 1878), 195.

81. Hiroyuki Matsubara, "Stratified Whiteness and Sexualized Chinese Immigrants in San Francisco: The Report of the California Special Committee on Chinese Immigration in 1876," *American Studies International* 41, no. 3 (October 2003): 32–59, uniquely reveals the intense focus on social and moral order rather than labor competition of the committee. I am indebted to her interpretation.

82. "Chinese Immigration," 103.
83. "Chinese Immigration," 196.
84. "Chinese Immigration," 47.
85. Shah, *Contagious Divides*, 87.
86. Willard B. Farwell, *The Chinese at Home and Abroad* (San Francisco: A. L. Bancroft, 1885), also quoted in Shah, *Contagious Divides*, 80.
87. Physicians understood how syphilis was spread long before they understood how it could be cured. It was not until 1904 that physician Prince Morrow described how common female complaints among young married women— sterility, congenital blindness in infants, syphilitic insanity, chronic uterine inflammation, and fatigue ("innocent infections")—could be traced "back to their original source in that irregular sexual commerce known as prostitution." Morrow blamed "masculine unchastity" rather than the female prostitute as the "chief malefactor." D'Emilio and Freedman, *Intimate Matters*, 204.
88. See Craddock, "Embodying Place," 351–71, for an astute discussion of how the pathologizing of the Chinese female in San Francisco in the mid-nineteenth century lent scientific authority to the "politics of normal" and the crucial role of medical theory in authorizing the superiority of Anglo-Saxon heritage.
89. Pfaelzer, *Driven Out*, 97–99.

Chapter Twelve. "She Had Stolen Nothing from Him but Herself"

Epigraph: Susie Baker Fountain Scrapbook Clippings, May 1871, vol. 74:143, Humboldt State University Library, Arcata; *Daily Standard*, n.d.

1. Susie Baker Fountain Scrapbook Clippings.
2. 487 U.S. 931, 108 S. Ct. 2751, 100 L. Ed. 2d 788, and 18 U.S.C.A. § 1584. See also "The Thirteenth Amendment," National Constitution Center, https://constitutioncenter.org/interactive-constitution/interpretation/amendment-xiii/interps/137.
3. A. W. Loomis, "Chinese Women in California," *Overland Monthly and Out West Magazine* 2, no. 4 (April 1869): 345–51; *Daily Evening Bulletin* (San Francisco), August 27, 1874.
4. Benson Tong, *Unsubmissive Women: Chinese Prostitutes in Nineteenth-Century San Francisco* (Norman: University of Oklahoma Press, 1994), 74n62; Ira Condit, *The Chinaman as We See Him* (New York: Arno, 1978).
5. Loomis, "Chinese Women in California," 345–51.
6. For an analysis of the relationship of the Mission Home to white women's empowerment, see Peggy Pascoe, *Relations of Rescue: The Search for Female Moral Authority in the American West, 1874–1939* (New York: Oxford University Press, 1993), xvii.
7. Tong, *Unsubmissive Women*, 74n62; Condit, *Chinaman as We See Him*.

8. Loomis, "Chinese Women in California," 345–51; *Daily Evening Bulletin* (San Francisco), August 27, 1874.

9. Tong, *Unsubmissive Women*, 184.

10. *Daily Evening Bulletin* (San Francisco), February 4, 1888.

11. Tong, *Unsubmissive Women*, 160, 174.

12. *Daily Evening Bulletin* (San Francisco), March 4, 1891, cited in *Daily Alta California*, October 23, 1876.

13. Michele Walfred, "Illustrating Chinese Exclusion," Thomas Nast Cartoons, https://thomasnastcartoons.com/author/michelewalfred/.

14. For contemporary images of the Chinese in America in the late nineteenth century, see Michele Walfred's outstanding and extensive web exhibit on Thomas Nast's cartoons in *Harper's Illustrated Magazine*, "Illustrating Chinese Exclusion."

15. Lucie Cheng Hirata, "Free, Indentured, Enslaved: Chinese Prostitutes in Nineteenth-Century America," in *History of Women in the United States: Historical Articles on Women's Lives and Activities*, ed. Nancy F. Cott (Munich: K. G. Saur, 1993), 133. See also *Daily Alta California*, January 31, 1875; *Daily Evening Bulletin* (San Francisco), March 28, 1876; Richard H. Dillon, *The Hatchet Men: The Story of the Tong Wars in San Francisco's Chinatown* (New York: Coward-McCann, 1962), 319–21.

16. *The Statutes of California Passed in the 18th Session of the Legislature, 1869–1870*, ch. 230 (Sacramento, 1870), 330.

17. *Ex Parte Ah Fook* 49. Cal 402. 1874 Cal. Lexis (1874), 350.

18. Decision reproduced in *Daily Alta California*, September 22, 1874.

19. Cited in Loomis, "Chinese Women in California," 345–51. See also *Daily Alta California*, September 22, 1874.

20. *Chy Lung v. Freeman*, 92 U.S. 275 (1876).

21. Kerry Abrams, "Polygamy, Prostitution, and the Federalization of Immigration Law," *Columbia Law Review* 105, no. 3 (April 2005): 694.

22. *Report of the United States Industrial Commission* (1901), vol. 15, cited in Hirata, "Free, Indentured, Enslaved," n41; Him Mark Lai, "The Chinese Experience at Angel Island," *East/West* 10 (1976): 7–9.

23. In 1870, 3,536 Chinese women lived in California; 61 percent of these women were listed in the census as "prostitute." The number of Chinese in California rose from forty-nine thousand in 1870 to seventy-six thousand in 1880. Ronald Takaki, *Strangers from a Different Shore* (New York: Little, Brown, 1998); Sucheng Chan, "The Exclusion of Chinese Women, 1870–1943," in *Entry Denied: Exclusion and the Chinese Community in America, 1882–1943*, ed. Chan (Philadelphia: Temple University Press, 1991), 94; Hirata, "Free, Indentured, Enslaved," 149.

24. Chan, "Exclusion of Chinese Women," 103–4, 109–10; Judy Yung, *Unbound Feet: A Social History of Chinese Women in San Francisco* (Berkeley: University of California Press, 1995), 27. For an astute summary of the case, see "22

Lewd Chinese Women: Chy Lung v. Freeman," Asian American Bar Association of New York Trial Reenactments, https://reenactments.aabany.org/wp-content/uploads/2015/11/7.-22-LCW-FINAL.pdf.

25. Tong, *Unsubmissive Women*, 74n62; Condit, *Chinaman as We See Him*; Hirata, "Free, Indentured, Enslaved," 132.

26. *Inter Ocean*, September 4, 1874.

27. Albert Dressler, *California Chinese Chatter* (San Francisco: A. Dressler, 1927), with verification letter from Milton J. Ferguson, State Librarian, California State Library, Sacramento, dated March 21, 1927.

28. The 1870 census listed 2,157 of the 3,536 adult Chinese women as prostitutes; the 1880 census enumerators listed only 759. In 1890 there were only 37 Chinese women per one thousand men.

29. Tong, *Unsubmissive Women*, 119–20.

30. An Act to Execute Certain Treaty Stipulations Relating to the Chinese (May 6, 1882); Enrolled Acts and Resolutions of Congress (1789–1996); General Records of the United States Government, Record Group 11, National Archives. The Chinese Exclusion Act was approved on May 6, 1882.

31. Jean Pfaelzer, *Driven Out: The Forgotten War against Chinese Americans* (New York: Random House, 2007), 259.

32. Susan Craddock, "Embodying Place: Pathologizing Chinese and Chinatown in Nineteenth-Century San Francisco," *Antipode* 31, no. 4 (1999): 351–71. See Pfaelzer, *Driven Out*, for a discussion of the purges and Chinese resistance to *Pai Hua*.

33. *Daily Evening Bulletin* (San Francisco), May 20 and May 25, 1882.

34. *New York Times*, May 15, 1910. See W. E. B. Du Bois, "Race Amalgamation in Georgia Based on a Study of 40,000 Individuals of Negro Descent," LOT 11931, no. 13 [P&P], Library of Congress, Washington, DC.

35. Cited in Yong Chen, *Chinese San Francisco, 1850–1943: A Trans-Pacific Community* (Stanford, CA: Stanford University Press, 2000), 86. Stout would modify his views, and by the time of the Fifteenth Amendment, he advocated the naturalization of Chinese immigrants and rented property to the Chinese at a 200 percent profit. Chen, *Chinese San Francisco*, 293n91.

36. Nancy Cott, "Marriage and Women's Citizenship in the United States, 1830–1934," *American Historical Review* 103, no. 5 (December 1999): 1456.

37. See Pfaelzer, *Driven Out*, passim; Nayan Shah, *Contagious Divides: Epidemics and Race in San Francisco's Chinatown* (Berkeley: University of California Press, 2001), 28; Earl Hohlmayer, "Chinese Were Treated as Lesser Human Beings," *Antioch Daily Ledger*, April 2, 1990.

38. See Pfaelzer, *Driven Out; El Dorado County Republican*, October 11, 1877.

39. Humboldt County, *California Census Index* (1880), 53–58.

40. *Eureka Daily Times-Telephone*, February 13, 1885; Pfaelzer, *Driven Out*, 199.

41. *Wing Hing v. The City of Eureka* (1886); see Pfaelzer, *Driven Out*, 198–209.

42. *Daily Alta California*, September 22, 1877.

43. I am indebted to Benson Tong for his groundbreaking work, *Unsubmissive Women: Chinese Prostitutes in Nineteenth Century San Francisco*, and, in partic-ular, for his research on the role of missions and missionaries in buffering the police, in providing safe houses, and for his analysis of the contradictions of the pressure toward white domesticity in the safe houses in chap. 6, "Leav-ing the Trade," 159–91. See Chan, "Exclusion of Chinese Women," 94.

44. *Daily Evening Bulletin* (San Francisco), January 23, 1875.

45. In 1880 about 75,000 Chinese lived in California out of a total population of 865,000. In 1890 about 110,000 Chinese lived in California. "Population of Chinese in the United States 1860–1940 (48 Contiguous States Only)," in The Chinese Experience in 19th Century America, http://teachingresources .atlas.illinois.edu/chinese_exp/resources/resource_2_9.pdf.

46. *Act to Prohibit the Coming of Chinese Persons into the United States* of May 1892 (27 Stat. 25).

47. *San Francisco Morning Call*, March 30, 1893.

48. *San Francisco Chronicle*. See in particular February 8, March 1, and April 22, 1894.

49. Pfaelzer, *Driven Out*, 313–15.

50. Pfaelzer, *Driven Out*, 292–307.

51. Tong, *Unsubmissive Women*, 64.

52. Scott Reynolds Nelson, *A Nation of Deadbeats: An Uncommon History of America's Financial Disasters* (New York: Alfred Knopf, 2012), 189; Melvyn Dubofsky, *Industrialism, and the American worker: 1865–1920* (New York: Thomas Crowell, 1975), 16; Robert H. Wiebe, *The Search for Order, 1877– 1920* (New York: Hill and Wang, 1967), 14–15.

53. Charles Frederick Holder, "Chinese Slavery in America," *North American Re-view* 165, no. 490 (September 1897): 288–94.

54. *Daily Evening Bulletin* (San Francisco), October 30, 1889; March 29, 1890; March 4, 1891. Holder, "Chinese Slavery in America," 288–304.

55. Holder, "Chinese Slavery in America," 289.

56. Julia Flynn Siler, *The White Devil's Daughters: The Women Who Fought Slavery in San Francisco's Chinatown* (New York: Vintage, 2019), 82–94.

57. "UC Land Grab—University of California, Berkeley," UC Berkeley Centers for Educational Justice and Community Engagement, https://cejce.berkeley .edu › uc-land-grab.

58. Mae M. Ngai, "San Francisco's Survivors," *New York Times*, April 18, 2006.

59. Alexander McLeod, *Pigtails and Gold Dust: A Panorama of Chinese Life in Early California* (Caldwell, ID: Caxton, 1947), 69, 71–85, 58, 182–83. Elinor H. Stoy, "Chinatown and the Curse that Makes It a Plague-Spot in the Nation," *Arena* 38 (October 1907): 360–65.

60. *San Jose Evening News*, September 4, 1900; *Boston Journal*, February 19, 1898.

61. Gail Hershatter, *Women and China's Revolutions* (New York: Rowan and Little-field, 2019), passim; Yuhui Li, "Women's Movement and Change of Women's

Status in China," *Journal of International Women's Studies* 1, no. 1 (2000): 30–40.

62. Peter C. Hennigan, "Property War: Prostitution, Red-Light Districts, and the Transformation of Public Nuisance Law in the Progressive Era," *Yale Journal of Law and the Humanities* 16, no. 1 (2004): 123–98; Stephanie Foote, *Regional Fictions: Culture and Identity in Nineteenth-Century American Literature* (Madison: University of Wisconsin Press, 2001), 136–37.

63. Tong, *Unsubmissive Women*, 163.

64. "Yoke Leen from California," Tuolumne County Museum.

Chapter Thirteen. "Except as a Punishment for Crime"

1. Kenneth Lamott, *Chronicles of San Quentin* (New York: Ballantine, 1972), 3.
2. *Daily Alta California*, January 25, 1849.
3. Herbert Asbury, *The Barbary Coast: An Informal History of the San Francisco Underworld* (New York: Capricorn, 1968), 39.
4. Lucille Eaves, *A History of California Labor Legislation* (Berkeley: University of California Press, 1910), 3, 5. "San Francisco Population," San Francisco History, https://www.sfgenealogy.org.
5. Roger D. McGrath, "A Violent Birth: Disorder, Crime, and Law Enforcement, 1849–1890," *California History* 81, no. 3–4 (2003): 35.
6. Frank Soulé, John H. Gihon, and Jim Nisbet, *The Annals of San Francisco: Containing a Summary of the History of California, and a Complete History of Its Great City: to Which Are Added, Biographical Memoirs of Some Prominent Citizens* (New York: D. Appleton, 1855), 560.
7. *Daily Alta California*, August 2, 1849.
8. Stephen John Hartnett, *Incarceration Nation: Investigative Prison Poems of Hope and Terror* (Walnut Creek, CA: AltaMira, 2003), 50.
9. See Martin Ridge, "Disorder, Crime, and Punishment in the California Gold Rush," *Montana: The Magazine of Western History* 49, no. 3 (Autumn 1999): 12–27. Ridge argues that absent a nascent legal system, miners in California sought informally to reproduce familiar legal structures from the East and South.
10. "Charles Cora and James Casey are Hanged by the Committee of Vigilance, San Francisco, 1856," Wikipedia, https://en.wikipedia.org/wiki/San_Francisco_Committee_of_Vigilance#/media/File:Lynching-of-casey-and-cora.jpg.
11. Ward M. McAfee, "A History of Convict Labor in California," *Southern California Quarterly* 72, no. 1. (Spring 1990): 19.
12. Tony Platt, *Beyond These Walls: Rethinking Crime and Punishment in the United States* (New York: St. Martin's, 2018), 60.
13. *San Quentin Prison Registers*, 1851–1880, California State Archives, Sacramento; Clare V. McKanna, Jr., "The Origins of San Quentin, 1851–1880," *California History* 66, no. 1 (March 1987): 49–54n3.
14. *Weekly Alta California*, October 11, 1849.

15. *Daily Alta California*, March 15, 1851.

16. Tessa M. Gorman, "Back on the Chain Gang: Why the Eighth Amendment and the History of Slavery Proscribe the Resurgence of Chain Gangs," *California Law Review* 85, no. 2 (1997): 441. Gorman's pioneering work on chain gangs describes the slide between slavery, chain gangs, and convict labor, yet with no mention of California's evolving penal system.

17. McAfee, "History of Convict Labor," 19–40.

18. Rosaura Sánchez, *Telling Identities: The Californio Testimonios* (Minneapolis: University of Minnesota Press, 1995), 51; Benjamin Madley, "California's First Mass Incarceration System: Franciscan Missions, California Indians, and Penal SIN 14ervitude, 1769–1836," *Pacific Historical Review* 88, no. 1 (Winter 2019): 14–47.

19. Kelly Lytle Hernández, *City of Inmates: Conquest, Rebellion, and the Rise of Human Caging in Los Angeles, 1771–1965* (Chapel Hill: University of North Carolina Press, 2017), 1.

20. Benjamin Madley, "California's First Mass Incarceration System: Franciscan Missions, California Indians, and Penal Servitude, 1769–1836," *Pacific Historical Review* 88, no. 1 (Winter 2019): 14–47, argues that the missions in themselves launched the carceral state in California; I view them as hybrid sites with commonalities akin to the traditions of agrarian slave plantations in the Americas. Hernández, *City of Inmates*, 28–31.

21. Richard Steven Street, *Beasts of the Field: A Narrative History of California Farmworkers, 1769–1913* (Stanford, CA: Stanford University Press, 2004), 26, 49–50, 72, 74; Mary Floyd Williams, "Mission, Presidio and Pueblo: Notes on California Local Institutions under Spain and Mexico," *California Historical Society Quarterly* 1, no. 1 (July 1922): 23–35. See also Damian Basich, "Soldiers and Presidios in Alta California," California Frontier Project, August 9, 2017, https://www.californiafrontier.net/soldiers-presidios/.

22. Hernández, *City of Inmates*, 33, 37.

23. James P. Delgado, *Gold Rush Port: The Maritime Archaeology of San Francisco's Waterfront* (Berkeley: University of California Press, 2009), app. 2.

24. Greg Miller, "New Map Reveals Ships Buried below San Francisco," *National Geographic*, June 2017; Brad Smithfield, "San Francisco Was Built on the Abandoned and Buried Ships of the Gold Rush," The Vintage News, November 10, 2016, https://www.thevintagenews.com/2016/11/10/san-francisco -was-built-on-the-abandoned-buried-ships-of-the-gold-rush; Asbury, *Barbary Coast*.

25. *Weekly Alta California*, November 15, 1849; *Daily Alta California*, February 19, 1851; *Richmond Inquirer*, September 24, 1850; Soulé, Gihon, and Nisbet, *Annals of San Francisco*, 233.

26. Bryan Finoki, "Floating Prisons, and Other Miniature Prefabricated Islands of Carceral Territoriality," Subtopia, January 6, 2008, http://subtopia.blog spot.com/2008/01/floating-prisons-and-other-miniature.html.

27. *Weekly Pacific News*, May 15, 1851; *Daily Alta California*, May 23, 1851; The-

odore Henry Hittell, *History of California* (San Francisco: N. J. Stone, 1898), 4:72–78.

28.   Records of the Prison Industries Reorganization Administration, 1937:1, National Archives.

29.   William B. Secrest, *Behind San Quentin's Walls: The History of California's Legendary Prison and Its Inmates, 1851–1900* (Fresno, CA: Craven Street, 2015), 8–13.

30.   Secrest, *Behind San Quentin's Walls*, 22.

31.   Ward M. McAfee, "San Quentin: The Forgotten Issue of California's Political History in the 1850s," *Southern California Quarterly* 72, no. 3 (Fall 1990): 237–38; "Report of the Assembly Committee on the State Prison," *California Assembly Journal*, 4th sess. (1853): 2–4; *California Senate Journal*, 10th sess. (1859): 262.

32.   "State Prison Contract," *Sacramento Daily Union*, October 21, 1852.

33.   Cited in Hartnett, *Incarceration Nation*, 52.

34.   Certain escapes were actually arranged by low-paid prison guards to rid themselves of the more troublesome criminals. Calif. Stat., ch. 59 (1852). "Ships Served as First Prisons for Fledgling State," California Department of Corrections and Rehabilitation, https://www.cdcr.ca.gov/insidecdcr/2018 /06/06/ships-served-as-first-prisons-for-fledgling-state.

35.   Michael D. Brown, *History of Folsom Prison, 1878–1978* (Folsom, CA: Folsom Graphic Arts, 1978), 2; Glen A. Gildemeister, *Prison Labor and Convict Competition with Free Workers in Industrializing America, 1840–1890* (New York: Garland, 1987), 1–3.

36.   *Daily Alta California*, December 20, 1851.

37.   *Daily Alta California*, December 20, 1851.

38.   Secrest, *Behind San Quentin's Walls*, 17.

39.   The building ultimately cost $135,000, and the money was paid directly to Estell's San Francisco Manufacturing Company. Lamott, *Chronicles of San Quentin*, 31–33, 66; Brown, *History of Folsom Prison*, 3.

40.   *Sacramento Daily Union*, April 5, 1855.

41.   McAfee, "San Quentin," 239.

42.   Madley, "California's First Mass Incarceration System."

43.   Testimony of William H. White and Thomas Young, in "Report of Committee," in *Appendix to Senate Journal*, 6th sess. (1855): 20–23.

44.   *Sacramento Daily Union*, May 1, 1855. Bonnie L. Petry and Michael Burgess, eds., *San Quentin: The Evolution of a State Prison* (Rockville, MD: Borgo, 2004), reprints early key documents, a list of names of early convicts, and James Harold Wilkins's early report, *The Evolution of a State Prison* (1970).

45.   Report of the Visiting Physician, Alfred W. Taliaferro, in app. to *Journals of Senate and Assembly*, 18th sess. (Sacramento, 1870), 1:46.

46.   Gildemeister, *Prison Labor and Convict Competition*, 15–18.

47.   Arline Wilson, "Gothic Eruptions, Anti-Childhood and the Prison's Weap-

onization of Time" (PhD diss., University of Delaware, 2022), n.p.; Austin Reed, *The Life and Adventures of a Haunted Convict*, ed. Caleb Smith and David Blight (New York: Random House, 2016), passim.

48. McKanna, "Origins of San Quentin," 50, 54n10.

49. Barbara Jeanne Yaley, "Habits of Industry: Labor and Penal Policy in California, 1849–1940" (PhD diss., University of California, Santa Cruz, 1980); Secrest, *Behind San Quentin's Walls*, 30; Brown, *History of Folsom Prison*.

50. "Report of the State Prison," *Daily Alta California*, February 22, 1855.

51. San Quentin, "Daily Logs," 1854–1860, and Turnkey's "Biennial Report," in *Biennial Report of the Board of Directors of the California State Prison* (1879), in *Appendix to the Journals of Senate and Assembly*, 23rd sess. (Sacramento, 1879), 1:38, 27.

52. *Daily Alta California*, February 22, 1855.

53. *Daily Alta California*, May 14, 1855.

54. *Daily Alta California*, February 2, 1876.

55. Lamott, *Chronicles of San Quentin*, 68, 107. See Yaley, "Habits of Industry," 72.

56. McKanna, "Origins of San Quentin," 49–54, register n3.

57. George Hodak, "Congress Bans Maritime Flogging," *ABA Journal*, September 1, 2010. See also Amy Tikkanen, s.v. "San Quentin State Prison," in *Encyclopedia Britannica*, https://www.britannica.com/topic/San-Quentin-State-Prison.

58. Yaley, "Habits of Industry," 123; Brown, *History of Folsom Prison*, 5.

59. "Report of the State Prison to the Legislature of California," published in *Daily Alta California*, February 22, 1855.

60. Lamott, *Chronicles of San Quentin*, 34–39.

61. Shelley Bookspan, *A Germ of Goodness: The California State Prison System: 1851–1944* (Lincoln: University of Nebraska Press, 1991), 15.

62. *San Quentin State Prison Records*, 1850–1950, ID #R135, California State Archives, Office of the Secretary of State, Sacramento, Department of Corrections, Inventory of the Department of Corrections Records. Processed by the California State Archives staff, supplementary encoding and revision supplied by Xiuzhi Zhou. Ward M. McAfee, "A History of Convict Labor in California," *Southern California Quarterly* 72, no. 1 (Spring 1990): 19.

63. Lamott, *Chronicles of San Quentin*, 34–39; McKanna, "Origins of San Quentin," 50.

64. Bookspan, *Germ of Goodness*, 20–22.

65. *Report on State Prison Conditions* (April 5, 1862), Dr651:LP5, California State Archives, Sacramento.

66. Bookspan, *Germ of Goodness*, 15.

67. *Daily Placer Times and Transcript*, November 9, 1855, An Act to Punish Vagrants, Vagabonds, and Dangerous and Suspicious Persons, Calif. Stat. § 2, ch. 175 (1855), 227.

68. *Daily Evening Bulletin* (San Francisco), November 11, 1856.

69. *Daily Evening Bulletin* (San Francisco), September 13 and October 22, 1856.
70. *Daily Evening Bulletin* (San Francisco), January 13, 1858.
71. *Daily Evening Bulletin* (San Francisco), August 23, 1856.
72. *Daily Evening Bulletin* (San Francisco), October 15 and November 11, 1856, and January 20, March 7, November 24, 1858.
73. *Weekly California Express* (Marysville, CA), September 11, 1858; *Daily Evening Bulletin* (San Francisco), November 3, 1858.
74. Ruth Wilson Gilmore, *Golden Gulag: Prisons, Surplus, Crisis, and Opposition in Globalizing California* (Berkeley: University of California Press, 2007), 12–13, 70–71.
75. See *Sacramento Daily Democratic State Journal*, November 15, 1856; *Daily Evening Bulletin* (San Francisco), November 26, 1858.
76. *Daily Evening Bulletin* (San Francisco), October 20, 1857.
77. Wendy Sawyer, "How Much Do Incarcerated People Earn in Each State?," Prison Policy Initiative, April 10, 2017, https://www.prisonpolicy.org/blog/2017/04/10/wages/.
78. Yaley, "Habits of Industry," 98.
79. See Secrest, *Behind San Quentin's Walls*, 109.
80. *Sacramento Daily Union*, February 22, 1856; Eaves, *History of California Labor Legislation*, 256–68, 361, 359. See also McAfee, "History of Convict Labor in California," n6.
81. *Biennial Report of the Board of Directors of the California State Prison Board of Directors*, 1873, 12–13; *San Francisco Chronicle*, January 27, 1872, and January 15, 1874; Ira Cross, *A History of the Labor Movement in California* (Berkeley: University of California Press, 1974), 134n14.
82. *Daily Alta California*, February 2, 1876.
83. *California Prison Commission Report* (1874), 13; *California Penal Commission Report* (1887), 160.
84. Calif. Const. of 1879, art. X, § 6; *Daily Alta California*, July 13 and July 16, 1881.
85. An Act to Define and Regulate and Govern the State Prisons of California, § 25 (1880). See also *Daily Alta California*, August 18 and August 19, 1880.
86. *California Prison Commission* (1874), 13; *California Penal Commission* (1887), 160.
87. Paul Takagi and Tony Platt, "Behind the Gilded Ghetto: An Analysis of Race, Class and Crime in Chinatown," *Crime and Social Justice*, no. 9 (Spring–Summer 1978): 2–25; see Cross, *History of the Labor Movement*, chap. 8, nn13–14. See Eaves, *History of California*, chap. 15. Between 1858 and 1875, the population of the state rose from 12,700 to 65,500.
88. McAfee, "History of Convict Labor in California," 24.
89. *Daily Alta California*, December 7, 1881.
90. McAfee, "History of Convict Labor in California," 22; Kenneth Lamott, *Chronicles of San Quentin, The Biography of a Prison* (New York: David McKay, 1961), 13.

91. Brown, *History of Folsom Prison*.

92. McAfee, "History of Convict Labor in California," n8.

93. Brown, *History of Folsom Prison*, 16, 18.

94. Yaley, "Habits of Industry," 125; Brainard Smith, *Compendium of Statutes and Codes Relating to the State Prisons and Prisoners* (Sacramento: State Printer, 1909), 15; Frederick S. Wythe, *The Prison Laws of California 1909* (Sacramento: W. W. Shannon, 1909), 86.

95. Lamott, *Chronicles of San Quentin*, 107; *California Prison Commission* (1867–1874); Yaley, "Habits of Industry," 74.

96. For an early survey of these options, see Arthur H. Schwartz, "Legal Aspects of Convict Labor," *Journal of the American Institute of Criminal Law and Criminology* 16, no. 2 (August 1925): 272–77. McAfee, "History of Convict Labor in California," 20.

97. *Daily Alta California*, January 15, 1881.

Chapter Fourteen. A Fortress Economy

1. This discussion is based on Donald Lowrie's memoir, *My Life in Prison* (London: John Lane, 1912), 68, 72, 85.

2. Wheat production in California grew from seventeen thousand bushels in 1850 to four hundred thousand bushels in 1890. William Cronin, *Nature's Metropolis: Chicago and the Great West* (New York: Norton, 1991), 100, 104–9; Craig Canine, *Dream Reaper: The Story of an Old-Fashioned Inventor in the High-tech, High Stakes World of Modern Agriculture* (Chicago: University of Chicago Press, 1995), 82–85; James J. Rawls and Walton Bean, *California: An Interpretive History* (New York: McGraw Hill, 1968), 271.

3. Calif. Const. of 1879, art. X, § 6.

4. *California State Penological Commission* (1887), 124–25.

5. *California Assembly Committee on Prisons* (1881), 3–4, 6–7. See also Barbara Jeanne Yaley, "Habits of Industry: Labor and Penal Policy in California, 1849–1940" (PhD diss., University of California, Santa Cruz, 1980), 85.

6. *Daily Alta California*, August 26, 1881.

7. *Daily Alta California*, December 7, 1881.

8. Ward M. McAfee, "A History of Convict Labor in California," *Southern California Quarterly* 72, no. 1 (Spring 1990): 25.

9. Appendix to *Journals of the Senate and Assembly of the Twenty-Ninth Session of the Legislature of the State of California*, vol. 8 (1891); *Daily Alta California*, June 9, 1980; McAfee, "History of Convict Labor."

10. *San Francisco Call*, September 19, 1891; *Sacramento Daily Union*, July 18, 1895; *San Francisco Call*, April 10, 1892.

11. Lowrie, *My Life in Prison*, 63–69, 138; Yaley, "Habits of Industry," 275n85. See *New York Times*, April 18, 1915; *Daily Alta California*, December 7, 1881; McAfee, "History of Convict Labor," 25; Griffith J. Griffith, *Crime and Crim-*

inals (Los Angeles: Prison Reform League, 1910), 55–60; Walter Wilson, *Forced Labor in the United States* (New York: International, 1933), 37–57.

12. See Orlando Patterson, *Slavery and Social Death: A Comparative Study* (Cambridge, MA: Harvard University Press, 1982), 55, 58; Jim McManus, "Special Issue Book Reviews," *Punishment and Society* 2, no. 3 (July 2000): 350–54; Louis Harris, *The Story of Crime* (New Haven: Literary, 1929); John T. Parry, "Torture Nation, Torture Law," *Georgetown Law Journal* 97, no. 4 (2009): 135–36, 139; Jacob Bronsther, "Torture and Respect," *Journal of Criminal Law and Criminology* 109, no. 3 (Summer 2019): 423.

13. Lowrie, *My Life in Prison*, 62, 64, 67.

14. After Lowrie's release, he worked toward California's repeal of capital punishment, urged the state to open a bureau for the relief and guidance of ex-convicts, and exposed the risks of overcrowded police courts. In *My Life Out of Prison* he describes hiring former convicts who faced post-prison risks of alcoholism and refused to prosecute three men who assaulted him outside a theater, aware that he felt "bitterness" toward the men but no desire for them to face his "revenge" in San Quentin. Donald Lowrie, *My Life Out of Prison* (New York: Mitchell Kennerley, 1915). See *New York Times*, April 18, 1915.

15. Griffith, *Crime and Criminals*, 75. In 1912 the legislature limited the "jacket" to six consecutive hours.

16. Griffith, *Crime and Criminals*, 49.

17. Griffith, *Crime and Criminals*, 78, 82–83.

18. Griffith, *Crime and Criminals*, 79.

19. Kenneth Lamott, *Chronicles of San Quentin* (New York: Ballantine, 1972), 77, 110.

20. Lamott, *Chronicles of San Quentin*, 106–14.

21. *Daily Evening Bulletin* (San Francisco), October 11 and 18 and November 14, 1887; March 3, 1889.

22. *Daily Evening Bulletin* (San Francisco), October 11, 1887.

23. *Daily Evening Bulletin* (San Francisco), March 17, 1888.

24. Lamott, *Chronicles of San Quentin*, 253.

25. Linda S. Parker, "Murderous Women and Mild Justice," *Journal of San Diego History* 28, no. 1 (Winter 1992), passim, https://sandiegohistory.org/journal/1992/january/women-5/.

26. See Parker, "Murderous Women and Mild Justice," for an effective summary of attitudes toward criminality in the late nineteenth century, with specific references to data from San Quentin. Parker notes that "seventy-three percent of the female inmates, including foreign-born Europeans, were Anglos. However, the minority portion increased rapidly from 1900 to 1910. Although San Francisco County accounted for only twenty-one percent of the women in California between 1890 and 1910, the area contributed fifty percent of prisoners, most of whom were convicted of grand larceny." See also:

San Quentin Prison Register, California State Archives, Sacramento; U.S. Department of Commerce, Bureau of Census, *Eleventh Census, 1890: Population of the United States*, vol. 1, pt. 1 (Washington, DC, 1895), 756; *Thirteenth Census, 1910: Population of the United States*, vol. 2 (Washington, DC, 1913), 169, 175.

27. In Griffith, *Crime and Criminals*, 99–100. This exposé prompted white women from the California Reform Club to gather testimony from women who had been released and publish the long testimony of one woman who managed to get paroled.

28. Griffith, *Crime and Criminals*, 101.

29. Griffith, *Crime and Criminals*, 94–113. This report is corroborated by the *Los Angeles Branch of the Prison Reform League* (1909), cited in Griffith, *Crime and Criminals*, 94.

30. "Uren Pressing Gland Charges," *Los Angeles Times*, May 16, 1928.

31. Ethan Blue, "The Strange Career of Leo Stanley: Remaking Manhood and Medicine at San Quentin State Penitentiary, 1913–1951," *Pacific Historical Review* 78, no. 2 (May 2009): 211.

32. Blue, "Strange Career," 210–41, 221.

33. Calif. Stat., ch. 720 (1909). For a review of the evolution of California's sterilization laws, see Alexandra Minna Stern, "Sterilized in the Name of Public Health: Race, Immigration, and Reproductive Control in Modern California," *American Journal of Public Health* 95, no. 7 (2005) 1128–38. See also Alexandra Minna Stern, *Eugenic Nation: Faults and Frontiers of Better Breeding in Modern America* (Berkeley: University of California Press, 2005). See Shilpa Jindia, "Belly of the Beast: California's Dark History of Forced Sterilizations," *Guardian*, June 30, 2020: "There are an estimated 455 survivors of eugenic sterilizations and 244 survivors of prison sterilizations. Many of them are highly vulnerable to Covid-19 because of their age and medical history."

34. Tony Platt and Alex Stern, "Sterilization Abuse in State Prisons: Time to Break with California's Long Eugenic Patterns," *Huffington Post*, September 22, 2013; Leo Stanley, *Men at Their Worst* (New York: D. Appleton-Century, 1940), 154, 157.

35. See the well-documented overview "Eugenics in California," Eugenics in America, http://eugenicsinamerica.weebly.com/eugenics-in-california.html.

36. Stanley, *Men at Their Worst*, 160.

37. Leo Stanley, "Oral History: Stanley, Dr. Leo L., August 7, 1974," interview by Carla Ehat and Anne Thompson Kent, Anne T. Kent California Room, Marin County Free Library, quoted in Blue, "Strange Career," 216, 226, 232.

38. Blue, "Strange Career"; Leo L. Stanley, "An Analysis of One Thousand Testicular Substance Implantations," *Endocrinology* 6 (1922): 788–89.

39. Blue, "Strange Career," 235; *Biennial Report of the State Board of Prison Directors of the State of California, 1931–1932* (Sacramento, 1931–32), 50.

40. Milton Chernin, "Convict Road Work in California" (PhD diss., University

of California, Berkeley, 1938), 53, 56, 67; "Road Camps," The Black Prisoners Project, https://blackprisonersproject.omeka.net/exhibits/show/road-camps.

41. Pub. L. No. 74–215, 49 Stat. 494 (1935), codified at 18 U.S.C. §§1761–62, 5.

42. U.S. Department of Justice, *Bureau of Justice Statistics Bulletin* (June 1997): 4, 5.

43. Julie Light, "Look for That Prison Label," *Progressive* 64, no. 6 (June 2000): 21; Matt Potter, "Green and Made in the U.S.A.," *San Diego Reader*, August 25, 2014; "Prisons Punish Inmates Because of 'Negative' News Stories," *Prison News Service*, Proposition 1, http://prop1.org/legal/prisons/press.htm; Marc Belton, "Small Business: Captive Labor Force Filling Labor Gaps," *Los Angeles Times*, September 22, 1999; Chris Levister, "A Sweatshop behind Bars," AlterNet, https://www.alternet.org/2006/09/a_sweatshop_behind_bars/; David Leonhardt, "Labor Crunch Solution Seen in Prison Inmates," *Contra Costa Times*, March 19, 2000.

44. Nathan James, "U.S. Prison Labor at Home and Abroad: The Debate over Captive Labor," Congressional Research Service, National Institute for Corrections, U.S. Department of Justice, https://nicic.gov/authors/nathan-james. Laws that still adhere today were created during the Depression to protect the fragile jobs of free citizens. The 1935 Hawes-Cooper Act and the 1940 Ashurst-Sumners Act made interstate trading of prison-made goods illegal. During the 1970s, however, many of these laws were amended. In 1979 the Justice System Improvement Act allowed for privatization of prisons and for the transport of their goods across state boundaries. After this change in law, prison industry profits jumped from $392 million to $1.31 billion. However, the Depression legislation still holds true for state- and federally run prisons. See Martin B. Miller, "At Hard Labor: Rediscovering the 19th Century Prison," *Issues in Criminology* 9, no. 1 (Spring 1974): 91–114; Reese Erlich, "Prison Labor: 'Working' for the Man," *Covert Action Quarterly* 54 (Fall 1995): 3.

45. *Cristina Vasquez v. State of California*, 41 Cal. Rprt. 3d 556. No. D045592 (August 16, 2006). Vasquez, filing on behalf of the two men, was the international vice president for the Union of Needletrades, Industrial and Textile Employees. See also David Leonhardt, "As Prison Labor Grows, So Does the Debate," *New York Times*, March 19, 2000.

46. Potter, "Green and Made in the U.S.A."; *San Diego Business Journal*, January 2015; "Pierre Sleiman," LinkedIn, https://www.linkedin.com/in/pierresleiman.

47. Anita Sarah Jackson et al., "Toxic Sweatshop: How UNICOR Prison Recycling Harms Workers, Communities, the Environment, and the Recycling Industry," *Center for Environmental Health*, October 2006.

48. Anne-Marie Cusac, "Toxic Prison Labor," *Progressive*, March 28, 2009. See Diana Ceballos and Elena Page, "Occupational Exposures at Electronic Scrap Recycling Facilities," Centers for Disease Control and Prevention, September 30, 2014, https://blogs.cdc.gov/niosh-science-blog/2014/09/30/escrap/; "Justice OIG: Prison E-Waste Recycling Endangered Inmates, Staff," Envi-

ronment News Service, October 23, 2010, https://ens-newswire.com/justice
-oig-prison-e-waste-recycling-endangered-inmates-staff/.

49. Jackson et al., "Toxic Sweatshop," 39.

50. Tony Platt calls these prisons "human silos": *Beyond These Walls: Rethinking Crime and Punishment in the United States* (New York: St Martin's, 2018), 134–36.

51. California's prisons morphed into shell companies for corporations, and then into private prisons—an industry that increased 1,600 percent nationally between 1990 and 2010. In dangerous synchronicity, California's prison population swelled, but rather than commute sentences or parole convicts—mostly urban poor, Latino, and Black—California splurged on building more prisons and depleted the state's resources. In the two decades between 1984 and 2005, California built another two dozen prisons and two dozen "detention facilities." The "War on Drugs," "Just Say No," "Law and Order," and "Tough on Crime" opened the prison gate to more and more African Americans and Latinos. "Close the Border" built the Imperial Regional Detention Facility, the Otay Mesa Detention Center, and the Adelanto ICE Processing Center, owned by the monolithic GEO Group. Immigrants held at Adelanto must work for only one dollar a day or extra food. Throughout, the prisons created jobs for prison guards and built the prison guard unions, the largest donor to Governor Jerry Brown's campaign. In 2020 California banned private prisons from entering into any new contracts, with a countdown to 2028. There are loopholes: a private prison can remain in business if it provides educational, vocational, or medical services, or if the state operates it.

52. "Rape is never the sentence for a crime" comes from *Farmer v. Brennan*, 511 U.S. 825, 834 (1994). See Jeannine DeLombard, *In the Shadow of the Gallows: Race, Crime, and American Civic Identity* (Philadelphia: University of Pennsylvania, 2012), for a sustained and capacious discussion of convict labor.

53. U.S. Department of Justice, "Initial Regulatory Impact Analysis. Proposed National Standards to Prevent, Detect, and Respond to Prison Rape Under the Prison Rape," Elimination Docket No. OAG-131 RIN 1105-AB34 (January 24, 2011): 64–65.

54. Allen Beck, Marcus Berzofsky, Rachel Caspar, and Christopher Krebs, *Sexual Victimization in Prisons and Jails Reported by Inmates, 2011–12* (Washington, DC: U.S. Department of Justice, Bureau of Justice Statistics, 2013), https://www.bjs.gov/content/pub/pdf/svpjri1112.pdf.

55. Joan Petersilia, "California's Correctional Paradox of Excess and Deprivation," *Crime and Justice* 37, no. 1 (2008): 207–78.

56. *Giraldo v. CDCR*, 168 Cal. App. 4th 231, Cal. App. 1 Dist. (2008).

57. Petersilia, "California's Correctional Paradox," 232.

58. Beck, Berzofsky, Caspar, and Krebs, *Sexual Victimization in Prisons and Jails*, 115: "Sexual assault is 13 times more prevalent among transgender inmates in

California, with 59% reporting being sexually assaulted while in a California correctional facility." Valerie Jenness, Cheryl L. Mason, Kristy N. Matsuda, and Jennifer Macy Sumner, "Violence in California Correctional Facilities: An Empirical Examination of Sexual Assault," *Bulletin of the Center for Evidence-Based Corrections* 2, no. 2 (June 2007): 2.

59.   U.S. Const. amend. XIII: "Neither slavery nor involuntary servitude, except as a punishment for crime whereof the party shall have been duly convicted, shall exist within the United States, or any place subject to their jurisdiction."

Chapter Fifteen. Native American Boarding Schools

Epigraph: Kevin Whalen, *Native Students at Work: American Indian Labor and Sherman Institute's Outing Program, 1900–1945* (Seattle: University of Washington Press, 2018), 47.

1.   Clifford E. Trafzer, Matthew Sakiestewa Gilbert, and Lorene Sisquoc, "Introduction: The Indian School on Magnolia Avenue," in *The Indian School on Magnolia Avenue: Voices and Images from Sherman Institute*, ed. Trafzer, Gilbert, and Sisquoc (Corvallis: Oregon State University Press, 2012), 8.

2.   It is impossible to determine how many Indian children were kidnapped. Michael F. Magliari, "Masters, Apprentices, and Kidnappers: Indian Servitude and Slave Trafficking in Humboldt County, California, 1860–1863," *California History* 97, no. 2 (2020): 3.

3.   U.S. Statutes at Large, 39th Cong., sess. II, Ch. 187 (1867): 546.

4.   For reliable demographic data, see Benjamin Madley, "'Unholy Traffic in Human Blood and Souls': Systems of California Indian Servitude under U.S. Rule," *Pacific Historical Review* 83, no. 4 (November 2014): 626–67; Sherburne F. Cook, *The Conflict between the California Indian and White Civilization* (Berkeley: University of California Press, 1976), 61; Magliari, "Masters, Apprentices, and Kidnappers," 3. See also Robert F. Heizer, "Indian Servitude in California," in *Handbook of North American Indians*, vol. 4, *History of Indian-White Relations*, ed. William C. Sturtevant and Wilcomb E. Washburn (Washington, DC: Smithsonian, 1988), 415–16; Robert F. Heizer and Alan F. Almquist, *The Other Californians: Prejudice and Discrimination under Spain, Mexico, and the United States to 1920* (Berkeley: University of California Press, 1977), 53. Brendan Lindsay drew upon the annual and biennial reports of the superintendent of public instruction of the state of California, *Journals of the Senate and Assembly of the State of California, 1864–1880*, to compile these statistics, noting that based on incomplete and sporadic data from school districts, these numbers should be considered conservative: Brendan Lindsay, *Murder State: California's Native American Genocide, 1846–1873* (Lincoln: University of Nebraska Press, 2012), 267. Stacey L. Smith, *Freedom's Frontier: California and the Struggle over Unfree Labor, Emancipation, and Reconstruction* (Chapel Hill: University of North Carolina Press, 2013),

190–91; William J. Bauer, Jr., *We Were All Like Migrant Workers Here: Work, Community, and Memory on California's Round Valley Reservation, 1850–1941* (Chapel Hill: University of North Carolina Press, 2012), 68–69.

5. "Indentures as Apprentice Carpenter to F. H. Mellus," May 9, 1876, BANC C-Y 299, Box V, 1800–1899, Bancroft Library, University of California, Berkeley.

6. George Tinker, "Tracing a Contour of Colonialism: American Indians and the Trajectory of Educational Imperialism," in *Kill the Indian Save the Man: The Genocidal Impact of American Indian Residential Schools,* ed. Ward Churchill (San Francisco: City Lights, 2004), xiii–xlii.

7. Clifford Trafzer, ed., *American Indians American Presidents: A History* (Washington, DC: National Museum of the American Indian, Smithsonian, 2009), 101–7. "In reality the [peace] policy rested on the belief that Americans had the right to dispossess Native peoples of their lands, take away freedoms, and send them to reservations, where missionaries would teach them how to farm, read and write, wear Euro-American clothing, and embrace Christianity. If Indians refused to move to reservations, they would be forced off their homelands by soldiers": "Timeline: 1868," Native Voices: National Library of Medicine, https://www.nlm.nih.gov/nativevoices/timeline/342.html.

8. "The Lake Mohonk Conference," Native American Roots, April 26, 2011, http://nativeamericannetroots.net/diary/937. Jeffrey D. Schultz, Kerry L. Haynie, Anne M. McCulloch, and Andrew L. Aoki, eds., *Encyclopedia of Minorities in American Politics,* vol. 2, *Hispanic Americans and Native Americans* (Westport, CT: Greenwood, 2000), 608; Bauer, *We Were All Like Migrant Workers Here,* 120.

9. Report of the Commissioner, Indian Affairs, *Annual Reports of the Department of the Interior* (Washington, DC: Government Printing Office, 1902), 9–10. See Jana R. Noel, "Education toward Cultural Shame: A Century of Native American Education," *Educational Foundations* (Winter 2002): 19–32.

10. "Trigger Points: Current State of Research on History, Impacts, and Healing Related to the United States' Indian Industrial/Boarding School Policy," Native American Rights Fund, https://www.narf.org/nill/documents/trigger-points.pdf.

11. These include Fort Bidwell Indian School, Fort Yuma Indian School, Greenville Indian Industrial School, Hoopa Valley School, Perris Indian School, Round Valley Indian School, Sherman Institute, St. Anthony's Industrial School, St. Boniface Indian Industrial School, and St. Turibius Industrial School. See "Indian Boarding Schools by State," National Native American Boarding School Healing Coalition, https://secureservercdn.net/198.71.233 .187/ee8.a33.myftpupload.com/wp-content/uploads/2021/06/NABS -Boarding-school-list-2021-acc.pdf.

12. Tinker, "Tracing a Contour of Colonialism," xiii–xlii, xv.

13. "1887: Indian Affairs Commissioner Bans Native Languages in Schools," Na-

tive Voices: National Library of Medicine, https://www.nlm.nih.gov/native voices/timeline/369.html.

14. Richard H. Pratt, *Official Report of the Nineteenth Annual Conference of Charities and Correction* (1892), 46; Kevin Whalen, "Beyond School Walls: Race, Labor, and Indian Education in Southern California, 1902–1940" (PhD diss., University of California, Riverside, 2014), 21.

15. K. Tsianina Lomawaima and Jeffrey Ostler, "Reconsidering Richard Henry Pratt: Cultural Genocide and Native Liberation in an Era of Racial Oppression," *Journal of American Indian Education* 57, no. 1 (Spring 2018): 80–83.

16. Pratt, *Official Report* (1892), 46.

17. Lomawaima and Ostler, "Reconsidering Richard Henry Pratt," 80–83.

18. Tinker, "Tracing a Contour of Colonialism," xvi, 17; David Wallace Adams, *Education for Extinction: American Indians and the Boarding School Experience, 1875–1928* (Lawrence: University of Kansas Press, 1995), 11–15; Corey Dolgon, *Kill It to Save It: An Autopsy of Capitalism's Triumph over Democracy* (Bristol: Policy, 2018), 65.

19. "Boarding Schools," Northern Plains Reservation Aid, http://www.native partnership.org/site/PageServer?pagename=airc_hist_boardingschools.

20. Native American Rights Fund, "Trigger Points," 9 and nn45–46.

21. Native American Rights Fund, "Trigger Points," 13n66.

22. Mary Annette Pember, "Death by Civilization," *Atlantic*, March 8, 2019, https://www.theatlantic.com/education/archive/2019/03/traumatic-legacy -indian-boarding-schools/584293/.

23. Tinker, "Tracing a Contour of Colonialism," xiii–xlii, xv.

24. Whalen, "Beyond School Walls," 43.

25. Whalen, *Native Students at Work*, 29.

26. Whalen, *Native Students at Work*, 29–59.

27. Brenda J. Child (Ojibwe), *Boarding School Seasons: American Indian Families, 1900–1940* (Lincoln: University of Nebraska Press, 1998), 13.

28. Adams, *Education for Extinction*, 216.

29. Cathleen D. Cahill, *Federal Fathers and Mothers: A Social History of the United States Indian Service, 1869–1933* (Chapel Hill: University of North Carolina Press, 2013), 79.

30. Helen Carpenter, *Ukiah Republican Press*, April 2, 1897; Linda Pitelka, "Mendocino: Race Relations in a Northern California County, 1850–1949" (PhD diss., University of Massachusetts, Amherst, 1994), 296–97.

31. 25 USC 283: Regulations for Withholding Rations for Nonattendance at Schools (March 3, 1893), ch. 209, §1, 27 Stat. 628, 635.

32. William J. Bauer, Jr., "Family Matters: Round Valley Indian Families at the Sherman Indian Institute, 1900–1945," *Southern California Quarterly* 92, no. 4 (2010): 404–6.

33. Diana Meyers Bahr, *The Students of Sherman Indian School: Education and Na-*

tive Identity since 1892 (Norman: University of Oklahoma Press, 2014), 58–59. See also Diana Meyers Bahr, *Viola Martinez, California Paiute: Living in Two Worlds* (Norman: University of Oklahoma Press, 2003), 27, 58, 81, 140, 163. Note that the description of the Sherman Institute has radically changed, from standing at the forefront of the federal government's efforts to erase Indigenous cultures while providing an unpaid work force, to the modern Sherman Indian High School, where Indigenous languages and history, as well as sports and college prep, are at the core of the curriculum. See Whalen, "Beyond School Walls."

34. "Boarding Schools," Northern Plains Reservation Aid.
35. Child, *Boarding School Seasons*, 28. See also "1887: Indian Affairs Commissioner Bans Native Languages."
36. Bahr, *Students of Sherman Indian School*, 58–59. See also Bahr, *Viola Martinez*, 58.
37. Adams, *Education for Extinction*, 21.
38. "Dept. of the Interior Office of Indian Affairs, Washington January 13, 1902," repr. in Lynette Mullen, NorCal History Blog, https://lynette707.word press.com/?s=Dept.+of+the+Interior+Office+of+Indian+Affairs%2C+Wash ington+January+13%2C+1902.
39. William Jones, Commissioner of Indian Affairs to Superintendent, Round Valley, California, January 11, 1902, National Archives, Records of the Bureau of Indian Affairs, cited in Rebecca Onion, "The Infamous Government Order Mandating Forced Haircuts for Native Americans," Slate, August 20, 2013, https://slate.com/human-interest/2013/08/haircut-order-commissioner -jones-letter-demanding-that-supervisors-force-native-americans-to-cut -their-hair.html.
40. Kate Mook, "The Greenville Investigation: Missing and Murdered Indigenous Women and Boarding School Runaways" (master's thesis, California State University, San Bernardino, 2020), 48–76.
41. Alexandria L. Gough, "A Way Out: The History of the Outing Program from the Haskell Institute to the Phoenix Indian School" (master's thesis, University of Arkansas, Fayetteville, 2012).
42. Native American Rights Fund, "Trigger Points," 10.
43. Native American Rights Fund, "Trigger Points," 13n65.
44. Cahill, *Federal Fathers and Mothers*, 92–93; Robbie Ethridge, "Introduction: Mapping the Mississippian Shatter Zone," in *Mapping the Mississippian Shatter Zone: The Colonial Indian Slave Trade and Regional Instability in the American South*, ed. Ethridge and Sheri M. Shuck-Hall (Lincoln: University of Nebraska Press, 2009), 2.
45. See Herbert M. Hart, *Old Forts of the Far West* (Seattle: Superior, 1965); Justin Rughe, "Fort Gaston," Military Museum, http://www.militarymuseum.org /FtGaston.html.
46. Pember, "Death by Civilization."

47. Trafzer, Gilbert, and Sisquoc, *Indian School on Magnolia Avenue,* 112.
48. Gough, "Way Out"; "Dept. of the Interior Office of Indian Affairs, Washington January 13, 1902."
49. Bahr, *Students of Sherman Indian School,* 4–5; Pratt, *Official Report* (1892), 46.
50. See Beth Piatote, "Disciplinary Paternalism," lecture, Indigenous Enslavement and Incarceration in North America International Conference, Gilder Lehrman Center, Yale University, New Haven, November 15–16, 2013, and *Domestic Subjects: Gender, Citizenship, and Law in Native American Literature* (New Haven: Yale University Press, 2013); and Laura Wexler, *Tender Violence: Domestic Visions in an Age of U.S. Imperialism* (Chapel Hill: University of North Carolina Press, 2000), for discussions of the ways invasion, imperialism, aesthetic representations, and the law created, defined, and then sought to impose "disciplinary paternalism" through imposing visions of family and subjectivity that never existed outside the worlds of the law and the imagination. See also Trafzer, *American Indians/American Presidents.*
51. Richard H. Pratt, "The Advantages of Mingling Indians with Whites," *Proceedings of the National Conference of Charities and Correction: 1892,* ed. Isabel C. Barrows (Boston: Geo. H. Ellis, 1892), 45.
52. Whalen, *Native Students at Work,* 35.
53. In 1963 Sherman was revived and rebuilt, and in 1971 reaccredited as the Sherman Indian High School, recruiting Indigenous children from across the country who seek its Native orientation, competitive athletic program, and scholarships and links to California universities.
54. Leleua Loupe, *The Indian School on Magnolia Avenue: Voices and Images from Sherman Institute* (Corvallis: Oregon State University Press, 2012), 5.
55. Adams, *Education for Extinction,* 26–27.
56. Adams, *Education for Extinction,* 5–21, 23, 57, 62–63, 210–13, and passim. Trafzer, Gilbert, and Sisquoc, "Indian School on Magnolia Avenue," 6–7; Clifford E. Trafzer, Jean A. Keller, and Lorene Sisquoc, eds., *Boarding School Blues: Revisiting American Indian Educational Experiences* (Lincoln: University of Nebraska Press, 2006); Bahr, *Students of Sherman Indian School,* 21.
57. Adams, *Education for Extinction,* 26–27.
58. Whalen, *Native Students at Work,* 44.
59. Whalen, *Native Students at Work,* 32–34.
60. Whalen, *Native Students at Work,* 49–50, 52.
61. Trafzer, Gilbert, and Sisquoc, *Indian School on Magnolia Avenue,* 127; Katrina Paxton, "Learning Gender: Female Students at the Sherman Institute: 1907–1925," in *Boarding School Blues,* 174–86.
62. Whalen, *Native Students at Work,* 61–62, 66.
63. Don C. Talayesva, *Sun Chief: The Autobiography of a Hopi Indian,* ed. Leo. W. Simmons (New Haven: Yale University Press, 1970), 141.
64. Trafzer, Gilbert, and Sisquoc, *Indian School on Magnolia Avenue,* 112.
65. Whalen, *Native Students at Work,* 33.

66. Whalen, *Native Students at Work*, 44.

67. Trafzer, Gilbert, and Sisquoc, "Indian School on Magnolia Avenue," 6–7, 107.

68. Adams, *Education for Extinction*, 159; 163. See also Talayesva, *Sun Chief*, 109, 129; Trafzer, Keller, and Sisquoc, *Boarding School Blues*, 181–83; Bahr, *Students of Sherman Indian School*, 21.

69. Whalen, *Native Students at Work*, 49.

70. Whalen, *Native Students at Work*, 49–50, 52.

71. Cahill, *Federal Fathers and Mothers*, 79–80.

72. Whalen, *Native Students at Work*, 33.

73. Whalen, *Native Students at Work*, 38.

74. Paxton, "Learning Gender," 174–86.

75. Trafzer, Gilbert, and Sisquoc, *Indian School on Magnolia Avenue*, 113, 114, 117, · 118; Whalen, *Native Students at Work*, 35.

76. Whalen, *Native Students at Work*, 35.

77. Whalen, *Native Students at Work*, 44.

78. *Superintendent Ledger, Outing System* (February 20, 1900), 50–51, quoted in Trafzer, Keller, and Sisquoc, *Boarding School Blues*.

79. Whalen, "Beyond School Walls," 150–51.

80. Quoted in Pitelka, "Mendocino," 297.

81. Whalen, *Native Students at Work*, 49–50.

82. Whalen, *Native Students at Work*, 47.

83. Whalen, *Native Students at Work*, 48.

84. Trafzer, Gilbert, and Sisquoc, *Indian School on Magnolia Avenue*, 127; Paxton, "Learning Gender," 174–86.

85. Whalen, *Native Students at Work*, 48.

86. Bauer, "Family Matters," 411.

87. Whalen, *Native Students at Work*, 49, 81.

88. Child, *Boarding School Seasons*, 42.

89. Trafzer, Gilbert, and Sisquoc, *Indian School on Magnolia Avenue*, 124–27.

90. Pitelka, "Mendocino," 299; Bauer, *We Were All Like Migrant Workers Here*, 125.

91. Pitelka, "Mendocino," 303.

92. Pitelka, "Mendocino," 294, 302.

93. Lewis Meriam, *The Problem of Indian Administration: Report of a Survey Made at the Request of Honorable Hubert Work, Secretary of the Interior, and Submitted to Him, February 21, 1928/Survey Staff: Lewis Meriam . . . [et al.]* (Baltimore, MD: Johns Hopkins Press, 1928); Native American Rights Fund, "Trigger Points," 15.

94. Andrea A. Curcio, "Civil Claims for Uncivilized Acts: Filing Suit against the Government for American Indian Boarding School Abuses," *Hastings Race and Poverty Law Journal* 4, no. 1 (Fall 2006): 63.

95. Adams, *Education for Extinction*, 336–37.

96.   Whalen, *Native Students at Work*, 320.
97.   K. Tsianina Lomawaima, "Domesticity in the Federal Indian Schools: The Power of Authority over Mind and Body," *American Ethnologist* 20, no. 2 (1993): 236–37, quoted in Native American Rights Fund, "Trigger Points," 13.
98.   Native American Rights Fund, "Trigger Points," 14.
99.   See, for example, Bauer, *We Were All Like Migrant Workers Here*, xii, 11; Devra Weber, *Dark Sweat, White Gold: California Farm Workers, Cotton, and the New Deal* (Berkeley: University of California Press, 1996); and Colleen O'Neill and Brian Hosmer, "Introduction," in *Native Pathways: American Indian Culture and Economic Development in the Twentieth Century*, ed. Hosmer and O'Neill (Boulder: University Press of Colorado, 2004).
100.   See Philip J. Deloria, *Indians in Unexpected Places* (Lawrence: University Press of Kansas, 2004).
101.   John E. Echohawk, "Letter," in "Trigger Points," iv.
102.   Native American Rights Fund, "Trigger Points," 36.
103.   Whalen, *Native Students at Work*, 40.
104.   Indian Child Welfare Act of 1978. 25 U.S.C. ch. 21 § 1901. 25 U.S.C. §§ 1901–1963.

Chapter Sixteen. "We Are the Jury"

Epigraph: Elle Snow, conversation with the author.

1.   Phillip W. D. Martin, "Nail Salons and Human Trafficking," *WGBH News*, updated December 6, 2017.
2.   Kevin Bales and Ron Soodalter, *The Slave Next Door: Human Trafficking and Slavery in America Today* (Berkeley: University of California Press, 2009); Kevin Bales, *Disposable People: New Slavery in the Global Economy* (Berkeley: University of California Press, 2012). Sally Lieber, California Assembly member, asserted in signing the California Trafficking Victims Protection Act, AB 22 of 2005: "The problem of human trafficking has reached into neighborhoods throughout California."
3.   Narratives of other survivors of sex trafficking in California can be found at "Narratives," California Against Slavery, https://californiaagainstslavery.org/narratives/.
4.   UNODC, *Global Report on Trafficking in Persons 2014* (United Nations publication, Sales No. E.14.V.10), 34, https://www.unodc.org/documents/data-and-analysis/glotip/GLOTIP_2014_full_report.pdf. In 2012 the largest "sourcing" countries for global supply were Albania, Belarus, Bulgaria, China, Lithuania, Nigeria, Republic of Moldova, Romania, Russia, Thailand, and Ukraine.
5.   "California Spotlight; Arizona Spotlight 2019 National Human Trafficking Hotline Statistics," Polaris, https://polarisproject.org/wp-content/uploads/2020/11/2019-California-State-Report.pdf; "2019 U.S. National Human

Trafficking Hotline Statistics," Polaris, https://polarisproject.org/?s=statistics;
"National Human Trafficking Hotline Data Report," National Human Traf-
ficking Hotline, https://humantraffickinghotline.org/sites/default/files/Na
tional%20Report%20For%202020.pdf; "Hotline Statistics," National Human
Trafficking Hotline, https://humantraffickinghotline.org/states. See Britany
Anthony, Jennifer Penrose, and Sarah Jakiel, "The Typology of Modern
Slavery: Defining Sex and Labor Trafficking in the United States," Polaris,
https://issuu.com/polarisfreedom/docs/polaris-typology-of-modern-slavery.
See "Human Trafficking Statistics by State 2020," World Population Review,
http://worldpopulationreview.com/states/human-trafficking-statistics
-by-state/. In 2012 it was the fourth-highest site for human trafficking. See
Kamala D. Harris, *The State of Human Trafficking in California* (Sacramento:
California Department of Justice, 2012), 4; "Coalition to Abolish Slavery
and Trafficking A Serious Problem—Around the World and in the USA,"
Coalition to Abolish Slavery and Trafficking, https://www.castla.org/.

6. Siddharth Kara, *Modern Slavery: A Global Perspective* (New York: Columbia
University Press, 2017), 80.

7. I am very grateful to Professor Josh Meisel of the California State University
Humboldt Institute for Interdisciplinary Marijuana Research (https://hiimr
.humboldt.edu/), for many discussions about the economic and sociological
implications of the marijuana industry statewide.

8. Despite the legalization of medical marijuana in 1996 with Proposition 215
(the Compassionate Use Act of 1996) and recreational marijuana in 2016
with Proposition 64 (the Adult Use of Marijuana Act), marijuana growth,
sales, and consumption are illegal at the federal level, and numbers are per-
force inaccurate. Sean Williams, "The 10 Top-Selling Marijuana States in
2019," December 15, 2019, The Motley Fool, https://www.fool.com/investing
/2019/12/15/the-10-top-selling-marijuana-states-in-2019.aspx; Darco Jaci-
movic, "21 Astounding Cannabis Industry Statistics for 2020," Atheneum
Collective, https://atheneumcollective.com/21-astounding-cannabis-industry
-statistics-for-2020/.

9. Williams, "10 Top-Selling Marijuana States"; Al Olson, "Marijuana Is Officially California's Largest Cash Crop," Fresh Toast, January 5, 2017, https://
thefreshtoast.com/cannabis/you-wont-believe-how-massive-californias
-cannabis-crop-is/; Phillip Smith, "California's Six Largest Cash Crops: Marijuana Is a Monster," Oregon Cannabis Connection, January 23, 2017, www
.occnewspaper.com/californias-six-largest-cash-crops-marijuana-is-a-monster.

10. Bureau of Cannabis Control, California, "Strategic Plan, 2020–22," https://
bcc.ca.gov/about_us/documents/strategic_plan_2020-22.pdf.

11. Claire Heddles, "California's Largest Legal Weed Farms Face Conflict in
Wine Country," NPR, August 14, 2019, www.npr.org/2019/08/14/74744
1997/californias-largest-legal-weed-farms-face-conflict-in-wine-country.
See "Marijuana Production in the United States (2006)—Comparison with

other Cash Crops," Drug Science, https://www.drugscience.org/Archive/bcr2
/cashcrops.html.

12. Author interview with subject who wishes to remain anonymous. I am grateful to Professor Josh Meisel, director, who welcomed me to meetings at the
California State University Humboldt (now Cal Poly Humboldt) Institute
for Interdisciplinary Marijuana Research for many discussions about the economic and sociological implications of the marijuana industry statewide.

13. Patrick McGreevy, "California Now Has the Biggest Legal Marijuana Market in the World. Its Black Market Is Even Bigger," *Los Angeles Times*, August
15, 2019, https://www.latimes.com/california/story/2019-08-14/californias
-biggest-legal-marijuana-market.

14. "Unions [See] Worker Growth Potential in California's Marijuana Industry,"
Insurance Journal, December 27, 2017, https://www.insurancejournal.com
/news/west/2017/12/27/475386.htm.

15. Dwight K. Blake, "Marijuana Statistics 2020, Usage, Trends, and Data,"
https://americanmarijuana.org/marijuana-statistics/.

16. U.S. Department of Homeland Security Cybersecurity and Infrastructure
Security Agency, "Advisory Memorandum on Identification of Essential
Critical Infrastructure Workers During Covid-19 Response," May 19, 2020,
https://www.cisa.gov/sites/default/files/publications/Version_3.1_CISA
_Guidance_on_Essential_Critical_Infrastructure_Workers_0.pdf.

17. "H-2A Temporary Agricultural Workers," U.S Citizenship and Immigration
Services, October 2020, https://www.uscis.gov/working-in-the-united-states
/temporary-workers/h-2a-temporary-agricultural-workers; Lena Brook and
Juanita Constible, "Treat Farmworkers as Essential, not Sacrificial," NRDC,
September 14, 2020, https://www.nrdc.org/experts/lena-brook/treat-farm
workers-essential-not-sacrificial.

18. Kara, *Modern Slavery*, 78–94. See also: "Labor Trafficking in California's Central Valley Agricultural Industry," Cast, www.castla.org/wp-content/uploads
/2019/11/factsheetfromBookModernSlaveryonLabortraffickingin-Central
V.pdf.

19. "California Child Labor Law in Agriculture and Farming," Minimum Wage,
https://www.minimum-wage.org/california/agriculture-child-labor-laws.

20. Hoopa Valley Tribe, https://www.hoopa-nsn.gov/. See also "Cannabis Farms
Could Leave Salmon Runs Truly Smoked!" Hoopa Valley Tribe, www.arcgis
.com/apps/MapJournal/index.html?appid=7e3d3ee5c90544beadbdd46
e4608eea4%20; "Report to Congress on the Ninth Annual Government-to-
Government Violence against Women Tribal Consultation," U.S. Department of Justice, https://www.justice.gov/ovw/page/file/931816/download.

21. Kym Kemp, "'We Are Targeting the Illegal Grows,' Says Tribe Chairman as
Operation Yurok Restarts," Redheaded Blackbelt, July 19, 2016, https://kym
kemp.com/2016/07/19/we-are-targeting-the-illegal-grows-says-tribe-
chairman-as-operation-yurok-restarts/. Author interview with a grower who
wishes to remain anonymous.

22. Johnny Magdaleno, "Mexican Drug Cartels May Use Legal Marijuana to Increase Their Presence in Northern California," *Newsweek*, January 10, 2018; Madison Park, "Use of Federal Lands for Illegal Pot a Growing Concern, California Officials Say," CNN, May 30, 2018, https://www.cnn.com/2018 /05/30/us/california-illegal-marijuana-federal-lands/index.html; "California: Robots, Cannabis," *Rural Migration News*, July 2017; Paige St. John, "Hmong Pot Growers in Siskiyou County Seeking Identity, Profit or Both," *Los Angeles Times*, September 10, 2017; Joe Szydlowski, "Deputies: Legal Weed Grow Site under Investigation for Human Trafficking," *Californian* (*USA Today*), June 6, 2018; Jonah Raskin, "Cannabis Country: Memories of the Hmong Summer 2017," *Sonoma West*, May 30, 2018.

23. During the writing of this book, the author met with Sheriff William Honsal regarding sex and labor trafficking in the Emerald Triangle, and with District Attorney Investigator Kyla Baxley, Humboldt County. Quotations from Sheriff Honsal are from a report on NBC-5, November 21, 2016.

24. Author interview with subject who wishes to remain anonymous.

25. Mary Anastasia O'Grady, "Mexico Loses Its Sovereignty to Cartels," *Wall Street Journal*, November 10, 2019; "Humboldt Co. CA Investigates Human Trafficking at Illegal Marijuana Grows," KOBI-TV NBC5, November 22, 2016.

26. Author interview. The trucker and contractor wish to remain anonymous.

27. For further context see a similar case in forcibly importing skilled bakers into "French bakeries" in Los Angeles, *Ermita Alabado et al. v. French concepts, Inc., L'amande French Bakery, Analiza Moitinho de Almeida, and Goncalo Moitinho de Almeida*, Superior Court of the State of California, County of Los Angeles, Central District, Judicial District (March 19, 2015).

28. Shoshana Walter, "In Secretive Marijuana Industry, Whispers of Abuse and Trafficking," Reveal, September 8, 2016, https://revealnews.org/article/in -secretive-marijuana-industry-whispers-of-abuse-and-trafficking/.

29. Craigslist (Medford, CA), October 2020 (now deleted).

30. Walter, "Secretive Marijuana Industry." See also Lennon Bergland, "My Dreamy, Dangerous Season with the Weed Harvesters of California Cannabis Country," Narratively, November 5, 2015, https://narratively.com/my -dreamy-dangerous-season-with-the-weed-harvesters-of-california-cannabis -country/.

31. Author interviews with County Sheriff William Honsal, 2018–19; Madison Margolin cites the Humboldt Human Rights Commission: "Human Trafficking in Humboldt Still Hides among the Cannabis Farms," Herb, August 29, 2018, https://herb.co/news/culture/human-trafficking-humboldt-cannabis/.

32. Author interviews with County Sheriff William Honsal, 2018–19; Walter, "Secretive Marijuana Industry."

33. Author interviews with County Sheriff William Honsal, 2018–19. See also Will Houston, "Humboldt County Officials Seek a Unified Approach to Human Trafficking as Reports Rise," *Times-Standard* (Eureka), August 26, 2018.

34. Holly Austin Smith was trafficked during the summer after her eighth-grade

middle school graduation, lured from a mall in New Jersey. In *Walking Prey*, she writes from a survivor's and advocate's perspective and cites the 2013 U.S. State Department report that globally, 27 million men, women, and children are being trafficked at any given time. Smith makes an important distinction between human trafficking and human smuggling, bringing undocumented workers into the United States and harboring undocumented workers already in the United States: Holly Austin Smith, *Walking Prey: How America's Youth Are Vulnerable to Sex Slavery* (New York: Palgrave-MacMillan, 2014), 15, 19; Kara, *Modern Slavery*, 80.

35. Susan Abram, "Survivors of Slavery 'Still Fighting,'" *Los Angeles Daily News*, February 10, 2010.

36. Erin Blakemore, "20th-Century Slavery Was Hiding in Plain Sight," *Smithsonian*, July 31, 2020, https://www.smithsonianmag.com/smithsonian-institution /20th-century-slavery-california-sweatshop-was-hiding-plain-sight -180975441/. See also Julie Su, "What the El Monte Sweatshop Case Means to Me," U.S. Department of Labor Blog, August 2, 2021, https://blog.dol.gov /2021/08/02/what-the-el-monte-case-means-to-me; "Thai El Monte Garment Workers: The Return of Slavery and Trafficking in the Modern Era," DCA, https://culturela.org/event/thai-el-monte-garment-workers-the-return -of-slavery-and-trafficking-in-the-modern-era/2021-06-27/; "El Monte Garment Workers Case Sets Precedent," Asian Americans Advancing Justice, Los Angeles, https://www.advancingjustice-la.org; "El Monte Thai Garment Slavery Case," Wikipedia, https://en.wikipedia.org/wiki/El_Monte_Thai _Garment_Slavery_Case; U.S. Department of Justice, "Seven Thai Nationals Plead Guilty to Enslaving More Than 80 Female Laborers in an El Monte, California Garment Factory," February 9, 1996, https://www.justice.gov /archive/opa/pr/1996/February96/045.txt; "El Monte Sweatshop Tip Letter," State of California, Department of Industrial Relations, Division of Labor Standards Enforcement, Smithsonian National Museum of American History; Teresa Watanabe, "Human Trafficking Case Ends for 48 Thai Welders," *Los Angeles Times*, December 8, 2006.

37. Kent Wong and Julie Monroe, eds., *Sweatshop Slaves: Asian Americans in the Garment Industry* (Los Angeles: UCLA Center for Labor Research and Education, 2006), 94.

38. "El Monte Sweatshop Tip Letter."

39. See George White, "Workers Held in Near Slavery, Officials Say," *Los Angeles Times*, August 3, 1995; Teresa Watanabe, "Home of the Freed," *Los Angeles Times*, August 14, 2008; Wong and Monroe, *Sweatshop Slaves*, 93; Patrick McDonnell and Maki Becker, "7 Plead Guilty in Sweatshop Slavery Case," *Los Angeles Times*, February 10, 1996; "Seven Thai Nationals"; "El Monte Thai Garment Slavery Case"; "El Monte Garment Workers Case Sets Precedent."

40. Shyima Hall with Lis Wysocky, *Hidden Girl: The True Story of a Modern-Day Child Slave* (New York: Simon and Schuster, 2015), passim.

41. Sara Lin, "Pair Admit Keeping Girl, 12, as a Slave," *Los Angeles Times*, June 30, 2006.

42. *United States v. Abdel Nasser Youssef Ibrahim*, UNODC, https://sherloc.unodc .org/cld/case-law-doc/traffickingpersonscrimetype/usa/2006/united_states _v._abdel_nasser_youssef_ibrahim.html, cites her award as $122,000.

43. Martina E. Vandenberg, "Innovations," *New York Law School Law Review* 60, no. 3–4 (2015): 631–47.

44. Hall and Wysocky, *Hidden Girl*, passim.

45. *United States v. Abdel Nasser Youssef Ibrahim*; U.S. Court of Appeals for the Ninth Circuit, "Human Trafficking: The Reality, the Scope and the Conse- quences," YouTube, September 9, 2015, https://www.youtube.com/watch?v =qE9b6Lq5nYI.

46. In the course of my research on the study of sex trafficking, I interviewed Elle Snow. These were extensive conversations. I honor her expectations and legal agreement that these were privileged conversations and respect her need for safety, confidentiality, and anonymity. Elle Snow is not her real name. This history is based on our private conversations, court records of the criminal actions against David Bernard Anderson, *People of the State of California v. David B. Anderson, Case CR1 400854*; contemporary newspaper accounts, including by Shoshana Walter from the Center for Investigative Reporting (now Reveal), the *North Coast Journal*, the Eureka *Times-Standard*, KHSU/PBS Radio Station, Humboldt State University's newspaper the *Lum- berjack*, and the author's private interviews with the Humboldt County Dis- trict Investigator Kyla Baxley, County Sheriff William Honsal, Arcata Chief of Police Tom Chapman, the Humboldt County Board of Supervisors, and Second District Supervisor Estelle Fennell. In 2017 I attended Elle Snow's seminar in educating and advocating for survivors and victims of human trafficking, in Eureka, California, through her NGO Game Over.

47. Victor Cobo, "The Rise and Fall of RedBook, the Site That Sex Workers Couldn't Live Without," *WIRED*, February 2015. The "personals" section of Craiglist.com was removed in 2018 under the Online Sex Trafficking Act of 2017, which made the owners of a website liable if a third-party person or a user posted illegal content. The carnal ads on myRedBook were shut down in 2014 for facilitating prostitution and for twenty-four counts of money laundering.

48. Mickey Royal, *The Pimp Game: Instructional Guide* (Los Angeles: Sharif, 1998), 62, 66–74. See also Ken Ivy, *Pimpology: The 48 Laws of the Game* (New York: Simon and Schuster, 2007).

49. Royal, *Pimp Game*, 62, 66–74.

50. Ivy, *Pimpology*, 22.

51. "California," National Human Trafficking Hotline, https://humantrafficking hotline.org/state/california.

52. Backpage, www.backpage.com. See also Tom Porter, "Backpage Website Shut

Down, Founder Charged with 93 Counts by FBI in Sealed Indictment," *Newsweek*, April 7, 2018.

53. S.1693–115th Congress (2017–18).
54. CA Penal Code § 236.1.
55. H.R. 1865 (115), Allow States and Victims to Fight Online Sex Trafficking Act of 2017, 115th Cong. (2017–2018) Public Law No: 115-164 (April 11, 2018).

Epilogue

1. Lucy Young [T'tc~tsa], quoted in Erik Krabbe Smith, "Lucy Young or T'tc~tsa: Indian/White Relations in Northwest California, 1846–1944" (master's thesis, University of California, Santa Cruz, 1990), 1756–57.

2. James Walvin, "Freedom Fighters: The Enslaved People Who Fought for the Abolition of Slavery," History Extra, July 7, 2020, https://www.history extra.com/period/georgian/enslaved-people-who-how-fight-against-slavery -haiti-rebellion/?fbclid=IwAR0c-leJ-WG0-RkQ9_Y49qCcNd9i7JgJ6nMA _y5vymaLI-i56pz7dxEZiEI.

3. Freshman State Senator William Gwin, Jr., son of pro-slavery pioneer politician William Gwin, Sr., claimed that Congress did not have the power to give this right to African Americans. In endorsing the Fifteenth Amendment in 1969, California was only followed by the former slaveholding states of Maryland (1973), Kentucky (1976), and Tennessee (1997).

4. For this ongoing history, see, for example, Soumya Karlamangla, "California's Reparations Task Force Meets Again," *New York Times*, December 8, 2021; Christina Kim, "California Reparations Task Force Discusses Slavery, Housing Discrimination," KPBS, September 27, 2021, https://www.kpbs.org/news /2021/sep/24/taskforce-reparations-hears-witness-panels-selects/; Brandon Tensley, "A Closer Look at the Ongoing Reparations Movement in California and Beyond," CNN, November 11, 2021, https://www.cnn.com/2021/11 /11/politics/reparations-movement-race-deconstructed-newsletter/index .html; Adria Watson, "What Happens after George Floyd? California Looks to Reparations," Cal Matters, https://calmatters.org/politics/2020/06/cali fornia-reparations-committee-slavery-george-floyd; Sonali Kolhatkar, "California Forms a State-Level Reparations Task Force," Yes!, https://www.yes magazine.org/social-justice/2021/12/21/california-reparations-task-force; Antonio Ray Harvey, "California Reparations Task Force Votes to Replace Economic Advisor," National African-American Reparations Commission, December 17, 2021, https://reparationscomm.org/reparations-news/california -reparations-task-force-votes-to-replace-economic-advisor/; Soumya Karlamangla, "California's Reparations Task Force Meets Again," *New York Times*, December 8, 2021, https://www.nytimes.com/2021/12/08/us/californias-rep arations-task-force.html.

5. Achmat Dangor, *Bitter Fruit* (London: Atlantic, 2004), 86.

6. Sam Levin, "'This Is All Stolen Land': Native Americans Want More than California's Apology," *Guardian*, June 21, 2019, https://www.theguardian.com/us-news/2019/jun/20/california-native-americans-governor-apology-reparations.

7. "Federal Land Ownership by State (as of 2013)," Encyclopedia of American Politics, https://ballotpedia.org/Federal_land_ownership_by_state.

8. Alan Greenblatt, "History Matters: Debates about Monuments Reflect Current Divisions," March 5, 2021, https://www.governing.com/now/history-matters-debates-over-monuments-reflect-current-divisions.html.

9. "Congress Apologizes for Slavery, Jim Crow," National Public Radio, July 30, 2008.

10. Executive Department, State of California, Executive Order N-15-19; "About the California Truth and Healing Council," Office of the Tribal Advisor, https://tribalaffairs.ca.gov/cthc/about/.

11. Letter from Amah Mutsun Tribal Band of Costanoan/Ohlone Indians to Governor Gavin Newsom, October 21, 2019, https://divhff6x22264.cloudfront.net/wp-content/uploads/2019/12/Amah-Mutsun-Letter-to-Gov-Newsom.pdf.

12. "Land Acknowledgement," "Know the Land," and "What Does a Land Acknowledgement Mean to You?," Northwestern Native American and Indigenous Initiatives, https://www.northwestern.edu/native-american-and-indigenous-peoples/about/what-does-a-land-acknowledgement-mean-to-you.pdf.

13. Kaitlin Reed (Yurok/Hupa/Oneida), "It All Comes Back to the Land," *Humboldt Journal of Social Relations* 1, no. 42 (2020): 27–29, 37, 40.

14. Jean Pfaelzer, *Driven Out: The Forgotten War against Chinese Americans* (New York: Random House, 2008), 22–23, 31–33, 42–43, 45, 142.

15. *Wing Hing v. The City of Eureka* (1886).

16. Ta-Nehisi Coates, "The Case for Reparations," *Atlantic*, June 2014, https://www.theatlantic.com/magazine/archive/2014/06/the-case-for-reparations/361631/.

17. Aboriginal and Torres Strait Islander Social Justice, "National Sorry Day," Australian Human Rights Commission, https://humanrights.gov.au/about/get-involved/events/national-sorry-day.

18. Rohan Sullivan, "Noel Pearson: Australia Sorry for 'Loss, Grief,'" *Star*, February 13, 2008.

19. Robert L. Johnson, "Reparations for Slavery are the Only Way to Fix America's Racial Wealth Disparities," NBC News, June 5, 2020, https://www.nbcnews.com/think/opinion/reparations-slavery-are-only-way-fix-america-s-racial-wealth-ncna1225251.

20. Subramaniam Vincent, "Reparations: The Missing Chapter in America's 'Pragmatic' Quest for Justice to African Americans," Markkula Center for Applied

Ethics at Santa Clara University, March 4, 2019, https://www.scu.edu
/ethics/all-about-ethics/reparations-the-missing-chapter-in-americas-prag
matic-quest-for-justice-to-african-americans/.

21.   Gillian Brockell, "California Was a Free State. But There Was Still Slavery.
Now Reparations Are on the Table," *Washington Post*, October 1, 2020.

22.   In 1987, nearly forty-five years after the end of World War II, the U.S. government apologized to the descendants of Japanese prisoners who had been
rounded up and held in remote concentration or incarceration camps during
the war, and paid $20,000 to each *living* survivor under the Civil Liberties
Act of 1988, 100th Congress, S. 1009; see Karen Tumulty, "House Votes
Payments for Japanese Internees," *Los Angeles Times*, September 18, 1987,
https://www.latimes.com/archives/la-xpm-1987-09-18-mn-5750-story.html.
The U.S. government promised the fifty-two hostages held for 444 days by
Iran in 1979 payments of up to $4.44 million—$10,000 for each day of captivity; but hostages or their families have received only a small portion from
a special fund that administrators now say is out of money. There will be no
payments for 2022. See Anne Gearan, "Forty Years Later, a Dwindling Band
of Iran Hostages Awaits a Promised Payment," *Washington Post*, September
26, 2021, https://www.washingtonpost.com/politics/2021/09/26/40-years-later
-dwindling-band-iran-hostages-awaits-promised-payment/.

23.   Jack Norton, "'To Destroy in Whole or in Part,'" *Humboldt Journal of Social
Relations* 1, no. 42 (2020): 26.

24.   Lucy Young [T'tc~tsa] with Edith V. A. Murphey, "Out of the Past: A True
Indian Story Told by Lucy Young, of Round Valley Indian Reservation," *California Historical Quarterly* 20, no. 4 (December 1941): 358.

Index